BONES, STONES, AND BUDDHIST MONKS

Studies in the Buddhist Traditions

a publication of the
Institute for the Study of Buddhist Traditions
University of Michigan
Ann Arbor, Michigan

STUDIES IN THE BUDDHIST TRADITIONS

BONES, STONES, AND BUDDHIST MONKS

Collected Papers on the Archaeology, Epigraphy, and Texts of Monastic Buddhism in India

Gregory Schopen

UNIVERSITY OF HAWAI'I PRESS, HONOLULU

Printed in the United States of America

99 00 01 02 03 04 6 5 4 3 2

The Institute for the Study of Buddhist Traditions is part of the Department of Asian Languages and Cultures at the University of Michigan, Ann Arbor, Michigan. It was founded in 1988 to foster research and publication in the study of Buddhism and of the cultures and literatures that represent it. In association with the University of Hawai'i Press, the Institute publishes the series Studies in the Buddhist Traditions, a series devoted to the publication of materials, translations, and monographs relevant to the study of Buddhist traditions, in particular as they radiate from the South Asian homeland. The series also publishes studies and conference volumes resulting from work carried out in affiliation with the Institute in Ann Arbor.

Library of Congress Cataloging-in-Publication Data

Schopen, Gregory.
Bones, stones, and Buddhist monks : collected papers on the archaeology, epigraphy, and texts of monastic Buddhism in India / Gregory Schopen.
p. cm. — (Studies in the Buddhist traditions ; 2)
Includes index.
ISBN 0–8248–1748–6 (cloth : alk. paper). — ISBN 0–8248–1870–9 (paper : alk. paper)
1. Monastic and religious life (Buddhism)—India. 2. Buddhist antiquities—India. 3. Buddhism—India—History. I. Series.
BQ6160.I4S36 1996
294.3'657'0954—DC20 96–30844
CIP

University of Hawai'i Press books are printed on acid-free paper and meet the guidelines for permanence and durability of the Council on Library Resources.

Designed by Kenneth Miyamoto

Dedicated to the taxpayers
and working women and men of
Canada and Australia who paid
for this foreigner's education

CONTENTS

PREFACE

THE COLLEGIATE INSTITUTE for the Study of Buddhist Traditions of the University of Michigan is very pleased to be able to present this collection of papers by Professor Gregory Schopen as the second volume in its series. Through his meticulous studies of a wide range of neglected or forgotten sources, many of which are carved in stone, Professor Schopen has effected a major shift in the direction of Buddhist Studies, a shift away from the sometimes excessive focus upon the rarefied categories of the scholastic productions by monastic elites, and a shift toward a recognition of the importance of the materiality of "popular" practice. These practices not only occupied the concerns of a much larger segment of the Buddhist communities of India, both monastic and lay, but served as the inevitable context for the formulation and elaboration of scholastic doctrine.

Professor Schopen's work, published over the last fifteen years in a wide range of scholarly journals, has been focused broadly on two issues in the history of Indian Buddhism: monastic life and the rise of the various movements that we refer to as the Mahāyāna. Monastic Buddhism in India is the subject of the current volume. Professor Schopen's highly influential papers on the rise of the Mahāyāna, which have called into question both the coherence of the category as well as its date, are currently being edited for publication as the next volume in our series.

The present volume provides an essential foundation for a social history of Indian Buddhist monasticism. Challenging the popular stereotype that represented the accumulation of merit as the domain of the layperson while monks concerned themselves with more sophisticated realms of doctrine and meditation, Professor Schopen problematizes many assumptions about the lay-monastic distinction by demonstrating that monks and nuns, both the scholastic elites and the less learned, participated actively in a wide range of ritual practices and institutions that have heretofore been judged "popular," from the accumulation and transfer of merit; to the care of deceased relatives (a practice once assumed to have been part of "the Chinese transformation of Buddhism"); to serving as sponsors and donors, rather than always as the recipients, of gifts; to (possibly) the coining of counterfeit currency. A particular emphasis of the current volume is the role played by monks in the disposition of their own dead, combining a close examination of the various rules for monastic funerals contained in the *vinaya* with an analysis of the available epigraphical and archaeological evidence. In addition, Professor Schopen provides fascinating perspectives on the role of the deceased Buddha in the particulars of Indian Buddhist monastic life, both as a relic whose presence bestows sanctity on its environs and as a permanent resident and property holder in the monastic economy. Taken together, the studies contained in this volume represent the basis for a new historiography of Buddhism, not only for their critique of many of the *idées reçues* of Buddhist Studies but for the compelling connections they draw between apparently disparate details.

All of these papers have been published previously and have been revised slightly here to provide a greater consistency of style. Despite the fact that they have appeared elsewhere, it was the opinion of the faculty of the Institute for the Study of Buddhist Traditions that their importance warranted their being gathered from far and wide into a single volume because of the edification and intellectual stimulation they provide as we continue to call into question past assumptions and to ask increasingly difficult questions about the elusive category we call Buddhism.

DONALD S. LOPEZ, JR.
Institute for the Study of
Buddhist Traditions

ACKNOWLEDGMENTS

THE PERSON TO BLAME for this volume is Donald Lopez. He was, I think, abetted early on by Robert Sharf. When the former first proposed reprinting a collection of some of my articles, I thought that doing so would probably not unduly retard the progress of the human race and I saw at least one distinct advantage: it would give me the opportunity to acknowledge in a more enduring way the help and benefit I have received from a large number of people over a long period of time.

To start at the beginning, I have always liked the opening words of *The Life and Opinions of Tristram Shandy*: "I wish either my father or mother, or indeed both of them, as they were in duty both equally bound to it, had minded what they were about when they begot me . . ." It, and the rest of Sterne's first two chapters, make it wonderfully apparent how much depends on the fact that most parents don't. By not, I suspect, minding overmuch about what they were doing, my parents inadvertently assured that I would be part of a remarkable family. My mother is deeply devout and hopelessly irreverent; my father—who never finished grade school—had a wonderful collection of strange books (including, of course, *Tristram Shandy*) and begot a family of six. Of the four that made it three have Ph.D.s—the laggard is my youngest sister Barbara who is arguably the funniest and certainly the smartest. My brother Bernard has published three novels; my sister Ann skies marathons at over fifty. Though none of them has the quiet wisdom of my father, and though we all share his capacity for error, they have all encouraged me on my way. All have been, and continue to be, important teachers.

In terms of my formal education I owe a great deal to Professor Jan Yün-hua, now retired from McMaster University in Canada. Although I was working in a different field, he supported and encouraged me with humor and good sense in my early and very precarious years of graduate school. He embodies the very best of the Confucian Gentleman Scholar. I owe a great deal to Professor J. W. de Jong now retired from the Australian National University. A man of enormous knowledge, he tried to teach me not to be sloppy in source or sense. But perhaps more than for anything else I owe him deeply for having allowed and encouraged me to go my own way, although, again, he might now be inclined to reconsider the wisdom of it. Here too I must thank my Sensei in Tibetan: Professor Shoryu Katsura, now of Hiroshima University, then at the University of Toronto, taught me the rudiments of Classical Tibetan with a clarity and precision I will never forget, although, unfortunately, I frequently forget the actual Tibetan, through no fault of his.

I owe a great deal to two of my Ph.D. examiners, even though that particular ritual function was only the beginning. Professor David Ruegg not only read my dissertation and survived, but has for many years encouraged me at a distance in many ways. The other of my examiners continues to be one, not by his position so much as by his integrity, good sense and learning. Not only was Luis Gómez one of my examiners, he was also my first Sanskrit teacher at the University of Washington. He is, I think, fond of pointing out that I dropped the class. He also gave me the second job I had after I had finished my Ph.D.—the first was as a nightwatchman in a sawmill in Wyoming—and he has continued to be both a model, a teacher, and most importantly, a friend.

In terms of friends I have been lucky beyond any conceivable expectations. I owe a very great deal to a prematurely follicularly disadvantaged theologian with a terrible jumpshot: John Thiel of Fairfield University was the first to read several of the papers republished in this volume, and every one he read was improved through his reading. Especially the piece entitled "Archaeology and Protestant Presuppositions in the Study of Indian Buddhism" owes a great deal to his editorial skills and his eye for errant rhetoric. He continues to be an important teacher and a friend, and I am very grateful.

An equally old and important friend is Hal Roth. Many of the things in these papers were first forged in long conversations with him on the phone (usually at my expense—but then also to my profit), and his sense of humor and taste in clothes has been a constant source of amazement. He too remains a teacher and a friend.

Not long after making the acquaintance of these gentlemen I met my first real exotic: a Pacific islander who spoke a quaint dialect of what, he assured me, was English. In spite, though, of the language barrier, in spite of the intervening miles and misadventures—not to mention years—Paul Harrison has too remained a very important friend and teacher. His occasional good sense still astounds me.

There are still others. I am grateful to Phyllis Granoff who over the years has published my work and given me the consolation of good conversation and shared with me her observations and her always nimble wit. I am grateful to Charles Hallisey for his encouragement and for sharing some of his boundless capacity to be interested in almost everything; to Jonathan Silk for his enthusiasm and unwillingness to accept easy answers; to Jan Nattier for her early and continued encouragement, and her ability to fruitfully frame questions on just about everything; and to Richard Salomon for his skepticism about religious studies and his scholarly standards.

Further afield, I owe a great deal to several scholars in Europe who have helped me in many ways even though I had no claim on their time and generosity. Gérard Fussman has let me profit enormously from his work and taught me much by not being easily convinced. Oskar von Hinüber has done the same, has provided one model of solid scholarship, and has supported me by numerous letters at crucial points in my academic career. K. R. Norman has both provided yet another model of scholarly excellence and taught me much by his generous correspondence. Akira Yuyama not only made it possible for me to study for a year in Tokyo, but he also taught me how to wear a tie, how to keep things in perspective, and the value of precision. To all of these I am extremely grateful.

With colleagues in the more strictly institutional sense I have also been extremely lucky. Patrick Olivelle gave me my first permanent academic job more than ten years ago at Indiana. He was then—as he is now in Austin—not only a very fine Sanskritist but nothing short of the best chairman and the best colleague someone working on Classical India could have: I trust his judgment and his wisdom, and I gain from his learning almost daily—he does not come in on Mondays. He has supported me always, even on those occasions (and I fear they were not rare) when I tried his patience. Also at Texas Richard Lariviere has been a fine colleague, a needed teacher, and an almost inexhaustible source of tall tales. More recently Janice Leoshko has done what she could to educate my lack of visual acuity, though she has yet to get me to use a slide projector. All have been good friends.

Closest to home are three women. Lynn, in the early days, who put up with being a vagabond and sharing her life with boxes full of old books, has remained a very good friend—Lynn's parents also were crucial: one of the papers included here was dedicated to the memory of her father, a man I came to greatly admire. Alice, who has put up with even more boxes and still more moves, has kept me alive to the things of greater importance. She may yet get me up on her beloved high mountains where—I suspect—a good deal of her spirit comes from. I look forward to her attempts. And Morgan—without a doubt the finest accident to have occurred in my life because, yes, her father, too, did not mind what he was about, although he trusts that she will!

Finally, to come full circle, this volume owes most to those who put it together. The collection of papers it contains were written over many years and many moods. Few, if any, had benefited from the hands of a good copyeditor. It was therefore a final happy accident that the decision was made to reset the papers and that the project was taken on by Mimi Mayer and Reiko Ohnuma. The former went carefully through the papers and suggested many minor stylistic changes which have made, I think, a major improvement in their readability. The latter made even further refinements, brought some order to the chaos of my references, and put up with my long delays with good humor. I thank them both, and so should the reader. Given the enormity of their task, however, it should not be surprising that neither succeeded in imposing anything like an ordered consistency on what was inherently inconsistent material. In fact enough "variety" remains to excite even the moderately obsessive or anally retentive: hyphenation of Sanskrit compounds is erratic; the use of diacritics in place-names—especially in the titles of books and articles—is equally so, and there is even some variation in the spelling of such names; common terms involving *anusvāra* or nasals are spelled in every conceivable way (e.g., *saṅgha, saṃgha,* etc.); although Tibetan is usually transliterated using the so-called Wylie system, the discerning reader will occasionally find the older system that used diacritics; and so on. One can only hope that at least Emerson might approve.

Although the style of the papers, and their readability, have been improved, the content—alas—has not. I have silently corrected typos and misprints that I noticed in the original publications, but resetting the papers has probably created just as many new ones. And although I have inserted a few more recent references in square brackets into the notes, or added them at the end of the notes, I have made no attempt to revise any of the papers and no substantive changes have been made. Such changes—the important revisions and corrections—are, I think, rightly left to others. I have had my chance.

ABBREVIATIONS

AI	*Ancient India*
ABORI	*Annals of the Bhandarkar Oriental Research Institute*
ArA	*Artibus Asiae*
ARASI	*Annual Report of the Archaeological Survey of India*
ArO	*Ars Orientalis*
BEFEO	*Bulletin de l'école française d'extrême-orient*
BEI	*Bulletin d'études indiennes*
BHSD	F. Edgerton, *Buddhist Hybrid Sanskrit Dictionary* (New Haven: 1953)
BHSG	F. Edgerton, *Buddhist Hybrid Sanskrit Grammar* (New Haven: 1953)
BSOAS	Bulletin of the School of Oriental and African Studies
Derge	The Sde-dge Mtshal-par Bka'-'gyur, A Facsimile Edition of the 18th Century Redaction of Si-Tu Chos-kyi-'byuṅ-gnas. Prepared under the Direction of H. H. the 16th Rgyal-dbaṅ Karma-pa, Vols. 1–103 (Delhi: 1976ff). Cited by volume, folio number in the facsimile (not by original pagination), and line.
EI	*Epigraphia Indica*
EW	*East and West*
EZ	*Epigraphia Zeylanica*
Gilgit Buddhist Manuscripts	R. Vira and L. Chandra, eds., *Giglit Buddhist Manuscripts (Facsimile Edition)*, Sata-Piṭaka Series, Vol. 10, Part 6 (New Delhi: 1974). Cited

	by part number, folio number assigned in the facsimile, and line.
Gilgit Manuscripts	N. Dutt, ed., *Gilgit Manuscripts*, Vol. III, Part 1 (Srinagar: 1947); Vol. III, Part 2 (Srinagar: 1942); Vol. III, Part 3 (Srinagar: 1943); Vol. III, Part 4 (Calcutta: 1950). Cited by volume, part, page, and line.
Histoire du bouddhisme indien	Ét. Lamotte, *Histoire du bouddhisme indien, des origines à l'ére Śaka* (Louvain: 1958).
HJAS	*Harvard Journal of Asiatic Studies*
IA	*Indian Antiquary*
IIJ	*Indo-Iranian Journal*
IHQ	*The Indian Historical Quarterly*
IBK	*Indogaku bukkyōgaku kenkyū*
JA	*Journal asiatique*
JAIH	*Journal of Ancient Indian History*
JAOS	*Journal of the American Oriental Society*
JASBom	*Journal of the Asiatic Society of Bombay*
JBomBRAS	*Journal of the Bombay Branch of the Royal Asiatic Society*
JBORS	*The Journal of the Bihar and Orissa Research Society*
JESI	*Journal of the Epigraphical Society of India*
JIABS	*The Journal of the International Association of Buddhist Studies*
JIH	*The Journal of Indian History*
JIP	*Journal of Indian Philosophy*
JPTS	*Journal of the Pali Text Society*
JRAS	*Journal of the Royal Asiatic Society of Great Britain and Ireland*
MASI	*Memoirs of the Archaeological Survey of India*
MCB	*Mélanges chinois et bouddhiques*
Peking	D. T. Suzuki, ed., *The Tibetan Tripitaka, Peking Edition, Reprinted under the Supervision of the Otani University, Kyoto*, Vols. 1–169 (Tokyo and Kyoto: 1955–1961). Cited by volume, page, folio, and line.

RHR	*Revue de l'histoire des religions*
Saṅghabhedavastu	R. Gnoli, ed., *The Gilgit Manuscript of the Saṅghabhedavastu. Being the 17th and Last Section of the Vinaya of the Mūlasarvāstivādin*, Parts I–II, Serie Orientale Roma, XLIX, 1–2 (Roma: 1977–78). Cited by volume, page, and line.
Śayanāsanavastu and *Adhikaraṇavastu*	R. Gnoli, ed., *The Gilgit Manuscript of the Śayanāsanavastu and the Adhikaraṇavastu. Being the 15th and 16th Sections of the Vinaya of the Mūlasarvāstivādin*, Serie Orientale Roma, L (Roma: 1978). Cited by page and line.
StII	*Studien zur Indologie und Iranistik*
Tog	*The Tog Palace Manuscript of the Tibetan Kanjur*, Vols. 1–109 (Leh: 1975–1980). Cited by volume, folio number assigned in the reprint (not by original pagination), and line.
TP	*T'oung Pao*
UCR	*University of Ceylon Review*
WZKS	*Wiener Zeitschrift für die Kunde Südasiens*
ZDMG	*Zeitschrift der Deutschen Morgenländischen Gesellschaft*

CHAPTER I

Archaeology and Protestant Presuppositions in the Study of Indian Buddhism

THE WAY IN WHICH the history of Indian Buddhism has been studied by modern scholars is decidedly peculiar. What is perhaps even more peculiar, though, is that it has rarely been seen to be so. This peculiarity is most readily apparent in what appears at first sight to be a curious and unargued preference for a certain kind of source material. This curious preference, although it may not be by any means uniquely characteristic of the study of Indian Buddhism, is particularly evident there; so too is the fact that it has no obvious scholarly justification. We might first look at a small sample of statements expressing this preference and at its consequences. Then we must at least ask what can possibly lie behind it.

When Europeans first began to study Indian Buddhism systematically there were already two bodies of data available to them, and the same is true today. There was, and is, a large body of archaeological and epigraphical material, material that can be reasonably well located in time and space,[1] and material that is largely unedited and much of which was never intended to be "read."[2] This material records or reflects at least a part of what Buddhists—both lay people and monks—actually practiced and believed.[3] There was, and is, an equally large body of literary material that in most cases cannot actually be dated[4] and that survives only in very recent manuscript traditions.[5] It has been heavily edited,[6] it is considered canonical or sacred, and it was intended—at the very least—to inculcate an ideal.[7] This material records what a small, atypical part of the Buddhist community wanted that community to believe or practice. Both bodies of material, it is important to note, became available to Western scholars more or less simultaneously.[8] The choice of sources for the scholar interested in knowing what Indian Buddhism had been would seem obvious.

Originally published in *History of Religions* 31 (1991): 1–23. Reprinted with stylistic changes with permission of The University of Chicago Press.

But the choice made was, apparently, not based on an assessment of the two kinds of sources as historical witnesses, but on some other kind of an assumption. This assumption, it appears, more than anything else has determined the status and use of archaeological and epigraphical sources in the study of Indian Buddhism, and this assumption, apparently, accounts for the fact that an overriding textual orientation was in place very early in Buddhist studies.

In discussing Burnouf, who died in 1852 and whom he calls "the brilliant founder of the study of Buddhism," de Jong, himself the most recent historian of Buddhist studies, says: "Burnouf stressed the fact that Indian Buddhism had to be studied on the basis of the Sanskrit *texts* from Nepal and the Pāli *texts* from Ceylon. . . . Burnouf was well aware of the fundamental importance of the study of *texts* for the history of Buddhism. His idea with regard to India at the time of the Buddha, the doctrine of the Buddha and its later development, the relation of Buddhism to caste, etc., which he develops in the *Introduction,* are all based on a careful study of the *texts*" (emphasis added).[9]

De Jong himself has made a number of statements that clearly indicate that the position he ascribes to Burnouf in the first half of the nineteenth century is very much his own position in the second half of the twentieth: "Each of these vehicles [the three main "divisions" of Buddhism] has produced a rich literature. Undoubtedly, this literature is the most important source of knowledge of Buddhism. Buddhist art, inscriptions, and coins have supplied us with useful data, but generally they cannot be fully understood without the support given by the texts. Consequently, the study of Buddhism needs first of all to be concentrated on the texts. . . ."[10]

De Jong's statement is of interest both because it is recent and representative and because it makes explicit some of the assertions and assumptions that lie behind it. Notice first that de Jong gives a variant version of the all-too-common, simplistic view of archaeology as "the handmaiden of history."[11] But he goes even further: not only must archaeology be the handmaiden of literary sources, it and the evidence it brings forth can only be "fully understood" with "the support given by the texts"; not only must archaeology support and amplify the literary sources, it must also be supported and amplified by them; otherwise, it has no real use. It cannot be an independent witness. It cannot, therefore, tell a different story.

But notice too that this position, which gives overriding primacy to textual sources, does not even consider the possibility that the texts we are to study to arrive at a knowledge of "Buddhism" may not even have been known to the vast majority of practicing Buddhists—both monks and laity. It is axiomatically assumed that the texts not only were known but were also important, not only were read but were also fully implemented in actual practice. But no evidence in support of these assumptions, or even arguments for them, is ever presented.[12]

Notice too that no mention is made of the fact that the vast majority of the textual sources involved are "scriptural," that is to say, formal literary expressions of normative doctrine.[13] Notice, finally, that no thought is given to the fact that even the most artless formal narrative text has a purpose, and that in "scriptural" texts, especially in India, that purpose is almost never "historical" in our sense of the term.[14] In fact, what this position wants to take as adequate reflections of historical reality appear to be nothing more or less than carefully contrived ideal paradigms. This is particularly clear, for example, in regard to what these canonical texts say about the monk. But in spite of this, scholars of Indian Buddhism have taken canonical monastic rules and formal literary descriptions of the monastic ideal preserved in very late manuscripts and treated them as if they were accurate reflections of the religious life and career of actual practicing Buddhist monks in early India. Such a procedure has, of course, placed archaeology and epigraphy in a very awkward position. If, then, archaeology and epigraphy are to be in the service of a "history" based on written sources of this kind, then they are going to have to "support and amplify" something that very probably did not exist: they are going to have to sit quietly in the corner spinning cloth for the emperor's new clothes.

That this is largely what has happened and continues to happen is again not difficult to document. We might, as a simple example, cite a series of passages from a variety of scholars that address in one way or another the question of whether individual monks owned personal property—a question of considerable importance, since it bears on the character of Buddhist monasticism and because Buddhism has been presented as "the world-renouncing religion *par excellence*."[15]

Bühler, in discussing the second or first century B.C.E. donative inscriptions from Sāñcī, said: "Proceeding to the inscriptions which mention donations made by monks and nuns, the first point, which must strike every reader, is their great number, . . . *As the Buddhist ascetics could not possess any property,* they must have obtained by begging the money required for making the rails and pillars. This was no doubt permissible, as the purpose was a pious one" (emphasis added).[16] Discussing the Bhārhut donative inscriptions, which may slightly predate those from Sāñcī, Lüders said much the same thing: "It is perhaps striking to find monks and nuns making donations, *as they were forbidden to own any personal property* besides some ordinary requisites. Probably we have to suppose that they collected the money required for some pious purpose by begging it from their relatives and acquaintances" (emphasis added).[17]

Arguing that a "small jar" from Haḍḍa that had a Kharoṣṭhī inscription on it containing the name of a monk was not a gift made to that monk but rather "a funerary jar" intended to hold his ashes, Fussman said, in part: "Surtout il paraît surprenant que le don soit fait à un moine en particulier. *C'est contraire aux prescriptions du vinaya;* . . . On peut donc penser que la jarre était destinée à l'inhumation du moines"—to which he adds in a note: "*En ce cas il n'y aurait pas violation des règles du vinaya*" (emphasis added).[18] Marshall, commenting on one of the numerous hoards of coins found at the monastic site surrounding the Dharmarājikā at Taxila, said: "Probably the hollow block of kañjūr was merely a secret hiding place where one of the monks hid his store of coins . . . the possession of money by a monk *was contrary, of course, to the rule of the Church,* but the many small hoards that have been found in monasteries of the early medieval period leave little room for doubt that by that time the rules had become more or less a dead letter."[19] Finally, Spink, in an overview of Ajaṇṭā, said: "A number of inscriptions at Ajaṇṭā also prove that some of the caves, and numerous separate images, were donated by the monks themselves. This is an interesting commentary on the changing of Buddhism in India, for it suggests that monks, far from having renounced all worldly goods, were sometimes men of considerable wealth. It is doubtful that Buddhabhadra, the chief donor of the elaborate cave 26—a man who proclaims himself the friend of kings—spent very much time humbly wandering from village to village with his begging bowl *as his predecessors in the early days of Buddhism certainly did*" (emphasis added).[20]

The point here is not whether individual monks or nuns did or did not possess private property; the evidence we have, from all periods, indicates that they did. The point is that every time epigraphers, archaeologists, or art historians encountered evidence that even suggested the possibility that monks or nuns owned personal property, they first signaled their surprise ("It is perhaps striking, . . ." "Above all it appears surprising . . .") and then immediately invoked either explicitly or implicitly the rules in the canonical monastic codes against it to assert, in one way or another, that they were not really seeing what they saw. Either that, or they neutralized what they were seeing by attributing it to a "late change" or implied "decline" within the tradition. They all axiomatically assumed that the textual ideal either was or had been actually in operation, that if it said so in a text it must have been so in reality.

There appears to be, however, no actual evidence that the textual ideal was ever fully or even partially implemented in actual practice; at least none is ever cited. And even though the mere existence of rules against it might suggest that monks did own personal property,[21] and even though it is clear that in the textual ideal itself the infraction of those rules was a "minor offence,"[22] and even though it is almost certain that in a strictly legal sense "the monk might retain the ownership of the property that he had abandoned,"[23] still all material evidence that monks did have personal property must be explained away: Bühler's "they must have obtained by begging," Lüders' "Probably we have to suppose." This is an archaeology truly in the service of written sources, no matter how idealized the latter may be, an archaeology that will find itself forced to retire in the face of frequently indelicate situations. One example must suffice.

We know that Longhurst's Monastery 1 at Nāgārjunikoṇḍa was the gift of a lay-sister (*upāsikā*) named Bodhiśrī, and that it was the property of "the Theravādin teachers of Ceylon." These same "teachers" are further described in the epigraphy of Nāgārjunikoṇḍa as "skilled in the exegesis of both the letter and meaning of the ninefold instruction of the teacher and the preservers of the tradition of the holy lineage."[24] It is of some significance that it was in this monastery, belonging to this group, that Longhurst discovered in one of the cells "a large number of small lead coins of the usual South Indian type of about the second century A.D." But he also found, together with these coins, "a lump of lead ore and an earthenware die for the manufacture of coins of this size and pattern." Longhurst says simply that this indicates "that the monks made their own coins."[25] No mention is made of the fact that the authority for minting coins in early India was vested in the state, or in guilds of traders or "moneyers" by the power of the state.[26] This would suggest either that the monk or monks who lived in Monastery 1 at Nāgārjunikoṇḍa were involved in trading and commercial enterprises and were empowered by the state to do so, or that they were involved in counterfeiting. It is difficult to say which possibility is the more likely, but either alternative is interesting for what it might say about the character of actual, historical Buddhist monasticism. Evidence for such activities is, moreover, by no means limited to Nāgārjunikoṇḍa.[27]

The question of ownership by Buddhist monks of private wealth is, of course, not the only question that has been handled in this curious way. Another important example we might look at concerns the so-called doctrine of *karma.*

There are hundreds of short, simple donative inscriptions on the railings surrounding the *stūpas* at Sāñcī and Bhārhut that have been assigned to the second or first century B.C.E. Almost every one of them says something like *vajigutasa dānaṃ,* "the gift of Vajiguta," or *ghosāye dānaṃ,* "the gift of Ghosā," or one or another of hundreds of names, frequently with a title added indicating the donor's religious or secular status. That is all. The intention of the donor, the reason behind the gift, is—with only one exception—simply never stated. Confronted with this situation, Lamotte, in a book entitled *Histoire du bouddhisme indien,* a book that is *the* standard authority in the field, was able to say: "At this time the mentality remains strictly orthodox, that is to say it conforms to the spirit of the Buddha. By their charity, the generous donors [at Bhārhut and Sāñcī] never hope to reach the level of *Nirvāṇa,* but simply intend to benefit from the five advantages of the gift signaled by the *Aṅguttara* (III p. 38–41)."[28] Putting aside the fact that it is difficult to know how Lamotte knew exactly what "the spirit of the Buddha" was, still it is interesting to notice what happens here. The inscriptions themselves—again with one exception—say nothing about intention, nothing about what the donors' "hope" or what they "intended." There is, moreover, no evidence that the *Aṅguttara* was ever known at either Bhārhut or Sāñcī. Nevertheless, Lamotte not only imputes to actual individuals very specific intentions where none are actually expressed, he also assigns these intentions to a very specific text that he cannot, in fact, actually place at either site. This is at best a curious kind of history, a kind of history that—to put it most simply—seems to assume if it says so in a canonical text, it must have been so in reality. It does not seem to matter, again, that there is no actual evidence that this formal doctrine was ever a part of actual Buddhist practice.[29]

If this assumption is able to override the absence of evidence, it is also important to notice that it is also able to override the presence of contrary evidence. After ascribing to the donors at Bhārhut and Sāñcī the very specific intention of "benefiting from the five advantages" described in the canonical *Aṅguttara,* Lamotte goes on to say: "There can be no question [at Bhārhut and Sāñcī] of transferring the merit [of their gift] to someone else, nor moreover of formulating intentions which the mechanism of the retribution of acts would render inoperative."[30] Notice again that there can be no question either of transferring the merit or even of formulating a particular intention because, by implication, the mechanism of the retribution of acts would render both inoperative: that is to say, real donors—actual people—could only intend or want what was in conformity with a textual doctrine. There are, of course, a number of problems here, not the least of which is that it has never been established that a strict doctrine of retribution of acts was ever actually recognized outside of texts; it has never been established that it had any impact on actual behavior. In fact, what we know from contemporary anthropological studies of both Buddhist and Hindu communities where this doctrine is officially recognized suggests otherwise. It suggests that, where the doctrine is known at all, it is generally invoked in very limited and specific contexts, and people's behavior and their motivations are largely governed by other ideas or forms of a doctrine of *karma* that differ, sometimes very markedly, from the classical, textual doctrine.[31] Moreover, epigraphical data suggest that this has always been the case. Oddly enough, this is clear even at Bhārhut and Sāñcī, the sites Lamotte is specifically referring to.

As we have seen, the vast majority of donors at both sites do not record their intentions. There is only one exception. But in this single case in which the donor actually states his own intention, that intention is exactly what Lamotte says is impossible: it is exactly what the textual doctrine of the retribution of acts would render inoperative. However, Sagharakhita, the donor in question, does not seem to know that. He makes his gift *mātāpituna aṭhāyā,* "for the benefit of his mother and father."[32] This, in fact, is one of the earliest expressions of and the *only* actually attestable form of the actual—as opposed to the ideal—Buddhist doctrine of *karma* and giving current at Bhārhut and Sāñcī. But because it does not conform to and confirm the existence of the textual doctrine, it is said, "It cannot possibly be." Textuality overrides actuality. And actuality—as expressed by epigraphical and archaeological material—is denied independent validity as a witness. It may not be altogether surprising to note that the more we come to know about what real donors actually did, the clearer it becomes how defective our textual sources can be as historical witnesses.

Since Lamotte wrote the remarks quoted above, a number of important early inscriptions have come to light. In 1968 a number of donative inscriptions on what was a railing surrounding a *stūpa* were discovered at Pauni in Maharashtra. In both style and paleography they are very similar to the inscriptions found at Bhārhut and Sāñcī, and like them, have been assigned to the second or first century B.C.E. At Pauni, again as at Bhārhut and Sāñcī, the majority of donors do not express their intentions, but there is at least one exception. This exception indicates that the donor, one Visamitā, gave her gift "for the happiness of all beings" (. . . *{yā}ya visamitāya dana sukhāya hotu savasātāna*).[33] The other early inscriptions of interest to us come from Sri Lanka and are almost certainly even earlier than those from Bhārhut, Sāñcī, and Pauni. One of these inscriptions, according to Paranavitana, is among "the earliest in Ceylon that can be definitely attributed to a particular ruler" and dates to the period between 210 and 200 B.C.E. It reads: *gamaṇi-uti-maharajhaha{jhita abi-ti}śaya leṇe daśa-diśaśa sagaye dine mata-pitaśa aṭaya:* "The cave of the princess (Abi) Tissā, daughter of the great king Gāmaṇī-Uttiya, is given to the Saṅgha of the ten directions, for the benefit of (her) mother and father."[34] Additionally, we now have four virtually identical inscriptions that record gifts of caves and that may even predate Abi Tissā's inscription. All four end by saying that the gift was given *aparimita-lokadatuya śatana śita-śukaye,* ("for the welfare and happiness of beings in the boundless universe").[35]

Known epigraphical evidence, therefore, proves that the earliest actually attestable Buddhist doctrine of *karma* and giving—and this is now attested from the third century B.C.E. and at very widely separated geographic sites—always involves exactly what Lamotte, on the basis of textual sources, said "could not possibly be the case." The intentions of actual donors at Bhārhut, Pauni, and very early Sri Lanka, whenever they are actually expressed, indicate that they all wished in one sense or another "to transfer the merit to another": to their parents, or to all beings, or to "all beings in the boundless universe." These same inscriptions give no indication that any other doctrine, textual or otherwise, was ever known at these sites.

A final example we might cite concerns the disposal of the dead. Here, the assigning of primary status to literary sources has not so much determined how the archaeological record should be read. It has, rather, determined that it should not be read at all.

We know from the scholarly secondary literature on literary sources the precise views of several obscure monk-scholars on exactly how many angels can dance on the head of an abhidharmic pin, and yet that same literature tells us nothing about how the Indian Buddhist community disposed of its dead. Even de La Vallée Poussin, in writing the entry entitled "Death and Disposal of the Dead (Buddhist)" for Hastings' *Encyclopaedia of Religion and Ethics,* was able to say almost nothing about disposal of the dead and filled the entry instead with scholastic definitions and descriptions of the process of death itself.[36] Again, the reasons for this are not difficult to determine. T. W. Rhys Davids says: "Nothing is known of any religious ceremony having been performed by the early Buddhists in India, whether the person deceased was a layman, or even a member of the Order. *The Vinaya Pitaka, which enters at so great length into all the details of the daily life of recluses, has no rules regarding the mode of treating the body of a deceased bhikkhu*" (emphasis added).[37] Rhys Davids, writing in 1900, makes it clear at least why nothing is known about the ritual disposal of the monastic dead: because the canonical literature known to him says nothing about it, the inference being, of course, that it therefore did not occur. But evidence that it did occur, that early Buddhist monastic communities were, in fact, preoccupied not only with disposing of their dead but with ritually and elaborately housing them as well, had been published nearly fifty years before Rhys Davids and sixty before de La Vallée Poussin. But this was only material, physical evidence of what actually occurred—archaeological evidence—not canonical evidence.

As early as 1854, Cunningham published the results of his cursory excavations of the Central Indian monastic sites around Sāñcī. Here already was clear evidence that indicated the existence of an extensive "cemetery" associated with the Buddhist monastic site at Bhojpur before the common era; here too at Sāñcī itself and at Sonārī and Andher was clear evidence for the elaborate housing and worshiping of the remains of the monastic dead.[38] The epigraphical material we have makes it clear that the construction and embellishing of the monumental reliquaries that contained these remains resulted from activity undertaken and paid for by a disproportionately large number of monks and nuns.[39] Only eight years later, in 1862, West published the first description of what he correctly identified as an extensive monastic cemetery that formed a part of the Buddhist monastic complex at Kānheri on the western coast of India.[40] In 1883 Burgess published a description of what is clearly another monastic cemetery in the midst of the monastic cave complex at Bhājā.[41] All of this evidence was available to both Rhys Davids and de La Vallée Poussin, but for them, it seems, Indian Buddhism and Indian Buddhist practice were contained in canonical texts. What

Indian Buddhists actually did was of no consequence. And since this was true, Buddhist archaeology and epigraphy also were of no consequence.

It would appear, then, that the ascription of primacy to textual sources in Buddhist studies not only effectively neutralizes the independence of archaeological and epigraphical sources as witnesses, it also effectively excludes what practicing Buddhists did and believed from the history of their own religion. We can see something more of this in, for example, another statement of de Jong's:

> Missionaries came into contact with Theravāda Buddhism in Ceylon, Burma, Siam, and Indochina and with different forms of Mahāyāna Buddhism in China and Japan. Their knowledge was based upon what they observed, and on discussions with Buddhist priests, but very rarely on the study of Buddhist literature itself. For these reasons it must have been very difficult to gain a clear notion of the main Buddhist ideas. A religion like Buddhism which is based upon principles which are very different from the guiding principles of Christianity cannot be understood without a thorough study of its scriptures.[42]

Without wanting in any sense to defend "missionaries," still there are a number of statements here that one would like to unpack, although we can deal with only a few of the most important. Notice only that it is again clear that, for this position, Buddhism is based on texts, that it can be really—do we dare to say "correctly"?—understood only by a study of its scriptures. The implicit judgment, of course, is that real Buddhism is textual Buddhism. Notice that "Buddhist ideas"—at least "correct" "Buddhist ideas"—apparently do not reside in what Buddhists actually did or in what their "priests" said in conversation. Notice that knowledge based on observation of actual behavior is not adequate. But if actual religious behavior cannot tell us about religious "ideas" then this, again of necessity, has radical implications for the uses of archaeology and epigraphy: since archaeology and epigraphy tell us what people actually did, they cannot tell us about "real" or "correct" religion. "Real" or "correct" religion, we are given to understand, and it is assumed, resides in scriptural texts, in formal doctrine.

It is precisely this curious assumption concerning the location of real religion that lies behind the equally curious history of the study of Indian Buddhism. But the fact that it is so firmly fixed in Buddhist studies, and was operational from the very beginning, and the fact that this is a discipline largely formed—if not fully founded—within the Western intellectual tradition, might well suggest that this assumption too is rooted there, and that it might occur elsewhere as well. And indeed it does. It is not only found in fact in a variety of similar disciplines, it is much more nakedly expressed in other fields. I cite here only three examples.

Charles Thomas, one of the foremost figures in the archaeology of Early Britain, starts his book entitled *The Early Christian Archaeology of North Britain* with some important observations. He says:

> It would now be possible to build, slowly, a reliable framework for the Christian events of those centuries [the fifth to the sixth], using no more than archaeological, artistic and architectural data . . . So much that we can today detect through the exercise of archaeological methods—the primacy of the Christian cemetery, the direct Mediterranean contacts, the introduction of full monasticism, and the interplay of art styles in different media—is nowhere explicitly described in what literature has survived. Conversely, much that *is* contained in literary guise alone is not, as yet, reflected in visible or tangible evidence from this period.[43]

These observations—all of which point toward the importance of archaeological remains as independent sources for the history of a religion—are, however, followed by an otherwise curious *apologia:*

> The Christian reader may find many features of insular Christianity explained below in terms of pagan or prehistoric monuments. . . . This requires, perhaps, a short clarification. The central message of the New Testament, that redemption and the means of grace were provided for us, the priesthood of all believers, through God's assumption of manhood and his crucifixion in the person of Jesus Christ, remains untouched. It is a message conveyed by the Gospels, by patristic writing, and additionally through the means of symbols; these apart, it does not and cannot require any material reflection. On the other hand, the outward and visible form assumed by humanly constructed burials or burial-grounds, by the commemoration of dead humans by living humans, by the retention of skeletal fragments and like trivia as relics, and by the building of structures specially designed for the ceremonies of worship, are man's accretions in response to this message. As such, they are independent of the Word, and for the most part devoid of direct biblical authority. They are no more than the handiworks of what Professor Mircea Eliade has called "religious man." They are, moreover, the Christian versions of certain ideas . . . which prove, upon examination, to occur widely and commonly in the outward manifestations of most known religions both past and present.[44]

Thomas' statements, taken from a work of historical archaeology published in 1971 by Oxford University Press, provide us with a startling example of how the assumption as to where religion is located neutralizes the significance of material remains and, *ipso facto,* the role of human behavior in the history of a religion. Thomas makes it very clear that because "they are independent of the Word, and for the most part devoid of direct biblical authority," the material remains that characterize the early *Christian* archaeology of North Britain—"the primacy of the *Christian* cemetery" (emphasis added), etc.—cannot be, paradoxically, in any way essentially and historically *Christian.* In fact, he hastens to assign them to some bloodless, ahistorical abstraction called "religious man" who seems to have behaved much the same everywhere and at all times.

Virtually the same position—though made even more explicit—is maintained by Snyder in an even more recent work on "the archaeological evidence of church life before Constantine." Snyder makes a number of moves that are similar to those of Thomas, although they are more neutral in their expression. He too seems anxious to make sure that "the central message of the New Testament . . . remains untouched," but he goes about it in a somewhat different way: "In this study," he says, "there is a resolve to use only archaeological data as derived from the early Christians themselves. For a study of the New Testament, there is no such possibility. It is a basic assumption of this study that there never will be such data available for the study of the New Testament period."[45] This, of course, rather effectively neutralizes the significance of any material remains that might turn up from early first century Capernaum, for example, simply because they could not be Christian.[46]

If this suggests to the disinterested reader that what early Christian people did or how they lived has nothing to do with the history of early Christianity, Snyder is quick to confirm this when he finally encounters material remains that are clearly "derived from the early Christians themselves" and therefore indicative of what they actually did: they are, in the end, also not allowed any significance for the history of Christianity.

Snyder first asserts that "the interpretive edge today rests with the Bonn School, which proposes to study early Christian remains contextually as a *Volkreligion.*" He then goes on to say:

> If archaeological data belong to the realm of popular religious practice, the interpreter, or historian, must state clearly how the evidence of archaeology does relate to the literary material, or, to state it another way, how the popular religion relates to ecclesiastical tradition. The issue raised belongs not to the disciplines of patristics, history, or theology, but to the sociology of religion.[47]

The position here is as straightforwardly contradictory as was that of Thomas. The historian must clearly relate the archaeological evidence to the literary material, but that relationship—"The issue raised"—does not belong to the discipline of history. Early Christian remains and archaeological data belong, according to Snyder, "to the realm of popular religious practice." They must represent then, at the very least, what early Christian people actually did. But again according to Snyder, the relationship of what early Christian people actually did, or actually believed, to "the literary material" falls outside the purview of the historian of Christianity. Christianity, like Buddhism, apparently only exists in texts.

It is here also worth noting incidentally that, as Thomas' reference to Eliade suggests, the same assumption concerning religion and where it is located occurs in widely different kinds of work. The fact that a scholar like Eliade, whose concerns differ widely from those of Thomas and Snyder, also implicitly accepts this is only confirmation of how pervasive and perverse it has been.

Eliade, in speaking about "the customs and beliefs of European peasants," says:

> It is true that most of these rural European populations have been Christianized for over a thousand years. But they succeeded in incorporating into their Christianity a considerable part of their pre-Christian religious heritage, which was of immemorial antiquity. It would be wrong to suppose that for this reason European peasants are not Christians. But we must recognize that their religion is not confined to the historical forms of Christianity. . . . We may speak of a primordial, ahistorical Christianity; becoming Christian, the European cultivators incorporated into their new faith the cosmic religion that they had preserved from prehistoric times.[48]

Although there is much here that would require clarification, for our purposes it is sufficient to notice that like Thomas and Snyder—but toward a very different end—Eliade separates what Christians actually did or do, their "customs and beliefs," from "the historical forms of Christianity." What European Christian peasants do or believe is excluded from the history of their own religion and is assigned to something called "ahistorical Christianity." Once again the implications are clear: the historical forms of Christianity—whatever they are, and these are assumed to be self-evident—have little to do with actual Christians.

It is a curious fact that Thomas, Snyder, and Eliade—although each deals with a different period, a different location, and different kinds of evidence—all end by doing the same thing: they all want to exclude in one way or another actual Christian behavior and belief from the history of Christianity. Thomas wants to assign it to generalized "religious man"; Snyder assigns it to "popular religious practice," the domain of the sociologist of religion; and Eliade attributes it to "immemorial antiquity" or "ahistorical Christianity." None of them will admit it into the history of Christianity, and this can only be because they all share a common conception of where "essential," "real," or true Christianity is located. For them it appears to reside in texts. It would appear, then, that Buddhist scholars, archaeologists of early Britain, and historians of religion are all working from the same assumption as to where religion is located. But at least in its origin, this may not be an assumption at all.

Although most Buddhist scholars, archaeologists, or historians would probably resist the suggestion, this assumption in regard to the sources for the understanding of religions looks, on closer inspection, very much like it might itself be a religious or theological position. Embedded, for example, in apparently neutral archaeological and historical method might very well be a decidedly nonneutral and narrowly limited Protestant assumption as to where religion is actually located.[49]

The methodological position frequently taken by modern Buddhist scholars, archaeologists, and historians of religion looks, in fact, uncannily like the position taken by a variety of early Protestant reformers who were attempting to define and establish the locus of "true religion." The unknown author of the tract "On the Old and the New God" proposes, according to Eire, "that Christians should not seek religion in outward things, but rather in scripture."[50] Karlstadt, again according to Eire, "began to strike out against the prevailing religious externalism of his day, hoping he would be able to reassert the primacy of the Word." His position "is clearly revealed in this dictum: Only the Spirit vivifies, and the Spirit works through the Word, not through material objects. 'The Word of God is spiritual, and it alone is useful to believers.' "[51] In his *Commentary on True and False Religion,* Zwingli declared that "we ought to be taught by the word of God externally, and by the spirit internally, those things that have to do with piety, and not by sculpture wrought by the artist's hands."[52] Calvin too saw material things—"images and like things"—not as integral and vital parts of "religion," but as "innumerable mockeries . . . which pervert religion" and must be excluded from it. They are not "spiritually ordained by the Word."[53]

There are other and probably better passages that could be cited, but the point at least, I think, is clear: there is a remarkable similarity between the value assigned literary sources in modern historical and archaeological studies and the argument of Protestant reformers concerning the location of true religion. This suggests, at least, the distinct possibility that historical and archaeological method—if not the history of religions as a whole—represents the direct historical continuation of Reformation theological values; it further suggests that if Karlstadt's hope was to "reassert the primacy of the Word," he may have succeeded in doing just that in some very unlikely and unforeseen ways.

There are other considerations that point in the same direction. It is not just the assigning of primacy to literary materials in the study of religion in both modern archaeological and historical studies that shows several signs of possibly being rooted in sixteenth-century Protestant tracts. The concomitant disinclination of archaeologists and historians to consider material remains as independent, critical sources for the history of a religion also looks very much like a more recent manifestation of the sixteenth-century Protestant distrust and devaluation of actual religious and historical human behavior. Sixteenth-century material objects—reliquaries, shrines, and images—were for Protestant reformers apparently irrefutable evidence of what Christian people were actually doing.

They refer to them constantly in their polemics: Calvin, in fact, drew up "an inventory of relics" to show, from his point of view, just how bad things were.[54] This inventory, ironically, is an extremely valuable historical document because it allows us to see what was actually occurring during his lifetime in specific geographical locations. But what is a boon for us was a bane for Calvin. In fact, the problem for the reformers was, in part at least, precisely what was actually occurring and what had been historically practiced. Given the nature of the case they were trying to advance, they did not—more pointedly, could not—allow actual religious practice to have any meaningful place in defining the nature of true religion. To have done so would have been to concede to their perceived opponents the validity of a substantial portion of the argument from "tradition." Proponents of this new and historically peculiar conception of religion, therefore, were of necessity forced to systematically devalue and denigrate what religious people actually did and to deny that it had any place in true religion.[55] This devaluation, not surprisingly but in fact almost obsessively, focused on material objects. The religious power and importance of these objects are, however, only underlined by the fact that they frequently had to be forcefully removed and destroyed and always had to be fulsomely denounced with an otherwise curious ardor. We, it seems, may have inherited both tendencies: the unwillingness to allow actual practice a meaningful place in the definition of religion and the devaluation of any sources that express it.

Merely stating the striking similarity between the arguments of sixteenth-century Protestant reformers and the assumptions of modern Buddhist scholars, archaeologists, and historians of religion, does not, of course, prove anything. It does, however, suggest some possibilities. It is possible that the curious history of the study of Indian Buddhism is neither curious nor unique. It begins to appear as only one instance in which a particular assumption concerning the location of religion has dictated and determined the value assigned to various sources.[56] It is possible that what originated as a sixteenth-century Protestant polemical conception of where "true" religion is located has been so thoroughly absorbed into the Western intellectual tradition that its polemical and theological origins have been forgotten and now it is taken too often entirely as a given.[57] It is possible then, that it is this conception that has determined the history of the study of Indian Buddhism and that—as a consequence—our picture of Indian Buddhism may reflect more of our own religious history and values than the history and values of Indian Buddhism. It is possible, finally, that the old and ongoing debate between archaeology and textual studies is not—as is frequently assumed—a debate about sources. It may rather be a debate about where religion as an object of investigation is to be located. It is possible, perhaps, that the Reformation is not over after all.

Notes

1. There is, of course, no single, systematic survey of Buddhist archaeological remains in India. The best attempt so far is D. Mitra, *Buddhist Monuments* (Calcutta: 1971). It, however, was not only not intended to be exhaustive but is now also some twenty years out of date. For inscriptional remains we have, for the period up to 1910, H. Lüders, *A List of Brahmi Inscriptions from the Earliest Times to about* A.D. *400 with the Exception of Those of Aśoka,* Appendix to *EI* 10 (Calcutta: 1912). It is, though, by now badly outdated and, as its title indicates, does not list material beyond "about A.D. 400." Both more comprehensive and much more recent is Shizutani Masao, *Indo bukkyō himei mokuroku* (Catalog of Indian Buddhist Inscriptions) (Kyoto: 1979), but it too is already dated and contains serious omissions—cf. Shizutani's listings of the Kharoṣṭhī inscriptions, e.g., with those in G. Fussman, "Gāndhārī écrite, gāndhārī parlée," *Dialectes dans les littératures indo-aryennes,* ed. C. Caillat (Paris: 1989) 444–451. Shizutani is especially unreliable now for important sites like Mathurā (only one of the finds from Govindnagar is included) and like Amarāvatī (none of the early inscriptions brought to light in the "clearance-operation" in 1958–1959, e.g., are included; see A. Ghosh, "The Early Phase of the Stupa at Amaravati, Southeast India," *Ancient Ceylon* 3 [1979] 97–103).

2. On the curious fact, e.g., that a considerable number of Buddhist inscriptions were never intended to be seen, let alone read, see H. Lüders, "The Manikiala Inscription," *JRAS* (1909) 660; S. Konow, *Kharoshṭhī Inscriptions with the Exception of Those of Aśoka,* Corpus Inscriptionum Indicarum, Vol. II, Pt. 1 (Calcutta: 1929) 31; A. V. Naik, "Inscriptions of the Deccan: An Epigraphical Survey (*circa* 300 B.C.–1300 A.D.)," *Bulletin of the Deccan College Research Institute* 11 (1948) 3–4; etc.

3. This point in regard to archaeological evidence in general has been made a number of times. See, for example, R. Grenet, *Les pratiques funeraires dans l'asie centrale sedentaire de la conquete grecque à l'islamisation* (Paris: 1984) 7, who, in referring to Zoroastrianism, contrasts "canonical or clerical texts—always untiringly scrutinized although the narrowness of the milieux which produced them is ever more clearly evident," with archaeological materials "which allow us the most direct access to the religion as it was lived and practised by all social classes." Much the same has also been said of epigraphical sources. For example, L. H. Kant, in speaking of Jewish inscriptions from the Greco-Roman world, says "inscriptions, in contrast to most other written records, reflect a broad spectrum of society—from nearly illiterate poor, who wrote many of the Roman catacomb inscriptions, to the apparently wealthy patrons of funerary poetry and from tradesmen such as shoemakers and perfume sellers to educated persons such as rabbis and disciples of sages. It is also striking that, unlike many written texts, the inscriptions express for us religious views that have not been filtered by a subsequent normative literary tradition" ("Jewish Inscriptions in Greek and Latin," *Aufstieg und Niedergang der römischen Welt: Geschichte und Kultur Roms in Spiegel der Neueren Forschung,* Teil 2, *Principat,* Band 20, Halbband 2, ed. W. Haase [Berlin: 1987] 674). Likewise, in regard to "les inscriptions latines chrétiennes," Sanders has said: "De la sorte, les inscriptions nous renseignent aussi de manière privilégiée sur la masse, sur la majorité oubliée par la littérature à hauts talons, le majorité silencieuse, l'homme de la rue, sa vie privée, son imbrication dans son monde à lui, telle qu'elle fut définie par les coordonnées du temps, de l'espace, des conditions sociales, du climat religieux et émotionnel . . ." (G. Sanders, "Les chrétiens face à l'épigraphie funéraire latine," *Assimilation et résistance à la culture gréco-romaine dans le monde ancien: Travaux du VIe congrès international d' études classiques,*

ed. D. M. Pippidi [Paris: 1976] 285). For the points of view represented in Indian Buddhist inscriptions and the role of the "lettré," whether "moine ou sculpteur," see the important remarks in G. Fussman's review of *Epigraphical Hybrid Sanskrit,* by Th. Damsteegt, *JA* (1980) 423–424. It should be noted, finally, that inscriptions are, of course, written sources, but they are most easily and clearly distinguishable from literary sources by the simple fact that they were not meant to be circulated.

4. For some representative recent views, see K. R. Norman, "The Value of the Pali Tradition," *Jagajjyoti Buddha Jayanti Annual* (Calcutta: 1984) 1–9. He points out that it is now known that "the Pali canon is a translation from some earlier tradition" (4), that, in fact, "all traditions which we possess have been translated at least once" (5). See also L. O. Gómez, "Buddhism in India," *Encyclopedia of Religion,* ed. M. Eliade (London: 1987) 352ff ("Textual sources are late, dating at the very least five hundred years after the death of the Buddha"); G. Schopen, "Two Problems in the History of Indian Buddhism" Ch. II below, 23–25.

5. This, ironically, is especially true for the so-called early canonical literature. For Pāli, see O. von Hinüber, "Pāli Manuscripts of Canonical Texts from North Thailand—a Preliminary Report," *Journal of the Siam Society* 71 (1983) 75–88 ("most of the surviving [Pāli] manuscript material is hardly older than the late 18th century" [78]); and the material cited in G. Schopen, "The *Stūpa* Cult and the Extant Pāli *Vinaya,*" Ch. V below, n. 23. For Central Asian Sanskrit material, see L. Sander, *Paläographisches zu den Sanskrithandschriften der Berliner Turfansammlung,* Verzeichnis der orientalischen Handschriften in Deutschland, Supplementband 8 (Wiesbaden: 1968) 51 ("Unter den in die Tausende gehenden, von den vier preussischen Expeditionen [1902–1914] im Norden Ostturkistans gefundenen fragmentarischen Sanskrithandschriften gibt es, soweit mir bekannt ist, nur sieben mit den charakteristischen Merkmalen der Kuṣāṇa-Brāhmī," and so on).

6. I. B. Horner, *Women under Primitive Buddhism* (London: 1930) xx: "Still another inherent difficulty in dealing with the Pāli texts arises from the various editions, glosses, and revisions which they have undergone at the hands of the monks"; etc.

7. A. K. Warder, e.g., starts his discussion of the Pāli Canon as a "historical record" by saying "the Buddhists . . . were ready to turn everything to account in developing and popularizing their ideas and in presenting a comprehensive 'world view,' " and ends it by saying: "The bias of the repeaters [of the canon] sometimes intrudes itself, often very clumsily"; see "The Pali Canon and Its Commentaries as an Historical Record," *Historians of India, Pakistan and Ceylon,* ed. C. H. Philips (London: 1961) 46–47.

8. For the history of the study of the archaeological and epigraphical material, see D. K. Chakrabarti, *A History of Indian Archeology: From the Beginning to 1947* (New Delhi: 1988); there is also some interesting material for the earliest period in P. Mitter, *Much Maligned Monsters: History of European Reactions to Indian Art* (Oxford: 1977); and some useful data in A. Imam, *Sir Alexander Cunningham and the Beginnings of Indian Archaeology* (Dacca: 1966). For the study of literary sources, the most recent and reliable work is J. W. de Jong, *A Brief History of Buddhist Studies in Europe and America,* 2nd rev. ed. (Delhi: 1987); see also H. de Lubac, *La recontre du bouddhisme et de l'occident* (Paris: 1952); R. Schwab, *The Oriental Renaissance: Europe's Rediscovery of India and the East, 1680–1880,* trans. G. Patterson-Black and V. Reinking (New York: 1984); W. Halbfass, *India and Europe: An Essay in Understanding* (Albany, N.Y.: 1988).

9. J. W. de Jong, "The Study of Buddhism: Problems and Perspectives," *Studies in Indo-Asian Art and Culture,* Vol. IV, ed. P. Ratnam (New Delhi: 1975) 21, and *A Brief History of Buddhist Studies in Europe and America,* 20.

10. De Jong, "The Study of Buddhism," 14.

11. Archaeologists themselves have contributed heavily to the currency of this view; see G. Daniel, *A Short History of Archaeology* (London: 1981) 13; J. A. Alexander, "The Archaeological Recognition of Religion: The Examples of Islam in Africa and 'Urnfields' in Europe," *Space, Hierarchy and Society,* ed. B. C. Burnham and J. Kingsbury, British Archaeological Reports, No. 559 (Oxford: 1979) 215; cf. D. P. Dymond, *Archaeology and History: A Plea for Reconciliation* (London: 1974).

12. Epigraphical evidence, at least, does not support the idea that Buddhist literature was widely known in actual Buddhist communities, but in fact points in the opposite direction; see, most recently, G. Schopen, "A Verse from the Bhadracarīpraṇidhāna in a 10th Century Inscription Found at Nālandā," *JIABS* 12.1 (1989) 149–157, and the sources cited in the notes there.

13. In speaking about "early Christian archaeology," G. F. Snyder refers to "three mistaken assumptions" about "sacred" literature: "It is assumed the literature represents rather accurately the historical situation when actually it may have a tendentious purpose. . . . It is assumed the literature speaks *cum solo voce* when actually other voices have been ignored, repressed, or assimilated. . . . It is assumed the literature represents a reflective or literary level of popular religion whereas actually literature and practice often stand in tension with each other" (*Ante Pacem: Archaeological Evidence of Church Life before Constantine* [Macon, Ga.: 1985] 8). Snyder's formulation is, of course, suggestive of what has been assumed in Buddhist studies as well; but cf. below pp. 11–12.

14. It is worth noting that even those South Asian Buddhist literary sources that have been taken to most closely approximate "historical" documents in our sense of the term were intended, by their authors or transmitters, to fulfill a very different function. The chapter colophons of the *Mahāvaṃsa,* e.g., uniformly say: Here ends such and such a chapter "in the *Mahāvaṃsa,* compiled for the faith and exhilaration of good men" (*sujanappasādasaṃvegatthāya*). See W. Geiger, *Mahāvaṃsa* (London: 1908) 11, 15, 20, etc.; see also the opening exhortatory verses in H. Oldenberg, *The Dīpavaṃsa: An Ancient Buddhist Historical Record* (London and Edinburgh: 1879) 13.

15. So R. C. Zaehner in his foreword to P. Olivelle's *The Origin and Early Development of Buddhist Monasticism* (Colombo: 1974).

16. G. Bühler, "Votive Inscriptions from the Sānchi Stūpas," *EI* 2 (1894) 93; cf. J. Marshall, A. Foucher, and N. G. Majumdar, *The Monuments of Sāñchī,* Vol. I (Delhi: 1940) 34 and n. 2.

17. H. Lüders, *Bharhut Inscriptions,* Corpus Inscriptionum Indicarum, Vol. II, Pt. 2, rev. by E. Waldschmidt and M. A. Mehendale (Ootacamund: 1963) 2. Like Bühler before him, and in similar terms, Lüders points out that a comparison of Buddhist with Jain inscriptions makes it very difficult to avoid the fact that, in Buddhist inscriptions, the monks themselves appear as donors—they are not acting as organizers or agents of others: "The wording of the Bhārh[ut] inscriptions refers to the Buddhist clergyman in such a way, as if he himself had made the donation" (2).

18. G. Fussman, "Une inscription Kharoṣṭhī à Haḍḍa," *BEFEO* 56 (1969) 8–9.

19. J. Marshall, *Taxila: An Illustrated Account of Archaeological Excavations Carried out at Taxila under the Orders of the Government of India between the Years 1913 and 1934,* Vol. I (Cambridge: 1951) 240. Such hoards are, in fact, found in Buddhist monasteries that are very much earlier than "the early medieval period"; see R. B. D. R. Sahni, *Archaeological Remains and Excavations at Bairat* (Jaipur: 1937) 21–22; D. B. Diskalkar, "Excavations at Kasrawad," *IHQ* 25 (1949) 12ff; etc.

20. W. Spink, "Ajanta: A Brief History," *Aspects of Indian Art: Papers Presented in a Symposium at the Los Angeles County Museum of Art, October 1970,* ed. P. Pal (Leiden: 1972) 51. For yet other examples, see D. D. Kosambi, "Dhenukākaṭa," *JASBom* 30.2 (1955) 52–53; R. A. L. H. Gunawardana, *Robe and Plough: Monasticism and Economic Interest in Sri Lanka* (Tucson: 1979) 81–86; N. A. Falk, "The Case of the Vanishing Nun: The Fruits of Ambivalence in Ancient Indian Buddhism," *Unspoken Worlds: Women's Religious Lives in Non-Western Cultures,* ed. N. A. Falk and R. M. Gross (San Francisco: 1980) 223, n. 2; H. P. Ray, *Monastery and Guild: Commerce under the Sātavāhanas* (Delhi: 1986) 104.

21. Compare W. Wassilieff, "Le bouddhisme dans son plein développement d'après les vinayas," *RHR* 34 (1896) 321: "pour le vie en communauté, même dans les autres religions, les règles établies ne peuvent sortir du cadre connu."

22. See, for the sake of convenience, C. S. Prebish, *Buddhist Monastic Discipline: The Sanskrit Prātimokṣa Sūtras of the Mahāsāṃghikas and Mūlasarvāstivādins* (University Park, Pa.: 1975) 13–14, 70–71; I. B. Horner, "The Pattern of the Nissaggiyas," *IHQ* 16 (1940) 268–291; M. Wijayaratna, *Le moine bouddhiste selon les textes du Theravāda* (Paris: 1983) 93–104.

23. R. Lingat, "Vinaya et droit laïque: Études sur les conflits de la loi religieuse et de la loi laïque dans l'indochine hinayaniste," *BEFEO* 37 (1937) 415–477, esp. 431ff; cf. H. Oldenberg, *Buddha: His Life, His Doctrine, His Order,* trans. W. Hoey (London: 1882) 355 and n.

24. J. Ph. Vogel, "Prakrit Inscriptions from a Buddhist Site at Nagarjunikonda," *EI* 20 (1929–1930) 22–23.

25. A. H. Longhurst, *The Buddhist Antiquities of Nagarjunakonda, Madras Presidency,* MASI, No. 54 (Delhi: 1938) 10; cf. I. K. Sarma, "A Coin Mould-Piece from Nāgārjuna-koṇḍa: New Light on the Silver Coinage of the Sātavāhanas," *Journal of the Economic and Social History of the Orient* 16 (1973) 89–106, which deals with an even earlier mold from the site.

26. K. D. Bajpai, "Authority of Minting Coins in Ancient India," *Journal of the Numismatic Society of India* 25 (1963) 17–21; D. C. Sircar, "Note on Chinchani Plate of Krishna III," *EI* 37 (1968) 277–278; etc.

27. Evidence for the manufacture of coins at Buddhist monastic sites is both early and widespread. For such evidence at Kasrawad, see Diskalkar, *IHQ* 25, 15; for Nālandā, B. Kumar, *Archaeology of Pataliputra and Nalanda* (Delhi: 1987) 212; S. S. P. Sarasvati, *Coinage in Ancient India: A Numismatic, Archaeochemical and Metallurgical Study of Ancient Indian Coins,* Vol. I (Delhi: 1986) 202ff; and so on.

28. *Histoire du bouddhisme indien,* 456. I have elsewhere discussed this same passage from a somewhat different point of view; see my "Two Problems in the History of Indian Buddhism," Ch. II below, 41–42.

29. There has been very little discussion of the assumptions and method that lie behind this important book. The only serious attempt to get at some of the problems involved is, as far as I know, M. Pye, "Comparative Hermeneutics in Religion," *The Cardinal Meaning: Essays in Comparative Hermeneutics, Buddhism and Christianity,* ed. M. Pye and R. Morgan (The Hague: 1973) 1–58, esp. 31ff. At least some of the problems, moreover, appear to be directly related to Lamotte's declared intentions, which, on the surface, appear to be mutually contradictory. He first says, "Notre premier souci a été de replacer le bouddhisme dans le cadre historique qui lui manquait, de le retirer du monde des idées où il se confinait volontairement pour le ramener sur terre," but then says: "En laissant au merveilleux la place qu'il a toujours occupée dans les sources, on

pense donner un reflet plus fidèle de la mentalité des disciples du Buddha. C'est cette mentalité qui constitue l'objet propre de notre enquête et non une fuyante et insaisissable certitude historique" (Lamotte, vi, x). Note that H. Durt has already pointed out that "certes, l'*Histoire du bouddhisme indien* n'est pas une 'histoire des mentalités' au sense contemporain du terme" in "Étienne Lamotte, 1903–1983," *BEFEO* 74 (1985) 14.

30. *Histoire du bouddhisme indien,* 456.

31. Even the most steadfastly conservative have had to admit this in regard to contemporary Buddhism. See, for example, R. F. Gombrich, *Precept and Practice: Traditional Buddhism in the Rural Highlands of Ceylon* (Oxford: 1971) 243: "The canonical theory of *karma* survives intact—cognitively; affectively its rigour is sometimes avoided. Similarly, though the doctrine of *anatta* can be salvaged by the claim that the personality continuing through a series of births has as much reality as the personality within one life, *prārthanā* for happy rebirths and the transfer of merit to dead relatives show that the *anatta* doctrine has no more affective immediacy with regard to the next life than with regard to this, and that belief in personal survival after death is a fundamental feature of Sinhalese Buddhism in practice." Interestingly, something very like this had been pointed out more than a hundred years ago; see P. E. de Foucaux, *Le Lalitavistara: Devéloppement des jeux, contenant l'histoire du Bouddha Çakya-muni, depuis sa naissance jusqu' à sa prèdication,* Vol. I (Paris: 1884) xvi, n. 2, and xvii, nn. 1 and 2. For the Hindu context, see, among many possibilities, U. Sharma, "Theodicy and the Doctrine of Karma," *Man* 8 (1973) 347–364.

32. Lüders, *Bharhut Inscriptions,* 55 (A 108).

33. V. B. Kolte, "Brahmi Inscriptions from Pauni," *EI* 38 (1969) 174 (D); S. B. Deo and J. P. Joshi, *Pauni Excavation (1969–1970)* (Nagpur: 1972) 38, no. 2.

34. S. Paranavitana, *Inscriptions of Ceylon,* Vol. I, *Containing Cave Inscriptions from 3rd Century* B.C. *to 1st Century* A.C. *and Other Inscriptions in the Early Brahmi Script* (Ceylon: 1970) no. 34; see also lii–liii.

35. Paranavitana, *Inscriptions of Ceylon,* Vol. I, nos. 338–341; see also lii–liii.

36. L. de La Vallée Poussin, "Death and Disposal of the Dead (Buddhist)," *Encyclopaedia of Religion and Ethics,* ed. J. Hastings, Vol. IV (Edinburgh: 1911) 446–449.

37. T. W. Rhys Davids, *Buddhist Suttas,* Sacred Books of the East, Vol. XI (Oxford: 1900) xliv–xlv.

38. A. Cunningham, *The Bhilsa Topes: Or, Buddhist Monuments of Central India* (London: 1854) 211–220, Bhojpur—at which *Stūpa* 8c, e.g., contained numerous large bones; 184–189, Sāñcī, *Stūpa* no. 2; 203–205, Sonārī, *Stūpa* no. 2; 223–226, Andher, *Stūpas* nos. 2 and 3.

39. This is beyond doubt, for example, in regard to Sāñcī *Stūpa* no. 2; see Schopen, "The *Stūpa* Cult and the Extant Pāli *Vinaya,*" Ch. V below, 92 and n. 32. M. Bénisti has recently argued that this *stūpa* is older even than Bhārhut in "Observations concernant le stūpa no. 2 de Sāñcī," *BEI* 4 (1986) 165–170.

40. W. West, "Description of Some of the Kanheri Topes," *JBomBRAS* 6 (1862) 116–120; S. Gokhale, "The Memorial Stūpa Gallery at Kanheri," *Indian Epigraphy: Its Bearing on the History of Art,* ed. F. M. Asher and G. S. Gai (New Delhi: 1985) 55–59; etc.

41. J. Burgess, *Report on the Buddhist Cave Temples and Their Inscriptions,* Archaeological Survey of Western India, Vol. IV (London: 1883) 7; see Mitra, *Buddhist Monuments,* 153.

42. De Jong, *A Brief History of Buddhist Studies in Europe and America,* 11.

43. C. Thomas, *The Early Christian Archaeology of North Britain* (London: 1971) 1.

44. Ibid., 3–4.

45. Snyder, *Ante Pacem,* 10.

46. This same assumption also makes it impossible for archaeological investigation to critically comment on the nature of the New Testament as a historical document; cf. the remarks in E. M. Meyers and J. F. Strange, *Archaeology, Rabbis and Early Christianity* (Nashville: 1981) 58–59, on the absence of a first-century synagogue at Capernaum in spite of the fact that Mark 1:21 places one there. For other problems concerning Capernaum in the New Testament, see J. Blenkinsopp, "The Literary Evidence," in V. Tzaferis, *Excavations at Capernaum, Vol. I, 1978–1982* (Winona Lake, Ind.: 1989) 201ff.

47. Snyder, 7, 9.

48. M. Eliade, *The Sacred and the Profane: The Nature of Religion* (San Diego: 1959) 164.

49. "Protestant" is used here in the broadest and most general sense, and the assumption involved is probably only meaningfully so-called in regard to its origins. It has, it seems, been so generalized and fully assimilated into Western intellectual and cultural values that, in its present form, it is probably most simply characterized as "Western." Elements of this assumption were, of course, much older. There was, to begin with, the "Second Commandment" and its long and convoluted history; see J. Gutmann, "The 'Second Commandment' and the Image in Judaism," *Hebrew Union College Annual* 32 (1961) 161–174, and "Deuteronomy: Religious Reformation or Iconoclastic Revolution?" in *The Image and the Word: Confrontations in Judaism, Christianity and Islam,* ed. J. Gutmann (Missoula, Mont.: 1977) 5–25. There was Vigilantius, of whom Saint Jerome, at least, was not fond and the later Iconoclastic controversies; see W. H. Fremantle, *The Principal Works of St. Jerome,* Select Library of Nicene and Post-Nicene Fathers of the Christian Church, Ser. 2, Vol. 4 (Grand Rapids, Mich.: 1983) 417–423, and, among an immense bibliography, D. J. Sahas, *Icon and Logos: Sources in Eighth-Century Iconoclasm* (Toronto: 1986) along with the select bibliography given there. There was Guibert of Nogent's *De Pignoribus sanctorum;* see K. Guth, *Guibert von Nogent und die hochmittelalterliche Kritik an der Reliquienverehrung* (Ottobeuren: 1970), but see also J. F. Benton's discussion of Guibert's character in *Self and Society in Medieval France: The Memoirs of Abbot Guibert of Nogent* (New York: 1970) 1–33; and even Erasmus in *Ten Colloquies,* trans. C. R. Thompson (Indianapolis: 1979) 56–91. But none of these in and of themselves had lasting cultural influence, and almost all are more significant in retrospect—that is to say, in the way in which they were perceived and used during and after the Reformation.

50. C. M. N. Eire, *War against the Idols: The Reformation of Worship from Erasmus to Calvin* (Cambridge: 1986) 76.

51. Ibid., 55, 59.

52. Ulrich Zwingli, *Commentary on True and False Religion,* ed. S. M. Jackson and C. N. Heller (Durham, N.C.: 1981) 331–332.

53. "The Lausanne Articles," No. 7, *Calvin: Theological Treatises,* ed. J. K. S. Reid, Library of Christian Classics, Vol. 22 (Philadelphia: 1954) 36.

54. "An Admonition, Showing the Advantages which Christendom might Derive from an Inventory of Relics," *Tracts Relating to the Reformation by John Calvin,* trans. H. Beveridge (Edinburgh: 1844) 289–341.

55. This can be illustrated by a number of passages from the *Institutes of the Christian Religion by John Calvin,* ed. J. Allen, Vol. II, 4th ed. (Philadelphia: 1843). In reference to the intercession of saints, 3.20.21: "Therefore, since the Scripture calls us away from all others to Christ alone . . . it would be a proof of great stupidity, not to say insanity, to be so desirous of procuring an admission by the saints, as to be seduced from him, without whom they have no access themselves. But that this has been practised in some

ages, and is now practised wherever Popery prevails, who can deny?"; 4.9.14: "Of purgatory, the intercession of saints, auricular confession, and similar fooleries, the Scriptures contain not a single syllable. But, because all these things have been sanctioned by the authority of councils, or, to speak more correctly, have been admitted into the general belief and practice, therefore every one of them is to be taken for an interpretation of Scripture"—a position Calvin, of course, denies; 4.10.1: "Whatever edicts have been issued by men respecting the worship of God, independently of His word, it has been customary to call *human traditions.* Against such laws we contend."

56. This, of course, is not to deny that other factors were involved. P. C. Almond, for example, has recently discussed the textualization of Buddhism as an instrument of colonialist ideology: a "Victorian Buddhism . . . constructed from textual sources increasingly located in and therefore regulated by the West" (*The British Discovery of Buddhism* [Cambridge: 1988] 24ff). A striking example of the effects of this textualization may be seen in S. Hardy, *A Manual of Buddhism in Its Modern Development,* 2d ed. (London: 1880) 412: "The difficulties attendant upon this peculiar dogma [the textual conception of *anatta*] may be seen in the fact that it is almost universally repudiated. Even the sramana priests, at one time, denied it; but when the passages teaching it were pointed out to them in their own sacred books, they were obliged to acknowledge that it is a tenet of their religion." See also L. Rocher, "Max Müller and the Veda," *Mélanges Armand Abel,* ed. A. Destrée, Vol. III (Leiden: 1978) 221–235. That the textualization of Hinduism by Indian "reformers"—in imitation of the Protestant missionary model of religion—had the same consequences for the evaluation of Indian religious practice as the Protestant location of religion had had on the evaluation of European practice, at least at the intellectual level, is painfully clear from a number of sources. Rāmmohan Roy said, e.g., "My constant reflections on the inconvenient, or rather injurious rites introduced by the peculiar practice of Hindoo idolatry which more than any other pagan worship, destroys the texture of society, together with compassion for my countrymen, have compelled me to use every possible effort to awaken them from their dream of error; and *by making them acquainted with their Scriptures,* enable them to contemplate with true devotion the unity and omnipresence of nature's God"; quoted in G. Richards, *A Source-Book of Modern Hinduism* (London: 1985) 5 (my emphasis); see also 6–9, 24, 30–33, 45, 48–50, etc. It is undoubtedly and notoriously difficult to separate the religious and the political in colonialist ideology, but since both were also at work in founding the Archaeological Survey of India (Imam [n. 8 above] 40–41), the ideological concern could not itself have been a sufficient cause for the dominance of the textual orientation.

57. This, again, is not to say that there were not powerful competing conceptions, but only to say that they did not culturally win. Early on, the "Catholic" conception held its own and produced, as a consequence, some important scholarly works: "Catholic scholars tended to anchor their investigation of Christian religious observance in ancient tradition. It was the study of this tradition that inspired the monumental and often reprinted *Annales Ecclesiastici* and the work on the Roman martyrs by Cesare Baronio, as well as Bosio's *Roma sotterranea,* the first major archaeological account of the Roman catacombs. On the other hand, when Protestants discussed the practice of Christian piety, they most often appealed to reason and to theological and philosophical principles. . . . In the words of John Calvin, a Christian should have 'no use [for] place apart from the doctrine of godliness' which could be taught anywhere at all"; see S. MacCormack, "Loca Sancta: The Organization of Sacred Topography in Late Antiquity," *The Blessings of Pilgrimage,* ed. R. Ousterhout (Urbana, Ill., and Chicago: 1990) 8–9. But recent scholar-

ship, which has tended to see "the Counter-Reformation and the Protestant Reformation as analogous social and religious processes" (so Badone in her introduction to *Religious Orthodoxy and Popular Faith in European Society,* ed. E. Badone [Princeton, N.J.: 1990] 12), has also pointed clearly to the strong textualizing responses in the former; so J. Delumeau, in *La Catholicisme entre Luther et Voltaire* (Paris: 1971): "De l'extraordinaire intérêt qu'on marqua pour les choses de la religion, au moins dans le public qui savait lire, témoignent les statistiques concernant l'édition . . . l'histoire religieuse et celle des mentalités ne peuvent négliger ce fait quantitatif: jamais autant les livres de spiritualité—souvent de petits formats et en langue vulgaire—, jamais autant d'éloges de la vierge n'avaient été mis en circulation" (84); "Surtout, l'époque de l'humanisme vit l'essor de la théologie *positive* . . . qui est l'étude de l'Ecriture, aidée par les interprétations des Pères et des conciles" (85); "En 1654, Godeau, évêque de Vence, donna dans ses mandements des listes de livres à lire à ses prêtres. En 1658 l'archevêque de Sens, Godrin, demanda à ses curés de se procurer 47 ouvrages qu'ils devaient, le cas échéant, présenter lors des visites pastorales et, parmi eux, une Bible, le catéchisme romain" (271); cf. also B. Baroni, *La contre-réforme devant la Bible: La question biblique* (Lausanne: 1943). Delumeau's remarks raise, as well, the question of the sheer influence of the development of printing on the location of religion in texts, and it undoubtedly played a role. But any argument contending that printing in itself is a sufficient explanation must take into account the fact that printing served a very different function in the Far East—especially in the earlier periods. There, sacred texts were printed not so they could be read, but so they could empower sacred objects. The earliest extant examples of printing in Japan, e.g., contain "versions of Sanskrit charms [*dhāraṇīs*] transliterated into Chinese characters," and, even if they had been seen, they would have had little or no literal meaning for a literate Japanese. But they, in fact, were never intended to be seen. They were meant to be inserted into miniature *stūpas;* see J. Needham, *Science and Civilization in China,* Vol. V, *Chemistry and Chemical Technology,* Pt. 1, *Paper and Printing,* by Tsien Tsuen-hsuin (Cambridge: 1985) 336–337; see also 321–322.

* * *

[For some further observations on the early inscriptions from Sāñcī see now: G. Schopen, "What's in a Name: The Religious Function of the Early Donative Inscriptions," *Unseen Presence: The Buddha and Sanchi,* ed. V. Dehejia (Bombay: 1996) 58–73. For monks and private property, see Schopen, "Monastic Law Meets the Real World: A Monk's Continuing Right to Inherit Family Property in Classical India," *History of Religions* 35 (1995) 101–123. For Buddhist disposal of the dead, see chs. VII, IX, and X below.]

CHAPTER II

Two Problems in the History of Indian Buddhism

The Layman/Monk Distinction and the Doctrines of the Transference of Merit

I.

IN AN AREA like Indian Buddhist doctrinal history, where there is constant discussion but little proof, it might sometimes be useful if we try to draw up lists of what we actually know. Such lists might be even more useful if we distinguish clearly, in so far as this is possible, what we know from what we have conjectured or reconstructed or hypothesized. This is what I have tried to do here in regard to two particular problems: the problem of the Layman/Monk Distinction in Indian Buddhism, and the problem of the Doctrine, or Doctrines, of the Transference of Merit in Indian Buddhism. If, however, we begin with the purpose of limiting ourselves to what we can actually know in regard to these problems, then the conventional evaluation and use of literary sources in discussions of Buddhist doctrinal history becomes, in fact, our first problem, and it is here that we must begin.

II.

We know, and have known for some time, that the Pāli canon as we have it—and it is generally conceded to be our oldest source—cannot be taken back further than the last quarter of the first century B.C.E., the date of the Alu-vihāra redaction, the earliest redaction that we can have some knowledge of,[1] and that—for a critical history—it can serve, at the very most, only as a source for the Buddhism of this period. But we also know that even this is problematic

Originally published in *Studien zur Indologie und Iranistik* 10 (1985):9–47. Reprinted with stylistic changes with permission of *Studien zur Indologie und Iranistik*.

since, as Malalasekera has pointed out: ". . . how far the *Tipiṭaka* and its commentary reduced to writing at Alu-vihāra resembled them as they have come down to us now, no one can say."[2] In fact, it is not until the time of the commentaries of Buddhaghosa, Dhammapāla, and others—that is to say, the fifth to sixth centuries C.E.—that we can know anything definite about the actual contents of this canon.

We also know that there is no evidence to indicate that a canon existed prior to the Alu-vihāra redaction. Although Aśoka in his Bhābrā Edict specifically enjoined both monks and laymen to recite certain texts, which he named,[3] he nowhere in his records gives any indication that he knew of a canon, or the classification of texts into *nikāyas.*[4] We do know, however, that the epithet *pañcanekāyika* occurs in the Bhārhut and Sāñcī inscriptions, but we also know that Lamotte has shown that it is unlikely that this refers to the five collections of the *Suttapiṭaka.*[5] And even if it could be shown to refer to the *nikāyas* as codified collections, this would still not push the data for the collection of at least some texts into *nikāyas* much beyond the first century B.C.E., the approximate date of the inscriptions from Bhārhut and Sāñcī. The earliest known reference to the *Tripiṭaka* is still later. It is found in an inscription published in 1974 by Fussman that is dated by him to year 5 of Kaniṣka.[6] And finally, we also know that it is not until Nāgārjunikoṇḍa and Amarāvatī—and then only in the South—that we find specific reference to the *Dīgha-, Majjhima-,* and, probably, to the *Saṃyutta-nikāyas* in inscriptions.[7]

The occurrence of the titles *sutaṃtika, sutātika,* etc., "one who knows the *sutta*" (once at Bhārhut, three times at Sāñcī), or *vinayadhara,* "one who knows the *vinaya*" (once at Sāñcī), or *peṭakin,* "one who knows the *Piṭaka*" (once at Bhārhut),[8] proves that just prior to, or contemporaneous with, the date of the Alu-vihāra redaction at least some Buddhist literature had been classified as *sutta* and *vinaya,* and that some idea of a *Piṭaka* had already emerged. But we have no idea what these classifications included.

What we definitely know of the Pāli texts that preceded the Alu-vihāra redaction, or perhaps better, the *Aṭṭhakathā* redaction—the redaction known to Buddhaghosa, et al.—is limited. We do know that at least two collections of texts, the *Aṭṭhakavagga* and the *Pārāyaṇavagga,* preceded the first redaction of the canon that we have; both collections are quoted or referred to by name in other texts of that canon; both collections have already received commentaries by the time of the earliest known redaction, and they are the only texts that have; finally, the commentaries on both collections are themselves already considered canonical in that early redaction.[9] We also know that at least seven texts (*dhaṃma-paliyāya*) were known to Aśoka since he refers to them by name in his Bhābrā Edict, but unfortunately only three of these have been identified with anything approaching unanimity (*Muni-Gāthā* = *Suttanipāta* vss. 207–221; *Moneya-Sūte*

= *Nālaka-sutta, Suttanipāta* vss. 699–723; *Upatisa-pasine* = *Sāriputta-sutta, Suttanipāta* vss. 955–975) and even these are not certain.[10] If, however, we can take the *Aṭṭhakavagga,* the *Pārāyaṇavagga* and perhaps the three Aśokan texts as we now have them as representing something like their original form, then we know, in addition, that those texts that are demonstrably old are all short texts in verse, and that none of them in form and—it now appears—in content are anything like the finished *suttas* of the *nikāya/āgamas,* especially the first and second *nikāyas.*[11] This is of importance for the study of doctrinal history, since the majority of proof texts cited usually come from these two *nikāyas.*

We also know that Lüders has argued that the reliefs and their accompanying labels on the railings of Bhārhut presuppose actual texts,[12] but this, again, has been called into question by Lamotte.[13] An interesting point, however, is that if Lüders were to be correct, then the texts that we would once again have early evidence for are, again, unlike the finished *suttas* of the *nikāyas:* if the Bhārhut railings give evidence of actual texts, those texts are in content almost entirely *jātaka* or *avadāna* texts.[14] And it is interesting to note that the donors who commissioned illustrations from these "texts" were—as we shall see in a considerable number of cases—monks or nuns.

We know too that the earliest source we have in an Indian language other than Pāli—and this, according to Norman, is a translation[15]—appears to be the Gāndhārī *Dharmapada,* the manuscript of which may date to the second century C.E.[16] Of our Sanskrit sources, almost all from Central Asia, probably none is earlier than the fifth century,[17] and the Gilgit Manuscripts, which appear to contain fragments of an *Ekottarāgama,*[18] are still later. Our Chinese sources do not really begin until the second half of the second century, and it is, in fact, probably not until we arrive at the translations of the *Madhyamāgama* and the *Ekottarāgama* by Dharmanandin in the last quarter of the fourth century that we have the first datable sources which allow us to know—however imperfectly—the actual doctrinal content of at least some of the major divisions of the *nikāya/āgama* literature.[19] It is from this period, then, from the end of the fourth century, that some of the doctrinal content of Hīnayāna canonical literature can finally be definitely dated and actually verified. Not before.

III.

I am, of course, aware of the fact that it has been maintained that "higher criticism" is able to take us back to a point considerably before our earliest known redaction. Unfortunately, I am also aware of the fact that there are certain fundamental problems involving the cardinal tenet of this "higher criticism" and that tenet's application, which have not been critically examined. The cardinal tenet of this criticism states, in effect, if all known sectarian versions of a text or passage agree, that text or passage must be very old; that is, it must come from a presectarian stage of the tradition. This principle, in one form or another, underlies virtually all of the important historical and chronological statements formulated by Bareau, Frauwallner, et al.[20] But in applying this principle, almost no account has been given to two important sets of facts.

First, we do not actually know when the sectarian period began. We do know, as Bareau says, that "Les ouvrages qui nous ont transmis les tableaux et listes de sectes ne sont pas très anciens. Aucun ne remonte avec certitude au delà de 300 ap. J.-C., c'est-à-dire quelque 500 ans après les événements qu'ils rapportent."[21] There is, as Bareau clearly shows, a good deal of agreement between these late sources, and they have much in common. One of the most striking common elements, however, is that they all give different dates for the appearance of the schisms. Of those sources that Bareau classifies as "Les traditions de la première époque," the *Dīpavaṃsa* says that "tous les schismes se seraient produits dans la courant du IIᵉ s. après la Nirvāṇa"; the Sammatīya tradition says that the first took place in 137 E.N. (= "ère du Nirvāṇa"), the second in 200 E.N., and the third in 400 E.N.; "La tradition cachemirienne" has schisms taking place in 100 E.N. and in the IIᵉ, IIIᵉ, and IVᵉ centuries E.N., but according to the *Mañjuśrīparipṛcchāsūtra* "tous les schismes auraient eu lieu dans la Iᵉʳ s. de l'ère du Nirvāṇa."[22] We also know, again as Bareau says, that on the basis of epigraphical sources "l'existence de la quasi-totalité des sectes est un fait certain," but that "nous n'avons plus d'autres renseignements avant le IIᵉ s. de notre ère. A cette époque, les inscriptions nous apprennent la présence des Sarvāstivādin: près de Peshawer, dans l'Ouest du Cachemire, à Mathurā et à Çrāvastī; des Mahāsāṅghika: à Mathurā, à Karle, etc." We know, in other words, that it is not until the second century C.E. that we begin to find references to actual "schools" in inscriptions.[23] They simply do not occur in the earlier periods of known Buddhist inscriptions. Not at Bhārhut and Sāñcī—although both sites testify to the existence of the beginnings of the division of labor (*sutaṃtika, vinayadhara,* etc.) that some have argued was an important precondition to the eventual emergence of the sects.[24] And not in the known Aśokan inscriptions. In spite of the fact that there appears to have been some kinds of internal problems within the *Saṃgha,* Aśoka always speaks of it as "the *Saṃgha*" or "the *Bhikṣu-Saṃgha.*"[25] We know, therefore, that there is no actual evidence for the emergence of the schools prior to the second century C.E. The precise value of the literary tradition—especially the *vinayas*—in regard to this question leads us to the second group of problems involved in the application of this particular method of criticism.

In applying the principle that says, in effect, if all known versions of a text or passage agree, that text or passage must be very old, almost no account has been given to the fact that all the material to which it is applied is very late:

the Pāli sources, as we have already seen, cannot be taken back beyond 29 to 17 B.C.E. (the Alu-vihāra redaction), and we cannot know anything definite about their actual contents until the fifth or sixth centuries (the *Aṭṭhakathā* redaction); probably none of the Chinese sources go back beyond the second century C.E. and most are considerably later; the Sanskrit sources for the early literature—and here we are talking about manuscripts—are, with few exceptions, even later (from the fifth century on); and the Tibetan sources later still (not before the seventh century). The textual critic is therefore comparing texts from uniformly late stages of the literary tradition. Once this is taken fully into account, any agreement between the sources is open to a very different, if not the very opposite interpretation. The cardinal tenet may then have to be framed in the following form: If all known versions of a text or passage agree, that text or passage is probably late; that is, it probably represents the results of the conflation and gradual leveling and harmonization of earlier existing traditions.

This idea, of course, is not new. Wassilieff, for example, in an old paper which raised a number of points that have never been answered, says:

> Ordinairement pour établir l'ancienneté de la composition des Vinayas on insiste sur ce trait que, dans toutes les rédactions ou dans toutes les écoles ils sont à peu près identiques. . . . Mais à notre avis ce trait même prouve que les Vinayas parvenus à nous ont été rédigés à une époque tardive, quand la question de la vie ascétique ne constituait plus un sujet de discussion, et que toutes les écoles étaient déjà fort tranquillement établies dans des monastères, et avaient pris en conséquence une teinte monotone, parce que pour la vie en communauté, même dans les autres religions, les règles établies ne peuvent sortir du cadre connu.[26]

More recently Lamotte has said in his remarks on Frauwallner's *The Earliest Vinaya and the Beginnings of Buddhist Literature* that

> Si dans le canevas de ces derniers [i.e., the various *vinayas*]—et nous songeons surtout aux Vinaya Pāli, Mahīśāsaka et Dharmagupta—on constate de remarquables similitudes, le fait s'explique par un développement parallèle. Les communautés bouddhiques ne vivaient pas en vase clos; elles suivaient avec intérêt les travaux exécutés par leurs voisins. Il n'y a donc rien d'étonnant à ce qu'elles aient travaillé selon les mêmes méthodes et en suivant pratiquement le même plan.[27]

And Bareau himself notes that "les exemples de bonne entente entre moines de sectes différentes abondent." He then says, as an example, that "Dans l'Uḍḍiyāṇa, les Mahāsāṅghika, les Sarvāstivādin, les Mahīśāsaka, les Dharmaguptaka, et les Kāśyapīya vécurent durant des siècles en parfait accord et meme en véritable symbiose . . ."[28] But perhaps even more important than these general considerations is the fact that something like what I have suggested can, I think, actually be shown to be the case in those instances where we are fortunate enough to have an unrevised version of a text or passage still preserved.

The fact, for example, that the Pāli version as well as the Mahāsāṅghika, Mahīśāsaka, and Dharmaguptaka versions of the account of the remains of the Buddha Kāśyapa studied by Bareau all agree in placing a *stūpa* of Kāśyapa at Toyikā cannot result from the fact that this is an old, presectarian tradition. On the contrary, the fact that they all agree in this seems to result from the very opposite; it seems to result from the fact that they all represent later, revised, and conflated versions of an earlier tradition that knew nothing of a *stūpa*. Here, unfortunately, I can give only a very condensed summary of this important case, but it is clear that we have in this instance a fine example of how the accepted principle of this "higher criticism" is supposed to work, and—as we shall see—when we can actually check it, it is also clear that it does not seem to work very well at all.

To begin with what Bareau has collected, we have three versions of what is clearly the same text: a Mahāsāṅghika, a Mahīśāsaka, and a Dharmaguptaka version. These three versions, according to Bareau, "sont étroitement apparentées et proviennent manifestement d'un même récit antérieur."[29] We also have a Pāli version of this text, which appears to be the latest of all the versions and is also obviously related to the other three.[30] These four versions have a number of elements in common, and although each has been padded out with one or more of a variety of subplots and literary clichés taken from the common stock of Buddhist story literature,[31] the basic elements of the text are, in each version, still clearly visible and can be separated out: the Buddha is traveling in Kosala; he reaches a spot near a village called Tou-i, Tou-tseu, Todeyya (all = Skt. Toyikā); he has an encounter with a man working in a nearby field as a result of which it becomes known that the *stūpa* of the Buddha Kāśyapa lies buried under this spot; the Buddha then makes the *stūpa* appear momentarily and, after it disappears, he and/or the monks construct a *stūpa* on that spot from mud ("boue", "boule de boue"; in the Pāli account a *stūpa* of stone appears; the Mahīśāsaka account adds "ce fut le premier *stūpa* élevé alors sur le territoire du Jambudvīpa"); this then is followed—in one case preceded—by instructions on how a *stūpa* should be built and/or by verses praising the merit of building or worshipping *stūpas*. Since all four versions agree on these basic elements of the text, and since each version belongs to a separate school, we can conclude—according to the accepted principle—that the essential elements of this account must go back to a very old or presectarian stage of the tradition. As a matter of fact, on the basis of the agreement between the three Chinese versions set alongside his interpretation of the Nigālī Sāgar Edict of Aśoka, Bareau concludes that "cette légende paraît antérieure à Aśoka."[32] Here, however, unlike in the overwhelming majority of such cases, we can actually check both the conclusion and procedure, since yet another version of this text—a version of an unusual kind—is in this case also available.

What is clearly a fifth version of this account of the remains of the Buddha Kāśyapa is now found once in the *Mūlasarvāstivāda-vinaya* from Gilgit[33] and twice in the *Divyāvadāna.*[34] And, although this version clearly belongs to the same group and has the same basic narrative structure (the Buddha going to Toyikā, his encounter with the man working in the field, his "miraculous" raising of the relics for the monks to see, etc.) it differs from the other four in at least two important ways. First, it has none of the various subplots found in the other versions—a fairly sure sign of priority[35]—and, second, it knows absolutely nothing about a *stūpa* at Toyikā or its construction. Here, it is not a *stūpa* that the Buddha makes appear, but only "the undivided mass of relics of the Saṃyaksaṃbuddha Kāśyapa (*kāśyapasya samyaksaṃbuddhasyāvikopitaḥ śarīrasaṃghāta ucchrāpitaḥ*)." The text, in fact, knows only these relics, *which are buried in the ground,* and is concerned solely with the sacralization of that otherwise unmarked piece of ground by acts of worship and the establishment of a festival (*maha*). The merit it praises arises, first of all, from activities undertaken in regard to this *pṛthivīpradeśa* and, secondly, in regard to *buddhacaityas* (always plural), a term which here quite clearly has nothing to do with *stūpas.* This version, in short, reflects a tradition—apparently later revised—that only knew a form of the relic cult in which the *stūpa* did not yet have a part.[36]

The existence of this version is somewhat puzzling, but I think it is impossible to see it as anything else but an old account that, for some reason, was never revised. The simple narrative structure, the absence of the well-known subplots and literary clichés, the absence, especially, of any reference to a *stūpa*—all make it impossible, I think, to put it any place but at the beginning of the known history of this particular text. We have, then, what appears to be the earliest known account that knows nothing of a *stūpa* at Toyikā—and this is an important *stūpa*—set over against the versions of the Mahāsāṅghika, Mahīśāsaka, Dharmaguptaka, and the Theravāda, all of which must be later and all of which agree that there was a *stūpa* of Kāśyapa at Toyikā. It would appear, then, that the original version, represented now by the Mūlasarvāstivāda account, was revised at some point in time, and that once this revision was made in one school's account, it was accepted and incorporated into the accounts of all schools other than—and here probably only by an oversight—the Mūlasarvāstivāda. In any case, here it appears in one of the very few cases where we actually have the means to check the conclusions that would be generated by our "higher criticism," that the Mahāsāṅghika, Mahīśāsaka, Dharmaguptaka, and Theravāda accounts agree not because they represent the old presectarian version, but because they almost certainly represent later, conflated, and fundamentally altered versions of an earlier tradition.[37]

IV.

But if we know that we cannot know anything definite about the actual doctrinal content of the *nikāya/āgama* literature much before the fourth century C.E., we also know that a very considerable number of Buddhist inscriptions predate by several centuries the old Chinese translations of the *Madhyamāgama* and the *Ekottarāgama,* and that if we want to look at the oldest verifiable sources for the question of the layman/monk distinction in Indian Buddhism—and this is one of the questions we are concerned with here—we must look first at these inscriptions.

This inscriptional material has at least two distinct advantages. First, much of it predates what we can definitely know from literary sources. Second, and perhaps of greater importance, this material tells us not what some literate, educated Indian Buddhist wrote, but what a fairly large number of practicing Buddhists actually did. In Buddhist studies, scholars intent on generating historical statements have consistently used textual sources as if they were somehow descriptions of actual behavior, and little explicit consideration has been given to the almost certain noncongruency between an ideal and the actual. This is particularly well illustrated in a long series of statements concerning the Monk. Implicit in almost everything that has been said about him is the assumption that the scheme of the religious life for the monk preserved in our literary sources is not a normative and carefully contrived ideal paradigm, but an adequate historical reflection of the actual career of the typical Buddhist monk of the early centuries. I think we need cite here only a single example—enormously influential—which is particularly germane to our topic. In the sole paragraph devoted to the *stūpa*/relic cult in his classic *Buddha, sein Leben, seine Lehre, seine Gemeinde,* Oldenberg stated flatly in reference to the *stūpa* cult that "the order of monks as such has nothing to do with this pompous show of veneration; the old rules of the order have not a word to say about it."[38] Our donative inscriptions, however, would seem to indicate otherwise.

V.

The earliest donative inscriptions that we have come from the railings of Bhārhut and Sāñcī and date from about 120 to 80 B.C.E.[39] Here already, we know for certain that a considerable proportion of the donors—those donors actively involved with establishing and embellishing sacred objects and sacred sites, those donors actively involved with the *stūpa* cult and donative, merit-making activity—were monks or nuns. At Bhārhut, for example, almost 40 percent of the donors were either monks (twenty-four) or nuns (fourteen).[40] We also know that a considerable proportion of these individuals were not simply monks, but doctrinal specialists: six are called *bhānakas,* "reciters"; one is called *sutaṃtika,* "one who knows the *sutta*"; one is called a *peṭakin,* "one who knows the *Piṭaka*"; and one is referred to as a *pacanekāyika,* "one who [according to Lamotte] was versed in the canonical doctrine taken as a whole."[41]

A very similar picture emerges from an analysis of the Kharoṣṭhī inscriptions edited by Konow. Here, if we restrict ourselves to donations that are connected with the *stūpa* cult or the cult of images, we find that again more than 40 percent of the donors are monks (sixteen) and the rest laymen of different categories (nineteen).[42] Here too, although titles are much less common in the Kharoṣṭhī inscriptions, at least one of the monk-donors is called a *venaea,* a *vainayika,* "one who knows the *vinaya,*" and another is called a *trepiḍaka,* "one who knows the *Tripiṭaka.*"[43]

We also know from other donative inscriptions that the proportion of monastic donors increases. For example—and it is a representative example—in the Mathurā inscriptions collected by Lüders, which are certainly Buddhist and in which the name of the donor is given or preserved, well over 50 percent of those donors are monks or nuns.[44] Among these we find a monk who is called both a *bhānaka* and a *caturvidya* (which Lüders takes to mean one "who knows the fourfold scriptures"); another who is called a *dharmakathika,* "a preacher of the *Dharma*"; and two monks who are called *prāhaṇīkas* or, according to Lüders, "practisers of meditation"; we also find a nun-donor who is said to be the niece of another nun who is a *trepiṭaka* and the pupil of a monk who is given the same title.[45]

In the inscriptions from the "Buddhist cave temples" collected by Burgess, if again we restrict ourselves to donations connected with cult forms (images, *caityagṛhas,* relics, etc.) and exclude gifts of residences (cells, caves, cisterns) and endowments for the material support of the residences and the monks living there, we find that slightly more than 65 percent of the donors were monks or nuns (twenty-eight) and fewer than 35 percent were laymen.[46]

Finally, if we go further and look at those inscriptions that, as I have recently attempted to show, are probably Mahāyāna, the figures are even more striking. In those inscriptions that appear to be Mahāyāna—and here we are talking about nearly eighty individual inscriptions—the donors in more than 70 percent of the cases are monks or nuns, mostly the former, and only 20 percent are laymen.[47]

None of this accords very well, if at all, with received views on the matter, with the views that maintain that there was a sharp distinction between the kinds of religious activities undertaken by monks and the kinds of religious activity undertaken by laymen, and with the view that cult and religious giving were essentially and overwhelmingly lay concerns in the Indian Buddhist context.[48] In fact, if we stick to what we can actually know, it would appear that something very like the opposite was the case: we know for certain from inscriptions that from ca. 150 B.C.E.—that is to say, from our earliest knowable donative inscriptions and well before we can have any definite knowledge of the textual tradition—monks and nuns formed a substantial proportion of those involved in donative, merit-making activities connected with the *stūpa* cult and, somewhat later, the cult of images, and that this proportion increased continually as time passed. We also know that, in a considerable number of cases, these individuals were not just ordinary monks, but doctrinal specialists (*trepiṭakas, vainayikas,* etc.) and the acknowledged transmitters of Buddhist teaching (*bhānakas*). Finally, it is also worth noting that the Mahāyāna figures are particularly significant. We know on the basis of these figures that, from its first appearance in inscriptions, the Mahāyāna was a monk-dominated movement, and that it continued to be so until the thirteenth century, the date of our last known Mahāyāna inscription. But this is not all that we can know from these donative inscriptions.

VI.

The donations recorded at Bhārhut and Sāñcī concern gifts of posts, railings, sculpted medallions, and the like—that is to say, gifts intended to embellish and mark the *stūpa* as an object of worship. The Kharoṣṭhī inscriptions too, at least in their earlier phases, are often connected with the *stūpa*/relic cults, although we also find a number of inscriptions connected with images. But the donations recorded in the Mathurā inscriptions as well as the inscriptions from the "cave temples," while still including gifts connected with *stūpas* and the so-called establishment of relics, are increasingly more concerned with the setting up of images, and the Mahāyāna inscriptions are almost exclusively so. So, while the purely epigraphic evidence of the monastic control and dominance of the *stūpa* cult—at least in our samples—is perhaps not quite so clear, there is absolutely no doubt that the cult of images was overwhelmingly a monastic concern. In the eighteen Kharoṣṭhī inscriptions edited by Konow that record the setting up of an image and in which the name of the donor is given or preserved, almost two-thirds or thirteen of eighteen of the donors are monks.[49] The figures for Lüders' Mathurā inscriptions are almost exactly the same: in the twenty-eight inscriptions that have or preserve a name and that record the gift of an image, eighteen of twenty-eight of the donors are monks and nuns—again almost two-thirds.[50] In the seventeen "cave temple" inscriptions collected by Burgess that are connected with an image, the donor in every case but one is a monk.[51] In the inscriptions I have identified as Mahāyāna, virtually all of which are concerned with the making or setting up of images, more than 70 percent of the donors are monks or nuns (mostly, again, the former).[52]

But we know even more than this. We know that not only was the image cult overwhelmingly a monastic concern, it was also, on the basis of the available information, a monastically initiated cult. We know that the earliest Buddha images accompanied by a dated donative inscription—and these are some of the earliest datable examples of both Mathurā and Gandhāra art—were all set up by monks or nuns. We can cite, for example, the images set up by the ubiquitous *Bhikṣu* Bala or his pupils at Kosam, Sārnāth, Set-Mahet, and Mathurā,[53] or the image set up by Buddhānanda in the fifth year of Kaniṣka.[54] Note too that, once again, we know for certain that in many cases these monastic donors were not just average monks. Both Bala and Buddhānanda are specifically said to be *trepiṭakas,* that is to say, "those who know the *Tripiṭaka*"; a little later at Jauliāñ we find an image that was the gift "of the friar versed in the Vinaya" (*v{e}naе(i)asa bhikshusa*).[55] All of these monks were doctrinal specialists, and they were all actively engaged in and concerned with popular cult practice.

VII.

The earliest donative inscriptions that we know clearly establish the active and sizable participation of monks in the *stūpa* cult from at least 150 B.C.E. This again, we know, is fully confirmed by archaeology and the history of monastic architecture. We know, again from the very beginning of our actual evidence (e.g., the early cave complexes at Kondivte, Nadsur, Pitalkhorā, Ajaṇṭā, and so forth) that, as Nagao has inadvertently shown, "the caitya was already part of the monastic complex," and that "the stūpa was not merely approved and accepted by the monastic community but actually adopted by it, integrated into cenobitic life as one of its most important elements."[56] I think, however, it is only fair to say that Nagao probably did not intend to show that from the very beginning of our actual evidence, the *caitya* was already part of the monastic complex, etc. Like a number of other authors, he posits several earlier phases for the development of monastic architecture. Unfortunately, that there is evidence for these phases is less than clear. For example, for the first of these phases, Nagao takes several passages from the *vinaya* as evidence for the fifth or fourth century B.C.E. after he himself has already said that the *vinaya* "took its present textual form only about the beginning of the Christian era," and that "these texts [the *vinayas*], though they refer to many incidents contemporaneous with the Buddha himself, reflect the thinking of a much later time, the time of their own redaction." He bases the next of his phases on an overstatement of the archaeological facts. He refers to what might or might not be the Jīvakāmravaṇa—or Jīvakārāma (Pāli: Jīvakāmbavana), the *ārāma* supposedly given to the Buddha by the famous physician Jīvaka—and draws a number of conclusions from what he sees there. But again, we do not know anything definite about the nature or purpose of the building in question; we do not even know whether it was a monastery, let alone whether it was *the* Jīvakāmravaṇa, and we still do not have anything like a full report on what the excavation brought to light. There are, as a matter of fact, a number of other "Elliptical Structures" similar to the so-called Jīvakāmravaṇa, and, according to Sarkar who has made a study of them, at least two of these buildings, "are identified as *stūpas*"![57] Nagao's discussion of actual, verifiable monastic architecture begins then only with his remarks on the "cave temples" and, importantly, the place of the *stūpa* at those sites.

The history of Buddhist monastic architecture, however, does not simply confirm the active participation of monks in the *stūpa*/relic cult. It would also seem to indicate something more than this; it would seem to indicate that the cult was, from the very beginning of our evidence, both monastically controlled and monastically dominated. That this was the case seems to follow from the fact that the *stūpas* that we know are almost always found in close association with monastic complexes and very frequently fully incorporated into such complexes. The significance of this relationship is reinforced when we note that only very rarely do we find *stūpas* or *caityagṛhas* disassociated from monastic establishments. The only instance, in fact, that I am able to cite is Sirkap.[58]

We can also add to this two pieces of epigraphical evidence not yet specifically mentioned. First, everywhere, but especially noticeable in the Kharoṣṭhī inscriptions, even when relics or *stūpas* are given by laymen, they are almost always given "in the acceptance of" or "for the acceptance of" (*parigrahe, pratigrahe*) one or another monastic community or school.[59] Either that or they are specifically said to be given in conjunction with a *saṃghārāma* or *vihāra* or to a particular *vihāra.*[60] Second, we might note an interesting Kharoṣṭhī inscription that is yet to be fully understood. This particular inscription seems to record that, on the date that "the pole of the *stūpa* was erected" (*yaṭhiṃ aropayata*), "a laywoman" (*upasika*) gave in addition to—assuming Konow's interpretation of *ṭhapa(ï)chaṃ* is right—the "setting up of the pole" (*yaṭhipratiṭhana*), the "surrounding structure" as well. It is clear that the erection of the *yaṣṭi* was a significant event; the inscription is dated on the day that this took place, and it probably indicated the completion of the *stūpa* and signaled its inauguration as an object of worship. The significant point here is that although both the setting up of the *yaṣṭi* and the "surrounding structure" were the gifts of a laywoman, it was expressly stated that it was a monk, a "preacher of the *Dharma*" (*dharmakathika*), who performed the ceremony that appears to have officially marked the *stūpa* as an object of worship.[61]

VIII.

We also know a few more specific things about doctrinal history on the basis of our donative inscriptions. We read, for example, in an inscription dated in the year 51 of Huveṣka from Mathurā:

(I) . . . {a}sya {p}u{rva}yā {bhi}kṣu{ṇā} {b}uddh{a}varmaṇā {bhagava}taḥ {śāk}y{am}u . . . pratimā pratiṣṭāpita sarva{b}uddhapūjārt{th}a{m} anana d{e}yadharmaparityāgen{a} upadhy{ā}yasya saghadāsasya {n}irvā{n}ā{va}ptaye = {s}t{u} mātāp{it} . . . buddh{a}varmas{y}a sarvad(u)khopaśamāya sarvasatvahitasukh{ā}r{th}a . . .

Lüders, *Mathurā Inscriptions* §29

. . . on this date an image of the Blessed One Śākyamuni was set up by the Monk Buddhavarman for the worship of all Buddhas. Through this religious gift may his Preceptor Saṅghadāsa attain *nirvāṇa,* (may it also be) for the cessation of all suffering of his parents . . . (and) for the welfare and happiness of all beings.

In another inscription on an image pedestal, again from Mathurā, we find:

(II) bhikhusa budhav{ā}lasa dān{a} māt{ā}pit{r}in{a} pujāye savasav{ā}n{a} ca

Lüders, *Mathurā Inscriptions* §90

(This is) the gift of the Monk Buddhapāla (which is made) as an act of *pūjā* for his parents and all beings.

Even more interesting are two inscriptions, one on a pillar base from the Jamālpur Mound, the other a Kharoṣṭhī inscription on an image "said to have come from near Peshawar":[62]

(III) +[63] *{d}ā{na}ṃ bh{ik}ṣus{y}a b . . . + . . . m{i}trasya v{o}jya + {vaśi}kasya — {mātap}i + {tṛ}ṇa {abhyat}itaka + laga{tā}nāṃ pujāy{e} + bhavatu sa{dh}yivi + harīsya dharma{d}ev{a}s{y}a + ar{o}g{a}dākṣiṇ{a}y{e} {bha}vat{u}*

Lüders, *Mathurā Inscriptions* §44

(This is) the gift of the Monk . . . mitra, the Vojyavaśika (?).[64] May it be an act of *pūjā* for his deceased parents. May it (also) be for the granting of health to his companion Dharmadeva.

(IV) sa{ṃ} 4 1 phagunasa masasa di paṃcami budhanadasa trepiḍakasa danamukhe madapidarana adhvadidana puyaya bhavatu

Fussman, *BEFEO* 61 (1974) 54

Year 5, on the fifth day of the month Phalguna. This is the gift of Buddhānanda who knows the *Tripiṭaka.* May it be an act of *pūjā* for his deceased parents.

Finally, we might cite yet another inscription on a pillar base found at the Jamālpur Mound:

(V) *ayaṃ ku{ṃ}bhako dānaṃ bhikṣunaṃ śurīyasya buddharakṣitasya ca prāhaṇīk{ā}-n{aṃ} an{e}n{a} deryadharmmaparītyāgen{a} sarvveṣ{a}ṃ pr{ā}haṇīkānaṃ arogyadakṣiṇ{ā}ye bhavat{āṃ}*

Lüders, *Mathurā Inscriptions* §46

This pillar base is the gift of the Monks Śurīya and Buddharakṣita who are practisers of meditation.[65] May this offering of a religious gift be for granting health to all practisers of meditation.

What we want to note are the basic ideas expressed in these records. It is, for example, clear that it was held that someone could be expected to obtain *nirvāṇa* as the result of an act of *pūjā* undertaken on his behalf by another. It was held that acts of *pūjā* could be undertaken for one's parents, whether living or dead. It was also held that acts of *pūjā* could be undertaken for the sake of conferring health on others. These are the expressed ideas and intentions of the individual donors. And we know beyond the shadow of a doubt that these ideas and goals were held and, more importantly, acted upon by members of the monastic community, that these were, in fact, monastic ideas and goals. We can add to this that, here again, the members of the monastic community in question were not, at least in two cases, just average monks. In one case they refer to themselves and the intended beneficiaries of their act as "practisers of meditation"; in another the donor is said to be one "who knows the *Tripiṭaka.*"

IX.

Fussman, in his remarks on the Kharoṣṭhī inscription cited above (no. IV), introduces our second problem. He explicitly recognizes that this inscription is a concrete expression of "la doctrine . . . du transfert des mérites." In fact, the same is true for all of the inscriptions just cited. All of these are individual applications of a single basic idea, the idea that the results of a religious act undertaken by one individual may be assigned or "transferred" to others, and even to all others—an act is undertaken "for the welfare and happiness of all beings" (*sarvasatvahitasukhārthaṃ*), or "as an act of *pūjā* for one's parents" (*mātāpitrina pujāye*), or "for the granting of health" (*arogyadakṣiṇāye*) to one or another individual. But in recognizing this fact, Fussman makes a number of statements that are more difficult to accept. He says:

> Je crois plutôt qu'il [the gift made in honor of the donor's deceased parents in IV cited above] implique l'existence de la doctrine mahāyāniste du transfert des mérites . . . Si notre interprétation est correcte, ce relief a été offert par un sectateur du Mahāyāna . . . Nous avons, donc, pour la première fois, une preuve de l'existence de courants mahāyānistes dans l'Inde du Nord-Ouest, à la fin du premier siècle de n.e.[66]

Fussman is almost certainly right in seeing here a doctrine of the transference of merit, but I think—and I think it can be shown—that the doctrine of the transference of merit which occurs in these inscriptions is not a Mahāyāna doctrine, and that none of the inscriptions I have cited, including his Kharoṣṭhī inscription, are Mahāyāna inscriptions.

We know that the formula "May it be an act of *pūjā* for his deceased parents" (*madapidarana adhvadidana puyaya bhavatu*) found in Fussman's inscription is also found elsewhere. He himself refers to the similar formula found in the inscription from the Jamālpur Mound that I have cited above (III), and Damsteegt refers to at least fifteen examples (including Fussman's and the Jamālpur inscription) of what he calls the "shorter" and "extended" forms of this expression.[67] From a survey of these we know that, in at least five instances, this formula appears in conjunction with a specifically named school and that in every instance that school is a Hīnayāna school: in a Mathurā inscription edited by Sircar that records a gift to the Mahāsāṅghikas, we find the expression *mātāpitraṇa abhatita-na{ṃ}. . . .*[68] In an inscription from Kānheri dating from the Sātavāhana period in which we find the phrase *{mā}tapitūnaṃ abhatītā{naṃ} . . . pūjāya,* the donation is made in conjunction with the Bhādrāyaṇīyas.[69] Three instances of what Damsteegt calls the "shorter" form—*mātāpit{r}ina pujāya,* etc.,—also occur in association with the name of a school: at Nāgārjunikoṇḍa we find *mātāpituno pūjā* . . . in conjunction with the Aparamahāvinaseliyas (Aparaśailas);[70] at Kārli *mātapituna pūjā{ya}* in association with the Mahāsāṅghikas;[71] and the shorter form also occurs in a Kharoṣṭhī inscription from Wardak, again in association with the Mahāsāṅghikas.[72] It is, I think, clear from this that whenever expressions like *madapidarana adhvadidana puyaya, mātapituna pūjāya,* occur in any inscription that also contains the name of a school, that school is always a Hīnayāna school (the Bhādrāyaṇīyas once, the Aparaśailas once, and the Mahāsāṅghikas three times). The other side of this is that the expression *madapidarana adhvadidana puyaya* or any of its variants is never found in association with the name Mahāyāna, or with the titles *Śākyabhikṣu/-bhikṣuṇī* or *Paramopāsaka/-opāsikā* (which, as I have tried to show, were used at first by the group we now call the Mahāyāna), and here again we are talking about nearly eighty inscriptions from several periods and from almost all parts of India.[73] Exactly the same pattern recurs if we look at any of the other formulae found in the five inscriptions I have cited above.

In the second inscription of this group, the Monk Buddhapāla makes his donation "as an act of *pūjā* for his parents and all beings" (*māt{ā}pit{r}in{a} pujāye savasav{ā}n{a} ca*). In the first, the Monk Buddhavarman sets up an image and specifies that this act—that is to say, the resulting merit—is to be for, in part, "the welfare and happiness of all beings" (*sarvasatvahitasukh{ā}r{th}a*). This latter formula, which again clearly "implique l'existence de la doctrine . . . du transfert des mérites," is found very frequently in Buddhist inscriptions of almost all periods, and in a number of instances it is also found in conjunction with a specifically named school, but never in conjunction with the name *mahāyāna* or the titles *śākyabhikṣu* and the like. At Mathurā it occurs in conjunction with the Sarvāstivādins once and twice with the Mahāsāṅghikas;[74] at Kārli it again occurs in association with the Mahāsāṅghikas,[75] and in yet another Kharoṣṭhī inscription edited by Fussman it occurs in association with the Dharmaguptakas;[76] it occurs in two inscriptions from Kānheri in connection with the Bhādrāyaṇīyas;[77] and in one inscription from Nāgārjunikoṇḍa published by Vogel it occurs in conjunction with the Mahīśāsaka,[78] while in another from the same place it is associated with the Vibhajyavādins;[79] finally, it appears again associated with the Sarvāstivādins in a Kharoṣṭhī inscription published by Konow[80] and in an inscription from Kāman published by Bühler.[81] We know, therefore, that whenever the expression *sarvasatvahitasukhārtha,* or some variant thereof, occurs in any inscription that also contains the name of a school, that school is always a Hīnayāna school, and that the expression is never found in inscriptions associated with the groups we now call the Mahāyāna.[82]

I think that, in light of this material, Fussman's remarks on the possible Mahāyāna character of his inscription must be put aside. But in the process of testing his hypothesis, we have discovered at least one very important fact: we know now, beyond any doubt, that virtually all of the Hīnayāna schools mentioned in inscriptions accepted gifts that were given with an implicit doctrine of the transference of merit explicitly attached to them, that they accepted gifts that were expressly stated to have been made, for example, "as an act of *pūjā* for one's dead parents." This, coupled with the fact that, in at least some cases, the donors were monks presumably belonging to the same schools, would seem to indicate that we can legitimately conclude that all of these schools, the Mahāsāṅghikas, Sarvāstivādins, Bhādrāyaṇīyas, and so on, had and held a doctrine of the transference of merit. But at the same time, we also know that the groups we now call the Mahāyāna did not have and did not hold this same doctrine of the transference of merit. We know this from the fact that the formulae that express this doctrine are completely absent from what appear to be Mahāyāna inscriptions. We also know it from the formulae actually found in inscriptions that appear to belong to the Mahāyāna group.

X.

As we have seen above, the doctrine of the transference of merit, which in inscriptions is explicitly associated with the named Hīnayāna schools, is expressed in a number of formulae. An act may be undertaken "for the welfare and happiness of all beings," or "as an act of *pūjā* for . . . (deceased) parents," or more specifically "for the granting of health" to one individual or another.[83] We might also note that the act might also be undertaken, as in the first inscription from Mathurā cited above, for the attainment of *nirvāṇa* by someone other than the donor, or, as in the Taxila Silver Scroll Inscription, for a generalized, nonspecific attainment of *nirvāṇa.*[84] But this is not a frequently expressed intention of religious donations in Hīnayāna inscriptions.[85] The actual transference in the doctrine of the transference of merit associated with the Sarvāstivādins, Mahāsāṅghikas, and so on, is, therefore, not consistently oriented toward one specific goal. In most cases, it seems to simply involve the assignment of merit by one individual (the donor) to another (the expressed beneficiary) for no specific purpose other than, presumably, increasing the recipient's store of merit. When a more specific purpose is also stated, it is, on occasion, the attainment of *nirvāṇa,* but more frequently, it is something less than the religious goal sanctioned by the literary tradition: granting health or conferring long life on some specified individual, for example.[86] In what appear to be Mahāyāna inscriptions, by contrast, apart from a very small number of questionable exceptions,[87] the act or gift recorded is always undertaken, first of all, for "all beings"—even if, as we shall see, certain individuals within the category of "all beings" are, in many cases, particularly singled out. And, again in virtually every case, the transference of merit to "all beings" in the Mahāyāna inscriptions is explicitly stated to be for a single, specific purpose, the simplest form of this being *yad atra puṇyaṃ tad bhavatu sarvasatvānām anuttarajñānāvāptaye:* "what here is the merit, may that be for the obtaining of supreme knowledge by all beings." That is to say, the merit of the act in Mahāyāna inscriptions is always said to be intended specifically for the attainment of *anuttarajñāna.*[88] This is apparent from the very beginning of our Mahāyāna inscriptions and is found even in what might be called, from a purely epigraphical point of view, an early proto-Mahāyāna inscription from Mathurā.

This proto-Mahāyāna inscription, published first by Nakamura and more recently by Mukherjee,[89] is of importance for a number of reasons, not the least of which is the fact that it contains the earliest, indeed the only, reference to the Buddha Amitābha in Indian inscriptions and is, therefore, one of the few hard facts we have concerning this Buddha and his cult in India proper.[90] The inscription records the fact that in the year 26 of Huveṣka an "image of the Blessed One, the Buddha Amitābha, was set up for the worship of the Buddha" (*bhagavato buddha amitābhasya pratimā pratiṣṭhapita buddha pūjāye*) by an individual named Nāgarakṣita or Sāmrakṣita.[91] He is not given a title, although his son is called a *sārthavāha*, "caravan merchant" or "itinerant trader," and his grandfather is called a *śreṣṭhin*, "banker" or the "head of a guild." The record then concludes with the words *imena kuśalamulena sarva(satana)anuttarajñānaṃ prātp(i)m* (rd:*prāptim) (bha) (va) (tu):* "through this root of merit may there be the attainment of supreme knowledge by all beings."

Although this inscription does not yet have all of the features that characterize those inscriptions that can, I think, be shown to be Mahāyāna, it is clearly related to them: its donor, unlike the donors of the majority of our typical Mahāyāna inscriptions,[92] does not refer to himself as a *paramopāsaka* or a *śākyopāsaka* (he appears to be, by the way, almost certainly a layman); where the typical Mahāyāna inscriptions always use the phrase *yad atra puṇyaṃ tad . . . ,* the present inscription uses the phrase *imena kuśalamulena* (a phrase that, according to Damsteegt, also occurs in three Kharoṣṭhī inscriptions and one from Bodh-Gayā, but one which does not occur elsewhere, even at Mathurā);[93] finally, the present inscription, instead of the final construction standard in our Mahāyāna inscriptions—*tad bhavatu . . . anuttarajñānāvāptaye*—has *anuttarajñānaṃ prāptiṃ bhavatu.* In spite of these differences, I think it is obvious that the present inscription represents a stage in the development toward the classical form of Mahāyāna inscriptions. When we bear in mind that it is earlier by at least two centuries than the earliest of our typical Mahāyāna inscriptions, I think that we can legitimately see it as an early prototype of the latter. It is significant, therefore, that this early prototype already contains the two features which distinguish the doctrine of the transference of merit associated with the group now known as the Mahāyāna from that associated with the Hīnayāna schools: it explicitly declares that the merit from the act undertaken is to be assigned to "all beings," and that merit so assigned is intended specifically for "the attainment of supreme knowledge" by those beings.[94]

We can compare one other formula found in inscriptions associated with the Hīnayāna schools with its counterparts in Mahāyāna inscriptions. In the former inscriptions, as we have seen, donors frequently present their gift "as an act of *pūjā* for their parents" or "as an act of *pūjā* for their deceased parents." This, again, is always expressed simply as a "transference" of merit from donor to parent; the merit is never said to be for any specified end. The corresponding formula found in the Mahāyāna inscriptions—and it is very frequently found—is once again quite different. The simplest forms of the expression are *yad atra puṇyaṃ tad bhavatu mātāpitṛpūrvaṅgamaṃ kṛtvā sarvasatvānāṃ anuttarajñānāvāptaye,* "What here is the merit, may that, having placed my parents in the forefront, be for the obtaining of supreme knowledge by all beings"; or *yad atra puṇyaṃ tad bhavatu mātāpitroḥ sarvasatvānāñ cānuttarajñānāvāptaye,* "What here is the merit, may that be for the obtaining of supreme knowledge by my parents and all beings." Here again, using the same basic formula as before, the donor declares that he wishes that the merit from his act should go for the obtainment of *anuttarajñāna* by the category "all beings," but here he adds a kind of subclause to the formula specifically singling out certain individuals within that category. Either that, or he simply joins the specific individuals he wants to mention and the larger category with an "and." But in any case, whenever parents or other specific individuals are mentioned in Mahāyāna inscriptions as the intended beneficiaries of a donor's act, they are never mentioned by themselves as they are in Hīnayāna inscriptions, but always in conjunction with the category of "all beings," either together with that category (*mātāpitroḥ sarvasatvānāñ ca*) or, more commonly, as a subgroup within it (*mātāpitṛpūrvaṅgamaṃ kṛtvā sarvasatvānāṃ*). And note again that, in inscriptions associated with the Mahāyāna, whether the donor directs his merit only to the general category "all beings" or whether in addition he specifically singles out his parents or other individuals within that larger group, the merit from his act is *always* explicitly stated to be for the obtainment of "supreme knowledge."[95] Finally, we might note that in none of our Mahāyāna inscriptions is merit ever transferred to deceased parents or for such things as conferring health or granting long life. These seem to have been—at least epigraphically—exclusively Hīnayāna ideas.

XI.

There is very little doubt about which of the two basic forms of the doctrine of the transference of merit found in inscriptions is—epigraphically—the oldest. If we put aside the proto-Mahāyāna inscription from Mathurā, none of our Mahāyāna inscriptions are earlier than the fourth century C.E.[96] This means that a very considerable number of the inscriptions associated with the Hīnayāna predate them by at least one or more centuries. As a matter of fact, we know that at least some form of the doctrine of the transference of merit associated in later inscriptions with the various schools of the Hīnayāna is as old as Bhārhut. We know because, in the single instance where the intention of a donor is actually stated, it is said, as Lamotte has pointed out, that the act was undertaken *mātāpituna aṭhāyā,* "pour le bénéfice de sa mère et de son père." It should be noted, however, that Lamotte draws from this somewhat different conclusions.

Lamotte says:

> A cette époque [of Bhārhut and Sāñcī], la mentalité demeure strictement orthodoxe, c'est-à-dire conforme à l'esprit du Buddha. Par leurs aumônes, les généreux donateurs n'espèrent nullement accéder de plain-pied au Nirvāṇa, mais entendent simplement bénéficier des cinq avantages du don signalés par l'*Aṅguttara* (III. p. 38–41) . . . Bien plus, ils savent que ces oeuvres méritoires sont leur bien propre . . . et qu'ayant été seuls à les accomplir, ils devront seuls en recueillir le fruit. Il ne peut être question de transférer ce mérite à des tiers, ni même de formuler des intentions que le mécanisme de la rétribution des actes rendrait inopérantes.[97]

This, however, is conjecture and the imputation of very specific views where almost none are expressed. In actual fact, we simply do not know what the intentions of the vast majority of donors at Bhārhut and Sāñcī were. What we do know is that in the lone case in which a donor himself expresses his intentions, they are just exactly what Lamotte says is out of the question: "Parmi les nombreux donateurs de Bhārhut et de Sāñcī de l'époque Śuṅga, Sagharakhita fut le seul à avoir accompli son oeuvre pie 'pour le bénéfice de sa mère et de son père.' " The rest of the donors—and, as Lamotte says, "ils sont des centaines"—simply do not express their intentions.[98] Lamotte's views have also been implicitly queried from yet another point of view. Agasse, after quoting the above passage from *Histoire,* says:

> Pourtant si 'innovation' il y a eu, ce n'est pas sans que les textes y aient invité et Sagharakhita, pour isolé qu'il soit, aurait pu lui aussi après tout, prétendre à quelque 'orthodoxie'. Car cette pratique [the transference of merit] . . . appartient bel et bien au corps de doctrine originel et les textes canoniques en portent témoignage en plusieurs endroits.[99]

Now, however, several important inscriptions have come to light that were not available to Lamotte. Although none of these were found at Bhārhut or Sāñcī, one appears to be contemporaneous with the inscriptions from these sites, and several others may be considerably earlier. The first of these comes from Pauni and palaeographically seems to belong to the "late Maurya/early Śuṅga" period. It is found on a coping stone and appears to be missing a few *akṣaras* at the beginning: . . . *ya visamitāya dana(ṃ) sukhāya hotu savasatānaṃ,* "the gift of Visamitā . . . may it be for the happiness of all beings."[100] The other inscriptions, interestingly enough, all come from Ceylon. The first of these inscriptions is one of "the earliest inscriptions in Ceylon that can be definitely attributed to a particular ruler" and dates, according to Paranavitana, "to the period between 210 and 200 B.C.": *gamaṇi-uti-maharajhaha[jhita abi-ti]śaya leṇe daśa-diśaśa sagaye dine mata-pitaśa aṭaya,* "The cave of princess (Abi) Tissā, daughter of the great king Gāmaṇī-Uttiya, is given to the Saṅgha of the ten directions, for the benefit of (her) mother and father."[101] In addition to this, we find four virtually identical inscriptions recording the gifts of caves to the *Saṅgha* by "Princess (Abi) Anurādhī, daughter of King Nāga and wife of King Uttiya, and King Uttiya," all of which end by saying that the act was done *aparimita-lokadatuya śatana śita-śukaye,* "for the welfare and happiness of beings in the boundless universe." Although less certain, it is possible that these four inscriptions are even slightly earlier than the record of the Princess Tissā.[102]

All of this renders Lamotte's interpretation less and less likely: the occurrence of the formula *mātāpituna aṭhāyā* at Bhārhut, of *sukhāya hotu savasatānaṃ* at Pauni, of *mata-pitaśa aṭaya* and *aparimita-lokadatuya śatana śita-śukaye* in third century B.C.E. Ceylon, clearly proves that the doctrine of the transference of merit associated with the Hīnayāna schools in later inscriptions was both very old and very widespread.

XII.

In concluding, we can note that all of this is of some interest in regard to the problem of the transference of merit in the Pāli canon and in modern Theravāda Buddhism in Southeast Asia. Bechert, among others, has written extensively on the subject and, although his exact position is not always immediately clear, he seems to want to say that the doctrine of the transference of merit is a "Mahāyāna idea." He says, for example:

> The fact that the possibility of transferring merit—a concept originating from the very beginnings of Mahāyāna Buddhism—has been acknowledged by all Buddhists—by the adherents of the 'Great Vehicle' as well as the Theravādins—confirms clearly to what extent this theory has to be considered as a logical consequence of the doctrines of early Buddhism. Thus we must not be astonished if we find traces of the Bodhisattva ideal in many texts of the Sarvāstivādins, e.g., the Avadānaśataka. These traces are not to be explained as outside influences; i.e., influences from Mahāyāna doctrines. On the contrary, these ideas followed quite naturally from the dynamics of early Buddhist thought—and Mahāyāna was based on these (the earlier German version of this passage says simply "Vielmehr ergaben sich diese Gedanken zwanglos aus der Entwicklung der buddhistischen Lehre").[103]

The position here is, as I have said, not altogether clear, although in a later paper Bechert appears to be a little more straightforward.[104]

If then, in the end, Bechert wants the doctrine of the transference of merit to be a "Mahāyāna idea" in the Theravāda Buddhism of Ceylon, there appear to be only two problems. The first is that this ignores the early and massive presence of *the* doctrine in Hīnayāna inscriptions. The second is that he does not give us the means by which we could know where what he presents as the "Mahāyāna idea" of the transference of merit actually comes from. His references are always in the form "in den Mahāyāna-Texten," but those texts are never cited nor are we ever given specific references. Moreover, the implication here is that there is a single, unified, and unchanging conception of the "idea" in Mahāyāna texts. But on the basis of a limited acquaintance with Mahāyāna *Sūtra* literature, this does not, to me, seem very likely, and in any case is yet to be demonstrated. What we need is a thorough study of the idea (or ideas) of the transference of merit in Mahāyāna literature. Then we will have something to compare and contrast with the material presented most recently by Agasse. For the moment, we can only observe that we know that the Pāli material that Agasse has analyzed is quite clearly much closer to the doctrine of the transference of merit which is associated epigraphically with the Hīnayāna schools than it is to the doctrine found in Mahāyāna inscriptions. But again, Bechert, by formulating an interesting hypothesis, has opened up new ground for what promises to be some very interesting exploration.

Notes

The research and writing of this paper were made possible by a grant from the Translations Program of the National Endowment for the Humanities, to which I will always be grateful. I should like to thank Professors L. O. Gómez and H. Durt for having read this paper and for allowing me to benefit from their observations. Also I must especially thank my friend Dr. John Thiel for having made a heroic attempt—not always successful—to make it more readable.

1. See, most recently, O. von Hinüber, "On the Tradition of Pāli Texts in India, Ceylon and Burma," *Buddhism in Ceylon and Studies on Religious Syncretism,* Abhandlungen der Akademie der Wissenschaften in Göttingen, Phil.-Hist. Klasse. Dritte Folge. Nr. 108, ed. H. Bechert (Göttingen: 1978) 48–49.

2. G. P. Malalasekera, *The Pāli Literature of Ceylon* (Colombo: 1928) 44.

3. J. Bloch, *Les inscriptions d'Aśoka* (Paris: 1950) 154.

4. Cf. E. Senart, *Les inscriptions de Piyadasi,* T. II (Paris: 1886) 103; *Histoire du bouddhisme indien,* 258–259.

5. *Histoire du bouddhisme indien,* 157; cf. 164–165; cf. H. Lüders, *Bharhut Inscriptions,* Corpus Inscriptionum Indicarum, Vol. II, Pt. 2 (Ootacamund: 1963) 71; B. M. Barua and K. G. Sinha, *Barhut Inscriptions* (Calcutta: 1926) 28–30. Note too that the epithet *pacanikāyika* also occurs once in the Brāhmī inscriptions from Pauni that appear to date from approximately the same period as the Bhārhut and Sāñcī inscriptions; see V. B. Kolte, "Brahmi Inscriptions from Pauni," *EI* 38 (1969) 171–172, 173 (A); S. B. Deo and J. P. Joshi, *Pauni Excavation (1969–1970)* (Nagpur: 1972) 39, no. 8.

6. G. Fussman, "Documents épigraphiques kouchans," *BEFEO* 61 (1974) 54–61. [This is incorrect. The earliest reference actually occurs in an inscription of the year 2 of Kaniṣka; cf. G. Schopen, "On Monks, Nuns, and 'Vulgar' Practices: The Introduction of the Image Cult into Indian Buddhism," Ch. XI below, and the sources cited there in n. 18.]

7. J. Ph. Vogel, "Prakrit Inscriptions from a Buddhist Site at Nāgārjunikoṇḍa," *EI* 20 (1929) C1; J. Burgess, *The Buddhist Stūpas of Amarāvatī and Jaggayyapeta,* Archaeological Survey of Southern India, Vol. I (London: 1887) 35; C. Sivaramamurti, *Amarāvatī Sculptures in the Madras Government Museum,* Bulletin of the Madras Government Museum, N. S., Vol. IV (Madras: 1956) 34.2; cf. N. Dutt, "Notes on the Nāgārjunikoṇḍa-Inscriptions," *IHQ* 7 (1931) 633–653; D. L. Barua, "On Some Terms in the Nāgārjunikoṇḍa Inscriptions," *Indian Culture* 1 (1934) 107–111. It should also be noted here that the title *majhimabaṇaka* occurs three times, the title *ekautirika-baṇaka (=Ekottarika°-)* once, and the title *śayutaka-baṇaka (=Saṃyuttaka)* once in the Brāhmī inscriptions of Ceylon; see S. Paranavitana, *Inscriptions of Ceylon,* Vol. I, *Containing Cave Inscriptions from 3rd Century B.C. to 1st Century A.C. and Other Inscriptions in the Early Brāhmī Script* (Ceylon: 1970) nos. 330, 708, 852; 407; 666. Unfortunately, none of these titles occur in inscriptions that also contain the name of a king, so it is impossible to date them with any precision. They could date anywhere from the third or second century B.C.E. to the first century C.E., or even much later; cf. P. E. E. Fernando, "Palaeographical Development of the Brahmi Script in Ceylon from the 3rd Century B.C. to the 7th Century A.D.," *UCR* 7 (1949) 282–301. It is interesting to note that the title *pacanikāyika* does not seem to occur anywhere in the Ceylonese Brāhmī inscriptions. Finally, it is worth noting that

Lévi at least has seen in the epithet *saṃyuktāgaminaḥ* found in "L'inscription de Mahānāman à Bodh-gaya" a clear reference to the *Saṃyuktāgama,* but this epithet, indeed the whole of this inscription, is associated with monks from Ceylon; see S. Lévi, "L'inscription de Mahānāman à Bodh-gaya, Essai d'Exêgèse appliquée à l'épigraphie bouddhique," *Indian Studies in Honor of Charles Rockwell Lanman* (Cambridge, Mass.: 1929) 46.

8. Cf. *Histoire du bouddhisme indien,*. 164–165. Note that the title *sutata-pāḷi-bāṇaka* occurs once, and the title *vinayadhara* twice in the Ceylonese Brāhmī inscriptions (Paranavitana, *Inscriptions of Ceylon,* Vol. I, nos. 1202; 1178, 1207), but all three occurrences are found in inscriptions that Paranavitana classifies as "Later."

9. For details see, at least, S. Lévi, "Sur la recitation primitive des textes bouddhiques," *JA* (1915) 401–447; B. M. Barua, "Aṭṭhakavagga and Pārāyaṇavagga as Two Independent Buddhist Anthologies," *Proceedings and Transactions of the Fourth Oriental Conference* (Allahabad: 1928) 211–219; "Some Points Concerning the Mahāniddesa," *Fifth Indian Oriental Conference, Proceedings,* Vol. I (Lahore: 1930) 603–615; N. A. Jayawickrama, "The Sutta Nipāta: Its Title and Form," *UCR* 6 (1948) 78–86; "The Vaggas of the Sutta Nipāta," *UCR* 6 (1948) 229–256; "Sutta Nipāta: Some Suttas from the Aṭṭhaka Vagga," *UCR* 8 (1950) 244–255; "The Sutta Nipāta: Pucchās of the Pārāyaṇa Vagga," *UCR* 9 (1951) 61–68; "A Critical Analysis of the Pāli Sutta Nipāta Illustrating its Gradual Growth: General Observations," *UCR* 9 (1951) 113–124.

10. N. A. Jayawickrama, "The Vaggas of the Sutta Nipāta," *UCR* 6 (1948) 229–232; *Histoire du bouddhisme indien,* 256–259.

11. See the two interesting articles published by L. O. Gómez ("Proto-Mādhyamika in the Pāli Canon," *Philosophy East and West* 26 [1976] 137–165) and H. Nakamura ("A Process of the Origination of Buddhist Meditations in Connection with the Life of Buddha," *Studies in Pali and Buddhism* [*Kashyap Volume*], ed. A. K. Narain [Delhi: 1979] 269–277). The doctrinal discontinuity noted especially by Nakamura, but also by Gómez, between the *Aṭṭhaka-* and the *Pārāyaṇa-vaggas* and the Pāli canon as a whole is also suggested from yet another angle by the lack of parallels to the former in the latter; cf. R. Otto Franke, "Die Suttanipāta-Gāthās mit ihren Parallelen," *ZDMG* 63 (1909) 1–64, 255–286, 551–586; 64 (1910) 760–807; 66 (1910) 204–260, 706–708 (= *Kleine Schriften* [Wiesbaden: 1978] 474–777).

12. H. Lüders, *Bhārhut und die buddhistischen Literatur,* Abhandlungen für die Kunde des Morgenlandes, XXVI.3 (Leipzig: 1941) 136–176.

13. *Histoire du bouddhisme indien,* 444–445.

14. It could be argued that there is at least one exception to this. It could be argued that the relief labeled *ajātasata bhagavato vaṃdate* in which "three stages of the visit of the king to Buddha are shown, as described in the *Sāmaññaphala-sutta*" presupposes the existence of this particular text; see E. J. Thomas, *The Life of Buddha as Legend and History,* 3rd ed. (London: 1949) x. In fact, however, it seems to presuppose only the text's narrative frame since it appears very likely that, as Thomas says, the doctrinal content of the *Sāmaññaphala-sutta* has been "inserted in a legend of king Ajātasattu, who is said to have come to Buddha after having inquired of the leaders of six rival schools" (ibid., 179). The inscription and the relief presuppose only this "legend." Note that the essential doctrinal components of this text occur verbatim again and again throughout the *Sīlakkhandha-vagga* of the *Dīgha* (*Suttas* 1–13) and almost certainly had an independent existence (178). Note too that essentially the same narrative frame—although with different characters—was also used by the author of the *Milindapañha.*

15. K. R. Norman, "The Gāndhārī Version of the Dharmapada," *Buddhist Studies in Honour of I. B. Horner,* ed. L. Cousins et al. (Dordrecht/Boston: 1974) 171–179.

16. J. Brough, *The Gāndhārī Dharmapada,* London Oriental Series, Vol. VII (Oxford: 1962) 55–56.

17. J. W. de Jong, "The Study of Buddhism. Problems and Perspectives," in J. W. de Jong, *Buddhist Studies,* ed. G. Schopen (Berkeley: 1979) 19. [This is in reference to canonical texts only; see also p. 16 n. 5 above.]

18. O. von Hinüber, "Die Erforschung der Gilgit-Handschriften (Funde buddhistischer Sanskrit-Handschriften I)," *Nachrichten der Ak. d. W. in Göttingen,* I. Phil.-hist. Kl., Jahrgang 1979, Nr. 12 (Göttingen: 1979) 341, no. 4a.

19. E. Zürcher, *The Buddhist Conquest of China, The Spread and Adaptation of Buddhism in Early Medieval China,* Vol. I (Leiden: 1959), notes, however, that "the versions [of the *Madhyamāgama* and *Ekottarāgama*] which now figure in the canon seem to be a later redaction of Dharmanandin's translation, executed by Saṅghadeva at the very end of the fourth century" (204). This statement must be supplemented by the more detailed remarks in Ét. Lamotte, "Un sūtra composite de l'Ekottarāgama," *BSOAS* 30 (1967) 104ff; see also E. Waldschmidt, "Central Asian Sūtra Fragments and their Relation to the Chinese Āgamas," *Die Sprache der ältesten buddhistischen Überlieferung,* Abhandlungen der Akademie der Wissenschaften in Göttingen, Phil.-Hist. Klasse. Dritte Folge. Nr. 117, ed. H. Bechert (Göttingen: 1980) 169ff. There were, of course, isolated pieces of the *nikāya/āgama* literature translated prior to this time; cf. *L'inde classique,* T. II (Paris: 1953) 2070, 2082–2083.

20. For Bareau, see especially *Recherches sur la biographie du Buddha dans les Sūtrapiṭaka et les Vinayapiṭaka anciens: de la quête de l'éveil à la conversion de Śāriputra et de Maudgalyāyana* (Paris: 1963); *Recherches sur la biographie du Buddha dans les Sūtrapiṭaka et les Vinayapiṭaka anciens: les derniers mois, le parinirvāṇa et les funérailles,* T. I (Paris: 1971); T. II (Paris: 1971); see also n. 36 below. For Frauwallner, *The Earliest Vinaya and the Beginnings of Buddhist Literature,* Serie Orientale Roma, VIII (Rome: 1956); "The Historical Data We Possess on the Person and the Doctrine of the Buddha," *EW* 7 (1957) 309–312. For a few typical examples of the invocation of this principle, see Ét. Lamotte, "Lotus et buddha supramondain," *BEFEO* 69 (1981) 32–33; Brough, *The Gāndhārī Dharmapada,* xviii; K. R. Norman, "Four Etymologies from the Sabhiya-Sutta," *Buddhist Studies in Honour of Walpola Rahula,* ed. S. Balasooriya et al. (London: 1980) 179 (§ 8.1). But note too that the acceptance of this principle is not limited to textual scholars but has been taken up by a wide variety of modern scholars dealing with Buddhism; see, for example, J. Ph. Vogel, "The Past Buddhas and Kāśyapa in Indian Art and Epigraphy," *Asiatica, Festschrift Friedrich Weller* (Leipzig: 1954) 808; F. E. Reynolds, "The Many Lives of Buddha: A Study of Sacred Biography and Theravāda Tradition," *The Biographical Process, Studies in the History and Psychology of Religion,* ed. F. E. Reynolds and D. Capps (The Hague: 1976) 41; etc.

21. A. Bareau, *Les sectes bouddhiques du petit véhicule* (Paris: 1955) 16.

22. Bareau, *Les sectes bouddhiques,* 16–19.

23. Bareau, *Les sectes bouddhiques,* 27, 36. The second century date is Bareau's. It may be possible to push it somewhat further back, but this depends on the date of the famous Mathurā Lion Capital Inscription, which is highly controversial. See, for example, R. Salomon, "The Kṣatrapas and Mahākṣatrapas of India," *WZKS* 17 (1973) 11; A. K. Narain, *The Indo-Greeks* (Oxford: 1957) 142ff.

24. N. Dutt, *Early Monastic Buddhism,* Vol. II (Calcutta: 1945) 14.

25. For some of the hypotheses that Aśoka's "Schismenedikt" has generated, see L. Alsdorf, "Aśoka's Schismen-Edikt und das dritte Konzil," *IIJ* 3 (1959) 161–174 (= *Kleine Schriften* [Wiesbaden: 1974] 414–427); H. Bechert, "Aśoka's 'Schismenedikt' und der Begriff Sanghabheda," *WZKS* 5 (1961) 18–52; H. Bechert, "The Importance of Aśoka's So-called Schism Edict," *Indological and Buddhist Studies. Volume in Honour of Professor J. W. de Jong on his Sixtieth Birthday,* ed. L. A. Hercus et al. (Canberra: 1982) 61–68.

26. W. Wassilieff, "Le bouddhisme dans son plein développement d'après les vinayas," *RHR* 34 (1896) 318–325. It is interesting to note that, in 1896, S. Lévi, who translated Wassilieff's paper into French, added a short preface to it in which he found it necessary to say that Wassilieff's "opinions . . . puissent choquer les idées courantes," and to add: "Il va sans dire que le traducteur n'entend pas se solidariser avec l'auteur: comme indianiste, il se voit même obligé d'exprimer les réserves les plus formelles sur les conclusions hardies de M. Wassilieff." But about ten years later in an article of his own Lévi, after quoting with approval the conclusions of Wassilieff's article, says "A mon tour, je me pose la même question"; then follows nearly a page of questions of almost exactly the same purport as Wassilieff's—none of which, again, have been answered. See S. Lévi, "Les éléments de formation du Divyāvadāna," *TP* 8 (1907) 116–117 and n. 1.

27. *Histoire du bouddhisme indien,* 197.

28. Bareau, *Les sectes bouddhiques,* 48. See also L. Renou and J. Filliozat, *L'inde classique. Manuel des Études indiennes,* T. II (Paris-Hanoi: 1953) 517 (§ 2245); H. Bechert, "Notes on the Formation of Buddhist Sects and the Origins of Mahāyāna," *German Scholars on India,* Vol. I (Varanasi: 1973) 10, 11.

29. A. Bareau, "La construction et le culte des stūpa d'après les Vinayapiṭaka," *BEFEO* 50 (1960) 257–261, esp. 260.

30. H. C. Norman, *The Dhammapadaṭṭhakathā,* Vol. III (London: 1906–1915) 250–255; cf. E. W. Burlingame, *Buddhist Legends,* Pt. 3, Harvard Oriental Series, Vol. 30 (Cambridge, Mass.: 1921) 68–69.

31. For example, "the smile of the Buddha," found also at *Aṅguttara,* iii, 214; *Majjhima,* ii, 45, 74 (cf. *Saṃyutta,* ii, 254; *Vinaya,* iii, 105—all references to the Pāli texts are to the Pali Text Society editions); *Mahāvastu* (Senart ed.), i, 317; *Divyāvadāna* (Cowell and Neil ed.), 67ff, 138ff, 265ff, etc. Or the stories of King Kṛkin and Kāśyapa found also at *Mūlasarvāstivāda-vinaya, Gilgit Manuscripts,* iii 1, 191, 195, 200; iii 2, 77–78; iii 4, 190–193 = *Divyāvadāna* (Cowell and Neil ed.), 22–24; *Avadānaśataka* (Speyer ed.), II, 76, 124–125; *Avadānakalpalatā* (Vaidya ed.), i, 95 (vss. 147–148), 145 (vss. 132–133), 279 (vss. 16–17); *Ratnamālāvadāna* (Takahata ed.), 132; etc.

32. Bareau, "La construction et le culte des stūpa," 261.

33. *Gilgit Manuscripts,* iii 1, 73.16–79.2; *Peking,* 41, 179-3-6 to 180-4-2. In light of what follows, it is of some significance to note that the *Mūlasarvāstivāda-vinaya* appears to be a fairly late compilation; cf. *Histoire du bouddhisme indien,* 187, 196; Ét. Lamotte, "La légende du Buddha," *RHR* 134 (1948) 61–62. See, however, the more recent observations in *Saṅghabhedavastu,* i, xxff. Note that neither the Chinese versions nor the Pāli version of this account are noted in J. L. Panglung, *Die Erzählstoffe des Mūlasarvāstivāda-vinaya analysiert auf Grund der tibetischen Übersetzung,* Studia Philologica Buddhica, Monograph Series III (Tokyo: 1981) 34; nor has he noted that the verses of the text are also found elsewhere; see H. Lüders, "Weitere Beiträge zur Geschichte und Geographie von Ostturkestan," *Philologica Indica* (Göttingen: 1940) 612; E. Waldschmidt, "Der Buddha preist die Verehrungswürdigkeit seiner Reliquien," *Von Ceylon bis Turfan* (Göttingen: 1967) 424–427.

34. E. B. Cowell and R. A. Neil, *The Divyāvadāna* (Cambridge: 1886) 76.10–80.9, 465.10–469.18.

35. Particularly significant in this regard is the absence of any reference to the King Kṛkin since Buddhist Sanskrit literary tradition consistently associates the Buddha Kāśyapa, and especially his funeral and the deposition of his bodily remains, with this king; cf. M. Hofinger, *Le congrès du lac Anavatapta I: Légendes des anciens* (*Sthavirāvadāna*) (Louvain: 1956) 225, n. 1. Not only is this association consistent, but—as a glance at the references in n. 31 will reveal—it is also widespread. The fact that our Sanskrit text knows nothing of this association is, therefore, as I have said, particularly significant.

36. Note that the existence of a text which knew only a "pre-*stūpa*" form of the relic cult creates some problems for Bareau's recent attempts to reconstruct the origin of the *stūpa* and its cult. This is particularly so since the text in question appears to represent perhaps the oldest tradition we have that is connected with one of the Previous Buddhas, and since we know from the Nigālī Sāgar Edict that the cult of the Previous Buddhas was, at the very least, pre-Aśokan. Cf. A. Bareau, "Sur l'origine des piliers dits Aśoka, des stūpa et des arbres sacrés du bouddhisme primitif," *Indologica Taurinensia* 2 (1974) 9–36; "Le parinirvāṇa du Buddha et la naissance de la religion bouddhique," *BEFEO* 61 (1974) 275–299; "Les récits canoniques des funérailles du Buddha et leurs anomalies: nouvel essai d'interprétation," *BEFEO* 62 (1975) 151–189.

37. Note that there appears to be at least one other instance in Buddhist literature where a "text" appears to have undergone a process of revision similar to that which we have found here. The "text" in question is the *Vyāghrī-jātaka,* and although the various versions of this "text" have yet to be systematically studied from this point of view, it is clear that at one stage, represented by the *Jātakamālā* version (Ch. I), the "text" knew nothing of a *stūpa,* and that at another stage, represented by the *Suvarṇabhāsottama* (Ch. XVIII), reference to a *stūpa* had been fully incorporated into the tale and has become an integral part of it. In fact, the manuscript tradition of the *Suvarṇabhāsottama* by itself seems to preserve two distinct stages of the revision.

In a more general vein, we must also note that there have, of course, been other more purely philological attempts to get beyond the earliest known redaction of the canon; cf. S. Lévi, "Observations sur une langue précanonique du bouddhisme," *JA* (1912) 495–514; H. Lüders, *Beobachtungen über die Sprache des buddhistischen Urkanons,* Abh. d. Deutschen Akad. d. Wiss. zu Berlin, Kl. f. Sprachen, Lit. u. Kunst. Jg. 1952 Nr. 10, Hg. v. E. Waldschmidt (Berlin: 1954); but see also the more recent work of O. von Hinüber, "Pāli Kaṭhati: ein Beitrag zur Überlieferungsgeschichte des Theravāda-Kanons," *IIJ* 21 (1979) 21–26, and the paper cited in n. 1 above. Unfortunately, the results of these important studies—when not controverted—have so far been rather limited from a larger historical point of view.

38. H. Oldenberg, *Buddha, sein Leben, seine Lehre, seine Gemeinde* (Stuttgart: 1923; first pub. 1881) 424; trans. *Buddha: His Life, His Doctrine, His Order* (London: 1882) 377.

39. R. P. Chanda, *Dates of the Votive Inscriptions on the Stupas at Sanchi,* MASI, No. 1 (1919); A. H. Dani, *Indian Palaeography* (Oxford: 1963) 62–65; V. Dehejia, *Early Buddhist Rock Temples, A Chronological Study* (London: 1972) 35–36, 186–188. I follow Dehejia here.

40. *Histoire du bouddhisme indien,* 455. Lüders, *Bharhut Inscriptions,* 1–2, counts twenty-five monk donors, sixteen nuns, and ninety-four lay. The figures for Sāñcī are virtually the same: out of a total of four hundred thirty seven (nineteen are either

fragmentary or nondonative), there are one hundred sixty three monastic donors. See G. Bühler, "Votive Inscriptions from the Sānchi Stūpas," *EI* 2 (1899) 87–116; Bühler, "Further Inscriptions from Sānchi," *EI* 2 (1899) 366–408.

41. M. Shizutani, *Indo bukkyō himei mokuroku* [*Catalogue of Indian Buddhist Inscriptions*] (Kyoto: 1979) §§ 206, 210, 217, 223, 231, 254; 226; 277; 288; *Histoire du bouddhisme indien,* 157.

42. S. Konow, *Kharoshṭhī Inscriptions with the Exception of Those of Aśoka,* Corpus Inscriptionum Indicarum, Vol. II, Pt. 1 (Calcutta: 1929). Monks: XXXV.1, XXXVI.1, 2, 4, 5, 6, 7, 8, XL, XLII, XLIII, XLIV, LII, LVIII, LXXXVIII, plus the inscription edited by Fussman, *BEFEO* 61 (1974) 54–58. Note that the donors in XL, XLII, XLIII, and XLIV are taken as monks on the basis of the terms *sadaviyarisa, sadayarisa,* etc.; cf. H. Lüders, *A List of Brāhmī Inscriptions from the Earliest Times to about* A.D. *400 with the Exception of Those of Aśoka,* Appendix to *EI* 10, 1909/10 (Calcutta: 1912) 223; Brough, *The Gāndhārī Dharmapada,* 177 and xx–xxi; Konow (107) equates the terms with *sārdhaṃchara* or *sārdhaṁvihārin.* Note that all these donors appear to have monastic names and that, in at least one case (XLIII), Konow has reconstructed the reading as *sa[dharmarataśamanasa sadayarisa]* although this is admittedly somewhat odd. Laymen: I, II, XIII, XV, XVII, XXI, XXVII, XXXI, XXXII, XXXV.4, XLVI, XLVII, XLIX, LXXIV, LXXVI, LXXVII, LXXX, LXXXII, LXXXVI.

43. Konow, *Kharoshṭhī Inscriptions,* XXXVI.7; Fussman, *BEFEO* 61 (1974).

44. H. Lüders, *Mathurā Inscriptions,* Abh. d. Akad. d. Wiss. in Göttingen, Philo-Hist. Klasse, Dritte Folge, Nr. 47, ed. K. L. Janert (Göttingen: 1961) §§ 4(?), 8, 24, 29, 31, 32, 33a, 33b, 35a, 35b, 36, 37, 38, 39a, 39b, 40a, 40b, 41, 44, 45, 46, 52, 53, 54, 55, 56, 58, 59, 67, 80 (?), 90, 103, 121, 126, 152, 154, 157, 179, 185, 186.

45. Lüders, *Mathurā Inscriptions,* §§ 33a, 33b, 35b; 46 [on *prāhaṇīka* cf. *BHSD,* 389 s.v. *prahāṇa;* 390 s.v. *prahāṇika* ("characterized by religious strenuosity"); 394 s.v. *prāhāṇika* ("engaging in [ascetic] exertion"); Th. Damsteegt, *Epigraphical Hybrid Sanskrit, Its Rise, Spread, Characteristics and Relationship to Buddhist Hybrid Sanskrit* (Leiden: 1978) 247; Lüders, *Mathurā Inscriptions,* 83, n. 2]; 24.

46. J. Burgess, *Report on the Buddhist Cave Temples and Their Inscriptions,* Archaeological Survey of Western India, Vol. IV (London: 1883; repr. Varanasi: 1975) IV.7, 8, 9, 10, 20 (?); VI.2; VII.3, 8, 9, 12, 13, 14, 16, 17; VIII.17; XI.6, 7, 9; XII.1, 3, 5, 7, 8, 10, 11, 12, 13, 14, 15, for monastic donors.

47. G. Schopen, "Mahāyāna in Indian Inscriptions," *IIJ* 21 (1979) 1–19, esp. 9. It should be noted that there is a certain amount of overlap among the "Mathurā Inscriptions," the "Cave Temple Inscriptions," and those grouped under the heading "Mahāyāna." A number of inscriptions from the first two groups are also included in the third.

48. See Oldenberg's statement quoted above. That this position is still very much current is clear, for example, from H. Bechert, "Contradictions in Sinhalese Buddhism," *Religion and the Legitimation of Power in Sri Lanka,* ed. B. L. Smith (Chambersburg, PA: 1978) 192–193. We can, however, also cite two recent exceptions to these views: R. F. Gombrich, *Precept and Practice. Traditional Buddhism in the Rural Highlands of Ceylon* (Oxford: 1971) 319, and D. Seyfort Ruegg, "A Recent Work on the Religions of Tibet and Mongolia," *TP* 61 (1976) 313–314.

49. Konow, *Kharoshṭhī Inscriptions,* monastic: XXXVI.1, 2, 4, 5, 6, 7, 8, XL, XLII, XLIII, XLIV, LVIII, LXXXVIII; an inscription reported by Fussman, *BEFEO* 61 (1974), would be one more. Konow's lay inscriptions are: XXI, XXXV.4, XLVI, XLVII, XLIX.

50. Lüders, *Mathurā Inscriptions,* monastic: §§ 4, 8, 24, 29, 41, 67, 80, 90, 103, 121, 126, 152, 154, 155, 157, 179, 185, 186; lay: §§ 1, 74, 76, 81, 135, 136, 150, 167, 172, 180. Note that §§ 8, 67, 152, 179, 185, 186 also fall into the inscriptions grouped under the heading "Mahāyāna."

51. Burgess, *Report on the Buddhist Cave Temples,* IV.7, 8, 9, 10; XI.7, 9; XII.1, 3, 5, 7, 8, 11, 12, 13, 14, 15, all monastic; XII.2 is the one exception. Here, the overlap with the Mahāyāna group is much greater. Only five of the seventeen inscriptions considered here are non-Mahāyāna: XII.2, 3, 7, 11, 13.

52. Schopen, "Mahāyāna in Indian Inscriptions," 9.

53. Lüders, *A List of Brāhmī Inscriptions,* §§ 918, 919, 925, 926, 927; K. G. Goswami, *EI* 24 (1938) 210ff; Lüders, *Mathurā Inscriptions,* § 24; Damsteegt, *Epigraphical Hybrid Sanskrit,* 152, 178–180; A. K. Coomaraswamy, *History of Indian and Indonesian Art* (London: 1927) 58–59; O. Takata, "On the Dated Buddha Images in the Kushan Art of Mathurā," *Bijutsu Kenkyu* 184 (1956) 223–240.

54. J. C. Harle, "A Hitherto Unknown Dated Sculpture from Gandhāra: A Preliminary Report," *South Asian Archaeology 1973,* ed. J. E. van Lohuizen-De Leeuw and J. M. M. Ubaghs (Leiden: 1974) 128–135. The inscription on this image is the same one published by Fussman in *BEFEO* 61; see n. 6; cf. K. W. Dobbins, "Gandhāra Buddha Images with Inscribed Dates," *EW* 18 (1968) 281–288.

55. Konow, *Kharoshṭhī Inscriptions,* XXXVI.7.

56. G. Nagao, "The Architectural Tradition in Buddhist Monasticism," *Studies in History of Buddhism,* ed. A. K. Narain (Delhi: 1980) 194, 195; cf. G. Nagao, *The Ancient Buddhist Community in India and its Cultural Activities* (Kyoto: 1971); D. Mitra, *Buddhist Monuments* (Calcutta: 1971) 20–52; Dehejia, *Early Buddhist Rock Temples,* 71–113.

57. H. Sarkar, *Studies in Early Buddhist Architecture of India* (Delhi: 1966) 15–24, esp. 22.

58. Sarkar, *Studies,* 53, 55; note, however, that there has been some doubt expressed as to whether these are Buddhist *stūpas;* cf. Mitra, *Buddhist Monuments,* 124.

59. Konow, *Kharoshṭhī Inscriptions,* XV, LXXII, LXXX, LXXXVI.

60. Konow, *Kharoshṭhī Inscriptions,* XIII, XXVII, LXXVI, etc.

61. See Konow, *Kharoshṭhī Inscriptions,* 140, where he discusses the interpretations of Hoernle and Majumdar as well as his own. There can, however, be little doubt that *yaṭhi* here refers to the "pole" *(yaṣṭi)* of the *stūpa.* There are textual parallels for both *yaṭhipratiṭhana* and *yaṭhiṃ aropayata.* We find *yūpa-yaṣṭir abhyantare pratipāditā,* for example, in the much-studied *stūpa* passage at *Divyāvadāna* (Cowell and Neil ed.), 244.7; see most recently G. Roth, "Bemerkungen zum Stūpa des Kṣemaṃkara," *StII* 5/6 (1980) 181–190, esp. 184–186; cf. F. B. J. Kuiper, "Yūpayaṣṭi- (Divy. 244.11)," *IIJ* 3 (1959) 204–205. And *yaṣṭim āropayed* occurs repeatedly in a short text, three copies of which I have identified among the Gilgit Manuscripts, entitled the *Adbhutadharmaparyāya.* See O. von Hinüber, "Die Erforschung der Gilgit-Handschriften. Nachtrag," *ZDMG* 130.2 (1980) *25*–*26* nos. 11, 13d, and 18; here in the repeated description of a miniature *stūpa,* we read *yo vā . . . mṛtpiṇḍād āmalakapramāṇaṃ stūpaṃ pratiṣṭhāpayet sūcīmātrāṃ yaṣṭim āropayed,* etc. [See G. Schopen, "The Ritual Obligations and Donor Roles of Monks in the Pāli *Vinaya,*" Ch. IV, below; and Y. Bentor, "The Redactions of the *Adbhutadharmaparyāya* from Gilgit," *JIABS* 11.2 (1988) 21–52.]

62. Harle, "A Hitherto Unknown Dated Sculpture from Gandhāra," 128.

63. The crosses mark an interesting feature of this inscription. Lüders says, "The

text contains eight *maṅgala* symbols which are engraved generally after the seventh *akṣara* irrespective of the meaning of the words" (*Mathurā Inscriptions,* 80).

64. According to Lüders, "Vojyavaśika (?) probably refers to the native place of the donor" (*Mathurā Inscriptions,* 80).

65. This is Lüders' translation of *prāhaṇīka;* see n. 45 above.

66. Fussman, "Documents épigraphiques kouchans," *BEFEO* 61 (1974) 56.

67. Damsteegt, *Epigraphical Hybrid Sanskrit,* 164–165 and notes.

68. D. C. Sircar, *EI* 30 (1953–1954) 184; Damsteegt, *Epigraphical Hybrid Sanskrit,* 164, n. 50; Shizutani, *Indo bukkyō himei mokuroku,* § 639. Here, I follow Damsteegt.

69. J. Burgess, *Report on the Elura Cave Temples and the Brahmanical and Jaina Caves of Western India,* Archaeological Survey of Western India, Vol. V (London: 1883) II. Kānheri Inscriptions, no. 7; Damsteegt, *Epigraphical Hybrid Sanskrit,* 186.

70. D. C. Sircar, *EI* 35 (1963–1964) 7ff, no. 2 (A, B); Shizutani, *Indo bukkyō himei mokuroku,* 715.

71. Burgess, *Report on the Buddhist Cave Temples,* IX.21.

72. Konow, *Kharoshṭhī Inscriptions,* LXXXVI; Damsteegt, *Epigraphical Hybrid Sanskrit,* 160, 165, n. 51.

73. Schopen, "Mahāyāna in Indian Inscriptions," 17, n. 24.

74. Lüders, *Mathurā Inscriptions,* §§ 2; 125, 157.

75. Burgess, *Report on the Buddhist Cave Temples,* IX.21.

76. Fussman, "Documents épigraphiques Kouchans," *BEFEO* 61 (1974) IV. "Vase inscrit de Qunduz," 58–61.

77. Burgess, *Report on the Elura Cave Temples,* II.4, 27; Shizutani, *Indo bukkyō himei mokuroku,* §§ 464, 482.

78. J. Ph. Vogel, *EI* 20 (1929–1930) H; Shizutani, *Indo bukkyō himei mokuroku,* § 708.

79. D. C. Sircar, *EI* 33 (1959–1960) 250; Shizutani, *Indo bukkyō himei mokuroku,* § 712.

80. Konow, *Kharoshṭhī Inscriptions,* LXXII; Shizutani, *Indo bukkyō himei mokuroku,* § 1775.

81. G. Bühler, *EI* 2 (1892) 212, no. 42; Shizutani, *Indo bukkyō himei mokuroku,* § 460.

82. There is one possible, though I think doubtful, exception to this. Lüders gives his Mathurā Inscription § 135 as: *{Ś}ā{ky}opāsakasya Suṣasya Hāruṣasya—dānaṃ Budhaprat{i}mā Ūttarasya H{ā}ruṣa{sya} vihāre sahā mātāpitihi—sarvasatvānaṃ hitasukhartha{ṃ}.* Note that what Lüders reconstructed as *{Ś}ā{ky}opāsakasya,* Cunningham and Vogel read as *upāsakasya.* Note too that if Lüders' reconstruction were to be accepted, this would be the only instance in the forty-five inscriptions associated with *Śākyabhikṣu/-bhikṣuṇīs, Śākyopāsikas,* etc., where the formula *sarvasatvānaṃ hitasukharthaṃ* occurs. And it is not only the occurrence of this formula which is odd here. The whole structure of Mathurā § 135 differs from what we find everywhere else associated with *Śākyabhikṣus,* etc. *Dānaṃ* never occurs with the latter, but always *deyadharmo 'yaṃ,* and neither the term *budhapratimā,* nor the phrase *sahā mātāpitihi* is ever found in their inscriptions. All of this, I think, puts Lüders' reconstruction in doubt.

83. The direct evidence for the affiliation of the formula *arogyadakṣiṇāye* is not so abundant as for some other formulae. It occurs three times in the Mathurā inscriptions (§§ 44, 46, 180) and, according to Damsteegt, in seven Kharoṣṭhī inscriptions (*Epigraphical Hybrid Sanskrit,* 162). Unfortunately, the name of a school appears to occur in only one of these inscriptions, the Wardak Vase Inscription (Konow, *Kharoshṭhī Inscriptions,*

LXXXVI) where *sarvasatvaṇa arogadakshiṇae* is found in association with the Mahāsāṅghikas. We also find the phrase *atmaṇasya arogada{kṣ}i{ṇa . . .}* in an inscription from Haḍḍa published more recently by Fussman in association with the Sarvāstivādins (*BEFEO* 66 [1969] 5–9). We can say only that, in the two instances in which the formula occurs in association with a specifically named school, that school is a Hīnayāna school, and that the formula never occurs in inscriptions associated with the Mahāyāna or *Śākyabhikṣus*, etc.

84. Konow, *Kharoshṭhī Inscriptions,* XXVII; S. S. Ram, "Taxila Silver Scroll Inscription, Year 136," *Indological Studies* 2 (1974) 45–52.

85. In addition to Mathurā Inscription § 29 cited above, it is also found, for example, at Konow, *Kharoshṭhī Inscriptions,* XXVII and LXXXII; in an inscription from Kalawān edited by Konow, *JRAS* (1932) 949ff (cf. Shizutani, *Indo bukkyō himei mokuroku,* § 1745); and in several inscriptions from Nāgārjunikoṇḍa in Vogel, *EI* 20 (1929–1930) C3, B4, B5, C2, C5; Sircar, *EI* 35 (1963–1964) 11–13, no. 4; cf. N. Dutt, *Buddhist Sects in India* (Calcutta: 1970) 124–125.

Since we have traced the affiliation of all the other formulae that occur in the five inscriptions I have quoted above, we might note that the formula *sarvabuddhapūjārtham* is also consistently associated with the Hīnayāna schools. It occurs three times in the Mathurā Inscriptions in association with the name of a school: once with the Sammitīyas (§ 80) and twice with the Mahāsāṅghikas (§§ 86, 157); it occurs in the Mathurā Lion Capital Inscription in association with the Sarvāstivādins in Konow, *Kharoshṭhī Inscriptions,* XV; and again it occurs in association with the Mahāsāṅghikas in a Mathurā inscription published by Sircar in *EI* 30 (1953–1954) 181; Shizutani, *Indo bukkyō himei mokuroku,* § 639.

86. Health and longevity are mentioned, for example, in two inscriptions from Nāgārjunikoṇḍa associated with the Aparamahāvinaseliyas (Vogel, *EI* 20 [1929–1930] E; and Sircar, *EI* 35 [1963–1964] 7ff, no. 2 [A, B]; Shizutani, *Indo bukkyō himei mokuroku,* §§ 684, 715), and in an inscription from Tor Ḍherai in conjunction with the Sarvāstivādins (Konow, *Kharoshṭhī Inscriptions,* XCII).

87. There are four possible exceptions: MadP i, Aj iii 4, Bih ii, and Sa i B(b)59; the key to any abbreviations used here (e.g. MadP i) and in what follows will be found in Schopen, "Mahāyāna in Indian Inscriptions," *IIJ* 21 (1979) 2–4. Of these, MadP i is very carelessly done and is full of omissions as can be seen in the text it gives for the *Pratītyasamutpādagāthā,* and it is therefore safe to assume that our formula—which makes up the second half of the inscription and which reads only *yad atra puṇyaṃ tat bhavatu mātāpitarebhyaḥ*—has suffered the same mutilation. Aj iii 4 reads: *deyadharmo 'yam śākyabhi(kṣor) bhadanta-dha{rma} devasya /// mātāpitro{:} -dasya ya{d atra} pu{ṇyaṃ tad bha}vatu cā(nutta)rājñanāvāptaye.* But again this has obviously been badly written and is corrupt. Note that the *yad atra* clause and the *mātāpitṛ* clause have been inverted. But note especially the *ca* preceding *anuttara-.* This is a good indication that *sarvasatvānām* has probably been inadvertently omitted. Bih ii, which reads *deyadharmo 'yaṃ pravaramahāyāna-yāyinyā(ḥ) paramopāsikā-śau(śrī)-santoṣa-vadhu-maharokāyā yad atra puṇyaṃ tad bhavatv iti,* is—in spite of the *iti,* or perhaps because of it (*iti* = etc.)—obviously incomplete. There is neither person nor thing for which the merit is supposed to be. The last case, Sa i B(b)59, is in the main well written and correct: *deyadharmo 'yaṃ śākyabhikṣo{r} buddhapṛi(ri)yasya yad atra puṇyaṃ tad bhavatu anuttarajñānāvātma(pta)ye.* But in light of the fact that in every other occurrence of our formula *sarvasatvānām* is either present or its absence can be accounted for, it is probably safe to assume that it has simply been accidentally omitted here.

These remarks concerning the presence of both *sarvasatva-* and *anuttarajñāna-* in virtually all instances of the formula do not agree with some statements made in my earlier paper. The latter, however, must be corrected. Cf. the following note.

88. There are again some apparent exceptions in which *anuttarajñānāvāptaye* appears to be omitted: MadP i, Bih ii, Ma i 185, MadP ii B, Aj iii 3, and Aj iii 5. But the first two of these are, as we have already seen, faulty or incomplete (cf. n. 87), and Ma i 185 also, according to Lüders, is probably incomplete (*Mathurā Inscriptions,* 211, n. 4). MadP ii B is one of four inscriptions on a set of seven images from Phophnar Kalan, two of which are very short, and two of which contain a formula. One of these formulae—*yad atra puṇyam tad bhavatu aparimita-lokadhātustha-sarvv-ānuśaya-{ba}ndhan-āvabaddha-satva-lokasy-ānāvaraṇa-jñān-āvāptaye*—is very unusual and, as Gai has pointed out, "is not met with anywhere else in epigraphs" (G. S. Gai, Post-script to M. Venkataramayya and C. B. Trivedi, "Four Buddhist Inscriptions from Phophnar Kalan," *EI* 37 [1967] 150). We have, therefore, some grounds for suspecting that the other formula—which reads only *yad atra puṇya{ṃ} tad {bhavatu sa}rvva-{sa}tvānām,* omitting *anuttarajñānāvāptaye*—is also unusual, since it too is found nowhere else in complete and otherwise unproblematic inscriptions. Finally, Aj iii 3 and 5 are perhaps somewhat more complicated. Aj iii 5 has *yad atra (puṇyam) tad bhavatu mā(tāpitroḥ) sarvvasatvā(nān) ca,* but Dhavalikar says, "The inscription consists of three lines while there are traces of some letters in the fourth line" (M. K. Dhavalikar, "New Inscriptions from Ajaṇṭa," *ArO* 7 [1968] 151). Aj iii 3 has virtually the same reading, but here Dhavalikar says that the second sentence of the inscription states "that the merit accruing to the pious act of Mitradharma was meant for the attainment of the supreme knowledge by all sentient beings including his parents and others" (150). On the basis of this remark it would seem that Dhavalikar has probably omitted one line in his transcription.

After having looked at the same material from a different point of view it is clear, as I said in the previous note, that a number of statements in my earlier paper "Mahāyāna in Indian Inscriptions" must be corrected. Without going into details here, let me simply say that lines 8–17 on p. 5 of that paper should be deleted, as well as the related statement at lines 32–33. And it should be noted that the simplest, certainly attestable form of the formula appears now to be *yad atra puṇyaṃ tad bhavatu sarvvasatvānām anuttarajñānāvāptaye,* found for example at Ma i 186, Bo i 72, and Na ii.

89. Cf. Shizutani, *Indo bukkyō himei mokuroku,* § 1823; B. N. Mukherjee, "A Mathura Inscription of the Year 26 and of the Period of Huvishka," *JAIH* 11 (1977–1978) 82–84. The same inscription was also published in R. C. Sharma, "New Buddhist Sculptures from Mathura," *Lalit Kalā* 19 (1979) 25–26; R. C. Sharma, *Buddhist Art of Mathurā* (Delhi: 1984) 232, n. 169. Neither of these editions appear to be altogether satisfactory and the publication of both a good facsimile and a critical edition is very much needed. [See now G. Schopen, "The Inscription on the Kuṣān Image of Amitābha and the Character of the Early Mahāyāna in India," *JIABS* 10.2 (1987) 99–134.]

90. For what appears to be "the earliest datable literary reference" to Amitābha, see P. Maxwell Harrison, "Buddhānusmṛti in the Pratyutpannabuddhasammukhāvasthita-samādhi-sūtra," *JIP* 6 (1978) 42–44, and for a recent view on at least certain aspects of the "cult" of Amitābha in India, see G. Schopen, "Sukhāvatī as a Generalized Religious Goal in Sanskrit Mahāyāna Sūtra Literature," *IIJ* 19 (1977) 177–210, esp. 204–205, and the additions and corrections to this in G. Schopen, "The Five Leaves of the Buddhabalādhānaprātihāryavikurvāṇanirdeśa-sūtra Found at Gilgit," *JIP* 5 (1978) 335, n. 2. See also J.

C. Huntington, "A Gandhāran Image of Amitāyus' Sukhāvatī," *Annali dell' Instituto Orientale di Napoli* 40 (1980) 651–672; Huntington, "Mathurā Evidence for the Early Teachings of Mahāyāna," to be published in a volume of papers read at an International Seminar on Mathurā at Mathurā in January 1980 [since published in D. M. Srinivasan, ed., *Mathurā. The Cultural Heritage* (New Delhi: 1988) 85–92] (I should like to thank Prof. Huntington for sending me copies of his papers, but I also must add that I think that there are a number of things in both papers that require further discussion); J. Brough, "Amitābha and Avalokiteśvara in an Inscribed Gandhāran Sculpture," *Indologica Taurinensia* 10 (1982) 65–70. (This, too, I think requires further discussion.)

91. Nakamura reads *nāgarakṣita* (cf. Shizutani, *Indo bukkyō himei mokuroku,* § 1823), Mukherjee, *sāmrakṣita* (cf. *JAIH* 83.3).

92. There are, however, at least six inscriptions where the Mahāyāna donative formula is also used by a donor who does not use a title, but gives only his name. Cf. Schopen, "Mahāyāna in Indian Inscriptions," 9, and the parenthetical statement at the bottom of 11.

93. Damsteegt, *Epigraphical Hybrid Sanskrit,* 185. A phrase very like it, however, occurs frequently in Sanskrit literary sources; e.g., *Ajitasenavyākaraṇanirdeśa, Gilgit Manuscripts,* i, 129.10: *anena kuśalamūlena sarvasatvā anuttarāṃ samyaksaṃbodhim abhisaṃbudhyante;* S. Bagchi, *Mūlasarvāstivādavinayavastu,* Vol. I (Darbhanga: 1967) 210.18: *yan mayā bhagavataḥ kāśyapasya samyaksaṃbuddhasya {sat}kārāḥ kṛtāḥ / anena mama kuśalamūlena bahavaḥ putrā bhaveyur iti;* Bagchi, *Mūlasarvāstivādavinayavastu,* Vol. II (Darbhanga: 1970) 170.20; P. L. Vaidya, *Avadānaśataka* (Darbhanga: 1958) 2.15, 5.11, 12, 16, etc.

94. Although they cannot be discussed here, it should be pointed out that Shizutani has collected six inscriptions from the Gupta period which he thinks belong to the Mahāyāna (M. Shizutani, "Mahāyāna Inscriptions in the Gupta Period," *IBK* 10.1 [1962] 47–50). However, apart from the first two of these, which I also have classified as Mahāyāna, there appears to be no direct evidence for their affiliation. They do, though, certainly merit fuller discussion. I might also add that after writing the paper "Mahāyāna in Indian Inscriptions," an inscription published by Bühler ("The New Inscription of Toramana Shaha," *EI* 1 [1890] 238–241) came to my attention in which, if we could accept Bühler's reconstruction, the formula *yad atra puṇyaṃ,* etc. would seem to appear in conjunction with the Mahīśāsakas. But there are some serious doubts about the text and Bühler's reconstruction, which in the end make his interpretation, I think, unacceptable. (This, too, must be discussed at a future time.)

95. Although it is usually the donor's parents who are thus singled out, references to his *upādhyāyācārya,* his "teacher and preceptor," are not rare, and it can occur that they are mentioned even where his parents are not. We can find, then, either *ācāryopādhyāye mātāpitṛpūrvaṅgamaṃ kṛtvā* as at Bih iii 69, Bo i 76, Ma i 67, etc., or simply *upādhyāyācāryapūrvaṃgamaṃ kṛtvā* as at Bih iii 51. The transference of merit to *upādhyāyācāryas* found in these inscriptions is interesting. Something like it occurs less frequently in non-Mahāyāna inscriptions; cf. *Mathurā Inscriptions,* § 29 cited above, and *upajayasa* + name + *puyae* in Konow, *Kharoshṭhī Inscriptions,* LXXXVIII. And yet, according to Woodward, one of the earliest references in Pāli to the doctrine of the transference of merit is in the *Upasampadakammavaca* where the candidate for ordination transfers his merit to the ordaining monk; see F. L. Woodward, "The Buddhist Doctrine of Reversible Merit," *The Buddhist Review* 6 (1914) 38–50, esp. 38–39; see also, however, R. Gombrich, "Merit Transference in Sinhalese Buddhism. A Case Study of the Interaction between Doctrine and Practice," *History of Religions* 11 (1971) 205. For a more detailed discussion of the

place of parents in Indian Buddhist inscriptions, see G. Schopen, "Filial Piety and the Monk in the Practice of Indian Buddhism," Ch. III below (which was written after this paper).

96. See the very approximate chronological summary in Schopen, "Mahāyāna in Indian Inscriptions," 13–14.

97. *Histoire du bouddhisme indien,* 456.

98. For some views on the development of the formulae by which donors express their intentions and some of the concepts found in them, see E. Senart, "Notes d'épigraphie indienne," *JA* (1890) 119–123, and Damsteegt, *Epigraphical Hybrid Sanskrit,* Ch. III.

99. J.-M. Agasse, "Le transfert de mérite dans le bouddhisme pāli classique," *JA* (1978) 311–332, esp. 312–313. On Agasse and on the transfer of merit, see the short but important paper by J. Filliozat, "Sur le domaine sémantique de *puṇya,*" *Indianisme et Bouddhisme, Mélanges offerts à Mgr. Étienne Lamotte* (Louvain-La-Neuve: 1980) 101–116.

100. Deo and Joshi, *Pauni Excavation,* 38, no. 2; Kolte, *EI* 38 (1969) 174 (D).

101. Paranavitana, *Inscriptions of Ceylon,* Vol. I, no. 34; see also lii–liii; cf. W. S. Karunaratne, "The Date of the Brāhmī Inscriptions of Ceylon," *Paranavitana Felicitation Volume* (Colombo: 1965) 243–250.

102. Paranavitana, *Inscriptions of Ceylon,* Vol. I, nos. 338–341; see also lii–liii.

103. H. Bechert, "Notes on the Formation of Buddhist Sects and the Origins of Mahāyāna," *German Scholars on India,* Vol. I (Varanasi: 1973) 17–18; "Zur Frühgeschichte des Mahāyāna-Buddhismus," *ZDMG* 113 (1964) 535.

104. H. Bechert, "Buddha-feld und Verdienstübertragung: Mahāyāna-ideen im Theravāda-Buddhismus Ceylons," Académie Royale de Belgique, *Bulletin de la Classe des Lettres et des Sciences Morales et Politiques,* 5e série, T. 62 (1976) 27–51, esp. 48–49. Bechert cites and discusses most of the previous discussions of the problem of the transference of merit in a Theravāda context on 37ff; but see in addition D. S. Ruegg's review of N. A. Jayawickrama, *The Sheaf of Garlands of the Epochs of the Conqueror, JAOS* 92 (1972) 180–181, and his "Pāli Gotta/Gotra and the Term Gotrabhū in Pāli and Buddhist Sanskrit," *Buddhist Studies in Honour of I. B. Horner,* ed. L. Cousins et al. (Dordrecht: 1974) 207 and n. 37. It is also worth pointing out that two old papers by H. S. Gehman have been consistently overlooked in discussion of the transfer of merit: "Ādisati, anvādisati, anudisati, and uddisati in the Petavatthu," *JAOS* 43 (1923) 410–421; "A Pālism in Buddhist Sanskrit," *JAOS* 44 (1924) 73–75.

* * *

[For some critical remarks on some aspects of this paper, see H. Bechert, "Buddha-Field and Transfer of Merit in a Theravāda Source," *IIJ* 35 (1992) 95–108, esp. 104–106; see also G. Fussman, "Documents épigraphiques kouchans (V). Buddha et bodhisattva dans l'art de mathura: deux bodhisattvas inscrits de l'an 4 et l'an 8," *BEFEO* 57 (1988) 5–25, esp. 10–11; L. Schmithausen, "An Attempt to Estimate the Distance in Time between Aśoka and the Buddha in Terms of Doctrinal History," *The Dating of the Historical Buddha / Die Datierung des historischen Buddha,* ed. H. Bechert (Göttingen: 1992) Pt. 2, 111 and n. 9; 113 and nn. 15, 17, 18; 130, n. 142; 143, n. 231.]

CHAPTER III

Filial Piety and the Monk in the Practice of Indian Buddhism

A Question of "Sinicization" Viewed from the Other Side

In memory of my father-in-law, V. L. Thorpe

IN HIS CATALOG of Indian Buddhist epigraphical material, the final version of which was published in Kyoto in 1979, Shizutani Masao lists more than two thousand separate inscriptions.[1] These inscriptions come, of course, from all periods and virtually every part of India and have been thoroughly mined by historians, but not, unfortunately, by Buddhist scholars. Buddhist scholars, in fact, have shown very little interest in this material, especially those scholars writing on the development of Buddhist doctrine—this in spite of the fact that this material contains considerable information about such important matters as the conception of the Buddha or Buddhas, the conception or conceptions of merit and religious acts, and the nature of the actual, as opposed to the ideal goals of religious activity among practicing Indian Buddhists. In fact, this epigraphical material has, as I have said elsewhere, at least two distinct advantages. First, much of it predates by several centuries our earliest actually datable literary sources. Second, it tells us what a fairly large number of Indian Buddhists actually did, as opposed to what—according to our literary sources—they might or should have done.[2] But in addition to these two advantages, there is a third: this material, in a considerable number of cases, tells us what individuals themselves—whether laymen or monks—hoped to accomplish by those religious acts which they chose to record.

Originally published in *T'oung Pao, Revue internationale de sinologie* 70 (1984):110–126. Reprinted with stylistic changes with permission of E. J. Brill.

The failure of Buddhist scholars to take this epigraphical material into account has generated a number of distortions both within the realm of Indian studies and beyond. One particular example will concern us here.

Ch'en, in his deservedly well known book on Buddhism in China, says in reference to the Lung-men inscriptions that date from the very end of the fifth to the beginning of the sixth century that:

> . . . the frequent references to filial piety in the inscriptions testify to the change that had taken place in Buddhism after its introduction into China. Buddhism started as a religion renouncing all family and social ties, yet in the inscriptions one meets again and again with prayers for the well-being of deceased ancestors, uttered even by monks and nuns. These expressions of piety indicate that although the monks and nuns had joined the monastic order, their ties to family and ancestors still remained strong and enduring. *This is a specific example of how Buddhism had adapted itself to contemporary social conditions in China* (emphasis added).[3]

It should be noted here that I have not cited Ch'en's remarks because they are in any way unique. Quite the contrary. I cite them because they are a particularly clear formulation of a very widely held notion concerning the transformation of Indian Buddhism in China,[4] and because they so clearly reflect the conception of the Indian Buddhist monk presented by even our best modern authorities. The implications of Ch'en's remarks are clear: there is not supposed to be in Indian Buddhism anything like the kind of "filial piety" he finds expressed in the Lung-men inscriptions, and even if there were, Indian Buddhist monks most certainly would not be involved in it. This second point, of course, accords very well with the accepted view of the Indian Buddhist monk. The Indian monk is rather consistently presented as a radical ascetic who had severed all ties with his family and who was not involved in cult activity and, especially, not in religious giving. According to the accepted view, these practices were the province of the laity.[5] Questions remain, however, whether Ch'en's interpretation of his material is acceptable, whether there is not comparable material in India, and whether the current conception of the practicing Indian Buddhist monk accurately reflects what we can actually know about him. We want to know, then, two things: first, do our sources for Indian Buddhism give any indication of a concern similar to that expressed at Lung-men for the "well-being of deceased ancestors," or for departed or living parents; and second, if such a concern is, in fact, attested, is there any indication that this was an active concern of Indian monks and nuns. If we look at Indian epigraphical material, the answer to both of our questions is, I think, quite clear.

Most of our very earliest Buddhist donative inscriptions do not indicate the intentions of the donor. They say, for example, only *ghosāye dānaṃ*, "the gift of Ghosā" (Bhārhut),[6] or *vajigutasa dānaṃ*, "the gift of Vajiguta" (Sāñcī).[7] There are, however, exceptions, two of which are of particular interest. The first of these exceptions comes from Ceylon. I cite it here as Indian evidence because it is in effect an Indian inscription: it is written in early Brāhmī script and dates from a period during which an indigenous Ceylonese Buddhism could not have been developed. It is, in fact, one of "the earliest inscriptions in Ceylon that can be definitely attributed to a particular ruler" and dates, according to Paranavitana, "to the period between 210 and 200 B.C."[8] The inscription concerns the gift of a cave and reads: *gamaṇi-uti-maharajhaha{jhita abi-ti}śaya leṇe daśa-diśaśa sagaye dine mata-pitaśa aṭaya,* "The cave of princess (Abi) Tissā, daughter of the great king Gāmaṇī-Uttiya, is given to the Saṅgha of the ten directions, for the benefit of (her) mother and father."[9] The second exception comes from Bhārhut and is probably to be dated about a hundred years later than the Ceylonese inscription. Here on a *suci* we read: *sagharakhitasa mātāpituna aṭhāyā dānam:* "The gift of Sagharakhita, for the benefit of (his) mother and father."[10]

Here already in very early Buddhist Ceylon and at Bhārhut, we have inscriptions in which the donors themselves say that they performed acts of religious giving for the "benefit" or profit of their parents. In either case, we do not know if the parents were deceased when the gifts were made, although we do know that these inscriptions are six- and seven-hundred years older than those found at Lung-men. We also know that wording very like that which we find in our Ceylonese and Bhārhut inscriptions is also frequently found in the Kharoṣṭhī inscriptions.

Our Kharoṣṭhī inscriptions come predominantly from Northwest India. The earliest of them may date from around the middle of the first century B.C.E., but most appear to fall in the first few centuries of the Common Era. Of the Kharoṣṭhī inscriptions edited by Konow—and this is our single, most important collection—twenty-nine contain statements in which the individual donors express the intentions for which they undertook the religious act recorded in the inscription.[11] Of these twenty-nine, fourteen, or almost exactly one-half, indicate that the religious act was in whole or in part undertaken on behalf of the donors' parents.[12] Similar statements are also found in at least five additional Kharoṣṭhī inscriptions published after Konow's collection.[13] The donors' intentions may be expressed in as simple a form as . . . *matapitu puyae,* "(this is done) as an act of *pūjā* for my parents" (XXXVII. 6),[14] or they might add in addition to reference to their parents any number of other elements. They might say . . . *kue karite matapitae puyae sarvasatvaṇa hidasuhae,* ". . . this well was made as an act of *pūjā* for my parents (and) for the advantage and happiness of all beings" (XXIII), or . . . *par{i}vara {sha}dhadana . . . mira boyaṇasa erjhuṇa kapasa puyae madu pidu puya{e},* "(this) chapel is the religious gift of . . . (name) . . . as an act of *pūjā* for Mira, the Saviour [a royal title] (and) Prince Kapa, as an act of *pūjā* for my mother and father" (XX). We can note here, however, that although these and other additional elements occur in the donors' expressions of their intentions, reference to benefiting their parents is the single most frequent element. We can also note at least one more additional fact: in one of our Kharoṣṭhī inscriptions, it is specifically said that the gift recorded was made for the donor's *deceased* parents (. . . *danamukhe madapidarana adhvadidana puyaya bhavatu*).[15]

It is clear then that "benefiting" parents, both living and dead, was, in the Kharoṣṭhī inscriptions, the most frequently mentioned purpose for religious giving. It was, it seems, a major preoccupation of those who engaged in such activities. But this means that this preoccupation occurs already in inscriptions that predate those found at Lung-men by several centuries. Again in regard to China, we might also note that, already more than twenty years ago, Brough published a Kharoṣṭhī inscription—which he would date "with some reservations . . . towards the end of the second century A.D.,"—that was found at or around Lo-yang. This might suggest that we are dealing here with a case of direct contact between two widely separated bodies of Buddhist inscriptions.[16]

This same preoccupation also appears elsewhere in Indian inscriptions which predate Lung-men. In the Mathurā inscriptions published by Lüders, there are thirty-nine Buddhist inscriptions in which the donors' intentions are expressed. Of these thirty-nine at least one-fourth or nine indicate that the donation was made in whole or in part for the sake of the donors' parents;[17] and in at least two other inscriptions not included in Lüders' collection, the donors' parents are, again, the intended beneficiaries of the religious act.[18] Here again the intentions of the donors can be expressed in a number of ways. The donor may say that the gift was made "as an act of *pūjā* for his mother and father and all living beings" (*māt{ā}pit{r}in{a} pujāye savasav{ā}n{a} ca* § 90);[19] or he may conclude his inscription by declaring that "what here is the merit {of my act} may that be for my parents" (*yad attra puṇyaṃ mātāpi{t}tra sya* § 78). And here again, although in the majority of cases we do not know if the donors' parents were living or dead, in at least one of our Mathurā inscriptions the donor explicitly says that he intends his act "as an act of *pūjā* for his *deceased* parents" (*{mātāp}i{tṛ}ṇa {abhyat}itakalaga{tā}nāṃ pujāye bhavatu* § 44). And another fragmentary Mathurā inscription also appears to make explicit reference to deceased parents (*mātāpitraṇa abhatitana{ṃ}* . . .).[20]

Like the Kharoṣṭhī inscriptions, the inscriptions from Mathurā also predate those found at Lung-men by several centuries. Although Lüders classifies a few as belonging to the Śuṅga period, the majority belong to the Kṣatrapa, the Kuṣāṇa, and—to a lesser extent—the Gupta periods.[21] But we also find a considerable number of inscriptions that fall into these same periods elsewhere in India in which an act of religious giving is expressly stated to have been undertaken for the benefit of the donors' parents. This is the case, for example, at Bodh-Gayā, where a donor ends the record of his gift by saying "by this root of merit may it be as an act of *pūjā* for my mother and father" (*imenā kuśala-mūlena mātāpitṛṇā{ṃ} pūjāye bhavatu* . . .),[22] or again at Bodh-Gayā, but in a record more nearly contemporaneous with Lung-men: "Whatever merit may have been acquired by me by all this, may this be for the benefit of my parents at first . . ." (*tad etat sarvvaṃ yan mayā puṇyopacitasambhāraṃ tan mātāpitroḥ p(ūrvaṃgamaṃ kṛtvā* . . .).[23] This is also the case at Nāgārjunikoṇḍa, where the donors frequently state that they made their gifts so that, first, they could "transfer" their act of giving to their mothers or to their families by birth and marriage. In several instances it is specifically said that the "transfer" is to be made to past, present, and future members on both sides of the donors' families. We find, for example,

> . . . this stone pillar was set up in order to transfer [it, i.e., the act and the fruit of the act] to her mother and for procuring the attainment of *nirvāṇa* for herself . . .
>
> . . . *apano mātaraṃ haṃmasiriṇikaṃ parinamatuna atane ca nivāṇasaṃpatisaṃpādake imaṃ selathaṃbhaṃ patithapitaṃ* . . .
>
> C2; cf. C4[24]

or, more elaborately,

> . . . this pillar was set up in order to transfer (it) to past, future, and present members of both of her families for the attainment of benefits and ease in both worlds, and for the procuring of the attainment of *nirvāṇa* for herself, and for the attainment of benefits and ease by all the world . . .
>
> . . . *apano ubhayakulasa atichhitam-anāgata-vaṭamānakānaṃ parināmetunaṃ ubhayalokahitasukhāvahathanāya atano ca nivāṇasaṃpatisaṃpādake savalokahitasukhāvahathanāya ca imaṃ khaṃbhaṃ patithapitaṃ ti* . . .
>
> C3; cf. B2, B4, E

We also have a comparatively large number of inscriptions from Sārnāth and Ajaṇṭā that either predate or are nearly contemporaneous with the Lung-men inscriptions. And here again the donors frequently state that their intention in making their religious gift was, in whole or in part, to benefit their parents. Among the inscriptions from Sārnāth that have been taken as belonging either to the Gupta period or, more specifically, to the fourth, fifth, or sixth centuries, I have noticed at least ten inscriptions in which the donors' parents are specifically listed among the intended beneficiaries.[25] We find donors saying:

> What here is the merit acquired by me after having had this image made, may that be for the obtainment of cessation for my parents and *gurus* and the world.
>
> *yad atra puṇyaṃ pratimāṃ kārayitvā mayā bhṛtam/mātāpittror gurūṇāṃ ca lokasya ca śamāptaye.*[26]

or, perhaps more typically,

> What here is (my) merit, may that be for the obtaining of supreme knowledge by my mother and father and all living beings.
>
> *yad atra puṇyaṃ tad bha{va}tu mātāpi{tro(ḥ)} sarvva{sattvā}nāñ ca anuttarajñānāvāptaye.*[27]

This second formula is, in fact, also very common at Ajaṇṭā.

The inscriptions from Ajaṇṭā, the last group of inscriptions we shall look at here, are of particular interest. If Spink is right—and the chances of this seem to be very good—most, if not all, activity ceased at Ajaṇṭā in the last quarter of the fifth century.[28] This would mean that the inscriptions at Ajaṇṭā are close in time to those at Lung-men and yet clearly predate them. Moreover, Ajaṇṭā and Lung-men are not only close in time, they are also sites of essentially the same kind. Both are complexes of excavated cave shrines; both received royal patronage, and yet a large number of individual, nonroyal donative inscriptions have been found at both sites.

I have been able to find twenty-one inscriptions from Ajaṇṭā that have a donative formula. Of these more than 90 percent, or nineteen inscriptions, declare that the intended beneficiaries of the gifts recorded are, in whole or in part, the donors' parents.[29] In eleven, or slightly more than half of these, the donors' intentions are expressed by means of variants of a single basic formula. In its simplest form at Ajaṇṭā it occurs as

> What here is his merit, may that be for the obtaining of supreme knowledge by his mother and father and all living beings.
>
> *yad atra {pu}ṇyaṃ tad bhavatu mātāpitro{ḥ} sarvva{sa}tvānāñ cānuttarajñānāvāp{t}aye.*[30]

This, of course, is almost exactly the same version of the formula as in our second example found at Sārnāth, and this or some other variant of the basic formula occurs, as I have said, in eleven of the nineteen inscriptions from Ajaṇṭā in which the donors name their parents as beneficiaries. But other donors at Ajaṇṭā express their intentions without having recourse to this particular formula. We find, for example, the donor saying simply: "This is the religious gift of . . . Śīlabhadra (made) in the name of his father and mother" (*deyaddharmmo yam . . . śīlabhadrasya mātāpitaram udi{śya}*).[31] The expression used here, *mātāpitaram uddiśya,* "in the name of his mother and father," is of particular interest and occurs in at least four other inscriptions from Ajaṇṭā.[32] In fact, the use of the term *uddiśya* seems to imply—as Senart appears to have suggested some time ago, and as its occurence in a variety of literary sources also would suggest—that the individuals concerned are deceased.[33] This would seem to be more clearly the case in The *Praśasti* of Buddhabhadra in Cave XXVI. Here Buddhabhadra says his gift was made "in the name of Bhavvirāja and also his [Buddhabhadra's] mother and father" (*taṃ bhavvirājam uddiśya mātāpitaram eva ca*), and then a little later he says "what merit is here, may that be for them [i.e., Bhavvirāja and his parents] and for the world for the attainment of the fruit of great awakening and the accumulation of all pure qualities" (*yad atra puṇyaṃ tat teṣā{ṃ} jagatāṃ ca bhavatv idaṃ sarvvāmalaguṇavyāta-*[read *vrāta-*] *mahābodhiphalāptaye*). But Buddhabhadra has already specifically indicated right before the *uddiśya* passage that Bhavvirāja, at least, was dead (. . . *pitaryy uparate*).[34]

We are now in a position to answer our first question. Indian epigraphical sources prove beyond any doubt that the basic elements of the inscriptions from Lung-men, which Ch'en interpreted as indications of "filial piety," occur already in Indian Buddhist inscriptions that predate those from Lung-men by as much as seven centuries. They prove that concern for the "well-being" of both deceased and living parents was a major preoccupation of Buddhist donors in India; that one of the most frequently stated reasons for undertaking acts of religious giving was to benefit the donors' parents, both living and dead; and that this concern was both very old and very widespread in India.[35] But if we have answered our first question, we still must discover whether there are any indications that this concern for the well-being of their parents was an active concern of Indian Buddhist monks. This, perhaps, is an even more interesting question and, once again, I think our answer can be unequivocal.

Our two earliest donative inscriptions that refer to benefiting the donors' parents both record the gifts of laymen. We know, however, that the Bhārhut inscription is only one of a large number from that site recording similar gifts, and that in thirty-six cases, or almost 40 percent of these inscriptions, the donors were monks or nuns. In several instances the individual monks involved are specifically said to be *bhānakas* or "reciters"; one is called a *sutaṃtika,* "one who knows the sutta", another a *peṭakin,* "one who knows the Piṭaka," and yet another is referred to as a *pacanekāyika,* "one who is versed in the canonical doctrine as a whole."[36]

We also know that perhaps as many as one-fourth of the Kharoṣṭhī inscriptions that refer to benefiting the donors' parents record the gifts of monks.[37] One of these inscriptions, interestingly enough, is also the single Kharoṣṭhī inscription in which there is specific reference to deceased parents. The whole inscription reads:

> Year 5, on the fifth day of the month Phalguna. This is the gift of Buddhānanda who is one who knows the *Tripiṭaka.* May it be an act of *pūjā* for his deceased parents.
>
> *sa{ṃ} 4 1 phagunasa masasa di paṃcami budhanadasa trepiḍakasa danamukhe madapidarana adhvadidana puyaya bhavatu.*[38]

Here, then, not only is a gift given by an individual for the benefit of his deceased parents, but this individual, to judge by his title, is not a simple, uneducated, village monk. He appears to have been, like many of the monk-donors at Bhārhut, a religious specialist. He is "one who knows the *Tripiṭaka,*" one who has mastered the Buddhist literature of his time.

Our Mathurā inscriptions present us with a similar—and perhaps even more definite—set of facts. There are eight inscriptions from Mathurā that record gifts made for the benefit of the donors' parents in which the donors' names or titles have been preserved. In six cases, or in 75 percent of these inscriptions, the donors were monks.[39] In the one instance where reference is specifically made to deceased parents, the donor is again a monk:

> (This is) the gift of the monk . . . mitra, the Vojyavaśika (?). May it be an act of *pūjā* for his deceased parents. May it (also) be for the granting of health to his companion Dharmadeva.
>
> *{d}ā{na}ṃ bh{ik}ṣus{y}a b . . . + . . . m{i}trasya v{o}jya + {vaśi}kasya – {mātap}i + {tṛ}ṇa {abhyat}itaka + laga{tā}nāṃ pujāy{e} + bhavatu sa{dh}yivi + harīsya dharma{d}ev{a}s{y}a + ar{o}g{a}dākṣiṇ{ā}y{e} {bha}vat{u}.*[40]

At least one other of the monk-donors at Mathurā who intended their gifts for the benefit of their parents is given a title that appears to indicate that he was a learned monk, a religious specialist: he is referred to as a *dha{r}mma{kathi}ka,* "a preacher of the Dharma."[41]

In one of the two inscriptions I have cited above from Bodh-Gayā the donor is, again, a monk. Here, the donor who declares that his act was intended to benefit his parents describes himself as either "a monk who preserves the Vinaya" (*vinayadhara*) or the "companion" or "co-resident" of such a monk (*sadhevihārī*), and as a "preacher of the *Dharma*" (*dharmakathika*).[42]

If the evidence in all of these inscriptions is clear, it is equally if not more clear in those Indian inscriptions from the Gupta period—especially those from the fourth and fifth centuries—or in those inscriptions that are in date near to, though somewhat earlier than, the inscriptions found at Lung-men. At Sārnāth, for example, in the ten inscriptions that record gifts made for the benefit of the donors' parents, four-fifths or eight of the donors were monks.[43] In the nineteen inscriptions from Ajaṇṭā that express a similar intention, thirteen of the donors were certainly monks, two more were probably monks, and in one case it is impossible to say. In only three of the nineteen inscriptions were the donors certainly laymen.[44]

We have looked so far at the Kharoṣṭhī inscriptions, at inscriptions from Mathurā, Bodh-Gayā, Sārnāth, and Ajaṇṭā, and we have found a recurring pattern. Before, however, we can summarize our findings, we must deal briefly with an apparent exception: in none of the fairly numerous inscriptions from Nāgārjunikoṇḍa in which the merit of the act is transferred to the donors' parents or family is the donor a monk. At first sight, this could be significant. But seen in a larger context it is probably only another indication of the atypical character of all the Nāgārjunikoṇḍa inscriptions connected with the Ikṣvaku dynasty. There is, first of all, the atypical character of the vocabulary of these inscriptions. Several set expressions and terms are found in these inscriptions that are not found anywhere else in Indian inscriptions. This is the case with *ubhayakula*, with the expression *dhātuvaraparigahita* used to describe a *stūpa*, with the verb *parināmetuna* that is always used to express the intended "transfer." This is also the case with the formula *ubhayalokahitasukha* and the formula *atano ca nivāṇasaṃpatisaṃpādake.* All of these elements are found again and again in inscriptions of this period at Nāgārjunikoṇḍa but nowhere else at any period in India.[45] An equally atypical characteristic of the Ikṣvaku inscriptions from Nāgārjunikoṇḍa is the fact that monastic donors are extremely rare.[46] This is in marked contrast with what—as I have said elsewhere—we find everywhere else in India. From Bhārhut and Sāñcī and thereafter, monks and nuns everywhere constituted a considerable portion of the active donors at religious sites: almost 40 percent of the donors at both Bhārhut and Sāñcī were monks or nuns; well over 50 percent of the donors in the Mathurā inscriptions were also monks or nuns; 40 percent of the donors in the Kharoṣṭhī inscriptions, 65 percent of the donors in the inscriptions of the Western Cave Shrines, and 70 percent of the donors in those inscriptions that I have argued belong to the Mahāyāna were members of the monastic community.[47] Even at Amarāvatī, also in the South, twenty-four of the sixty-five individual donors were either monks or nuns.[48] Clearly then, Ikṣvaku Nāgārjunikoṇḍa is atypical and should be treated as such. It represents an isolated, very narrowly localized aberration both in terms of geography and in terms of time; all three of the Sanskrit inscriptions from this area published by Ramachandran date from the fifth century and record the gifts of monks.[49]

Having established the purely local and markedly atypical character of the material from Ikṣvaku Nāgārjunikoṇḍa, we can now summarize our findings. Indian epigraphical material establishes that not only was one of the most frequently stated reasons for undertaking acts of religious giving in Buddhist India to benefit the donors' parents—both living and dead—and that this was a major preoccupation of Buddhist donors in India, it also clearly establishes that this concern for the well-being of deceased and living parents was an active concern and major preoccupation of Indian Buddhist monks in particular. In the Kharoṣṭhī inscriptions, as many as one-fourth of the donors who indicated that their act was undertaken to benefit their parents were monks; at both Mathurā and Ajaṇṭā 75 percent of such donors were monks. At Sārnāth the percentage is even higher: there, in eight out of the ten inscriptions in which the donors indicated that their acts were undertaken to benefit their parents, those donors were monks. In fact, if we take the total number of inscriptions in our sample, it would appear that not only was the concern for their parents—both living and dead—a major preoccupation among our monk-donors, *but it was perhaps a special concern of this group:* in more than 60 percent of all of the Indian inscriptions in our sample in which acts were undertaken to benefit the donors' parents, the donors were monks, and the percentage of monk-donors is considerably higher, as we have seen, at Mathurā, Ajaṇṭā, and Sārnāth. It is also worth noting again that at least three of the monk-donors who made religious gifts for the benefit of their parents, or their deceased parents, were not average, uneducated village monks: one is called a *trepiḍaka;* one is called a *dharmakathika;* and a third was either a *vinayadhara,* or the "co-resident" of a *vinayadhara,* as well as a *dharmakathika.* These monks appear to have been the teachers and transmitters of "official" Buddhist literature.[50]

In light of what we have found in Indian epigraphical material, and in light of the fact that all of the material we have looked at predates—in some cases by five or more centuries—the inscriptions from Lung-men, it hardly seems necessary to emphasize the fact that Ch'en's interpretation of his Lung-men data is unacceptable. Clearly, "the frequent references to filial piety in the inscriptions" from Lung-men do not testify to any "change that had taken place in Buddhism after its introduction into China"; nor is the fact that monks make up a considerable number of the donors at Lung-men who are concerned with deceased or living parents "a specific example of how Buddhism had adapted itself to contemporary social conditions in China." But the merit of Professor Ch'en's interpretation of the Lung-men data is that it forces us to focus on an aspect of the practice of Indian Buddhism that has been almost completely ignored by Buddhist scholars: in answering the questions raised by Professor Ch'en's remarks, we have come to see that "filial piety" was an old, an integral, and a pervasive part of the practice of Indian Buddhism from the earliest periods of which we have any definite knowledge, and that in actual practice the idea of benefiting one's parents, whether living or dead, by making religious gifts on their behalf was a major, if not a specific preoccupation of Indian Buddhist monks. Once again, the actual monk of the first to the fifth centuries C.E. in India turns out to be—when we can catch a glimpse of him—something quite different from the picture of the monk that has been abstracted from our textual sources.[51] This is, in fact, the second point of merit in Ch'en's interpretation: it makes clear the very real dangers that arise when making historical statements on the basis of textual sources alone, when treating literary elaborations of doctrine as if they were records of actual description. We have just seen that it is clear from Buddhist inscriptions beginning from the time of Bhārhut that the donation of religious gifts was as much a part of the monk's religious life as it was of the layman's. And although this is contrary to what virtually all our modern authorities want us to believe, and although it receives no very definite support in early textual sources, it is nevertheless a demonstrable fact.

But there are also at least two curious qualities found in the inscriptions that reveal this fact, both of which bear on how we are to understand this type of religious giving in an Indian Buddhist context. First, although our inscriptions constantly refer to the objects made or presented as "gifts" (*dāna, deyadharma*), there is at least one essential component of the classic Indian definition of the "gift" which is missing: although there is always a giver and an object given, there is, in the vast majority of epigraphical cases, no recipient. Moreover, in the great majority of the inscriptions we have looked at here, the thing given is of no economic value: it is not land, housing, clothing, or food. On the contrary, the gifts recorded are almost all relics or *stūpas* or images or paintings. We have then a giver and items of no economic value given to no specific recipient. Clearly, there seems to be little here which even approaches the classic definition of a "gift" as a "transaction": there is no exchange; no conception of incurred debt; no notion of reciprocity. In itself this might seem somewhat odd, but the situation appears even stranger when we add to this the fact that the inscriptions that record these gifts were in a considerable number of cases—as Lüders and Konow pointed out long ago—never meant to be read by anyone.[52] These factors combine to leave only more questions. For example, if our inscriptions were never meant to be read, why did the individual donors take such care in recording not only their names, titles, and their places of residence, but also the exact date on which the donations were made?

The answer to at least some of these puzzles may be found, I think, in a fuller understanding of what our donors were giving and in the conceptions of merit which they held. It is true that, on one level, the laymen and monks who made these gifts were giving objects, but because these objects were of a specific kind, they were actually giving more than mere objects: they were giving objects of worship, objects that, in fact, made worship possible. They were, then, really giving to any of their fellow beings who ritually approached those objects both the means and the opportunity to make merit; they were providing for all both the opportunity and the means to further their religious lives. But this would also seem to suggest that the initial gift of the actual object only marked the first moment in the donor's act of giving. Each time the object was approached, he or the persons to whom he transferred his act of giving was to be credited with having provided an additional opportunity for someone else to make merit. Each opportunity was a separate act of giving. The donor's act of giving and its consequent merit, then, were continually repeated over time in every act of worship directed toward the object he had provided.[53] It was the donor's initial act that in a very concrete sense made each consecutive act of worship possible.

It was because the donor's act was continually repeated over time, because it took place again and again long after the donor himself had disappeared, that it was necessary to clearly record the donor's name, the moment of the initial act, and—most importantly—the donor's intentions. And it was no small matter to transfer such an act to the donor's parents. By doing so, the donor denied to himself but provided for his parents a source of merit which would continue and be maintained long after the donor himself was dead. This, it would seem, is true filial piety.

Notes

1. Shizutani Masao, *Indo bukkyō himei mokuroku* (Kyoto: 1979).

2. G. Schopen, "Two Problems in the History of Indian Buddhism," Ch. II above.

3. K. K. S. Ch'en, *Buddhism in China, A Historical Survey* (Princeton: 1964) 179; cf. K. K. S. Ch'en, "Filial Piety in Chinese Buddhism," *HJAS* 28 (1968) 81–97, and *The Chinese Transformation of Buddhism* (Princeton: 1973) 14ff. These last two works deal with filial piety in Chinese Buddhism on the basis of literary sources, and it is from the second of these (p. 5) that I have borrowed the term "sinicization" that occurs in my title. It is perhaps worth pointing out that in the appendix on *yü-lan-p'en* in the same volume (61–64) Ch'en has overlooked at least two important papers: J. Przyluski, "Les rites d'avalambana," *MCB* 1 (1931–1932) 221–225, and J. Jaworski, "L'avalambana sutra de la terre pure," *Monumenta Serica* 1 (1935–1936) 82–107. For the inscriptions from Lung-men, see E. Chavannes, *Mission archéologique dans la Chine septentrionale,* T. I, deuxième partie (Paris: 1915) 320–561, and Mizuno Seiichi and Nagahiro Toshio, *Ryūmon sekkutsu no kenkyū* (Tokyo: 1941).

4. Cf. P. Demiéville, "Le bouddhisme chinois," *Encyclopédie de la Pléiade, Histoire des Religions,* T. I (Paris: 1970) 1273 (repr. in *Choix d'études bouddhiques* [Leiden: 1973] 389); A. F. Wright, *Buddhism in Chinese History* (New York: 1969) 59; etc.

5. *Histoire du bouddhisme indien,* 59, 68, 81, 698f; cf. more recently, J. Holt, "Assisting the Dead by Venerating the Living, Merit Transfer in the Early Buddhist Tradition," *Numen* 28 (1981) 1–28. Unfortunately, even apart from the fact that he ignores the epigraphical material, Holt's analysis is rather badly distorted since he unaccountably chose to ignore the fact that the *Petavatthu*—the text on which his paper is supposed to be based—contains a number of stories in which it is not a layman who gives a gift to release his deceased kinsmen, but a monk. The most striking instance of the monk-donor occurs in the story of Sāriputta's mother in N. A. Jayawickrama, *Vimānavatthu and Petavatthu,* Vol. II (London: 1977) 2.14, but there are several others.

6. B. Barua and K. G. Sinha, *Barhut Inscriptions* (Calcutta: 1926) 31, no. 56.

7. G. Bühler, "Further Inscriptions from Sānchi," *EI* 2 (1892) 370, no. 25.

8. S. Paranavitana, *Inscriptions of Ceylon,* Vol. I, *Containing Cave Inscriptions from 3rd Century* B.C. *to 1st Century* A.C. *and Other Inscriptions in the Early Brāhmī Script* (Ceylon: 1970) lii–liii.

9. Paranavitana, *Inscriptions of Ceylon,* Vol. I, no. 34.

10. Barua and Sinha, *Barhut Inscriptions,* 22, no. 28; for several different views of the significance of this inscription, see *Histoire du bouddhisme indien,* 456; Schopen, "Two

Problems in the History of Indian Buddhism," now Ch. II above; J-M. Agasse, "Le transfert de mérite dans le bouddhisme pāli classique," *JA* (1978) 312–313. On Agasse, and the question of the transfer of merit generally, see the important paper by J. Filliozat, "Sur le domaine sémantique de puṇya," *Indianisme et buddhisme, Mélanges offerts à Mgr Étienne Lamotte* (Louvain-La-Neuve: 1980) 101–116.

11. S. Konow, *Kharoshṭhī Inscriptions with the Exception of Those of Aśoka,* Corpus Inscriptionum Indicarum, Vol. II, Pt. 1 (Calcutta: 1929) I, II, XIII, XV, XX, XXIII, XXIV, XXVI, XXVII, XXXI, XXXV.2, XXXVII.6, XLVI, LV.c, LVII, LVIII, LX, LXIII, LXXII, LXXIV, LXXV, LXXVI, LXXX, LXXXI, LXXXII, LXXXV, LXXXVI, LXXXVII, XCII.

12. Konow, *Kharoshṭhī Inscriptions,* II, XIII, XX, XXIII, XXVII, XXXI, XXXV.2, XXXVII.6, LV.c, LXXV, LXXVI, LXXXV, LXXXVI, XCII.

13. These five Kharoṣṭhī inscriptions are: 1. S. Konow, "Charsadda Kharoṣṭhī Inscription of the Year 303," *Acta Orientalia* 20 (1947) 107–119; 2. G. Fussman, "Documents épigraphiques kouchans," *BEFEO* 61 (1974) 54–58 (the same inscription read and translated by J. Brough was published in J. C. Harle, "A Hitherto Unknown Dated Sculpture from Gandhara: A Preliminary Report," in J. E. van Lohuizen-De Leeuw and J. M. M. Ubaghs, *South Asian Archaeology 1973* [Leiden: 1974] 128–136); 3. G. Fussman, "Documents épigraphiques kouchans (II)," *BEFEO* 67 (1980) 55; 4. G. Fussman, "Nouvelles inscriptions śaka: ère d'Eucratide, ère d'Azès, ère Vikrama, ère de Kaniṣka," *BEFEO* 67 (1980) 6; 5. H. W. Bailey, "Two Kharoṣṭhī Casket Inscriptions from Avaca," *JRAS* (1978) 3. This same inscription has also been published in B. N. Mukherjee, "An Interesting Kharoṣṭhī Inscription," *JAIH* 11 (1977–1978) 93–114; G. Fussman, *BEFEO* 67 (1980) 3–4; R. Salomon, "The 'Avaca' Inscription and the Origin of the Vikrama Era," *JAOS* 102 (1982) 59–68. [See now also R. Salomon and G. Schopen, "The Indravarman (Avaca) Casket Inscription Reconsidered: Further Evidence for Canonical Passages in Buddhist Inscriptions," *JIABS* 7.1 (1984) 107–23.]

14. All parenthetical roman numerals refer to the inscription numbers in Konow, *Kharoshṭhī Inscriptions.*

15. Fussman, *BEFEO* 61 (1974) 54; Brough in Harle's *South Asian Archaeology 1973,* 129 and n. 1.

16. J. Brough, "A Kharoṣṭhī Inscription from China," *BSOAS* 24 (1961) 517–530.

17. H. Lüders, *Mathurā Inscriptions,* ed. K. L. Janert, Abhandlungen der Akademie der Wissenschaften in Göttingen, Philologisch-Historische Klasse, Dritte Folge, Nr. 47 (Göttingen: 1961) 1, 2, 3, 8, 24, 29*, 31, 35, 41, 44*, 46, 50, 60, 61, 62, 67*, 73, 76, 78*, 80, 81, 86, 87, 89, 90*, 125*, 126, 128, 135, 136, 153, 154, 157, 179*, 180*, 184*, 185, 186, 187. Here and in the notes that follow, those inscriptions in which the donations were made for the sake of the donors' parents are marked with an asterisk.

18. D. C. Sircar, "Mathura Image Inscription of Vasudeva," *EI* 30 (1953–1954) 181–184 (cf. n. 20 below); Sircar, "Brahmi Inscriptions from Mathura," *EI* 34 (1961–1962) 9–13, no. 1.

19. All numbers marked with § refer to the inscription numbers in Lüders, *Mathurā Inscriptions.*

20. Sircar, *EI* 30 (1953–1954) 184, reads *mātāpitreṇa abha(s)i(ta)naṁ;* the reading cited above, however, is that proposed by Th. Damsteegt, *Epigraphical Hybrid Sanskrit, Its Rise, Spread, Characteristics and Relationship to Buddhist Hybrid Sanskrit* (Leiden: 1978) 164 and n. 50; cf. 119.

21. Lüders, *Mathurā Inscriptions,* 22–23.

22. B. M. Barua, "A Bodh-Gayā Image Inscription," *IHQ* 9 (1933) 419.

23. B. M. Barua, "Old Buddhist Shrines at Bodh-Gayā," *IHQ* 6 (1930) 27–28. The translation here is Barua's; the end of the line is missing and he has supplied a *bhavatu,* although it is possible that more than just a *bhavatu* has been lost.

24. All the letter and number references refer to J. Ph. Vogel, "Prakrit Inscriptions from a Buddhist Site at Nagarjunikonda," *EI* 20 (1929–1930) 1–37.

25. D. R. Sahni, *Catalogue of the Museum of Archaeology at Sarnath* (Calcutta: 1914) 53(B[b]60)*, 85(B[b]292), 85(B[b]293)*, 239(D[f] 1)*; H. Hargreaves, "Excavations at Sārnāth," *ARASI 1914–1915* (Calcutta: 1920) XIV*, XV*, XVI*, XVII*, XVIII*, XIX.

26. Hargreaves, *ARASI 1914–1915,* XVI, XVII.

27. Sahni, *Catalogue of the Museum of Archaeology at Sarnath,* 85(B[b]292).

28. W. Spink, "Ajanta: A Brief History," *Aspects of Indian Art* (Leiden: 1972) 49–58, esp. 56–59; Spink, "The Splendours of Indra's Crown: A Study of Mahāyāna Developments at Ajaṇṭā," *Journal of the Royal Society for the Encouragement of Arts, Manufactures, and Commerce* (1974) 743–767; cf. J. G. Williams, *The Art of Gupta India, Empire and Province* (Princeton: 1982) 181ff.

29. J. Allan, "A Note on the Inscriptions of Cave II," Appendix to G. Yazdani, *Ajanta,* Part II: Text (Oxford: 1933) Cave II.11 (fragmentary, note . . . *pitṛm;*) N. P. Chakravarti, "A Note on the Painted Inscriptions in Caves VI–XVII," Appendix to G. Yazdani, *Ajanta,* Part III: Text (Oxford: 1946) Cave VI; Cave IX.1*, IX.6*; Cave X.2, X.10*, X.11*, X.12, X.17, X.21*; Cave XVI.1*, XVI.2*, XVI.3*; N. P. Chakravarti and B. Ch. Chhabra, "Notes on the Painted and Incised Inscriptions of Caves XX–XXVI," Appendix to G. Yazdani, *Ajanta,* Part IV: Text (Oxford: 1955) Cave XX(Inc.) n. 3*; Cave XXII(P) n. 4*; Cave XXVI.1*, XXVI.2*; D. C. Sircar, "Inscription in Cave IV at Ajanta," *EI* 33 (1960) 262; M. K. Dhavalikar, "New Inscriptions from Ajaṇṭā," *ArO* 7 (1968) nos.3, 4*, 5*. The two inscriptions that do not make reference to the donors' parents are Cave VI, and X.2.

30. Yazdani, *Ajanta,* Part III, Cave XVI .3. On this formula, see G. Schopen, "Mahāyāna in Indian Inscriptions," *IIJ* 21 (1979) 1–19, and corrections to this in the second half of Schopen, "Two Problems in the History of Indian Buddhism," Ch. II above.

31. Yazdani, *Ajanta,* Part III, Cave X.21.

32. Yazdani, *Ajanta,* Part III, Cave X.10, 11, 12; Yazdani, *Ajanta,* Part IV, Cave XXVI.1.

33. E. Senart, "The Inscriptions in the Caves at Nasik," *EI* 8 (1905) 64; L. de La Vallée Poussin, "Staupikam," *HJAS* 2 (1935) 283; H. Kern and B. Nanjio, *Saddharmapuṇḍarīka* (St. Petersburg: 1908–1912) 50.9, 241.6, 340.6; C. Bendall, *Śikṣāsamuccaya* (St. Petersburg: 1897–1902) 309.6.

34. Yazdani, *Ajanta,* Part IV, Cave XXVI.1.

35. It should be noted here that there are a considerable number of other Indian inscriptions in which we find reference to parents, but the interpretation of these inscriptions is uncertain. They almost always contain a formula, the key element of which is *sahā.* Lüders, *Mathurā Inscriptions,* § 126 is a typical example: . . . *bh{i}khuṇiye budhadevāye bodhisatvo pratithāpito sahā mātāpitīhi sarvasat{v}ahitasukh{a}ye.* Lüders translates: ". . . the Bodhisattva was set up by the nun Budhadevā (Buddhadevā), . . . together with her parents for the welfare and happiness of all sentient beings." But there are at least three possible interpretations here. First, the inscription may record a donation that was actually made jointly by the nun and her parents. Secondly, it may be that the nun-donor simply

used the *sahā* formula as a way of sharing the merit of her act with her parents by associating them with that act. That is to say, she shares or transfers the act rather than the merit, although the end result is the same. Thirdly, it is possible that the syntax of the formula has not been properly understood and that we should translate: ". . . the Bodhisattva was set up by the nun Budhadevā for the welfare and happiness of all sentient beings together with her parents" (cf. *yad atra puṇyaṃ tad bhavatu mātāpitṛpūrvaṅgamaṃ kṛtvā sarvasatvānāñ anuttarajñānāvāptaye* or *yad atra puṇyaṃ tad bhavatu mātāpitroḥ sarvasatvānāñ cānuttarajñānāvāptaye;* Schopen, "Two Problems in the History of Indian Buddhism," Ch. II, above). There are a number of cases where the first interpretation is almost certainly impossible. This is the case, for example, at Sahni, *Catalogue of the Museum of Archaeology at Sarnath,* 35 (B[a]1), where, if we adopted the first interpretation, we would have a single image that was the actual gift of a monk named Bala, his parents, his preceptors, teachers, fellow monks, pupils, a nun, the Satrap Vanaṣpara, and the fourfold Buddhist community (i.e., all monks, nuns, laymen, and laywomen). This appears rather unlikely, and we must adopt either the second or third interpretation. But adopting either of these last two interpretations would mean that all such inscriptions would then have to be added to our list of inscriptions that record an act undertaken—in whole or in part—for the benefit of the donor's parents. This, of course, would only further and more fully confirm the observations we have already made. [See G. Schopen, "On Monks, Nuns and 'Vulgar' Practices," Ch. XI, below; and Fussman, *BEFEO* 57 (1988) 10, n. 27.]

36. Cf. Schopen, "Two Problems in the History of Indian Buddhism," Ch. II above, and the sources cited there in nn. 40 and 41.

37. Konow, *Kharoshṭhī Inscriptions,* XXIII (cf. 64), LV.c, XCII; Fussman, *BEFEO* 61 (1974) III.

38. Fussman, *BEFEO* 61 (1974) III.

39. Lüders, *Mathurā Inscriptions,* §§ 29, 44, 67, 90, 179; Sircar, *EI* 34 (1961–1962) no. 1.

40. Lüders, *Mathurā Inscriptions,* § 44.

41. Sircar, *EI* 34 (1961–1962) no. 1.

42. Barua, *IHQ* 9 (1933) 419.

43. I.e., those inscription numbers marked with an asterisk in n. 25 above.

44. In those inscriptions marked with an asterisk in n. 29 above, the donors are definitely monks.

45. For occurrences of these terms and formulae, see the glossary in Vogel, *EI* 20 (1929–1930) 26–35.

46. Cf. Vogel, *EI* 20 (1929–1930) C1 (p. 17).

47. Schopen, "Two Problems in the History of Indian Buddhism," now Ch. II above.

48. G. Sivaramamurti, *Amarāvati Sculptures in the Madras Government Museum,* Bulletin of the Madras Government Museum, N.S., Vol. IV (Madras: 1956) 271–304. There are one hundred and twenty six inscriptions collected here, but six are nondonative, in eleven the donor has no title, and forty are too fragmentary to be intelligible. In four a *nigama* is given as a collective donor.

49. T. N. Ramachandran, *Nāgārjunakoṇḍa 1938,* MASI, No.71 (Calcutta: 1953) 28–29.

50. The fairly massive participation of monks in cult activity and religious giving that our inscriptions document raises a number of interesting points. In this regard it is well to note—as Bühler noted many years ago—that the role of the monk in Jaina inscriptions differs very markedly from the role of the monk in Buddhist inscriptions.

Bühler says, in specific reference to Sāñcī: "Proceeding to the inscriptions which mention donations made by monks and nuns, the first point, which must strike every reader, is their great number . . . But it is interesting to note the different proceedings of the Jaina ascetics, who, according to the Mathurā and other inscriptions, as a rule, were content to exhort the laymen to make donations and to take care that this fact was mentioned in the votive inscriptions" (G. Bühler, "Votive Inscriptions from the Sānchi Stūpas," *EI* 2 [1892] 93). For examples of the kind of thing Bühler is referring to in Jaina inscriptions, see Lüders, *Mathurā Inscriptions,* §§ 13, 14, 93, 140, where the key term is *nirvartana-* (on which, see Damsteegt, *Epigraphical Hybrid Sanskrit,* 75, 171, 173, 252). Other Jaina inscriptions express the same thing with a different vocabulary; cf. D. C. Sircar, "Indological Notes 7, Vidiśa Jain Image Inscriptions of the Time of Rāmagupta," *JAIH* 3 (1969–1970) 150–151. It is also worth quoting a wise old art historian here. Walter Spink says: "A number of inscriptions at Ajanta also prove that some of the caves, and numerous separate images, were donated by the monks themselves. This is an interesting commentary on the changing of Buddhism in India, for it suggests that monks, far from having renounced all worldly goods, were sometimes men of considerable wealth. It is doubtful that Buddhabhadra, the chief donor of the elaborate Cave 26—a man who proclaims himself the friend of kings—spent very much time humbly wandering from village to village with his begging bowl as his predecessors in the early days of Buddhism certainly did" (Spink, "Ajanta: A Brief History," *Aspects of Indian Art,* 51). The question, of course, is whether the facts from Ajaṇṭā that Spink refers to reflect any change at all. In fact, we simply do not know what Buddhabhadra's "predecessors in the early days of Buddhism" *actually* did. We do know, however, that from the very beginning of our actual epigraphical evidence (Bhārhut, Sāñcī, etc.), a large number of monks were doing exactly what the data indicate they were doing at Ajaṇṭā; cf. Schopen, "Two Problems in the History of Indian Buddhism," Ch. II above. What we do not know is what else they were doing.

51. Cf. Schopen, "Two Problems in the History of Indian Buddhism," Ch. II above.

52. H. Lüders, "The Manikiala Inscription," *JRAS* (1909) 660 (repr. H. Lüders, *Kleine Schriften,* hrsg. O. von Hinüber [Wiesbaden: 1973] 335); Konow, *Kharoshṭhī Inscriptions,* 31.

53. Cf. the eighth verse of the *praśasti* of the monk Buddhabhadra from Cave XXVI at Ajaṇṭā: *yāvat kīrttir lloke tāvat svarggeṣu modati ca dehī / candrārkkakālakalpā kāryyā kīrttir mahīdhreṣu//:* "And as long as the shrine (he built) remains in the world, so long does that man enjoy the heavens. So a shrine equal in duration to the sun and moon should be built on the mountains." Text cited from Yazdani, *Ajanta,* Part IV, 115.

CHAPTER IV

The Ritual Obligations and Donor Roles of Monks in the Pāli *Vinaya*

MORE THAN ONCE recently it has again been suggested that Buddhist monks had little or no role in life-cycle ceremonies in early India.[1] I do not know on what evidence these suggestions are based, but it does not seem that it could be the Pāli texts. In fact, Buddhist *vinaya* texts in Pāli, Sanskrit, and what Roth calls "Prākrit-cum-Sanskrit" seem to suggest quite otherwise. They seem to suggest and assume that monks regularly had a role in such ceremonies and that their ritual presence and performance at such ceremonies was of some importance. Most passages, indeed, employ language that suggests "obligation" (*karaṇīya*). The same texts suggest and assume that Buddhist monks were active donors to their own monastic community.

Ironically, the one life-cycle ceremony in which a significant place for monks has been explicitly conceded—the funeral—is also the one which is not explicitly included in the list of such ceremonies that appears in the Pāli *Vinaya* passage that seems most concerned with such matters. But although the funeral is not explicitly mentioned there, the passage may allude at least to death rituals as Edgerton sometime ago seemed to surmise: it speaks of "illness" (*gilāna*), and the illness in question seems to be, to judge by context, terminal.[2]

The passage occurs in the *Vassupanāyika-khandhaka,* the section dealing with the "beginning of the rains." In the Pali Text Society edition, the only one available to me, this passage is rather badly chopped up in an apparent attempt by editor or scribe to abbreviate repetitions. It deals in general with the occasions or situations when a monk could legitimately break the rain-retreat during which he was otherwise strictly forbidden to travel. One of these reasons—but only one—has been widely cited: a monk may be away for up to seven days if he goes to learn from a lay-brother (*upāsaka*) a "recognized *sūtra*" (*abhiññātaṃ . . . suttantaṃ*) that might otherwise be in danger of being lost. There are, however, a number of other equally legitimate reasons.[3]

Originally published in *Journal of the Pali Text Society* XVI (1992):87–107. Reprinted with stylistic changes with permission of the Pali Text Society.

The enumeration of these reasons begins in Horner's translation as follows:

> This is a case, monks, where a dwelling-place for an Order comes to have been built by a layfollower (*idha pana bhikkhave upāsakena saṃghaṃ uddissa vihāro kārāpito hoti*). If he should send a messenger to monks, saying: "Let the revered sirs come, I want to give a gift and to hear *dhamma* and to see the monks" (*āgacchantu bhaddantā, icchāmi dānañ ca dātuṃ dhammañ ca sotuṃ bhikkhū ca passitun ti*), you should go, monks, if you are sent for (*pahita*) and if the business (*karaṇīya*) can be done in seven days, but not if you are not sent for.
>
> (I, 139.27; IV, 186.16)

This is followed by a long list of the kinds of buildings, including "bathrooms" and other constructions ("a lotus pond"), which a lay-brother has built for "an Order," or "for several monks" or "for one monk," and so on, in regard to which the same instructions are given. Since in these cases the order or the monks are the recipients of the constructions, it is perhaps not remarkable that their presence on these occasions was considered important enough to justify breaking the rain-retreat. The same considerations, however, will not account for their presence on other occasions.

The passage continues:

> This is a case, monks, where a dwelling comes to have been built by a layfollower for himself (*idha pana bhikkhave upāsakena attano atthāya nivesanaṃ kārāpitaṃ hoti*) . . . a sleeping room (*sayanighara*) . . . a stable (*uddosita*) . . . a hall in the bathroom . . . a lotus pond . . . a shed . . . a park . . .
>
> (I, 140.27; IV, 187.22)

This list—an abbreviation of an already abbreviated text—is much longer and contains almost every conceivable kind of domestic construction. Here, there is no question of these constructions being presented to the monks; they are explicitly said to have been made for the lay-brother himself. The monks in these cases cannot be there as recipients, and their presence must have been sought, and allowed, for other reasons. Since the text expresses the lay-brother's request using the formula "I want to give a gift and to hear *dhamma* and to see the monks," it would seem reasonable to assume that not just here, but even in the prior cases where the monks were the intended recipients, the reason for the monks' presence was essentially ritualistic. It would appear that the text allows as legitimate and even requires the presence of the monks at some sort of ceremony marking the completion (the verbal form is *kārāpita*) of construction of all sorts of domestic structures owned by laymen at which monks would receive gifts and recite religious texts. It is, in fact, hard to interpret the text otherwise. But two further points should be noted: it appears to have been assumed by the redactors of the text that monks would regularly receive such requests, and that their compliance with such requests was important enough to justify their temporary absence from the rain-retreat.

If what we see here looks very much like sanctioned and assumed monastic participation in the domestic house-dedication rituals that are frequently found in traditional cultures, then what follows in the passage can only verify this impression. To the list of house-dedications the text then adds at least three other occasions of traditional domestic rituals:

> This is the case, monks, where a dwelling comes to have been built by a layfollower for himself . . . a sleeping room . . . a park . . . , or there comes to be his son's marriage (*puttassa vā vāreyyaṃ hoti*), or there comes to be his daughter's marriage (*dhītuyā vā vāreyyaṃ hoti*), or he becomes ill (*gilāno vā hoti*) . . .
>
> (I, 140.35; IV, 188.3)

In each of these cases—as in those that precede them—monks, if requested through the formulaic request, are required to go. Since the reason or occasion that immediately follows concerns preserving "a recognized *sūtra*" that is in danger of being lost, and since no distinction is made between it and the marriages of sons or daughters, for example, it would seem that the redactors of the *Theravāda-vinaya* considered the latter occasions to have the same importance as the former; in other words, the presence of monks at weddings was as important as the preservation of *sūtras*. It is, moreover, difficult to avoid the impression that this passage presupposes something like a client relationship between monks and lay-brothers. That there was some sense of obligation in this relationship seems virtually certain: the text does not say the monk *may* go, but that—if sent for and if it can be accomplished in seven days—he "*must* go" (*gantabba*).

The clarity of the text here renders elaborate discussion, I think, unnecessary. It is all but self-evident that the redactors of the Pāli *Vinaya* assumed and insisted upon monastic presence at and participation in a whole series of purely domestic or life-cycle rituals. Our passage is not simply of interest for its clear articulation of a set of ritual obligations bearing on Buddhist monks, however, because it also assumes that requests for the ritual presence of monks will not be made by laymen only. It goes on to enumerate in very nearly the same language another series of individuals who have dwelling places and monasteries built for the order and themselves, and who also request the ritual presence of the monks on such occasions:

> This is a case, monks, where a dwelling place . . . a site for a monastery for an Order . . . for several monks . . . for him-(her-)self is built by a monk . . . a nun . . . a probationer . . . a novice (*idha pana bhikkhave bhikkhunā saṃghaṃ uddissa, bhikkhuniyā saṃghaṃ uddissa . . . attano atthāya vihāro kārā-*

> *pito hoti*). If he (she) should send a messenger to monks, saying: "Let the revered sirs (masters) come. I want to give a gift and to hear *dhamma* and to see the monks," you should go, monks, if you are sent for and if the business can be done in seven days . . .
>
> (I, 141.31; IV, 189.11)

Here too, I think, the text has an elegant clarity. The redactors of our passage could only have assumed and taken very much for granted that—exactly like laymen—monks, nuns, "probationers" (*sikkhamānā*), and novices (*sāmaṇera*) all had monasteries and monastic buildings regularly constructed both for the order and for themselves, and—again like laymen—all had on such occasions need for the ritual presence of fellow monks. The text does not rule on, but assumes, that monks and nuns can and do act as major donors. We need not again belabor the fact that this kind of assumption by the redactors of the *Theravāda-vinaya* fits awkwardly, if at all, in the picture of monastic Buddhism found in our handbooks but very nicely with the actions of monks and nuns recorded in Indian inscriptions.[4] Nor is the role of monks in domestic rituals a commonplace in modern presentations of monastic Buddhism. The apparent discordancy—since we prefer so often the pictures in our *own* books—might suggest some suspicion in regard to the present passage, or perhaps that it is just another aberration peculiar to the Pāli *Vinaya.*[5] That such suspicions are unfounded seems to follow from two further quite different texts.

The *Mūlasarvāstivāda-vinaya* found at Gilgit has a section—the *Varṣāvastu*—that corresponds in the main to the Pāli *Vassupanāyika-khandhaka.* There is, as well, in the Gilgit *Varṣāvastu* a long passage that corresponds to the Pāli passage cited above and enumerates the occasions on which the monks may legitimately be away during the rain-retreat. Both the enumeration and language here are similar to what occurs in the Pāli *Vinaya,* but by no means are they the same. The *Varṣāvastu* passage starts with a list of obligations (*karaṇīya*) owed to *upāsakas* or lay-brothers. Unfortunately, the description of the very first of the occasions on which a monk must go when sent for by a layman involves a textual—and perhaps lexical—problem that I cannot solve. It is, however, virtually certain that it had something to do with the marriage of the lay-brother.[6] I therefore cite what is, in fact, the last occasion enumerated to give an example of the formulaic character of the language used in the *Varṣāvastu:*

> There is moreover a further obligation to a lay-brother (*upāsakasya karaṇīyam*). It may occur that a lay-brother has a sickness, suffering, a serious illness. He will send a messenger to the monks (saying) "Will the Venerable Ones give a recitation" (*āryā vācaṃ dāsyanti*). A monk should go, having been authorized for seven days, through this obligation to a lay-brother (*gantavyaṃ bhikṣuṇā saptāham adhiṣṭhāya upāsakasya karaṇīyena*).[7]

The *Mūlasarvāstivāda-vinaya,* like the *Vinaya* of the Theravāda, then assumes and requires the presence of monks at certain lay, domestic life-cycle ceremonies. It does not list all of the same occasions, however, referring explicitly only to marriage and serious, if not terminal, illness. The *Mūlasarvāstivāda-vinaya* does not seem to refer to house-dedication rituals; it certainly does not contain the long list of different kinds of structures found in the Pāli. But it does contain some of the same occasions found in the Pāli that are more specifically Buddhist. It refers, for example, to a lay-brother having a *vihāra* constructed, although here too it uses a different language: "It may occur that a lay-brother wishes to have erected a monastery for the community of monks from the four directions" (*yathāpi tad upāsakaś cāturdiśe bhikṣusaṃghe vihāraṃ pratiṣṭhāpayitukāmo bhavati*). It also lists a number of more specifically Buddhist occasions not found in the Pāli *Vinaya:* a lay-brother "desiring to donate bedding and seats to that monastery" (. . . *asminn eva vihāre śayanāsanam anupradātukāmo bhavati*), "wanting to designate a permanent alms-giving" in it (. . . *asminn eva vihāre dhruvabhikṣāṃ prajñapayitukāmo bhavati*), and, interestingly, "wanting to have erected a *stūpa* for the body of the Tathāgata in that monastery" (. . . *tasminn eva vihāre tathāgatasya śarīrastūpaṃ pratiṣṭhāpayitukāmo bhavati*).[8] In all of these cases—as in the case of marriage and illness—if the monks are sent for, and if they can return within seven days, they are, of course, required to go. One such occasion, however, may be particularly important because we may be able to connect it with a record that can be much more securely placed in time and place.

The Gilgit text gives one of the more specifically Buddhist occasions in the following form:

> There is moreover a further obligation to a lay-brother. It may occur that a lay-brother wants to donate the raising of a staff on that *stūpa,* the raising of an umbrella, the raising of a flag, the raising of a banner . . . he sends a messenger to the monks . . . a monk should go . . .
>
> *aparam apy upāsakasya karaṇīyam. yathāpi tad upāsakas tasminn eva stūpe yaṣṭy-āropaṇaṃ chatrāropaṇaṃ dhvajāropaṇaṃ patākāropaṇam . . . anupradātukāmo bhavati . . . sa bhikṣūṇāṃ dūtam anupreṣayati . . . gantavyaṃ bhikṣuṇā . . .*[9]

Admitting that the exact sense of *yaṣṭi*—although much discussed[10]—is uncertain, it is still difficult not to see in this passage a regulation that corresponds almost exactly to the record of an actual event that appears to have occurred at a *stūpa* near Bahāwalpur in the first century of the Common Era. This event was recorded in a Kharoṣṭhī inscription, the language of which one might call "a Sanskritized Prākrit." Although there have been some differences of opinion in regard to its interpretation, Konow's—as usual—appears to be basically correct:

> The eleventh year—year 11—of the Great King, the King Surpassing Kings, the Son of Devas, Kaniṣka, in the month of Daisios, on the eighteenth

> day—day 18—when the monk (*bhikṣu*) Nāgadatta, a narrator of *Dharma* (*dha{rma}kathi*), the student (*śiṣya*) of the teacher (*acarya*) Damatrāta, the student's student of the teacher Bhava, raised the staff (*yaṭhiṃ aropayata*) here in Damana, the mistress of the monastery (*viharasvamiṇi*), the lay-sister (*upasika*) Balānandī and the matron, her mother Balajayā, also gave, in addition to the setting up of the *yaṣṭi* (*imaṃ yaṭhipratiṭhanaṃ*), the enclosure (*parivara*). May this be for the benefit and ease of all living beings.[11]

Here we seem to have the record of almost precisely the kind of occasion envisioned in the text. A lay-sister donates "the setting up of the *yaṣṭi*" at a *stūpa,* but the presence of a monk—if not his actual direction of the event—is carefully recorded, using in at least one case exactly the same wording as the *Vinaya* passage. The importance of the epigraphical record lies, of course, in the fact that it allows us to say that what was promulgated, in at least this *Vinaya,* appears to actually have been occurring by the first century.[12]

Apart from these points, and apart from noting that the Mūlasarvāstivāda passage also lists as one occasion the recitation of texts by a lay-brother, we need only note that this *Vinaya* not only confirms the kind of participation of monks in the domestic rituals that was taken for granted in the Pāli *Vinaya,* it also assumes—again as in the Pāli—that monks will regularly act as donors. The first of a monk's obligations to fellow monks occurs in the following form:

> What is the obligation to a monk (*bhikṣoḥ karaṇīyam*). It may occur that a monk wants to present a park to the community of monks from the four directions (*yathāpi tad bhikṣuś cāturdiśe bhikṣusaṃghe ārāmaṃ niryātayitukāmo bhavati*). By him there an abundance of material things and worldly things are brought together (*tena tatra prabhūto vastulābha āmiṣalābhaś ca samupānīto bhavati*). He sends a messenger to the monks (saying) "Come! The Reverends will enjoy." A monk should go, having been authorized for seven days, through this obligation to a monk.[13]

In referring to bringing together "material things and worldly things," the text uses exactly the same formulaic wording it had used several times previously in regard to lay-brothers. Moreover, immediately after this passage the text also lists in abbreviated form virtually all the occasions it had enumerated in detail in regard to obligations to lay-brothers: *yathāpi tad bhikṣur asminn evārāme vihāraṃ śayanāsanaṃ dhruvabhikṣāṃ tathāgatasya śārīrastūpam, . . .*[14] As in the section dealing with lay-brothers, so here the section ends with reference to a monk's obligation to attend to a sick or dying fellow monk by giving a recitation: *yathāpi tad bhikṣur ābādhiko duḥkhito vāḍhaglāno bhavati. sa bhikṣūṇāṃ dūtam anupreṣayati. āgacchantv āyuṣmanto vācāṃ bhā{ṣi}ṣyanti, . . .*[15]

We have then two apparently distinct *vinaya* traditions—the Theravāda and Mūlasarvāstivāda—that both assume and enjoin monastic participation in at least some domestic, lay life-cycle rituals and take as a given the fact that monks—exactly like laymen—make both major and minor religious donations, and that when they do, other monks are obliged to be present. There is, moreover, at least a third *vinaya* tradition in which we find something very similar.

The *Abhisamācārikā,* the "Prākrit-cum-Sanskrit" text of which was discovered in Tibet by Sankrityayana, belongs to the Mahāsāṅghika-Lokottaravāda monastic tradition. In its formal structure it does not contain divisions corresponding to the Pāli *Vassupanāyika-khandhaka* nor to the Gilgit *Varṣāvastu* and, as a consequence, we do not find in it a passage that formally corresponds to those we have discussed. We do find, however, the expression of the same sorts of assumptions and ideas. Its first chapter,[16] for example, which deals in large part with the duties of a senior monk (*saṃgha-sthavira*), says that one of the duties of such a monk is to determine, when an invitation to a meal has been received by the monks, what the occasion for the meal is (*jānitavyaṃ. kim ālambanaṃ bhaktaṃ*). He is to determine whether, significantly, the invitation is "connected with a birth, connected with a death, connected with a marriage, connected with a housewarming" (*jātakaṃ mṛtakam vā vevāhikam vā gṛha-praveśakam vā*).[17] These are the occasions, apparently, on which it was assumed monks would receive and accept invitations from the laity, and they, as in the Pāli and Gilgit *Vinayas,* are all connected with domestic life-cycle rituals. The text goes on to say that, in addition to the occasion, the senior monk must also determine the source of the invitation; he must determine whether it comes from "a visitor, a villager, a householder, or a renunciant" (*āgantukasya gamikasya gṛhasthasya pravrajitasya*). It is clear from the instructions given by the senior monk to the person sent to determine these matters that when the invitation is made by a householder, he is generally assumed to be a lay-brother or *upāsaka: tena gacchiya pṛcchitavyam, koci imaṃ hi itthannāmo nāma upāsako.* It is equally clear from similar instructions that the inviter could be a monk or nun: *ko nimantreti, bhikṣu bhikṣuṇī upāsakopāsikā āgantuko gamiko vāṇijako sārthavāho.*[18]

After indicating how all of this should be determined, the text goes on to specify how on each occasion the transfer of merit apparently expected from the monks should be performed, citing—curiously—both an inappropriate and an appropriate verse to be recited that in every case is tailored to the specific occasion. Typical are the instructions concerning an invitation "connected with a death":

> Now, then, when it is an occasion connected with a death, it is not permissible to direct the reward thus (*nāyaṃ kṣamati evaṃ dakṣiṇā ādiśituṃ*):
>
> "Today for you is a very good day, very efficacious. At present has arrived an auspicious moment.
> Today for you in the well-ordained, through the well-ordained, the reward in the most excellent vessel shines."

> Not in this way is the reward to be directed, but rather the reward should be directed (*atha khalu dakṣiṇā ādiśitavyā*):
>
> > "All living beings will die. Indeed life ends in death. As was their action so they will go, going towards the result of good or bad.
> > There is hell for those of bad action; good being done, they go to heaven.
> > Having developed the noble path they without further consequences enter *nirvāṇa*."
>
> In this way the reward is to be directed.[19]

The monks on each occasion are required to recite an appropriate verse and "to direct the reward" that results from this. Although not frequently, the expression used here to refer to the "transfer of merit"—*dakṣiṇā ādiś*—does occur in the Pāli canon, and there, as here, is also associated with the recitation of verses. It is far more frequent and firmly anchored in the *Mūlasarvāstivāda-vinaya* and related sources, where again it is frequently connected with the recitation of verses or *Dharma*. And it is referred to as well in other Mahāsāṅghika sources.[20] The appropriate verse here, as in most other cases, occurs elsewhere in canonical literature.[21] But for our present purposes the most important point to be noted is, of course, that the *Abhisamācārikā,* though representing yet another distinct *vinaya* tradition, assumes, and makes rules to govern, the participation of monks in domestic life-cycle rituals, and assumes as well that monks and nuns act as donors. Though minor details may vary, it has in common a set of basic assumptions and ideas with both the Theravāda and Mūlasarvāstivāda monastic traditions and codes. All share the assumption and acceptance of a monk's obligation to be present at, and to have an active role in, a variety of domestic, life-cycle rituals connected with birth, marriage, house construction, sickness, and death. All promulgate rules governing such obligations.[22] All recognize as perfectly regular that monks and nuns will act as donors. The texts, I think, are unambiguous on these points, although there is, as well, an important qualification in all of them.

The qualification or restriction that appears to apply to the obligations monks owe to others is highlighted in, for example, another discussion in the Pāli *Vinaya.* The case involves a monk whose mother falls ill and sends for him during the rain-retreat. The monk is made to recall the Buddha's ruling on the matter, but it apparently does not cover this particular case because the monk says: *ayañ ca me mātā gilānā sā ca anupāsikā. kathaṃ nu kho mayā paṭipajjitabban ti,* "This is my mother who is fallen ill, *but she is not a lay-sister.* How now should I proceed?" The Buddha responds by adding the monk's mother and father to the previously established list of individuals—all otherwise formally connected with the Buddhist community—to whom a monk had a clear obligation in such circumstances: a monk, a nun, a probationer, a novice, a woman novice, and lay-brothers and -sisters.[23]

This case confirms and makes explicit what all of our texts, whether Theravāda, Mūlasarvāstivāda, or Mahāsāṅghika, seem to imply: the obligation of monks to attend and participate in lay life-cycle ceremonies is not owed to the *total* lay population, but only to individuals who are formally designated as lay-brothers (*upāsakas*) or lay-sisters (*upāsikās*). To which the Pāli tradition, at least, adds a monk's mother and father, even if the parents are not formally connected with the Buddhist community. This restriction is significant for understanding the social dynamics of the Buddhist community as it was understood by *vinaya* masters. It is also significant because epigraphical material seems strongly to suggest that only a small number of those people who made gifts at Buddhist sites identified themselves as *upāsakas* or *upāsikās*.[24] The ritual clientele of Buddhist monks may necessarily have been limited in early India. The problem that remains, then, is determining what "early" can mean here.

This situation is not new. It recurs repeatedly in the study of early Buddhist canonical sources, especially when textual sources transmitted by more than one Buddhist monastic order are consulted. In this instance, we have texts redacted and transmitted by the Theravāda, Mūlasarvāstivāda, and Mahāsāṅghika that, although they differ in regard to detail, share or have in common a set of rules and a common assumption in regard to monastic participation in domestic ritual. To account for such shared or common elements, two basic theories have been used: one says that common elements in discrete textual and monastic sources must go back to a period which predates the development of schisms; the other says that such common elements result from contamination, mutual borrowing, and a process of leveling, and, therefore, are late.[25] The first theory depends on the assumption that Buddhist monastic groups can be meaningfully treated as so-called sects—this has been repeatedly questioned.[26] It depends on the assumption that, once developed, these sects existed in isolation, hermetically sealed, with no significant contact or interchange—this is contrary to all our evidence.[27] It depends on the assumption that we actually know when the splits or schisms occurred—but we do not. The textual sources, all very late, give a variety of discordant dates, and epigraphical sources suggest that discrete monastic orders appeared centuries later than our textual sources say.[28] Finally, this theory assumes that "orthodoxy" or uniformity among related religious groups is established first and then, only over time, do significant differences develop—this is contrary to almost everything church historians and sociologists have discovered: if uniformity is ever achieved, it is achieved over more or less long periods of time through a complex process of mutual influence, borrowing, and sometimes violent leveling that works on originally discrete and competing groups and voices.[29] The second theory seems to avoid these problems.

A similar, in fact related, set of questions concerns the date of the various *Vinayas.* But it too seems that the old observations and arguments of Wassilieff and Lévi remain unrefuted and best account for what seem to be the facts. The former said some years ago that it appears that "les Vinayas parvenus à nous ont été rédigés à une époque tardive," and the evidence seems to be mounting in his favor.[30]

Fortunately, however, the dates of the *vinayas* need not here be decided. It is probably true that, in terms of absolute chronology, *all* of the *vinayas* are late. But from the point of view of relative chronology, they also represent the earliest codification of monastic rules that we have. For our specific purposes, this means that monastic presence and participation in a range of domestic life-cycle rituals is assumed, judged important, and prescribed in the earliest *vinaya* literature that we have, and that our earliest *vinaya* sources assume that monks and nuns will regularly act as donors and rule on the obligations of fellow monks when they do.

We still, of course, do not know if monks actually participated in domestic rituals. We only know that the monk redactors of several *vinayas* assumed they did and said they should. That monks and nuns acted as donors, however, is certain. Not only do those same monk redactors assume they did, and formulate rules for governing the behavior of other monks when they would, but Indian inscriptions put this beyond any doubt. Once again, the isolated, socially disengaged "early" Buddhist monk of modern scholars and Mahāyāna polemics is difficult to find.[31]

Notes

1. H. Bechert and R. Gombrich, eds., *The World of Buddhism: Buddhist Monks and Nuns in Society and Culture* (London: 1984) 14; R. Gombrich, *Theravāda Buddhism. A Social History from Ancient Benares to Modern Colombo* (London: 1988) 124. That these sorts of remarks represent the received wisdom probably does not require documentation. Similar—if not stronger—suggestions have also been frequently made in regard even to monks' participation in more specifically "Buddhist" ritual and cult practice, but see G. Schopen, "Monks and the Relic Cult in the *Mahāparinibbāna-sutta:* An Old Misunderstanding in Regard to Monastic Buddhism," Ch. VI below.

2. F. Edgerton, "The Hour of Death. Its Importance for Man's Future Fate in Hindu and Western Religions," *Annals of the Bhandarkar Institute* 8.3 (1926–1927) 234; for the participation of monks in monastic funerals in both the Pāli and, especially, the Mūlasarvāstivāda *Vinayas,* see G. Schopen, "On Avoiding Ghosts and Social Censure: Monastic Funerals in the *Mūlasarvāstivāda-vinaya,*" Ch. X below.

3. All the Pāli citations below come from H. Oldenberg, *The Vinaya Piṭakaṃ,* Vol. I (London: 1879) 139–142; the translations are from I. B. Horner, *The Book of The Discipline,* Vol. IV (London: 1951) 185–189.

4. See G. Schopen, "Filial Piety and the Monk in the Practice of Indian Buddhism," Ch. III above; Schopen, "Two Problems in the History of Indian Buddhism," Ch. II above; Schopen, "On Monks, Nuns, and 'Vulgar' Practices," Ch. XI below.

5. The presence in the Pāli canonical *Vinaya* of rules governing the obligatory presence of monks at weddings, for example, is particularly intriguing in light of what has recently been said about the modern "change" and "transformation" of Buddhism in Sri Lanka; see R. Gombrich and G. Obeyesekere, *Buddhism Transformed. Religious Change in Sri Lanka* (Princeton: 1988) 265–273; H. L. Seneviratne, *Rituals of the Kandyan State* (Cambridge: 1978) 129.

6. *Gilgit Manuscripts,* iii 4, 138.9, prints the text as follows: *kim upāsakasya karaṇīyena / yathāpi tad upāsakasya gṛha-kalatraṃ pratyupasthitaṃ bhavati ātmano veṣṭanaṃ . . . sa bhikṣūṇāṃ dūtam anupreṣayati. . . .* On at least two occasions immediately prior to this passage, a householder is described in similar terms: *tatra . . . gṛhapatiḥ prativasati / tasya gṛha-kalatraṃ pratyupasthitam / ātmano veṣṭanaṃ. . .* (136.15, 137.13; see also 140.22). Unfortunately, in all of these cases, the manuscript seems to read not *gṛha-kalatram,* but *gṛha-kanutram* (*Gilgit Buddhist Manuscripts,* vi, 733.8, 734.3, 734.7, 736.1), and I do not know what *-kanutram* means. I suspect that Dutt also did not and—as he so often did—silently "corrected" the text on the basis of the Tibetan: *dge bsnyen gyi bya ba gang zhe na / 'di ltar yang dge bsnyen gyis khyim du rang gi 'ching ba bag ma blangs te / (Tog,* I, fol. 692.2; cf. fols. 689.2, 690.6, 696.1). Although, again, I do not fully understand the phrase *khyim du rang gi 'ching ba,* the Tibetan text has certainly understood its text to be referring to the lay-brother's marriage.

7. *Gilgit Manuscripts,* iii 4, 140.17.

8. *Gilgit Manuscripts,* iii 4, 138.14–139.11.

9. *Gilgit Manuscripts,* iii 4, 139.11–139.17.

10. For *yaṣṭi,* see F. Weller, "Divyāvadāna 244.7f," *Mitteilungen des Instituts für Orientforschung* 1 (1953) 268–276; L. Alsdorf, "Der Stūpa des Kṣemaṃkara," *Studia Indologica (Festschrift für Willibald Kirfel)* (Bonn: 1955) 9–16; M. Bénisti, "Étude sur le stūpa dans l'Inde ancienne," *BEFEO* 50 (1960) 37–116, esp. 76f; F. B. J. Kuiper, "Yūpayaṣṭi- (Divy. 244,11)," *IIJ* 3 (1959) 204–205; G. Roth, "Bemerkungen zum Stūpa des Kṣemaṃkara," *StII* 5/6 (1980) 181–192; etc.

11. For Konow's edition and translation, see S. Konow, *Kharoshṭhī Inscriptions with the Exception of Those of Aśoka,* Corpus Inscriptionum Indicarum, Vol. II, Pt. 1 (Calcutta: 1929) 139–141 (no. LXXIV), pl. XXVI—my translation is heavily indebted to his. For some earlier interpretations of the record, see A. F. R. Hoernle, "Readings from the Arian Pāli," *IA* 10 (1881) 324–331; B. Indraji, "A Baktro-Pāli Inscription of Sui Bāhāra," *IA* 11 (1882) 128–129; N. G. Majumdar, "The Suë Vihar Copper-plate of the Reign of Kaniṣka," *Sir Asutosh Mookerji Silver Jubilee Volumes,* III, 1 (Calcutta: 1922) 459–474.

12. If our *Mūlasarvāstivāda-vinaya* passage strongly argues for Konow's interpretation of the Kharoṣṭhī inscription, it is less helpful for understanding the references to *yaṣṭis* or *laṣṭis* in a series of records from Western India. See B. Indraji, "The Western Kshatrapas," *JRAS* (1890) 652; R. D. Banerji, "The Andhau Inscriptions of the Time of Rudradaman," *EI* 16 (1921–1922) 19–25 (two of these *might* be Buddhist); S. Gokhale, "Andhau Inscription of Caṣṭana, Śaka 11," *JAIH* 2 (1969) 104–111; D. C. Sircar, "Andhau Fragmentary Inscription of Caṣṭana, Year 11," *JIH* 48 (1970) 253–257; S. Sankaranarayanan, "A New Early Kushana Brahmi Inscription," *Śrīnidhiḥ. Perspectives in Indian Archaeology, Art and Culture. Shri K. R. Srinivasan Festschrift,* ed. K. V. Raman et al. (Madras: 1983) 277–284; etc. Although the references that I know are late, it is

worth noting that—like our *Mūlasarvāstivāda* passage—Hindu inscriptions also refer to a ritual *dhvajāroha* or *dhvajārohaṇa.* See R. Sharma, "Udayapur Inscription of Paramara Udayaditya, Vikrama 1137," *EI* 38 (1970) 281ff; S. L. Katare, "Kalanjara Inscription of V. S. 1147," *EI* 31 (1955–1956) 163ff; etc.

13. *Gilgit Manuscripts,* iii 4, 141.1f.

14. *Gilgit Manuscripts,* iii 4, 141.6f. It will have been noticed that where the *Mūlasarvāstivāda-vinaya* makes full reference to *stūpas* the *Theravāda-vinaya* has none. On this pattern, see G. Schopen, "The *Stūpa* Cult and the Extant Pāli *Vinaya,*" Ch. V below, and the responses to it in O. von Hinüber, "*Khandhakavatta.* Loss of Text in the Pali Vinaya," *JPTS* 15 (1990) 127–138; C. Hallisey, "Apropos the Pāli Vinaya as a Historical Document. A Reply to Gregory Schopen," ibid, 197–208; R. Gombrich, "Making Mountains Without Molehills: The Case of the Missing *Stūpa,*" ibid, 141–143. What has come out of this discussion—apart from some light entertainment provided by Professor Gombrich—seems to be: an increased awareness of the complexity and extent of Pāli *Vinaya* literature, and a promising suggestion that there is something like an "ideal" *Vinaya* (the canonical *Vinaya*) and an "actually used" *Vinaya* (the various summaries and "different monastic handbooks"), with the consequent confirmation of the suggestion "that the canonical *Vinaya* text is not as useful as once thought as a ready source for extracting usable historical data" (Hallisey, 207). It seems too that the suggestion of "the loss of text" is weaker even than I thought, but some problems remain. Though the *Katikāvata* passage might be neutralized by invoking the *du* or *ca,* this will not affect the *Visuddhimagga* passages. They, as Hallisey says, "are more difficult to explain." There is, moreover, what appears to be a much more likely case of "loss of text"—here again concerning "relics"—in the Sri Lankan manuscripts of the *Saṃyutta;* see G. Schopen, "An Old Inscription from Amarāvatī and the Cult of the Local Monastic Dead in Indian Buddhist Monasteries," Ch. IX below, 191–192 and 203, n. 111. Finally, it seems absolutely certain—given Professor Gombrich's agreement—that it can no longer be said that the Pāli *Vinaya* does not contain any references to *stūpas.* He seems to have been so convinced by my suggestion that the references to *cetiyas* in the *Sutta-Vibhaṅga* are to be understood as referring to *stūpas* that he wants to use them against me (140). But the presence of such rules in one part of the Pāli *Vinaya,* but not in another, does not seem to puzzle.

15. *Gilgit Manuscripts,* iii 4, 142.5. Elsewhere in the *Mūlasarvāstivāda-vinaya*—in its *Cīvaravastu*—there are even more specific rules governing the performance of a "worship of the Teacher (= Buddha)" (*śāstuś ca pūjā*) for a sick and dying monk and how that *pūjā* should be financed; see *Gilgit Manuscripts,* iii 2, 124.11–125.9.

16. The whole text was first edited in B. Jinananda, *Abhisamācārikā {Bhikṣuprakīrṇaka}* (Patna: 1969). The first chapter has been again edited and translated—though the latter, at least, is far from satisfactory—in S. Singh and K. Minowa, "A Critical Edition and Translation of Abhisamācārikā Nāma Bhikṣu-Prakīrṇakaḥ," *Buddhist Studies. The Journal of the Department of Buddhist Studies, University of Delhi* 12 (1988) 81–146; see also M. Prasad, *A Comparative Study of Abhisamācārikā* (Patna: 1984).

17. Singh and Minowa, 91.26; Jinananda, 17.8.

18. Singh and Minowa, 91.27, 89.32, 95.27; Jinananda, 17.9, 14.9, 25.1.

19. Singh and Minowa, 92.15f; Jinananda, 18.13f.

20. For references in both primary and secondary sources and some discussion concerning the expression *dakṣiṇā ādiś-*, see Schopen, "On Avoiding Ghosts and Social Censure," Ch. X below, esp. n. 43. It has yet, however, to be fully studied. {See also

G. Schopen, "Doing Business for the Lord: Lending on Interest and Written Loan Contracts in the *Mūlasarvāstivāda-vinaya*," *JAOS* 114 (1994) 527–554; esp. 545f.]

21. This verse or variants of it occur at *Mahāvastu,* ii, 66; *Saṃyutta,* i, 97; etc.

22. The various *vinayas* obviously do not list all the same ritual occasions. The *Abhisamācārikā* list is the most inclusive, and the Pāli *Vinaya* puts considerable emphasis on "house dedication" rituals. The *Mūlasarvāstivāda-vinaya* is noticeably the most restrictive in terms of the kind of domestic rituals at which monks are obliged to be present. The explanation for these differences is not yet determined. It may be related to the cultural and geographical milieu in which the various codes were redacted rather than to chronology. We may see in the restrictive character of the *Mūlasarvāstivāda-vinaya,* for example, another indication that it was redacted by, and for, a Buddhist monastic community in close contact with brahmanical or significantly brahmanized groups in which domestic ritual was already in the hands of other religious specialists. The needs or requirements of a monastic group in "tribal" or partially brahmanized areas could differ markedly. Cf. Schopen, "On Avoiding Ghosts and Social Censure," Ch. X below.

23. Pāli *Vinaya,* i, 147.20ff.

24. A thorough study of *upāsakas* and *upāsikās* in Indian Buddhist inscriptions has yet to be done. But at Sāñcī *Stūpa* no. 1, for example, only eighteen of the more than three hundred twenty-five lay donors call themselves *upāsakas* or *upāsikās;* at Bhārhut none do; at Nāsik only four of twenty-three; at Kārli only two of twenty-two; and I very much suspect a similar pattern will hold throughout until at least the fifth or sixth century.

25. Cf. L. O. Gómez, "Buddhism in India," *Buddhism and Asian History,* ed. J. M. Kitagawa and M. D. Cummings (New York: 1989) 64, and L. Schmithausen, Preface, *Earliest Buddhism and Madhyamaka,* Panels of the VIIth World Sanskrit Conference, Vol. II (Leiden: 1990) 1–2.

26. See H. Bechert, "Zur Geschichte der buddhistischen Sekten in Indien und Ceylon," *La nouvelle clio* 7–9 (1955–1957) 311–360; Bechert, "On the Identification of Buddhist Schools in Early Sri Lanka," *Indology and Law; Studies in Honor of Professor J. Duncan M. Derrett,* ed. G. D. Sontheimer and P. K. Aithal (Wiesbaden: 1982) 60–76.

27. *Histoire du bouddhisme indien,* 197.

28. See Schopen, "Two Problems in the History of Indian Buddhism," Ch. II above, 26.

29. See, for example, the now classic W. Bauer, *Orthodoxy and Heresy in Earliest Christianity* (Philadelphia: 1971). Something similar has occasionally been argued in the development of Indian Buddhism—but only occasionally. J. Przyluski, for example, in discussing the *pratītyasamutpāda* formula said many years ago: "En somme, nous ne pouvons admettre qu'il y eût à l'origine du Bouddhisme une série de douze 'conditions' dont les autres listes ne seraient que des déformations récentes. Plus haut nous remontons dans le passé, plus grande est la diversité que nous constatons. C'est probablement à une époque assez tardive qu'on s'efforça de concilier les thèses divergentes et que finit par prévaloir la série: *avidyā . . . jarāmaraṇa*" (J. Przyluski, "La roue de la vie à Ajaṇṭā," *JA* [1920] 327–328).

30. W. Wassilieff [V. Vasilyev], "Le bouddhisme dans son plein développement d'après les vinayas," *RHR* 34 (1896) 318–325, esp. 321ff; S. Lévi, "Les éléments de formation du Divyāvadāna," *TP* 8 (1907) 116–117 and n. 1; Lévi, "Les saintes écritures du bouddhisme," *Mémorial Sylvain Lévi* (Paris: 1937) 82–84: "De plus, la vie du couvent, qui allait en se développant sans cesse, proposait ainsi sans cesse des problèmes pratiques

qu'il fallait résoudre au nom du fondateur de l'ordre. Les couvents les plus riches, les mieux fréquentés, se créaient ainsi des collections qui se perpétuaient en s'accroissant. Les religieux errants, qui circulaient toujours nombreux de couvent en couvent, maintenaient dans ce vaste ensemble une communication constante qui tendait à niveler les divergences trop accusées. Réduits par élagage à leurs éléments communs, les Vinaya de toutes les écoles se ramènent sans effort à une sorte d'archétype unique, qui n'est pas le Vinaya primitif, mais la moyenne des Vinaya."

31. The influence of the characterizations of "early" monks found in Mahāyāna *sūtra* literature on modern scholarly characterizations is a subject not yet studied, but one which may well be of particular significance. There are cases, for example, where what appears to be Mahāyāna polemical caricature has been used to account for historical development. Dayal has said that ". . . it seems that the Buddhist monks . . . in the second century B.C. . . . emphasized a few duties to the exclusion of others. They became too self-centered and contemplative, and did not evince the old zeal for missionary activity among the people. They seem to have cared only for their own liberation from sin and sorrow. They were indifferent to the duty of teaching and helping all human beings. . . . The *bodhisattva* ideal can be understood only against this background of a saintly and serene, but inactive and indolent monastic order" (H. Dayal, *The Bodhisattva Doctrine in Buddhist Sanskrit Literature* [London: 1932] 2–3). This explanation of a historical occurrence has, in a variety of forms, often been repeated (see *Histoire du bouddhisme indien,* 73, 78, 699), but no evidence for it is ever cited, and it appears to be little more than a paraphrase of the polemical position taken in Mahāyāna *sūtras.* There is, moreover, little, if any, indication in Indian inscriptions that monks—either before or after the beginning of the Common Era—were "self-centered," "cared only for their own liberation," and "were indifferent to . . . helping all human beings." In fact, the indications are quite otherwise. They suggest a monk very active in giving, concerned with benefiting parents, teachers, friends, and "all beings," and very much engaged in the social world; see the references in n. 1 above. We see this monk in Indian inscriptions that date to almost exactly the period during which we think Mahāyāna *sūtras* were first composed. Obviously, much remains to be learned here.

* * *

[For a short response to this paper see R. Gombrich, "The Monk in the Pāli Vinaya: Priest or Wedding Guest?" *JPTS* 21 (1995) 193–197. For more on the title translated here as "mistress of the monastery," see now G. Schopen, "The Lay Ownership of Monasteries and the Role of the Monk in Mūlasarvāstivādin Monasticism," *JIABS* 19.1 (1996) 81–126.]

CHAPTER V

The *Stūpa* Cult and the Extant Pāli *Vinaya*

One of the more curious things about the Pāli *Vinaya* as we have it is that it contains no rules governing the behavior of monks in regard to *stūpas.* In this respect it is, among the various *vinayas* that have come down to us, unique: "tous les *Vinayapiṭaka . . . à la seule exception du vinaya pāli,* contiennent," according to Bareau, "d'intéressantes données concernant la construction et le culte des *stūpa*" (emphasis added).[1] Bareau seems to see the absence of such "données" in the Pāli *Vinaya* as a function of the chronology of the compilation of the various *vinayas* and seems to suggest that the absence of such material results from the relatively earlier date of the closing of its compilation.[2] Roth explains the absence of such rules in the Pāli *Vinaya* in a somewhat different way: "The Pāli tradition apparently did not include such a section, as the compilers of the ancient Pāli canon were governed by a tradition according to which the construction and worship of a *stūpa* was the concern of laymen and not of monks. Therefore, there was felt to be no need for a particular *stūpa*-section to be included in the *Khandhaka*-section of the Pāli *Vinaya.*"[3] There is, however, a passage in a twelfth century Sinhalese *Katikāvata,* or monastic code, a passage in the *Visuddhimagga,* and several passages in the *Sutta-vibhaṅga,* that might suggest quite a different possible explanation.

The *Mahā-Parākramabāhu Katikāvata,* which has come down to us in a twelfth century inscription from Galvihāra,[4] was promulgated as a part of one of the many attempts to "purify" or "reform" the Sri Lankan *Saṅgha,* and its authors claim that it "was formulated also without deviating from the tradition of the lineage of preceptors [*ädurol* = *ācārya-kula*] and after the consultation of Dhamma and Vinaya."[5] One of the sections intended to regulate the daily life of the monks says, in part, in Ratnapala's translation:

Originally published in *Journal of the Pali Text Society* XIII (1989):83–100. Reprinted with stylistic changes with permission of the Pali Text Society.

> They should rise at dawn and pass the time walking up and down (for the sake of bodily exercise). Thereafter they should wear the cīvara covering themselves properly with it and after they have finished cleaning the teeth and have attended to *the duties specified in the Khandhaka such as the duties pertaining to Stūpas,* the great bodhi-tree, the temple terrace, the teachers, the Theras, the sick and the lodging places (*dahagab mām̆bo an̆gaṇa-vatu-du äduru-vat tera-vat gilan-vat senasun-vat ä kandu-vatu-du sapayā*), should if need arise enter the refectory . . . (emphasis added).[6]

It would appear from his translation that Ratnapala understood the *Katikā-vata* to be saying that all the "duties" enumerated here were "specified" in the *Khandhaka,* and that he assumes that *Khandhaka* here refers to the portion of the *Vinaya* so named. But this would suggest, *if* Ratnapala's interpretation of the text is correct, that the authorities who drafted this *Katikāvata* in the twelfth century knew—and presupposed that their intended audience knew—a *Khandhaka* which contained rules concerning "duties pertaining to Stūpas." The *Khandhaka-vatta,* or duties specified in the *Khandhaka,*" were, again according to Ratnapala, specifically identified by Mahāsvāmi Śāriputra, a leading figure and *vinaya* authority contemporary with the promulgation of the *Katikāvata,* with "the major and minor duties enumerated in the *Vatta-khandhaka,* i.e., *Vinaya* ii 207–230."[7] Śāriputra, then, also understood *Khandhaka-vatta* to refer to the text of the *Vinaya,* and his specificity, in fact, should make it easy to locate these rules. But when we look at *Vinaya* ii 207–230, it becomes clear that, although there are now rules there regarding "the teachers, the Theras, the sick and the lodging places," *Vinaya* ii 207–230, *as we have it,* does not contain a word about *stūpas.* This might suggest either that Śāriputra was wrong in his identification of the *Khandhaka-vatta* with these specific pages, or that the compilers of the *Katikāvata* knew—and expected contemporaries to have—a *Vinaya* different from the one we have, a *Vinaya* which had a fuller text of *Vinaya* ii 207–230 than the one that has come down to us. Oddly enough, even if Śāriputra was wrong in his specific identification, we are still left in much the same position: even if the *Katikāvata* is not specifically referring to *Vinaya* ii 207–230, it must at least be referring to the *Vinaya.*[8] And it is not in just *Vinaya* ii 207–230 that there are no references to "duties pertaining to Stūpas"; there are no references to such duties anywhere in the Pāli *Vinaya* that we know. It is, however, not just the authors of our *Katikāvata* who appear possibly to have known a Pāli *Vinaya* different from the one we have.

Buddhaghosa refers on several occasions in his *Visuddhimagga* to the *Khandhaka* and there is, I think, no doubt about what he understood by the term. In one place he says: *ubhato-vibhaṅgapariyāpannaṃ vā ādibrahmacariyakaṃ, khandhakavattapariyāpannaṃ ābhisamācārikaṃ,* which Pe Maung Tin translates as "Or, that which is included in both the Vibhangas is the 'major precept'; that which is included in the Khandhaka duties is the 'minor precept'."[9] At another place he refers to the "proper duties" promulgated by the Blessed One in the *Khandhaka* (*yan taṃ bhagavatā . . . khandhake sammāvattaṃ paññattaṃ*) and then quotes a passage similar to that found in our *Katikāvata* that is found now in *Vinaya* ii 231.[10] It seems fairly obvious, then, that when Buddhaghosa uses the terms *Khandhaka* or *Khandhaka-vatta,* he is always referring to the text of the canonical *Vinaya* which he knew. This is of some importance because in yet another passage in his *Visuddhimagga,* he refers his readers to the *Khandhaka* for rules regarding many of the same things that the *Mahā-Parākramabāhu-Katikāvata* refers to. The passage in question reads:

> *āgantukaṃ pana bhikkhuṃ disvā āgantukapaṭisanthāro kātabbo va. avasesāni pi cetiyaṅgaṇavatta-bodhiyaṅgaṅavatta-uposathāgāravatta-bhojanasālājantāghara-ācariyupajjhāya-āgantuka-gamikavattādīni sabbāni khandhakavattāni pūretabbān' eva*

which Pe Maung Tin translates as:

> On seeing a guest-monk, he should give him the greetings due to a guest. All the remaining *Khandhaka* duties should be performed, such as the duties of the shrine-yard, the yard of the Bo-tree, the sacred-service hall, the dining-hall, the fire-room, the duties towards the teacher, the preceptor, guests.[11]

It is clear from his translation that Pe Maung Tin understood *Khandhaka* in the *Visuddhimagga* to be a proper name or the title of a work. T. W. Rhys Davids and Stede before him understood the term in the *Visuddhimagga* in the same way. Citing the same passages we have cited above from the *Visuddhimagga,* Rhys Davids and Stede defined *khandhaka-vatta* as "duties or observances specified in the v. khandha or chapter of the Vinaya which deals with these duties."[12] But if these scholars are correct, then it is hard to avoid concluding from the passage just cited that, like the authors of the *Katikāvata* who knew a *Khandhaka* containing rules "pertaining to *Stūpas,*" Buddhaghosa knew a *Khandhaka* that contained rules concerning "the shrine-yard" or *cetiyaṅgaṇa.* Since he was—like the authors of the *Katikāvata*—giving practical instructions to his readers, it is again difficult to avoid the assumption that he assumed that they would know or be able to consult a similar *Khandhaka.* But, although the Mahāsāṅghika *Vinaya* preserved in Chinese, for example, has rules concerning what Bareau translates as "l'enceinte du *stūpa,*"[13] and although the Sanskrit version of the *Mūlasarvāstivāda-vinaya* has rules regarding the *stūpāṅgaṇa,*[14] the Pāli *Vinaya as we have it* does not have a single reference to the *cetiyāṅgaṇa* or *stūpāṅgaṇa.*[15]

Unless Ratnapala, Pe Maung Tin, Rhys Davids, and Stede are all wrong in their interpretations of the compound *khandhakavatta,* unless, in short, we do not understand what the term actually refers to, these two passages—one from the fifth century *Visuddhimagga,* the other from a twelfth century Sinhalese

Katikāvata—seem to suggest that there is a distinct probability that the Pāli *Vinaya,* like virtually all the other *vinayas* known to us, had once contained specific "duties pertaining to *Stūpas*" and "duties of the shrine-yard." It is, moreover, not just sources external to the Pāli *Vinaya* like the *Visuddhimagga* and *Mahā-Parākramabāhu Katikāvata* that seem to suggest that this *Vinaya* may have originally contained such rules. There are indications within the Pāli *Vinaya* itself that would seem to point to much the same conclusion.

Although, as we have already noted, the Pāli *Vinaya* as we have it, and more particularly the *Khandhaka,* have no rules specifically governing behavior in regard to *stūpas, stūpas*—or at least *cetiyas*—are taken for granted as an integral part of the monastic life in at least four passages in the *Sutta-vibhaṅga.* We might look briefly at these.

In discussing the passage from the *Visuddhimagga* above, I have assumed that Buddhaghosa's *cetiyaṅgaṇa* was the Pāli equivalent of the Mūlasarvāstivādin *stūpāṅgaṇa* and of the "l'enceinte du *stūpa*" found in the Chinese *vinayas.* Given the narrative uses and descriptions of the *cetiyaṅgaṇa* in Buddhaghosa, it would be hard to argue otherwise. But if this equivalence of *cetiya* and *stūpa* holds here, it may hold elsewhere as well. Two of the four passages from the *Sutta-vibhaṅga* that concern us, for example, deal with property rights in, and the tripartite economic structure of, Buddhist monastic establishments. The first of these, *Vinaya* iii 266, reads:

> *saṃghassa pariṇataṃ aññasaṃghassa vā cetiyassa vā pariṇāmeti, āpatti dukkaṭassa. cetiyassa pariṇataṃ aññacetiyassa vā saṃghassa vā puggalassa vā pariṇāmeti, āpatti dukkaṭassa. puggalassa pariṇataṃ aññapuggalassa vā saṃghassa vā cetiyassa vā pariṇāmeti, āpatti dukkaṭassa.*

And Horner translates the passage as:

> If he appropriates what was apportioned to the Order for another (part of the) Order or for a shrine, there is an offence of wrong-doing. If he appropriates what was apportioned to a shrine for another shrine or for an Order or for an individual, there is an offence of wrong-doing. If he appropriates what was apportioned to an individual for another individual or for an Order or for a shrine, there is an offence of wrong-doing.[16]

This passage, and the virtually identical passage at *Vinaya* iv 156, can, I think, only represent the Pāli versions of similar discussions of property rights found in Sanskrit in the *Mūlasarvāstivāda-vinaya* and in several *vinayas* now preserved in Chinese. In the *Mūlasarvāstivāda-vinaya,* for example, we find:

> *bhagavān āha / sarvasaṃghaṃ sannipātyāsau lakṣitavyaḥ / kiṃ sambhinnakārī na vā iti / yadi sambhinnakārī / sāṃghikaṃ staupikaṃ karoti / staupikaṃ vā sāṃghikam / evam adhārmikam /*

> The Blessed One said: 'Having assembled the whole community, this is to be considered: is this a (case for) making a full division [or: mixed distribution], or is it not? If there is a full division (and) it takes what belongs to the *Saṅgha* as what belongs to the *stūpa,* or what belongs to the *stūpa* as what belongs to the *Saṅgha*—such (a procedure) is not in conformity with the *Dharma* (*de lta bu chos dang mi mthun pa yin pas*).[17]

In regard to the Chinese *vinayas,* Bareau notes, for example, that "les Sarvāstivādin parlent aussi des biens inépuisables du *stūpa,* qui sont inaliénables. Les biens qui sont donnés en offrande au *stūpa* ne peuvent être utilisés à d'autres fins. On ne doit pas les mélanger avec les biens de la Communauté des quatre directions, ni avec les biens consistant en nourriture, ni avec les biens à partager."[18]

It would seem fairly certain that the *Sutta-vibhaṅga* passage, the *Mūlasarvāstivāda-vinaya* passage, and the Sarvāstivādin material summarized by Bareau are all dealing with the same basic concern: the distribution of property to, and the ownership rights of, the different corporate or juristic entities within a monastic establishment. The fact that, in exactly similar contexts, the Sarvāstivādin and Mūlasarvāstivādin *Vinayas* speak of *stūpas* or that which "belongs to the *stūpas*" (*staupika*) and the Pāli *Sutta-vibhaṅga* speaks of *cetiyas* would seem again to suggest that the two terms are equivalent, that *cetiya* in these contexts is the Pāli equivalent for *stūpa.* It is interesting to note that the Pāli preference for *cetiya* may, in fact, represent a relatively late South Indian influence on the vocabulary of the Pāli *Vinaya.* At Nāgārjunikoṇḍa, for example, what elsewhere would be called a *stūpa* is, in the inscriptions, consistently referred to as a *cetiya.*[19]

But if *cetiya* in these contexts and in the compound *cetiyaṅgaṇa* is the Pāli equivalent of *stūpa,* then it is equally possible that it is being used in the same way in the two remaining passages we must mention from the *Sutta-vibhaṅga. Saṅghādisesa* V prohibits monks from acting as "go-betweens" (*sañcaritta*) but notes that "there is no offence if it is for the Order, or for a shrine, or if he is ill; if he is going on business, if he is mad, if he is a beginner" (*anāpatti saṃghassa vā cetiyassa vā gilānassa vā karaṇīyena gacchati, ummattakassa, ādikammikassā ti*).[20] Similarly, in the *Bhikkhunīvibhaṅga, Pācittiya* XLIV, which prohibits nuns from doing household work, cooking, etc., it is said that "there is no offence if it [cooking, etc.] is a drink of conjey, if it is for the Order; if it is for worship at a shrine . . ." (*anāpatti yāgupāne saṃghabhatte cetiya-pūjāya* . . .).[21] If Pāli *cetiya* in these two passages does not refer to what in other *Vinayas* would be called *stūpas,* it is hard to know what it could refer to. The *cetiya* in these passages is an "object" for whose worship nuns can properly prepare food and for whose sake monks can engage in activities otherwise forbidden to them. It is unlikely, therefore, that the term here could be referring to local or non-Buddhist "shrines"—the only other "objects" generally referred to by the term in Pāli canonical literature.[22] These considerations, and the fact that the use of Pāli *cetiya* for *stūpa* is virtually assured, as we have seen, elsewhere in the *Sutta-vibhaṅga* would certainly support the possibility that it is so used here as well.

If we keep in mind, then, the equivalence of *cetiya* and *stūpa* that seems virtually certain in two cases in the Pāli *Sutta-vibhaṅga,* and likely in two more, it would appear that the Pāli *Sutta-vibhaṅga* (although it has no rules specifically governing behavior in regard to *stūpas* or *cetiyas)* takes such behavior and the existence of *stūpas* or *cetiyas* very much for granted when it deals with other matters. The rules governing the division of property, acting as a "go-between," cooking foods, etc., take the *stūpa* or *cetiya* and activity undertaken in regard to it as established and fully integrated elements of the monastic life. This, of course, makes the complete absence of rules specifically concerned with *stūpas* or *cetiyas* in the *Khandhaka* even more striking and would seem to provide yet another argument for concluding that the Pāli *Khandhaka* must originally have contained such rules. But if—as the *Mahā-Parākramabāhu Katikāvata,* the *Visuddhimagga,* and the *Sutta-vibhaṅga* seem to suggest—the Pāli *Vinaya* had originally contained such rules, then the fact that they are no longer found in the *Vinaya* known to us could, apparently, only be explained by assuming that either they had inadvertently dropped out of the manuscripts or, perhaps, that they were intentionally written out.

The comparatively recent date of the vast majority of the surviving manuscripts for texts in the Pāli canon,[23] coupled with the long and troubled history of their transmission—especially after the twelfth century—could easily account for the loss of material from these texts on a fairly large scale and makes an uninterrupted transmission of our Pāli texts extremely unlikely. In fact, the historical situation would suggest that the transmission was probably interrupted not once but on several different occasions.[24] It is, therefore, possible to think that the loss of "the duties pertaining to Stūpas" could have occurred in just this way. There is at least one consideration, however, that renders this possibility less forceful and may, in fact, suggest quite a different process.

In the *vinayas* surveyed by Bareau—those of the Mahīśāsaka, Dharmaguptaka, Mahāsāṅghika, Sarvāstivādin, and Mūlasarvāstivādin—the rules regarding *stūpas,* although concentrated in the various *Kṣudrakavastus,* are scattered throughout this *vastu* and, in some of the collections, in other *vastus* or divisions of the *vinaya* as well.[25] They do not occur as a single block. Assuming that much the same held for the Pāli *Vinaya,* and that although concentrated in a single *vastu,* rules regarding *stūpas* would have been scattered throughout it and elsewhere in the *Skandhaka,* it would be easy enough to see how some of these scattered rules could have been lost through accidents of transmission. But that all such rules would have been lost in this way seems very unlikely. In light of this, the total absence of rules regarding *stūpas* in the Pāli *Vinaya* would seem to make sense only if they had been systematically removed.

But acknowledging the possibility—if not the likelihood—of such a systematic removal having actually occurred is one thing; knowing why it might have occurred is something else again. One might be tempted to try to explain any removal from the Pāli *Vinaya* of rules regarding *stūpas* by referring to the purported prohibition of monastic participation in the *stūpa*/relic cult that is supposed to occur in the *Mahāparinibbāna-sutta.* This, however, will raise many more questions than answers and, in fact, leads us to much the same conclusion that consideration of the *Katikāvata,* the *Visuddhimagga,* and the *Sutta-vibhaṅga* suggests. First of all—as I hope to show in some detail elsewhere—the injunction addressed to Ānanda concerning *sarīra-pūjā* has nothing to do with an ongoing cult of relics or *stūpas.*[26] Not only can this be shown from the *Mahāparinibbāna-sutta* and related texts, but it is equally clear from other sources that any discomfiture with monastic participation in *stūpa* or relic cult activity is distinctly modern. In the *Udāna* version of the story of "Bāhiya of the Bark Garment," for example, there is a clear directive to monks to build *stūpas:*

> . . . having seen (the body of Bāhiya, the Blessed One) addressed the monks: 'You, monks, must take up the body of Bāhiya of the Bark Garment! Having put it on a bier, having carried it out, you must cremate it, and you must build a *stūpa* for it! For monks, a fellow-monk has died.'
>
> . . . *disvāna bhikkhū āmantesi: gaṇhatha bhikkhave Bāhiyassa dārucīriyassa sarīrakaṃ mañcakaṃ āropetvā nīharitvā jhāpetha thūpañ c'assa karotha, sabrahmacārī vo bhikkhave kālaṅkato ti.*[27]

The *Apadāna* version of the same story has the Buddha saying to the monks: . . . *thūpaṃ karotha pūjetha,* "You must build a *stūpa!* You must worship it!"[28]

That these texts give expression to very early practice concerning the disposal of the monastic dead is confirmed by some of the earliest archaeological and epigraphical evidence that we have. There are, for example, the group of *stūpas* of the local monastic dead at the monastery complex at Bhājā, "probably one of the oldest Buddhist religious centres in the Deccan";[29] or the old *stūpa* of the "forest-dweller" Gobhūti built by his monk pupil at Bedsā;[30] or *Stūpa* no. 2 at Sāñcī, which held the mortuary remains of the local monastic dead, and which Bénisti has recently argued is older even than Bhārhut:[31] this *stūpa* appears to have been established and largely funded by monks and nuns.[32] The same early kind of evidence proves the early and massive monastic participation in the cult of the relics and *stūpas* of the historical Buddha at Bhārhut, Sāñcī, and Pauni.[33] Clear evidence for the active participation of monks and nuns in the *stūpa*/relic cult is found as well at other sites. At Pangoraria in Madhya Pradesh at a very old monastic site, the *yaṣṭi,* or shaft, and umbrella of the main *stūpa,* both of which were very finely worked, were the gift of a *bhikṣuṇī* and her disciples according to the inscription on the shaft that dates to the second century B.C.E.[34]

The inscriptions on the Bhaṭṭiprolu relic caskets, which have been dated variously from the third to the first centuries B.C.E., show that monks (*samana*) took an active and prominent part in the enshrinement of the relics of the Buddha (*budhasarira*) there, both as donors and members of the *gothi* or "committee" that undertook the project.[35] Of the many early inscriptions from Amarāvatī recording gifts of monks connected with the *stūpa* cult, we might note the one "in Maurya characters" that records the gift of a *dhamakathika* or "preacher of the Dharma."[36] An inscription dating from the second or first century B.C.E. from Guṇṭupalle indicates that the "steps leading to the circular brick chaitya-griha" were the gift "of the pupil of the Thera, the Venerable Namda."[37] An early first century C.E. inscription from Kārli says: "a pillar containing a relic (*sasariro thabho*), the gift of the Venerable Satimita, a reciter (*bhāṇaka*) belonging to the Dharmottariya School, from Soparaka."[38] A Kharoṣṭhī inscription from 32 B.C.E. records the gift of relics made by a monk that were given to "the Mahīśāsaka teachers."[39] If it is true, therefore, as T. W. Rhys Davids asserted long ago, that the Pāli *Vinaya* "enters at so great length into *all* the details of the daily life of the recluses" (emphasis added),[40] then, oddly enough, this archaeological and epigraphical evidence would seem to argue for the fact that either the Pāli *Vinaya* must have originally contained rules referring to such activity, or that the Pāli *Vinaya* was unknown or had no influence at these early Indian sites—and they are among the earliest sites that we can know.

Sri Lankan literary data also suggests monastic concern with and involvement in the *stūpa*/relic cult from the very beginning and, in so doing, would strongly suggest that premodern Sri Lankan tradition could not have understood the injunction in the *Mahāparinibbāna-sutta*—or any other passage in the canon—as prohibiting monastic participation in the cult. Mahinda, the monk *par excellence* and nominal founder of Sri Lankan monasticism, is presented by the tradition itself as intending to leave the island because "it is a long time since we have seen the Perfect Buddha, the Teacher . . . There is nothing here for us to worship." The reigning king is puzzled and responds, "But, sir, did you not tell me that the Perfect Buddha has entered *nirvāṇa?"*; to which the Monk Mahinda responds in turn: "When the relics are seen [or: "are present"], the Buddha is seen [or: "is present"]". The king promises to build a *stūpa;* the Monk Mahinda appoints another monk to fly to India to procure relics; he succeeds; and Mahinda stays.[41] The moral of this tale, written by a monk about a monk, seems obvious: the continuance of Buddhist monasticism in Sri Lanka depended on procuring a relic and building a *stūpa* so that the monks would have an object of worship. The relic and *stūpa* cults were, therefore, seen by the author of the *Mahāvaṃsa* as a primary concern of the monastic community and a necessary prerequisite for its continuance. That such a pivotal part of the institution would have been left out of the rules that governed the early community seems very unlikely.

It would seem, then, that there is much to suggest the likelihood of the interpretation of the *Katikāvata* and *Visuddhimagga* passages, and of the data in the *Sutta-vibhaṅga,* presented here. But even if this interpretation turns out not to be entirely correct, in considering it we have come upon further considerations that seem to indicate, at least, that the absence of rules regarding *stūpas* in the Pāli *Vinaya* is much more problematic for the historian than has heretofore been recognized. If the interpretation presented here is correct, the Pāli *Vinaya,* like all the *vinayas,* had such rules, and they were removed at a comparatively recent date. If this interpretation is not correct, and if the Pāli *Vinaya* did not contain such rules, then it either could not have been the *Vinaya* which governed early Buddhist monastic communities in India, or it presents a very incomplete picture of early and actual monastic behavior and has, therefore, little historical value as a witness for what we know actually occurred on a large scale at all of the earliest monastic sites in India that we have some knowledge of. The whole question clearly deserves further consideration.

Notes

1. A. Bareau, "La construction et le culte des stūpa d'après les Vinayapiṭaka," *BEFEO* 50 (1960) 229.

2. Bareau, *BEFEO* 50 (1960) 230, 267–268, 273–274.

3. G. Roth, "Symbolism of the Buddhist Stūpa according to the Tibetan Version of the Caitya-vibhāga-vinayodbhāva-sūtra, the Sanskrit Treatise Stūpa-lakṣaṇa-kārikā-vivecana, and a Corresponding Passage in Kuladatta's Kriyāsaṃgraha," *The Stūpa. Its Religious, Historical and Architectural Significance,* ed. A. L. Dallapiccola and S. Z. Lallemant (Wiesbaden: 1980) 186. K. R. Norman, *Pāli Literature. Including the Canonical Literature in Prakrit and Sanskrit of all the Hīnayāna Schools of Buddhism,* A History of Indian Literature, ed. J. Gonda, Vol. VII, Fasc. 2 (Wiesbaden: 1983) 23, cites Roth's explanation as probable.

4. This inscription was first published in E. Müller, *Ancient Inscriptions in Ceylon,* 2 Vols. (London: 1883) Text: 87–90, 120–124, pl. 137. It was reedited in D. M. de Zilva Wickremasinghe, "Polonnaruva, Gal-Vihara: Rock-Inscription of Parakrama Bahu I," *Epigraphia Zeylanica* 2 (1928) 256–283, and most recently in N. Ratnapala, *The Katikāvatas. Laws of the Buddhist Order of Ceylon from the 12th Century to the 18th Century,* Münchener Studien zur Sprachwissenschaft, Beiheft N (München: 1971) 37–44, 127–135.

5. Ratnapala, *The Katikāvatas,* 38, 129, 304.

6. Ratnapala, *The Katikāvatas,* 40, § 12 (text); 131–132 (translation). Exactly the same reading of the text was given earlier by de Zilva Wickremasinghe, and his translation of it differs only very slightly: ". . . and have attended to the duties specified in the Khandhaka, such as those rules of conduct in respect of the Dāgābas, etc." (*Epigraphia Zeylanica* 2 [1928] 271, 275). The version of this passage repeated in the *Daṁbadeṇi Katikāvata,* which "belongs to the reign of king Parākramabāhu II (1236–1270 A.D.)," differs slightly: *dahagab mahabō aṅgana-vatu-du äduru-vat tera-vat gilan-vat senasun-vat ä vatu-du sapayā* (61, § 96). It is hard to know for certain whether the omission here of

kandu- is anything but scribal. It is not noted by Ratnapala nor reflected in his translation, 158, § 96.

7. Ratnapala, *The Katikāvatas,* 193, 197; cf. 290. References to the Pāli *Vinaya* are here and throughout to the Pali Text Society edition by H. Oldenberg.

8. Cf. T. W. Rhys Davids and W. Stede, *The Pali Text Society's Pali-English Dictionary* (London: 1921–1925) 234; Pe Maung Tin, *The Path of Purity,* Pali Text Society Translation Series, Nos. 11, 17, 21 (London: 1923–1931; repr. 1971) 14, n. 4; 117, n. 3; etc.; these are discussed more fully below.

9. H. C. Warren and D. Kosambi, *Visuddhimagga of Buddhaghosācariya,* Harvard Oriental Series, Vol. 41 (Cambridge: 1950) I.27, 10; Pe Maung Tin, *The Path of Purity,* 14. In addition to the instances in the *Visuddhimagga,* Buddhaghosa frequently refers to the *Khandhakavatta* in the *Samantapāsādikā;* see H. Kopp, *Samantapāsādikā. Buddhaghosa's Commentary on the Vinaya Piṭaka,* Vol. VIII, Indexes to Vols. I–VII, Pali Text Society Text Series, No. 167 (London: n.d.) 1511. Although these references add some detail, they do not seem to suggest a referent for the term other than the text of the *Vinaya.* It should, however, be noted that the "conclusions" drawn in what follows about the *Khandhaka* known to Buddhaghosa raise some serious questions about the relationship of the *Samantapāsādikā* to the text of the *Vinaya* it was commenting on, and the nature and extent of that text. Such problems will only be resolved by a careful and thorough study of this massive commentary in comparison with the *Vinaya* as we have it. Such a study remains to be done.

10. Warren and Kosambi, *Visuddhimagga,* III. 71, 82; Pe Maung Tin, *The Path of Purity,* 117. For other similar *Vinaya* passages, see *Vinaya,* ii, 223; i, 46ff.

11. Warren and Kosambi, *Visuddhimagga,* VI.60, 153; Pe Maung Tin, *The Path of Purity,* 215.

12. Rhys Davids and Stede, *The Pali Text Society's Pali-English Dictionary,* 234.

13. Bareau, *BEFEO* 50 (1960) 251, 253.

14. *Śayanāsanavastu and Adhikaraṇavastu,* 38.29, 39.2.

15. Questions concerning "duties in regard to the yard of the Bo-tree" in the Pāli and other *Vinayas* will also have to be investigated, but given our ignorance in regard to the place of "Bo-trees" in Indian monastic communities, and given the great importance assigned to their presence in Sri Lanka, this will require a separate study. It is, however, perhaps worth noting here that the only clear reference I know in Indian inscriptional sources to a shrine connected with a Bo-tree explicitly connects that shrine with a Sri Lankan monastic community. The Second Apsidal Temple Inscription F from Nāgārjunikoṇḍa records the benefactions of the Upāsikā Bodhisiri. One of these is said to have been the construction of "a shrine for the Bodhi-tree at the Sīhaḷa-vihāra" (*sīhaḷa-vihāre bodhi-rukha-pāsādo*); see J. Ph. Vogel, "Prakrit Inscriptions from a Buddhist Site at Nagarjunikonda," *EI* 20 (1929–1930) 22–23.

16. I. B. Horner, *The Book of the Discipline,* Vol. II (London: 1940) 162.

17. *Gilgit Manuscripts,* iii 2, 145.15–146.1; *Peking,* 41, 284-2-2ff. I am not altogether sure I have completely understood this passage. The text is extremely terse, and the technical meaning of *sambhinnakārī* is not well established. I have followed my understanding of the Tibetan translation, and the problems do not, in any case, affect my point here: discussions of property rights similar to those in the Pāli *Sutta-vibhaṅga* occurring in the *Mūlasarvāstivāda-vinaya* refer frequently to *staupika* or indicate that what is *buddhasantaka* is to be used for the *stūpa;* cf. *Gilgit Manuscripts,* iii 2, 143.11; *Peking,* 44, 95-3-4ff; etc.

18. Bareau, *BEFEO* 50 (1960) 257; cf. J. Gernet, *Les aspects économiques du bouddhisme dans la société chinoise du Ve au Xe siècle* (Paris: 1956) 61ff, 159ff. For the persistence in Mahāyāna *sūtra* literature of both the vocabulary and conception of ownership found in the various *Vinayas,* see G. Schopen, "Burial *Ad Sanctos* and the Physical Presence of the Buddha in Early Indian Buddhism", Ch. VII below, 128–131.

19. Cf. G. Schopen, "On the Buddha and His Bones" Ch. VIII below, 159–160. Apart from the odd rule, "qui interdisent de faire un *stūpa* avec la nourriture puis de le démolir et de le manger," that the Pāli *Vinaya* shares with that of the Mūlasarvāstivāda according to Bareau in *BEFEO* 50 (1960) 271 (if that is what *thūpikata* actually means), the only actual occurrence of the term *stūpa* in the Pāli *Vinaya* occurs in the bizarre story concerning "the group of six nuns" found at *Vinaya,* iv, 308–309. Here it is said that "the Venerable Kappitaka, the Venerable Upāli's preceptor" destroyed the *stūpa* that "the group of six" had built for one of their deceased members. This story of an uncharacteristically violent and almost sacrilegious act may be particular to the Pāli *Vinaya*. The same rule appears to be explained by a very different story in the *Mahāsāṃghika-Bhikṣuṇī-Vinaya,* for example, in A. Hirakawa, *Monastic Discipline for the Buddhist Nuns. An English Translation of the Chinese Text of the Mahāsāṃghika-Bhikṣuṇī-Vinaya,* Tibetan Sanskrit Works Series, No. XXI (Patna: 1982) 284–286. [For reference to a Mūlasarvāstivādin story about a monk destroying a *stūpa* built by a group of nuns, see G. Schopen, "Ritual Rights and Bones of Contention: More on Monastic Funerals and Relics in the *Mūlasarvāstivāda-vinaya,*" *JIP* 22 (1994) 71 and n. 85.] It may also be related to what appears to be an explicitly local Sri Lankan resistance to *stūpas* for the local monastic dead. At least, the argument against the erection of *stūpas* for "virtuous puthujjana monks" found in the Sri Lankan commentaries is a purely local one: *puthujjanabhikkhūnaṃ hi thūpe anuññāyamāne tambapaṇṇadīpe gāmapaṭṭanānaṃ okāso ca na bhaveyya tathā aññesu ṭhānesu,* "for were a *stūpa* to be allowed for *puthujjana* monks there would be no room for any villages or cities in Tambapaṇṇadīpa (Ceylon), likewise in other places"; see P. Masefield, *Divine Revelation in Pali Buddhism* (London: 1986) 23. To what degree this resistance was purely literary remains to be seen, although Longhurst already long ago noted that "the *stūpas* erected over the remains of ordinary members of the Buddhist community were very humble little structures. The ashes of the dead were placed in an earthenware pot and covered with a lid, and the humble little *stūpa* erected over it. Plenty of Buddhist *stūpas* of this class may still be seen in the Madras Presidency and also in Ceylon"; see A. H. Longhurst, *The Story of the Stūpa* (Colombo: 1936) 14.

20. I. B. Horner, *The Book of the Discipline,* Vol. I (London: 1938) 243; *Vinaya,* iii, 143.

21. I. B. Horner, *The Book of the Discipline,* Vol. III (London: 1942) 329; *Vinaya,* iv, 301.

22. Cf. B. C. Law, "Cetiya in the Buddhist Literature," *Studia Indo-Iranica. Ehrengabe für Wilhelm Geiger,* hrsg. v. W. Wüst (Leipzig: 1931) 42–48. That *cetiya* is *always* used in Pāli literature to refer to a *stūpa* is, of course, not being asserted here.

23. See, at least, O. von Hinüber, "On the Tradition of Pāli Texts in India, Ceylon and Burma," *Buddhism in Ceylon and Studies on Religious Syncretism in Buddhist Countries,* Abhandlungen der Akademie der Wissenschaften in Göttingen, Phil.-Hist. Klasse. Dritte Folge. Nr. 108, ed. H. Bechert (Göttingen: 1978) 48–57; O. von Hinüber, "Notes on the Pāli Tradition in Burma," *Nachrichten der Akademie der Wissenschaften in Göttingen,* I. Phil.-Hist. Klasse Jg. 1983, Nr. 3, 67–79; O. von Hinüber, "Pāli Manuscripts of Canonical Texts from North Thailand—A Preliminary Report," *Journal of the Siam Society* 71 (1983)

75–88; O. von Hinüber, "Two Jātaka Manuscripts from the National Library in Bangkok," *JPTS* 10 (1985) 1–22; O. von Hinüber, "The Pāli Manuscripts Kept at the Siam Society, Bangkok. A Short Catalogue," *Journal of the Siam Society* 75 (1987) 9–74; O. von Hinüber, "The Oldest Dated Manuscript of the Milindapañha," *JPTS* 11 (1987) 111–119; P. E. E. Fernando, "A Note on Three Old Sinhalese Palm-Leaf Manuscripts," *The Sri Lanka Journal of the Humanities* 8 (1982, actually 1985) 146–157.

24. As one of the many possible sources for the troubled history—both internal and external—of the Sri Lankan Saṅgha from the twelfth century on, see Ratnapala, *The Katikāvatas,* 219–232; for Burma, see E. M. Mendelson, *Sangha and State in Burma. A Study of Monastic Sectarianism and Leadership* (Ithaca and London: 1975) 31–118; for Thailand, Y. Ishii, *Sangha, State and Society. Thai Buddhism in History* (Honolulu: 1986) 59–66; etc.

25. Bareau, *BEFEO* 50 (1960) 229–230.

26. The supposed injunction occurs, of course, at *Dīgha,* ii, 141.18 (= *Mahāparinibbānasutta,* V.10). Although the details will have to be given elsewhere, it can, I think, be convincingly shown both that *sarīra-pūjā* does not refer to "worship of the relics" but to what we might call "preparation of the body" prior to cremation, and that even as late as the *Milindapañha* the injunction at *Dīgha,* ii, 141 was not understood to apply to all monks. Moreover, if this injunction, by itself, were to account for the absence of rules regarding *stūpas* in the Pāli *Vinaya,* we would expect to find that other schools who had a similar text of the *Mahāparinirvāṇa-sūtra* would also have no such rules in their *Vinayas.* But this is not the case. [See G. Schopen, " Monks and the Relic Cult in the *Mahāparinibbāna-sutta,*" Ch. VI below.]

27. P. Steinthal, *Udāna* (London: 1885) 8, 21 (I.10).

28. Bhikkhu J. Kashyap, *The Apadāna (II)—Buddhavaṃsa-Cariyāpiṭaka* (*Khuddakanikāya,* Vol. VII), Nālandā-Devanāgarī-Pāli-Series (Bihar: 1959) 125.16 (54.6.216).

29. See S. Nagaraju, *Buddhist Architecture of Western India (c. 250* B.C.*–c.* A.D. *300)* (Delhi: 1981) 113–130, 329–330. On the inscriptions associated with these *stūpas,* see also D. D. Kosambi, "Dhenukākaṭa," *JASBom* 30.2 (1955) 70–71.

30. Nagaraju, *Buddhist Architecture of Western India,* 107–108, 329.

31. M. Bénisti, "Observations concernant le stūpa n° 2 de Sāñcī," *BEI* 4 (1986) 165–170.

32. For the donative inscription connected with the mortuary deposit, see J. Marshall, A. Foucher, and N. G. Majumdar, *The Monuments of Sāñchī,* Vol. I (Delhi: 1940) 294, although its interpretation there is perhaps not entirely free of problems. Of the ninety-three donative inscriptions from *Stūpa* no. 2 at Sāñcī published by Majumdar, nearly 60 percent, or fifty-two, record the gifts of monastics: monks, nos. 631, 638, 640, 644, 646, 647, 648, 655, 656, 657, 669, 675, 677, 688, 691, 693, 694, 695, 702, 709, 716, 719, Büh xvii, xviii, xix, xx, 803, 820; nuns, nos. 662, 663, 664, 668, 672, 674, 678, 700, 703, 706, 708, 713, 714, Büh xxi, 759, 812; female disciples, nos. 637, 645, 673, 704; male disciples, nos. 632, 633, 634, 671.

33. For monastic donors at Bhārhut and Sāñcī, see G. Schopen, "Two Problems in the History of Indian Buddhism," Ch. II above, 30–31 and notes, although the Sāñcī count there is based on the old publications. For Pauni, see S. B. Deo and J. P. Joshi, *Pauni Excavation (1969–1970)* (Nagpur: 1972) 37–43.

34. H. Sarkar, "A Post-Asokan Inscription from Pangoraria in the Vindhyan Range," *Sri Dinesacandrika. Studies in Indology. Shri D. C. Sircar Festschrift,* ed. B. N. Mukherjee et al. (Delhi: 1983) 403–405.

35. G. Bühler, "The Bhattiprolu Inscriptions," *EI* 2 (1894) 323–329; H. Lüders, "Epigraphische Beiträge. I Die Inschriften von Bhaṭṭiproḷu," *Philologica Indica* (Göttingen: 1940) 213–229; D. C. Sircar, *Select Inscriptions Bearing on Indian History and Civilization,* Vol. I, 2nd ed. (Calcutta: 1965) 224–228.

36. J. Burgess, *The Buddhist Stūpas of Amaravati and Jaggayyapeta in the Krishna District, Madras Presidency, Surveyed in 1882,* Archaeological Survey of Southern India, Vol. I (London: 1887) 94, pl. LVI no. 3.

37. I. K. Sarma, "Epigraphical Discoveries at Guntupalli," *JESI* 5 (1975) 51.

38. E. Senart, "The Inscriptions in the Caves at Karle," *EI* 7 (1902–1903) 55, no. 9.

39. G. Fussman, "Nouvelles inscriptions—śaka (iv)," *BEFEO* 74 (1985) 47–51.

40. T. W. Rhys Davids, *Buddhist Suttas,* Sacred Books of the East, Vol. XI (Oxford: 1900) xlv.

41. W. Geiger, *The Mahāvaṃsa* (London: 1908) XVII.2–XVII3. On the conception of a relic articulated here, see E. W. Adikaram, *Early History of Buddhism in Ceylon* (Colombo: 1946) 136ff; Schopen, "Burial *Ad Sanctos* and the Physical Presence of the Buddha in Early Indian Buddhism," now Ch. VII below; Schopen, "On the Buddha and His Bones," Ch. VIII below.

* * *

[At least three responses to this paper were quickly published; for references, see above, Ch. IV, n. 14. For both the rule and the stories about destroying *stūpas* referred to in n. 19, see now also G. Schopen, "The Suppression of Nuns and the Ritual Murder of Their Special Dead in Two Buddhist Monastic Texts," *JIP* 24 (1996) 563–592.]

CHAPTER VI

Monks and the Relic Cult in the *Mahāparinibbāna-sutta*

An Old Misunderstanding in Regard to Monastic Buddhism

IT IS ALMOST always instructive to look at the actual evidence for what are taken to be established facts in the history of Indian Buddhism. If nothing else, such an exercise makes it painfully obvious that most of those established facts totter precariously on very fragile foundations. One example only will concern us here.

It is—and has been—consistently asserted that there was in early Buddhism a fundamental difference between the religious activities of monks and the religious activities of lay persons, especially in regard to worship and participation in cult. Moreover, this fundamental difference is said to distinguish not only the religious lives of monks from the religious lives of lay persons in early Buddhism, it is also said to distinguish the Mahāyāna monk from his non-Mahāyāna coreligionists. All of this is, of course, asserted as fact, and far-reaching implications are made to follow from it. But this so-called fact—as I have pointed out several times now—stands in jarring contrast to everything we know from Indian epigraphy and archaeology.[1] It is, indeed, the accumulating weight of this epigraphical and archaeological material that, in the first instance, forces us to reexamine the evidence on which the fact of this asserted difference is founded. That evidence—not surprisingly given the history of Buddhist Studies—turns out to be exclusively literary. But it is not just exclusively literary evidence on which this fact rests: it rests entirely, it seems, on a less-than-careful

Originally published in Koichi Shinohara and Gregory Schopen, eds., *From Benares to Beijing: Essays on Buddhism and Chinese Religion* (Oakville, Ontario: Mosaic Press, 1991), pp. 187–201. Reprinted with stylistic changes with permission of the editors.

reading of a single passage of a single text. The passage in question is, of course, *Mahāparinibbāna-sutta* V.10:

> *kathaṃ mayaṃ bhante tathāgatassa sarīre paṭipajjāmāti*
> *avyāvaṭā tumhe ānanda hotha tathāgatassa sarīra-pujāya, iṅgha tumhe ānanda sadatthe ghaṭatha, sadattham anuyuñjatha, sadatthe appamattā ātāpino pahitattā viharatha. sant' ānanda khattiya-paṇḍitā pi brāhmaṇa-paṇḍitā pi gahapati-paṇḍitā pi tathāgate abhippasannā te tathāgatassa sarīra-pūjaṃ karissantīti.*[2]

This, in T. W. Rhys Davids' still-standard English translation of the passage, appears as:

> 'What are we to do, lord, with the remains of the Tathāgata?'
> 'Hinder not yourselves, Ānanda, by honouring the remains of the Tathāgata. Be zealous, I beseech you, Ānanda, in your own behalf! Devote yourselves to your own good! Be earnest, be zealous, be intent on your own good! There are wise men, Ānanda, among the nobles, among the brahmins, among the heads of houses, who are firm believers in the Tathāgata; and they will do due honour to the remains of the Tathāgata.'[3]

This single, short passage, probably one of the most frequently quoted passages of Buddhist canonical literature, has been taken to establish, for example, that "śarīrapūjā, the worship of relics, is the concern of the laity and not the bhikṣusaṃgha,"[4] that "advanced monks were not to occupy themselves with such worship of stūpas," and that "the worship of stūpas should be left to the laity alone."[5] But, even if we bracket the distinct possibility raised by Bareau that this passage—and a number of related passages—are to be considered as interpolations in the *Mahāparinibbāna-sutta,*[6] the passage *as we have it* simply will not support the conclusions modern scholars have drawn from it.[7] First of all, nowhere in the passage is there a reference to monks. The injunction, if it is an injunction, is addressed to Ānanda, not to all monks. It is true that plural pronominal and verbal forms are used in the Pāli version of this passage. But if the plural forms are used there as inclusive of the category "monk," then they should be used in that same way at, for example, *Mahāparinibbāna* V.7, where the same thing occurs. That, however, as the context makes absolutely clear, is out of the question since the plural *mayaṃ,* "we," is actually used there in such a way as to *exclude* "monks in different districts." Likewise in VI.1, where a first person plural form of the pronoun is used, Rhys Davids himself recognized that it could not be intended to include all monks: he translates *siyā kho pan' ānanda tumhākam evam assa* as " 'It may be, Ānanda, that *in some of you* the thought may arise' " (emphasis added). Moreover, when in the *Mahāparinibbāna-sutta* we actually find explicit reference to rules governing the *Saṅgha* as a whole—as we do in the passage dealing with the abolition of the "lesser and minor precepts" at VI.3—it is explicitly stated to be a matter for the entire *Saṅgha.* But these considerations, although consistently overlooked, may not necessarily be, in the end, the most important ones. The fact would remain that, even if it could somehow be argued that the injunction was intended for the entire *Saṅgha,* it would still be difficult to establish that that injunction had anything to do with the *stūpa*/relic cults.

There has been more than the usual degree of inconsistency in translating the text of the injunction and virtually no attempt to determine the precise meaning of the term *śarīra-pūjā* as it is used there. Even the great de La Vallée Poussin gives at least four different translations of the injunction, two of them in the same book:

> "Ne vous occupez pas du culte de mes reliques."[8]
> "Ne vous occupez pas des funérailles."
> "Ne vous occupez pas du culte des reliques."[9]
> "Ne vous préoccupez pas d'honorer mon corps."[10]

This kind of inconsistency, which can slip so easily into confusion, is still with us. Recently, for example, Hirakawa said:

> During the early period of Buddhism offerings to the Buddha's relics (*śarīra-pūjā*) were made by laymen. According to the Mahāparinibbāna Suttanta, the Buddha was asked by Ānanda what type of ceremony should be held for the Buddha's remains. The Buddha replied, 'you should strive for the true goal [*sadattha*] of emancipation [*vimokṣa*].' The Buddha thus prohibited monks from having any connection with his funeral ceremonies and instead called upon wise and pious lay believers to conduct the ceremonies.[11]

Here in four sentences, *śarīra-pūjā* is glossed in three different ways: as offerings to relics, as ceremony for remains, and as "funeral ceremonies."

The problem, of course, with de La Vallée Poussin's and with Hirakawa's treatments is, as it is with virtually all treatments of the passage, that they make no attempt to establish the precise meaning of *śarīra-pūjā* and, as a consequence, may be inadvertently conflating what are typologically two quite distinct phenomena: funeral ceremonies and cult activity directed toward relics or reliquaries are fundamentally different forms of religious behavior. In this instance the texts—*as we have them*—seem clearer than their interpreters.

In arguing for his interpretation of the curious statement at the end of the Ahraurā version of Aśoka's First Minor Rock Edict, Norman says "that in Sanskrit *śarīra* means 'body,' not 'relics,' which is its meaning in the plural."[12] That the same holds for the Pāli *sarīra* in the *Mahāparinibbāna-sutta* is, uncharacteristically, beyond doubt. Before a certain point in the narrative, the term is never used in the plural, always in the singular, and can only mean "body": in V.2, for example, the trees burst into bloom out of season and scatter their flowers on the *body* of the dying, but not yet dead, Buddha (*te tathāgatassa sarīraṃ okiranti*); in V.11 the *body* of a *cakkavattin* is said to be wrapped in a new cloth (*cakkavattissa sarīraṃ ahatena vatthena veṭhenti*); in VI.13 the Mallas are said to have approached the *body* "with dancing and hymns, and music, and with garlands and perfumes" (*yena bhagavato sarīraṃ ten' upasamkamiṃsu, upasaṃkamitvā bhagavato sarīraṃ naccehi gītehi . . . pūjentā*); in VI.18 the *body* is said to have been wrapped (*bhagavato sarīraṃ veṭhetvā*), "placed on the pyre" (*bhagavato sarīraṃ citakaṃ āropesuṃ*), etc. Wherever, therefore, the term *sarīra* occurs in the singular in the *Mahāparinibbāna,* it unambiguously means *body,* and it occurs in the singular throughout the entire description of the actual funeral. It is, in fact, only after the funeral proper, only after the cremation, that we find *sarīra* in the plural, and it is only here that the text could be speaking about "relics." We can actually watch—in VI.23—the transition in both grammatical number and meaning as it takes place in a single paragraph. The only question that remains, then, is which of the two possible meanings of *sarīra* is in play in the injunction delivered to Ānanda.

Since the text of the injunction uses *sarīra* in compound—*avyāvaṭā tumhe ānanda hotha tathāgatassa sarīra-pujāya*—we have no formal indication of the implied grammatical number and, therefore, of the intended meaning of *sarīra.* But even in the absence of a formal indicator, the contextual indication is virtually certain. The injunction is not an unsolicited declaration; it is a response or answer to a very specific question, and the question itself does have the formal indication of grammatical number that we need. The question is put in the following form: *kathaṃ mayaṃ bhante tathāgatassa sarīre paṭipajjāmāti. Sarīre* here is almost certainly a locative singular used in the sense of "in regard to" exactly as in the immediately preceding *mātugāme,* which is constructed with the same verb: *kathaṃ mayaṃ bhante mātugāme paṭipajjāmāti* (V.9). Rhys Davids translates the latter as "How are we to conduct ourselves, lord, with regard to womankind?" If the construction of the question leading to our injunction is analogous, and if *sarīre* there is in the locative singular, it would accordingly have to be translated: "How are we to conduct ourselves in regard to the body of the Tathāgata?" To argue that *sarīre* is not a locative singular, moreover, would be difficult. The only other thing it could be, as far as I know, is an accusative plural, but there is much evidence against this. A neuter accusative plural in *-e,* though found on occasion elsewhere, would be distinctly out of place in the language of the *Mahāparinibbāna-sutta;*[13] when *sarīra* occurs elsewhere in the *Mahāparinibbāna-sutta* in the accusative plural—and it does so at least five times—it always occurs with the normal neuter plural ending, *-āni;* in the one other instance where *sarīre* occurs in the final sections of the *Mahāparinibbāna-sutta,* it forms a part of a locative absolute so there can be no doubt about its interpretation: *daḍḍhe kho pana bhagavato sarīre,* VI.23.

All of this is only to say that it seems virtually certain that Ānanda, in his question, was not asking about his or anyone else's participation in the relic cult. He was asking about how the *body* of the Buddha should be treated *immediately* after his death, about that which we would call "the funeral arrangements."[14] But if the question is about funeral arrangements, it is at best disingenuous to suggest that the answer and the injunction is about something else. In fact, the text of the injunction itself also seems to indicate that *sarīra-pūjā,* the activity Ānanda was not to be preoccupied with, was intended to refer to only funeral activities.

The text says in V.11 that "the body of the Tathāgata" is to be treated in the same way as "the body of a wheel-turning king" is treated. It is this that the "wise men . . . among the nobles, among the brahmins, among the heads of houses" are to do, and it is this that Ānanda is not to be overly concerned with. But the treatment accorded to the body of a dead king that is detailed in the Pāli text makes no reference either to relics or to an ongoing cult. The *sarīra-pūjā* of a dead king's body described in the text involves the following steps: the body is wrapped elaborately in cloth; the body is then placed in an "oil vessel of iron"; a funeral pyre is built; the body is cremated; and a *stūpa* is built. That is all. "This is the way they treat the body of a wheel-turning king, Ānanda," the text says, and then goes on:

> *yathā kho ānanda rañño cakkavattissa sarīre paṭipajjanti evaṃ tathāgatassa sarīre paṭipajjitabbaṃ. cātummahāpathe tathāgatassa thūpo kātabbo. tattha ye mālaṃ vā gandhaṃ vā vaṇṇakaṃ vā āropessanti abhivādessanti vā cittaṃ vā pasādessanti tesaṃ taṃ bhavissati dīgharattaṃ hitāya sukhāya.*
>
> As indeed, Ānanda, they proceed in regard to the body of a wheel-turning king, so in regard to the body of the Tathāgata the procedure is to be followed. At the main crossroads a *stūpa* of the Tathāgata is to be made. Who will take a garland or perfume or paint there, or will salute, or will cause their mind to be tranquil, that will be for their benefit and ease for a long time.

It may be of some importance to note the shift in verbal forms that takes place in this passage, since that shift would seem to indicate that the final sentence was not intended as a part of the instructions concerning the treatment of the Buddha's body and that, therefore, the activities it describes were not thought to form a part of *sarīra-pūjā*. When the text refers to what is to be done in regard to the body of the Buddha, it uses future passive participles to indicate what must be done by the wise laymen who will perform the *sarīra-pūjā:* the procedure followed in regard to a deceased king *is to be followed* in regard to the Buddha; a *stūpa of the Tathāgata is to be made.* These are clear injunctions in both grammar and sense. But the injunctions end here. The final sentence, which contains the only references in the passage to what might be called cult practices, constitutes not an injunction, but a statement about the future. The text shifts from future passive participles with an imperative sense to simple futures, from "it is to be done" to "those who will do." Notice too that the final sentence also introduces a new grammatical subject: context suggests that the injunctions are addressed to the wise laymen who will perform the *sarīra-pūjā,* but the subject of the final sentence is the indefinite *ye* which Rhys Davids renders by "whosoever." All of this, again, would appear to indicate that all of those activities that we associate with an ongoing relic cult did not—for the author of our text—form a part of *sarīra-pūjā,* and that *sarīra-pūjā* was used to refer only to funeral activities that began with the wrapping of the body and ended with cremation and constructing a *stūpa* and had—like the injunction as a whole—nothing to do with relics.

That this was indeed the original meaning of *sarīra-pūjā* is, in fact, further demonstrated by a number of passages in Hīnayāna literature where we have clear references to monastic funerals. In an interesting passage from the *Mūlasarvāstivāda-vinaya* we find, for example:

> Again on that occasion another monk, being sick, died in his cell. Having brought him to the burning ground, having performed *the worship of the body,* that monk was burnt. Then the monks returned to the monastery (. . . *sa bhikṣur ādahanaṃ nītvā śarīra-pūjāṃ kṛtvā dagdhas, tato vihāram āgatā*).[15]

To that passage from the *Mūlasarvāstivāda-vinaya* we might add another from the same source:

> Again on that occasion another monk died. The monks, having carried out his body, having simply thrown it into the burning grounds (. . . *tan 'bhinirhṛtya evam eva śmaśāne chorayitvā*), returned to the monastery. The distributor of robes entered the dead monk's cell saying 'I distribute the bowl and robe.' He—the dead monk—having been reborn among nonhuman beings appeared there wielding a club. He said: 'Until you perform *the worship of the body* for me (*yāvan mama śarīra-pūjāṃ kurutha*), do you now distribute (my) bowl and robe?'
>
> The monks asked the Blessed One concerning this matter.
>
> The Blessed One said: 'By the monks *the worship of the body* for the deceased is first to be performed (*bhikṣubhis tasya pūrvaṃ śarīra-pūjā karttavyeti*). After that the bowl and robe are to be distributed.'[16]

Both of these passages enumerate a sequence of activities involved in the disposal of the body of a monk who has died in his cell. In both it is clear that *śarīra-pūjā*—whatever it involved—took place after the body had been removed and taken to the cremation ground, but before it was cremated, before there could have been anything like what we call "relics." It is again fairly certain that *śarīra-pūjā* involved the ritual handling or treatment of the body prior to cremation since the second passage contrasts it with—and insists that it replace—"having simply thrown the body into the burning grounds." That it is the body and not relics that is the object of this treatment is both clear here and made even more explicit elsewhere.

The forty-eighth *avadāna* of the *Avadānaśataka* looks very much like a literary elaboration of the much simpler narratives concerning the disposal of the monastic dead found in the *Mūlasarvāstivāda-vinaya,* two examples of which have already been cited. It leaves us in no doubt as to the object toward which *śarīra-pūjā* is directed. It says a certain monk:

> *. . . kālagataḥ svake layane preteṣūpapannaḥ / tato 'sya sabrahmacāribhir muṇḍikāṃ gaṇḍīṃ parāhatya śarīrābhinirhāraḥ kṛtaḥ / tato 'sya śarīre śarīrapūjāṃ kṛtvā vihāram āgatāḥ /*
>
> . . . died and was reborn in his own cell as a hungry ghost (*shi nas rang gi gnas khang du yi dags su skyes so*). Then his fellow monks, having struck the *muṇḍikā* gong ("la cloche funèbre"), performed the removal of the body. Then, having performed the worship of the body on his body, they returned to the monastery.[17]

Virtually every element of this passage from the *Avadānaśataka* also occurs in the *Mūlasarvāstivāda-vinaya.* The "*muṇḍikā* gong," or "cloche funèbre,"[18] for example, is referred to in the latter more intelligibly as the *mṛta-gaṇḍī* or "gong for the dead."[19] It is, however, not just the elements of the funeral procedure that are essentially the same in the two works; the sequence in which they are said to occur is also basically the same. It is, therefore, significant that where the *Mūlasarvāstivāda-vinaya* has *śarīra-pūjāṃ kṛtvā,* "having performed the worship of the body," the *Avadānaśataka* has corresponding to it the even more explicit *śarīre śarīra-pūjāṃ kṛtvā,* "having performed the worship of the body on his body." This construction leaves no doubt about the object of the *pūjā* involved.[20] Nor is this in doubt in another instance where the construction is used. In the Sanskrit version of the *Mahāparinirvāṇa-sūtra* (48.8) when Mahākāśyapa meets an Ājīvika coming from Kuśinagarī, he asks him if he knows his teacher. The Ājīvika answers:

> *jāne / śramaṇo gautamaḥ / parinirvṛtas te āyuṣmañ chāstā / adya (gate saptāhe va)rtate śarīre śarīra-pūjā.*
>
> I know him. He is the *Śramaṇa* Gautama. But sir, your teacher is dead. For seven days now the worship of the body on his body is performed.[21]

But since the Buddha had not yet been cremated, it is here not just the construction, but the context too that makes it certain that *śarīra-pūjā* was understood to be an activity directed toward the body of the deceased that took place after the individual's death, but before or as a part of his cremation. It could not, therefore, have anything to do with relics for the simple reason that there were no relics.

All of this is richly confirmed by a variety of other passages as well. In the account of the funeral of Mahāprajāpatī and her companions found in the *Vinaya-kṣudraka-vastu* of the *Mūlasarvāstivāda-vinaya,* for example, in which prominent monks come from afar to undertake the full performance of the worship of her body (*de'i lus la mchod pa lhag par bya ba la brtson par byas*), the text says: "Then, having performed the great worship and having removed the bodies, they set the biers down at an appropriate and isolated spot" (*de nas mchod pa chen po byas te khyer nas sa phyogs bar skabs dben par khyogs rnams bzhag go*). Only after the great worship was performed and the bodies were removed did the cremation take place (*de nas . . . bsregs so*).[22] In the terse account of the end of Aśoka found in the *Divyāvadāna,* the text says that the ministers thought of enthroning the new king only "after having carried out (Aśoka's body) on dark blue and yellow biers, after having performed the worship of the body, and after having cremated him" (*yāvad amātyair nīlapītābhiḥ śivikābhir nirharitvā śarīra-pūjāṃ kṛtvā dhmāpayitvā rājānaṃ pratiṣṭhāpayiṣyāma iti*).[23] Here again, "worship of the body" precedes cremation; it takes place before there could be any relics.

Still other passages make it clear that *śarīra-pūjā* also took place prior to the erection of a *stūpa.* The *Saṅghabhedavastu* of the *Mūlasarvāstivāda-vinaya,* describing the events that followed the death of a former Buddha, says:

> A great crowd of people, after having performed the worship of the body in regard to his body, established a great *stūpa* on an isolated spot.
>
> *tasya mahājanakāyena śarīre śarīra-pūjāṃ kṛtvā viviktāvakāśe pṛthivīpradeśe mahān stūpaḥ pratiṣṭhāpitaḥ.*[24]

Similarly, in the description of events that followed the death of a series of former Buddhas found in the *Avadānaśataka*—a description that is repeated at least eleven times—the text says:

> The king . . . , after having performed the worship of the body in regard to the body of the Blessed One, established a *stūpa* a *yojana* in circumference, etc.
>
> *tato rājñā . . . bhagavataḥ śarīre śarīra-pūjāṃ kṛtvā samantayojanastūpaś catūratnamayaḥ pratiṣṭhāpitaḥ krośam uccatvena.*[25]

Significantly, in several instances, this statement is completed with the phrase "and a festival of the *stūpa* was instituted" (*stūpamahaś ca prajñaptaḥ*). In all of these cases then, *śarīra-pūjā* could not possibly have been thought to be connected with activity in regard to *stūpas* since it was only after *śarīra-pūjā* had been completed that a *stūpa* was established. Moreover, in those cases in which it was said that "a festival of the *stūpa* was instituted"—and, therefore, something like an ongoing cult is referred to—this too took place after *śarīra-pūjā* had been performed. *Śarīra-pūjā* did not form a part of any ongoing activity.

We might consider here one final and perhaps particularly interesting passage from the Sanskrit text of the *Mahāparinirvāṇa-sūtra* (49.15). In this version, when Mahākāśyapa approaches the funeral pyre of the Buddha, he takes the lid off the oil vessel, removes the cloths wrapped around the body, and "pays reverence to the uncovered body of the Blessed One" (*bhagavataḥ śarīram avigopitaṃ vandate*). Then the following thought occurs to him: *yan nv ahaṃ svayam eva bhagavataḥ śarīra-pūjāyām autsukyam āpadyeya,* "What if I myself, indeed, were to be zealous in regard to the worship of the body of the Blessed One." Having thought this, he brings other cloths, wraps the body with them, puts it back into the vessel, closes the lid, makes a(nother) pyre, and stands to one side. That is all. It is apparently just this sequence of activities that the text intends by the term *śarīra-pūjā.* Although it looks to us like "worship," what Mahākāśyapa does in regard to the body when he has initially uncovered it is not even included; that activity is expressed by a completely different word: *vandate.*

It is also important to note that, in the Sanskrit text, Mahākāśyapa does precisely what Ānanda is earlier told not to be concerned with, and the two passages use virtually the same words. Ānanda's question is expressed as *kathaṃ vayaṃ . . . bhagavataḥ śarīra-pūjāyām autsukyam āpadyemahi* (36.2) and the injunction as *alpotsukas tvam ānanda bhava śarīra-pūjāyāḥ* . . . (36.3), while Kāśyapa's intention appears as *yan nv ahaṃ svayam eva bhagavataḥ śarīra-pūjāyām autsukyam āpadyeya* (49.19). Since we know what Kāśyapa did when he involved himself in *śarīra-pūjā,* we also know quite precisely what Ānanda was not to be concerned with and, again, it has nothing to do with the relic cult.[26] But since the Sanskrit text goes to the trouble to point out that Kāśyapa was a monk of the highest standing, one of only four *Mahāsthaviras* alive at the time (49.16), and since it is precisely this *Mahāsthavira* who is said to have engaged in *śarīra-pūjā,* we also know that it is extremely unlikely that the authors of the text understood the earlier injunction addressed to Ānanda to apply to all monks or to forbid monastic involvement in such activity. In fact, if there were any restrictions on participation in *śarīra-pūjā,* they appear from the Sanskrit text to have been of a very different order. Since, again, the Sanskrit text takes the trouble to point out that Kāśyapa was not only one of only four *Mahāsthaviras,* but was also—in Buddhist monastic terms—rich and famous,[27] and since he involved himself actively in behaviors Ānanda was counseled not to be concerned with, the text may be suggesting almost the opposite of what we would expect: it may be suggesting that participation in that part of monastic funerals known as *śarīra-pūjā* was—in, at least, important funerals—the prerogative of advanced monks of high status.[28] Since Ānanda, at this stage, appears to have been neither, this may only confirm from an unexpected angle that the injunction addressed to him was fundamentally *ad hominem.*

All of the evidence we have, then, would seem to argue for the fact that *śarīra-pūjā* did not originally mean "the worship of relics" and did not have anything to do with a relic cult. It would seem to strongly suggest—if not establish—that, originally, it referred to that part of the funeral ceremony that took place primarily between the time of death and the cremation and construction of a *stūpa,* and involved primarily what we would call "preparation of the body." The construction of a *stūpa*—if it is included at all—signaled the end of *śarīra-pūjā,* not its beginnings.

But if the available evidence suggests that *śarīra-pūjā* was not connected with an ongoing relic cult, that same evidence suggests the injunction concerning it as it was delivered to Ānanda was not intended to apply to all monks. The restricted range of the injunction is confirmed from an unexpected source.

The injunction delivered to Ānanda created problems, apparently, for the later Theravāda tradition. It reappears as one "lemma" of an interesting dilemma in the Fourth Book of the *Milindapañha.* This dilemma is particularly important for our discussion since it allows us to see at least something of how the injunction was understood in Sri Lanka in about the fifth century C.E.[29] In presenting the dilemma Milinda points out that the Buddha said both "Do not you, Ānanda, be occupied with honouring the Tathāgata's bodily remains," and—in the *Vimānavatthu* 82, vs. 8—"Venerate that relic of him who is to be venerated (*pūjetha naṃ pūjaniyassa dhātuṃ*); by doing so, you will go from here to heaven."[30] It is clear from the conjunction of these two passages that by the time this Book was added to the *Milinda* a change in the meaning of *sarīra-pūjā* had occurred; it is clear by the way in which the dilemma is framed that *sarīra-pūjā* was now considered equivalent to "venerating a relic," and could now mean that. But it is also clear from Nāgasena's response that even then, and even when taken to refer to relic worship, the injunction addressed to Ānanda had not yet been understood to apply to all monks. If the injunction had already been understood to apply to all monks, or if this interpretation had been widely or fully accepted, Milinda's dilemma could not have arisen and Nāgasena's response would have made no sense.

The response of Nāgasena comes in the following form:

bhāsitam p'etaṃ mahārāja bhagavatā: abyāvaṭā tumhe ānanda hotha tathāgatassa sarīrapūjāyāti. puna ca bhaṇitaṃ:
pūjetha naṃ pūjaniyassa dhātuṃ
evaṃkarā saggam ito gamissathāti
tañ ca pana na sabbesaṃ. jinaputtānaṃ yeva ārabbha bhaṇitaṃ: abyāvaṭā tumhe ānanda hotha tathāgatassa sarīrapūjāyāti. akammaṃ h'etaṃ mahārāja jinaputtā-

> *naṃ yad idaṃ pūjā; sammasanaṃ saṅkhārānaṃ, yoniso manasikāro, saṭipaṭṭhānā-nupassanā, ārammaṇa-sāraggāho, kilesayuddhaṃ sadatthamanuyuñjanā, etaṃ jinaputtānaṃ karaṇīyaṃ; avasesānaṃ devamanussānaṃ pūjā karaṇīyā.*

Taking into account the new meaning attributed to *sarīra-pūjā,* this can be translated as:

> Great King, this was indeed spoken by the Blessed One: 'You, Ānanda, should not be concerned with worshipping the relics of the Tathāgata!' And again it was said (by him):
>
> 'Worship the relic of one who is to be worshipped!
> Acting thus, you will go from here to heaven.'
>
> But that (which was said) was not (intended) for everyone. Only in reference to the sons of the Conqueror was it said: 'You, Ānanda, should not be concerned with worshipping the relics of the Tathāgata!' For this, Great King, is not an action for the sons of the Conqueror, namely, worship. Thoroughly understanding the conditioned; concentrating the mind; realizing the establishment of mindfulness; taking hold of the most excellent foundations; destroying the impurities; pursuing the highest goal—this is what is to be done by sons of the Conqueror. By the remainder of gods and men worship is to be performed.

The primary purpose of this passage and of the elaborate series of metaphors that follow it is readily apparent. Its primary, if not its sole purpose was to establish the meaning of the injunction delivered to Ānanda by establishing to whom that injunction was to apply. The mere fact that this was a dilemma can, again, only mean that, at the time that this passage was written, it had not yet been established for whom the injunction was meant; it had not been determined that—as modern scholarship would have it—the injunction was meant for all monks. In fact—and this is the significance of the passage—even this late book of the *Milinda* does not understand the passage in this way.

According to the *Milinda,* the injunction did not apply to monks but to what it calls *jinaputtas,* "sons of the Conqueror." But, first of all, this could not have been the intention of the original injunction since the *Dīgha* as a whole is completely ignorant of such a group. "The compound [*jinaputta*] appears to occur," according to Horner, "three times in Buddv. [= *Buddhavaṃṣa*], but nowhere else in the Pāli Canon."[31] Moreover, what little we know about this term comes from a single passage in the *Madhuratthavilāsinī,* a commentary on the *Buddhavaṃsa,* which in Horner's words "is late."[32] It says simply *jinaputtā ti dīpaṅkarassa satthuno sāvakā,* "the sons of the Conqueror means the disciples of the Teacher Dīpaṅkara."[33] The equation *jinaputta* = *sāvaka* is, of course, not terribly helpful. It has recently been pointed out that it is not always easy to determine who was understood to be included in the category *sāvaka,* that it certainly included monks—but by no means, perhaps, all monks—and certainly, at times, included some laymen.[34] The group designated *sāvaka* is not, therefore, certainly coterminous with the group designated *bhikkhu* and, given its vagueness, the group designated *jinaputta* seems even less so. It would, as a consequence, be difficult to argue even that the author of this Book of the *Milinda* was moving *toward* the modern interpretation, which wants to see in the injunction a prohibition of monastic involvement in the relic cult. But even if this argument were to be made, it would have to be conceded that even that author is yet a long way from articulating it with any precision. That interpretation, even as late as the Fourth Book of the *Milinda,* simply has not been made. Had it been, the dilemma would not have arisen; had it been, the author of Book Four, instead of using a term like *jinaputta,* could have simply used the word *bhikkhu.* The fact that he did not is important; the fact that he used a metaphoric epithet rather than an ecclesiastical title may also be important.

Bhikkhu and *jinaputta* are fundamentally different kinds of designations. *Bhikkhu* is a title conferred on an individual as a result of having undergone a set of formal ecclesiastical procedures for induction into a particular group. It designates his formal membership in that group. That membership is not subject to interpretation or opinion; it is subject to recognized procedure. Anyone who undergoes the procedure is a monk. The same, of course, is not true of an epithet like *jinaputta,* if for no other reason than it obviously cannot be taken literally. An individual so designated cannot literally be "a son of the Conqueror." Moreover, there are no formally recognized procedures that make one such a "son" and no formally recognized criteria for determining membership in this group. It, in effect, does not designate membership in a particular group, but conformity to an ideal notion of what the religiosity of a follower of the Buddha—whether that follower be a layman or a monk—ought to be. This, of course, is decidedly a matter of interpretation and not a matter of ecclesiastical procedure. It may well be, then, that the author of the Fourth Book of the *Milinda* saw in the injunction addressed to Ānanda support for *his* view that *pūjā* was not an activity of what he thought was a *true* monk, but even he could not see in the injunction support for the view that it prohibited all monks from such activity. The contrast for him, in fact, continues to be not that between social groups (laymen and monks), but that between different styles of religiosity (meditative and devotional), and a particular religious style had not yet been identified exclusively with any particular group.

It would seem, then, that if the arguments and observations presented here turn out to be even approximately correct, we will be required to admit that a good deal of what has been said about early monastic Buddhism is based on a misunderstanding. If *sarīra-pūjā* in the *Mahāparinibbāna-sutta* has nothing to do with relics or an ongoing cult of relics, then the only textual basis for asserting that monks were not allowed to be involved with either activity disappears. If the injunction concerning *sarīra-pūjā*—however the latter be precisely understood—was not addressed to all monks, then, once again, we are left without any warrant for one of our favorite claims, and we must rethink what we thought we knew about the acultic character of early monastic Buddhism. Once again, it seems, we have encountered material—this time literary—that appears to suggest that our view of the Indian Buddhist monk is in need of more than a little revision.[35]

Notes

1. See especially G. Schopen, "Two Problems in the History of Indian Buddhism," Ch. II above, 30ff; Schopen, "The *Stūpa* Cult and the Extant Pāli *Vinaya,*" Ch. V above, 92ff.

2. T. W. Rhys Davids and J. E. Carpenter, *The Dīgha Nikāya,* Vol. II (London: 1903) 141. All references to the Pāli text are to this edition.

3. T. W. and C. A. F. Rhys Davids, *Dialogues of the Buddha,* Part II (London: 1910) 154.

4. A. Hirakawa, "The Rise of Mahāyāna Buddhism and Its Relationship to the Worship of Stupas," *Memoirs of the Toyo Bunko* 22 (1963) 102.

5. N. Dutt, "Popular Buddhism," *IHQ* 21 (1945) 250–251.

6. A. Bareau, "La composition et les étapes de la formation progressive du mahāparinirvāṇa-sūtra ancien," *BEFEO* 66 (1979) 45–103.

7. As a small sample—and it is only that—of these "conclusions," see H. Oldenberg, *Buddha. Sein Leben, seine Lehre, seine Gemeinde* (Berlin: 1897) 428; N. Dutt, "Place of Laity in Early Buddhism," *IHQ* 21 (1945) 164; Ét. Lamotte, "Le bouddhisme des läics," *Studies in Indology and Buddhology. Presented in Honour of Professor Susumi Yamaguchi on the Occasion of his Sixtieth Birthday* (Kyoto: 1955) 80; *Histoire du bouddhisme indien,* 81; D. L. Snellgrove, "Śākyamuni's Final Nirvāṇa," *BSOAS* 36 (1973) 410; A. Bareau, "Le parinirvāṇa du buddha et la naissance de la religion bouddhique," *BEFEO* 61 (1974) 283–284; G. Nagao, "The Architectural Tradition in Buddhist Monasticism," *Studies in History of Buddhism,* ed. A. K. Narain (Delhi: 1980) 193–194; M. Wijayaratna, *Le moine bouddhiste. Selon les textes du theravāda* (Paris: 1983) 183; R. Gombrich, *Theravāda Buddhism. A Social History from Ancient Benares to Modern Colombo* (London and New York: 1988) 119–124. See also the works cited in nn. 4 and 5 above and nn. 8–11 below; etc.

8. L. de La Vallée-Poussin, *Nirvāṇa* (Paris: 1924) 7.

9. L. de La Vallée-Poussin, *Le dogme et la philosophie du bouddhisme* (Paris: 1930) 64, 191.

10. L. de La Vallée-Poussin, *L'inde aux temps des mauryas et des barbares, grecs, scythes, parthes et yue-tchi* (Paris: 1930) 141.

11. A. Hirakawa, "Stupa Worship," *The Encyclopedia of Religion,* ed. M. Eliade, Vol. 14 (New York: 1987) 93.

12. K. R. Norman, "Notes on the Ahraurā Version of Aśoka's First Minor Rock Edict," *IIJ* 26 (1983) 278.

13. W. Geiger, *Pāli Literature and Language,* trans. by B. Ghosh (Calcutta: 1943) § 78.7; see also *Mahāparinibbāna* V.11 quoted below.

14. This seems clear, as well, in *Mahāparinibbāna* V.17, where Ānanda tries to dissuade the Buddha from passing away in Kusinārā.

15. *Gilgit Buddhist Manuscripts,* vi, fol. 852.8; *Gilgit Manuscripts,* iii 2, 127.13; *Peking,* 41, 281-1-1: *de'i tshe dge slong nad pa zhig gnas khang du shi nas de dge slong rnams kyis dur khrod du khyer te ro la mchod pa byas bsregs nas de nas gtsug lag khang du lhags pa dang /.*

16. *Gilgit Buddhist Manuscripts,* vi, fol. 852.6ff; *Gilgit Manuscripts,* iii 2, 127.4ff; *Peking,* 41, 280-5-6ff: *de'i tshe dge slong zhig shi nas dge slong rnams kyis de phyung ste / dur khrod du de bzhin du bor nas . . . re shig kho bo'i ro la mchod pa yang ma byas par . . . dge slong rnams kyis sngar de'i ro la mchod pa byas la. . . .* This and the preceding passage are two of a series of interesting passages dealing with monastic funerals that occur in the *Mūlasarvāstivāda-vinaya;* I am now working on a detailed study of this material. [See G. Schopen, "On Avoiding Ghosts and Social Censure," Ch. X below; and Schopen, "Ritual Rites and Bones of Contention: More on Monastic Funerals and Relics in the *Mūlasarvāstivāda-vinaya,*" *JIP* 22 (1994) 31–80.]

17. J. S. Speyer, ed., *Avadānaçataka. A Century of Edifying Tales belonging to the Hīnayāna,* Vol. I (St. Petersburg: 1906–1909; repr. The Hague: 1958) 271.15ff; *Peking,* 40, 184-1-8ff. On the sectarian affiliation of the *Avadānaśataka,* see, most recently, J.-U. Hartmann, "Zur Frage der Schulzugehörigkeit des Avadānaśataka," *Zur Schulzugehörigkeit von Werken der Hīnayāna-Literatur,* hrsg. H. Bechert, Erster Teil (Göttingen: 1985) 219–224.

18. So L. Feer, *Avadāna-Çataka. Cent légendes bouddhiques,* Annales du musée guimet, T. XVIII (Paris: 1891) 185.

19. *Gilgit Manuscripts,* iii 2, 120.6ff.

20. For similar cognate constructions, see *Saṅghabhedavastu,* i, 59.18: *atithīnām atithipūjā kartavyā* (the reading here, however, is not absolutely certain; see 59, note b); *Gilgit Manuscripts,* iii 4, 177.9: *jñātīnāṃ vā jñātipūjā na kriyate,* etc.

21. For the Sanskrit text of the *Mahāparinirvāṇa-sūtra,* I refer throughout to the edition in E. Waldschmidt, *Das Mahāparinirvāṇasūtra. Text in Sanskrit und Tibetische, verglichen mit dem Pāli nebst einer Übersetzung der chinesischen Entsprechung im Vinaya der Mūlasarvāstivādins,* T. I–III (Berlin: 1950–1951). All references are to the paragraph numbers imposed on the text by Waldschmidt.

22. For the Tibetan text of the *Vinaya-kṣudraka-vastu,* I have used the *Derge* edition. The account of the death of Mahāprajāpatī is found at *Derge,* 10, 224.6ff.

23. E. B. Cowell and R. A. Neil, eds., *The Divyāvadāna. A Collection of Early Buddhist Legends* (Cambridge: 1886) 433.13–433.16; S. Mukhopadhyaya, ed., *The Aśokāvadāna. Sanskrit Text compared with Chinese Versions* (New Delhi: 1963) 132.7. The text is cited from the latter; for variants, see 132, n. 6.

24. *Saṅghabhedavastu,* i, 161.14.

25. Speyer, *Avadānaśataka,* i, 349.6, 352.16, 357.3, 361.14, 365.13, 369.18, 373.10, 377.12, 383.2, 387.5; ii, 5.17.

26. It is worth noting here that in the Sanskrit text of the injunction, singular pronominal and verbal forms are used, and it is clearly addressed to Ānanda alone.

27. . . . *āyuṣmān mahākāśyapo jñāto ma(hā)puṇyo lābhī cīvarapiṇḍapātaśayan(āsana)-gl(ā)napratyayabhaiṣajyapariṣkārāṇāṃ,* 49.17.

28. On Mahākāśyapa's place in the text as a whole, see Bareau, "La composition et les étapes de la formation progressive du mahāparinirvāṇasūtra ancien," 70ff; Bareau refers to the incidents involving Kāśyapa as "la série des récits inventés par les auteurs de *Vinayapiṭaka* pour glorifier Mahākāśyapa."

29. In dating the section in the *Milinda* in which our passage occurs, I follow P. Demiéville, "Les versions chinoises du milindapañha," *BEFEO* 24 (1924) 34–35; *Histoire du bouddhisme indien,* 465; I. B. Horner, *Milinda's Questions,* Vol. I (London: 1963) xxx–xxxi; cf. the discussion in K. R. Norman, *Pāli Literature. Including the Canonical Literature in Prakrit and Sanskrit of All the Hīnayāna Schools of Buddhism,* A History of Indian Literature, ed. J. Gonda, Vol. VII, Fasc. 2 (Wiesbaden: 1983) 110–113.

30. The text cited here and throughout is from V. Trenckner, ed., *The Milindapañho. Being Dialogues between King Milinda and the Buddhist Sage Nāgasena* (London: 1880) 177ff; the translation here is from Horner, *Milinda's Questions,* i, 249ff.

31. Horner, *Milinda's Questions,* i, 250, n. 1.

32. I. B. Horner, ed., *Madhuratthavilāsinī. The Commentary on Buddhavaṃsa of Bhadantācariya Buddhadatta Mahāthera* (London: 1946) vi.

33. Horner, *Madhuratthavilāsinī,* 99; I. B. Horner, *The Clarifier of the Sweet Meaning (Madhuratthavilāsinī). Commentary on the Chronicle of Buddhas (Buddhavaṃsa) by Buddhadatta Thera* (London: 1978) 142.

34. P. Masefield, *Divine Revelation in Pali Buddhism* (London: 1986) 1–36. Masefield's conclusions are not infrequently overstated and problematic, but he clearly shows that the Pāli texts will not support a simple equation of *sāvaka* and *bhikkhu.*

35. Cf. G. Schopen, "Filial Piety and the Monk in the Practice of Indian Buddhism," Ch. III above; Schopen, "On Monks, Nuns, and 'Vulgar' Practices," Ch. XI below.

CHAPTER VII

Burial *Ad Sanctos* and the Physical Presence of the Buddha in Early Indian Buddhism

A Study in the Archaeology of Religions

IT IS HARDLY REVOLUTIONARY to suggest that, had the academic study of religions started quite literally on the ground, it would have been confronted with very different problems. It would have had to ask very different questions, and it would have produced very different solutions. It would, in short, have become not the History of Religions—which was and is essentially text-bound—but the Archaeology of Religions. It would have used texts, of course, but only those that could be shown to have been actually known or read at a given place at a given time, or to have governed or shaped the kind of religious behavior that had left traces on the ground. In fact, texts would have been judged significant only if they could be shown to be related to what religious people actually did. This Archaeology of Religions would have been primarily occupied with three broad subjects of study then: religious constructions and architectures, inscriptions, and art historical remains. In a more general sense, though, it would have been preoccupied *not* with what small, literate, almost exclusively male and certainly atypical professionalized subgroups wrote, but rather, with what religious people of all segments of a given community actually did and how they lived.

All of this—since it did not happen—is, of course, totally academic. But—and this is the beauty of it—since the History of Religions is also totally academic, it still might. In fact, what I will present here is meant as a small push in that direction. In what follows, I want to look at Indian Buddhism on the ground. It is, however, very clear to me that, since this is something of a

Originally published in *Religion* 17 (1987): 193–225. Reprinted with stylistic changes with permission of Academic Press Limited.

first attempt,[1] the results that it will produce will necessarily be somewhat tentative. My data can and should be supplemented. My methods may have to be refined. My conclusions and interpretations may have to be modified and perhaps, in part, rejected. But it should be an interesting discussion, and once the discussion is engaged, I very much suspect it will become an unavoidable part of Buddhist Studies and, I hope, of the academic study of religions in general.

Starting on the Ground

If, then, our study of Indian Buddhism is to start on the ground, the first and most noticeable things we encounter are Buddhist sacred sites. Like so many sacred sites elsewhere, these sites immediately appear to be connected, at least in part, with the way in which the early Buddhist tradition disposed of and behaved toward its "very special dead."[2]

From two inscriptions of Aśoka we know that, already in the third century B.C.E., the Buddhism that he knew had developed two geographically fixed sacred sites. In fact, both of these sites are probably pre-Aśokan. One of them most certainly is. Although these two sites appear to us to be different in kind, Aśoka himself behaves in regard to both in exactly the same way. In both inscriptions when he initially describes what he did, he uses exactly the same wording: "King Priyadarśī . . . came in person (and) worshipped (here)" (*devānapiyena . . . attana āgācca mahīyite,* Rummindei; and *devānaṃpiyena . . . attana āgacca mahīyite,* Nigliva).[3] The places in question are Lumbini, the birthplace of the Buddha Śākyamuni, and the *stūpa* or monumental reliquary of the past Buddha Konākamana.[4] In regard to the latter, it should be noted that some years before "coming in person," Aśoka had the reliquary doubled in size (*thube dutiyaṃ vaḍḍhite).* In regard to the former, he also effected some construction at the site, and he describes it in an important way. He says:

> King Priyadarśī . . . came in person (and) worshipped, saying 'Here the Buddha was born, Śākyamuni,' he had a stone wall made and erected a stone pillar. Saying 'Here the Blessed One was born,' the village of Lummini was freed from tax and put at one-eighth.
>
> *devānapiyena . . . attana āgācca mahīyate hida buddhe jāte sakyamunī ti silāvigaḍabhī cā kālāpita silātthabhe ca ussapāpite hida bhagavaṃ jāte ti luṃminigāme ubbalike kaṭe aṭṭhabhāgiye ca.*

The statement "here the Blessed One was born," however, is almost certainly not Aśoka's, but an old ritual formula that was to be spoken by any individual upon arriving at the sacred site. It is almost certainly an actual quotation or direct paraphrase as is indicated, at least in part, by the particle *ti* (Skt. *iti*), although this has not always been understood.[5] This quotation, or direct paraphrase, makes it highly likely that Aśoka knew some version of a short text now preserved in somewhat different forms in the various versions of the *Mahāparinirvāṇa-sūtra.* The earliest actually datable Indian version—which is also closest to the wording found in Aśoka—has the Buddha say:[6]

> After I have passed away, monks, those making the pilgrimage to the shrines, honoring the shrines, will come [to these places], they will speak in this way: 'Here the Blessed One was born,' 'here the Blessed One attained the highest most excellent awakening,' etc.
>
> *āgamiṣyanti bhikṣavo mamātyayāc caityaparicārakāś caityavandakās* (Tib. *mchod rten bskor ba dan̄ mchod rten la phyag 'tshal ba;* cf. Pāli, though not here, *cetiyacārika) ta evaṃ vakṣyanti / iha bhagavāñ jātaḥ /,* etc., 41.7–41.8.

The similarity in context and wording between the *Mahāparinirvāṇa* text and the Aśokan inscription is too close to be coincidental.

If Aśoka knew a version of the text that was similar to the one that has come down to us—and the fact that Aśoka quotes or paraphrases what he does indicates that some version of it was very old and predated him—then we are able to recover a number of other points. First, there is the question as to whether or not Aśoka's action was unique and purely individual in its motivation; a predated text would suggest otherwise. It would suggest that he was only doing what was prescribed for "a devout son of good family." The extant Sanskrit version of the old text says:

> Monks, there are these four places which are to be/must be visited by a devout son or daughter of good family during their life.
>
> *catvāra ime bhikṣavaḥ pṛthivīpradeśāḥ śrāddhasya kulaputrasya kuladuhitur vā yāvajjīvam anusmaraṇīyā* (but read with the ms. *abhigamanīyā*[7]) *bhavanti,* 41.5.

The Pāli text is, interestingly, even stronger. It says:

> Ānanda, there are these four places that a devout son of good family must do *darśan* of, and powerfully experience.
>
> *cattār' imāni ānanda saddhassa kulaputtassa dassanīyāni saṃvejanīyāni ṭhānāni.*

In both cases, there are future passive participles that blend into and frequently replace the imperative in both languages. Both versions make it clear that there must be direct contact with these places, and the verbs in the Pāli version are particularly striking.[8] It is worth noting that, despite the fact that it has dropped out of the English translations in particular, the final sections of the Pāli version of the *Mahāparinibbāna-sutta* are clearly marked with the notion and importance of *darśan,* and *darśan* is about direct, intimate contact with a living presence.[9] In fact, the idea that Bodh-Gayā was a place at which one did *darśan* must have persisted for a very long time. We find reference to it again in an inscription written in Devanāgarī that may be as late as the fifteenth century.[10]

It is also worth noting, in light of a common misconception, to whom these injunctions were directed. A *kulaputra,* "a son of good family," was no more the actual son of a family of a certain socioeconomic class than an *ārya* was a member of a specific racial group. "Son of good family" was simply an honorific title, a title applied as frequently to monks as to laymen. Note that in the Sanskrit version the injunction is delivered to monks and in the Pāli version to a specific monk. A few lines later in the same passage, the Sanskrit version replaces "devout son of good family" with two other titles: "one who makes the pilgrimage to the shrines," and an "honorer of shrines"—and we know from early inscriptions from Amarāvatī that the second of these, at least, was a monastic title.[11] The Pāli version makes an even more specific substitution. For its "devout son of good family," it substitutes later in the same passage "devout monks, nuns, laymen, and laywomen" (*saddhā bhikkhubhikkhuniyo upāsaka-upāsikāyo*).[12] In fact, all of the early epigraphical material confirms a predominately monastic preoccupation with Bodh-Gayā. The greater part of the surviving first century B.C.E. railing appears to have been the gift of a single nun; all of the Kushan and Gupta inscriptions in which the status of the donor is clear record the donations of monks—monks from as far away as Sri Lanka.[13]

Again, if we can assume that Aśoka knew a version of the old text that was similar to the oldest actually datable version we have, then we can make at least two other important statements about the early Buddhist conception of sacred sites. After having the Buddha say "After I have passed away, monks, those making the pilgrimage to the shrines . . . will come, they will speak in this way, . . . " that version has him then say:

> Those who during that time die here with a believing mind *in my presence,* all those who have *karma* still to work out, go to heaven.
>
> *atrāntarā ye kecit prasannacittā mamāntike kālaṃ kariṣyanti te sarve svargopagā ye kecit sopadhiśeṣāḥ,* 41.9 and 14.

First, it seems fairly clear that the monk redactor of the text thought that the Buddha was, after his *parinirvāṇa,* in some sense actually present at the places where he is known to have formerly been. The text is hard to read in any other way. Second, it is equally clear that the monk redactor of the text accepted as fact that a devout death that occurred within the range of this presence assured for the individuals involved—and these were both monks and laymen—rebirth in heaven. The Pāli version of the text, while it differs somewhat in articulation, confirms the essentials:

Indeed, Ānanda, whosoever being engaged in visiting the shrines with a devout mind dies, they all after the breakup of their body, after death, will be reborn in heaven.

ye hi keci ānanda cetiyacārikaṃ āhiṇḍantā pasannacittā kālaṃ karissanti sabbe te kāyassa bhedā param maraṇā sugatiṃ saggaṃ lokaṃ uppajjissantīti.

One cannot help but suspect that both of these ideas are somehow connected with a curious but consistent pattern clearly observable in the archaeological record of Buddhist sacred sites.[14]

An Archaeological Pattern

Everywhere in the Indian Buddhist archaeological record, the exact spot at which the former presence of the Buddha was marked had a clear and pronounced tendency to draw to it other deposits. Bodh-Gayā, although a much disturbed site, is a fine example. Crowded in a jumbled mass around the central point of the site, the exact point of former contact, are hundreds and thousands of small *stūpas* of various sizes, and what we see today is only the lowest strata. Above this strata, according to Cunningham, were at least:

> four tiers of similar monuments . . . carved stones of an early date were frequently found in the bases of the later monuments, and as the soil got silted up, the general level of the courtyard was gradually raised, and the later stūpas were built over the tops of the earlier ones in successive tiers of different ages . . . so great was the number of these successive monuments, and so rapid was the accumulation of stones and earth that the general level of the courtyard was raised about 20 feet above the floor of the Great Temple.[15]

However, it is not just at spots at which the former presence of the Buddha was marked that we find this pattern; exactly the same configuration occurred around *stūpas* containing relics. Here, the presence of the relic has had exactly the same effect that the presence of the point of former contact with the Buddha's physical body had. It has drawn to it a jumble of minor *stūpas* which crowd around it in an ever increasing state of disarray. The Dharmarājikā *Stūpa* in Taxila is a good, early example. Although, as Marshall himself admits, there is no surviving evidence to actually prove that the main *stūpa* is Mauryan, it is unlikely that it is much later; a second century B.C.E. date is not unlikely.[16] Within a century this main *stūpa* was surrounded by a tight circle of smaller *stūpas* crowding around it, some of which can be dated by coin finds more specifically to the first century B.C.E. A similar situation is found at Jauliāñ, a later but particularly well-preserved site that had not been overwhelmed by successive layers of building. Here, there is a central *stūpa* on a well-planned oblong plinth, but crowded around it are at least twenty-one smaller *stūpas* of varying size that, by their irregular placement, were clearly not a part of the original plan, and that were clearly added at different times wherever space allowed. When space ran out, these *stūpas* spilled down to a lower level where five more are found.[17] Likewise at Mīrpūr-Khas in Sind—a site both badly preserved and badly reported—around the main *stūpa* at the upper level was "a regular forest of smaller stūpas" that, much like at Bodh-Gayā, had been built directly on top of still earlier levels of still earlier minor *stūpas*. Cousens thinks that the main *stūpa* at least cannot be later than 400 C.E. and may be earlier.[18]

This clustering apparently occurred even at sites where it is no longer visible. The main *stūpa* at Sāñcī, for example, today rises somewhat awesomely straight out of the flat, clear ground that surrounds it. This, however, was not always the case. Marshall says "Time was when the Great Stūpa was surrounded, like all the more famous shrines of Buddhism, by a multitude of *stūpas* of varying sizes crowded together on the face of the plateau. The majority of these appear to have been swept away during the operations of 1881–1883, when the ground around the Great Stūpa was cleared for a distance of some 60 feet from the outer rail."[19] Only a very few of these smaller *stūpas* survived the destruction.

The Mortuary Associations of the Pattern

These smaller *stūpas* have, by habit, been taken to be votive *stūpas* and a number of imaginative scenarios created to explain their presence. But in a significant number of cases this simply cannot be so. These cannot be "votive" in any meaningful sense of the term because these smaller *stūpas* contain things, and the things they contain are of particular interest. All of the earliest smaller *stūpas* crowding around the Dharmarājikā described by Marshall contained "relic" deposits; that is, anonymous bones and ashes.[20] That these bones and ashes did not belong to Śākyamuni may be inferred from the fact attested almost everywhere, that, when his relics were deposited, they were accompanied with an inscriptional label of some sort indicating that they were his.[21] Moreover, his relic was already present in the main *stūpa*. Likewise at Jauliāñ, where only the bases of most of the smaller *stūpas* survive, still, at least three of these contained anonymous burial deposits or chambers that once contained such deposits.[22] At Mīrpūr-Khas "all the smaller stūpas of the upper level, which had been opened, had funerary associations, as they contained urns with pieces of bone. Below the floor of these stūpas were found some earlier minor stūpas, which included two of clay, one with bones."[23] Even at Sāñcī, at least one of the very few surviving "votive" *stūpas* contained such an anonymous burial deposit.[24]

The situation at Bodh-Gayā is a little more complex, but equally interesting. Cunningham says in regard to the "votive" *stūpas* found in such large numbers at Bodh-Gayā that "the pinnacles of the tall mediaeval stūpas were always more or less broken, and even the solid hemispheres of the earlier structural stūpas were mostly displaced."[25] That is to say that almost all of these *stūpas* had no "pinnacle" or elaborate finial. Cunningham attributes this "loss" to the construction of new structures on top of the old, but there is now evidence to suggest that his explanation may not be correct.

Excavations of the site at Ratnagiri in Orissa have revealed very similar "votive" *stūpas* in numbers equaling, if not surpassing, those found at Bodh-Gayā.[26] Here, it is even more clear than at Bodh-Gayā that a considerable number of these *stūpas* were portable; that is they were brought from somewhere else and deposited near the main *stūpa.* But here—to judge by the photographs—most of these *stūpas* appear never to have had pinnacles. Most appear to have a socket on top into which plugs of various shapes were inserted.[27] Indeed, a very considerable number of these so-called votive *stūpas* from both sites seem to correspond in form, at least, to what I-tsing in his *Record of The Buddhist Religion as Practised in India and the Malay Archipelago* called a *"kula."* However, these *kulas* had a very specific use. I-tsing says: "They [Buddhist monks in India] sometimes build a thing like a stūpa for the dead, to contain his *śarīra* (or relics). It is called a *'kula,'* which is like a small stūpa, but without the cupola on it."[28] That at least some of the monolithic "votive" *stūpas* at Ratnagiri corresponded, not only in form but also in function, to I-tsing's *kula* is beyond doubt. Mitra, in referring to the smaller monolithic *stūpas* at Ratnagiri, says: "They are mostly votive in nature, with or without some inscribed texts in their cores, but in a few cases their funerary character was obvious, for they contained charred bone relics either within sockets plugged by stone lids or in urns."[29] It may not be these cases only that are funerary. If, as appears likely, the sockets on the top of these *stūpas* that previously have been taken to be meant for the insertion of some kind of finial were actually intended for and held ash or bone, then the funerary character of a very large number of these *stūpas* is established.[30] But there is still something more of interest in what Mitra says.

The Mortuary Associations of Inscribed *Dhāraṇīs*

Mitra refers here, and elsewhere, to the presence of "inscribed texts" in the cores of some of these *stūpas,* and the same thing has been noticed at Bodh-Gayā, Nālandā, Paharpur, and at other sites. A significant number of these texts are *dhāraṇīs,* at least in later *stūpas.* Although largely ignored, it has recently been shown that these are not *ad hoc* compositions but specific *dhāraṇīs* taken from a specific group of texts. And these texts tell us quite explicitly why these *dhāraṇīs* were placed in *stūpas.*[31] Although this group of texts is only now beginning to be studied, even a preliminary survey makes it clear that all of them are preoccupied with the problem of death and with either the procurement of a means to avoid rebirth in the hells or other unfortunate destinies, or with the release of those already born there. The latter, in fact, is one of the primary reasons for placing *dhāraṇīs* in *stūpas.* I cite here a typical example from the Tibetan translation of the *Raśmivimalaviśuddhaprabhādhāraṇī:*

> Moreover, if someone were to write this *dhāraṇī* in the name of another (who is deceased) and were to deposit it in a *stūpa* and earnestly worship it, then the deceased, being freed (by that) from his unfortunate destiny, would be reborn in heaven. Indeed, being reborn in the region of the Tuṣita gods, through the empowering of the Buddha he would (never again) fall into an unfortunate destiny.
>
> *yaṅ gaṅ la la źig gis gsaṅ sṅags yi ger bris pa gźan gyi miṅ nas smos te / mchod rten gyi naṅ du bcug la nan tan du mchod pa byas na śi ba gaṅ yin pa de naṅ soṅ gi gnas nas thar te mtho ris su skye bar 'gyur ro / yaṅ na dga 'ldan gyi lha'i ris su skye bar 'gyur te / saṅs rgyas kyi byin gyis brlabs kyis ṅan soṅ du ltuṅ bar mi 'gyur ro /*[32]

But these *dhāraṇīs* are also connected with Buddhist mortuary practices in a variety of other ways as well. Again, a typical example can be seen in the *Sarvakarmāvaraṇaviśodhanidhāraṇī:*

> If one, reciting (this *dhāraṇī*) over earth or sesame or white mustard or water, were to scatter it over the corpse, or if, having washed (the body), one afterwards were to either cremate it or deposit and preserve it in a *stūpa,* writing this *dhāraṇī* and attaching it to the top (or head), then the deceased—although already reborn in an unfortunate destiny—being freed, would without a doubt after seven days be reborn in a blessed heaven, or else he would be reborn through the power of his own vow.
>
> *sa 'am til lam yuṅs kar ram chu gaṅ yaṅ ruṅ ba la bzlas brjod byas te śi ba'i lus la gtor ram/khrus byas nas de'i 'og tu bsreg pa 'am/yaṅ na mchod rten gyi naṅ du bcug ste bźag la/rig sṅags kyaṅ bris te mgo bo la btags na de naṅ soṅ du skyes pa yaṅ źag bdun gyis gnod mi za bar thar te bde 'gro mtho ris kyi 'jig rten du skye bar 'gyur ba am/yaṅ na raṅ gi smon lam gyi dbaṅ gis skye bar 'gyur ro/*[33]

Finally, it is perhaps worth noting that similar, although more complicated, funerary rituals involving the same kinds of uses of written *dhāraṇīs* are to be found in the *Sarvadurgatipariśodhanatantra* published in 1983 by Skorupski—a text which, though a fully developed *tantra,* is clearly related both narratively and doctrinally to our group.[34]

That the *dhāraṇīs* found at Ratnagiri and elsewhere had funerary associations is suggested not only by the texts that they were taken from, but also by the fact that they are almost always found in exactly the same archaeological contexts as are the anonymous deposits of bone and ash. This again is particularly clear at Ratnagiri. In addition to the small *kula*-like monolithic *stūpas,* there are also a considerable number of small structural *stūpas* crowded around the main *stūpa* at Ratnagiri, and an even larger number of them still contained undisturbed their original deposits of anonymous bones. Mitra specifically mentions that in *Stūpas* 3, 4, 23, 24, 25, and 115—all structural—bone deposits were found; however, she then adds that "there is every reason to believe that there were many more *śārīrika stūpas* (i.e., those containing bone or ash). For, stray bones with or without reliquaries were found in the *Stūpa* area. Apparently, they must have got dislodged from structural *stūpas,* many of which are reduced to the lowest part of the base or platform."[35] All eight of the *dhāraṇīs* found at Ratnagiri—exactly like the anonymous bone deposits—were found in the cores of structural *stūpas.*[36]

The Archaeological Pattern Recapitulated

The archaeological record of Buddhist sacred sites exhibits, then, from the very beginning of our actual evidence, at least one curious but consistent pattern. This pattern, significantly, is most distinctly and directly visible at our very earliest undisturbed sites. The Dharmarājikā at Taxila, which dates to the second century B.C.E., is a fine example. But there are also clear indications that the same pattern held at other very early sites like Sāñcī and Bhārhut until these sites, by different agents, were irrevocably altered or virtually destroyed. It continues to hold through the fourth and fifth centuries C.E.—for example, at Jauliāñ and Mīrpūr-Khas—and is found at Ratnagiri still in its full disorderly effervescence in the tenth and twelfth centuries. What we find is a large central structure that marks one of two things: either the presence of a spot that was formerly in direct contact with the physical body of the Buddha, or—more commonly—the presence of an actual physical piece of that body. Around this structure, closely packed, in increasing disorder, are a large number—increasingly so—of other smaller structures that frequently contain anonymous bones or bone ash or other items connected with mortuary deposits. That these smaller structures were added at different times is apparent from the fact that they are not part of any discernible original or ordered plan. In fact, they frequently appear to violate any preexisting orderly plan of the sites. The only concern that appears to have governed their placement was an apparent desire to have them as close as possible to the main structure. All of this would suggest, in turn, that these mortuary deposits were purposely brought here, again at different times, from somewhere else. In fact, a considerable number of the smallest of these structures were obviously portable.[37] This, in outline, is what we see. What we want to know, of course, is what it means.

Some Archaeological Parallels

It is worth noting, however briefly, some remarkably similar archaeological configurations found elsewhere. In at least some of these other instances, we know a considerable amount about the ideational systems that produced these parallel configurations, and they are, therefore, at least suggestive of what the configuration in Buddhist India might have meant.

Ariès condensed into a few sentences a large body of archaeological literature that is of interest to us. He says:

> Over the saint's tomb a basilica would be built . . . Christians sought to be buried close to this structure. Diggings in the Roman cities of Africa or Spain reveal an extraordinary spectacle concealed by subsequent urban growth: piles of stone sarcophagi in disorder, one on top of the other, several layers high, especially around the walls of the apse, close to the shrine of the saint.[38]

This, again according to Ariès, "is what one finds in Tipasa, Hippo, and Carthage. The spectacle is just as striking in Ampurias, in Catalonia . . . [and] . . . the same situation is found in our Gallo–Roman cities, but it is no longer visible to the naked eye and has to be reconstructed beneath the successive deposit of history."[39]

Notice that, apart from the technical vocabulary ("basilica," "sarcophagi," etc.), Ariès' description of the archaeological record in the Roman cities of Africa, Spain, and France could almost serve equally well as a description of what was seen at Bodh-Gayā, Taxila, and other South Asian sites. Another site of interest to us differs from these two groups in only one significant way: the successive waves of mortuary deposits, rather than being heaped one on top of the other, have spread out in horizontal layers to cover an immense area, to produce in effect what has been called "the greatest cemetery of Japan." This is the cemetery on Mount Kōyasan. Here, a dense jumble of graves and markers covering many acres crowds around the tomb of Kōbō Daishi, the eighth or ninth century monk who, among a multitude of other accomplishments, founded Shingon Buddhism. Casal notes that "the number of graves . . . is indeed very large . . . But not all the graves contain a body or its ashes; it suffices to bury a bone, or even some hair or a tooth. The important thing is that one's symbol be interred near the great teacher. . . ."[40]

It is interesting to note that the ideas that produced the configuration of crowding or clustering of mortuary deposits around a central structure in both the Roman cities of Africa and Spain and on Mount Kōyasan appear to be reducible—in both cases—to two basic sets. The first set is perhaps the easier to describe because there is an established vocabulary that can be applied to it. The ideas grouped here are essentially eschatological: in the Christian case, they concern the Doctrine of the Resurrection of the Dead; in the case of Kōyasan, they concern the coming of Maitreya, the Future Buddha. The Christian case can be illustrated by some remarks of Geary: "Early Christians took literally Christ's promise of the resurrection and thus expected that on the last day the martyrs' physical bodies would be taken up again by their owners . . . Christians believed that physical proximity to these bodies was beneficial, and that those buried near a saint's tomb would be raised up with the saint on the day of judgment."[41] Similar ideas were also certainly associated with the tomb of Kōbō Daishi, although one might dispute the exact wording of those scholars who have described them. Lloyd, for example, says: "The Shingon are firm believers in Maitreya . . . It is their conviction that the body of Kōbō Daishi, which never decays, is awaiting the advent of Maitreya in his tomb at Kōya San, and Shingonists often send the bones of their dead, after cremation, to Kōya San, so as to be near to Kōbō at the resurrection, which will take place when Maitreya makes his appearance."[42]

The eschatological set, although clearly present in both cases, is only one of two sets and probably is not the most important. The second set—again present in both cases—is based on the notion that the tomb or shrine contains an actual living presence. It was thought, to quote Hakeda, that "Kukai had not died but had merely entered into eternal Samādhi and was still quite alive on Mt. Kōya as a savior to all suffering people."[43] Here, there is no preoccupation with some distantly future eschatological event. Burial in close physical proximity to the living presence, in fact, effects an immediate result: it assures that the individual whose bones or ashes are placed there will gain rebirth in paradise, in the Pure Land of Amitābha, in Sukhāvatī.[44] Christian notions that fall into this second set are much more richly documented. "It was commonly believed," says Wilson, ". . . that, far from inhabiting any distant heaven, the saint remained present in his shrine. Delehaye wrote that, for those who followed his cult, St. Menas 'resided, invisible, in his basilica' in the Mariut, near Alexandria."[45] Here too, eschatological notions are largely absent, and a different set of functions comes into play. Ariès first quotes St. Paulinus, who had had the body of his son buried beside the Saints at Aecola. Paulinus writes: "We have sent him [his dead son] to the town of Complutum so that he may lie with the martyrs in the union of the grave, and so that from the blood of the saints he may draw that virtue that refines our souls like fire." Ariès himself then adds the following observation: "We see here that the saints not only grant protection from the creatures of Tartarus, they also communicate to the deceased who is associated with them a little of their virtue, and post-mortem, redeem his sins."[46]

The Buddhist Conception of Relics as "Living Entities"

We know, then, that the above ideas produced the essentially similar archaeological configurations that are to be seen at Carthage and Kōyasan, and we might well expect that similar thinking produced the same configuration at Bodh–Gayā and Taxila. In India, however, the first set seems not to have been operational. There is no evidence of any kind of a connection between the presence of the relic—whether it be a contact relic, like a spot of earth, or an actual bone—and any eschatological event.[47] In fact, if there is any eschatological thinking in India, it takes a decidedly different form. This would seem to suggest that if the configuration found at Bodh–Gayā and Taxila was produced by ideas similar to those that produced Carthage and Kōyasan, then the ideas involved would probably belong not to the first set, but to the second. But if this were the case, we might expect to find at least some indications that the relic in early Buddhist India was thought of as an actual living presence. And we have some evidence for this.

The first piece of evidence that might be brought forward is the old text we started with, which is now preserved in the various versions of the *Mahāparinirvāṇa-sūtra.* Notice that the redactor of the Sanskrit version seems clearly to have thought that the Buddha, although dead, was somehow actually present at the places where he was formerly known to have been. Notice too that he explicitly indicates that a death in physical proximity to that actual presence produces specific and positive results, that it, like burial near a Saint or close to Kōbō Daishi, resulted in "heaven." In other words, death at Bodh–Gayā and burial *ad sanctos* at Carthage and Kōyasan have exactly the same result, although the heaven in each case is somewhat differently appointed. In fact, the key concept in this old text—only very slightly extended—is probably able to account by itself for what is seen in the archaeological record of several Buddhist sacred sites in India. The extension would only be from *death* to *deposition of the already dead* in close physical proximity to that actual presence.[48]

However, strictly speaking, the old text is referring only to geographically fixed points of former contact with the physical body of the Buddha: Bodh–Gayā, Sārnāth, and so on. The text says he is present at these places, and yet the archaeological pattern appears to indicate burial *ad sanctos* not just at these sites, but also at sites where there is only a bodily relic. This archaeological evidence, if we are correct in our interpretation of it, would suggest that, at these sites too, the Buddha was thought to be actually present and alive. There is, again, some evidence that would indicate this to be the case.

One of the earliest Indian inscriptions after Aśoka is written on the broken lid of a relic casket that came from Shinkot. It records, very laconically, the deposition of a relic of the Buddha Śākyamuni in the reign of the Indo-Greek king, Menander, who ruled in the second century B.C.E. All are agreed—Majumdar, Konow, Sircar, Narain, and Lamotte[49]—that it said on the rim:

> . . . [on] the 14th day of the month Kārttika, the relic of the Blessed One Śākyamuni which is endowed with life was established.
> *kārttikasya {māsasya} divase 14 prāṇasametaṃ {śarīraṃ} {bhagavataḥ śākyamuneḥ} pratiṣṭhāpitam.*[50]

Similar wording to this also occurs on the inner face of the lid:

> [This is] a relic of the Blessed One Śākyamuni which is endowed with life.
>
> *prāṇasametaṃ śarīraṃ bhagavataḥ śākyamuneḥ.*

What this seems to mean is, of course, what Konow and Lamotte have already said: "The relics were looked upon as living entities"; "la relique corporelle . . . c'est un être vivant 'doué de souffle.' " However, neither of these authors noted—perhaps because it did not seem germane to their particular point—that this is the earliest actually datable reference to the relics of the historical Buddha, and that, in fact, the conception of the relic as "un être vivant" is the earliest actually attestable conception that we have.

Other early sources indicate that the physical relics of Śākyamuni were endowed with more than just "life" or "breath." They were "informed," "parfumée," "saturated," "pervaded," "imbued" with just those characteristics that defined the living Buddha. Statements to this effect are found in a wide variety of sources. The Inscription of Senavarma is a good example. This inscription, which dates to the early first century C.E., is "la plus longue des inscriptions Kharoṣṭhī jusqu' ici connues," and has proven to be difficult.[51] The portion which concerns us, however, is clear. Senavarma says in part:

> I establish these relics which are infused with morality, infused with concentration, wisdom, emancipation, and knowledge and vision.
>
> *ima dhadu śila(pari)bhavita samasiprañavimutiñaṇadra(śa)paribhavita . . . pratiṭhavemi.*

The list of faculties and qualities given here looks very much as though it may have been intended for, or is perhaps a haplography of what the Pāli tradition calls the five *sampadās* or "attainments" and, of course, normally only a living person can be "infused" with such "attainments." Yet another Kharoṣṭhī inscription, which can be dated more exactly to 25 to 26 C.E., has a similar characterization of the relics of Śākyamuni. Here, the relics are said to be *śilaparibhavida sama(s)iparibhaveṃtu prañaparibhavida* or "infused with morality, infused with concentration, infused with wisdom."[52] That is to say, the relics themselves were thought to retain—to be "infused with," impregnated with—the qualities that animated and defined the living Buddha.

Something of the same vocabulary found in these two inscriptions is also found in Aśvaghoṣa's *Buddhacarita.* In fact, both of these inscriptions and Aśvaghoṣa may have been closely contemporaneous. Johnston dates the latter to "between 50 B.C. and 100 A.D. with a preference for the first half of the first century A.D."[53] It is not, however, just his date that makes Aśvaghoṣa important for us. Both of our inscriptions record the gifts of laymen, although they, or the redactors of their inscriptions, had some apparent familiarity with accepted Buddhist doctrines.[54] Aśvaghoṣa, on the other hand, was most decidedly a monk, an extremely literate and very widely learned monk, and his conception of relics is important because of that: they are the conceptions of a monk exceptionally well-versed in Buddhist doctrine.[55] In the passage that concerns us, Aśvaghoṣa says, for example, that the relics of Śākyamuni, like "the sphere (*dhātu*) of the chief of the gods (*Brahmā*) in heaven at the end of the aeon," cannot be destroyed by the final cosmic conflagration, that these relics "cannot be carried even by Viṣṇu's Garuda," that "though cool, they burn our minds" (*bsil ba yin kyaṅ bdag cag rnams kyi yid rnams sregs).* But Aśvaghoṣa also uses less overwrought expressions, like those found in our inscriptions. The relics, he says, are "full of virtue" (*dge legs gaṅ ba*), and "informed (*paribhāvita?*) with universal benevolence (*maitrī*)" (*byams pas yoṅs su rnam par bsgoms pa).*[56]

There are also other witnesses, at least one of which is hostile. The *Aṣṭasāhasrikāprajñāpāramitā* is one of the earliest Mahāyāna texts translated into Chinese, and some version of it was very probably contemporaneous with both our inscriptions and Aśvaghoṣa.[57] Like the *Suvarṇaprabhāsottama,* the *Buddhabalādhāna,* the *Saddharmapuṇḍarīka,* and a number of other, later texts, it is in part preoccupied with sometimes sustained arguments intended to devalue—if not altogether deny the value—of relics.[58] In fact, it devotes large parts of at least three chapters to such arguments. As a part of these arguments, the *Aṣṭasāhasrikā* on two occasions concedes that there are good reasons for worshipping relics, and, in so doing, uses much the same vocabulary as is found in our two inscriptions and in Aśvaghoṣa's *Buddhacarita.* It is stated quite explicitly that:

> the relics of the Tathāgata are worshipped because they are saturated with the Perfection of Wisdom.
>
> *api tu khalu punar bhagavaṃs tāni tathāgataśarīrāṇi prajñāpāramitāparibhāvitatvāt pūjāṃ labhyante.*[59]

The final instance that we might cite here where relics are said to be "saturated" or "infused" or "pervaded" with specific qualities comes from the Fourth Book of the *Milindapañha,* a book which Demiéville has shown was almost certainly added to the *Milinda* in Ceylon at a date not much earlier than the fifth century C.E.[60] It is, therefore, noteworthy that despite the fact that it is separated from the Senavarma Inscription by 500 years, the *Milindapañha*—as Fussman has already pointed out—contains an almost exact verbal parallel to that inscription. Here too, the relic is described as "infused with morality, concentration, wisdom, emancipation, and the knowledge and vision of emancipation" (*sīlasamādhipaññāvimuttivimuttiñāṇadassanaparibhāvitaṃ dhāturatanañ).*

Each of these passages comes from a distinctly different kind of source, and yet they all use exactly the same participle, *paribhāvita,* in characterizing the relics of the Buddha. The same participle is, of course, used elsewhere, and its characteristic usages are worth noting. One of the most common usages of the term in canonical Pāli, oddly enough, has to do with chicken's eggs. In a frequently found simile, eggs are described as "sat on" (*adhisayita*), "heated" (*parisedita*), and "pervaded or infused" (*paribhāvita*) by a hen. It is this that makes the eggs "live." In fact, the point of the simile is that, if this is not done properly, the chicks do not live.[61] Apart from this, the term is more usually applied to living persons. A particularly interesting usage occurs twice in the *Sarvatathāgatādhiṣṭhānasattvāvalokanabuddhakṣetrasandarśanavyūha-sūtra* from Gilgit. Here, the negative *aparibhāvitakāya,* "having an unpervaded or uninvigorated body" is twice paired with *alpāyuṣka,* "having little life."[62] In the *Mahāvastu* [Senart ed., Vol. i, 153.12], *bodhisattvas,* like relics in Aśvaghoṣa, are said to be "completely saturated with virtue" (*kuśalaparibhāvita*); likewise in *Milindapañha* 361.23, those who fulfill the ascetic practices, like the relics in our two inscriptions, are said to be "saturated with the lovely and excellent unparalleled sweet perfume of morality" (*sīlavarapavara-asamasucigandha-paribhāvito hoti).* Again like relics in Aśvaghoṣa, a *bodhisattva* is said in the *Saddharmapuṇḍarīka* [Kern-Nanjio ed., 3.1] to "have his body and mind saturated with benevolence" (*maitrīparibhāvitakāyacitta).* From these and other passages, it seems evident that *paribhāvita* implies "filled or infused with life," "invigorated," "strengthened or made strong," "impregnated," "animated," and that, according to our passages, is what relics are.

The *Stūpa* as a "Legal Person"

A set of three imprecatory inscriptions on the gateways of *Stūpa* no. 1 at Sāñcī also deserves our attention. The substance of these three inscriptions—which are very much alike and which are as early as at least the first century B.C.E.—is fully expressed in the following passage from the inscription on the West Gateway:

> He who dismantles, or causes to be dismantled, the stone work from this Kākaṇāva [i.e., the old name for the *Stūpa* at Sāñcī], or causes it to be transferred to another house of the teacher, he shall go to the [same terrible] state as those who commit the five sins that have immediate retribution.
>
> *pac-ānatariya-kārakāna gati{ṃ} gacheya yo ito kākaṇāvāto selakame upā{ḍeya} upāḍ{ā}peya vā anaṃ vā ācariyakulaṃ saṃkāmeyā. . . .*[63]

There are two points that should be noted here. First, the *Stūpa* or reliquary at Sāñcī appears to be implicitly classified as an *ācariya-kula,* a "house of the teacher" [i.e., the Buddha]. Bühler long ago suggested that this is a comparable expression, a parallel expression, to the common Indian term for a temple, *devakula,* "a house of the *deva.*" But if this is the case, we know that *devakula* was taken quite literally, that is, it was the place where the *deva* lived, where he was actually and powerfully present, and it is rather unlikely that an *ācariya-kula* would have been conceived of any differently.[64]

The second point to be noted here is that these inscriptions indicate that a set of important ideas known only from later literary sources was already operational at Sāñcī in the first century B.C.E. In a very useful study of the material found in the various monastic codes (*vinayas*) dealing with "la construction et le culte des *stūpas*" Bareau noted that "comme toute personne, le *stūpa* a le droit de possession . . . et ce droit doit être protégé." He goes on to say, for example:

> Les Sarvāstivādin parlent aussi des biens inépuisables du *stūpa,* qui sont inaliénables. Les biens qui sont donnés en offrande au *stūpa* ne peuvent être utilisés à d'autres fins. On ne doit pas les mélanger avec les biens de la Communauté des quatre directions, ni avec les biens consistant en nourriture, ni avec les biens à partager.[65]

From these same texts, it is clear that the property belonging to the *stūpa* or reliquary included real property such as land in the form of gardens with productive fruit and flowering trees and ponds.

What Bareau did not note was that "le droit de possession" of the *stūpa* was referred to and elaborated in sources other than the *Vinayas.* These other sources are important for two reasons: first, they are still later than the *Vinayas* and, therefore, indicate the long continuity of these ideas; second, at least some of these sources must be considered, again, as hostile witnesses since they are Mahāyāna *Sūtras,* the majority of which perhaps are at best ambivalent in regard to the value of relics and *stūpas,* if they are not explicitly engaged in actually devaluing them.[66] The number of these references in Mahāyāna literature is also impressive. Edgerton, under the term *staupika,* cites two passages from the *Śikṣāsamuccaya,* two from the *Bodhisattvabhūmi,* and one each from the *Rāṣṭrapāla* and *Gaṇḍavyūha.*[67] However, there are at least four more in the *Śikṣā* and two also now available in the *Upālipariprcchā.*[68]

The strength of the ideas concerning the *stūpa's* rights of ownership is clear from a long passage from the *Ratnarāśi-sūtra* quoted in the *Śikṣā* (56.9). The substance of this passage is this: although funds of the local order—if there is a surplus and unanimous agreement—can be used to make up a deficit in the ecumenical order (normally such funds must be kept strictly separated), funds belonging to the *stūpa,* even if there is an excess, must never be handed over to either the local or ecumenical order (*yadi punaḥ kāśyapa kiyad bahur api staupiko lābho bhavet / sa vaiyāvṛtyakareṇa na saṃghe na cāturdiśasaṃghe upanāmayitavyaḥ*). The text, in fact, goes so far as to say that "a robe (or piece of cloth) given to the *stūpa must* be allowed to go to ruin on the *stūpa* through the wind and sun and rain," that such a robe cannot be exchanged for a sum of money, and that nothing that belongs to a *stūpa* can have a commercial price set on it (*yac ca stūpe cīvaraṃ niryātitaṃ bhavati tat tatraiva tathāgatacaitye vātātapavṛṣṭibhiḥ parikṣayaṃ gacchatu / na punaḥ staupikaṃ cīvaraṃ hiraṇyamūlyena parivartayitavyaṃ / na hi staupikasya kaścid argho*).[69] The reason given for this is of some interest: "Whatever belongs to a *stūpa,* even if it is only a single fringe that is given . . . that itself is a sacred object for the world together with its gods" (*yā staupikā antaśa ekadaśāpi . . . niryātitā bhavati / sā sadevakasya lokasya caityaṃ*). That is to say, an object given to a *stūpa* becomes itself a sacred object (*caitya*). However, we know that there is only one way for objects to become sacred in a Buddhist context: they must be owned or used by a sacred *person.* In fact, the Chinese version of the above passage translates *staupika* or "belonging to the *stūpa*" by characters which mean "belonging to the Buddha."[70]

We should also notice that some of these Mahāyāna texts—exactly like the gateway inscriptions at Sāñcī—explicitly associate or equate taking property belonging to the *stūpa* with "the five acts with immediate retribution"; for example, this is true of the *Ākāśagarbha-sūtra* and the *Upālipariprcchā.*[71] This, if nothing else, indicates the extremely serious nature of such an act, as these five acts are the most serious offenses known to the Indian Buddhist tradition. However, the association of theft or destruction of property belonging to a *stūpa* with this set of five offenses is probably more than just a way of indicating its terrible seriousness. "The five acts with immediate retribution" are: taking the life of one's mother; taking the life of one's father; taking the life of an *arhat;* causing a division within the *Saṅgha;* and wounding or causing physical harm to a Buddha. Four of the five, then, have to do with seriously harming living persons of rank. That harm done to a *stūpa* or reliquary is explicitly equated with acts of this kind would suggest, again, that the *stūpa* was cognitively classified as a "living person of rank." If this were not the case, it would be difficult to understand the extreme seriousness with which such harm was viewed.

In noting that the *stūpa* or reliquary "comme toute personne" had the right to, and did in fact, possess personal real property, and in noting that the ideas surrounding this right were both old and markedly tenacious, it is of some interest to point out that we find ourselves again in front of a phenomenon noted elsewhere. In discussing the "Thefts of Relics in the Central Middle Ages," Geary repeatedly insists that "in a very basic sense, men in the Central Middle Ages perceived relics as being alive . . . relics were actually the saints themselves, continuing to live among men." One body of evidence he uses to establish this view parallels exactly at least a part of what we have just seen in regard to the Buddhist *stūpa.* He says, "Relics even had legal rights; they received gifts and offerings made specifically to them and owned churches and monasteries, which were technically the property of the saints who lay in their crypts."[72]

The Functional Equivalence of the Relic and the Living Buddha

If Buddhist reliquaries and the relics they contained were legal persons, that is to say, if they had and exercised the rights of living persons, and if harm done to them was explicitly equated with harm done to living persons of rank, then the reverse of the second equation in particular should also hold: honor or worship done to them should be explicitly equated with honor or worship done to living persons. And so it is. An instance of exactly this equation is found, for example, in a text now preserved in the Gilgit *Mūlasarvāstivādin-vinaya,* which has the appearance of being very old. This text, in fact, seems to reflect a period prior to the development of the monumental *stūpa* when relics were simply buried in the ground at specific places.[73]

The text says the Buddha in company with Ānanda went to a place called Toyikā. When he arrived there, there was a *brahmin* plowing his field. This gentleman saw the Buddha and said to himself, "If I approach the Blessed One Gautama and pay honor to him, my work will suffer; but if I do not approach him and pay honor to him, my merit will suffer. What can I do to avoid both a loss of work and a loss of merit?" He decided—being a clever *brahmin*—to remain where he was, but to pay honor to Gautama from a distance, which he did still—as the text pointedly notes—holding his goad. Gautama, of course, was not terribly impressed with this expedient—the text calls it an *upāya*—and he said, in part, to Ānanda:

> 'Mistaken, Ānanda, is this brahmin. Had he approached this spot then when he did honor here, he would himself have known "on this spot the undisturbed mass of relics of the Perfect Buddha Kāśyapa is present." Had he approached I would have been honored by him, indeed honor would have been done by him to two Perfect Buddhas. Why is that? Because, Ānanda, at this spot the undisturbed mass of relics of the Perfect Buddha Kāśyapa is present.'

> *kṣūṇa ānanda eṣa brāhmaṇaḥ / {anenopakramyāsmin pradeśe abhivādane kṛte} sati pratyātmaṃ jñānadarśanaṃ pravartate / etasmin pradeśe kāsyapasya samyaksaṃbuddhasyāvikopito 'sthisaṃghātas tiṣṭhatīti / aham anenopakramya vandito bhaveyam / evam anena dvābhyāṃ samyaksaṃbuddhābhyāṃ vandanā kṛtā bhavet / tatkasya hetoḥ / asminn ānanda pradeśe kāśyapasya samyaksaṃbuddhasyāvikopito 'sthisaṃghātas tiṣṭhati /*[74]

The implications here are that there is no distinction between a living Buddha and a collection of relics—both make the sacred person equally present as an object of worship, and the presence of either makes available the same opportunity to make merit. In case his reader missed the point, the redactor of the text adds a set of verses that make it explicit in slightly different terms:

> He who would worship a living (Buddha), and he who would worship one who has entered final *nirvāṇa,* having made their minds equally devout—between them there is no distinction of merit.
>
> *tiṣṭhantaṃ pūjayed yaś ca yaś cāpi parinirvṛtam / samaṃ cittaṃ prasādyeha nāsti puṇyaviśeṣatā /* 78.8.

That such ideas were both common and durable would seem to be suggested by the fact that this same verse, or close variants of it, occurs in what Waldschmidt calls a "sondertext" of the Sanskrit *Mahāparinirvāṇa-sūtra,* in the *Caityapradakṣiṇa-gāthā* manuscripts of which have been found at Gilgit, in the "Schenkungsformular" manuscript from Turkistan published by Lüders, and in the Khotanese text of the *Pradakṣiṇa-sūtra.*[75] Yet another version of this verse has come down to us in the work of the learned Monk Aśvaghoṣa:

> The learned should know the qualities of the Buddha, and that if one worships with similar devotion the Seer when he is present, or if one worships his relic after he has entered final Nirvāṇa, the result is the same.
>
> *draṅ sroṅ bźugs ba la ni mchod pa sbyaṅ nas sam / yoṅs su mya ṅan 'das pa'i gduṅ la phyag byas nas / yid kyi daṅ ba mñam na 'bras bu mñan pa ste / saṇs rgyas yon tan rnams ni mkhas rnams śes par mdzod /*[76]

Notice that all of these texts emphasize that the individual is to "make his mind equally devout" in regard to the actual presence and the relic (*samaṃ cittaṃ prasādya; same cittaprasāde hi; sems dge ba ni mtshuṅs 'gyur na; yid kyi daṅ ba mñam na;* etc.). That is to say, one is to adopt the same frame of mind toward the relic as is adopted in regard to the living presence. For the believer they are to be taken as the same. They have the same function. They make possible the same result.

It is interesting too to note that one of the clearest expressions of these ideas is to be found in the *Mahāvaṃsa,* the fifth century Pāli chronicle of

Buddhism in Sri Lanka written by the Monk Mahānama. The passage concerned is supposed to be the record of a conversation which took place in the third century B.C.E. between the Monk Mahinda, who is credited with the conversion of Sri Lanka, and the reigning Sri Lankan king, Devānaṃpiyatissa. Mahinda, who according to the *Dīpavaṃsa* is on the verge of leaving Sri Lanka, complains to the king: "For a long time O King, we have not seen the Perfect Buddha, the Teacher. We have lived without a Master. There is nothing here for us to worship"; to which the king replies: "But, sir, did you not tell me that the Perfect Buddha has entered *nirvāṇa?*" The Monk Mahinda answers—and his answer perfectly condenses much of our discussion—"when the relics are seen [or: are present], the Buddha is seen [or: is present]" (*ciradiṭṭho hi saṃbuddho satthā no manujādhipa / anāthavāsaṃ vasimha natthi no pūjiyaṃ idha // bhāsittha nanu bhante me: saṃbuddho nibbuto iti / āha dhātusu diṭṭhesu diṭṭho hoti jino iti*). The king, of course, promises to build a *stūpa,* and Mahinda appoints another monk to fly to India to procure relics.[77]

The Public Value Placed on Relics

Before our findings up to this point are summarized, it is worth looking briefly at one final piece of evidence, not because it provides further indications that the relic was thought of as a living presence—that, I think, is already sufficiently clear—but because it is an early piece of evidence for what we might call, in the absence of a better term, the communal or public value placed on relics. The evidence in question is an old tradition concerning what has come to be called the War of the Relics. Already in the oldest surviving Buddhist art—at Sāñcī, Bhārhut, Amarāvatī, and in Gandhāra—we have illustrations of this episode,[78] although the narrative details are now known only from later texts. After the cremation of the Buddha, the Mallas of Kusinārā "surrounded the bones of the Exalted One in their council hall with a lattice work of spears, and with a rampart of bows." Seven other groups representing distinct and apparently competing political entities also came, however, armed for war to claim a share of the relics. They were initially refused. Interestingly enough, imminent conflict was avoided only by the intervention of a brahmin who pointed out the incongruency of waging war over the remains of one who was a teacher of forbearance (*khantivāda*).[79]

We might note that this old tradition, however the details might fall, forcefully articulates in the strongest possible contemporary political idiom the extreme value placed on these remains. Bareau has noted:

> Qu'elle [this tradition] raconte un fait historique ou qu'elle soit pure légende, peu importe ici, l'essentiel pour notre propos est que . . . les fidèles, dont les hagiographes reflètent l'esprit, ont cru à la réalité de cet épisode,

> ont regardé comme parfaitement vraisemblable que la dévotion de leurs prédécesseurs ait poussé ces derniers à se disputer les restes corporels du bienheureux, les armes à la main. Cela prouve qu'au temps où la première version de ce récit fut composée, les fidèles trouvaient normal et même édifiant un tel excès de zèle . . .[80]

And, but for one small detail, Bareau's remarks are very much to the point: unless he wants to assert that it was written by a layman—and I doubt that he would—"la première version de ce récit," or any other for that matter, can tell us nothing directly about some hypothetical and generalized "fidèles." What it can and does prove, however, is what "les hagiographes" who composed it—almost certainly monks—"trouvaient normal et même édifiant." This, of course, is a very different matter.

Conclusions

Several different kinds of data have been presented here. There are the archaeological data that show a seemingly characteristic, repeatedly encountered configuration of material remains at Buddhist sacred sites. This configuration consists of a central structure marking either a spot known to have been formerly in direct contact with the physical body of the Buddha, or housing an actual part of that physical body. Around this central structure are crowded in increasing disarray large numbers of smaller structures, a considerable number of which contain anonymous mortuary deposits—bone and ash—or other objects known to be associated with mortuary practices. These mortuary deposits have been purposely brought and placed here at different times. They do not form a part of an original or ordered plan.

In addition, an old literary tradition exists that indicates that the Buddha was thought to be actually present at certain spots with which he was known to have had direct physical contact. There is also a whole series of epigraphical and literary documents that prove that the physical relic of the Buddha was thought to be possessed of "life" or "breath," and to be impregnated with the characteristics that defined and animated the living Buddha, that show that the relic or the reliquary that contained it had and exercised the right to own personal property—that it was legally a person—and that it was cognitively classified with living persons of rank. Some of these literary documents, at least one of which is very old, also establish that the presence of the relic was thought to be the same thing as the presence of the actual Buddha, that the two were religiously the same, and that the same behavior was required in regard to both.

This, in turn, means that the central structures at both types of Buddhist sacred sites contained or located the actual living presence of the Buddha, and it was this presence that drew to it the secondary mortuary deposits and a host of subsidiary structures.

Another part of the same old literary tradition proves that it was thought that a death in the presence of the Buddha resulted in rebirth in heaven. In addition, there are the parallels in conception and mortuary practice in the Roman cities of Spain and Africa and on Mount Kōyasan.

We have, it would seem, reason to believe that Indian Buddhists also practiced and believed in some form of what in the Latin West was called *depositio ad sanctos,* and that—regardless of what some canonical texts might occasionally suggest and what some scholastic texts definitely state—the Buddha was and continued to be an actual living presence in the midst of the Buddhist community.

Notes

I would like to thank my colleagues Gérard Fussman and Patrick Olivelle for their helpful comments on different drafts of this paper.

1. There have been other attempts to draw archaeological and art historical sources into the mainstream of Buddhist Studies, most notably those of P. Mus. See the bibliography in G. Moréchand, "Paul Mus (1902–1969)," *BEFEO* 57 (1970) 25–42, but note that Mus' *Barabuḍur. Esquisse d'une histoire du bouddhisme fondée sur la critique archéologique des textes* (Hanoi: 1935), deux tomes, has since been reprinted by Arno Press (New York: 1978), both volumes in one. There are, however, some very real problems with Mus' work. He ignored Indian epigraphy—which is surprising in light of the work he did in Indo-China—and he was very little concerned with chronology. He also used textual material very indiscriminately, citing texts of widely different periods and widely different provenances without ever asking if this material could ever have been known to any actual Buddhist in the premodern period. In religious studies, generally, the last published work of S. G. F. Brandon was also clearly moving in the direction of what I would call the Archaeology of Religions; see Brandon's *Man and God in Art and Ritual. A Study of Iconography, Architecture and Ritual Action as Primary Evidence of Religious Belief and Practice* (New York: 1975).

2. The category "the very special dead" is, of course, borrowed from Peter Brown, *The Cult of the Saints. Its Rise and Function in Latin Christianity* (Chicago: 1981) 69ff. Although he applied it to Christian saints as a whole, I will here be almost exclusively concerned not with Buddhist "saints" as a group, but with the historical Buddha Śākyamuni. This is not to say that there was not a "cult of the saints" or other "very special dead" in Indian Buddhism. There is both epigraphical and archaeological evidence that indicates otherwise, but a discussion of this material must await another time. [See G. Schopen, "An Old Inscription from Amarāvatī," Ch. IX below.]

3. J. Bloch, *Les inscriptions d'Asoka* (Paris: 1950). The Prakrit cited here and below all comes from Bloch's edition. The two inscriptions in question are from Rummindei (Paderia), 157, and Nigālī Sāgar (Nigliva), 158. Unlike the bulk of the Aśokan material, these two inscriptions are not edicts. They, at least together with the Barabar Inscription,

constitute the earliest surviving Indian donative inscriptions. Whether or not the Aśokan material establishes that Bodh–Gayā was an established sacred site at the time of Aśoka depends very much on how one interprets the word *saṃbodhi* in the 8th Rock Edict. Since A. L. Basham reopened the question, it has yet to be resolved; see "Saṃbodhi in Aśoka's 8th Rock Edict," *JIABS* 2 (1979) 81–83. Therefore, this is not taken into account here, although my own position is much closer to the one most recently expressed by R. Lingat, "Encore *ayāya saṃbodhim* à propos de l'inscription gréco-araméenne d'Aśoka," *JA* (1967) 195–198.

4. On the Past Buddhas, see J. Ph. Vogel, "The Past Buddhas and Kāśyapa in Indian Art and Epigraphy," *Asiatica Festschrift Friedrich Weller* (Leipzig: 1954) 808–816; R. Gombrich, "The Significance of Former Buddhas in the Theravādin Tradition," *Buddhist Studies in Honour of Walpola Rahula,* ed. S. Balasooriya et al. (London: 1980) 62–72; A. Vergati, "Le culte et l'iconographie du buddha dīpankara dans la vallée de Kathmandou," *Arts asiatiques* 37 (1982) 22–27.

5. See, for example, Bloch, *Les inscriptions d'Asoka,* 49, 157, nn. 2 and 4. Note that Aśoka here uses the absolutive form of *ā√gam* to describe his coming to Lummini, and, according to Bloch's index, this root is used only here and in the related Nigālī Sāgar inscription. Both the Sanskrit and Pāli versions of our passage also use forms of *ā√gam.* Note too that while neither of the two instances of the *hida* statement in Aśoka corresponds with the Pāli, the second, *hida bhagavaṃ jāte,* corresponds exactly with the Sanskrit *iha bhagavāñ jātaḥ.*

6. I here refer to, and cite throughout, the Sanskrit version of the *Mahāparinirvāṇa-Sūtra* edited by E. Waldschmidt (*Das Mahāparinirvāṇasūtra,* Teil I, II, III, Abh. DAW Berlin, Kl. f. Spr., Lit. u. Kunst, Jg. 1949, No. 1; Jg. 1950, No. 2 und Jg. 1950, No. 3 [Berlin: 1950, 1951, 1951]; I cite the text according to Waldschmidt's paragraph numbers). Since the Sanskrit text is based primarily on the Turfan materials, this means that we have actual manuscripts for it that are centuries earlier than anything we have for the Pāli text, and, in this sense at least, its readings are the earliest actually attestable readings that we have for the text in an Indian language. On the Turfan manuscript material, see L. Sander, *Paläographisches zu den Sanskrithandschriften der Berliner Turfan-sammlung,* Verzeichnis der Orientalischen Handschriften in Deutschland, Supplementband 8 (Wiesbaden: 1968). For Pāli manuscripts, see H. Smith, *Saddanīti, La grammaire palie d'aggavaṃsa* (Lund: 1928) v; O. von Hinüber, "On the Tradition of Pāli Texts in India, Ceylon and Burma," *Buddhism in Ceylon and Studies on Religious Syncretism in Buddhist Countries,* Abh. d. Akad. d. Wiss. in Göttingen, Phil.-Hist. Kl. Dritte Folge. Nr. 108, ed. H. Bechert (Göttingen: 1978) 48: "The big gap between the first redaction of our Pāli canon and the basis of the texts as we have them today, becomes evident at once, if we bear in mind that there is no manuscript older than about 400 years, with the only exception, as far as I know, of a tenth century Vinaya-fragment in Pāli found in Nepal." [See O. von Hinüber, *The Oldest Pāli Manuscript. Four Folios of the Vinaya Piṭaka from the National Archives, Kathmandu,* Akademie der Wissenschaften und der Literatur, Mainz, Abhandlungen der Geistes- und Sozialwissenschaftlichen Klasse, Jahrgang 1991, Nr. 6 (Stuttgart: 1991).] More recently, von Hinüber has said "that most of the surviving manuscript material [for the Pāli canon] is hardly older than the late 18th century." He also refers to "an extremely old manuscript dated as early as A.D. 1412," and adds "if this date is correct, this would be the oldest dated Pāli manuscript known so far" in "Pāli Manuscripts of Canonical Texts From North Thailand—A Preliminary Report," *Journal of the Siam Society* 71 (1983) 78. Note too that, in terms of Pāli literature, a

slightly shorter version of the *Mahāparinibbāna* passage on pilgrimage also occurs at *Aṅguttara,* ii, 120. In light of these passages, it is difficult to understand what A. Bharati meant when he said, "Although pilgrimage figures importantly in the religions of India, it never had any canonical status in non-tantric traditions" (*The Tantric Tradition* [London: 1965] 85).

7. Waldschmidt's *anusmaraṇīyā* appears to be reconstructed on the basis of Tibetan *rjes su dran par 'gyur bar bya.* In fact, in neither of the two manuscript fragments for 41.5 has the actual reading been preserved. But in the restatement of 41.5 that occurs in 41.10, the one manuscript in which the actual reading has been preserved has quite clearly *abhigamanīyā;* see Teil I, 43, 113.2. Note that this passage of the *Mahāparinirvāṇa-Sūtra* has been reedited by F. Edgerton in *Buddhist Hybrid Sanskrit Reader* (New Haven: 1953) 34–35; cf. n. 14 below.

8. For the range of meanings of *saṃvejanīya,* "to be powerfully experienced," see A. K. Coomaraswamy, "*Saṃvega:* Aesthetic Shock," *HJAS* 7 (1943) 174–179, repr. in *Coomaraswamy* 1. *Selected Papers. Traditional Art and Symbolism,* ed. R. Lipsey (Princeton: 1977) 179–185. He translates *saṃvejanīya* from our passages of the *Mahāparinibbāna-sutta* as "should be deeply moved." For an interesting use of *vega/pravega* in early Mahāyāna *sūtra* literature, see *Vajracchedikā Prajñāpāramitā* (Conze ed.) 14A: *atha khalv āyuṣmān subhūtir dharmavegenāśrūṇi* [the Gilgit text has *-pravegenā-*] *prāmuñcat,* etc.

9. J. Gonda has clearly demonstrated the antiquity of many of the ideas that most secondary literature associates only with the much later "classical" *bhakti* conception of *darśan* in *Eye and Gaze in the Veda,* Verhandelingen der Koninklijke Nederlandse Akademie van Wetenschappen, Afd. LetterKunds. Nieuwe Reeks-Deel 75 (Amsterdam: 1970). On *darśan* generally, see the fine little book by D. L. Eck, *Darśan. Seeing the Divine Image in India* (Chambersburg: 1981). In light of the pervasiveness and age of these Indian ideas about "seeing" and what it entails, it would appear that many of our translations, at the very least, miss the nuance and may, in fact, miss the whole point. The exhortation that Ānanda was directed by the Buddha to deliver to the Mallas is a good example. Ānanda was told to go and tell the Mallas that the Buddha would enter *parinibbāna* during the last watch of that night, and he was supposed to say to them: *abhikkhamatha . . . abhikkhamatha . . . mā pacchā vippaṭisārino ahuvattha: amhākañ ca no gāmakkhette tathāgatassa parinibbānaṃ ahosi, na mayaṃ labhimhā pacchime kāle tathāgataṃ dassanāyâti,* which Rhys Davids translates as: "Be favourable . . . be favourable. Give no occasion to reproach yourselves hereafter, saying: 'In our own village did the death of our Tathāgata take place, and we took not the opportunity of visiting the Tathāgata in his last hours' "; see T. W. and C. A. F. Rhys Davids, *Dialogues of the Buddha,* Pt. II (London: 1910) 162. The Rhys Davids' translation is, of course, not really wrong, but unless the reader has the etymology of the English word clearly in mind, to translate *dassana* by "visit," from Latin, *visere* "to go to see," *videre, visum* "to see," is at best terribly flat. In a culture where "casting one's eyes upon a person and touching him were related activities" (Gonda, 19), where there was strong "belief in the beneficial results of visual contact" (46), and where there were large numbers of old "ritual texts prescribing a conscious and directed look by which the spectator was . . . believed to benefit, or ritual acts performed to derive some advantage from looking on a mighty being . . . to participate in its nature or essence, to be purified or raised to a higher level of existence by being *vis-à-vis* with such a man" (55)—in such a culture, to go to "see" a man, especially an exceptionally holy man, clearly involves much more than a "visit." In fact, the Upavāṇa Incident in the *Mahāparinibbāna-sutta* makes it absolutely clear that, for this text, the important

aspect of *dassana* was direct visual contact and that such contact was very highly valued. In this remarkable incident, the Buddha is lying on his deathbed and the Monk Upavāṇa is standing in front of him fanning him. But then the Buddha "spoke harshly" to Upavāṇa (*apasādesi*—a very strong verb and an action very uncharacteristic of the textual Buddha), saying "Get away, Monk! Don't stand in front of me!" (*apehi bhikkhu mā me purato aṭṭhāsīti*). Ānanda is puzzled (shocked, cf. Skt. 35.4) and asks about the Buddha's behavior. The latter calmly explains that the *devas* from all the ten directions have come together to gaze upon/behold/see him (*devatā sannipatitā tathāgataṃ dassanāya*), but they are "grumbling" (*ujjhāyanti*), saying "we have come from great distances to gaze upon/etc. the Tathāgata . . . but this eminent Monk standing in front of the Blessed One is preventing it and we do not get to gaze on the Tathāgata in his final moments" (*na mayaṃ labhāma pacchime kāle tathāgataṃ dassanāyâti*). Clearly, here again the *devas* did not come simply "to visit," and, in fact, here Rhys Davids was almost forced to translate *dassana* as "behold." It is also worth noting that there is Buddhist evidence for other aspects of the conception of *darśan* usually associated with mediaeval *bhakti* which is, relatively speaking, much earlier. Both Coomaraswamy (*Mediaeval Sinhalese Art,* 2nd ed. [New York: 1956] 70–75) and Gombrich ("The Consecration of a Buddhist Image," *The Journal of Asian Studies* 26 [1966] 23–36) have pointed out that Buddhaghosa, already in the fifth century C.E., refers to the ritual empowerment of an image by painting in its eyes, and there is a clear allusion to the same idea in the *Ratnaguṇasaṃcayagāthā* (Yuyama ed.) VII.2 that is almost certainly several centuries earlier than Buddhaghosa.

10. A. Cunningham, *Mahābodhi or the Great Buddhist Temple under the Bodhi Tree at Buddha-Gaya* (London: 1892) 82–83; B. M. Barua, "Old Buddhist Shrines at Bodh-Gayā," *IHQ* 6 (1930) 30–31. There may, in fact, have been several more inscriptions of roughly the same period that refer to *darśan,* but it is not possible to be sure from Cunningham's presentation. He says that in Slabs F and G, "The pilgrim offers his adoration to Mahābodhi, for the benefit of his father and mother," but he does not give the actual reading of the inscriptions. Since, however, he translates . . . *jina dasakena sri man mahābodhi bhandāraka darsana kritam yadatra punyam tad bhavati mātapittri purvaga* . . . as " . . . Jina Dasaka . . . adoration was made at the Temple of Sri-man Mahābodhi, for the benefit of his father and mother, etc." (83), it is possible that F and G also had this same reading; see Barua for a much better reading of Slabs F and G.

11. In H. Lüders, *A List of Brahmi Inscriptions from the Earliest Times to about A.D. 400 with the Exception of Those of Aśoka,* Appendix to *EI* 10 (Calcutta: 1912) no. 1223, a gift made by "The Elder *(thera),* the Chaitya worshipper *(Chetiyavaṃdaka) bhayaṃta (bhadanta)* Budhi"; no. 1263, a gift made by "Papin (Pāpin), brother of *bhayaṃta (bhadanta)* Budhi (Buddhi), the Chaitya worshipper *(Chetiavadaka).*" As both of these inscriptions come from Amarāvatī and are roughly contemporaneous, there is a good chance that the monk named Budhi referred to in both is the same person. But if this is true, there is an equally good chance that the Monk Budhi who is called a *cetiyavandaka* in these two inscriptions is the same Monk Budhi who is called a *mahāvinayadhara,* "a great preserver/knower of the Vinaya," in two other contemporaneous Amarāvatī inscriptions found in Lüders, no. 1270, and in H. Sarkar, "Some Early Inscriptions in the Amarāvatī Museum," *JAIH* 4 (1970–1971) 9, no. 63, and a *dhamakathika,* "a preacher of Dharma," in a third inscription in Lüders, no. 1267. This would seem to indicate that some, at least, of the "honorers of shrines" were the acknowledged transmitters of Buddhist doctrine and monastic rules and monks of considerable standing.

12. In the Pāli canon, in the *Araṇavibhaṅgasutta* (*Majjhima,* iii, 237), the Monk Subhūti is called a *kulaputta;* in the *Dhātuvibhaṅga-sutta* (*Majjhima,* iii, 238–247), the Monk Pukkasāti is repeatedly referred to as a *kulaputta;* in a recurring "arhat formula," *kulaputtas* are the ones said to properly go forth from the house to the houseless state (*Aṅguttara,* i, 282; *Dīgha,* ii, 153; etc.); etc. In very early Mahāyāna *sūtra* literature, it is clear that not only did the title *kulaputra* apply both to monks and laymen, but it was also a title that could be applied to followers of both what we usually call the Mahāyāna and the Hīnayāna. In the *Pratyutpannabuddhasaṃmukhāvasthitasamādhisūtra, byaṅ chub sems dpa' khyim pa 'am/ rab tu byuṅ ba,* "both householder and renunciant bodhisattvas," are equated with *rigs kyi bu 'am rigs kyi bu mo,* "sons and daughters of good family"; see P. M. Harrison, *The Tibetan Text of the Pratyutpannabuddhasaṃmukhāvasthitasamādhisūtra* (Tokyo: 1978) 7B; see also 8G, where *kulaputras* who seek arhatship are referred to; 9E, which refers to *kulaputras* who are "adherents of the *Śrāvakayāna*"; etc. Likewise, in the equally early *Akṣobhyatathāgatasya-vyūha,* we find *byaṅ chub sems dpa'i theg pa pa daṅ ñan thos kyi theg pa pa'i rigs kyi bu 'am/rigs kyi bu mo gaṅ dag khyim gyi gnas nas ṅes par byuṅ źiṅ rab tu byuṅ bar gyur pa dag . . . Peking,* 22, 132-5-4; cf. 137-1-2, 154-4-6, 156-1-7, 2-3, 3-1, etc. On this important but until recently little studied text, see now J. Dantinne, *La splendeur de l'inébranlable (Akṣobhyavyūha),* T. I (Louvain-la-neuve: 1983). For a much later occurrence, see *Suvikrāntavikrāmiparipṛcchā* (Hikata ed.) 64.14.

13. See Barua's "Old Buddhist Shrines at Bodh-Gayā," 6ff, esp. 20, and his "A Bodh-Gayā Image Inscription," *IHQ* 9 (1933) 416–419. A Kushan inscription records the gift of a monk who is called a *dharmakathika,* "preacher of *Dharma,*" and who is associated with a *vinayadhara,* a "preserver/transmitter of the Vinaya"; see J. F. Fleet, *Inscriptions of the Early Gupta Kings and Their Successors,* Corpus Inscriptionum Indicarum, Vol. III (Calcutta: 1888) nos. 71, 72, 76.

14. A. Wayman translates the Sanskrit *atrāntarā ye kecit prasannacittā mamāntike kālaṃ kariṣyanti,* etc., as "among these places, whoever with pure thought will die in my presence, all those belong to heaven *(svarga),* whoever are with remainder" in "Buddhism," *Historia Religionum. Handbook for the History of Religions,* Vol. II, ed. C. J. Bleeker and G. Widengren (Leiden: 1971) 401, taking *kālaṃ kariṣyanti* as that which takes place *mamāntike* and not *prasannacittā.* This is worth noting because the Tibetan translation appears to do just the opposite: *kha cig ṅa la sems dad pas dus byas pa* (v. 1. *te*) *de thams cad mtho ris su 'gro'o / kha cig ni phuṅ po lhag ma daṅ bcas par ro,* "Some with devout thoughts in regard to me die, they all go to heaven. Some are possessed with a substratum (i.e., still have *karma* to work out)." But the Tibetan is either translating a Sanskrit text that differs from the one we have, or it is only a very loose rendering. It has nothing corresponding to *atrāntarā,* and it suggests a text that read: *ye kecin mamāntike prasannacittāḥ kālaṃ kariṣyanti.* The genitive + *antike* can of course mean "in regard to," but Edgerton's examples in *BHSD,* 40, make it clear that the genitive + *antike* is always followed by and never preceded by the action concerned: *daridrapuruṣas tasya gṛhapater antike pitṛsaṃjñāṃ utpādayet,* SP 107.4; *devānām . . . antike cittāni pradūṣayitvā,* Mv i 30.9; etc. This is the construction regardless of the sense in which *antike* is used, and this makes it difficult to see in *mamāntike kālaṃ kariṣyanti* anything but "those who will die in my presence." To say "those who will die in regard to/in reference to me" makes no sense. It is possible, however, that the Tibetan translation did not result from the fact that it was based on a different original, nor from a misunderstanding. It may represent an intentional alteration of the text. Notice that the Tibetan corresponding to 41.9, as well as—if not more so than—that corresponding to 41.14 (*kha cig ni ṅa la sems dad pas dus byas pa* [v. 1. *te*]

de thams cad mtho ris su 'gro'o / kha cig ni phuṅ po lhag ma daṅ bcas par ro / ji ltar mṅon du 'gro bar bya ba de ltar rjes su dran par bya'o) looks very much like an attempt to retain the benefit of rebirth in heaven while no longer requiring an actual pilgrimage. The Tibetan appears to want to make a *mental* pilgrimage equal to the *actual* pilgrimage, or at least to make the former an option. Notice that its *ji ltar mṅon du 'gro bar bya ba de ltar rjes su dran par bya'o* is clearly an addition. There is nothing corresponding to it in either Sanskrit or Pāli and, while we do not actually have manuscript readings for the Sanskrit of 41.5, where the Pāli has *dassanīyāni saṃvejanīyāni,* i.e., a reference to direct visual contact, the Tibetan has *rjes su dran par 'gyur bar bya'o* = *anusmaraṇīya,* meaning "mental recalling" or "visualization." When we do have an actual manuscript reading for the Sanskrit, as in 41.10, it is *abhigamanīya.* The substitution or option that the Tibetan translation appears to be introducing is also clearly visible in the Chinese version of the text translated by Waldschmidt: "Wenn man an diesen vier Plätzen entweder persönlich seine Verehrung bezeigt oder (ihnen) aus der Ferne seine Achtung übermittelt, sehnsuchtsvoll und aufrichtig reinen Glauben entstehen lässt und beständig die Gedanken daran heftet, wird man nach Lebensende Geburt im Himmel erlangen." Here too, one can *either* go in person to the four places *or* call them to mind from afar; cf. A. Bareau, *Recherches sur la biographie du Buddha dans les sūtrapiṭaka et les vinayapiṭaka anciens: II Les derniers mois, le parinirvāṇa et les funérailles,* T. II (Paris: 1971) 29–32. Bareau, however, takes Waldschmidt's reconstructed *anusmaraṇīya* at 41.5 without comment, and this affects some of what he says. All of this would seem to suggest that, as long as the text remained in India, the original readings like *dassanīya, saṃvejanīya,* and probably *abhigamanīya*—all of which required actual pilgrimage—were not a problem, but that when the texts moved outside of India—where actual pilgrimage would have been extremely difficult—new readings, like *anusmaraṇīya,* and new options, like visualization "aus der Ferne," had to be introduced into the text. It is in this light, I think, that the Tibetan translation and some of the Chinese translations of our passage are to be viewed. There were, of course, other ways of dealing with the problem of actual pilgrimage. See, for example, the interesting paper by A. B. Griswold, "The Holy Land Transported: Replicas of the Mahābodhi Shrine in Siam and Elsewhere," *Paranavitana Felicitation Volume,* ed. N. A. Jayawickrama (Colombo: 1965) 173–222.

15. Cunningham, *Mahābodhi,* 46–49; for a recent study of the surviving "minor" *stūpas* at Bodh-Gayā, see M. Bénesti, *Contribution à l'étude du stūpa bouddhique indien: les stūpa mineurs de Bodh-gayā et de Ratnagiri,* T. I and II (Paris: 1981).

16. J. Marshall, *Taxila: An Illustrated Account of Archaeological Excavations Carried Out at Taxila under the Orders of the Government of India between the Years 1913 and 1934,* Vol. I (Cambridge: 1951) 235; see Vol. III, pl. 45, for a clear ground plan of the whole Dharmarājikā complex.

17. Marshall, *Taxila,* Vol. I, 368–387; see Vol. III, pl. 101, for the ground plan of Jauliāñ. A slightly fuller acccount of the excavations at Jauliāñ had been published earlier in J. Marshall, *Excavations at Taxila: The Stūpas and Monasteries at Jauliāñ,* MASI, No. 7 (Calcutta: 1921).

18. H. Cousens, *The Antiquities of Sind,* Archaeological Survey of India, Vol. XLVI, Imperial Series (Calcutta: 1929) 82–97; D. R. Bhandarkar, "Excavations near Mirpur Khās," *Progress Report of the Archaeological Survey of India, Western Circle, for the Year Ending 31st March, 1917,* 47–48; D. Mitra, *Buddhist Monuments* (Calcutta: 1971) 132–133.

19. J. Marshall, *A Guide to Sanchi* (Calcutta: 1918) 87–88.

20. Marshall, *Taxila,* Vol. I, 240ff. Marshall does not specifically describe all the earliest smaller *stūpas,* but of those that he does all contain bone or ash (i.e., R5, S8, S9, B6, B3). Other contemporary *stūpas* that contain bone or ash are J2, N7, and Q1. *Stūpas* of varying date scattered around the complex that are specially said to contain "relic" deposits are G4, G5, T12, K3, P6, S10, N11, N10, N9, P10, P12, U1.

21. See, for example, "The Piprāhwā Buddhist Vase Inscription" in Lüders, *List,* no. 931, with bibliography; G. Bühler, "The Bhattiprolu Inscriptions," *EI* 2 (1894) 323–329; J. Ph. Vogel, "Prakrit Inscriptions from a Buddhist Site at Nagarjunikonda," *EI* 20 (1929–1930) 1–36 (where the *stūpa* itself appears to be repeatedly described as containing the relics of the Buddha, although Vogel, I think, has misunderstood this and the construction is somewhat odd; see Āyaka Pillar Inscriptions C3, B2, B4, B5, C2, C4, C5. The key instance for the correct interpretation of the construction appears to be the First Apsidal Temple Inscription E: *saṃma-saṃbudhasa dhātuparigahitasa mahāchet-iya-pādamūle*); R. Salomon and G. Schopen, "The Indravarman (Avaca) Casket Inscription Reconsidered: Further Evidence for Canonical Passages in Buddhist Inscriptions," *JIABS* 7 (1984) 107–123; P. R. Srinivasan, "Devni-Mori Relic Casket Inscription of Rudrasena, Kathika Year 127," *EI* 37 (1967) 67–69; etc.

22. Marshall, *Taxila,* Vol. I, 373, A11; 373, D5; 374, A16. There was also at least one reliquary found in the debris between *Stūpas* A7 and A8.

23. Mitra, *Buddhist Monuments,* 133; Cousens, *The Antiquities of Sind,* 97.

24. Marshall, *A Guide to Sanchi,* 88.

25. Cunningham, *Mahābodhi,* 48–49.

26. A. Ghosh, ed., *Indian Archaeology 1957–58—A Review* (New Delhi: 1958) 39–41, pls. XLIX–LIII; D. Mitra, "Ratnagiri. Unearthing of a New Buddhist Site in Orissa," *Indo-Asian Culture* 9 (1960) 160–175; D. Mitra, *Ratnagiri (1958–61),* Vol. I, MASI, no. 80 (New Delhi: 1981). For the configuration and numbers of the smaller *stūpas* around the main *stūpa* at Ratnagiri, see the siteplan of the *stūpa* area, Mitra, *Ratnagiri,* 26, fig. 3; this can be compared with that for Bodh-Gayā published by Cunningham, *Mahābodhi,* pl. XVIII. For a study of the smaller *stūpas* at Ratnagiri, see M. Bénisti, *Contribution à l'étude du stūpa bouddhique indien,* T. 1, 93ff, figs. 119ff, and Mitra, *Ratnagiri,* 44–138, pls. LX–LXXXI.

27. See Mitra, *Ratnagiri,* pls. IX, XX–XXI, XXXIV, XLII, LVI–LVIII, etc.

28. I-tsing, *A Record of the Buddhist Religion as Practised in India and the Malay Archipelago (A.D. 671–695),* trans. J. Takakusu (London: 1896; repr. 1966) 82. An additional, but I do not think an alternative, explanation for the absence of a finial on *some* Buddhist votive *stūpas* is suggested by U. Wiesner in "Nepalese Votive Stūpas of the Licchavi Period: The Empty Niche," *The Stūpa—Its Religious, Historical and Architectural Significance,* Bieträge zur Südasien-Forschung Südasien-Institut Universität Heidelberg 55, ed. A. L. Dallapiccola et al. (Wiesbaden: 1980) 170–172. What Wiesner says about an intentional sectarian "revision" of the form of the *stūpa,* however, *could* only apply to those found on the surface. The vast majority of the *stūpas* we are concerned with only came to light during excavation, having been covered over by newer levels of building.

29. Mitra, *Indo–Asian Culture* 9 (1960) 166.

30. Notice that Mitra, in the final excavation report published (*Ratnagiri,* 31–32), comes close to suggesting something similar. She says first that "a limited number of these monolithic *stūpas* were doubtless used for enshrining the bone-relics of the departed: for this purpose they were provided with sockets, usually at the base, to hold charred bones." However, she then adds that "most of the sockets of these *śārīrika stūpas* were

found empty, and only a few (*stūpas* 112 and 188 for instance), which were found plugged by stone blocks, retained the relics." This raises the real possibility that many more might have contained relics, a possibility that she clearly states in discussing the structural *stūpas,* as we will see below. Notice too that she incidently notes (44n) that "the relics were noticed mostly during the conservation of the *stūpas,*" i.e., the possibilities of the presence of bone deposits were not in any way systematically studied.

31. G. Schopen, "The Text on the 'Dhāraṇī Stones from Abhayagiriya': A Minor Contribution to the Study of Mahāyāna Literature in Ceylon," *JIABS* 5 (1982) 100–108; G. Schopen, "The Bodhigarbhālaṅkāralakṣa and Vimaloṣṇīṣa Dhāraṇīs in Indian Inscriptions: Two Sources for the Practice of Buddhism in Medieval India," *WZKS* 29 (1985) 119–149. In the second of these papers, I was able to show that the "*dhāraṇī*-text" on the Cuttack Stone Inscription published by A. Ghosh (*EI* 26 [1941] 171–174) was an incomplete Sanskrit version of a text called the *Bodhigarbhālaṅkāralakṣadhāraṇī.* Although Mitra refers to Ghosh (*Ratnagiri,* 31), she apparently did not recognize that the two *dhāraṇīs* found on eight plaques at Ratnagiri that she transliterated (43, 99) were the same *dhāraṇī* that he had transliterated. The same *dhāraṇī* is also found on at least two plaques from Nālandā and on a "cachet" from Qunduz.

32. *'Phags pa 'od zer dri ma med pa rnam par dag pa'i 'od ces bya ba'i gzuṅs, Peking,* 7, 190-1-4. It is interesting to note that the two earliest known examples of printing—one from Korea and one from Japan—both contain the *Raśmivimala,* and in both countries were found inside *stūpas;* see L. Carrington Goodrich, "Printing: Preliminary Report on a New Discovery," *Technology and Culture* 9 (1967) 376–378; T. F. Carter, *The Invention of Printing in China and Its Spread Westward,* 2nd ed. rev. L. Carrington Goodrich (New York: 1955) 46–53; B. Hickman, "A Note on the Hyakumantō Dhāraṇī," *Monumenta Nipponica* 30 (1975) 87–93.

33. *'Phags pa las kyi sgrib pa thams cad rnam par sbyoṅ ba źes bya ba'i gzuṅs, Peking,* 11, 252-1-6. It is very likely that the *dhāraṇī* from this text was one of the *dhāraṇīs* deposited by the Monk Bu Ston in the *stūpa* he built for his deceased mother; see D. S. Ruegg, *The Life of Bu Ston Rin Po Che, With the Tibetan Text of the Bu Ston rNam Thar,* Serie Orientale Roma, XXXIV (Rome: 1966) fol. 29a, 5 and 136.

34. T. Skorupski, *The Sarvadurgatipariśodhana Tantra* (Delhi: 1983). Notice that, although the *dramatis personae* and the setting differ in each case, the *Raśmivimalaviśuddhaprabha,* the *Samantamukhapraveśaraśmivimaloṣṇīṣaprabhāsasarvatathāgatahṛdayasamayavilokita* (*Peking,* 7, no. 206), and the *Sarvadurgatipariśodhanī-uṣṇīṣavijaya* (*Peking,* 7, no. 198) *dhāraṇīs* and the *Sarvadurgatipariśodhana Tantra* (Skorupski, 4, 122.29ff) are all introduced by essentially the same thematic kind of narrative. The introductions to the *dhāraṇīs* are summarized in *Mkhas Grub Rje's Fundamentals of the Buddhist Tantras. Rgyud sde spyiḥi rnam par gźag pa rgyas par brjod,* trans. F. D. Lessing and A. Wayman (The Hague: 1968) 104–107, 115–117. On *dhāraṇīs* in funerary rites in the *Sarvadurgati Tantra,* see Skorupski, 81, 242.22ff.

35. Mitra, *Ratnagiri,* 28. For a brief description of three of the "dislocated reliquaries," see 28–29.

36. Mitra, *Ratnagiri,* 43, 98–99. It should be noted that a more complete and systematic survey of Buddhist sites than the one I have been able to present here promises—despite the deficiencies of much of the published archaeological literature—to produce much fuller evidence for the funerary functions of the minor *stūpas* found at almost all Buddhist sites. For now I can only mention the following points. It is possible that "les stūpa à avancée" or "les stūpa à cella" which occur at both Bodh-Gayā

(Cunningham, *Mahābodhi,* 48, pl. XXIII.k; Bénisti, *Contribution à l'étude du stūpa,* T. i, 20–22; T. ii, figs. 23–26, 28, 29, 31, 33) and Ratnagiri (Mitra, *Ratnagiri,* pls. XXIa. 102, XXIb. 107, XLVIIA.228) and which have been taken—on very weak evidence—to have been meant for images, may, in fact, have been intended and used for funerary deposits. It has been reported, at least at Mainamati, that "the hoard of miniature baked and unbaked clay stūpas" found there "contained bone relics or small sealings or sometimes both" ("Mainamati Excavations," *Pakistan Archaeology* 5 [1968] 173). These miniature *stūpas* have a very wide distribution indeed; see M. Taddei, "Inscribed Clay Tablets and Miniature Stūpas from Gaznī," *EW* 20 (1970) 85–86. Finally, G. Fussman has already published two Kharoṣṭhī inscriptions that he thinks are funerary in "Une inscription kharoṣṭhī à Haḍḍa," *BEFEO* 56 (1969) 5–9, and "Documents épigraphiques kouchans," *BEFEO* 61 (1974) 58–61. There are, according to a personal communication from Prof. Fussman, also a number of similar inscriptions from Haḍḍa that have yet to be published. A. H. Dani has also published a number of Kharoṣṭhī inscriptions that appear to be funerary in "Shaikhan Dheri Excavation (1963 and 1964 Seasons)," *Ancient Pakistan* 2 (1965–1966) 109–113. All of these things deserve to be studied much more fully.

37. Mitra, however, has indicated that, at Ratnagiri at least, there is some evidence to indicate that the "portable monolithic *stūpas*" were made locally (*Ratnagiri,* 32).

38. P. Ariès, *Western Attitudes Towards Death: From the Middle Ages to the Present* (Baltimore: 1974) 16–17.

39. P. Ariès, *The Hour of Our Death* (New York: 1981) 34.

40. U. A. Casal, "The Saintly Kōbō Daishi in Popular Lore (A.D. 774–835)," *Journal of Far Eastern Folklore. Folklore Studies* 18 (1959) 143.

41. P. Geary, *Furta Sacra. Thefts of Relics in the Central Middle Ages* (Princeton: 1978) 33–34; see also S. Wilson's Introduction to *Saints and Their Cults. Studies in Religious Sociology, Folklore and History,* ed. S. Wilson (Cambridge: 1983) 10.

42. A. Lloyd, "Death and Disposal of the Dead (Japanese)," *Encyclopaedia of Religion and Ethics,* Vol. 4, ed. J. Hastings (Edinburgh: 1911) 491; see also Casal, "The Saintly Kōbō Daishi," 139, 143.

43. Y. S. Hakeda, *Kukai: Major Works* (New York: 1972) 60.

44. O. Statler, *Japanese Pilgrimage* (New York: 1983) 94–96, 128, 175, etc., taking as his "basic source" S. Gorai, *Koya Hijiri* (Tokyo: 1965).

45. Wilson, *Saints and Their Cults,* 11; see also P. Brown, *The Cult of the Saints. Its Rise and Function in Latin Christianity* (Chicago: 1981) 3–4.

46. Ariès, *The Hour of Our Death,* 33.

47. There is, of course, the old story of Kāśyapa awaiting the coming of Maitreya entombed in the "Kukkuṭapada" or "Gurupada" mountain that has some obvious similarities with some of the ideas connected with Kōbō Daishi; see T. Watters, *On Yuan Chwang's Travels in India,* Vol. II (London: 1905) 143ff, and literature cited therein, but this has nothing to do with relics as such. Outside of India, G. Obeyesekere refers to a "Sinhalese myth which states that in the flood that heralds the destruction of this age all the Buddha *dhātu* found in various parts of the world will assemble together through *ridhi* and the Buddha himself will be refashioned out of these substances. He will then utter a last sermon" ("The Buddhist Pantheon in Ceylon and Its Extensions," *Anthropological Studies in Theravada Buddhism* [New Haven: 1966] 9). M. E. Spiro cites several instances of a similar "myth" in Burma: "Just prior to his [Maitreya's] arrival, the relics of the present Buddha, Gautama, will be recombined to form his physical body. By worshiping him, the *weikza* will automatically achieve nirvana" (*Burmese Supernaturalism. A Study in the*

Explanation and Reduction of Suffering [Englewood Cliffs: 1967] 231, 165–66, 191). The Indian antecedents of the Sri Lankan and Burmese materials are very vague. Both are undoubtedly related to the *Anāgatavaṃsa;* see J. Minayeff, "Anāgatavaṃsa," *JPTS* (1886) 36; cf. H. C. Warren, *Buddhism in Translation* (Cambridge: 1896) 484–485, but this text is itself sometimes presented as a *sutta* (e.g., Minayeff's Ms. B from Rangoon) while at other times it is considered an authored work attributed to a Coḷiyan monk named Kassapa who probably lived between 1160 and 1230 C.E.; see J. Minayeff, "The Gandha-Vaṃsa," *JPTS* (1886) 60–61, 66, 70; A. P Buddhadatta and A. K. Warder, *Mohavicchedanī Abhidhammamātikatthavaṇṇanā* (London: 1961) x–xi, xvi–xviii. The *Anāgatavaṃsa* itself clearly owes much to Buddhaghosa's *Manorathapūraṇī* (*Histoire du bouddhisme indien,* 216). To complicate matters even further, two versions of an *Anāgatavaṃsa* exist in the Tibetan Kanjur (*Peking,* nos. 751 and 1010), both of which were co-translated by a Sri Lankan Monk, Ānandaśrī, in the thirteenth century; see G. Schopen, "Hīnayāna Texts in a 14th Century Persian Chronicle: Notes on Some of Rashid al'Din's Sources," *Central Asiatic Journal* 26 (1982) 231, n. 9, and sources cited therein; and S. Lévi, "Maitreya le consolateur," *Études d'orientalisme publiées par le musée guimet à la mémoire de Raymonde Linossier,* T. II (Paris: 1932) 379–380; Lévi's discussion of the Tibetan translations, 377, needs, in part, to be corrected. Sorting all this out requires and deserves a good deal of future work, but it would appear at this stage that the ideas expressed in the *Anāgatavaṃsa,* etc., are too late to have had any real formative role in producing the archaeological configuration that concerns us.

48. See D. L. Eck, *Banaras: City of Light* (New York: 1982) 215: "Those who die in Kāshī, assured of liberation, will be cremated on the banks of the river of Heaven at this most sacred of *tīrthas.* If one cannot die in Kāshī, then cremation by the Ganges anywhere along her banks is desirable. If even this is impossible, then relatives might later bring the ashes of the deceased to the Ganges at Kāshī, or even send them to Kāshī parcel post."

49. N. G. Majumdar, "The Bajaur Casket of the Reign of Menander," *EI* 24 (1937) 1–8; S. Konow, "New Traces of the Greeks in India," *New Indian Antiquary* 2 (1939/40) 639–648; Konow, "Note on the Bajaur Inscription of Menandros," *EI* 27 (1947–1948) 52–58; D. C. Sircar, "A Note on the Bajaur Casket of the Reign of Menander," *EI* 26 (1942) 318–321; Sircar, *Select Inscriptions Bearing on Indian History and Civilization,* Vol. I, 2nd ed. (Calcutta: 1965) 102–106; A. K. Narian, *The Indo-Greeks* (Oxford: 1957) pl. VI; Ét. Lamotte, "De quelques influences grecques et scythes sur le bouddhisme," *Académie des inscriptions et belles-lettres. Comptes rendus des séances de l'année 1956,* 485–504, esp. 494; *Histoire du bouddhisme indien,* 464, 474ff. Essentially a reworking of the first paper, much of what Lamotte says in both places in regard to "influences grecques et scythes" is highly conjectural, and some of it can now be shown to be wrong. On the historical setting of the Bajaur Inscription, see most recently R. Salomon, "The 'Avaca' Inscription and the Origin of the Vikrama Era," *JAOS* 102 (1982) 62–65. [See G. Fussman, "L'indo-grec Ménandre ou Paul Demiéville revisité," *JA* (1993) 61–138.]

50. I cite here, and below, Sircar's Sanskritized text from *Select Inscriptions,* 105. It should be noted that this inscription is very fragmentary, and not all of the inscriptions on the lid go back to the time of Menander.

51. First edited by H. W. Bailey, "A Kharoṣṭhī Inscription of Senavarma, King of Oḍi," *JRAS* (1980) 21–29; edited anew, with much better results, by G. Fussman, "Documents épigraphiques kouchans (III). L'inscription kharoṣṭhī de Senavarma, roi d'Oḍi: Une nouvelle lecture," *BEFEO* 71 (1982) 1–46; yet another edition, by R.

Salomon, is forthcoming. I quote below Salomon's edition (Bailey line 7; Fussman 7a–7d). [See R. Salomon, "The Inscription of Senavarma, King of Oḍi," *IIJ* 29 (1986) 261–293.]

52. G. Fussman, "Nouvelles inscriptions śaka (II)," *BEFEO* 73 (1984) 38 ('5. reliquaire [en l'honneur de?] Kopśakasa'); Fussman translates: "ces reliques . . . parfumées de moralité, parfumées de concentration, parfumées de discernement."

53. E. H. Johnston, *The Buddhacarita or Acts of the Buddha,* Pt. II (Calcutta: 1935–1936; repr. Delhi: 1972) xvii; cf. F. Wilhelm, "Kanika and Kaniṣka—Aśvaghoṣa and Mātṛceta," *Papers on the Date of Kaniṣka,* ed. A. L. Basham (Leiden: 1968) 337–345; B. Bhattacharya, *Aśvaghoṣa: A Critical Study* (Santiniketan: 1976) 20.

54. On the important question of the role of "le rédacteur" in Buddhist inscriptions, see Fussman, *BEFEO* 56 (1969) 7, and his review of Th. Damsteegt, *Epigraphical Hybrid Sanskrit, JA* (1980) 424.

55. See Johnston, *Buddhacarita,* Pt. II, xxiv–lxxix.

56. Cantos XV–XXVIII of the *Buddhacarita* are known to us only in the Tibetan and Chinese translation. Johnston has published an English translation of the Tibetan text in "The Buddha's Mission and Last Journey; Buddhacarita, XV–XXVIII," *Acta Orientalia* 15 (1937) 26–111, 231–292. For the passage that concerns us, XXVII, 77–79, I follow Johnston, 276. The Sanskrit equivalents in parentheses are his; the Tibetan in parentheses is cited from *Peking,* 129, no. 5656, 169-4-8 to 169-5-3, the only version that was available to me.

57. See L. R. Lancaster, "The Oldest Mahāyāna Sūtra: Its Significance for the Study of Buddhist Development," *The Eastern Buddhist* 8 (1975) 30–41.

58. See G. Schopen, "The Phrase 'sa pṛthivīpradeśaś caityabhūto bhavet' in the Vajracchedikā: Notes on the Cult of the Book in Mahāyāna," *IIJ* 17 (1975) 147–181, esp. 163–167, for the *Saddharmapuṇḍarīka;* also J. Nobel, *Suvarṇabhāsottamasūtra. Das Goldglanz Sūtra. Ein Sanskrittext des Mahāyāna Buddhismus* (Leipzig: 1937) 6–19; G. Schopen, "The Five Leaves of the Buddhabalādhānaprātihāryavikurvāṇanirdeśa-sūtra Found at Gilgit," *JIP* 5 (1978) 329ff, and *Peking,* 34, 191-4-6ff. The translation offered in *JIP* 5 is a rather awful piece of English. This is, in part at least, because I tried to translate the Sanskrit and Tibetan at the same time—an exercise I would now never repeat—and because I tried to be unnaturally literal. But I also occasionally did not understand the text. One instance of this occurs on 332, where the passage beginning "As-so-ever he sees . . ." up to "does not (exist in the Tathāgata)" should be translated from the Tibetan: "As he sees those beings who will not honor the Teacher, who do not have faith in the Tathāgata, who are the lowest dregs (*kaśaṭṭaka*) and who can (only) be trained through (his manifesting) a final *nirvāṇa* and through relics, as he sees those, just so he manifests a final *nirvāṇa,* but a Tathāgata does not come and does not go." I am now working on a revised edition of the Sanskrit fragments and an edition of the complete Tibetan translation of the *Buddhabalā.* [Unfortunately, I am still working on it.]

59. U. Wogihara, *Abhisamayālaṃkārālokā Prajñāpāramitāvyākhyā,* fasc. 3 (Tokyo: 1934) 272.16, 273.5.

60. The passage in question is *Milindapañho* (Trenckner ed.) 98; see P. Demiéville, "Les versions chinoises du Milindapañha," *BEFEO* 24 (1924) 29, 34–35.

61. *Majjhima,* i, 104, 357; *Saṃyutta,* iii, 153; *Aṅguttara,* iv, 125, 176; *Vinaya,* iii, 3.

62. *Gilgit Manuscripts,* i, 50.19, 51.6.

63. The text is cited from Majumdar's edition published in J. Marshall, A. Foucher,

and N. G. Majumdar, *The Monuments of Sāñchī,* Vol. I (Delhi: 1940) 342, no. 404; see also nos. 389 and 396.

64. There is disagreement about the meaning of *ācariya-kula* here. I have followed G. Bühler, "Further Votive Inscriptions from the Stūpas at Sāñchi (II)," *EI* 2 (1894) 396 and n. 1; Lüders, *A List of Brahmi Inscriptions,* nos. 340 and 350; and Sircar, *Indian Epigraphical Glossary* (Delhi: 1966) 4. In *Monuments of Sāñchī,* Vol. I, 298, however, Majumdar connects the term found in the Sāñcī inscriptions with the *ācariyavāda* found in the much later *Mahāvaṃsa* in a very different context (see W. Geiger, *The Mahāvaṃsa* [London: 1908] 5.4 and 5.11, and *ācariya-kulavādakathā niṭṭhitā* which occurs as a kind of sectional colophon on 29). Majumdar then makes a number of very tenuous assertions concerning the demography of early Buddhist sects on the basis of his "connection." In "Buddhist Schools as Known from Early Indian Inscriptions," *Bharati. Bulletin of the College of Indology* 2 (1957/58) 28–29, A. M. Shastri questions some of the assertions but not Majumdar's basic "connection." The whole question needs further study in light, especially, of other epigraphical imprecations and the now much richer inscriptional materials in which named "schools" appear. [See also G. Schopen, "Doing Business for the Lord: Lending on Interest and Written Loan Contracts in the *Mūlasarvāstivāda-vinaya,*" *JAOS* 114 (1994) 527–554, esp. 550–551.]

65. A. Bareau, "La construction et le culte des stūpa d'après les Vinayapiṭaka," *BEFEO* 50 (1960) 253, 257; cf. J. Gernet, *Les aspects économiques du bouddhisme dans la société chinoise du Ve au Xe siècle* (Paris: 1956) 61ff, 159ff. For literature other than the *Vinayas,* see the remarks of M. Hofinger, "Le vol dans la morale bouddhique," *Indianisme et bouddhisme. Mélanges offerts à Mgr. Étienne Lamotte* (Louvain-La-Neuve: 1980) 185, which indicate the existence of a broader range of opinions.

66. In "La construction et le culte des stūpa," Bareau did, however, point out that these interdictions were maintained regardless of whether a given sect maintained "que le don au Buddha ou le culte rendu à un *stūpa* ne produisent pas de grands fruits." In fact, of the schools that he named as holders of such a view—Mahīśāsaka, Vetullaka, Caitika, Pūrvaśaila, and Aparaśaila—at least the last three are Mahāsāṅghika, and it is just the Mahāsāṅghika who most explicitly and with the greatest detail "interdisent de prendre ou d'utiliser les biens du stūpa" (253).

67. *BHSD,* 608–609; *Śikṣā,* 56.5, 170.3; *Bbh,* 163.11, 166.20; *RP,* 29.8; *Gv,* 228.21.

68. *Śikṣāsamuccaya* (Bendall ed.) 59.13, 63.15, 169.3, 269.4; P. Python, *Vinaya-Viniścaya-Upāli-Paripṛcchā. Enquête d'Upāli pour une exégèse de la discipline* (Paris: 1973) paragraphs 22 (*Śikṣā,* 169.3) and 25 (*Śikṣā,* 170.3).

69. Bendall's text here is mispunctuated; as a consequence the translation by Bendall and Rouse (*Śikshā-Samuccaya. A Compendium of Buddhist Doctrine* [London: 1922; repr. 1971] 57) is also off the mark; cf. *Ratnarāśi-Sūtra, Peking,* 24, 212-4-7ff.

70. Bendall and Rouse, *Śikshā-Samuccaya,* 57, n. 2; cf. Gernet, *Les aspects économiques du bouddhisme,* 67 and n. 5.

71. *Śikṣāsamuccaya* (Bendall ed.) 54.13ff (*Ākāśagarbhasūtra*); *Vinaya-Viniścaya-Upāli-Paripṛcchā* (Python ed.) paragraph 22.

72. Geary, *Furta Sacra,* 152–53.

73. I have discussed this interesting text in more detail in G. Schopen, "Two Problems in the History of Indian Buddhism," Ch. II above, 28–29.

74. *Gilgit Manuscripts,* iii 1, 73.9 (*Bhaiṣajyavastu* of the *Vinaya* of the Mūlasarvāstivādin; the same text also occurs twice in the *Divyāvadāna* [Cowell and Neil ed.]), 76.10–80.9, 465.10–469.18.

75. E. Waldschmidt, "Der Buddha preist die Verehrungswürdigkeit seiner Reliquien. Sondertext I des Mahāparinirvāṇasūtra," *Von Ceylon bis Turfan* (Göttingen: 1967) 426; *Caityapradakṣiṇagāthā, Peking,* 39, 86-2-8; cf. O. von Hinüber, "Die Erforschung der Gilgit-Handschriften, Neue Ergebnisse," *ZDMG* 131 (1981) nos. 13b, 13d, 60; H. Lüders, "Weitere Beiträge zur Geschichte und Geographie von Ostturkestan," *Philologica Indica* (Göttingen: 1940) 613; H. W. Bailey, "The Pradakṣiṇa-Sūtra of Chang Tsiang-Kuin," *Buddhist Studies in Honour of I. B. Horner,* ed. L. Cousins et al. (Dordrecht: 1974) 16.

76. *Buddhacarita,* XXVIII.69; Tibetan text, *Peking,* 129, 171-5-4; cf. Johnston, *Acta Orientalia* 15 (1937) 285.

77. *Mahāvaṃsa* (Geiger ed.) XVII.2–.3; cf. W. Geiger, *The Mahāvaṃsa or the Great Chronicle of Ceylon* (London: 1912) XVII.2–.3; H. Oldenberg, *The Dīpavaṃsa. An Ancient Buddhist Historical Record* (London: 1879; repr. New Delhi: 1982) XV 1–5. It should be noted that Pāli *diṭṭha,* though literally meaning "seen," blends into—like *dṛṣṭa* in Buddhist Hybrid Sanskrit—"visible," "present," "here," cf. the idiom *diṭṭhe dhamme, dṛṣṭe dharme,* in contrast to *saṃparāya.* The Sri Lankan Chronicles are rich in references to relics, and a careful study of them would undoubtedly produce interesting results. On the other hand, references to relics in the anthropological literature on Sri Lanka and Southeast Asia generally are few and rather disappointing. A notable exception, however, are the remarks of G. Obeyesekere, "The Buddhist Pantheon in Ceylon and Its Extensions" (see n. 47 above), 5–9.

78. Marshall et al., *The Monuments of Sāñchī,* Vol. I, 214, pl. 61.2; A. K. Coomaraswamy, *La Sculpture de Bharhut* (Paris: 1956) fig. 15, planche V; C. Sivaramamurti, *Amaravati Sculptures in the Madras Government Museum* (Madras: 1977) pls. xiv.2, xliii.1; A. Foucher, *Les bas-reliefs gréco-bouddhiques du gandhāra* (Paris: 1905) figs. 31, 288, 289, 291–295, 297–300; H. Ingholt, *Gandhāran Art In Pakistan* (New York: 1957) figs. 149–154, 158; etc.

79. For the literary sources and an analysis of them, see A. Bareau, *Recherches sur la biographie du buddha dans les sūtrapiṭaka et les vinayapiṭaka anciens: II. Les derniers mois, le parinirvāṇa et les funérailles,* T. II (Paris: 1971) 265ff.

80. A. Bareau, "Le parinirvāṇa du buddha et la naissance de la religion bouddhique," *BEFEO* 61 (1974) 287.

* * *

[See now also G. Schopen, "*Stūpa* and Tīrtha: Tibetan Mortuary Practices and an Unrecognized Form of Burial Ad Sanctos at Buddhist Sites in India," *The Buddhist Forum, Volume III, 1991–93, Papers in Honour and Appreciation of Professor David Seyfort Ruegg's Contribution to Indological, Buddhist and Tibetan Studies,* ed. T. Skorupski and U. Pagel (London: 1994) 273–293.]

CHAPTER VIII

On the Buddha and His Bones

The Conception of a Relic in the Inscriptions of Nāgārjunikoṇḍa

NĀGĀRJUNIKOṆḌA, WHICH LIES NOW at the bottom of a man-made lake, was a rich source not only of Buddhist and Hindu archaeological and art historical remains, but also of inscriptions. It has proved to be, as a consequence, an equally rich source of conundrums and a well-watered ground for speculation. There has been a persistent series of attempts, for example, to see elements of the Mahāyāna in the early phases of Nāgārjunikoṇḍa, in spite of the fact that there is no actual epigraphical or art-historical evidence for this movement anywhere in the Andhra area prior to the fifth or sixth centuries C.E., and in spite of the fact that what epigraphical and art-historical evidence we actually have richly documents the presence there of non-Mahāyāna groups.[1]

The inscriptions from Nāgārjunikoṇḍa are difficult. They are difficult because of "the want of precision of which they show ample evidence." Vogel has noted that, "considering that these inscriptions were meant to be perpetual records of pious donations made by ladies of royal blood, the careless manner in which they have been recorded is astonishing." [2] They are also difficult because they are, in many ways, atypical. They contain a number of phrases and formulae not found elsewhere in Indian Buddhist inscriptions so that we do not have, in many cases, parallels to assist us.[3] This difficulty is offset in part by the fact that these inscriptions tend to be highly repetitive; there are frequently numerous "copies" of the same basic inscription. I would like here to look at one of these atypical phrases that has important implications for Buddhist doctrinal history and to exploit the advantage that the existence of multiple copies presents us with.

Most of the pillar inscriptions connected with the *Mahācetiya*[4] are structured

Originally published in *Journal of the American Oriental Society* 108 (1988):527–537. Reprinted with stylistic changes with permission of American Oriental Society.

in exactly the same way. They begin with (1) the word *sidhaṃ,* "success!"; this is followed usually by (2) an invocation to the Buddha, which consists of the word *namo,* "adoration to," followed by a string of epithets of the Buddha in the genitive. Then come (3) the name of the place at which the gift recorded was made, put in the locative; (4) the name of the donor, her pedigrees and relationships; (5) the purpose or intent behind her gift; (6) the nature of the gift, etc. We will be concerned here only with the second and third elements: the invocation consisting of the *namo* plus the string of epithets in the genitive, and the name of the place at which the gift was made in the locative.

The first thing to notice is that the number of epithets in the string of genitives following *namo* varies. The fullest form of the formula containing the invocation and the name of the location at which the gift was made is, in the Prakrit original:

> *namo bhagavato deva-rāja-sakatasa supabudha-bodhino savaṃñuno sava-sat-ānukaṃpakasa jita-rāga-dosa-moha-vipamutasa mahāgaṇi-vasabha-gaṃdha-hathisa saṃma-saṃbudhasa dhātuvara-parigahitasa mahācetiye . . .*(C3)

Sircar translates this into Sanskrit as:

> *namaḥ bhagavate devarājasatkṛtāya suprabuddhabodhaye sarvajñāya sarvasattvānukampakāya jitarāgadoṣamoha- (= āsaktighṛṇājñāna-)-vipramuktāya mahāgaṇi-vṛṣabhagandhahastine (= bahusaṅkhyakaśiṣya-mahācāryeṣu pradhānaḥ) samyaksaṃbuddhāya dhātuvara-parigṛhītāya (= nirvāṇaprāptāya) {asmin} mahācaitye . . .*[5]

and Vogel puts it into English as:

> Adoration to the Lord, the Supreme Buddha, honoured by the Lord of the gods, omniscient, compassionate towards all sentient beings, freed from lust, hatred and delusion which have been conquered by him, the bull, and musk-elephant among great spiritual leaders, the perfectly Enlightened One, who is absorbed by the best of the elements (i.e., by Nirvāṇa). At the Mahāchetiya . . .[6]

At least four "copies" of this same inscription omit everything after *deva-rāja-sakatasa* up to *saṃma-saṃbudhasa,* reading as a consequence:

> *namo bhagavato deva-rāja-sakatasa saṃma-saṃbudhasa dhātuvara-parigahitasa mahācetiye . . .*[7]

Vogel's interpretation of what he takes to be the last of the string of epithets—*dhātuvara-parigahita,* "absorbed by the best of the elements (i.e., by Nirvāṇa)" —was suggested to him by de La Vallée Poussin, who added: "If the inscriptions belonged to the Mahāsanghikas, a conjectural explanation of *dhātu-*

vara as *Dharmadhātu* would not be excluded. The *Dharmadhātu* was sometimes a kind of Buddhist Brahman for the followers of the Mahāyāna."[8] Sircar also has taken the term in much the same way, glossing it with *nirvāṇaprāpta,* and Dutt, who translates the compound by "possessed of the excellent *dhātu,*" wants to see in it evidence that raises "the presumption that the Andhaka conception of *Nirvāṇa* was different from that of the Theravādins or their subsect the Mahīśāsakas,"[9] which de La Vallée Poussin, at least, does not query.[10] A. M. Shastri, finally, sees in the expression evidence indicating that "the Andhakas . . . upheld the docetic theory and believed that the Buddha was supramundane," and, following de La Vallée Poussin, that it "most probably alludes to the Kāya doctrine of the Mahāyānists for whom the Buddha was not a historical personality."[11]

This line of interpretation, which connects the expression with the development of Mahāyāna scholastic definitions and conceptions of the Buddha, did not go unquestioned. In editorial notes added to Vogel's initial publication of the inscriptions in *Epigraphia Indica,* Sastri said, "to me it does not appear to be impossible that the Mahāchetiya has been specified in these inscriptions as 'protected by the corporeal remains of the Buddha' and that the genitive case is used here to discriminate this *stūpa* from others not similarly consecrated."[12] Longhurst too was inclined toward this interpretation.[13] Even Dutt, three years before his "notes" on Vogel's treatment of the inscriptions, seems to have gone in this direction: he refers to one of the inscriptions and says it records "the gift of a pillar . . . to the *caitya,* enshrining a *dhātu* of Sammāsambuddha."[14]

There are basically two problems here. The interpretation of Vogel et al. takes *dhātuvara-parigahita* as one of the series of epithets governed by the initial *namo.* Sastri et al. want it rather to be a kind of "partitive" genitive constructed with the following *mahācetiye.* This is the first problem. The second, quite simply, is the meaning of *dhātuvaraparigahita,* the discussion so far having turned almost entirely on the significance of the final member of the compound.

The first problem arises in large part from the fact that the inscriptions are not punctuated. To quote again only the short form, we find:

> *namo bhagavato deva-rāja-sakatasa saṃma-saṃbudhasa dhātuvara-parigahitasa mahācetiye . . .*

Vogel et al. understand a *daṇḍa* or full stop after *dhātuvaraparigahitasa.* Sastri's interpretation, however, implies a full stop after *saṃma-saṃbudhasa.* But at least two other inscriptions from Nāgārjunikoṇḍa indicate that neither of these constructions of the text is correct. Āyaka-pillar Inscription B2 opens not with the invocation to the Buddha but with several lines praising the donor's father. The reference to the site at which the gift was made does not occur until almost the very end of the inscription and reads:

> *bhagavato saṃma-sa{ṃ}budhasa dhātuvaraparigahītasa mahācetiye imaṃ khaṃbhaṃ patidhapaṃta* {rd. *patiṭhāpitaṃ*} *ti* . . .

Here, where the *namo* construction does not interfere, it is clear that the genitives are constructed with *mahācetiye* and that *dhātuvaraparigahīta* is an adjective modifying *saṃma-saṃbudhasa.* This is fully confirmed by the First Apsidal Temple Inscription E. This inscription also opens, like Āyaka-pillar Inscription B2, with the praise of a relative of the donor. Here, the gift recorded is said to have been made at:

> *saṃma-saṃbudhasa dhātu-*{*vara*}[15]*-parigahitasa mahācetiya-pādamūle* . . .

Once again, without the *namo* plus genitive construction, there is no doubt as to how the text is to be constructed. In light of these two unambiguous cases, it seems fairly sure that *dhātuvaraparigahitasa* everywhere must be an adjective modifying *saṃma-saṃbudhasa,* and that *saṃma-saṃbudhasa dhātuvaraparigahitasa* everywhere must be taken, not as a part of the string of epithets in the genitive governed by *namo,* but as a separate adjectival phrase modifying *mahācetiye.* This is only more fully confirmed if we notice that, although almost all of our Nāgārjunikoṇḍa inscriptions open with or contain a *namo* invocation consisting of strings of *different* epithets of the Buddha, the collocation *saṃma-saṃbudhasa dhātuvara-parigahitasa* occurs *only* in inscriptions that make reference to the *mahācetiya* and *always* immediately precedes the noun *mahācetiya* in the locative. Just this observation allows some improvement in our understanding of the text that, in the short form of the formula, might now be read:

> *namo bhagavato deva-rājasakatasa* {*|*} *saṃma-saṃbudhasa dhātuvaraparigahitasa mahācetiya* . . .

> Homage to the Blessed One, he who is honored by the King of the Gods! At the Great Shrine of the Perfectly Enlightened One who is *dhātuvaraparigahita* . . .

While this is an improvement, it still leaves us, obviously, with the problem of the meaning of *dhātuvaraparigahita.* Although most previous discussions have concerned the meaning of the final member of the compound and, only correlatively, the first, the meaning of the middle term may also be of significance.

Dhātu- in our inscriptions has been taken by most interpreters—as we have seen—in the sense of "sphere," "state," "condition," and assimilated to *nirvāṇa-dhātu* or even *dharmadhātu.* This interpretation is, however, put forth without any justification—de La Vallée Poussin refers to his suggestion as "a conjectural explanation" —and it appears in fact to be unjustifiable. While not uncommon in this sense in abhidharmic, scholastic, and learned literature, or even in the technical vocabulary of the *sūtras,*[16] *dhātu* by itself is never certainly found with this meaning anywhere in Buddhist donative inscriptions dating prior to the medieval period, and even after this period one would be hard pressed to find a single unambiguous instance in donative inscriptions of this use.

Where it occurs in contemporaneous or—by Indian standards—nearly contemporaneous Buddhist donative inscriptions, *dhātu* always and unambiguously appears to mean "relic."[17] This is the case whether the term occurs in association with an explicit reference to the person of the Buddha—as it does in several Kharoṣṭhī inscriptions—or without such an association, as in a pillar inscription from Amarāvatī. We find, for example, *śastakhadhatu,* "the collar-bone relic of the Lord," in the Mathurā Elephant Inscription;[18] or *bhagavato śakamuni{sa} dhatuve pratiṭhavita,* "des reliques du Bienheureux Śākyamuni ont été déposées" in both the Bhagamoya and Kopśakasa Reliquary Inscriptions;[19] or, again, in both the Taxila Silver Scroll Inscription and the Taxila Gold Plate Inscription, we find reference to the deposition of *bhagavato dhatu,* "relics of the Blessed One."[20] The Amarāvatī pillar inscription already referred to records the gift of "a chaitya pillar with a relic," *cetiyakhabho sadhāduko dānaṃ,* without specifying to whom the relic "belongs."[21]

But if the term *dhātu* always appears to be used in the sense of "relic" in Buddhist inscriptions connected with shrines—*stūpas, caityas,* pillars, etc.—the same is true of its usage in literary texts wherever it occurs in narrative passages dealing with shrines. *Dhātu,* in the sense of "sphere," "condition," and so on, never appears to be found in such contexts unless it is specifically compounded with *nirvāṇa,* and *dhātu* alone is never used to stand for *nirvāṇa-dhātu.*[22] There would be little point in surveying all such passages, but it is worth noting an exact parallel to the first two members of our compound, *dhātuvara,* which occurs in an "historical" literary text that—again, by Indian standards—is quite close in time to our inscriptions, and quite near in geographical location. This parallel seems to render the equations *dhātuvara* = *dharmadhātu,* or *dhātuvara* = *nirvāṇa-dhātu,* altogether untenable.

We know from two inscriptions that there was during the period under discussion—the late third to the early fourth centuries C.E.—a community of Sri Lankan monks at Nāgārjunikoṇḍa.[23] It is, therefore, of some interest that the term *dhātuvara* occurs at least three times in the *Dīpavaṃsa,* which was "composed" sometime in the fourth century,[24] in a particularly important context. When Sumana was given instructions to go to Pāṭaliputta to get what would become one of the most important relics in Sri Lanka, an "object" which would make it possible for the monks living there "to see the Buddha," he was told to ask Aśoka: *dehi dhātuvaraṃ tassa,* "grant him the most excellent of relics." When Sumana arrives he says to Asóka: "Your friend, Great King, has faith in the teaching of the Buddha. Grant him the most excellent of relics. He is going to make a *stūpa* for the Teacher" (*sahāyo te mahārāja pasanno buddhasāsane / dehi dhātuvaraṃ tassa thūpaṃ kāhati satthuno*). Sumana then goes and makes a similar request to Kosiya (Indra) in almost exactly the same words: *devānampiyo rājā so pasanno buddhasāsane / dehi dhātuvaraṃ tassa karissati thūpam uttamaṃ.*[25]

Although seemingly a small point, it is worth noting the language used in the request Sumana was told to, and did, make to Aśoka: *dhātuvara* and "the Teacher" do not appear to have been thought of here as different things. The *stūpa* that was to be built to house the *dhātuvara* is specifically said to be "for the Teacher," not—be it noted—for a part of the Teacher or for something belonging to the Teacher. And if the language here only suggests that the relic was not thought of as merely a part of the physical remains of the Buddha, but was thought to be the Buddha himself, it—like so much else in the *Dīpavaṃsa*—is explicitly stated in the *Mahāvaṃsa.* In the *Mahāvaṃsa* account of the same events narrated in our passages from the *Dīpavaṃsa,* Mahinda complains to Devānaṃ-piya, saying: "For a long time, O King, we have not seen the Perfect Buddha, the Teacher" (*ciradiṭṭho hi saṃbuddho satthā no manujādhipa*); to which the King replies: "But did you not tell me, Revered Sir, that the Perfect Buddha is extinguished/dead?" (*bhāsittha nanu bhante me: saṃbuddho nibbuto iti*); to which Mahinda replies in turn: "When the relics are seen (or 'are present'), the Buddha is seen (or 'is present')" (*dhātusu diṭṭhesu diṭṭho hoti jino iti*).[26]

It is also worth noting that *dhātuvara* continues to be used in the *vaṃsa* literature. It occurs twice, for example, in the *Thūpavaṃsa,* which probably dates to the thirteenth century; once in the rather florid opening verse, and once to refer to the same relic that the *Dīpavaṃsa* also referred to as *dhātuvara.*[27] It occurs again in the *Chakesadhātuvaṃsa,* which, though of unknown author or date, is clearly later and yet gives clear expression to the same conception of a relic as is found at the very beginning of the *vaṃsa* literature in the *Dīpa-* and *Mahāvaṃsa.* In one passage, for example, we find the enshrinement of a relic described in the following terms:

> . . . having taken the relic of the Buddha from his head [where he had placed it out of respect], having bathed it with water from Sakka's jar, saying: 'May the Reverend Blessed One live/dwell at this place for five thousand years for the benefit of all living things,' he enshrined it.
>
> . . . *dasabalassa dhātuṃ sīsato oropayitvā sakkabhiṅkārodakena nhāpetvā bhante bhagavā imasmiṃ ṭhāne sakalajanahitatthaṃ pañcavassasahassapamāṇaṃ tiṭṭhā 'ti vatvā ṭhapesi.*[28]

We might notice again the language used in this passage from the *Chakesadhātu-vaṃsa.* Notice, for example, that in speaking to the relic, the same titles are used as are used in addressing the Buddha himself: *bhante bhagavā;* rephrased, the request to dwell or live for a long time at the place in question, although spoken to the relic, is addressed to the Buddha. Again, the relic and the Buddha do not appear to have been thought of as separate things.

Of course, the *Chakesadhātuvaṃsa* is a late text, but its conception of a relic is not. The same conception is already found, as we have seen, in the *Mahā-* and *Dīpavaṃsa,* the latter especially being only slightly later than our inscriptions from Nāgārjunikoṇḍa. Something like it is also found, as I have already pointed out elsewhere, in inscriptions and textual sources which are somewhat earlier than our Nāgārjunikoṇḍa epigraphs.[29] In the Kopśakasa Reliquary Inscription, for instance, which has been dated to 26 C.E. and which records the deposition of "reliques du Bienheureux Śākyamuni," these relics (*dhaduve*) are said to be *śila-paribhavida sama(s)i-paribhaveṃtu praña-paribhavida,* "saturated/invigorated/enlivened by morality, concentration, and wisdom." The Inscription of Senavarma, King of Oḍi, that also dates to the early first century C.E., also contains a very similar characterization of the relics of Śākyamuni. Here the relics (*dhadu*) are characterized as *śila(pari)bhavita samasiprañavimutiñaṇadra(śa)paribhavita,* "saturated/invigorated/enlivened by morality, saturated/invigorated/enlivened by concentration, wisdom, emancipation, knowledge, and vision."[30]

At the very least, this must mean that the relics are characterized by—full of—exactly the same spiritual forces and faculties that characterize, and, in fact, constitute and animate the living Buddha. To speak of an inanimate object in these terms, to speak of an inanimate object as "saturated or invigorated by morality or concentration" would at least require some explanation. But as a matter of fact, with one apparent exception, Buddhist sources do not speak of inanimate objects in such terms. When *paribhāvita,* the participle in these inscriptions, is used in literary sources, it is always used—again, with one apparent exception—in reference to two related categories of "things": (1) "living persons"—like ascetics or *bodhisattvas*—or that which distinguishes those persons from inanimate objects: their mental faculties, minds, or consciousness (*citta, manas, vijñāna,* etc.); and (2) "objects" that contain life or are capable of being enlivened, like a body or an egg that is being incubated.[31] It is, for example, as a result of being "sat on" (*adhisayita*), "heated" (*parisedita*), and "saturated/invigorated" by a hen that a chicken's egg "lives."[32] Conversely, in at least one text, *aparibhāvitakāya,* "having an uninvigorated body," is twice paired with *alpāyuṣka,* "having a short life."[33] The necessary connection suggested here between being *paribhāvita* by something and continuing to live is made even more explicit elsewhere. There is, in fact, at least one remarkable passage that has come down to us in both Pāli and Sanskrit that indicates that what is "invigorated with morality and wisdom"—as relics are said to be—is what continues to live after the breakup of the body. The Pāli version of this passage, which is now found in the *Saṃyutta-nikāya,* provides us the fullest indication of its setting: a devout layman from Kapilavatthu expresses to the Buddha the anxieties he has about what will happen to him after death (*imamhi cāhaṃ samaye kālaṃ kareyyaṃ kā mayhaṃ gati ko abhisamparāyo iti*). The Buddha reassures him (*mā bhāyi . . . mā bhāyi . . .*) and tells him that, after the destruction of the body:

> the mind that is for a long time saturated/invigorated/enlivened by faith, saturated/invigorated by morality, learning, renunciation, and wisdom, goes upward, goes to distinction.
>
> *cittaṃ dīgharattaṃ saddhāparibhāvitam sīla-suta-cāga{paññā}-paribhāvitaṃ, tam uddhagāmi hoti visesagāmi.*[34]

When *paribhāvita* is used in Buddhist literary sources, it appears, then, always to express something like "impregnated with active force," "invigorated or enlivened by," and is used—with one exception—in reference to living persons and to that which animates living persons, or to objects that contain life. The exception is, of course, relics, whether the term used is *dhātu* or *śarīra.* Literary sources too, like inscriptions, characterize relics as "saturated or invigorated with virtue and wisdom." We might look at just two examples that are somewhat earlier than the Nāgārjunikoṇḍa inscriptions, but probably nearly contemporaneous with the Senavarma and Kopśakasa Reliquary Inscriptions.

A particularly interesting example comes from the *Aṣṭasāhasrikāprajñāpāramitā,* which some have associated—though not necessarily convincingly—with South India and the area around Nāgārjunikoṇḍa.[35] Here we find it said that:

> *itaḥ prajñāpāramitāto nirjātāni tāni tathāgataśarīrāṇi pūjāṃ labhante yad uta prajñāpāramitāparibhāvitatvāt.*
>
> These relics of the Tathāgata, being born from the Perfection of Wisdom, receive worship—that is to say from the fact that they are invigorated by the Perfection of Wisdom.[36]

Here, *paribhāvita* is glossed by *nirjāta,* "to be born, given life." Elsewhere in the text it is, for example, the "all knowledge" of the Buddha that is said to be "born from the Perfection of Wisdom" (*prajñāpāramitānirjātā hi . . . tathāgatānām arhatāṃ samyaksaṃbuddhānāṃ sarvajñatā*).[37] What gives life to and animates the "all knowledge" of the Buddha, gives life to and animates the relic.

The second passage we might cite comes from a very different type of literature and is particularly significant because of that. Aśvaghoṣa in his *Buddhacarita* characterizes the relics (*khams, dhātu*) of Śākyamuni as "full of virtue" (*dge legs gaṅ ba*). He then intentionally plays on several senses of the word *dhātu:*

> The jars hold the great relics . . . like the jewelled ore (*dhātu*) of a great mountain, and the relics (*dhātu*) are unharmed by fire, just as the sphere (*dhātu*) of the chief of the gods (Brahmā) in heaven (is unharmed by the fire at the end of the aeon).

"These bones," he says, are "informed (*paribhāvita?*) with universal benevolence (*maitrī*)" (*byams pas yoṅs su rnam par bsgoms pa*).[38]

Notice that when *dhātu* is used here in the sense of "sphere," that sense is secondary and forced and occurs in a context of contrived and learned wordplay. This sort of learned artfulness is absent from our Nāgārjunikoṇḍa inscriptions. The primary meaning of *dhātu* in Aśvaghoṣa is, as everywhere in passages dealing with the physical remains of Śākyamuni, "relic." Notice too that Aśvaghoṣa, who can be dated fairly firmly to the first century C.E., characterizes relics as full of what can only be human qualities—"virtue" and "universal benevolence"—and, in doing so, appears to use at least once the same participle, or something very near to it, as was used by both contemporary or nearly contemporary canonical *sūtra* texts and Indian inscriptions.

Aśvaghoṣa was, of course, no ordinary monk. His work exhibits immense learning and broad culture. The range of sources he was able to draw upon is, as Johnston has shown, daunting.[39] For just that reason, the conception of relics articulated in the *Buddhacarita* is particularly important: it represents a conception current not among "the masses" or village monks, but a conception current among the most learned, cultured, and educated of monastic circles. The fact that there is a marked consistency in both conception and vocabulary with regard to relics in such diverse sources as Buddhist epigraphical records, canonical or paracanonical texts, historical or *vaṃsa* literature, and learned poetical works of "high" literature, makes it possible justifiably to assert that this conception of the relic—the conception that takes the relic as a living presence animated and characterized by the same qualities that animated and characterized the living Buddha—is the one conception that had general currency in the Buddhist world in the period that both preceded and followed the Nāgārjunikoṇḍa inscriptions. This same material also clearly establishes the wide currency of the term *dhātu* in the sense of "relic" for the same period. It is, therefore, virtually certain that it is this sense of the word *dhātu* and this conception of a relic that is to be expected in the Nāgārjunikoṇḍa inscriptions as well. To assert otherwise would require clear evidence, and this is not forthcoming.

The occurrence of the expression *dhātuvara* in the *vaṃsa* literature, where the sense of the second element is fairly obvious, supports the derivation of *vara,* the second member of the Nāgārjunikoṇḍa compound, from $\sqrt{2}$ *vṛ,* and suggests the likelihood that the interpreters of the Nāgārjunikoṇḍa inscriptions were correct in assigning to it there the sense of "the most excellent," "the best," etc. But in light of the fact that *dhātuvara* occurs in the inscriptions in close association with the term *mahācetiya,* the latter denoting a *stūpa* or monumental reliquary, one other *possible* derivation suggests itself. It is *possible*—but only that—to derive *-vara-* from $\sqrt{1}$ *vṛ* and see in it the meaning "enclosing," "surrounding," and, therefore, "room" or "chamber." *Dhātuvara-* would then be almost perfectly parallel to *dhātugarbha,* "relic chamber," which is, of course, well attested. This interpretation of *-vara-*, moreover, may receive some support from at least one other Buddhist inscription, the Sui Vihār Copper-Plate Inscription of the Year 11, which was recovered from the chamber of a ruined *stūpa. Although it is itself not without difficulties,* it appears to record in addition to the "foundation of the staff" [of the *stūpa*] (*yaṭhipratiṭhanaṃ ṭhapa[i]chaṃ*), the gift of the *pari-vara* or *anu-pari-vara* as well. As one possible meaning of the latter, Konow suggests that *anu-pari-vara* must have the same meaning as he assigned to *pari-vara*—"cover," "surrounding wall or hedge," "enclosure"—and must "refer to the chamber raised around the relics, after the *yaṭhi* had been put up."[40] That *vara* might have this sense in the Nāgārjunikoṇḍa inscriptions is possible and only that. To establish that it did would require much fuller and less uncertain evidence.

Parigahita, the final element of the Nāgārjunikoṇḍa compound, has been taken in one of two ways: either "absorbed (by)" or "protected (by)." But the participle occurs in several other compounds in the Nāgārjunikoṇḍa inscriptions. It occurs several times in an adjectival compound used to describe a male member of the ruling family. He is called *virūpakhapatimahāsena-parigahita,* which Vogel translates as "absorbed by Mahāsena the Lord of Virūpakhas" in one place, but as "favoured (absorbed?) by Mahāsena, etc." in another.[41] Although it proved awkward, since Vogel had translated *parigahita* in our compound by "absorbed," he appears to have felt it should have the same force in this compound. Others, like Sastri and Sircar, have taken the term here to mean "protected by."[42]

Parigahita also occurs in Vogel's C1 and C2:

> *ācariyānaṃ aparamahāvinas[e]liyāna[ṃ] suparigahitaṃ imaṃ mahācetiyana-vakaṃma[ṃ].*
>
> This new construction, the Great Shrine, was fully received (or 'taken possession of') by the Teachers of the Aparamahāvinaseliya sect.[43]

Yet another usage is attested in the First Apsidal Temple Inscription E, and in two other places where the gifts recorded are said to be *savaniyuta[ṃ] cātusala-parigahitaṃ sela-maṃṭava[ṃ];* Vogel translates as "a stone shrine [Skt. *maṇḍapa*] surrounded by a cloister and provided with everything."[44]

Having established with a fair degree of probability what *dhātuvara* means in our inscriptions allows us to eliminate some of the meanings ascribed to *parigahita.* Although the meaning "protected" fits well in several contexts, since our compound, *dhātuvaraparigahita,* describes the Buddha, and not the *Mahācetiya,* it seems unlikely there: the Buddha almost certainly would not be, nor need to be "protected" by "the most excellent relic." It also seems unlikely that he would be described as "taken possession of" by the relic. Vogel's "absorbed in," though not impossible, is a meaning that is both rather far from the primary meaning of *parigahita* and not easily attested. This would seem to leave only "surrounded by" or "enclosed in" —a sense that is quite close to the literal meaning of *parigahita* and, therefore, involves the least amount of conjecture.

Our discussion, then, generates at least one clear alternative to the previous interpretations of the formula found in the Nāgārjunikoṇḍa inscriptions, and one other interpretation that is at least possible. The short form of the formula might, in light of our discussion, be better translated as:

> Homage to the Blessed One, he who is honored by the king of the gods! At the Great Shrine of the Perfectly Enlightened One *who is enclosed within the most excellent relic* . . .

or possibly—but again only that—we might be able to translate *saṃma-saṃbudhasa dhātuvaraparigahitasa mahāchetiye* . . . as:

> At the Great Shrine of the Perfectly Enlightened One who is enclosed in the relic chamber . . .

If we adopt the first and most likely of these interpretations, the wording of our Nāgārjunikoṇḍa inscriptions would seem to indicate that their redactor *did not* think of the *dhātu* or "relic" as a piece or a part of the Buddha. He seems, in fact, to have thought of it as something that contained or enclosed the Buddha himself, something in which the Buddha was wholly present. But if the Buddha was present in the relic, the relic could not represent—as has sometimes been argued—a token or reminder of the past and "dead" Buddha: for the Buddha to be present, he would have to have been thought of as alive. And such a living "relic" could, of course, be characterized as "saturated or invigorated with morality, knowledge, and wisdom."

Even if we adopt the second interpretation, the resultant meaning is much the same. In this case, the inscriptions do not refer to the relic of the Buddha in the shrine but to the Buddha himself being enclosed within its "relic" chamber. The wording again would indicate that it is not a part or a piece of the departed Buddha that is there in the chamber but the Buddha himself who is wholly present there. In both interpretations the conception of a "relic" seems to be very much the same. Both interpretations are only variant forms of the conception of a "relic" already articulated in the Senavarma and Kopśakasa Reliquary Inscriptions, in Aśvaghoṣa and the *Aṣṭasāhasrikā,* and both suggest that the redactor of the Nāgārjunikoṇḍa inscriptions—almost certainly a monk—thought of the Buddha as a living presence dwelling in his shrine.

Although we do not necessarily know anything about the redactor of our inscriptions, we do know something about the individual who "completed" the construction of the shrine and the erection of the pillars on which the inscriptions are inscribed. He is described in two of the inscriptions where we find, in Vogel's translation:

> . . . this pious foundation of the Mahāchetiya has been completed by the Reverend Ānanda, who knows the *Dīgha-* and the *Majjhima-nikāyas* by heart, (who is) a disciple of the masters of the Ayira-haṃgha (Skt. *Ārya-saṅgha*) who are resident in Paṃṇagāma and who are preachers and preceptors of the *Dīgha,* the *Majjhima{-nikāya}* and of the five *Mātukas.* This pious work, the Mahāchetiya, was completed and the pillars were erected.[45]

The Reverend Ānanda—although not specifically designated as such here—appears to have been the *navakammika,* the monk appointed as the superintendent of construction of religious buildings.[46] The construction of the *cetiya* and the erection of the pillars was overseen by him. As a consequence, even if he was not himself the redactor of the inscriptions incised on the pillars, he would still have been responsible for their content, and they would have to have been approved by him. This would mean that the views expressed in the inscriptions—notably, the conception of a relic—must represent the view and conceptions that were either dictated by or redacted under the auspices of a very learned monk, a monk "who knew by heart both the *Dīgha-* and *Majjhima-nikāyas.*" They do not, again, represent the views of an uneducated village monk. They do not represent a popular conception of a relic, but an official, monastic conception.

We also know that the Mahācetiya at Nāgārjunikoṇḍa was "accepted or taken possession of by," or "belonged to," the Aparamahāvinaseliya teachers (*ācariyānaṃ aparamahāvinas{e}liyāna{ṃ} suparigahitaṃ imaṃ mahācetiyanavakaṃ-ma{ṃ},* C1, C2). But what little we think we know about the doctrinal position of the Aparamahāvinaseliya group—and this is on the generous assumption that it is the same as the Aparaśaila—*appears* not to set altogether well with this fact. Both Vasumitra and Vinītadeva maintain that one of the tenets of this school was: *mchod rten la mchod pa ni 'bras bu mchog tu gyur pa ma yin no,* "l'acte de vénérer (*pūjākara*) un reliquaire (*stūpa*) ne procure pas un grand fruit."[47] Rosen has taken the *appearance* at face value and offered the following explanation:

> Amongst their [the Aparamahāvinaseliyas'] doctrines, according to Vasumitra, we find it stated that the worship of a *stūpa* or the worship of a *caitya* does not produce much fruit. Nevertheless, the fact that one of the largest *stūpas* in India was built for the benefit of this sect, indicates that they were willing to alter their practices to fit more modern times.[48]

Rosen, in referring to both *stūpas* and *caityas,* has been misled in part by Bareau's paraphrase of Vasumitra.[49] The Tibetan text has only *mchod rten,* and, while it is true that we cannot be sure whether this translated *stūpa* or *caitya,* both Bareau and Masuda translate their texts by *stūpa.*[50] It is also true that one of the most notable characteristics of the Aparamahāvinaseliya inscriptions at Nāgārjunikoṇḍa is the complete avoidance of the term *stūpa.* Although it is used everywhere else in Buddhist inscriptions in India, the term never occurs at Nāgārjunikoṇḍa. There Buddhist "shrines" are always called *cetiyas.* This usage shows every sign of being intentional and very likely reflects a regional influence in the vocabulary applied to Buddhist sacred sites. In addition to these considerations, our inscriptions make it clear that the Mahācetiya at Nāgārjunikoṇḍa was not conceived of as "un reliquaire," but as a structure housing the living presence of the Buddha: any worship of "it" would actually be of *him.*

But these considerations aside, Rosen's argument is still—in at least one aspect—a little startling. It is not known who among the several Vasumitras who appear in the history of Buddhist scholasticism was the author of the work on "les sectes bouddhiques" assigned to that name. What appears to be known is that the first translation of the work into Chinese took place at "la fin du ive siècle ou début du ve siècle de notre ère." There is also general agreement that its author, whoever he was, was a Sarvāstivādin.[51] We have, then, an assertion by an unknown Sarvāstivādin author, of unknown geographic provenance, in a work of about the fourth century purporting to express the views of a group to which he did not belong. Over against this we have an historical record either written by, or redacted under the auspices of, a learned Aparamahāvinaseliya monk from Nāgārjunikoṇḍa in the third century that was intended to record what a community of Aparamahāvinaseliya monks there actually did. By any criteria, the historical value of the two sources for the history of the Aparamahāvinaseliya cannot be the same. It is, therefore, curious that Rosen takes as somehow more representative of the Aparamahāvinaseliya position not what Aparamahāvinaseliya monks in the third century actually did, but what a Sarvāstivādin author of the fourth century said. This perfunctory preference for formal literary sources—which is quite common in historical works on Indian Buddhism—can only result in histories of Buddhism that have little relationship to what practicing Buddhists actually did. At the very least, it rather effectively impedes an adequate appraisal or appreciation of other kinds of sources. But it is, in fact, precisely because our inscriptional formula from Nāgārjunikoṇḍa is one of these "other kinds of sources" that it is important.

If, for example, the phrase *saṃma-saṃbudhasa dhātuvaraparigahitasa mahācetiye* means what I have suggested it does, then it would appear to be another piece of nontextual evidence that indicates that we have not yet understood at all well the Buddhist conception of "relics" or the nature of Buddhist sacred sites. Elsewhere I have recently presented evidence indicating that the earliest actually attestable Buddhist conception of relics was that "la relique corporelle . . . c'est un être vivant 'doué de souffle' "; "that relics were thought to retain—to be infused with, impregnated with—the qualities that animated and defined the living Buddha"; that the *stūpa* or reliquary was cognitively classified as a "living person of rank" and that it was—like the Hindu image—a "juristic personality" and owned property; that, finally, the Indian Buddhist community practiced a form of what in the West was called "burial *ad sanctos*" and that this can only be accounted for by the belief that the *stūpa* contained a living presence.[52] The formula found in the Nāgārjunikoṇḍa inscriptions appears to be yet one more piece of this ever-more-clearly emerging complex of actual beliefs—as opposed to the formal literary doctrines—of practicing Indian Buddhists, both monastic and lay.

Notes

1. N. Dutt, "Discovery of a Bone-Relic at an Ancient Centre of Mahāyāna," *IHQ* 5 (1929) 794–796; Dutt, "Notes on the Nāgārjunikoṇḍa Inscriptions," *IHQ* 7 (1931) 633–653; H. Sarkar, *Studies in Early Buddhist Architecture of India* (Delhi: 1966) 74–96; E. S. Rosen, "Buddhist Architecture and Lay Patronage at Nāgārjunikoṇḍa," in A. L. Dallapiccola and S. Z. Lallemant, eds., *The Stūpa: Its Religious, Historical and Architectural Significance* (Wiesbaden: 1980) 112–126; A. and H. Wayman, *The Lion's Roar of Queen Śrīmālā* (New York: 1974) 1–4; A. Wayman, "The Mahāsāṃghika and the Tathāgatagarbha," *JIABS* 1 (1978) 42–43; etc. On the Mahāyāna in Andhra art, see D. Barrett, "The Later School of Amarāvatī and Its Influence," *Art and Letters* 28.2 (1954) 41–53; D. Barrett, *Sculptures from Amaravati in the British Museum* (London: 1954) 59; Ét. Lamotte, "Mañjuśrī," *TP* 68 (1960) 4; on the Mahāyāna in epigraphical sources, see G. Schopen, "Mahāyāna in Indian Inscriptions," *IIJ* 21 (1979) 1–19; Schopen, "The Inscription on the Kuṣān Image of Amitābha and the Character of the Early Mahāyāna in India," *JIABS* 10.2 (1987) 99–137. Since writing the first of these, I have come across a single instance of the Mahāyāna formula in an inscription from the Andhra area; it dates to the fifth century; see T. N. Ramachandran, *Nāgārjunikoṇḍa 1938,* MASI, No. 71 (Calcutta: 1953) 29 (III).

2. J. Ph. Vogel, "Prakrit Inscriptions from a Buddhist Site at Nāgārjunikoṇḍa," *EI* 20 (1929) 11–12.

3. Cf. G. Schopen, "Filial Piety and the Monk in the Practice of Indian Buddhism," Ch. III above, 63–64.

4. Vogel, *EI* 20 (1929) A2–A4, B1–B5, C1–C5, D2–D4, and X. Citations in the text are made following Vogel's letter/number system.

5. D. C. Sircar, *Select Inscriptions Bearing on Indian History and Civilization,* 2nd ed. (Calcutta: 1965) 230. I have silently corrected two misprints in the passage cited.

6. Vogel, *EI* 20 (1929) 17.

7. Vogel, *EI* 20 (1929) 16, n. 2; B3, C1, D2, and D4.

8. Vogel, *EI* 20 (1929) 29, n. 1.

9. Dutt, "Notes on the Nāgārjunikoṇḍa Inscriptions," 649–650, and N. Dutt, *Buddhist Sects in India* (Calcutta: 1970) 124–125.

10. L. de La Vallée Poussin, "Notes et bibliographie bouddhiques," *MCB* 1 (1931–1932) 383.

11. A. M. Shastri, *An Outline of Early Buddhism (A Historical Survey of Buddhology, Buddhist Schools and Sanghas Mainly Based on the Study of Pre-Gupta Inscriptions)* (Varanasi:

1965) 29–30; cf. A. M. Shastri, "The Legendary Personality of the Buddha as Depicted in Pre-Gupta Indian Inscriptions," *The Orissa Historical Research Journal* 8 (1960) 172–173.

12. Vogel, *EI* 20 (1929) 29, n. 1.

13. A. H. Longhurst, *The Buddhist Antiquities of Nāgārjunikoṇḍa, Madras Presidency,* MASI, No. 54 (Delhi: 1938) 18.

14. Dutt, "Discovery of a Bone-Relic at an Ancient Centre of Mahāyāna," 794.

15. The "scribe" has omitted *-vara-* here, but this is almost certainly only another instance of the "carelessness" in these records noted by Vogel; cf. also *EI* 20 (1929) 21, n. 2.

16. See the long entry on *dhātu* in *BHSD,* 282–284.

17. Cf. the very problematic passage in the Senavarma Reliquary Inscription, *ime śarireṇa tadagada-prava-diśaṇivaṇa-dhatu-gade ta pratiṭhavemi* (7c–7d), where, if *dhatu* were to be constructed with the preceding *ṇivaṇa-*, we might have an instance where the sense of "sphere," etc. was in play. But this passage, in spite of the efforts of Bailey, Fussman, and Salomon remains, as the last of these scholars says, "highly obscure"; H. W. Bailey, "A Kharoṣṭhī Inscription of Senavarma, King of Oḍi," *JRAS* (1980) 21–29; G. Fussman, "Documents épigraphiques kouchans (III). L'inscription kharoṣṭhī de senavarma, roi d'oḍi: une nouvelle lecture," *BEFEO* 71 (1982) 1–45; R. Salomon, "The Inscription of Senavarma, King of Oḍi," *IIJ* 29 (1986) 261–293.

18. S. Konow, *Kharoshṭhī Inscriptions with the Exception of Those of Aśoka,* Corpus Inscriptionum Indicarum, Vol. II, Pt. 1 (Calcutta: 1929) 49–50, XVI.

19. G. Fussman, "Nouvelles inscriptions śaka (II)," *BEFEO* 73 (1984) 33–38, 38–46; R. Salomon, "The Bhagamoya Relic Bowl Inscription," *IIJ* 27 (1984) 107–120.

20. Konow, *Kharoshṭhī Inscriptions,* 70–77, XXVII; 83–86, XXXI.

21. C. Sivaramamurti, *Amaravati Sculptures in the Madras Government Museum,* Bulletin of the Madras Government Museum, N.S. Vol. IV (Madras: 1977) 283, no. 47.

22. But see Aśvaghoṣa's use of *dhātu* cited below.

23. Vogel, *EI* 20 (1929) 22; D. C. Sircar and A. N. Lahiri, "Footprint Slab Inscription from Nagarjunikoṇḍa," *EI* 33 (1960) 247–250.

24. K. R. Norman, *Pāli Literature. Including the Canonical Literature in Prakrit and Sanskrit of All the Hīnayāna Schools of Buddhism,* A History of Indian Literature, ed. J. Gonda, Vol. VII, Fasc. 2 (Wiesbaden: 1983) 115ff.

25. H. Oldenberg, *The Dīpavaṃsa: An Ancient Buddhist Historical Record* (London and Edinburgh: 1879) 79.14, 79.21, 80.8.

26. W. Geiger, *The Mahāvaṃsa* (London: 1908) XVII.2–XVII.3; on the relationship of the *Mahāvaṃsa* to the *Dīpavaṃsa,* see Norman, *Pāli Literature,* 115.

27. N. A. Jayawickrama, *The Chronicle of the Thūpa and the Thūpavaṃsa,* Sacred Books of the Buddhists, Vol. XXVII (London: 1971) 147.1, 201.1; on the date of the *Thūpavaṃsa,* see Norman, *Pāli Literature,* 142–143.

28. I. P. Minayeff, "The Cha-kesa-dhātu-vaṃsa," *JPTS* (1885) 10.11, 8.15; cf. B. C. Law, "An Account of the Six Hair Relics of the Buddha (Chakesadhātuvaṃsa)," *JIH* 30 (1952) 193–204; on the date of the *Chakesadhātuvaṃsa,* see Norman, *Pāli Literature,* 143.

29. G. Schopen, "Burial *Ad Sanctos* and the Physical Presence of the Buddha in Early Indian Buddhism," Ch. VII above, 125–128.

30. Fussman, *BEFEO* 73 (1984) 38ff; Fussman, *BEFEO* 71 (1982) 4, 7a–7b; Salomon, *IIJ* 29 (1986) 265. There are several additional references to "relics" in the Senavarma Inscription that seem to point in the same direction. I hesitate to cite them, however, since in spite of the fine efforts of both Fussman and Salomon they remain obscure. Note

only that in 12b the "relic" deposited by Senavarma seems clearly to be characterized as "immortal" or "deathless" (*amudae dhatue*), and cf. n. 17 above.

31. Schopen, "Burial *Ad Sanctos* and the Physical Presence of the Buddha in Early Indian Buddhism," Ch. VII above, 128.

32. *Majjhima*, i, 104, 357; *Saṃyutta*, iii, 153; *Aṅguttara*, iv, 125, 176; *Vinaya*, iii, 3. All references to canonical Pāli sources are to the editions published by the Pāli Text Society.

33. *Gilgit Manuscripts*, i, 50.19, 51.6.

34. *Saṃyutta*, v, 369–370; the Sanskrit version of this passage is cited in L. de La Vallée Poussin, *L'Abhidharmakośa de Vasubandhu*, T. II (Paris: 1923–1931; repr. 1971) 95, n. 1. For Hindu and Jain instances of the use of the participle *-bhāvita* in similar contexts, see Edgerton, "The Hour of Death," *ABORI* 8.3 (1927) 225, 227.

35. See, for example, E. Conze, *The Prajñāpāramitā Literature*, 2nd ed. (Tokyo: 1978) 1ff.

36. P. L. Vaidya, *Aṣṭasāhasrikā Prajñāpāramitā*, Buddhist Sanskrit Texts, No. 4 (Darbhanga: 1960) 49.6.

37. Vaidya, *Aṣṭasāhasrikā*, 36.1.

38. *Buddhacarita*, XXVII.77–XXVII.79; I cite here the translation and Sanskrit equivalents given in E. H. Johnston, "The Buddha's Mission and Last Journey; Buddhacarita, XV–XXVIII," *Acta Orientalia* 15 (1937) 276; the Tibetan is cited from *Peking*, 129, no. 5656, 169-4-8 to 169-5-3.

39. For a discussion of both Aśvaghoṣa's date and his learning, see E. H. Johnston, *The Buddhacarita or Acts of the Buddha*, Pt. II (Calcutta: 1935–1936; repr. 1972) xvii, xxiv–lxxix; B. Bhattacharya, *Aśvaghoṣa: A Critical Study* (Santiniketan: 1976) 20; etc.

40. S. Konow, *Kharoshṭhī Inscriptions*, 141; see also—for other meanings of *parivara*—38, 60, 170. For earlier interpretations of the inscription, see the sources cited in Konow, 141, nn. 2–6; more recently, D. R. Patik, "The Origin of Memorial Stones," in S. Settar and G. D. Sontheimer, eds., *Memorial Stones. A Study of Their Origin, Significance and Variety* (Dharwad: 1982) 52–53; G. Schopen, "Two Problems in the History of Indian Buddhism," Ch. II above, 34. [See also G. Schopen, "Ritual Obligations and Donor Roles of Monks in the Pāli *Vinaya*," Ch. IV above.] There are at least two other sources that might also suggest that *dhātu-vara* was intended to refer to a structure holding relics. Sircar sees in vs. 16 of the Mandasor stone inscription of the time of Prabhākara the expression *dhātuvara*, and the term here—if this is the correct reading—is clearly used interchangeably with the term *stūpa*. Sircar says in a note: "*Dhātu-vara* really means the relics of the Buddha; but here it means a *stūpa* built on the Buddha's relics. Such *stūpas* were usually called *dhātu-garbha*" (Sircar, *Select Inscriptions*, 409 and n. 3). Unfortunately Garde, the first to read the inscription, read not *dhātu-vara*, but *dhātu-dhara* (M. B. Garde, "Mandasor Inscription of Malava Samvat 524," *EI* 27 [1947–1948] 15), although Agrawala, to whom we owe the most recent edition, reads—as did Sircar—*dhātuvara* in P. K. Agrawala, *Imperial Gupta Epigraphs* (Varanasi: 1983) 81. In fact, the reading in the published facsimiles is problematic. A comparison of the third *akṣara* of the compound with the *akṣara -va-* elsewhere in the inscription (line 1, eighth *akṣara;* line 5, fifteenth *akṣara;* etc.) would argue against reading the *akṣara* in our compound as *-va-*, but a comparison of it with the *-dhā-* of the immediately preceding *dhātu-* does not unambiguously support Garde either. On balance, all we can say is that the *akṣara* is uncertain, although it looks to me more like *-dha-* than *-va-*. (Incidentally, this verse in the Mandasor inscription, like the verse from the *Buddhacarita* cited above, seems to

contain a pun or wordplay involving the word *dhātu*). The second source that may use the compound *dhātu-vara* to refer to a structure holding relics is literary. In G. Sastri's edition of the *Rājavyākaraṇa-parivarta* of the *Mañjuśrīmūlakalpa,* the term *dhātu-vara* occurs repeatedly in contexts that make it certain that it is being used interchangeably with the term *stūpa,* and the Tibetan version supports this: it consistently translates *dhātu-vara* by *mchod rten.* But almost as consistently, Sāṅkṛtyāyana "corrects" every occurrence of *dhātu-vara* into *dhātu-dhara.* Since it is not clear if Sāṅkṛtyāyana's "corrections" are based on anything but the Tibetan, and since the manuscript tradition of the *Mañjuśrīmūlakalpa* is notoriously problematic, it is difficult to cite this material with confidence; see K. P. Jayaswal, *An Imperial History of India* (Lahore: 1934) vss. 427, 431, 531, 588, 589, etc.; cf. vss. 416, 574, etc.

41. Vogel, *EI* 20 (1929) 17, 21.

42. Vogel, *EI* 20 (1929) 29, n. 1; 30, n. 2 (notes marked "Ed."); Sircar, *Select Inscriptions,* 230, n. 3.

43. Elsewhere in the inscriptions from Nāgārjunikoṇḍa, *parigahe* (E; J. Ph. Vogel, "Additional Prakrit Inscriptions from Nāgārjunikoṇḍa," *EI* 21 [1931] M2, M3) is found in the same context—once (H) *suparigahe. Parigahe* is more in conformity with Buddhist epigraphical usage elsewhere.

44. *Cātusāla-parigahita* also occurs in Vogel, *EI* 21 (1931) M4, and in H. Sarkar, "A Note on Some Fragmentary Inscriptions from Nāgārjunikoṇḍa," *EI* 38 (1969) 176.

45. Vogel, *EI* 20 (1929) 17 (C1), 19 (C2).

46. Cf. M. Njammasch, "Der *navakammika* und seine Stellung in der Hierarchie der buddhistischen Klöster," *Altorientalische Forschungen* 1 (1974) 279–293.

47. E. Teramoto and T. Hiramatsu, *Vasumitra's (dByig-Gi bÇes-gÑen) Samaya-Bhedo-paracana-Cakra (gShuṅ-Lugs-kyi Bye-Brag bKod-Paḥi ḥKhor Lo),* etc. (Kyoto: 1935) 9 (V), 42; A. Bareau, "Trois traités sur les sectes bouddhiques attribués à Vasumitra, Bhavya et Vinītadeva," *JA* (1954) 248 (VIII.2), etc.

48. Rosen, "Buddhist Architecture and Lay Patronage at Nāgārjunikoṇḍa," 114.

49. A. Bareau, *Les sectes bouddhiques du petit véhicule* (Paris: 1955) 105.

50. Bareau, "Trois traités sur les sectes bouddhiques," 248; J. Masuda, "Origin and Doctrines of Early Indian Buddhist Schools," *Asia Major* 2 (1925) 38.

51. Bareau, *JA* (1954) 231.

52. Schopen, "Burial *Ad Sanctos* and the Physical Presence of the Buddha in Early Indian Buddhism," Ch. VII above.

* * *

[There is what appears to be a response to this paper in A. Wayman and E. Rosen, "The Rise of Mahāyāna Buddhism and Inscriptional Evidence at Nāgārjunakoṇḍa," *The Indian Journal of Buddhist Studies* 2.1 (1990) 49–65, but I cannot claim to have understood it.]

CHAPTER IX

An Old Inscription from Amarāvatī and the Cult of the Local Monastic Dead in Indian Buddhist Monasteries

ALTHOUGH THEY HAVE yet to be carefully studied, scattered throughout extant Buddhist literature are references to permanently housing the mortuary remains of deceased monks. In both the Pāli *Udāna* and *Apadāna,* for example, there is a clear injunction addressed to monks—and monks alone—directing them not only to perform the funeral rites for a "fellow-monk" (*sabrahmacārin*), but to build a mortuary *stūpa* for him as well and to worship it.[1] In the Pāli *Vinaya* there is an account that describes, in part, a group of nuns performing the funeral rites and building a *stūpa* for a deceased member of their group.[2] In the account of the deposition of the remains of Śāriputra preserved in the Tibetan version of the *Mūlasarvāstivāda-vinaya,* there is a passage in which the placement of the monastic dead within the monastery complex is directly addressed. Here, the Buddha first gives instructions concerning the form of mortuary *stūpa* appropriate to different categories of individuals, starting with a *buddha* and ending with "stream-winners" (*rgyun du zhugs pa*) and "ordinary good men" (*so so'i skye bo dge ba*). He then says:

> As Śāriputra and Maudgalyāyana sat (in relation to the Buddha) when the Tathāgata was sitting, just so should their mortuary *stūpas* be placed as well. Moreover, the *stūpas* of various elders (*sthavira*) should be aligned in accordance with their seniority. *Stūpas* of ordinary good men should be placed outside the monastery (*dge 'dun gyi kun dga' ra ba, saṃghārāma*).[3]

The *Mahāsāṃghika-vinaya*—according to de La Vallée Poussin—also contains such passages: "D'après le Mahāsāṃghikavinaya," he says, "des moines hommes du commun (*pṛthagjana*) ont aussi droit au *stūpa,* à savoir le Vinayadharadharmācārya, le Vaiyāpṛtyabhikṣu, le Vertueux-bhikṣu. Comme ils ne sont pas des Āryas,

---

Originally published in *Journal of the International Association of Buddhist Studies* 14.2 (1991) 281–329. Reprinted with stylistic changes with permission of the editor.

il n'y a pas de *lou-pan* ["dew-dish"] et [le stūpa] est dans un lieu caché. Péché à faire autrement."[4]

There is also—although, again, not yet systematically studied—an important body of independent evidence for the monastic preoccupation with permanently housing their dead from well preserved cave sites like Bhājā, Bedsā, and Kānheri. But with a few exceptions, little certain evidence has been noted for such activity at structural monastic sites. Evidence of this sort would, in fact, be difficult to detect at such structural sites for several reasons. The first and most general reason is, of course, that structural sites in India are far less well-preserved than the Western Cave Complexes. Those same cave complexes suggest, in addition, that the structures associated with the local monastic dead at structural sites would very likely have been small, and very well might have been situated some distance away from the main *stūpa* or center of the site. Neither of these factors would have favored the detection of such structures. Moreover, very few structural monastic sites in India have been extensively investigated or excavated horizontally; generally, attention and effort have been focused on the main *stūpa* of such sites. Anything not in the immediate vicinity would only accidentally have been noted.[5] The fact that such small structures would have required—and, therefore, would have left—no substantial foundations, that their superstructures would not only have been exposed to the elements, but also would have been easy prey for those who used such sites for building materials suggests that even horizontal surveys may have noted little. In such circumstances, stray epigraphical evidence for the housing of the local monastic dead is the most likely certain evidence to survive at structural sites; even then, such incidents of survival may not be numerous, and each possible piece should be carefully studied. The present essay concerns one such possible piece from Amarāvatī.

Amarāvatī must have been a striking monastic site. The main *stūpa* stood on a plain between the old city of Dharaṇikoṭa and the neighboring hills "where," said Burgess, "so many dolmans or rude-stone burying places are still to be seen."[6] "Upwards of 10,000 to 12,000 [carved] figures" were—according to Fergusson's calculations—associated with the *stūpa.* He calls it, perhaps without undue inflation, "a wonderful pictorial Bible of Buddhism as it was understood at the time of the erection of the monument."[7] But through the work of *zamindars,* zealous treasure seekers, and untrained if well-intentioned British civil servants, most of the complex—one of the longest lasting in India—has disappeared.[8] As a consequence, we know next to nothing about the monastic quarters there and very little about any secondary structures at the site. We do know that there were a number of mortuary *stūpas* clustered around the main *stūpa.* Burgess, in 1882, referred to two of these, in one of which he found "a small *chatti* [a type of pot] . . . and a quantity of calcined bones." A similar "*chatti*" had earlier been recovered from another.[9] Rea also excavated several secondary *stūpas,* one of which still had its lower portion encased in sculptural slabs,[10] as well as another that overlay a group of seventeen "megalithic" urn burials.[11] In fact, the site plan published by Rea in 1909 shows almost twenty small *stūpas* and at least one "earthenware tomb." We do not, unfortunately, know anything more about these *stūpas* except for the fact that their placement and contents conform to a pattern found at a considerable number of other Buddhist sites in India and seem to reflect the practice that I—on analogy with the Christian West—have called "burial *ad sanctos.*"[12] The inscription we will be primarily concerned with here may have been associated with one such *stūpa.*

The stone on which our inscription is inscribed was not found in its original position. It had already been displaced and could even have been moved a considerable distance, given its size and shape. Burgess describes it as "a circular slab 2 feet 1 inch in diameter . . . with a mortise hole in the centre surrounded by a lotus, and this again by a sunk area carved with rays. The outer border is raised . . ." and it is on this raised border that our record—"a well-cut inscription"—occurs.[13] This "circular slab"—a good photograph of which was also published by Burgess[14]—is clearly the "umbrella" (*chata, chattra*) referred to in the inscription. That this "umbrella" was intended for a shrine (*cediya*) or *stūpa* is clear as well from the inscription, and the comparatively small size of the *chattra* is sufficient to indicate that the *stūpa* was a small one. We do not, however, know exactly where this small *stūpa* stood.

With a few minor exceptions, the readings of this "well-cut" record were not difficult to establish, and, after something of a false start in the first transcription published in Burgess' *Notes,* the basic text was quickly established. In the "Additional Notes" added to that same volume, in fact, Hultzsch had already come very close to his final version, which appeared a year later.[15] The text is printed there as:

> *uvāsikāya cadaya budhiṇo mātuya saputikāya sadutukāya aïrānaṃ utayipabhāhīnaṃ cediyasa chata deyadhamaṃ*

and this is the basic text accepted by Lüders,[16] Franke,[17] and Sivaramamurti.[18] Sivaramamurti does, however, read *-pabhāhinaṃ* rather than *-pabhāhīnaṃ,* and notes that the "nasal"—he means *anusvāra*—"is not quite clear in *aïrānaṃ* and *utayipabhāhinaṃ,*" although this is more true of the latter than the former.

Hultzsch first translated the text as:

> An umbrella (*chhattra*), a meritorious gift to the Chaitya (?) of the venerable Utayipabhāhins by the female worshipper Chadā (Chandrā), the mother of Budhi, together with her sons, together with her daughters

He added as well the following note: "*Utayipabhāhin* seems to be the name of a school like *Dharmottarīya* . . . Perhaps *utara* (= *uttara*) is to be read for *utayi,* and *pabhāhin* = *prabhāsin*."[19] But a year later he published a slightly different rendering:

> Ein Sonnenschirm (*chattra*), die verdienstliche Gabe der Laiin *Cadā* (*Candrā*), der Mutter des Budhi (*Buddhi*), mit ihren Söhnen, mit ihren Töchtern, an die (Schule der) ehrwürdigen *Utayipabhāhis* (?) (und) an das *Caitya*[20]

The English translation of the record that appears in Burgess' later report looks like a somewhat garbled version of Hultzsch's second translation, and here too, *Utayipabhāhin* appears to have been taken as the name of a Buddhist school. Burgess adds to it the following note: "May this not be synonymous with Uttaraparvatas, or Uttaraśelas."[21] Although he proposed no emendation or equivalent, Lüders lists *Utayipabhāhi* in his index of personal names as the name of a Buddhist "school," and translates the portion of the record that most concerns us as: "Gift of a parasol (*chhata*) to the Chaitya (*chediya*) of the venerable (*aïra*) Utayipabhāhis, . . ."[22] In fact, Sivaramamurti alone *seems* to have considered other possible interpretations of the text, but his translation—as printed—is also garbled and without explanation or comment: "Meritorious gift of umbrella for the caitya (cediya) of the worthy airānam Utayipabhāhi, etc." What "*airānaṃ*," still carrying its case ending, is doing in the translation is, of course, far from clear, especially since it already seems to have been translated by "worthy." Moreover, Sivaramamurti lists *Utayipabhāhi* in his glossary as "probably Uttaraseliyas."[23]

The inclination to see in *utayipabhāhin* the name of a school has had, in fact, a wide currency. Lamotte says:

> Les donations religieuses signalées par les inscriptions proviennent, non seulement de particuliers, mais encore de clans (*kula*), de groupes (*gaṇa*) et d'associations (*sahaya*). Parmi ces dernières, quelques-unes peuvent avoir été des sectes bouddhiques, non mentionées en littérature,

and as one example of such a group he cites the "aïra (*ārya*) Utayipabhāhi" of our inscription.[24] In a later paper, Furtseva has said: "The epigraphic data gives evidence of the existence of the schools unknown to any tradition. These are such schools as, for example, Utayibhāhī in Amaravati, . . ." again citing our inscription.[25]

Although this interpretation of our record has received wide currency, and although Furtseva, for example, seems to take it as an established fact that the inscription refers to a Buddhist school, the evidence for this was never firm: Hultzsch had said *utayipabhāhin* only "*seems* to be the name of a school," Burgess, "may this not be . . . ," Sivaramamurti, "probably," and so on. In fact, there are a number of reasons to reject seeing in the inscription a reference to a shrine or *caitya* that "belonged" to a specific Buddhist school, and much evidence that suggests a much more supportable interpretation.

Although the evidence is sadly fragmentary, it appears, as has already been indicated, that the main *stūpa* at Amarāvatī was—as Marshall says of Sāñcī—"surrounded, like all the more famous shrines of Buddhism, by a multitude of *stūpas* of varying sizes crowded together."[26] The *stūpa* or *caitya* to which our umbrella was donated appears to have been just one of such a multitude and, to judge by the size of the *chattra,* a comparatively small one at that. That one of such a multitude of secondary *stūpas* close to—or in the vicinity of—the main shrine would have been claimed as the special property of a specific school seems very unlikely. That monastic orders accepted as gifts and, therefore, "owned," specific forms of property—relics, fields, buildings, images, and so on—is virtually certain. It is equally certain that specific schools "owned" the main *stūpa* at certain sites. But there is no other case, in so far as I know, where one of the small secondary *stūpas* was so "owned." Whether near the main shrine or situated elsewhere in the complex, secondary *stūpas* at Buddhist sites are almost always uninscribed and anonymous. There are, however, a small number of significant exceptions, and it is this group of exceptions that may point toward a better understanding of the record on our small umbrella from Amarāvatī.

The first exception may come from Amarāvatī itself. If we can accept Sivaramamurti's reading of his no. 103 as even approximately correct, then the one other secondary *stūpa* that had an associated inscription at Amarāvatī was "the small cetiya of the mendicant monk Nāgasena." Sivaramamurti gives the text of his no. 103 in the following form:

> *sidham (namo) bhagavato gāmmamahivathasa peṇḍavatikasa nāgasenasa khuda-cetiya . . . haghavāṇikiniya patiṭhapitam savasatamata a . . .*[27]

If we put aside *gāmmamahivathasa,* which is clearly wrong (although it just as clearly indicated the place of residence of Nāgasena), and if we follow—however reluctantly—Sivaramamurti's interpretation of . . . *haghavāṇikiniya* as "by the merchant's wife, Haghā," this could be translated as:

> Success. (Homage) to the Blessed One. The small *cetiya* of the mendicant monk Nāgasena who lived in . . . established by the merchant's wife Haghā for the . . . of all . . .

We do not know where the sculptured slab on which this record was inscribed was discovered. Already by the time of Burgess (1887), it had been removed to Bejwāḍā, "possibly," says Burgess, by Colonel Mackenzie.[28] On the basis of the expression *khudacetiya,* "small *cetiya*" in the record itself, Sivaramamurti assumes that the slab formed a part of one of what he calls the "smaller votive *stūpas.*" That the inscribed slab did, in fact, belong to a secondary *stūpa* appears likely. The problem remains, however, that Sivaramamurti's reading of the record cannot actually be verified with the published material at hand. Although Burgess and

Stern and Bénisti both provide illustrations of the slab on which the record occurs, in neither case is the photograph sufficiently clear to allow the inscription to be read with any confidence.[29] Sivaramamurti also reproduces the record reduced to such a degree that no certain reading is possible,[30] and in cases where his readings can be checked, they are by no means always as careful as one might wish. Given this situation, the most that one could say is that it appears—although it is not certain—that, in the one other case at Amarāvatī in which a secondary *stūpa* had an associated inscription, that inscription does not refer to the *stūpa* as "belonging" to a specific school, but seems to describe it as "belonging" to an individual monk, a monk who appears to have been of purely local stature and who is otherwise unknown.

But this itself raises some further questions that it would be well to deal with here. The exact sense of the genitive construction used here in *nāgasenasa khudacetiya,* and in other records connected with *stūpas* "of" local monks, is not at first sight immediately clear. This, in part at least, is related to the fact that in inscriptional Prakrits, much as in the Prakrits generally, the dative case—although it has not entirely disappeared—is very much attenuated, and dative functions have been taken over by an already elastic conception of the genitive. Given these linguistic realities, *nāgasenasa khudacetiya,* for example, can be understood, at least on one level, in two ways: "the small *cetiya of* Nāgasena," or "the small *cetiya for* Nāgasena." It could be argued that the intended meaning here is more like "the small *cetiya* built *for the merit* of Nāgasena by Haghā," but the one certain case I know of that does record something like this is not only late but articulated in a very different way. The case in point occurs in a tenth century inscription from Nālandā where the disciple of a monk is said to have raised "a *caitya* of the Blessed One, the Sugata" (*bhagavataḥ sugatasya caityaḥ*) with the expressed hope or intention that his teacher, through the merit of the disciple's act, might "obtain the unsurpassed station of a *buddha*" (*puṇyenānena labdhāsau bauddham padam anuttaraṃ*).[31] In fact, from the earliest Buddhist inscriptions that record acts undertaken for another, the statement of purpose almost always involves an explicit expression of that fact: the construction is usually something like *aṭhāyā* (*arthāya,* "for the sake of"), either in compound with the name of the person or persons involved, or with the latter in the genitive (*mātāpituna aṭhāyā*), or a construction like *sukhāya hotu savasatānaṃ* ("for the happiness of all beings") is used.[32] The transaction involved is very rarely, if at all, expressed by the simple genitive or dative. In the rare and still uncertain cases in which the simple genitive or dative might be used, it appears that the name of the person for whose benefit a gift is given is put not in the genitive, but in the dative. On what Rao calls "an āyaka pillar" found near the second *stūpa* at Sannati, for example, we find: *ahimarikāya nāganikāya arikā-bhātuno giridatanakasa.* This would appear to indicate that the "pillar" in question was the gift of Giridatanaka, brother of Arikā, "for or in honor of"—expressed by the simple dative—Nāganikā of Ahimara, the latter being a place name.[33] Considerations of this sort would seem to rule out *nāgasenasa khudacetiya* in our Amarāvatī inscription as being intended to convey "the small *cetiya* for the benefit or merit of Nāgasena"; so too does the fact that, although now fragmentary, there seems to have been a separate dedicative statement at the end of the record (compare the better-preserved record from Mathurā cited below).

If, then, *nāgasenasa khudacetiya* does not mean "the small *cetiya* for the benefit or merit of Nāgasena," it—and similarly constructed records elsewhere—must mean "the small *cetiya* of or for Nāgasena" in some other sense. Since *stūpas* or *cetiyas*—whether they were memorials or mortuary containers—were never, as far as we know, erected *for* anyone who was not physiologically dead,[34] this would mean, if our inscription in fact refers to "the small *cetiya* of or for Nāgasena," that Nāgasena must have been not just a local monk, but a *deceased* local monk. But in that case it is important to note that, although Nāgasena was "dead," the *cetiya* was not said to be "of" or "for" his relics or remains, but "of" or "for" him—period. Exactly the same thing is, of course, said elsewhere at Amarāvatī and at other Andhra sites in regard to the *cetiya* of the Buddha. On more than one occasion at Amarāvatī we meet with something like *bhagavato mahāc(e)tiyasa,* "for the Great Shrine of the Blessed One," or *bhagavato mahacetiya-padamale* [rd: *-mūle*], "at the foot of the Great Shrine of the Blessed One."[35] Similar phrasing is also found, for example, at Jaggayyapeṭa: *bhagavato budhasa mahācetiye,* "at the Great Shrine of the Blessed One, the Buddha."[36] In all of these cases, the genitive phrasing was almost certainly intended to express both the fact that the *cetiya* "belonged" to the Blessed One—that is to say, he "owned" it—and the fact that it contained, or was thought to contain, the Buddha himself.[37] It is again important to notice that where we might want to say the *cetiya* was "of" or contained the relics of the Buddha, these inscriptions themselves never use a term for "relics": they say the *cetiya* was "of" or "for" the Buddha himself. He—not his remains—was, apparently, thought to reside inside. But if this is true in regard to the *cetiyas* "of" the Buddha, it would be hard to argue that exactly the same genitive phrasing applied to the *cetiya* "of Nāgasena"—or to the *stūpa* "of" any other local monk—could have meant something different. This secondary *stūpa*—actually called a "small shrine" if we can accept Sivaramamurti's reading—must either have contained, or had been thought to contain, what we would call the "relics" of a local mendicant monk named Nāgasena, but what the composer of the inscription called Nāgasena himself.[38]

It would seem, then, that in the one other possible case at Amarāvatī where we have an inscription associated with a secondary *stūpa,* there is no support for the interpretation of the record on the small umbrella from the same site proposed by Hultzsch, Burgess, Lüders, and others. The former inscription makes no reference to a "school," but rather points towards a very different possibility and set of ideas. It suggests the possibility at least that *utayipabhāhin* in the umbrella inscription may not be the name of a "school" but the name of a deceased local monk. This possibility receives further support when we look elsewhere since, although there are no other instances where a secondary *stūpa* is said to be "owned" by a specific "school," there are a small but significant number of cases where secondary *stūpas* are explicitly said to be "of" or "for" the local monastic dead. At least one of these other cases comes from another sadly dismembered structural site.

It is ironic that, although we have a large number of inscriptions and a far larger number of sculptural and architectural pieces from Mathurā, we know very little really about the structures they were associated with, about what the Buddhist complexes at the site looked like, or how these complexes were laid out. We have only a large number of fragments and disassociated pieces.[39] On one such piece occurs an inscription which van Lohuizen-de Leeuw has read in the following fashion:

> *sa 90 2 he 1 di 5 asya pū(r)vvaye*
> *vi(or kha)ṇḍavihare vasthavyā bhikṣusa grāha-*
> *dāsikasa sthuva prāṣṭhāpāyati sa-*
> *rva sav(v)anaṃ hitasukhaye*

She translates the record as:

> In the year 92, the first (month of) winter, on the 5th day, on this occasion as specified, the inhabitants of the Viṇḍa Monastery erected a stūpa for the monk Grāhadāsika. May it be for the welfare and happiness of all beings.[40]

More than a dozen years later, this same inscription was edited again by Sircar, who seems to have been under the impression that the record was discovered in 1958. Although his reading differs on several minor points from van Lohuizen-de Leeuw's, it is significantly different in only one regard: where van Lohuizen-de Leeuw reads *vasthavyā* plural ("inhabitants"), Sircar reads *vastavya-* and takes it in compound with the following *bhikṣusa*. But this makes for an odd compound and, more importantly, results in a text in which there is no possible subject for the main verb, which Sircar reads as *pra{ti*}ṣṭhāpayati.*[41] The absence of such a subject renders Sircar's construction of the text highly problematic, and suggests that, for the moment, van Lohuizen-de Leeuw's is to be preferred. From the paleographic point-of-view, however, Sircar's *vastavya*—with short final *-a*—appears likely, and this would give a singular subject for the singular verb. The result would be a slight alteration of van Lohuizen-de Leeuw's translation: ". . . an inhabitant of the Viṇḍa Monastery erected a *stūpa* for the Monk Grāhadāsika."

Here, of course, there is no possibility of taking the text to mean "for the benefit or merit of the Monk Grāhadāsika." The text ends with an explicit statement indicating for whom the act was undertaken, and it was not Grāhadāsika, but "all beings." Sircar says: "the object of the inscription is to record the erection of a *stūpa* of the Buddhist monk Grāmadesika"; this is his reading of the name. But he adds: "In the present context, the word *stūpa* mean[s] a memorial structure enshrining the relics of the monk in question."[42] Such an interpretation seems very likely, although here too it is important to note that where Sircar speaks of "relics," the composer of our record—although he certainly could have—does not. For the composer, the *stūpa* does not seem to have been a structure for enshrining relics, but a structure for enshrining, in some sense, the monk himself.

We do not, again, know where the *stūpa* of Grāhadāsika stood. Van Lohuizen-de Leeuw assumes that it "was erected in the monastery," but that is not terribly helpful. The slab on which the inscription is inscribed appears to have been a small one—the writing covers a space that is only nine-and-one-half inches long and four inches high. More than anything else, it seems to resemble the small engraved slabs—to be discussed more fully below—associated with the brick *stūpas* of the local monastic dead at Kānheri, where the writing covers a space of almost the same dimensions. It would appear, then, that the *stūpa* at Mathurā was a small one situated somewhere within the confines of one of the monastic complexes. But in spite of the uncertainties concerning the exact location of the *stūpa* it mentions, this Mathurā record—like Sivaramamurti's Amarāvatī no. 103—does not lend any support to the view that sees in the inscription on the small *chattra* from Amarāvatī a reference to a *stūpa* "belonging" to a specific monastic school. On the contrary, both this Mathurā inscription and Amarāvatī no. 103 would seem to indicate that when secondary *stūpas* or *cetiyas* in this period are inscribed, those *stūpas* or *cetiyas* are *stūpas* or *cetiyas* "of" deceased local monks. That this is so, not just for this period but also for periods long before and after, will become evident below. But these two cases are already sufficient to establish the suspicion that the record on the Amarāvatī umbrella is, again, also referring to such a *stūpa.* Neither Amarāvatī no. 103 nor the Mathurā inscription, however, account for a peculiarity of the Amarāvatī umbrella record, which has undoubtedly exerted considerable influence on previous interpretations.

The Amarāvatī umbrella record does not at first sight appear to be referring to a *cetiya* of a *single* monk. The reading—which is virtually certain apart from the final *anusvāras*—is *aïrāna(ṃ) utayipabhāhīna(ṃ) cediyasa. Aïra,* a Prakrit form of *ārya,* is certainly in the plural, and the following *utayipabhāhin*—though the form is not so well recognized—was almost certainly also intended for a plural. But this use of the plural, rather than suggesting that the *cetiya* "belonged" to a group of monks, may in fact confirm the possibility that the reference is to a single, *deceased* individual.

There are more than a dozen inscriptions that can be cited to demonstrate that the name and titles of a monk for whom a *stūpa* was built were commonly put in the genitive plural. Two are particularly informative: one from Bedsā, which Nagaraju assigns to the first century B.C.E., and one from Kānheri, which he dates to the early second century C.E.[43] In both instances, we are dealing with small secondary *stūpas* whose precise location relative to the main shrine is known. In both instances, these small secondary *stūpas* are inscribed and can therefore be certainly identified as *stūpas* "of" local monks. And in both instances, the individual local monk in question is referred to in the plural.

Less than twenty-five feet to the left of the entrance to the main *caityagṛha* at Bedsā there is "a tiny apsidal excavation" containing a small *stūpa.* On the back wall of this "excavation" there is a short "much weatherworn" inscription in two lines. Some syllables at the beginning of both lines appear to have been lost, but what remains can be fairly certainly read, and the general sense of the record is clear in spite of the missing syllables. Burgess published the following reading in 1883:

> *. . . ya gobhūtinaṃ āraṇakāna peḍapātikānaṃ mārakuḍavāsinā thupo*
> *. . . {aṃte}vāsinā bhatāsāḷa{ḷha}mitena kārita {//}*[44]

In spite of the fact that Gobhūti's name and all his epithets are in the genitive plural, this can only mean:

> The *stūpa* of . . . Gobhūti, a forest-dweller, a mendicant monk who lived on Māra's Peak—caused to be made by his pupil, the devoted Asāḷamita.

At Kānheri as well we have to do with a small excavation containing a *stūpa*. The steps leading up to the chamber containing this *stūpa* are no more than twelve feet to the left of the steps that lead to the main "hall of worship" at the site. On the *harmika* of the small *stūpa* the following record occurs:

> *sidhaṃ heranikasa dhamanakasa bhayā-a*
> *sivapālitanikāya deyadhaṃma*
> *therāna bhayata-dhaṃmapālānaṃ*
> *thuba {//}*[45]

Likewise here we have the name of a monk and his title in the genitive plural, and this can only refer to a single individual:

> Success. The religious gift of Sivapālitanikā, the wife of the treasurer Dhamanaka—the *stūpa* of the Elder, the Reverend Dhaṃmapāla.

Bearing in mind again that *stūpas* were, in so far as we know, erected only for individuals who were dead, these two cases from Bedsā and Kānheri present us with two clear cases where a deceased local monk is referred to in the plural. These cases can only represent a specific application of the *pluralis majestaticus* or plural of respect, and it is important to note that in this regard they are not, apparently, exceptions, but represent something of a rule. Plurals of respect are certainly the rule in the numerous *stūpa* labels found in association with the two monastic "cemeteries" that have been identified at Western Cave sites.

At Bhājā, "probably one of the oldest Buddhist religious centres in the Deccan," a group of fourteen small *stūpas* are clustered together in what Mitra alone has explicitly noted "may be regarded as the cemetery."[46] Nagaraju suggests that these *stūpas* "belong to different dates ranging from late third century B.C. to about the end of the second century A.D."[47] Although Burgess seems to have been of the opinion that a larger number of these *stūpas* had originally been inscribed, in his day only five such inscriptions still remained, in part or in whole. One of the two inscriptions that appeared to be complete reads:

therānāṃ bhayaṃta-aṃpikiṇakānaṃ thūpo {//}

The *stūpa* of the Elder, the Reverend Aṃpikiṇaka.

The other complete record is of exactly the same form, and enough survives of the other three of the five inscriptions to show that, in every case, the name of the monk for whom the *stūpa* was built and his titles were always in the genitive plural.[48] The use of the *pluralis majestaticus* in referring to deceased local monks appears from the Bhājā cemetery labels, then, to have been both an early and a continuous practice over time. But the evidence from the Bhājā cemetery not only confirms this linguistic usage noted previously at Bedsā and Kānheri, it confirms as well the assumed character and contents—in at least one sense—of *stūpas* built "for" deceased local monks. Fergusson and Burgess note that on the capitals of at least four of these *stūpas* there were "holes on the upper surface as if for placing relics . . . and in two cases there is a depression round the edge of the hole as if for a closely fitting cover."[49] The fact that Deshpande discovered at Pitalkhorā exactly the same sort of "holes" still plugged with "a closely fitting cover" and—as a consequence—still containing their relic deposits, makes it highly likely that the "holes" in the *stūpas* at Bhājā—and perhaps all such "holes" in rock-cut *stūpas* in the Western Caves—originally held relics: such *stūpas* were, as a consequence, by no means simply "commemorative" but contained the mortuary deposits of the monks mentioned in their accompanying inscriptions.[50]

The Bhājā cemetery, however, is not the only monastic cemetery in the Western Caves that provides evidence for the use of the *pluralis majestaticus* in referring to deceased monks. The character of the large monastic cemetery at Kānheri was almost immediately surmised. In 1862, West had already said in regard to these groups of *stūpas:* "It seems likely that these topes have contained the ashes of the priesthood and that this gallery has been the general necropolis of the caves."[51] In 1883, Burgess had described this "gallery"—which at that time was assigned the number 38—in the following terms: "No. 38 is the long terrace under the overhanging rock on the brow of the hill, where are the bases of numerous brick stūpas, being the monuments over the ashes of numerous Bauddha sthaviras or priests who died there . . . a vast number fill this gallery"—more than a hundred according to the most recent count—"which is about 200 yards in length; many of them, however, are covered over with the débris of decayed bricks and rock and all seem to have been rifled long ago of any relics or caskets they contained."[52] Although West had already published in 1861 an eye-copy of at least one inscription connected with "the Kaṇheri Bauddha Cemetery"—his no. 58—it was never read;[53] it was not until 1974 or 1975 that further and fuller epigraphical data came in the form of a considerable number of small inscribed slabs, which had originally been inset into the brick *stūpas,* but which—after these *stūpas* had decayed—had either fallen or been thrown into the ravine on the edge of which the gallery sits. The exact number of inscribed insets recovered is not clear—Gokhale says in one place that there were nearly fifteen but in another nearly twenty; Gorakshkar put the number at about forty, but Rao at twenty-nine.[54] Gokhale has edited eight of these inscriptions, but not always well, and the published photographs are not always easy to read.

In spite of these problems, some important points are sufficiently clear. Like the inscriptions associated with the *stūpas* of the local monastic dead at Bhājā, none of the inscriptions so far available from the Kānheri cemetery are donative. They are all labels, and—like the Bhājā inscriptions although more elaborate—they are all consistently patterned. Both considerations are enough to indicate that these labels—like all labels at Buddhist sites—are not the result of individual donative activity but the results of endeavors by the monastic community or its "administration" at their respective sites. Again, as in the Bhājā labels, in all the Kānheri labels that are available—including that published long ago by West—the name and titles of each individual monk for whom a *stūpa* was erected are in the genitive plural. I cite here just two examples that can be checked against the photos:[55]

> *therāṇaṃ ayya-vijayaseṇāṇaṃ tevijāṇaṃ arahantāṇaṃ thūbhaṃ*
>
> The *Stūpa* of the Elder, the Venerable Vijayasena, One Possessed of the Three Knowledges, an Arhat
>
> *therāṇaṃ bhadata-dāmāṇaṃ anāgāmiṇam thū(bhaṃ)*
>
> The *Stūpa* of the Elder, the Reverend Dāma, a Nonreturner

These labels—obviously written by someone familiar with the technical textual terminology of Buddhist conceptions of "sainthood"—establish that at Kānheri, as at Bedsā and Bhājā, deceased local monks were individually referred to in the plural. The use of the *pluralis majestaticus* was, in fact, the rule in referring to such individuals. But if the Bhājā labels establish this usage long before our Amarāvatī umbrella inscription, those from Kānheri establish its continued currency for a long time after. Gokhale had first suggested a date of "between 550 A.D. and 700 A.D." for the Kānheri labels; later they are said to be "written in the late fifth- or early sixth-century boxheaded variety of Brāhmī."[56] In any case, they date from a period long after our Amarāvatī record.

The material presented so far from Amarāvatī itself and from Mathurā, Bedsā, Bhājā, and Kānheri must bear heavily on any interpretation of the Amarāvatī umbrella inscription. This material establishes at least two consistent patterns: first, it would appear that all secondary *stūpas* from Buddhist sites that have associated inscriptions and that date from well before the Common Era to at least the sixth century C.E. are—in every case—*stūpas* raised for deceased local monks; second, with some exceptions that prove the rule, the names and titles of deceased individual monks that occur in *stūpa* inscriptions or labels from this period are put in the genitive plural. The Amarāvatī umbrella record comes from the same period, was associated with a small secondary *stūpa,* and has a name in the genitive plural preceded by a title commonly given to monks. Since, therefore, it conforms in every other respect to records connected with the shrines of deceased local monks, and since *Utayipabhāhin* is nowhere certainly attested as the name of a "school," nor is there any other instance where a secondary *stūpa* is said to belong to such a "school," it is very difficult—if not impossible—to avoid the conclusion that *Utayipabhāhin* in the Amarāvatī umbrella inscription is the name of a local monk. Such a conclusion, it seems, must be accepted until there is clear and incontrovertible evidence to the contrary.[57]

There is, however, one further point in regard to this name that is worth noting, a point that involves us again with yet other *stūpas* of the local monastic dead. Sivaramamurti said that "the term *Utayipabhāhi* is puzzling," and there has, in fact, been some uncertainty in regard even to the stem form of what appears in the inscription as *utayipabhāhīnaṃ* or *utayipabhāhinaṃ.* Originally, Hultzsch seems to have preferred *utayipabhāhin,* but later he and almost everyone else seems to have preferred *utayipabhāhi.*[58] Given the morphological variation in inscriptional Prakrits, a genitive plural form that ends in *-īnaṃ* or *-inaṃ* could have been made from either an *i*-stem or a stem in *-in.* In the present case there is, therefore, no certain formal means of determining the stem, but this—in the end—may not pose a serious problem. It is perhaps more important to note that Hultzsch had proposed *-prabhāsin* as the Sanskrit equivalent of *-pabhāhin*[59] and this—the only equivalent that has been suggested—seems likely: the change of *s* to *h* is well attested in the South.[60] In fact, whether the stem form is taken to have been *-pabhāhin*—which seems preferable—or *-pabhāhi,* it seems fairly certain that, in either case, we would have a derivative from *pra√bhās,* "to shine, be brilliant," etc. It may, therefore, be of interest to note that other derivations from *pra√bhās* occur as the final element of a name or title in—interestingly enough—two other inscriptions connected with the local monastic dead.

Almost one hundred forty years ago, Cunningham published an account of his explorations and "excavations" of the Sāñcī ruins and the Buddhist monuments of central India. Much work has, of course, been done since on Sāñcī—its art, architecture, and inscriptions—but the other related sites in this complex, Sonārī, Satdhāra, Bhojpur, and Andher, have been almost completely ignored. In fact, it is hard to find a reference to them after Cunningham. Also ignored is the fact that this cluster of related sites, among the earliest structural sites that we know, produced some of the clearest and most concrete evidence for the monastic cult of the local monastic dead. Cunningham discovered that the remains of ten individual monks—representing at least three generations—had been deposited in *Stūpa* no. 2 at Sāñcī. The remains of some of these same monks also had been deposited in Sonārī *Stūpa* no. 2, which contained the relics of five individuals, and in *Stūpas* nos. 2 and 3 at Andher.[61] In all of these cases, the deposits had been carefully labeled, and the inscription on one of the Andher deposits reads: *sapurisasa gotiputasa kākanāvapabhāsanasa koḍiñagotasa,* which Majumdar renders as: "(Relics) of the saint Gotiputa, the Kākanāva-pabhāsana, of the Koḍiña-gota."[62] Majumdar notes as well that "the expression *kākanāva-pabhāsana* is used as an epithet of Gotiputa and means 'the Light of Kākanāva,' " Kākanāva being, of course, the old name for Sāñcī.[63] A variant of the epithet also occurs at Sāñcī itself in the one donative record connected with the deposits in *Stūpa* no. 2. Majumdar reads and translates the latter as *kākanava-pabhāsa-siha(n)ā dana,* "the gift of the pupils of the Light of Kākanava," and says here that *kākanava-pabhāsa* "may be taken as standing for Gotiputa himself."[64] If Majumdar is correct in his interpretation of these inscriptions—and the chances are good that he is[65]—they may provide a possible parallel for the "name" that occurs in the Amarāvatī umbrella inscription. *Kākanava-pabhāsana* or *-pabhāsa* is, at Sāñcī and Andher, used both as an epithet of a local monastic "luminary" named Gotiputa and—by itself—as an alternative designation or name of that same individual. This may suggest that *utayipabhāhin* too could have been both an epithet and an alternative name for a prominent deceased local monk from a place named Utayi, which was situated somewhere in the region of Amarāvatī, that *-Pabhāsa* or *-Pabhāsin* might have been an ecclesiastical title of some currency, and that *Utayipabhāsin* might be translated "the Light or Luminary of Utayi"—all of this, at least, would seem a reasonable possibility.

As a result of our discussion so far, we are, then, in a position to do two things: we can offer a new and defensible translation of the old inscription on the small umbrella found long ago at Amarāvatī, and we can make some preliminary and perhaps promising observations on the cult of the local monastic dead in Indian Buddhist monasteries.

The Amarāvatī record can now be translated—keeping close to the syntax of the original—as follows:

> Of the lay-sister Cadā, the mother of Budhi, together with her sons, together with her daughters, to the shrine of the Venerable Luminary from Utayi, the umbrella is a religious gift.

Interpreted and translated in this way, the Amarāvatī inscription takes its place as one among a limited series of significant inscriptions or labels associated with *stūpas* of the local monastic dead. It is significant in regard to Amarāvatī itself because it would provide a much more certain piece of evidence than Sivaramamurti's inscription no. 103 for the presence of such *stūpas* at the site. The presence of such *stūpas* at Amarāvatī is, in turn, significant because it allows us to add it to the list of structural sites for which we have firm epigraphical evidence to prove the presence of *stūpas* of the local monastic dead: epigraphical evidence for the presence of this type of *stūpa* at structural sites has come from Sāñcī, Sonārī, Andher, Mathurā, and now from Amarāvatī. But the Amarāvatī inscription has broader significance as well. It provides us with an especially clear case in which the *stūpa* of a deceased local monk is presented with "gifts" exactly like the *stūpas* of the Buddha himself were, a clear instance in which such a *stūpa* receives the same kind of accoutrement—an umbrella—as did the *stūpas* of the Buddha. This is welcome corroboration of what we learn from the donative inscriptions associated with *Stūpa* no. 2 at Sāñcī, which indicate that coping stones, crossbars, rail-pillars, and pavement slabs, etc., were donated to this *stūpa* of the local monastic dead, just as they were to the *stūpa* of the Buddha at the site. In neither form nor content do the inscriptions associated with *Stūpa* no. 2 differ from those associated with *Stūpa* no. 1. The two sets are virtually indistinguishable, and, in fact, may have had some of the same donors.[66] But in arriving at our interpretation and translation of the Amarāvatī umbrella inscription, we have had to look at virtually all the parallel records that are known, and even our limited discussion of this group of inscriptions allows for some interesting provisional generalizations.

The first and perhaps most obvious generalization might be stated as a simple fact: the remains of the local monastic dead were permanently housed at a significant number of monastic complexes, the majority of which are very early: we have epigraphical evidence from Sāñcī, Sonārī, Andher, Mathurā, Amarāvatī, Bedsā, Bhājā, and Kānheri. These remains, moreover, were permanently housed in the same type of architectural structure as were the remains of the Buddha. I have elsewhere collected epigraphical, archaeological, and literary evidence that suggests that the mortuary remains or relics of the Buddha were thought to be possessed of "life" or "breath," that—as Lamotte says—"la relique corporelle . . . c'est un être vivant,"[67] that they were thought "to be impregnated with the characteristics that defined and animated the living Buddha," that "relics" are addressed as persons and treated as persons.[68] Bareau had, in fact, already noted that the "culte bouddhique des reliques . . . s'inspire en effet d'abord des marques de vénération que l'on adresse aux personnes vivantes."[69] But the fact alone that the remains of the local monastic dead were both treated and housed in the same way as the remains of the Buddha makes it again very difficult to argue that they were thought to be, in any essential way, different. Bareau has also said that "dès avant notre ère, donc, le *stūpa* est plus que le symbole du Buddha, c'est le Buddha lui-même."[70] To argue that the *stūpa* of Utayipabhāhin or the *stūpa* of Gobhūti were thought of any differently would require clear evidence. What evidence is available does not now favor such an argument.

The parallelism between the remains of the Buddha and the remains of the local monastic dead is not limited to the kinds of structures used to house them. There is, as well, a strict parallelism in the way in which these similar structures are referred to. As we have already seen, although we might describe a *stūpa* as a structure "for" relics or a container "of" relics, our inscriptions do not. They refer to *stūpas* or *cetiyas* "for" *persons* or "of" *persons.* This—again as we have seen—is clearly the case for *stūpas* "of" or "for" the Buddha or Blessed One (*bhagavato mahāc(e)tiya-, bhagavato budhasa mahācetiye,* etc.). But it is also the case for *stūpas* "of" or "for" deceased local monks (*aïrānaṃ utayipabhāhīnaṃ cediya-, bhikṣusa grāhadāsikasa sthuva, gobhūtinaṃ āraṇakāna . . . thupo,* etc.). Exactly the same construction and phrasing are used without distinction and regardless of the person "for" whom the *stūpa* was intended. But if this genitive phrasing suggests that, in the case of the Buddha, the *stūpa* "of" the Buddha was thought to contain him, or to be owned or possessed by him, or to be—in some sense—the Buddha himself, then the *stūpas* "of" Utayipabhāhin or Grāhadāsika or Gobhūti, since they are referred to in exactly the same way, could hardly have been thought of differently. In other words, parallel linguistic usage points in the same direction as parallel architectural form.

There may be yet another parallel as well. If we stick to actually datable *stūpas* of the historical Buddha—and put aside the not infrequent assertions of an "Aśokan" date for what are usually hypothetical "earlier" or "original" forms of extant structures—then it will be possible to see that there may be few or no clear chronological gaps between the earliest actually datable *stūpas* of the historical Buddha and the earliest examples of *stūpas* for the local monastic dead that we know. We might take Bhārhut as an example. Scholarly consensus, at least, would place it at or very near the beginning of the known sequence of *stūpas* for the historical Buddha. But Bénisti has recently argued that at least the rail that surrounded the Bhārhut *stūpa* was not the earliest such rail. She has said:

> . . . la décoration qu'offre la *vedikā* qui entoure le *Stūpa* n° 2 de Sāñcī . . . remonte, dans sa quasi totalité, à la première moitié du IIe siècle avant notre ère; elle est donc, de peu, antérieure à celle du *stūpa* de Bhārhut . . . et, très sensiblement, antérieure à celle des *toraṇa* du grand *Stūpa* n° 1 de Sāñcī.[71]

Since "le *Stūpa* n° 2 de Sāñcī" is a *stūpa* of the local monastic dead, this would seem to mean either that this *stūpa* for the local monastic dead predates both the Bhārhut and Sāñcī *stūpas* of the historical Buddha "de peu" and "très sensiblement," or—at least—that it was the first of these to receive the kind of rail we associate with *stūpas* of the Buddha and, therefore, may have been considered, in some sense, more important. However this might ultimately be decided, it would appear—again, at the very least—that, at these early sites, there is no clear or considerable chronological gap between *stūpas* of the local monastic dead and *stūpas* for the historical Buddha; rather, in regard to these structural sites, there appears to be a broad contemporarity between the two types of *stūpas*. This same contemporarity appears to hold for the Western Caves as well. The main *caityagṛha* at Bhājā—Bhājā no. 12—has, for example, been called "the earliest of rock-cut chetiyagharas of [the] Western Deccan" and assigned by Nagaraju to the third century B.C.E.[72] But some of the labeled *stūpas* of the local monastic dead at Bhājā have been assigned to the same period. There is, again, no clear chronological gap. Even at somewhat later sites, *stūpas* for the Buddha and *stūpas* for the local monastic dead seem to appear simultaneously. The inscription in Cave 7—the main *caityagṛha* at Bedsā—is assigned by Nagaraju to his "series III" (60 B.C.E.), but that associated with Gobhūti's *Stūpa* he places in his "series IVa" (60 B.C.E. to 100 C.E.), and he says that it "probably" falls toward the end of the first century B.C.E.[73] Given the fact that paleography alone is rarely capable of making such fine distinctions, it is clear that the two inscriptions—and, therefore, the two *stūpas*—belong to the same broad period. Although the question requires and deserves much fuller study, it appears now that there is possibly little, if any, chronological gap between *stūpas* for the historical Buddha and *stūpas* for the local monastic dead, little clear evidence for the kind of gap that could suggest that practices connected with the former's remains were, over time, extended or generalized to the remains of the latter. Archaeologically and epigraphically, the two types of *stūpas* appear now as roughly contemporary with, in some cases, some indication that *stūpas* of the local monastic dead may actually have predated those of the Buddha. It is interesting to note, moreover, that if we look at the internal chronology or narrative time taken for granted in our Buddhist literary sources, it would appear that their redactors also considered *stūpas* for the local monastic dead to predate those of the Buddha. Both of the *stūpas* mentioned in the *Udāna* and *Apadāna,* and that referred to in the Pāli *Vinaya,* for example, long preceded—according to the narrative time assumed by our texts—those erected for the Buddha.[74] It might, in fact, some day be possible to argue that the relic cult and *stūpas* of the historical Buddha represent only a special and particularly well-known instance of what was a common and widespread monastic practice. It may, indeed, have been much more widespread than our certain evidence now indicates.

It is certain that there were *stūpas* of the local monastic dead at Sāñcī, Sonārī, Andher, Mathurā, Amarāvatī, Bhājā, Bedsā, and Kānheri. This is certain because, at all of these sites, we have either donative inscriptions or inscribed labels that prove it. These inscribed and, therefore, certain instances are, of course, important in themselves. But they also have an importance that goes beyond their respective individual sites. Given the poor state of preservation of most Buddhist sites in India and the virtually complete absence of contemporary documentation concerning them, we often must, and can, argue—as in archaeology in general—from those cases that are certain to those that are less so. In this situation, the individual labeled *stūpas* in their own small separate shrines placed near the main shrine at Bedsā and Kānheri, the clearly labeled *stūpas* in the ordered monastic cemeteries at Bhājā and Kānheri, and the multiple labeled deposits in *Stūpa* no. 2 at Sāñcī—all have considerable indexical or typological importance. They establish the important fact that *all* secondary *stūpas* at monastic sites situated in small separate shrines near the main *stūpa* or in ordered groups away from the hub of the complex or that contain multiple deposits are—in *every* case in which they are *labeled* and it can therefore be determined—mortuary *stūpas* of the local monastic dead. In light of this, it would seem that unless, and until there is evidence to the contrary forthcoming, we are obliged to assume that those *stūpas* found at monastic sites that are similar, but not actually labeled, are also *stūpas* of the local monastic dead. On this basis, we may be able to identify a considerable number of additional *stūpas* of this category.

We may note, for example, using Nagaraju's numbers, that Cave 1 at Bedsā, and Caves 2c, 2d, and 2e at Kānheri are all—like the shrines of Gobhūti at Bedsā and Dhaṃmapāla at Kānheri—excavations grouped around the main *caitya*-hall at their respective sites; they are all small chambers; they all contain a single *stūpa.*[75] If these are not mortuary *stūpas* for the local monastic dead like those of Gobhūti and Dhaṃmapāla, they have no readily explicable function. We may note as well that, at both cave and structural sites, there are groups of unlabeled small *stūpas* that look remarkably like the labeled monastic cemeteries at Bhājā and Kānheri.

Among the Western Caves, Sudhagarh provides an early example. Here, in "a large low-roofed cell," Kail found a group of eight *stūpas* ranging in height from three-and-one-half to four-and-one-half feet. Without citing his evidence or good illustration, Kail said these "are not devotional *stūpas* but are funerary mounds, the relics . . . of a Buddhist saint being enshrined in a hollow receptacle in the square abacus."[76] Nadsur also provides a good example. In Cave 3—which measures thirty-four by twenty feet—there are twelve *stūpas* differing somewhat in size, form, and type of construction, making it virtually certain that they were neither cut nor constructed at the same time. In fact, four of these *stūpas* were structural, and, in the most complete of these, Cousens found "a handful of old rice husks, and about as much grey ash."[77] We might cite Pitalkhorā as a final example from the caves. At Pitalkhorā, on the side of the ravine opposite the main *caityagṛha* and the living quarters, Deshpande describes a cluster of four excavations, all of which contain at least one small *stūpa* and one of which contains three, again dating to different periods. None of this cluster of small *stūpas* are well preserved, but in at least one, Deshpande noted "two holes," one with "a ledge . . . to receive a cover," that—in analogy with similar still-plugged holes containing relics in the *stūpa* of his Cave 3—could only have been used to hold mortuary deposits.[78]

There are no inscriptions associated with these *stūpas* at Sudhagarh or Nadsur or Pitalkhorā, but at all of these sites, we seem to see a number of common characteristics. In so far as we can tell from the reports, there is evidence at all three sites that these were mortuary *stūpas*. At all three sites, these *stūpas* had been placed together in orderly groups over more or less long periods of time. In so far as we can tell—and this is particularly clear at Pitalkhorā—these groups were situated well away from the public areas of their complexes. All three cases—in analogy with similar but inscribed and, therefore, certain cases at Bhājā and Kānheri—can only have been, it seems, cemetery shrines for the local monastic dead. This same kind of argument could be made for several structural sites as well.

This argument could be made for Bhojpur, for example, where at least fifty small *stūpas* whose mortuary character is strikingly evident—large deposits of bones being found in several—are placed together away from the hub of the complex in a way that parallels the placement of the local monastic dead in the cemeteries of the Western Caves and, significantly, at the structural site at Sāñcī.[79] It could be made for the orderly rows of mortuary *stūpas* at Guṇṭupalle in Andhra, which Longhurst long ago suggested could represent "the ruined tombs of monks who died" at the site.[80] It could be made for the area "to the east and north-east of monastery 19" at Śrāvastī, which "seems to have been specifically utilized for the erection of *stūpas*."[81] It could, as well, be made in regard to the still-curious orderly arrangement of secondary *stūpas* at Lauṛiyā Nandangaṛh, whose mortuary character is again clear and whose Buddhist affiliation now seems sure.[82] All of these sites—and a number of others—have all or several of the characteristics that define inscribed and, therefore, certain monastic cemetery shrines, and this would suggest that they too belong to this category.

It is, however, not just individual labeled shrines or labeled monastic cemeteries that have uninscribed parallels. The certain cases of the deposition of the mortuary remains of a number of local monks together in a single *stūpa* at Sāñcī, Sonārī, and Andher argue well for Longhurst's interpretation of the deposits he discovered in at least two *stūpas* at Nāgārjunikoṇḍa. Longhurst found in the spaces created by the "spokes" and crosswalls of the foundations of his *Stūpa* no. 4 "twelve water-pots covered with inverted food bowls . . . together with six large begging-bowls . . . placed on the floor of the chamber near the other vessels. The pots were in small groups of three or four and filled with a mixture of bone ash and fine red earth." By itself, in a separate space, he also found a distinctively shaped "globular" pot inside of which was a silver "casket" that contained in turn "a tiny gold reliquary." Longhurst suggests that this *stūpa* "was built to contain the remains of twelve monks and the ashes of some important divine" from the monastery in front of which it stands. In his *Stūpa* no. 5, Longhurst again discovered six "water-pots and bowls" of the same form and content, and again suggested that this *stūpa* too "was erected to contain the remains of monks or priests" belonging to its associated monastery.[83]

None of the deposits in the two *stūpas* at Nāgārjunikoṇḍa were labeled, and Longhurst does not cite the Sāñcī, Sonārī, and Andher deposits that are. The latter sites, however, establish a sure precedent for the deposition of the mortuary remains of a number of local monks together in a single *stūpa,* and they indicate again that, until we have equally sure evidence or examples to the contrary, we must assume—even in the absence of inscriptions—these *stūpas* at Nāgārjunikoṇḍa also contained, as Longhurst suggested, the remains of the local monastic dead. The same may apply as well to other instances. At Śrāvastī, for example, Marshall discovered in the northeast corner of a very early *stūpa* three "earthen jars . . . filled," he says, "with a mixture of sand and clay."[84]

To round out the range of the possible, we might cite several examples in which there are neither associated inscriptions nor parallels with such inscriptions, but that nevertheless have been interpreted as possible *stūpas* for the local monastic dead. For instance, in referring to the still badly reported Ghoṣitārāma monastery at Kauśāmbī, Ghosh has said:

> the portion presently excavated contained the foundations of a large number of small *stūpas* and pavements with numerous roughly circular postholes. It appears that ordinary monks were memorialized by the erection of small pillars, their relics being buried in earthen pots in the floors adjoining the small *stūpas.*[85]

In *vihāras* at Taxila, Kālawān, and Mohṛā Morādu, Marshall found small *stūpas* built in what originally could only have been the living quarters of individual monks. He suggested that these *stūpas* were funeral monuments intended "as memorials to signalise the sanctity of the cell where some specifically holy *bhikshu* had lived and died," that these *stūpas* "probably" contained the ashes of these monks, or "doubtless contained the bodily relics" of a former resident.[86]

It would appear, then, that the list of certain, probable, and possible monastic sites for which there is evidence for the permanent housing or enshrinement of the local monastic dead is already a long one: Sāñcī, Sonārī, Andher, Mathurā, Bedsā, Kānheri, Bhājā, Amarāvatī, Sudhagarh, Nadsur, Pitalkhorā, Bhojpur, Guṇṭupalle, Śrāvastī, Lauṛiyā Nandangarḥ, Nāgārjunikoṇḍa, Kauśāmbī, Taxila, Kālawān, and Mohṛā Morādu. This list—which is nothing more than preliminary and provisional—is startling if for no other reason than it reflects only what a superficial survey has turned up in reports of explorations and excavations that were almost completely unconcerned with, and uninformed about, the treatment of the local monastic dead. A good deal could be said about early archaeological methods in India and the character of the published reports, much of which would not be kind. One matter, however, is clear: Buddhist historical archaeology in India was from the beginning—and to a large degree remains—text bound.[87] Unfortunately, the texts that were, and to some degree continue to be, the best known are coming more and more to be seen as the least representative and—at least as they were interpreted—less-than-sure guides to actual practice.[88] This meant, of course, that investigators of Buddhist monastic sites often did not know what to look for or did not recognize what they were seeing. Since, for example, it was taken on good scholarly authority that "the *Vinaya*" contained no rules governing the disposal of the monastic dead,[89] it is hardly surprising that no attempt was made to survey sites for evidence of such practices. What is, however, surprising is that especially the early investigators sometimes actually noted such evidence, and in some cases accurately identified it for what it was. It is still more surprising that, in spite of the lack of anything even approaching a systematic attempt to locate evidence for the treatment of the monastic dead, our list of sites for which there is such evidence—however casually or incidentally reported—is as long as it is. Had there been any attempt to locate such evidence, it is reasonable to assume our list would have been far longer.

But this list is impressive not just by its length. It contains a considerable number of early sites and several of the earliest sites that we have certain knowledge of (Sāñcī, Sonārī, Andher, Bhājā, Bhojpur, Pitalkhorā); it includes some of the main Buddhist sites referred to in *nikāya/āgama* literature (Śrāvastī, Kauśāmbī); it includes sites from the South (Amarāvatī, Guṇṭupalle, Nāgārjunikoṇḍa), from the West (Bedsā, Kānheri, Sudhagarh, Nadsur, etc.), from the Northwest (Taxila, Kālawān, Mohṛā Morādu), from Central India (Sāñcī, Sonārī, etc.), and from the Buddhist heartland. In short, this list testifies to a preoccupation with permanently housing or enshrining the local monastic dead that was very early and very widespread geographically.

Again, if nothing else, this preoccupation with local monks forces us toward a long-overdue recognition of the limited character of the so-called great tradition, and an acknowledgment of the potential significance of the purely local in actual Buddhist communities. In an interesting sociological study of the monasteries and modern monks of Bhubaneswar, Miller and Wertz found that when people were asked to name a "holy man," by far the greatest number of them (38.2 percent) named contemporary ascetics *in the local community.* Only 11.3 percent named historical religious figures such as the Buddha, Guru Nanak, or Śaṅkara.[90] These figures must, at least, remind us of the distinct possibility that, whereas *we* tend to locate the "holy" almost exclusively in major historically known Indian religious men, actual Indian communities—including monastic communities—may never have done so. In fact, the mere existence of the architecturally marked presence of the local monastic dead in so many Buddhist monastic complexes already suggests that those who lived in such complexes located the holy at least as often in purely local figures as they did in pan-Buddhist figures such as the Buddha or Śāriputra and Maudgalyāyana. We are, moreover, already able to say a little more about who or what these local figures were, and about the individuals or groups who were preoccupied with preserving their permanent presence.

Information regarding the individual local monks whose remains were preserved at Buddhist monastic sites is, of course, limited to what is contained in the inscriptions and labels associated with their *stūpas* or the deposits of their relics. In some cases, there are indications of a monk's place of origin or residence, but, in all cases, the individual monk involved is given an ecclesiastical title or a title indicative of his religious practice and status or both. It is, however, almost immediately obvious that these titles—whether ecclesiastical or religious—are not, until very late, elaborate. There is little indication that these individuals were "great saints," at least in terms of what we might have expected from textual descriptions of religious achievements.[91] Nor is there much indication that they were high ecclesiastics or "pontiffs." Grāhadāsika in the Mathurā record is simply called a *bhikṣu,* a monk. Dhaṃmapāla at Kānheri, and all the monks in the Bhājā cemetery, are referred to only as "Elders" (*thera*) and given the title "Reverend" (*bhadanta*). The monks whose remains were deposited in *Stūpa* no. 2 at Sāñcī may be referred to collectively as *vināyakas,* which should mean "guide, leader, trainer, or discipliner," but it may be an alternative expression for *vinayadhara,* "preserver of the *vinaya,*" or "*vinaya* master." However, only one of the monks is individually so-called; two are called *ara,* but the significance of this term is unclear. Most scholars have taken it to be equivalent to *arhat,* although that is not likely.[92] The term *arhat* occurs in the Prakrit inscriptions of Central India not infrequently as *arahata, araha, ariha, arāha,* but never as *ara. Ara* could, in fact, just as easily be from *ārya,* although the common form of *ārya* in these same inscriptions is *aya.*[93] One of these monks is also called an *ācārya* and one is called an *ātevāsin,* "pupil." Most significantly, however, *all* of these monks are individually referred to as *sapurisa,* and, in eight out of the ten individual labels, that is all that they are called. At Sonārī, too, *sapurisa* is the only religious title that occurs in the four labels; and at Andher, although one individual is again called a "pupil" and another a *pabhāsana* or "luminary," both are called *sapurisa,* and the two other individuals named there are called only that. The one quality, then, that all of these monks had in common—in addition to the fact that their remains had been enshrined in a set of Central Indian *stūpas*—was classification as a *sapurisa.* Unfortunately, what such a classification meant is not very clear. *Sapurisa* in Pāli seems to mean little more than "a good, worthy man" and is cited as "equal to *ariya*";[94] in Sanskrit sources too, it is said to mean literally a "worthy or true man." Edgerton says that "they are evidently a lay category" and that "the term *satpuruṣa* may include monks."[95] Although the monk in our Amarāvatī umbrella inscription may have a title (*-pabhāhin*) that may be related to one of the titles that occurs at Andher (*-pabhāsana*), and although he is also referred to as an *ārya,* the title *sapurisa* occurs neither in this inscription nor in any of the other inscriptions or labels associated with the local monastic dead. It seems to reflect a purely local classification and—at the very least—one which has no demonstrable connection with canonical or textual definitions of religious achievement or "sainthood." In fact, only two of the early inscriptions connected with the local monastic dead contain references to a distinct type of religious practitioner recognized by the textual tradition. In Amarāvatī no. 103, Nāgasena is called a *peṇḍavatika,* a "mendicant monk," and in the *stūpa* inscription from Bedsā, Gobhūti is called both a *peḍapātika* and an *āraṇaka,* a "forest-dweller," as well. Both *piṇḍapātika* and *āraṇyaka* are, of course, known in the literature, primarily as two of the twelve or thirteen *dhutaṅgas* or *dhutaguṇas.* But the status and value placed on these "ascetic practices"—especially in Pāli sources—are less than clear. *The Pali Text Society Dictionary,* for example, refers to a passage that occurs twice in the *Parivāra* "deprecating such practices," and says that each of the *dhutaṅgas* is "an ascetic practice not enjoined in the Vinaya." It notes as well that "the Milinda devotes a whole book (chap. VI) to the glorification of these 13 *dhutaṅgas,*" but says "there is no evidence that they were ever widely adopted." That there was a certain amount of ambivalence toward these practices in at least some of the literary sources seems fairly sure, and it appears that nowhere were they considered obligatory or an integral part of the career of the *arhat.* It is therefore curious that they, and they alone, find mention in Buddhist epigraphs that refer to significant individuals in actual communities.[96] What is perhaps even more significant, however, is what is absent in these epigraphs. Nowhere in these early inscriptions that refer to local monks whose remains were treated like those of the Buddha is there any reference to the classical textual definitions of Buddhist "sainthood," no certain references to *arhats* or any of the levels of spiritual attainment associated with or preliminary to this ideal. There are, in fact, no indications—apart from references to *piṇḍapātikas* or *āraṇyakas*—that canonical or textual definitions of religious achievement or "sainthood" ever penetrated actual early monastic communities in India, no indications in these records that they were known at all.

The absence of such indications in early records connected with the local monastic dead is in itself striking. But it is even more so in light of the fact that such indications are frequently found—in spite of what might have been expected—in the latest series of such inscriptions, long after, one might have thought, the *arhat* ideal had lost its predominant place. It is not until the sixth or seventh century, and even then only at Kānheri, that we find in records associated with the local monastic dead certain references to *arhats*—seven of the eight Kānheri labels published by Gokhale in 1985 refer to monks who are called *arhats*—and to characteristics associated with textual definitions of "sainthood": *tevija, ṣaḍabhijñāna, anāgāmin,* etc. This situation is, again, not what might have been expected, and deserves fuller study. But it would appear, at the very least, that we have here yet another case indicating that we need not—and probably should not—assume that the presence of an idea in a canonical Buddhist text necessarily means that that same idea was current in actual Buddhist communities. The two need not—and probably often did not—have any necessary connection, chronological or otherwise. Our inscriptions, for example, suggest that the significance of the individual local monks whose remains were carefully and permanently preserved at early monastic sites was not linked to their having achieved the religious ideals articulated in what are taken to be early texts; such a linkage occurs, in fact, only later, long after we think those early texts were composed. Although it would lead too far afield to discuss it here, it is also at least worth noting that nowhere in these inscriptions—even very late and at Kānheri—is there the slightest hint or trace of the religious ideals we associate with the Mahāyāna. When we do finally encounter textual definitions of the ideal, they are definitions articulated in traditions firmly rooted in the *nikāyas* and *āgamas,* and show no influence of the Mahāyāna *Sūtras,* even though a very large number of the latter seem to have been composed long before.[97]

If, then, epigraphical data tell us something about the local monks for whom *stūpas* were raised and whose remains were preserved in early India, if these tell us that such monks were not thought—until very late—to have been *arhats,* but are instead said to be *theras* or *bhadantas* or, sometimes, *piṇḍapātikas,* these same materials also tell us something, finally, about the people who made considerable efforts to ensure the permanent presence of those *theras* and *bhadantas* in their midst, who established, honored, and adored the structures that housed them. Our best information concerning these matters comes, perhaps, from *Stūpa* no. 2 at Sāñcī.

Among the labels found on the deposits in *Stūpa* no. 2 at Sāñcī there is, as we have seen, one donative inscription. Majumdar reads the latter as: *kākanava-pabhāsa-siha{n}ā dana,* and translates it: "the gift of the pupils of the Light of Kākanāva"—"the Light of Kākanāva" being the monk and *sapurisa* Gotiputa mentioned also in an Andher label. If Majumdar's reading and interpretation are correct, then so too must be his conclusion:

> It may, therefore, be concluded that the casket on which this inscription occurs was the gift of the disciples of Gotiputa, the *Kākanava-pabhāsa.* It is highly probable that the other three caskets, which do not bear any donative inscription but were deposited along with this one in the stone box, were likewise contributed by the same persons.[98]

Although Majumdar's derivation of what he reads as *siha* from Sanskrit *śaikṣa* is not entirely free of problems,[99] his interpretation of the record appears to be the most satisfying to date, and it suggests that the deposition of the monastic remains in *Stūpa* no. 2 at Sāñcī was the result of monastic endeavors. But even if this suggestion cannot be taken as entirely certain, even if some doubt might remain concerning the donors of the deposit itself, there can be no doubt that the structure that housed this deposit was disproportionately paid for by monks and nuns. There are ninety-three donative records connected with *Stūpa* no. 2 at Sāñcī in which the status of the donor is clear, and which record the gifts of coping stones, crossbars, rail-pillars, pavement slabs, and berm and stairway balustrades. Forty-four of these inscriptions record the gifts of monks (twenty-eight) and nuns (sixteen), and eight more the gifts of pupils (*antevāsin*) of monks and nuns.[100] This means that well over half of the donors who contributed to the construction and adornment of this *stūpa* of the local monastic dead were monks and nuns, some of whom were *sutaṃtika,* "versed in the *Suttantas,*" and *bhāṇakas,* "reciters (of the *Dharma*)." Unless one would want to argue that monks and nuns made up more than half of the population in the area around Sāñcī, it would appear that monks and nuns not only made up an absolute majority of the donors concerned with *Stūpa* no. 2, but that their numbers were disproportionately large in light of the fact that they almost certainly constituted only a small percentage of the local population; Sāñcī, after all, was very near "the famous and populous city of Vidiśa" and, perhaps, a "nodal point" on an important commercial route between Andhra and the north.[101] It should, therefore, have had a large lay catchment area.

It is unfortunate that we do not have comparably rich data for other *stūpas* of the local monastic dead. But what data we do have point very much in the same direction. We know, for example, that the *stūpa* of Gobhūti at Bedsā was "caused to be made" by the monk-pupil of Gobhūti. It is also virtually certain that the *stūpa* of Grāhadāsika at Mathurā was erected either by a monk or by a group of monks who resided in the Viṇḍa Monastery. The labeled *stūpas* in the monastic cemeteries at both Bhājā and Kānheri could have been erected and maintained only—almost certainly—by the monks of their respective establishments. Had they had individual "donors," it is reasonable to assume that those donors would have been named—as they are at Bedsā, Mathurā, and elsewhere—in their associated inscriptions. But no donors are mentioned. Moreover, the labels at Kānheri especially could only have been written by persons familiar with the textual, technical definitions of "sainthood," and this too would suggest monks. Even in the case of the uninscribed *stūpas,* it is difficult to avoid the conclusion that the monks themselves were responsible for the deposit of the remains of what appear to be local monastic dead. At Nāgārjunikoṇḍa, for example, neither *Stūpa* nos. 4 nor 5 were the main *stūpas* at the site. Both appear to have been the private *stūpas* of the monasteries with which they are closely and physically associated. Again, it is unlikely that anyone but the monks could have established and maintained the orderly groups of *stūpas* at, for example, Sudhagarh and Nadsur. Moreover, and much more broadly, there is evidence to indicate that, from the very beginning, construction activities at monastic sites were—not surprisingly—under the supervision and control of specifically designated monks, and that, as a consequence, what we see at such sites is the reflection of monastic choices and monastic values. Already at Bhārhut and Sonārī, at Amarāvatī, Nāgārjunikoṇḍa, Kānheri, and so on, we find evidence for the presence of *navakammikas,* monks "appointed by the Chapter as a superintendent of the building operations."[102] Njammasch has, in fact, gone some ways toward showing that "Der *navakammika* war offenbar eine wichtige Persönlichkeit in der Struktur der indischen buddhistischen Klöster."[103] The earliest *navakammika* that we have reference to is Isipālita at Bhārhut, and he appears to have been by no means an average monk: in addition to being a "Superintendent of Works," he is also called a *bhadanta,* an *ārya,* and a "Reciter (of *Dharma*)" (*bhāṇaka*);[104] at Amarāvatī, the *Navakammika* Budharakhita is called both a *thera* and a *bhadanta*—that is to say, he belonged to the same class as did so many of the monks for whom *stūpas* were built;[105] at Nāgārjunikoṇḍa, the three *navakammikas* mentioned in the Second Apsidal Temple Inscription F are all called *theras,* the monk responsible for the construction of the *cetiya* and *vihāra* referred to in Detached Pillar Inscription H is called "the Master, the Great Preacher of the Law, the *Thera* Dhaṃma[gho]sa" (*acariyena mahādhaṃmakāthik{e}na dhaṃma{gho}sa-therena anuthitaṃ*), and the *Mahācetiya* was said to have been brought to completion by "the

Reverend Ānanda, who knows the *Dīgha-* and the *Majjhima-nikāyas* by heart" (*dīgha-majhima-nikāya-dharena bhajaṃtānadena nithapitaṃ*).[106] Monks—and oftentimes learned monks—supervised and controlled building activities at monastic sites; they determined, it would appear, what was and what was not built and where it was to be placed. Their choices and their values are, again, what we see expressed at Buddhist monastic sites. These monastic choices and monastic values have almost certainly determined the presence—whether they are inscribed or not—of the *stūpas* of the local monastic dead at so many sites in India.

Although the evidence that we have primarily points directly and indirectly to monastic initiative for the deposition of the remains of the local monastic dead and the establishment of permanent structures to house them, and although this same evidence suggests that monks would have been predominantly preoccupied with and active in any cult of the local monastic dead, there is, as well, some evidence to indicate that the laity were not entirely excluded. The Amarāvatī umbrella inscription, for example, records the gift of an *upāsikā* or "lay-sister" to the *stūpa* of a local monk, although the *stūpa* itself seems, obviously, already to have been in existence.[107] At Kānheri, however, "the *stūpa* of the Elder, the Reverend Dhaṃmapāla" is explicitly said to be "the religious gift of Sivapālitanikā, the wife of the treasurer Dhamanaka."[108] In addition to these records, there are the donative inscriptions from *Stūpa* no. 2 at Sāñcī that also reveal lay participation in activity connected with the local monastic dead. But that participation at Sāñcī, as everywhere else, seems to have been overshadowed by that of the monks. The place and participation of the laity in activity connected with the local monastic dead seems everywhere to have been restricted, and this, in turn, may be reflected in the literature.

Conflict—potential or actual—is a consistent theme in literary accounts of the deposition of the Buddhist dead. The War of the Relics, never actually launched, is an established element of the accounts of the death of the Buddha.[109] Ānanda's death and the deposition of his remains also takes place in a context marked by the threat of war between competing claimants for his remains.[110] But the conflict over the remains of Śāriputra may be of particular interest. Although the only canonical Pāli account of the death of Śāriputra has either suffered—or been intentionally altered—in transmission, still it is clear from the *Saṃyutta-nikāya* account that the collection and preservation of Śāriputra's remains was thought to have been an exclusively monastic affair.[111] The account of these same events in the *Mūlasarvāstivāda-vinaya,* however, presents a much more complicated situation.[112] Although, here too, the initial collection of Śāriputra's remains was undertaken by a monk, and they were taken possession of by the Elder Ānanda, another monk, in this account, the monastic claim to exclusive possession and access is challenged by the wealthy layman Anāthapiṇḍada. He approaches Ānanda and asks for the remains, but Ānanda flatly refuses. This conflict between the monastic and lay claims then has to be mediated by the Buddha himself, who initially seems to favor Anāthapiṇḍada, and instructs Ānanda to hand over the remains. But that the redactors of this version did not see this either as a happy solution or as signaling the end of monastic control seems apparent from what follows: Anāthapiṇḍada takes the remains and enshrines them in his own house, but this only restricts access to these relics in another way. People come to Anāthapiṇḍada's house, but find the door locked. They complain to the Buddha, who, as a result, indicates that *stūpas* for deceased monks—although they might be erected by laymen—have to be erected within the confines of the monastery.

Although this quick summary does not do justice to the text, a text which deserves to be translated in full, it at least suggests that its author assumed or asserted the priority of an exclusive monastic claim to the remains of the monastic dead; it suggests that that claim at some point had been challenged, and that the monastic response to the challenge had been, at best, ambivalent: it allowed lay participation and involvement, but it restricted it to the confines of the monastery and indicated that lay participation was to be governed by monastic rules.

The account of the deposition of the remains of Śāriputra in the *Mūlasarvāstivāda-vinaya* is—in so far as we can now tell—only a story; as such, it can only tell us what its compiler or redactor thought or wanted his intended audience to think. The same applies, as well, to the accounts in the Pāli *Udāna* and *Apadāna* in which the Buddha is presented as directing monks, and monks alone, to perform the funeral and build a *stūpa* for a deceased fellow monk, or to the account in the Pāli *Vinaya* concerning a group of nuns doing the same for one of their deceased members.[113] As of now there is, of course, no way to relate any of these geographically unlocalizable and largely undatable documents directly to any of our sites. The most that we can say is it appears that all of the compilers or redactors of these stories assumed or asserted that concern for the local monastic dead was originally and primarily a concern of monks and nuns, that the laity, if they were involved at all, were thought, or directed to be, only secondarily, even tangentially, involved. This assumption or assertion, moreover, would appear to have been widespread.

These and other passages from the canonical literature deserve to be much more carefully studied for what they can tell us about attitudes and ideas concerning the local monastic dead that various authors or redactors attributed to the Buddha. It is, however, very likely that they will not tell us very much, and this, perhaps, gives rise to the broadest generalization that we can make. The epigraphical and archaeological material we have looked at—although it too requires much fuller study—already tells us some important things about the limitations of our literary sources. We know from the epigraphical and archaeological sources, not only that the remains of the *local* monastic dead were housed in permanent structures that paralleled structures used to house the remains of the Buddha, but we know too that the relationship between the *local* dead and the structures that housed their remains was expressed exactly as was the relationship between the "dead" Buddha and his *stūpa*—that, in both cases, the structure was said to be "of" or "for" the person, not "of" or "for" his remains. We know that there was little, if any, chronological gap between *stūpas* for the Buddha and *stūpas* for the *local* monastic dead; that a considerable amount of effort and expenditure went toward ensuring the continuing presence of deceased purely *local* monks in their respective communities; that the remains of *local* monks were deposited in separate shrines near the main *stūpa* of some sites, or that the remains of several *local* monks were deposited together in a single *stūpa,* or—most commonly—in ordered groups of individual *stūpas* placed away from the central hub of the complex. We know that there were *local,* perhaps regional, definitions of "sainthood," and that the status of *bhadanta* or *thera* appears to have had more than merely ecclesiastical significance in *actual* communities; that the preoccupation with the *local* monastic dead was primarily and predominantly a monastic concern and activity. Finally—and perhaps most importantly—we know that these conceptions and practices concerning the *local* monastic dead were certainly current at Sāñcī, Sonārī, Andher, Mathurā, Amarāvatī, Bhājā, Bedsā, and Kānheri, and probably at a dozen or more widely separated *actual* sites, and that such activity was not only widespread, but in most cases very early. We know all of this from epigraphical and archaeological material.

But almost none of this could have been clearly perceived, precisely understood, or even known from our canonical sources for the simple reason that all of it took place at a *local* level in actual monastic communities, and our canonical sources know nothing of—or say nothing about—the vast majority of the actual local sites at which we know early monastic Buddhism was practiced. There is, moreover, for the vast majority of such sites, no evidence that the canonical sources we know were known or used by the communities that lived there. These sources have, in this sense, no *direct* documentary value at all. If the study of Indian Buddhism is ever to be anything other than a study of what appears to be an idealizing and intentionally archaizing literature, if it is ever to deal directly with how this religion was actually practiced in actual local monasteries, these facts will have to be fully confronted, however uncomfortable that might be.

Notes

1. P. Steinthal, *Udāna* (London: 1885) 8.21; Bhikkhu J. Kashyap, *The Apadāna (II)—Buddhavaṃsa-Cariyā-Piṭaka* (*Khuddakanikāya,* Vol. VII), Nālandā-Devanāgarī-Pāli-Series (Bihar: 1959) 125.16 (54.6.216).

2. H. Oldenberg, *The Vinaya Piṭakaṃ,* Vol. IV (London: 1882) 308–309; cf. G. Schopen, "The *Stūpa* Cult and the Extant Pāli *Vinaya,*" Ch. V above, n. 19.

3. For the Tibetan text, see *Peking,* 44, 95-2-1. Certain aspects of this text—largely shorn of their context—have been discussed several times: W. W. Rockhill, *The Life of the Buddha and the Early History of His Order Derived from Tibetan Works in the Bkah-hgyur and Bstan-hgyur* (London: 1884) 111; L. de La Vallée Poussin, "Staupikam," *HJAS* 2 (1935) 276ff; A. Bareau, "La construction et le culte des stūpa d'après les Vinayapiṭaka," *BEFEO* 50 (1960) 236, 240, 247, 264; G. Roth, "Symbolism of the Buddhist Stūpa According to the Tibetan Version of the Caitya-vibhāga-vinayodbhāva-sūtra, the Sanskrit Treatise Stūpa-lakṣaṇa-kārikā-vivecana, and a Corresponding Passage in Kuladatta's Kriyāsaṃgraha," *The Stūpa. Its Religious, Historical and Architectural Significance,* ed. A. L. Dallapiccola and S. Z. Lallemant (Wiesbaden: 1980) 183ff.

4. de La Vallée Poussin, "Staupikam," 288.

5. For a survey of the kind and character of the "excavation" work done on Buddhist sites up until the '50s—and comparatively little major work has been done on such sites since then—see D. K. Chakrabarti, *A History of Indian Archaeology from the Beginning to 1947* (New Delhi: 1988).

6. J. Burgess, "Is Bezawāḍa on the Site of Dhanakaṭaka?" *IA* 11 (1882) 97–98. There is a good drawing of the plan and elevation of one of these "dolmens or rude-stone burying places" at Amarāvatī in J. Fergusson, "Description of the Amarāvatī Tope in Guntur," *JRAS* (1868) 143, fig. 6. Amarāvatī is not the only Buddhist site in Andhra built on or near proto-historical burials. There is evidence of such burials at Nāgārjunikoṇḍa; see R. Subrahmanyam et al., *Nagarjunakonda (1954–60),* Vol. I, MASI, No. 75 (New Delhi: 1975) 165ff. For Yeleswaram, see M. A. W. Khan, *A Monograph on Yelleshwaram Excavations* (Hyderabad: 1963) 4ff; for Jaggayyapeṭa, see R. Sewell, *Quelques points d'archéologie de l'inde méridionale* (Paris: 1897) 5–6; for Goli, see K. P. Rao, *Deccan Megaliths* (Delhi: 1988) 23; etc. The association of Buddhist sites with proto-historical burials is also by no means limited to Andhra—see, for convenience's sake, D. Faccenna, *A Guide to the Excavations in Swat (Pakistan) 1956–62* (Roma: 1964) 62, 65—and deserves to be much more fully studied as a general pattern. [See G. Schopen, "Immigrant Monks and the Proto-Historical Dead: The Buddhist Occupation of Early Burial Sites in India," *Festschrift Dieter Schlingloff,* ed. F. Wilhelm (Reinbek: 1996) 215–238.]

7. Fergusson, "Description of the Amarāvatī Tope in Guntur," 138, 140.

8. For the modern history of the site and a summary account of the work done on it, see N. S. Ramaswami, *Amaravati. The Art and History of the Stūpa and the Temple* (Hyderabad: 1975) 14–23. There is epigraphical evidence of Buddhist devotional and donative activity at the site in the eleventh century (E. Hultzsch, "A Pallava Inscription from Amaravati," *Madras Journal of Literature and Science for 1886–87* [Madras: 1887] 59–62), in the twelfth and thirteenth centuries (E. Hultzsch, "Two Pillar Inscriptions at Amaravati," *EI* 6 [1900–1901] 146–160), and in the fourteenth century (S. Paranavitana, "Gaḍalādeṇiya Rock-Inscription of Dharmmakīrtti Sthavira," *EZ* 4 [1935] 90–110). Some of the earliest work on the site had already revealed stray sculptures, relief work, and plaques that belonged to a "late" period, and in 1954 D. Barrett had made an attempt to describe "the Later School of Amaravati," which he situated between the seventh and tenth centuries in "The Later School of Amaravati and its Influence," *Arts and Letters* 28.2 (1954) 41–53. More recently, a certain amount of attention has been focused on what is rather loosely called "tantric" material from Amarāvatī and other Andhra sites; see K. Krishna Murthy, *Iconography of Buddhist Deity Heruka* (Delhi: 1988)

and K. Krishna Murthy, *Sculptures of Vajrayāna Buddhism* (Delhi: 1989). Although the latter work is often careless and badly done, still it makes clear that we have much to learn about the later phases of Buddhism in Andhra and suggests that it persisted far longer than we are wont to think. There is, moreover, evidence for this persistence not just at Amarāvatī but at Sālihuṇḍam (R. Subrahmanyam, *Salihundam. A Buddhist Site in Andhra Pradesh* [Hyderabad: 1964] 91ff), Guṇṭupalle (I. K. Sarma, *Studies in Early Buddhist Monuments and Brāhmī Inscriptions of Āndhra Deśa* [Nagpur: 1988] 59–91), Gummaḍidurru (M. H. Kuraishi, "Trail Excavations at Alluru, Gummadidurru and Nagarjunakonda," *ARASI 1926–27* [Calcutta: 1930] 150–161), and at a number of other sites.

9. J. Burgess, *Notes on the Amaravati Stupa* (Madras: 1882) 4, 9.

10. A. Rea, "Excavations at Amarāvatī," *ARASI 1905–06* (Calcutta: 1909) 118–119 and pl. L. Rea's pl. XLVII.6 reproduces "evidently a late example" of the kind of sculpture referred to in n. 8.

11. A. Rea, "Excavations at Amarāvatī," *ARASI 1908–09* (Calcutta: 1912) 90–91 and figs. 1 and 2. Rea called these burials "neolithic pyriform tombs," but Rao (*Deccan Megaliths,* 46) has pointed out that ". . . taking into account the recent evidence, we can safely assign them to the megalithic period." Note the "late" sculptures illustrated in Rea's pls. XXVIIId and XXXId.

12. G. Schopen, "Burial *Ad Sanctos* and the Physical Presence of the Buddha in Early Indian Buddhism," Ch. VII above.

13. Burgess, *Notes on the Amaravati Stupa,* 49.

14. J. Burgess, *The Buddhist Stupas of Amaravati and Jaggayyapeta in the Krishna District, Madras Presidency, Surveyed in 1882* (London: 1887) pl. xlv.6.

15. Burgess, *Notes on the Amaravati Stupa,* 49 (no. 88b), 55 (88b). Hultzsch's final version appeared in E. Hultzsch, "Amarāvatī-Inschriften," *ZDMG* 37 (1883) 555–556, no. 24.

16. H. Lüders, *A List of Brahmi Inscriptions from the Earliest Times to about* A.D. *400 with the Exception of those of Aśoka,* Appendix to *EI* 10 (Calcutta: 1912) no. 1276.

17. R. O. Franke, "Epigraphische Notizen," *ZDMG* 50 (1896) 600.

18. C. Sivaramamurti, *Amaravati Sculptures in the Madras Government Museum,* Bulletin of the Madras Government Museum, N.S. Vol. IV (Madras: 1942) 295, no. 92.

19. Burgess, *Notes on the Amaravati Stupa,* 55 and n. 2.

20. Hultzsch, "Amarāvatī-Inschriften," 555–556, no. 24.

21. Burgess, *The Buddhist Stupas of Amaravati and Jaggayyapeta,* 87.

22. Lüders, *A List of Brahmi Inscriptions,* no. 1276.

23. Sivaramamurti, *Amaravati Sculptures in the Madras Government Museum,* 295, no. 92; 342.

24. *Histoire du bouddhisme indien,* 583–584.

25. O. R. Furtseva, "On the Problem of the Territorial Distribution of the Buddhist Schools in Kushana Age (According to the Epigraphic Data)," *Summaries of Papers Presented by Soviet Scholars to the VIth World Sanskrit Conference, October 13–20, 1984, Philadelphia, Pennsylvania, U.S.A.* (Moscow: 1984) 55; see also A. M. Shastri, "Buddhist Schools as Known from Early Indian Inscriptions," *Bhāratī, Bulletin of the College of Indology* 2 (1957/1958) 48; etc.

26. J. Marshall, *A Guide to Sanchi* (Calcutta: 1918) 87.

27. Sivaramamurti, *Amaravati Sculptures in the Madras Government Museum,* 298.

28. Burgess, *The Buddhist Stupas of Amaravati and Jaggayyapeta,* 72.

29. Burgess, *The Buddhist Stupas of Amaravati and Jaggayyapeta,* pl. xxxi.6; Ph. Stern and M. Bénisti, *Évolution du style indien d'Amarāvatī* (Paris: 1961) pl. lxvi.

30. Sivaramamurti, *Amaravati Sculptures in the Madras Government Museum,* pl. lxv.8.

31. G. Schopen, "A Verse from the Bhadracarīpraṇidhāna in a 10th Century Inscription found at Nālandā," *JIABS* 12.1 (1989) 149–157.

32. See for references G. Schopen, "Two Problems in the History of Indian Buddhism," Ch. II above, nn. 97–102.

33. M. S. Nagaraja Rao, "Brāhmī Inscriptions and their Bearing on the Great Stūpa at Sannati," *Indian Epigraphy. Its Bearing on the History of Art,* ed. F. M. Asher and G. S. Gai (New Delhi: 1985) 41–45, esp. 42, no. 8. There are a number of problems concerning the inscriptions from this recently discovered site in Karnataka, and their nature is not fully understood. For example, although Rao takes the record cited above as a donative inscription and says it occurs on "an āyaka pillar," it is very likely—to judge by the illustration in his pl. 62—that it is a memorial pillar, not an *āyaka* pillar, and the record might simply be a label.

34. Literary sources do, of course, refer to *keśanakha-stūpas, "stūpas* for the hair and nail clippings," and these are—as Feer has said—presented as a kind of "monument élevé à un Buddha de son vivant" (*Avadāna-Çataka. Cent légendes bouddhiques* [Paris: 1891] 482). References to this type of *stūpa* occur widely: in the *Avadānaśataka* (J. S. Speyer, *Avadānaçataka. A Century of Edifying Tales belonging to the Hīnayāna* [St. Petersburg: 1906–1909] i, 123.1, 307.1ff; ii, 71.3; etc.); in the *Divyāvadāna* (P. L. Vaidya, *Divyāvadāna* [Darbhanga: 1959] 122.1–122.25: *dharmatā khalu buddhānāṃ bhagavatāṃ jīvatāṃ dhriyamāṇānāṃ yāpayatāṃ keśanakhastūpā bhavanti* . . . —this is a particularly important passage, and a part of it is quoted as well by Śāntideva in C. Bendall, *Çikshāsamuccaya. A Compendium of Buddhistic Teaching* [St. Petersburg: 1897–1902] 148.13, where he attributes it to the Sarvāstivādins: *ārya-sarvāstivādānāṃ ca paṭhyate*); and scattered throughout the *vastus* of the *Mūlasarvāstivāda-vinaya:* the *Cīvaravastu* (*Gilgit Manuscripts,* iii 2, 143.12), the *Pārivāsikavastu* (*Gilgit Manuscripts,* iii 3, 98.4), the *Śayanāsanavastu* (*Śayanāsanavastu and Adhikaraṇavastu,* 28.1, 5), the *Kṣudrakavastu* (*Derge,* 10, 9.6, 7), etc. There are also a number of references to a *keśanakha-stūpa* in some of the versions of the meeting of the Buddha with Trapuṣa and Bhallika; for some of these—and for further references to *keśanakha-stūpas* in general—see A. Bareau, *Recherches sur la biographie du buddha dans les sūtrapiṭaka et les vinayapiṭaka anciens: de la quête de l'éveil a la conversion de śāriputra et de maudgalyāyana* (Paris: 1963) 106–123; A. Bareau, "La construction et le culte des stūpa d'après les Vinayapiṭaka," *BEFEO* 50 (1960) 261–263; de La Vallée Poussin, "Staupikam," 285–87; etc. But in spite of the fact that there are numerous references in literary sources to such *stūpas,* and in spite of the fact that the Chinese pilgrims refer to them (Li Yung-hsi, *A Record of Buddhist Countries by Fa-hsien* [Peking: 1957] 32; S. Beal, *Buddhist Records of the Western World,* Vol. II [London: 1884] 80, 173; etc.), there is as yet no archaeological or epigraphical evidence to confirm their actual existence. Moreover, the texts themselves indicate that though such *stūpas* were thought to have been built while the *buddhas* in question were still alive, such *stūpas* were built only for *buddhas,* certainly not for local monks like Nāgasena. Finally, it might be noted that the possibility of *cetiyas* being made during the lifetime of the Buddha is also explicitly raised in the Pāli *Kāliṅgabodhijātaka: Sakkā pana bhante tumhesu dharantesu yeva cetiyaṃ kātun* (V. Fausbøll, *The Jātaka together with its Commentary,* Vol. IV [London: 1887] 228.17), and—although the text is not entirely clear—what we normally think of as *stūpas, sāririka-cetiyas,* are clearly and obviously ruled out. Things like the *bodhi*-tree, which the Buddha had "used," are alone

clearly allowed; cf. de La Vallée Poussin, "Staupikam," 284–285. The classification of *cetiyas* into *sāririka, pāribhogika,* and *uddesika* found in the *Kāliṅgabodhijātaka* and other Pāli sources, although frequently cited, shows several signs of being very late; cf. E. W. Adikaram, *Early History of Buddhism in Ceylon* (Colombo: 1946) 135, but note that he has overlooked the *Jātaka* passage.

35. Sivaramamurti, *Amaravati Sculptures in the Madras Government Museum,* nos. 102, 118; cf. no. 51.

36. G. Bühler, "Inscriptions from the Stupa of Jaggayyapeṭā," *IA* 11 (1882) 258 (II.6), 259 (.6); also in Burgess, *The Buddhist Stupas of Amaravati and Jaggayyapeta,* 110, no. 2, 1.5; no. 3, 1.4.

37. For both ideas, see Schopen, "Burial *Ad Sanctos* and the Physical Presence of the Buddha in Early Indian Buddhism," Ch. VII above, esp. 128–131; Schopen, "The Buddha as an Owner of Property and Permanent Resident in Medieval Indian Monasteries," Ch. XII below, 272–274.

38. It is worth noting here that it is in Andhra alone that structures connected with the local monastic dead are called *cetiyas.* Elsewhere, even in the Deccan, they are referred to as *stūpas.* A similar—but not exactly the same—pattern seems to hold as well in regard to structures connected with the "dead" Buddha: in Andhra they are consistently called *cetiyas,* usually *mahā-cetiyas,* while elsewhere in inscriptions—apart from the Western Caves—such structures are usually called *stūpas.* In the Western monastic cave complexes there is evidence to suggest that the structures connected with the "dead" Buddha were called *cetiyas* (e.g. *caityagṛha*), while the word *stūpa* was used "primarily to denote" what Sarkar calls "small-sized memorial *stūpas* raised in honour of some elder *thera*" (H. Sarkar, *Studies in Early Buddhist Architecture of India* [Delhi: 1966] 4). Obviously these regional differences must be more fully studied and precisely plotted, but it is worth noting that some canonical Pāli literature—like Andhran epigraphy—shows a clear preference for the term *cetiya,* and that this shared preference may evidence mutual contact and influence; cf. Schopen, "The *Stūpa* Cult and the Extant Pāli *Vinaya,*" Ch. V above, 89–91.

39. Although it is neither well written nor well documented, C. Margabandhu, "Archaeological Evidence of Buddhism at Mathurā—A Chronological Study," *Svasti Śrī. Dr. B. Ch. Chhabra Felicitation Volume,* ed. K. V. Ramesh et al. (Delhi: 1984) 267–280, provides an overview of work on the site. For attempts to reconstruct even the basic outlines of the development of the site, see M. C. Joshi and A. K. Sinha, "Chronology of Mathurā—an Assessment," *Puratattva* 10 (1978–1979) 39–44; R. C. Gaur, "Mathura-Govardhana Region: An Archaeological Assessment in Historical Perspective," *Indological Studies. Prof. D. C. Sircar Commemoration Volume,* ed. S. K. Maity and U. Thakur (New Delhi: 1987) 103–113; S. C. Ray, "Stratigraphic Evidence of Coins from Excavations at Mathura," *Sraddhānjali. Studies in Ancient Indian History (D. C. Sircar Commemoration Volume),* ed. K. K. Das Gupta et al. (Delhi: 1988) 375–384; M. C. Joshi, "Mathurā as an Ancient Settlement," *Mathurā. The Cultural Heritage,* ed. D. M. Srinivasan (New Delhi: 1988) 165–170; etc. There are two papers that—for different reasons—are particularly important for the site, neither of which is directly connected with Buddhist material: K. W. Folkert, "Jain Religious Life at Ancient Mathurā: The Heritage of Late Victorian Interpretation," *Mathurā. The Cultural Heritage,* 103–112, which discusses some of the distortions in interpretation that have arisen, at least in part, from the piecemeal discovery and publication of the material from Mathurā; and H. Härtel, "Some Results of the Excavations at Sonkh. A Preliminary Report," *German Scholars on India. Contributions to Indian Studies,* Vol. II (New Delhi: 1976) 69–99, which establishes a clear, datable

stratigraphical sequence, and—by contrast—makes clear what could have been gained by systematic excavation of specific complexes at Mathurā.

40. J. E. van Lohuizen-de Leeuw, *The "Scythian" Period. An Approach to the History, Art, Epigraphy and Palaeography of North India from the 1st Century B.C. to the 3rd Century A.D.* (Leiden: 1949) 181–183; van Lohuizen-de Leeuw refers to a still earlier treatment of the record in V. S. Agrawala, "New Sculptures from Mathurā," *Journal of the United Provinces Historical Society* 11.2 (1938) 66–76, but I have been unable to consult this paper.

41. D. C. Sircar, "Brahmi Inscriptions from Mathurā," *EI* 34 (1961–1962) 9–13, esp. 10–11 and pl.

42. Sircar, "Brahmi Inscriptions from Mathurā," 11.

43. S. Nagaraju, *Buddhist Architecture of Western India (c. 250 B.C.—c. A.D. 300)* (Delhi: 1981) 113 (a reading of the Bedsā record is given on 329 as well); chart iii places the Kānheri inscription early in the period between A.D. 100 and A.D. 180 (see also 333, no. 6 under Kānheri). V. Dehejia, *Early Buddhist Rock Temples. A Chronology* (London: 1972) 177, assigns the record from Bedsā to "c. 50–30 B.C."; for Kānheri, see 183–184.

44. J. Burgess, *Report on the Buddhist Cave Temples and Their Inscriptions,* Archaeological Survey of Western India, Vol. IV (London: 1883) 89 (VI.2) and pl. xlvii; see also D. D. Kosambi, "Dhenukākaṭa," *JASBom* 30.2 (1955) 50–71, esp. 70. For the spatial location of this *stūpa* within the Bedsā complex, the most useful site plan is that published in A. A. West, "Copies of Inscriptions from the Caves near Beḍsa, with a Plan," *JBomBRAS* 8 (1864–1866) 222–224 and 2 pl.—this contains as well an eye-copy of the inscription.

45. J. Burgess, *Report on the Elura Cave Temples and the Brahmanical and Jaina Caves in Western India,* Archaeological Survey of Western India, Vol. V (London: 1883) 78, no. 10, and pl. li. For the position of this small "shrine" within the complex, see Nagaraju, *Buddhist Architecture of Western India,* 197–198 and fig. 39; J. Fergusson and J. Burgess, *The Cave Temples of India* (London: 1880) pl. liii.

46. D. Mitra, *Buddhist Monuments* (Calcutta: 1971) 153.

47. Nagaraju, *Buddhist Architecture of Western India,* 129. Dehejia, in *Early Buddhist Rock Temples,* 47–48, 154, assigns the inscriptions to c. 70–50 B.C.

48. For these records from Bhājā, see Burgess, *Report on the Buddhist Cave Temples and Their Inscriptions,* 82–83 (I.2–I.5); Kosambi, "Dhenukākaṭa," 70–71; Nagaraju, *Buddhist Architecture of Western India,* 330; etc.

49. Fergusson and Burgess, *The Cave Temples of India,* 228.

50. M. N. Deshpande, "The Rock-cut Caves of Pitalkhorā in the Deccan," *AI* 15 (1959) 66–93, esp. 72–73. On "relic" deposits in monolithic or rock-cut *stūpas,* see also Fergusson and Burgess, *The Cave Temples of India,* 186, n. 1; H. Cousens, *The Antiquities of Sind. With Historical Outline* (Calcutta: 1929) 105, referring to Kārli; etc.

51. W. West, "Description of Some of the Kānheri Topes," *JBomBRAS* 6 (1862) 116–120, esp. 120.

52. Burgess, *Report on the Buddhist Cave Temples and Their Inscriptions,* 67. On the same page there is a good woodcut illustrating what a part of the cemetery looked like in his day.

53. E. W. West, "Copies of Inscriptions from the Buddhist Cave-Temples of Kānheri, etc. in the Island of Salsette, with a Plan of the Kānheri Caves," *JBomBRAS* 5 (1861) 1–14, esp. 12, no. 58.

54. S. Gokhale, "New Inscriptions from Kānheri," *JESI* 5 (1975) 110–112, esp. 110; S. Gokhale, "The Memorial Stūpa Gallery at Kānheri," *Indian Epigraphy. Its Bearing on the History of Art,* ed. F. M. Asher and G. S. Gai (New Delhi: 1985) 55–59, esp. 55,

and pls. 94–101; S. Gorakshkar, "A Sculptured Frieze from Kānheri," *Lalit Kalā* 18 (1977) 35–38, esp. 35, and pls. xvi–xviii; M. S. Nagaraja Rao, ed., *Indian Archaeology 1983–84—A Review* (New Delhi: 1986) 154; cf. M. S. Nagaraja Rao, ed., *Indian Archaeology 1982–83—A Review* (New Delhi: 1985) 122.

55. Gokhale, "The Memorial Stūpa Gallery at Kānheri," 56, no. 1, pl. 95; 57, no. 4, pl. 98.

56. Gokhale, "New Inscriptions from Kānheri," 110; Gokhale, "The Memorial Stūpa Gallery at Kānheri," 56.

57. Before leaving the question of the use of plurals of respect in Buddhist inscriptions—a question that also requires further study—it is important to note that the use of such plurals, although characteristic of records referring to the local monastic dead, is not restricted to records of this kind. See, for example: E. Senart, "The Inscriptions in the Caves at Nasik," *EI* 8 (1905–1906) 76; Burgess, *Report on the Buddhist Cave Temples and Their Inscriptions,* 85, no. 7; 87, no. 22; 95, no. 17 (etc.); D. C. Sircar, *Epigraphic Discoveries in East Pakistan* (Calcutta: 1975) 11 (there is here, however, the additional problem that the inscription Sircar is referring to may not be Buddhist—cf. S. Siddhanta, "The Jagadishpur Copper Plate Grant of the Gupta Year 128 (A.D. 44–48)," *Journal of the Varendra Research Museum* 1.1 [1972] 23–37); Schopen, "The Buddha as an Owner of Property and Permanent Resident in Medieval Indian Monasteries," Ch. XII below, 264, referring to the Valabhī grants; etc.

58. Burgess, *Notes on the Amaravati Stupa,* 55, no. 88b and n. 2; Hultzsch, "Amarāvatī-Inschriften," 555–556; Burgess, *The Buddhist Stupas of Amaravati and Jaggayyapeta,* 87; Lüders, *A List of Brahmi Inscriptions,* no. 1276; Sivaramamurti, *Amaravati Sculptures in the Madras Government Museum,* 295, no. 92.

59. Burgess, *Notes on the Amaravati Stupa,* 55, n. 2.

60. M. A. Mehendale, *Historical Grammar of Inscriptional Prakrits* (Poona: 1948) 122 (§232, c ii); O. von Hinüber, *Das Ältere Mittelindisch im Überblick* (Wien: 1986) 111 (§221).

61. A. Cunningham, *The Bhilsa Topes; or Buddhist Monuments of Central India* (London: 1854) esp. 184–189, 203–205, 223–236. The local character of the monks whose remains were deposited in the *stūpas* at Sāñcī and related sites has been obscured by an early and persistent tendency to identify some of these monks with some of the monks involved in the so-called Third Council, which is known only from Sri Lankan sources. This sort of identification started with Cunningham himself (184–189) and has been reasserted—with variation and differing degrees of certitude—over the years: see J. F. Fleet, "Notes on Three Buddhist Inscriptions," *JRAS* (1905) 681–691; W. Geiger, *The Mahāvaṃsa or the Great Chronicle of Ceylon* (London: 1912) xix–xx; E. Frauwallner, *The Earliest Vinaya and the Beginnings of Buddhist Literature,* Serie Orientale Roma, VIII (Roma: 1956) 14–15; *Histoire du bouddhisme indien,* 333–334; etc. Such identifications have not, however, gone entirely unquestioned, and recently Yamazaki has presented an argument that has put the question of the "council" and the identification of the monks named on the Sāñcī area deposits in an entirely new light: see G. Yamazaki, "The Spread of Buddhism in the Mauryan Age—with Special Reference to the Mahinda Legend," *Acta Asiatica* 43 (1982) 1–16. It is important to note that even if we were to accept that *some* of the monks whose remains were deposited in *stūpas* at Sāñcī, Sonārī, and Andher were connected with a "Third Council," the majority were not. At least seven of the ten monks—like the named monks at Bedsā, Bhājā, Kānheri, Mathurā, and Amarāvatī—are completely unknown in the so-called Great Tradition and could only have been local monastic "saints."

62. J. Marshall, A. Foucher, and N. G. Majumdar, *The Monuments of Sāñchī,* Vol. I (Delhi: 1940) 294.

63. For more recent remarks on Kākanāva/Sāñcī, see P. H. L. Eggermont, "Sanchi-Kākanāda and the Hellenistic and Buddhist Sources," *Deyadharma. Studies in Memory of Dr. D. C . Sircar,* ed. G. Bhattacharya (Delhi: 1986) 11–27.

64. Marshall et al., *The Monuments of Sāñchī,* Vol. I, 294.

65. Majumdar's interpretation of *siha,* which he says "can be equated with Arddha-Māgadhī *seha,* corresponding to Sanskrit *śaiksha,*" remains, however, problematic; see below n. 99.

66. For the inscriptions from Sāñcī *Stūpa* no. 2, see Marshall et al., *The Monuments of Sāñchī,* Vol. I, 363–375, nos. 631–719, nos. xvi–xxi, and nos. 803, 812, 819–821.

67. *Historie du bouddhisme indien,* 474.

68. Schopen, "Burial *Ad Sanctos* and the Physical Presence of the Buddha in Early Indian Buddhism," Ch. VII above, 125–133; Schopen, "On the Buddha and His Bones," Ch. VIII above, esp. 152–156ff.

69. Bareau, "La construction et le culte des stūpa d'après les Vinayapiṭaka," 268.

70. Bareau, "La construction et le culte des stūpa d'après les Vinayapiṭaka," 269.

71. M. Bénisti, "Observations concernant le Stūpa n° 2 de Sāñcī," *BEI* 4 (1986) 165–170, esp. 165.

72. Nagaraju, *Buddhist Architecture of Western India,* 119, 129.

73. Nagaraju, *Buddhist Architecture of Western India,* 112–113.

74. For references, see nn. 1 and 2 above.

75. Nagaraju, *Buddhist Architecture of Western India,* 107, 191.

76. Very little work has been done on the Buddhist caves at Sudhagarh, the primary source of information on them being O. C. Kail, "The Buddhist Caves at Sudhagarh," *JASBom,* N.S. 41/42 (1966/1967) 184–189, figs. 1–7. Kail assigns the caves to a period ranging from 200 B.C.E. to 150 B.C.E. (188).

77. H. Cousens, *An Account of the Caves at Nadsur and Karsambla* (Bombay: 1891) esp. 3–4 and pl. II. See also J. E. Abbott, "Recently Discovered Buddhist Caves at Nadsur and Nenavali in the Bhor State, Bombay Presidency," *IA* 20 (1891) 121–123. Cousens says: ". . . I think we cannot be far wrong in ascribing to these caves as early a date as Bhājā or Kondāne, i.e., about B.C. 200" (10); Dehejia, *Early Buddhist Rock Temples,* assigns the sculpture at Nadsur to "the period of Sanchi II" (118), but the inscriptions to "around 70 B.C." (153).

78. Deshpande, "The Rock-cut Caves of Pitalkhorā in the Deccan," esp. 78–79. See also W. Willetts, "Excavation at Pitalkhorā in the Aurangabad District of Maharashtra," *Oriental Art,* N.S. 7.2 (1961) 59–65, and Mitra, *Buddhist Monuments,* 174. The latter says: "Curiously enough, all the four caves of this group are associated with *stūpas* . . . evidently made in memory of some distinguished resident-monks as at Bhājā."

79. A. Cunningham, *The Bhilsa Topes; or Buddhist Monuments of Central India,* 211–220.

80. A. H. Longhurst, "The Buddhist Monuments at Guntupalle, Kistna District," *Annual Report of the Archaeological Department, Southern Circle, Madras, for the Year 1916–17* (Madras: 1917) 30–36 and pls. xvii–xxvii, esp. 31 and 35; see also R. Sewell, "Buddhist Remains at Guṇṭupalle," *JRAS* (1887) 508–511; A. Bareau, "Le site bouddhique du Guntupalle," *Arts Asiatiques* 23 (1971) 69–78 and figs. 1–32. Bareau noted that "de tels alignements de petits *stūpa* se retrouvent sur d'autres sites bouddhiques," and evidence for the mortuary character of these *stūpas* is accumulating; see A. Ghosh, ed., *Indian*

Archaeology 1961–62—A Review (New Delhi: 1964) 97, and B. B. Lal, ed., *Indian Archaeology 1968–69—A Review* (New Delhi: 1971) 64. For other results of recent work on the site, see I. K. Sarma, "Epigraphical Discoveries at Guntupalli," *JESI* 5 (1975) 48–61 and pls. i–ix (pl. i gives a good photograph of the rows of *stūpas* on the middle terrace), and Sarma, *Studies in Early Buddhist Monuments and Brāhmī Inscriptions of Āndhradeśa,* 57–91.

81. See, for convenience's sake, M. Venkataramayya, *Śrāvastī* (New Delhi: 1981) 15.

82. T. Bloch suggested that "the funeral mounds in Lauriya go back to the pre-Mauryan epoch" and hinted at a "Vedic" connection in "Excavations at Lauriya," *ARASI 1906–07* (Calcutta: 1909) 119–126. Bloch's views are still occasionally referred to (e.g., P. V. Kane, *History of Dharmaśāstra,* Vol. IV [Poona: 1953] 234, 254), in spite of the fact that Majumdar's later work on the site (N. G. Majumdar, "Explorations at Lauriya-Nandangarh," *ARASI 1935–36* [Delhi: 1938] 55–66 and pls. xix–xxi; N. G. Majumdar, "Excavations at Lauriya Nandangarh," *ARASI 1936–37* [Delhi: 1940] 47–50 and pls. xxi–xxiv) "proved that many of the mounds at Lauriya are Buddhist in character, enclosing *stūpas*" (so G. N. Das, "Coins from Indian Megaliths," *Bulletin of the Deccan College Research Institute* 8 [1947] 208; cf. Mitra, *Buddhist Monuments,* 83–85). A good survey of work on the site may be had in J. E. van Lohuizen-de Leeuw, "South-East Asian Architecture and the Stūpa of Nandangarḥ," *ArA* 19 (1956) 279–290, esp. 281ff.

83. For both *stūpas* and Longhurst's comments, see A. H. Longhurst, *The Buddhist Antiquities of Nāgārjunakoṇḍa, Madras Presidency,* MASI, No. 54 (Delhi: 1938) 20–21. There may as well be a third *stūpa* of this type at Nāgārjunikoṇḍa—see A. Ghosh, ed., *Indian Archaeology 1955–56—A Review* (New Delhi: 1956) 25, under "Site XXV."

84. J. H. Marshall, "Excavations at Saheṭh-Maheṭh," *ARASI 1910–11* (Calcutta: 1914) 4.

85. A. Ghosh, ed., *Indian Archaeology 1955–56—A Review* (New Delhi: 1956) 9; see also G. R. Sharma, "Excavations at Kauśāmbī, 1949–55," *Annual Bibliography of Indian Archaeology* 16 (Leyden: 1958) xlii–xliii.

86. J. Marshall, *Taxila. An Illustrated Account of Archaeological Excavations carried out at Taxila under the Orders of the Government of India between the Years 1913 and 1934,* Vol. I (Cambridge: 1951) 246, 335, 361; J. Marshall, *Mohenjo-Daro and the Indus Civilization. Being an Official Account of Archaeological Excavations at Mohenjo-Daro carried out by the Government of India between the Years 1922 and 1927,* Vol. I (London: 1931) 120–121. See also R. D. Banerji, *Mohenjodaro. A Forgotten Report* (Varanasi: 1984) 59ff. The burial deposits in what has been taken to be a Buddhist monastery at Mohenjo-daro may also be connected with the local monastic dead, but the interpretation of these data remains controversial.

87. Cf. G. Schopen, "Archaeology and Protestant Presuppositions in the Study of Indian Buddhism," Ch. I above.

88. Schopen, "The *Stūpa* Cult and the Extant Pāli *Vinaya,*" Ch. V above, 92–93; Schopen, "Monks and the Relic Cult in the *Mahāparinibbāna-sutta,*" Ch. VI above.

89. See H. Oldenberg, *Buddha. Sein Leben, seine Lehre, seine Gemeinde* (Berlin: 1881) 384, n. 3; H. Oldenberg, *Buddha: His Life, His Doctrine, His Order,* trans. W. Hoey (London: 1882) 376 and note (which contains a significant addition); T. W. Rhys Davids, *Buddhist Suttas,* Sacred Books of the East, Vol. XI (Oxford: 1900) xliv–xlv; and G. Schopen, "On Avoiding Ghosts and Social Censure," Ch. X below.

90. D. M. Miller and D. C. Wertz, *Hindu Monastic Life. The Monks and Monasteries of Bhubaneswar* (Montreal: 1976) 100, table 8.

91. See most recently—although limited to Pāli sources—G. D. Bond, "The Ara-

hant: Sainthood in Theravāda Buddhism," *Sainthood. Its Manifestations in World Religions,* ed. R. Kieckhefer and G. D. Bond (Berkeley: 1988) 140–171.

92. Marshall et al., *The Monuments of Sāñchī,* Vol. I, 290, n. 5.

93. Mehendale, *Historical Grammar of Inscriptional Prakrits,* 169 (§294), 166 (§290 b, i).

94. T. W. Rhys Davids and W. Stede, *The Pali Text Society's Pali-English Dictionary* (London: 1921–1925) 680.

95. *BHSD,* 554.

96. These references to "ascetic" monks—one specifically called a "forest-dweller"—may suggest that what has been noted recently in regard to such monks in modern Thailand and Sri Lanka may have a long history; see S. J. Tambiah, *The Buddhist Saints of the Forest and the Cult of Amulets* (Cambridge: 1984); S. J. Tambiah, "The Buddhist Arahant: Classical Paradigm and Modern Thai Manifestations," *Saints and Virtues,* ed. J. S. Hawley (Berkeley: 1987) 111–126; M. Carrithers, *The Forest Monks of Sri Lanka. An Anthropological and Historical Study* (Delhi: 1983); etc.

97. There are also epigraphical references to the Mahāyāna, or related to what we call "the Mahāyāna," that almost certainly predate the Kānheri labels—at least two at Kānheri itself; see G. Schopen, "Mahāyāna in Indian Inscriptions," *IIJ* 21 (1979) 1–19; Schopen, "Two Problems in the History of Indian Buddhism," Ch. II above, 38–41; Schopen, "The Inscription on the Kuṣān Image of Amitābha and the Character of the Early Mahāyāna in India," *JIABS* 10.2 (1987) 99–134; Schopen, "The Buddha as an Owner of Property and Permanent Resident in Medieval Indian Monasteries," Ch. XII below, n. 49.

98. Marshall et al., *The Monuments of Sāñchī,* Vol. I, 294.

99. Elsewhere at Sāñcī itself we find *sijhā-* for *śaikṣā-,* and *sejha-* for *śaikṣa-,* which suggests a development different from that suggested by Majumdar; see Mehendale, *Historical Grammar of Inscriptional Prakrits,* 151 (§267.b, §286.a iv); also von Hinüber, *Das Ältere Mittelindisch im Überblick,* 114–116 (§§232–236).

100. See Schopen, "The *Stūpa* Cult and the Extant Pāli *Vinaya,*" Ch. V above, n. 32, for a detailed tabulation.

101. Marshall, *A Guide to Sanchi,* 2; H. P. Ray, "Bhārhut and Sanchi—Nodal Points in a Commercial Interchange," *Archaeology and History. Essays in Memory of Shri A. Ghosh,* ed. B. M. Pande and B. D. Chattopadhyaya, Vol. II (Delhi: 1987) 621–629. It should be noted that Ray's figures and remarks concerning the donors at both Sāñcī and Bhārhut are unreliable; they are entirely based on Lüders' *List* and do not take into account the much fuller and more complete collections of inscriptions from both sites published after 1912.

102. This is the definition of *navakammikas* given by J. Ph. Vogel, "Prakrit Inscriptions from a Buddhist Site at Nagarjunikonda," *EI* 20 (1929–1930) 30.

103. M. Njammasch, "Der *navakammika* und seine Stellung in der Hierarchie der buddhistischen Klöster," *Altorientalische Forschungen* 1 (1974) 279–293, esp. 293; but see also P. V. B. Karunatillake, "The Administrative Organization of the Nālandā Mahāvihāra from Sigillary Evidence," *The Sri Lanka Journal of the Humanities* 6 (1980) 57–69, esp. 61–63; G. Fussman, "Numismatic and Epigraphic Evidence for the Chronology of Early Gandharan Art," *Investigating Indian Art,* ed. W. Lobo and M. Yaldiz (Berlin: 1987) 67–88, esp. 80–81 and the sources cited there.

104. H. Lüders, *Bharhut Inscriptions,* Corpus Inscriptionum Indicarum, Vol. II, Pt. 2, ed. E. Waldschmidt and M. A. Mehendale (Ootacamund: 1963) 38 (A59).

105. Sivaramamurti, *Amaravati Sculptures in the Madras Government Museum,* 290, no. 69.

106. Vogel, "Prakrit Inscriptions from a Buddhist Site at Nagarjunikonda," 22, 24 (for an important correction to Vogel's reading of the "Detached Pillar Inscription H," see K. A. Nilakanta Sastri and K. Gopalachari, "Epigraphic Notes," *EI* 24 [1937–1938] 279, VI), 17.

107. See above 167–168; 179.

108. See above 174.

109. See, for convenience's sake, A. Bareau, *Recherches sur la biographie du buddha dans les sūtrapiṭaka et les vinayapiṭaka anciens: II. Les derniers mois, le parinirvāṇa et les funérailles,* T. II (Paris: 1971) 265–288.

110. *Peking,* 44, 243-3-5ff; cf. J. Przyluski, "Le partage des reliques du buddha," *MCB* 4 (1935–1936) 341–367, esp. 347ff.

111. The account of Śāriputra's death occurs at L. Feer, *Saṃyutta-nikāya,* Pt. V (London: 1898) 161–163, and is translated in F. L. Woodward, *The Book of the Kindred Sayings,* Pt. V (London: 1930) 140–143. The text as it appears in Pāli has a close parallel in the Tibetan *Kṣudrakavastu* (*Peking,* 44, 93-1-7ff) as well. The textual situation for the Pāli version is complicated. In the text as printed by Feer, when Cunda announces Śāriputra's death he says: *āyasmā bhante sāriputto parinibbuto idam assa pattacīvaran ti,* "Sir, the Venerable Sāriputta has passed away—here are his robe and bowl." This reading represents the Sri Lanka manuscripts, but Feer notes that one of his Burmese manuscripts has . . . *idam assa pattacīvaraṃ idaṃ dhātuparibhāvanan ti,* and Woodward's note suggests this reading is characteristic of the Burmese manuscripts. What *dhātuparibhāvana* means is not immediately obvious, but it almost certainly contains a reference to relics. In fact, the text of the *Saṃyutta* on which Buddhaghosa wrote his commentary—the *Sāratthappakāsinī*—also appears to have had a reference to relics. Buddhaghosa, citing the text, says: ***idam assa pattacīvaran*** *ti ayam assa hi paribhoga-patto.* ***idam dhātu-parissāvaṇan*** *ti evaṃ ekekam ācikkhi* (F. L. Woodward, *Sārattha-Pakāsinī,* Vol. III [London: 1937] 221.28): " 'This is his robe and bowl' [means] this is indeed the bowl [actually] used by him. 'This is the [or 'a' or 'his'] water strainer [full] of relics'—he described them thus one by one." Where the Burmese manuscripts have the difficult *dhātu-paribhāvana,* the text cited by Buddhaghosa had, then, the more immediately intelligible *dhātu-parissāvaṇa,* "water strainer [full] of relics." The latter, in fact, may well represent a "correction" introduced by a scribe who also had had difficulty with the meaning of *-paribhāvana.* The Tibetan version, though it has nothing corresponding to either *-paribhāvana* or *-parissāvaṇa,* also clearly refers to relics. When Śāriputra's death is announced it is done so in the following words: *btsun pa śā ri'i bu ni yongs su mya ngan las 'das te / de'i ring bsrel dang / lhung bzed dang / chos gos kyang 'di lags so /:* "The Venerable Śāriputra has passed away. These are his relics and his bowl and robe." All of this will require further study to sort out, but it seems virtually certain that the Pāli text as we have it is defective. It appears that in the only canonical Pāli account of the death of Śāriputra reference to the preservation of his relics has either dropped out, or been written out, of the Sri Lankan manuscripts of the *Saṃyutta.*

112. What follows here is based on the Tibetan translation—see above n. 3. [See now G. Schopen, "Ritual Rights and Bones of Contention: More on Monastic Funerals and Relics in the *Mūlasarvāstivāda-vinaya,*" *JIP* 22 (1994) 31–80, esp. 45ff.]

113. For references, see above nn. 1 and 2.

CHAPTER X

On Avoiding Ghosts and Social Censure

Monastic Funerals in the *Mūlasarvāstivāda-vinaya*

FUNERAL RITES and burial practices in Indian Buddhist monasteries have received very little scholarly attention. This is perhaps because such rites and practices, like those in so many other religious traditions, call clearly into question the degree to which purportedly official and purportedly central doctrines were known to the members of actual Buddhist monastic communities, or, if known, the degree to which they had actual impact on behavior. This may be particularly annoying to modern scholars of Buddhism because they seem to like official literary doctrine and seem to want to think—in spite of the apparent absence of good evidence—that it somehow had importance beyond a narrow circle of scholastic specialists. It is, however, perhaps more certainly true that certain statements made by early and good scholars did little to direct attention toward such rites and practices. Oldenberg, as early as 1881, said ". . . the Vinaya texts are nearly altogether silent as to the last honours of deceased monks. To arrange for their cremation was perhaps committed to the laity."[1] T. W. Rhys Davids went even further only eighteen years later. "Nothing is known," he said, "of any religious ceremony having been performed by the early Buddhists in India, whether the person deceased was a layman, or even a member of the order. The Vinaya Piṭaka, which enters at so great length into all details of the daily life of the recluses, has no rules regarding the mode of treating the body of a deceased Bhikkhu."[2]

That such statements would not have encouraged further research would hardly be surprising. If, too, they were entirely correct, there would be little need for it. But they are not. There are at least two things wrong with statements

---

Originally published in *Journal of Indian Philosophy* 20 (1992):1–39. Reprinted with stylistic changes with permission of Kluwer Academic Publishers.

of this kind. First of all, both Oldenberg and Rhys Davids—like so many scholars still—axiomatically assumed that evidence for Buddhist practices can only be found in texts, that texts and texts alone reflect what actually occurred. It does not seem to matter that there was and is clear epigraphical and archaeological evidence that proves that Buddhist monastic communities at Sāñcī, Sonārī, Andher, and Bhojpur, at Bhājā, Bedsā, and Kānheri, at Amarāvatī and Mathurā were concerned—even preoccupied—with ritually depositing and elaborately housing the remains of at least some of the local monastic dead. It does not seem to matter that a good deal of this evidence was available long before either Oldenberg or Rhys Davids were writing, or that a good deal of it dates to the earliest period of Buddhist monasticism of which we have certain knowledge.[3] But even if we put aside—as we must here—this epigraphical and archaeological evidence,[4] the fact remains that both Oldenberg's and Rhys Davids' statements are still distortive. Both refer to "*the Vinaya,*" which meant for them, as it still means for many, only the Pāli *Vinaya.* We now know, however, that the Pāli *Vinaya,* in fact the Pāli canon as a whole, is—in Norman's words—"a translation from some earlier tradition, and cannot be regarded as a primary source," that in some cases the Pāli *Vinaya* is "markedly inferior" to the other *Vinayas,* and in some cases appears decidedly later.[5] Moreover, Csoma's analysis of the Tibetan *'dul ba,* published almost fifty years before Oldenberg, contained enough in summary form to make it clear that if the Pāli *Vinaya* as we have it had "no rules regarding the mode of treating the body of a deceased *Bhikkhu,*" the *Mūlasarvāstivāda-vinaya* did.[6] Rockhill's extracts from the same *Vinaya,* which were published only two years after Oldenberg and six years before Rhys Davids, should have put this beyond all doubt.[7]

This Mūlasarvāstivāda material was, and has remained, largely ignored while Oldenberg's, and especially Rhys Davids', assertions—although demonstrably distorted, if not entirely wrong—have come to be taken as established fact. Kane, for example, in his influential *History of Dharmaśāstra,* simply paraphrases Rhys Davids' remarks concerning the Buddhist treatment of their dead.[8] This clearly will not do, and the Mūlasarvāstivāda material—available in part in Sanskrit in the Gilgit Manuscripts,[9] in part in a partial and far-from-perfect Chinese translation,[10] and in its entirety in the Tibetan Kanjur—needs to be brought into the discussion. There have already been limited and partial attempts to do this, notably by de La Vallée Poussin.[11] What follows, I hope, is a more concerted attempt to be added to those that have gone before though it remains very much in the category of the tentative: it is based on a far-from-full familiarity with two *Vinayas;* it does not take into account the important monastic codes preserved in Chinese (but I hope might stimulate others to do so); it does not solve—but, in fact, exiles to the forest of footnotes or ignores—numerous lexical, terminological, and textual problems encountered in these legalistic codes; it merely suggests and does not necessarily establish some possible lines of interpretation that might or might not prove fruitful. It does, I think, make more fully available some interesting data.

There are literally dozens of references to the death of a local monk in both the Pāli *Vinaya* and the *Vinaya* of the Mūlasarvāstivādins, but the bulk of these in both *Vinayas* occur in what at first sight might seem an unlikely place. In both *Vinayas,* the death of a local monk is treated most fully in their respective "section on robes or robe-material" (*Cīvara-vastu, Cīvarakkhandhaka*). The explanation for this, however, seems to be that the death of a local monk raised for the *vinaya* masters one of the same problems that death in almost every community, whether secular or religious, raises: the problem of property and inheritance. Since the "robe" was one of the primary pieces of personal property that belonged to a monk, and since inheritance might be an important means by which other monks might acquire robes, it is only natural that the disposition of a deceased monk's property would be discussed together with the other means of legitimately acquiring robes and the rules governing such acquisition. In the Pāli *Cīvarakkhandhaka,* inheritance of a monk's property is neither heavily legislated nor encumbered. The formal rules are kept to a minimum. Typical is the first promulgation in this regard: two monks tend to a sick monk who dies. They take the deceased monk's robe and bowl and report his death to the Buddha. The latter says:

> Monks, the Order is the owner of the bowl and robes of a monk who passed away. But truly those who tend the sick are of great service. I allow you, monks, to give through the Order the three robes and the bowl to those who tended the sick.[12]

The formal procedure is then explained. This relatively simple legislation becomes more complicated when the property of a dead monk is more extensive, when, for example, it involves both what the texts call "biens légers" (*lahu-bhaṇḍa, lahu-parikkhāra)* and "biens lourds" (*garu-bhaṇḍa, garu-parikkhāra*).[13] But on the whole, the Pāli *Vinaya* legislates far fewer situations than does the *Mūlasarvāstivāda-vinaya* and limits itself to the enunciation of a few general principles. The *Mūlasarvāstivāda-vinaya,* on the other hand, devotes nearly thirty-five pages to the disposition of a dead monk's property, taking pains to make detailed rulings on a large range of specific situations.[14]

There has been a clear tendency to explain differences of this sort in the *vinayas* as reflections of differences of chronology, to see an increase in number and specificity of rules as an indication of later composition. But this explanation—although a favorite of Western scholars—is only one explanation, and a very narrow one at that. It completely overlooks a number of other equally possible explanations. For example, what has been taken as a reflection of a chronological difference may, in fact, reflect "sectarian" differences in legal rigorism that need not involve any chronological component at all. Looked at in this light, the Pāli rules governing the disposition of a deceased monk's property may simply have been loose, if not lax. They would have allowed a fair amount of ambiguity and leeway for individual judgment. The compilers of the *Mūlasarvāstivāda-vinaya* appear to have intended to prevent both situations and to frame a far stricter and more comprehensive code, a code in which little was left to an individual's or local community's discretion. The *Mūlasarvāstivāda-vinaya* may, then, represent a far stricter rule rather than a later one.

The *Mūlasarvāstivāda-vinaya* also appears to be straightforward about the kind and range of problems that could have arisen in the distribution of a dead monk's property. It contains, for example, the following detailed case about a monk named Upananda, who had amassed a considerable estate.[15] After establishing its right to the estate, which was initially impounded by the King, the community at Śrāvastī proceeded to distribute it among its resident monks. But then the monks from Sāketā heard about Upananda's death and came to claim a share (*asmākam api bhadantopanandaḥ sabrahmacārī. asmākam api tatsantako lābhaḥ prāpadyata iti*). As a result, the text says: *bhikṣubhiḥ pātayitvā taiḥ sārdhaṃ punar api bhājitaḥ,* "after having brought (the estate) together again, the monks (of Śrāvastī) once more divided it together with those (monks from Sāketā)." But this was not the end. Monks from Vaiśālī, Vārāṇasī, Rājagṛha, and Campā came, and the whole procedure had to be repeated again and again. The situation reached the point that, according to the text: *bhikṣavaḥ pātayanto bhājayantaś ca riñcanty uddeśaṃ pāṭhaṃ svādhyāyaṃ yogaṃ manasikāram,* "the monks (because they were always) bringing together and dividing (estates), abandon (their) instruction, recitation, study, yoga, and mental concentration."[16] The Buddha is informed of the situation and as a consequence he declares:

> *pañca karaṇāni lābhavibhāge. katame pañca. gaṇḍī tridaṇḍakaṃ caityaṃ śīlākā jñaptiḥ pañcakam. yo mṛtagaṇḍyām ākoṭyamānāyām āgacchati, tasya lābho deyaḥ. evaṃ tridaṇḍake bhāṣyamāṇe caityavandanāyāṃ kriyamāṇāyāṃ śīlākā{yām ā}caryamāṇāyām. tasmāt tarhi bhikṣavaḥ sarvaṃ mṛtapariṣkāraṃ jñaptiṃ kṛtvā bhājayitavyam. akopyaṃ bhaviṣyati.*[17]

> There are five occasions for the distribution of (a deceased monk's) possessions. Which five? The gong; the *Tridaṇḍaka;* the *caitya;* the ticket; the formal motion is the fifth. Who, when the gong for the dead is being beaten, comes—to him something is to be given. It is the same for when the *Tridaṇḍaka* is being recited, when the worship of the *caitya* is being performed, when tickets are being distributed, {when a formal motion is being made}.[18] Therefore, then, monks, having made a formal motion concerning all of the personal belongings of the deceased, they are to be distributed. It will be a fixed procedure {which is then described}.[19]

A passage such as this is an explicit recognition that Buddhist monastic communities had a wide range of potentially conflicting concerns and preoccupations, all of which were accepted as legitimate. Notice that concern with the distribution of a deceased monk's property is not here—nor in the Pāli *Cīvarakkhandhaka*—in itself ever criticized. It is presented as perfectly legitimate. A problem arises or a situation requiring legislation appears only when that concern distracts monks or communities from other legitimate concerns. In the present case, there is no hint that one set of concerns was considered more important than the other; the problem was to accommodate both. Since there is no legislation in the Pāli *Vinaya* for the particular situation addressed in this Mūlasarvāstivādin passage, and yet we know that the kinds of activities involved were known to, and recognized as legitimate concerns of a monastic community by, the compilers of the Pāli *Vinaya,* we might be able to see in this Mūlasarvāstivādin passage another good example of the consistent tendency on the part of its compilers to insist on a far stricter and more comprehensive code than was framed in the Pāli *Vinaya.* Again, chronological considerations need not enter in. It is, finally, also important to note that this passage presents us with the first direct indication of the intimate connection in the *Cīvara-vastu* of the *Mūlasarvāstivāda-vinaya* between the distribution of a deceased monk's property and what it presents as the proper performance of his funeral: the first of the *occasions* for the distribution mentioned in this passage, and very probably the second and third as well, are—as we shall see—particular moments in a Mūlasarvāstivādin monastic funeral. We know—again as we shall see—from a variety of Mūlasarvāstivādin sources that the sounding of "the gong or bell for the dead" (called variously the *mṛta-, anta-* or *muṇḍikā gaṇḍī* in Sanskrit,[20] and *shi ba'i gaṇḍī* or *gaṇḍī mjug* (v.l. *'jug*) *med pa* in Tibetan[21]) was used "pour l'annonce d'une mort" and appears to have signaled the beginning of the formal funeral proceedings.[22] We also know that the recitation of the "Tridaṇḍaka,"[23] or giving a recitation of *Dharma* (*dharmaśravaṇaṃ dattaṃ*),[24] or of the *Dharma* connected with the impermanent" (*mi rtag pa dang ldan pa'i chos dag bshad nas*),[25] took place at the end of or during the cremation, and that "worshipping the *Stūpa* or *caitya*" (*mchod rten la phyag 'tshal bar bya'o*) appears to have formally terminated the proceedings as a whole.[26]

The moments chosen for the distribution of a dead monk's property do not appear to have been arbitrary but appear initially to have been closely linked to significant moments in his funeral. The order in which they occur also does not appear to be arbitrary; it seems to reflect a sequence of moments that are increasingly removed from the moment of death and would appear to involve a decreasing degree of participation in the funeral activities. He "who, when the gong for the dead is being beaten, comes" is present and participates from the very commencement of the funeral. But he who comes "when the worship of the *caitya* is performed" need only be present at the end, and he who comes only "when a formal motion is being made" need not have been present at all. That the first moment is first in more than just a numerical sense and involves both a priority in time and a priority of rights to inherit is virtually certain. If the distribution takes place at the first moment, there will be no others, and only those present at that moment could partake in the distribution. Priority of rights, therefore, seems directly linked to degree of participation in the funeral. Even if, it is important to note, one might argue that the recitation of the *Tridaṇḍaka* and "the worship of the *caitya*" referred to here need not necessarily refer to moments in the funeral (both activities, as we shall see below, occur in other contexts as well), still the principle holds: preference and priority are still given to those individuals "who, when the gong for the dead is being beaten, come"; there can be no doubt about whether this refers to participation in the funeral. It is also worth noting that the commencement of the funeral with the sounding of the gong significantly underlines its communal character; this means of summons is used only for activities that concern the entire community: it is used "pour la convocation des moines, . . . l'appel au travail, . . . pour le repas," and "pour annoncer un danger."[27] It is perhaps unnecessary to point out that by making physical presence at key moments of the funeral the determining factor in defining who had first rights to participate as a recipient in the distribution of the estate, the compilers of the *Mūlasarvāstivāda-vinaya* assured or reinforced the communal character of the proceedings.

The linkage between the distribution of a deceased monk's property and the performance of his funeral is, in fact, a central theme of one of the two promulgations of rules governing monastic funerals found in the *Mūlasarvāstivāda-vinaya* that we will look at here. This promulgation is the least known and consists of three interlocked texts that mark out individually what appear to have been considered the important elements of a monastic funeral. They are now found together, one after the other in the *Cīvara-vastu*. The edition of these texts published by Dutt is not always satisfactory; although I cite his edition here, I have inserted in brackets at least the more important "corrections" that a study of the manuscript itself has indicated are required. Occasionally, I have also inserted the corresponding Tibetan in parentheses:

I. *śrāvastyāṃ nidānam. tena khalu samayenânyatamo bhikṣur glāno layane kālagataḥ. amanuṣyakeṣūpapannaḥ. cīvarabhājako bhikṣus taṃ layanaṃ praveṣṭum ārabdhaḥ. pātracīvaraṃ bhājayāmîti. sa tīvreṇa paryavasthānena laguḍam ādāyôtthitaḥ kathayati: yāvan mām abhinirharatha* [but ms: *mamābhinirharatha*] *tāvat pātracīvaraṃ bhājayatheti (re zhig kho bo dur khrod du yang ma phyung bar lhung bzed dang gos 'ged par byed dam). sa saṃtrasto niṣpalāyitaḥ.*

etat prakaraṇaṃ bhikṣavo bhagavata ārocayanti.

bhagavān āha: pūrvaṃ tāvan mṛto bhikṣur abhinirhartavyaḥ; paścāt tasya pātracīvaraṃ bhājayitavyam iti.[28]

Although the sense of this text is generally clear, it is still not always easy to arrive at an altogether smooth or satisfying translation. This is in large part due to the language of the greater part of the *Mūlasarvāstivāda-vinaya,* to what Lévi calls "ses étrangetés," and to its "almost colloquial style."[29] There is, for example, a heavy reliance on pronouns, and sometimes the same pronominal form is used in close proximity with two entirely different referents. This, together with an even more general tendency toward elliptical expression, sometimes requires that a good deal of padding be added to any translation. The Tibetan translators have sometimes been forced in this direction. Moreover, each of the texts in this series employs a *yāvat . . . tāvat* construction, the exact sense of which is neither easy to determine nor easy to render into English, and there is some disquieting variation. The Tibetan translations—although sufficiently clear—seem to presuppose a slightly different text as well. Either that, or they have settled for a far looser translation than usual. With these provisos, the first text may be translated:

> I. The setting was in Śrāvastī. On this occasion a certain monk, being sick, died in his cell. He was reborn among the nonhuman beings. The monk who was the distributor-of-robes started to enter the cell (of the dead monk) saying "I distribute the bowl and robes." (But) he (the deceased monk) appeared there with intense anger wielding a club and said: "When you perform for me the removal of the body, (only) then do you effect a distribution of (my) bowl and robe" (Tibetan: "How could one who had not even carried me out to the cremation ground effect a distribution of (my) robe and bowl?").[30] He (the distributor-of-robes) was terrified and forced to flee.
>
> The monks ask the Blessed One concerning this matter.
>
> The Blessed One said: "Now first the removal of a dead monk is to be performed. Then his robe and bowl are to be distributed."

Here we have legislated what appears to be the minimum funereal procedure that must be effected before any distribution of a dead monk's property can take place. This procedure is here expressed by forms of the verb *abhi-nir-√hṛ.* This verb, or close variants of it with or without the initial *abhi-,* is in fact something of a technical expression for the initial act of funereal procedures described in a variety of Buddhist sources.[31] It also occurs in Jain texts dealing with funerals.[32] But even when this exact expression is not used, we find a whole series of parallel expressions—*ādahanaṃ nītvā, śmaśānaṃ nītvā, tam ādāya dahanaṃ gatāḥ, ro bskyal nas,* etc.[33]—that indicate that the removal of the body, undoubtedly ritualized, was a first and minimal procedure involved in carrying out a monastic funeral or a funeral of any kind. It would appear, however, that the compilers of the

Mūlasarvāstivāda-vinaya did not consider this minimum procedure to be necessarily sufficient. After the passage cited above, the second in the series immediately follows:

> II. *śrāvastyāṃ nidānam. tena khalu samayenânyatamo bhikṣuḥ kālagataḥ. bhikṣavas tam abhinirhṛtya evam eva śmaśāne chorayitvā vihāram āgataḥ. cīvarabhājakas tasya layanaṃ praviṣṭaḥ pātracīvaraṃ bhājayāmîti. so 'manuṣyakeṣûpapannaḥ; laguḍam ādāyotthitaḥ sa kathayati: yāvan mama śarīrapūjāṃ kurutha tāvat pātracīvaraṃ bhājayatheti (re zhig kho bo'i ro la mchod pa yang ma byas par chos gos dang lhung bzed 'ged par byed dam zhes).*
>
> *etat prakaraṇaṃ bhikṣavo bhagavata ārocayanti.*
>
> *bhagavān āha: bhikṣubhis tasya pūrvaṃ śarīrapūjā kartavyeti. tataḥ paścāt pātracīvaraṃ bhājayitavyam. eṣa ādīnavo {na} bhaviṣyatîti (nyes dmigs 'dir mi 'gyur ro,* supporting Dutt's *{na}).*[34]
>
> II. The setting was in Śrāvastī. On that occasion a certain monk died. The monks, having performed the removal of that one('s body), having simply thrown it into the burning ground, returned to the *vihāra.* The distributor-of-robes entered his (the dead monk's) cell saying "I distribute the bowl and robe." He (the dead monk) was reborn among the nonhuman beings. Wielding a club he appeared (in his cell) and said: "When you perform the worship of the body for me, (only) then do you distribute (my) bowl and robe?" (Tibetan: "How could one who had not even performed the worshipping of my body effect a distribution of (my) robe and bowl?").
>
> The monks asked the Blessed One concerning this matter.
>
> The Blessed One said: "By the monks the worship of the body for him (the deceased monk) is first to be performed. After that (his) bowl and robe are to be distributed. This will (otherwise) be a danger" (Tibetan: "There would not be in this case a calamity/fault").

This second text, while indicating that the first procedure was still required, indicates as well that it might not prove sufficient and provides separate legislation for what appears to have been considered a second necessary component of a Mūlasarvāstivādin monastic funeral. This procedure is called here—and in a considerable number of other places—*śarīra-pūjā.* And this is a term that, although widely cited, has not been carefully studied and perhaps, has been misunderstood. It has commonly been taken to refer to the worship of relics, but I have recently tried to demonstrate "that *śarīra-pūjā*—whatever it involved—took place after the body had been removed and taken to the cremation ground, but before it was cremated, before there could have been anything like what we call 'relics,'. . ." and that it is "fairly certain that *śarīra-pūjā* involved the ritual handling or treatment of the body prior to cremation . . ."[35] Not surprisingly, this second text played a part in that attempted demonstration: it, perhaps better than any other passage, points toward what *śarīra-pūjā* involved by clearly stating what its opposite was. *Śarīra-pūjā* is presented in our passage as the opposite of, and correct alternative for "having simply thrown the body into the burning ground," or unceremoniously dumping it. That this alternative involved what we understand by the term "worship" seems unlikely, and, from this point of view at least, "worship of the body" is undoubtedly not a very good translation of *śarīra-pūjā.* I have retained it only to maintain some consistency with the way in which the term *pūjā* is generally rendered.[36] The Pāli sources here offer little aid. In fact the term *śarīra-pūjā,* although found throughout Mūlasarvāstivāda literature, is curiously uncommon in Pāli canonical literature outside of the *Mahāparinibbāna-sutta* where it is not impossible that it—like several other lexical items there—may represent a borrowing from continental Sanskrit sources.[37] Although uncommon as well, a Pāli parallel expression may be had in the term *sarīra-kicca,* but it, too, lacks a precise definition, being defined only as "the duties of the body, i.e., funeral rites."[38]

We have, then, in these two texts the legislation of two distinct funereal procedures that appear to have been considered necessary to keep angry ghosts at bay and to allow the distribution of a dead monk's property to go forward unobstructed. These same two procedures, however, are by no means exclusive to a dead monk's funeral; they are also components of, for example, the funerals of the Kings Aśoka (*. . . śibikābhir nirharitvā śarīrapūjāṃ kṛtvā*) and Prasenajit (*. . . dur khrod du skyol cig . . . 'di'i khog pa la mchod pa lhag par bya ba*),[39] and, therefore, do not specifically define a monastic funeral. Something more would appear to be required, and this is precisely what we find in the third and final text of this series:

> III. *śrāvastyāṃ nidānam. tena khalu samayenânyatamo bhikṣur glāno layane kālagataḥ. sa bhikṣur ādahanaṃ nītvā śarīrapūjāṃ kṛtvā dagdhaḥ. tato vihāram āgataḥ* [but ms: *āgatā*]. *cīvarabhājakas tasya layanaṃ praviṣṭaḥ. sa laguḍam ādāyotthitaḥ, tat tāvan* [but ms. clearly *na tāvan,* in this instance agreeing with Tibetan] *māṃ uddiśya dharmaśravaṇam anuprayacchatha tāvac cīvarakāṇi bhājayatheti (re zhig bdag gi ched du chos bsgrags pa ma byas par chos gos rnams 'ged par byed dam).*
>
> *etat prakaraṇaṃ bhikṣavo bhagavata ārocayanti.*
>
> *bhagavān āha: tam uddiśya dharmaśravaṇaṃ dattvā dakṣiṇāṃ uddiśya paścāc cīvarakāṇi bhājayitavyānîti (de'i ched du chos bsgrags pa dang / de'i ched du yon bsngo ba byas nas chos gos rnams bgo bar bya'o).*[40]
>
> III. The setting was in Śrāvastī. On that occasion a certain monk, being sick, died in his cell. After having brought him to the burning ground, (and) having performed (for him) the worship of the body, that (deceased) monk was cremated. After that they (the monks who had performed these procedures) returned to the *vihāra.* The distributor-of-robes entered that

(dead monk's) cell. He (the dead monk) appeared wielding a club, saying "You do not yet give a recitation of *Dharma* for my sake, (but only) then are you to effect a distribution of my monastic robes" (Tibetan: "How could one who had not performed a recitation of *Dharma* for me effect a distribution of (my) robes?").

The monks ask the Blessed One concerning this matter.

The Blessed One said: "Having given a recitation of *Dharma* in his (the deceased's) name, having directed the reward (to him), after that his monastic robes are to be distributed."

In this third and final text of the series, the monks, although they have performed the removal of the body as well as "the worship of the body," are still confronted by the belligerent ghost. He still has not relinquished ownership rights to his property. For that to happen one further—and, by implication, final—procedure appears to be required. This procedure is the most distinctively Buddhist of those so far met and appears to be particularly—perhaps exclusively—associated with monastic funerals. Although, as we have seen, both the "removal" and "the worship of the body" occur in the descriptions of the funerals of the Kings Prasenajit and Aśoka, there is no reference in either account to a recitation of *Dharma* having been made for their sake or a transfer of the resulting merit to their account. This stands in clear contrast with what we often find in the accounts of funerals performed for monks or nuns. In the latter accounts, there is occasional reference either to a recitation of *Dharma* or to the transfer of merit or both.[41] The recitation and the transfer of merit are the last and apparently sufficient elements of a monastic funeral separately legislated here. They appear to achieve the definitive separation of the deceased monk from his property and to allow the distribution of that property to go forward unencumbered. It is important to note that the monks who participate in the funeral generate the merit by giving a recitation of *Dharma,* and it is the monks who assign the merit to the deceased. This appears to be a straightforward case of religious merit being transferred or assigned to one who did not produce it.[42] This straightforward transfer of merit is, in fact, characteristic of many parts of the *Mūlasarvāstivāda-vinaya,* and this *Vinaya* contains as well numerous indications of its compilers' concerns with making such transfers to several categories of the dead.[43] There is, however, more here.

It is, of course, not simply the merit itself that allows the distribution of a dead monk's property to go forward. It is perhaps more the proper and complete performance of his funeral by the monks in attendance. The distribution, therefore, would appear to turn on two points: one, before the property is unencumbered, before any distribution can take place, a set of ritual procedures must be performed or a set of ritual obligations owed to the deceased must be met; two, those who participate in these rituals or in meeting these obligations are—as the account of Upananda's estate makes clear—precisely the same individuals who have a first and prior claim on the estate: "Who, when the gong for the dead is being beaten, comes—to him something is to be given. . . ." It is, moreover, almost certainly not accidental that the monks who perform or participate in the dead monk's funeral are the monks who have the first rights and opportunities to receive or inherit the deceased's property. In fact, such an arrangement would appear to suggest that—at least—these Buddhist monastic regulations governing the distribution of a dead monk's property were framed to conform to, or be in harmony with, classical Hindu laws or Dharmaśāstric conventions governing inheritance. In his *History of Dharmaśāstra* Kane says, for example, that "there was a close connection between taking the estate of a man and performing the rites after death up to the 10th day," and "that it was obligatory on everyone who took the estate of another . . . to arrange for the rites after death and *śrāddha*."[44] The *Baudhāyana-Pitṛmedha-sūtra* says that "proper cremation-rites" should be performed not only for one's mother, father, preceptor, etc., but also for any "person who leaves inheritance for one, whether he belongs to one's gotra or not."[45] This congruency between Buddhist monastic rule and Hindu law is not only interesting,[46] it is also in striking contrast with the apparent lack of congruency between the same *Vinaya* rule and formal Buddhist doctrine.

There can be little question that the promulgation of this set of rules is based on a belief in an individual "personality" that survives after death. That "personality," moreover, was thought to retain an active interest in, and ownership rights to, his former possessions. The claims of that "person" had to be compensated before any distribution of those possessions could take place. This belief—it is important to keep in mind—was assumed and articulated by monks in a code of behavior meant to govern monks. It is not part of some ill-defined lay or popular Buddhism; it is an element of official monastic Buddhism, and, precisely for that reason, its seemingly total lack of congruency with the supposedly fundamental Buddhist doctrine of the absence of a permanent self is even more striking. In speaking of the "traditional Buddhism" of the rural highlands of modern Sri Lanka, Gombrich has said that:

> though the doctrine of *anatta* can be salvaged by the claim that the personality continuing through a series of births has as much reality as the personality within one life, *prārthanā* for happy rebirths and the transfer of merit to dead relatives show that the *anatta* doctrine has no more affective immediacy with regard to the next life than with regard to this, and that belief in personal survival after death is a fundamental feature of Sinhalese Buddhism in practice.[47]

The set of rules governing monastic funerals and inheritance that we have been looking at suggests the very real possibility that there is nothing new in the modern Sri Lankan case. It suggests, as well, the distinct possibility that purportedly "fundamental" Buddhist doctrine may not only have had little influence on lay Buddhist behavior, it may as well have had equally little influence on even highly educated, literate monks.[48] The implications of this possibility are, of course, far reaching, and there are some equally interesting implications for our understanding of monastic Buddhism in a second promulgation of rules concerning monastic funerals found in the *Mūlasarvāstivāda-vinaya.*

Unlike the set of rules for monastic funerals that occur in the *Cīvara-vastu,* the second promulgation, perhaps because it is preserved as well in Chinese, has been referred to several times in the scholarly literature. In fact, apart from short or incidental references, we also have several paraphrases or summaries of the text: the earliest, perhaps, by Rockhill, based on the Tibetan;[49] the fullest, based on the Chinese, by de La Vallée Poussin;[50] and the most recent, again based on the Chinese, by Seidel.[51] None of these paraphrases or summaries are, however, entirely satisfactory from at least one point of view. This text, which is preserved in Tibetan in the *Vinaya-kṣudraka-vastu,* does not link the proper performance of a monastic funeral with the distribution of a deceased monk's property as do the texts preserved in the *Cīvara-vastu.* The text in the *Kṣudraka-vastu* is, rather, preoccupied with yet another problem that the death of a local monk would have raised for a Buddhist community. Unlike the *Cīvara-vastu* texts, which appear to respond to the kind of problems that such a death would occasion within the group—to what might be called "internal problems"—the text in the *Kṣudraka-vastu* appears to have been intended to respond to the kind of problems that such a death could occasion between that group and the larger world that surrounded it and on which it was almost entirely dependent. These external problems are most fully articulated not so much in the rules themselves but in the frame story that accounts for their promulgation, and it is this frame story that has suffered the most in the paraphrases. As a consequence, there are good reasons for citing here the Tibetan text as a whole. The text I cite is based on the three Kanjurs available to me: the Derge, Peking, and Tog Palace:[52]

> *sangs rgyas bcom ldan 'das mnyan yod na rgyal bu rgyal byed kyi tshal mgon med zas sbyin gyi kun dga' ra ba na*[a] *bzhugs so /*
>
> *mnyan yod na khyim bdag cig*[b] *gnas pa des rigs mnyam pa las chung ma blangs te / de de dang lhan cig ces bya ba nas / bu pho zhig btsas te de*[c] *btsas*[d] *pa'i btsas ston zhag bdun gsum nyi shu gcig tu rgya cher byas nas rigs dang mthun*[e] *pa'i ming btags te bsrings bskyed*[f] *nas chen por gyur to zhes bya ba'i bar snga ma bzhin no /*
>
> *ji tsam dus gzhan zhig na legs par gsungs pa'i chos 'dul ba la rab tu byung ba dang / de'i khams ma*[g] *mnyam nas na bar gyur te / de rtsa ba dang / sdong bu dang / me tog dang / 'bras bu'i sman dag gis rim gro byas na ma phan te dus las 'das so /*

de dge slong dag gis lhung bzed dang bcas / chos gos dang bcas par[h] *lam dang nye ba zhig tu bor ro /*

ji tsam na lam de nas bram ze dang khyim bdag 'gro ba de[i] *dag gis de mthong ste / de ni*[j] *kha cig gis smras pa / shes*[k] *ldan dag śākya'i bu*[l] *zhig dus las 'das so / gzhan dag gis smras pa / tshur sheg*[m] *blta bar bya'o /* [n]*de dag gis mthong nas ngo shes te de dag gis smras pa / shes ldan dag 'di ni khyim bdag che ge mo'i bu yin te / dge sbyong śākya'i bu pa mgon med pa rnams kyi nang du rab tu byung bas gnas skabs 'di 'dra bar gyur to / 'di dag gi nang du rab tu byung bar ma gyur na de*[o] *nye du dag gis 'di rim gro byas par 'gyur ba zhig /*

skabs de bcom ldan 'das la dge slong dag gis gsol ba dang / bcom ldan 'das kyis bka' stsal pa / dge slong dag de lta bas na gnang gis dge slong shi ba'i rim gro bya'o / bcom ldan 'das kyis dge slong shi ba'i rim gro bya'o zhes gsungs[p] *pa dang / dge slong dag ji ltar rim gro bya ba mi shes nas / bcom ldan 'das kyis bka' stsal pa / bsreg*[q] *bar bya'o /*

bcom ldan 'das kyis bsreg par bya'o zhes gsungs pa dang / bcom ldan 'das la tshe dang ldan pa nye ba 'khor gyis zhus pa / btsun pa bcom ldan 'das kyis lus 'di la srin bu'i rigs brgyad khri yod do zhes gang gsungs pa de dag ji lta bu lags / bcom ldan 'das kyis bka' stsal pa / nye ba[r] *'khor de skyes*[s] *ma thag tu de dag kyang skye la / shi ba'i tshe de dag kyang 'chi mod kyi 'on kyang rma'i sgo rnams su brtags te bsreg par bya'o /*

bcom ldan 'das kyis bsreg par bya'o zhes gsungs[t] *ba dang / shing ma 'byor nas skabs de bcom ldan 'das la dge slong dag gis gsol ba dang / bcom ldan 'das kyis bka' stsal pa / chu klung dag tu dor bar bya'o / chu klung med nas bcom ldan 'das kyis bka' stsal pa / sa brkos te gzhug par bya'o / dbyar kha sa yang 'thas la shing yang srog chags can du gyur nas / bcom ldan 'das kyis bka' stsal pa / thibs po'i phyogs su mgo byang phyogs su bstan te sngas su rtsva'i*[u] *bam po bzhag la glo g-yas pas bsnyal te rtsva*[v] *'am lo ma'i tshogs kyis*[w] *g-yogs la yon bsngo zhing rgyun*[x] *chags gsum gyi chos mnyan pa byin nas 'dong bar bya'o /*

dge slong dag de bzhin du dong ba dang / bram ze dang khyim bdag dag śākya'i bu'i dge sbyong rnams ni ro bskyal nas khrus mi byed par de bzhin 'dong ste gtsang sbra med do / zhes 'phya bar byed nas / skabs de bcom ldan 'das la dge slong dag gis gsol ba dang / bcom ldan 'das kyis bka' stsal pa / de bzhin du 'dong bar mi bya'i 'on kyang khrus bya'o / de dag thams cad bkru bar brtsams pa dang / bcom ldan 'das kyis bka' stsal pa / thams cad krus mi bya'i gang dag reg pa de dag gis gos dang bcas te bkru bar bya'o / gzhan dag gis ni rkang lag nyi tshe bkru bar bya'o /

de dag mchod rten la phyag mi 'tshal nas / bcom ldan 'das kyis bka' stsal pa / mchod rten[y] *la phyag 'tshal bar bya'o*

NOTES

a. P omits *na.* b. P *gcig.* c. P omits *btsas te de.* d. P *bcas.* e. P *'thun.* f. P *bskyad.* g. T *mi.* h. P *bad.* i. P *da.* j. T *na.* k. P *shas.* l. T adds *pa* after *bu.*

m. T *shog.* n. T has an additional *de* before *de dag gis.* o. T omits *de.* p. P *gsangs.* q. P *bsregs.* r. P, T *bar*; the name is commonly spelled *nye bar 'khor.* s. T *skyed.* t. P *gsung.* u. P *rtsa'i.* v. P *rca.* w. P *kyas.* x. P, T *rgyud.* y. P, T both add *dag* after *rten.*

The Buddha, the Blessed One, dwelt in Śrāvastī, in Prince Jeta's Grove, in the park of Anāthapiṇḍada.

In Śrāvastī there was a certain householder. He took a wife from a family of equal standing and, having laid with her, a son was born. Having performed in detail for three times seven, or twenty-one, days the birth ceremonies for the newborn son, he was given a name corresponding to his *gotra (trīṇi saptakāny ekaviṃśatidivasāni vistareṇa jātasya jātimahaṃ kṛtvā; gotrānurūpaṃ nāmadheyaṃ vyavasthāpitaṃ).*[53] His upbringing, to his maturity, was as before.[54]

When, at another time, he (the householder's son)[55] had entered (the Order of this) well-spoken *Dharma* and *Vinaya,* his bodily humors having become unbalanced, he fell ill. Although he was attended with medicines made from roots and stalks and flowers and fruits, it was of no use and he died (*sa . . . mūlagaṇḍapatrapuṣpaphalabhaiṣajyair upasthīyamāno na svasthībhavati . . . sa ca kālagataḥ*).[56]

The monks left him (i.e., his body), together with his robe and bowl, near a road.

Later, brahmins and householders who were out walking saw him from the road. One said, referring to him: "Good Sirs, a Buddhist monk (*śākyaputra*) has died." Others said: "Come here! Look at this!" When they looked, they recognized the dead monk and said: "Good Sirs, this is the son of such and such a householder. This is the sort of thing that happens when someone joins the Order of those lordless Buddhist *śramaṇas.* Had he not joined their Order, his kinsmen would have performed the funeral ceremonies for him."[57]

The monks reported this matter to the Blessed One, and the Blessed One said: "Now then, monks, with my authorization, funeral ceremonies for a (deceased) monk are to be performed" ("Bhikṣus, il faut rendre les derniers devoirs au cadavre").[58] Although it was said by the Blessed One "funeral ceremonies for a deceased monk are to be performed," because the monks did not know how they should be performed, the Blessed One said: "(A deceased monk) is to be cremated."

Although the Blessed One said: "(A deceased monk) should be cremated," the Venerable Upāli asked the Blessed One: "Is that which was said by the Reverend Blessed One—that there are 80,000 kinds of worms in the human body—not so?" The Blessed One said: "Upāli, as soon as a man is born, those worms are also born, so, at the moment of death, they too surely die. Still, (only) after examining the opening of any wound, is the body to be cremated" ("Quand le corps présente des ulcères, on doit voir s'il n'y a pas d'animaux, et alors le brûler." "Si le cadavre a des plaies, on ne peut le brûler qu'après avoir vérifié s'il n'y a pas de vers").[59]

Although the Blessed One said (a deceased monk) is to be cremated, when wood was not at hand, the monks asked the Blessed One concerning this matter, and the Blessed One said: "The body is to be thrown into a river." When there is no river, the Blessed One said: "Having dug a grave, it is to be buried." When it is summer and both the earth is hard and the wood is full of living things ("En été, la terre est humide et fourmille d'animaux"; "[et] en été, [quand] la terre est humide et fourmille de vers et d'insects?"),[60] the Blessed One said: "In an isolated spot, with its head pointing north, having put down a bundle of grass as a bolster, having laid the corpse on its right side, having covered it with bunches of grass or leaves, having directed the reward (to the deceased),[61] and having given a recitation of the *Dharma* of the *Tridaṇḍaka,* the monks are to disperse."[62]

The monks dispersed accordingly. But then brahmins and householders derided them saying: "Buddhist *śramaṇas,* after carrying away a corpse, do not bathe and yet disperse like that. They are polluted." The monks asked the Blessed One concerning this matter, and the Blessed One said: "Monks should not disperse in that manner, but should bathe." They all started to bathe, but the Blessed One said: "Everyone need not bathe. Those who came in contact (with the corpse) must wash themselves together with their robes. Others need only wash their hands and feet."

When the monks did not worship the *stūpa,* the Blessed One said: "The *stūpa* (v.l. *stūpas*) is to be worshipped" ("Rentrés au couvent, ils ne vénéraient pas le *caitya.* Le Bouddha dit: 'Il faut vénérer le *caitya*' ").[63]

Anyone who has read even a little *Vinaya* will immediately recognize this promulgation of rules as yet another instance—although perhaps a particularly striking one—of the preoccupation of the compilers of these codes with avoiding social censure. This preoccupation—which not infrequently appears obsessive—has been described in a number of ways. Horner has said, for example, in referring to the Pāli *Vinaya:*

For the believing laity, though naturally not to the forefront in the *Vinaya,* are in a remarkable way never absent, never far distant . . . thus the *Vinaya* does not merely lay down sets of rules whose province was confined to an internal conventual life. For this was led in such a way as to allow and even to encourage a certain degree of intercommunication with the lay supporters and followers, no less than with those laypeople who were not adherents of the faith. What was important, was that the monks should neither abuse their dependence on the former, nor alienate the latter, but should so regulate their lives as to give no cause for complaint. With these aims in view, conduct that was not thought seemly for them to indulge in had to be carefully defined, and it became drafted in rule and precept.[64]

Elsewhere, Horner again says: "It must be remembered that it was considered highly important to propitiate these [lay followers], to court their admiration, to keep their allegiance, to do nothing to annoy them."[65] But she also raises another point that may be germane to our *Kṣudraka-vastu* passage and—when seen in a certain light—only underscores the curious absence of such a passage in the Pāli *Vinaya.* She says: "We cannot tell with any degree of accuracy the historical order in which the rules [in the *Vinaya*] were formulated," but she notes that "it is, however, more likely that the majority of the rules grew up gradually, as need arose, and are the outcome of historical developments that went on within the Order."[66]

Horner's observations concerning the monastic sensitivity to lay values are important for a full understanding of our passage because there can hardly be a doubt that this passage—and the rules promulgated there—concern two related topics on which any even partially brahmanized social groups would have been acutely sensitive: death and pollution. Malamoud has not only said that "le rituel funéraire est le *saṃskāra* par excellence," but has noted as well that "les injonctions, les instructions techniques et les justifications théologiques qui traitent de la manière dont les vivants doivent se comporter à l'égard des morts forment une part considérable de la littérature normative de l'Inde brâhmanique (hymnes védiques, Brāhmaṇa, Kalpasūtra, Dharmasūtra et Dharmaśāstra). Le rituel funéraire . . . frappe par sa richesse, sa complexité, sa cohérence." "Le service des morts," he says, "l'institution des morts pèsent d'un poids très lourd dans la vie des Indiens qui se rattachent en quelque manière au brâhmanisme."[67] Much the same, of course, has been said of "purity" and "pollution." "Normative literature," says Dumont, "the literature of the *dharma* or religious law, has purification *(śuddhi)* as one of its main themes, the impurity resulting from birth and death being specially designated *āśauca* . . . Family impurity is the most important: it is that of birth *(sūtaka)* and above all death."[68]

As the sources cited especially by Malamoud would indicate, the brahmanical preoccupation with the proper ritual treatment of the dead was not only broad but very old. It would presumably have informed and presumably have framed the attitudes of any brahmanical or brahmanized community that Buddhist monastic groups came into contact with, and such contact must have been early and frequent, at least in the middle Gangetic plains: the area including Śrāvastī, Kauśāmbī, Rājagṛha, Vaiśālī, etc. Any disregard of such set attitudes in the surrounding population, especially of those touching on the treatment of the dead and pollution, would have opened the Buddhist monastic community to immediate criticism and opprobrium. Such criticism would have been especially strong if the case involved a deceased individual who had originally been a member of the local group, an individual whose history and birth were widely known. The compiler of our *Kṣudraka-vastu* passage seems, in fact, to have encountered or envisioned just such a situation. He seems to have taken some pains to clearly indicate that the deceased monk had been born from a perfectly regular, normatively sanctioned marriage; that the full complement of normative birth rituals had been performed for him; that he had been named according to his *gotra.* The proper performance of ritual that accompanied his birth, however, only provides a stronger contrast for the initial total disregard of normative procedures in regard to his death on the part of the Buddhist monastic community. The response such disregard is said to have provoked seems entirely believable—even the language seems particularly appropriate here: "Come here! Look at this! . . . This is the sort of thing that happens when someone joins the order of those lordless Buddhist *śramaṇas.*" Such behavior would most certainly have alienated "those laypeople who were not adherents of the faith," and almost certainly would not have been long-tolerated by either that group or—importantly—the Buddhist community that had to interact with and depend on it. In fact, unless the extent and depth of brahmanical attitudes among actual communities have been badly overestimated—and this is not impossible—it is almost inconceivable that such blatant disregard of established custom and local feeling would not have been immediately checked and regulated "in rule and precept." But this would, in turn, suggest that such rules, regardless of where they now occur, would probably have been in place very early on, and would suggest that a *Vinaya* which—like the Pāli *Vinaya*—did not contain such rules would have been poorly equipped to deal with monastic communities in close contact with brahmanical societies. The first of these suggestions has historical implications: it may be that this set of rules—like much else in the *Mūlasarvāstivāda-vinaya*—is very old indeed.[69] The second may underscore the importance of geography for understanding the various monastic codes: a monastic code framed in a predominantly brahmanical area would almost certainly—regardless of chronological considerations—contain rules and sets of rules that may differ from or not be included in codes redacted in, or meant for, communities in, say, predominantly "tribal" areas. Local or regional standards may have determined a good deal.

But if this second promulgation of rules concerning the local monastic dead in the *Mūlasarvāstivāda-vinaya* was, unlike the first, intended to respond to a particularly sensitive concern of the larger social group with which Buddhist monastic communities had to interact, and from which they drew recruits and economic support, still the funereal procedures that it prescribed were essentially similar to those of the first promulgation. Formal removal of the body—*abhinirhāra*—though not explicitly mentioned in the rules, is taken for granted throughout: the body is not to be casually dumped by the road side; there is clear reference to the monks having carried away the corpse *(śākya'i bu'i dge sbyong rnams ni ro bskyal nas)* in the remarks of the brahmins and householders concerning monks not having washed. Although the term *śarīra-pūjā / ro la mchod pa* is not explicitly used, *rim gro bya ba*—which generally translates some form of *sat√kṛ*—is, contextually, clearly its equivalent here: whereas in *Cīvara-vastu* II *śarīra-pūjā* is the prescribed alternative to simply dumping the body in the burning ground, *satkāra* here is the prescribed alternative to throwing it unceremoniously alongside the road.[70] The *Kṣudraka-vastu* passage differs, to be sure, in stipulating certain contingencies when alternative means of disposal could be used, but, in doing so, it only emphasizes the fact that the first choice in normal circumstances was cremation. The two related elements in the *Cīvara-vastu* monastic funeral that appear to be both most peculiarly Buddhist and, perhaps, restricted to funerals for monks—the recitation of *Dharma* and the transfer of merit—are also both explicitly mentioned and taken for granted. Although only actually mentioned after the last of the series of alternative means of disposal, it seems fairly certain it was to be understood that both the recitation and the transfer of merit were to follow whichever alternative was undertaken.[71]

We have seen, then, in this quick look at these passages from the *Mūlasarvāsti-vāda-vinaya* two sets of similar and mutually supplementary rules meant to govern a monastic funeral. Contrary to the old and established conventional wisdom, they establish that Buddhist *Vinaya* texts are by no means "nearly altogether silent as to the last honours of deceased monks," and they point to yet another concern in regard to which the Pāli *Vinaya,* as we have it, appears to be markedly deficient and possibly unrepresentative. Together with various narrative accounts scattered throughout Mūlasarvāstivādin literature, they also allow us to reconstruct the complete outline of a Mūlasarvāstivādin monastic funeral, from the tolling of the bell to the postfuneral bath, and they indicate that the laity were allowed no place in these procedures, that the funeral of a local monk was an exclusively monastic affair where participation was limited to monks and monks alone.[72] Even more than this, they allow us entrée into the mentality and concerns of the *Vinaya* masters who framed this code. They allow us to see learned monks and *Vinaya* authorities framing rules that were intended to avoid ghosts[73] and were preoccupied with the problems of inheritance and estates; monks concerned with carefully regulating behavior to avoid social censure; and monks—perhaps most importantly—who appear to have been influenced and motivated as much by Indian mores, beliefs, and legal conventions as by specifically Buddhist doctrines. They allow us to see, in short, a Buddhist monk who is far more human, and far more Indian, than the monk we usually meet in the works of Western scholarship.[74]

Textual Sources Cited and Abbreviations

The following notes contain several abbreviated titles of textual sources that differ from the listing at xv–xvii. These include:

ACF = *Annuaire du collège de france*
Aṅguttara = R. Morris and E. Hardy, eds., *The Aṅguttara-Nikāya,* Vols. i–v (London: 1885–1900). Cited by volume number and page.
Avadānaśataka = J. S. Speyer, ed., *Avadānaçataka. A Century of Edifying Tales belonging to the Hīnayāna,* Bibliotheca Buddhica, III, Vols. i and ii (St.-Pétersbourg: 1906–1909). Cited by volume, page, and line.
Divyāvadāna = P. L. Vaidya, ed., *Divyāvadāna,* Buddhist Sanskrit Texts, 20 (Darbhanga: 1959). Cited by page and line.
JOIB = *Journal of the Oriental Institute, Baroda*
Mahāparinirvāṇa-sūtra = E. Waldschmidt, ed., *Das Mahāparinirvāṇasūtra. Text in Sanskrit und Tibetisch, verglichen mit dem Pāli nebst einer Übersetzung der chinesischen Entsprechung im Vinaya der Mūlasarvāstivādins,* Teil I, Abhandlungen der Deutschen Akademie der Wissenschaften zu Berlin, Philosophisch-Historische Klasse, Jahrgang 1949, Nr. 1 (Berlin: 1950); Teil II, Abhandlungen . . . zu Berlin, Klasse für Sprachen, Literatur und Kunst, Jahrgang 1950, Nr. 2 (Berlin: 1951); Teil III, Abhandlungen . . . und Kunst, Jahrgang 1950, Nr. 3 (Berlin: 1951). Cited according to the "Vorgänge" and section numbers imposed on his restored text by Waldschmidt.
Pāli *Vinaya* = H. Oldenberg, *The Vinaya Piṭakaṃ. One of the Principal Buddhist Holy Scriptures in the Pāli Language,* Vols. i–v (London: 1879–1885). Cited by volume, page, and line.
Pravrajyāvastu = C. Vogel and K. Wille, eds., *Some Hitherto Unidentified Fragments of the Pravrajyāvastu Portion of the Vinayavastu Manuscript found near Gilgit,* Nachrichten der Akademie der Wissenschaften in Göttingen I. Philologisch-Historische Klasse, Jahrgang 1984, Nr. 7 (Göttingen: 1984). Cited by page or folio number and line.
Rab tu 'byuṅ ba'i gźi = H. Eimer, ed., *Rab tu 'byuṅ ba'i gźi. Die tibetische Übersetzung des Pravrajyāvastu im Vinaya der Mūlasarvāstivādins,* Teil i–ii, Asiatische Forschungen, Bd. 82 (Wiesbaden: 1983). Cited by volume, page, and line.
Udāna = P. Steinthal, *Udāna* (London: 1885). Cited by page and line.

Notes

1. H. Oldenberg, *Buddha. Sein Leben, seine Lehre, seine Gemeinde* (Berlin: 1881) 384 n; H. Oldenberg, *Buddha. His Life, His Doctrine, His Order,* trans. W. Hoey (London: 1882) 376 n.

2. T. W. Rhys Davids, *Buddhist Suttas,* Sacred Books of the East, XI (Oxford: 1900) xliv–xlv. In light of the references by both Oldenberg and Rhys Davids to the *Vinaya,* it is worth noting that there is good evidence for suggesting that the *Mahāparinibbāna-sutta*—which contains, of course, elaborate rules for funerals—was originally a part of the Pāli *Vinaya;* see L. Finot, "Textes historiques dans le canon pāli," *JA* (1932) 158; Finot, "Mahāparinibbāna-sutta and Cullavagga," *IHQ* 8 (1932) 241–246; E. Obermiller, "The Account of the Buddha's Nirvāṇa and the First Councils according to the Vinayakṣudraka," *IHQ* 8 (1932) 781–784; E. Frauwallner, *The Earliest Vinaya and the Beginnings of Buddhist Literature,* Serie Orientale Roma, VIII (Roma: 1956) 42ff. There are also indications that when read as a piece of *vinaya,* a number of puzzling elements in the *Mahāparinibbāna-sutta* begin to make much better sense; see below nn. 46 and 72.

3. For a discussion of the differential treatment of archaeological/epigraphical and

textual sources, see G. Schopen, "Archaeology and Protestant Presuppositions in the Study of Indian Buddhism," Ch. I above. One might suspect, moreover, that the inclination to locate Buddhism in canonical texts has had an inhibiting influence even on anthropological investigations. C. F. Keyes, for example, says, quoting Rhys Davids: "Because both men [i.e. two modern Thai "Saints"] were considered to be Buddhist saints, their deaths were interpreted in terms of Buddhist ideas about death and its aftermath. *There is really only one source for these ideas,* particularly since nothing is said in the Vinaya, the discipline incumbent upon monks, about the disposal of the corpses of members of the Sangha (Rhys Davids: xlv); and that is in the account of the death of the Buddha himself as given in the *Mahāparinibbāna sutta*" (C. F. Keyes, "Death of Two Buddhist Saints in Thailand," *Charisma and Sacred Biography,* ed. M. A. Williams, JAAR Thematic Studies, XLVIII/3 and 4 [n.d.] 154; my emphasis). This seeming restriction of "Buddhist ideas" to canonical texts appears especially odd coming from an anthropologist. In fact, Keyes himself has done perhaps more than anyone else writing on Southeast Asia to show that "Buddhist ideas about death" can come from a variety of sources: C. F. Keyes, "Tug-of-war for Merit: Cremation of a Senior Monk," *Journal of the Siam Society* 63.1–63.2 (1975) 44–62; P. K. Anusaranaśāsanakiarti and C. F. Keyes, "Funerary Rites and the Buddhist Meaning of Death: An Interpretative Text for Northern Thailand," *Journal of the Siam Society* 68.1 (1980) 1–28; cf. S. J. Tambiah, "The Ideology of Merit and the Social Correlates of Buddhism in a Thai Village," *Dialectic in Practical Religion,* ed. E. R. Leach (Cambridge: 1968) 41–121, esp. 88–99; etc. To my knowledge there has been no work done on monastic funerals and little on the disposal of the dead in general in Sri Lanka, for example, in spite of the fact that we have a reasonably detailed description of a monastic funeral which took place there in the fifth century from Fa-hsien, *A Record of the Buddhist Countries,* trans. Li Yung-hsi (Peking: 1957) 83–84. (For some incidental references to monastic funerals in Tibet and Tibetan speaking areas, see T. Wylie, "Mortuary Customs at Sa-Skya, Tibet," *HJAS* 25 [1964–1965] 229–242; M. Brauen, "Death Customs in Ladakh," *Kailash* 9 [1982] 319–332; C. Ramble, "Status and Death: Mortuary Rites and Attitudes to the Body in a Tibetan Village," *Kailash* 9 [1982] 333–356; T. Skorupski, "The Cremation Ceremony according to the Byang-gter Tradition," *Kailash* 9 [1982] 361–376; etc.) It is, finally, worth noting that although an immense amount of work has been done on Medieval Christian monasticism, relatively little has been done on monastic funerals; see, however, for some interesting comparative and contrastive material, L. Gougaud, "Anciennes coutumes claustrales. La mort du moine," *Revue mabillon* (1929) 283–302; J. Leclercq, "Documents sur la mort des moines," *Revue mabillon* (1955) 165–179; (1956) 65–81; J.-L. Lemaitre, "L'inscription dans les necrologes clunisiens, XIe–XIIe siecles," *La mort au moyen âge. Colloque de l'association des historiens médiévistes français réunis à Strasbourg en juin 1975 au palais universitaire* (Strasbourg: 1977) 153–167; J.-L. Lemaitre, "La mort et la commémoration des défunts dans les prieurés," *Prieurs et prieurés dans l'occident médiéval,* ed. J.-L. Lemaitre (Genève: 1987) 181–190; L. Gougaud, *Dévotions et pratiques ascétiques du moyen age* (Paris: 1925) 129–142 ("Mourir sous le froc"); etc.

4. For a preliminary survey and discussion of this evidence, see G. Schopen, "An Old Inscription from Amarāvatī," Ch. IX above.

5. K. R. Norman, "The Value of the Pāli Tradition," *'Jagajjyoti' Buddha Jayanti Annual* (Calcutta: 1984) 1–9, esp. 4, 7; cf. K. R. Norman, "Pāli Philology and the Study of Buddhism," *The Buddhist Heritage,* Buddhica Britannica, Series Continua I (Tring,

U.K.: 1989) 29–53; also see the much earlier S. Lévi, "Observations sur une langue précanonique du bouddhisme," *JA* (1912) 495–514, esp. 511.

6. A. Csoma de Körös, "Analysis of the Dulva," *Asiatic Researches* 20 (1836) 41–93, esp. 71, 89; cf. A. Csoma de Körös, *Analyse du Kandjour,* traduite et augmentée par L. Feer, Annales du musée guimet, 2 (Lyon: 1881) 175, 192, 194.

7. W. W. Rockhill, *The Life of the Buddha and the Early History of His Order derived from Tibetan Works in the Bkah-hgyur and Bstan-hgyur* (London: 1884) 112, 116, 150, etc.

8. P. V. Kane, *History of Dharmaśāstra,* Vol. IV (Poona: 1953) 234–235. The idea that "the Vinaya" treats "all details of the daily life of the recluses" rather than simply the staggering number of areas in which there were problems remains with us: "As the *saṅgha* evolved, regulations developed governing the cenobitical life. These ordinances, preserved in the Vinaya Piṭaka of the Pāli Canon, detail every aspect of the lives of monks and runs [read: nuns] in the *saṅgha*"; K. G. Zysk, *Asceticism and Healing in Ancient India. Medicine in the Buddhist Monastery* (Oxford: 1991) 39. If such characterizations of the scope of "the Vinaya" are accepted, then we are stuck with an interesting irony: ". . . les *Vinayapiṭaka* . . . ne soufflent mot des nombreuses pratiques spirituelles, méditations, recueillements, etc., qui constituaient l'essence même de la 'religion' bouddhique" (A. Bareau, "La construction et le culte des stūpa d'après les Vinayapiṭaka," *BEFEO* 50 [1960] 249). To say that the *Vinayas* "ne soufflent mot" about such matters is too strong, but the point remains: if we had to judge by the *Vinayas,* we would have to conclude that "pratiques spirituelles" had little, if any, place in the daily life of monks and nuns.

9. See most recently A. Yuyama, *Systematische Übersicht über die buddhistische Sanskrit-Literatur.* Erster Teil. *Vinaya-Texte,* Hrsg. H. Bechert (Wiesbaden: 1979) 12–33; K. Wille, *Die Handschriftliche Überlieferung des Vinayavastu der Mūlasarvāstivādin,* Verzeichnis der Orientalischen Handschriften in Deutschland. Supplementband 30 (Stuttgart: 1990).

10. *Histoire du bouddhisme indien,* 187, for example, refers to the Chinese translation as "médiocre et incomplète"; E. Frauwallner, *The Earliest Vinaya and the Beginnings of Buddhist Literature,* 195, says it "is not only incomplete but also full of gaps." "The Chinese translation," he says, "is also much less exact than the Tibetan one." Lévi, *JA* (1912) 509, had even earlier said: "Du Vinaya des Mūla-Sarvāstivādins, nous avons deux traductions: une en chinois, par Yi-tsing, du type des 'belles infidèles'; une autre en tibétain, scrupuleusement littérale." J. W. de Jong, "Les *sūtrapiṭaka* des sarvāstivādin et des mūlasarvāstivādin," *Mélanges d'indianisme à la mémoire de Louis Renou* (Paris: 1968) 401, has, "en comparant les versions chinoise et tibétaine du *Vinaya* des Mūlasarvāstivādin," argued that some of these characterizations are unjustified, that some of the omissions in I-tsing's translation can be accounted for since "les manuscrits de Gilgit prouvent qu'il [I-tsing] a dû traduire une recension plus brève"; but see also E. Huber, "Études bouddhiques I.—Les fresques inscrites de Turfan," *BEFEO* 14 (1914) 13–14.

11. See below and n. 50.

12. Pāli *Vinaya,* i, 302ff; I. B. Horner, *The Book of the Discipline,* Vol. IV (London: 1951) 434ff; for some discussion on the problems of inheritance and the Pāli *Vinaya,* see U. Gaung, *A Digest of the Burmese Buddhist Law concerning Inheritance and Marriage,* Vol. I (Rangoon: 1908) 447–468; R. Lingat, "Vinaya et droit laique. Etudes sur les conflits de la loi religieuse et de la loi laïque dans l'indochine hinayaniste," *BEFEO* 37 (1937) 415–477, esp. 443ff.

13. See J. Gernet, *Les aspects économiques du bouddhisme dans la société chinoise du* v^{e} *au* x^{e} *siècle* (Paris: 1956) 61ff. Although dealing primarily with China, Gernet's study is

still probably the best thing we have on the economic structures of Indian Buddhist monasteries as they are described in texts of Indian origin.

14. *Gilgit Manuscripts,* iii 2, 113–148.

15. *Gilgit Manuscripts,* iii 2, 117ff.

16. For *yogaṃ manasikāram,* the Tibetan translation has only *yid la byed pa* (*Derge,* 3, 204; *Tog,* 3, 267; *Peking,* 41, 279-5). Compare the list of activities ignored in the Mūlasarvāstivāda passage with the similar but divergent list found at Pāli *Vinaya,* i, 190 (*riñcanti uddesaṃ paripucchaṃ adhisīlaṃ adhicittaṃ adhipaññaṃ*—said of monks preoccupied with making and ornamenting shoes), and iii, 235 (said of nuns preoccupied with washing, dyeing, and combing sheep's wool).

17. *Gilgit Buddhist Manuscripts,* vi, fol. 848.7–848.9; *Gilgit Manuscripts,* iii 2, 120.3–120.4—Tibetan: *Derge,* 3, 204; *Tog,* 3, 267; *Peking,* 41, 279-5.

18. Tibetan *gsol ba byed pa na,* and context, both suggest that something like *jñaptyāṃ kriyamāṇāyāṃ* has dropped out of the Gilgit manuscript; cf. the following note.

19. The *Cīvaravastu,* the *vastu* in which this passage occurs in the Sanskrit text, may not have been translated by I-tsing into Chinese; see Frauwallner, *The Earliest Vinaya and the Beginnings of Buddhist Literature,* 195. Durt, however, refers to a very similar list of "five occasions" that occurs in the *Vinaya-saṃgraha* (*Taishō* 1458): "1° battement de gong . . . 2° récitation du Sankei Mujōkyō . . . le sūtra tripartite . . . 3° salutation profonde . . . 4° distribution de Bâtonnets . . . 5° proclamation d'une motion . . ." in H. Durt, "Chū," *Hôbôgirin,* cinquième fascicule (Paris/Tokyo: 1979) 437; and I-tsing certainly knew the *Cīvaravastu.* At least one entire chapter of his *Record* is, in fact, a translation of a long passage from this *vastu,* as N. Dutt pointed out long ago (*Gilgit Manuscripts,* iii 2, x–xi). The chapter in question is number xxxvi; see *A Record of the Buddhist Religion as Practiced in India and the Malay Archipelago by I-tsing,* trans. J. Takakusu (London: 1896) 189–193. The failure to recognize that this chapter of the *Record* was a translation of part of the *Mūlasarvāstivāda-vinaya* has misled a number of scholars who have presented it as a reflection of actual monastic practice in India at the time of I-tsing's visit: cf. Lingat, *BEFEO* 37 (1937) 464; Gernet, *Les aspects économiques du bouddhisme dans la société chinoise du ve au xe siècle,* 71–73; A. Bareau, "Indian and Ancient Chinese Buddhism: Institutions Analogous to the Jisa," *Comparative Studies in Society and History* 3 (1961) 447; A. Bareau, "Etude du bouddhisme. Aspects du bouddhisme indien décrits par I-tsing," *ACF* 1989–1990, 631–640. The fact that the *Cīvaravastu* is not now found in the *Taishō* may only indicate that it was one of I-tsing's works that was lost after his death; cf. A. Hirakawa, *Monastic Discipline for the Buddhist Nuns* (Patna: 1982) 12. For a detailed description of the procedure involved in distributing "tickets" mentioned in our passage, see the article by Durt mentioned above.

20. *Gilgit Manuscripts,* iii 2, 120.6; *Gilgit Manuscripts,* iii 4, 79.13; *Avadānaśataka,* i, 272.1; cf. L. Feer, *Avadāna-çataka. Cent légendes bouddhiques* (Paris: 1891) 185, who translates *muṇḍikā gaṇḍī* as "la cloche funèbre."

21. *Peking,* 41, 279-5; *Gilgit Manuscripts,* iii 4, 79, n. 3; *Peking,* 40, 184-3.

22. This is especially clear in the monastic funeral described in *Avadānaśataka,* i, 271ff: *tato 'sya sabrahmacāribhir muṇḍikāṃ gaṇḍīṃ parāhatya śarīrābhinirhāraḥ kṛtaḥ / tato 'sya śarīre śarīrapūjāṃ kṛtvā vihāram āgatāḥ /.* It is almost equally clear that this *avadāna* is a narrative elaboration of the much simpler accounts in the *Cīvaravastu* of the *Mūlasarvāstivāda-vinaya* in which the first set of rules governing monastic funerals is presented; see below. On the "sectarian" affiliation of the *Avadānaśataka,* see J.-U. Hartmann, "Zur

Frage der Schulzugehörigkeit des Avadānaśataka," *Zur Schulzugehörigkeit von Werken der Hīnayāna-Literatur,* Hrsg. H. Bechert, Erster Teil (Göttingen: 1985) 219–224.

23. See below n. 62.

24. *Gilgit Manuscripts,* iii 2, 144.14, in the account of the death of a monk who had left his bowl and robe in the keeping of others: *viṣūcitaḥ kālagataḥ / sa bhikṣubhiḥ śmaśānaṃ nītvā dagdhaḥ / dharmaśravaṇaṃ dattam / anupūrveṇa vihāraḥ praviṣṭaḥ /.*

25. *Derge,* 10, 226.2, in an account of the funeral of Mahāprajāpatī in which the Buddha himself is given a prominent part.

26. See below n. 63.

27. M. Helffer, "Le gandi: un simandre tibétain d'origine indienne," *Yearbook for Traditional Music* 15 (1983) 112–125; I. Vandor, "The Gandi: A Musical Instrument of Buddhist India Recently Identified in a Tibetan Monastery," *The World of Music* 17 (1975) 24–27; cf. S. Lévi and Éd. Chavannes, "Quelques titres énigmatiques dans la hiérarchie ecclésiastique du bouddhisme indien," *JA* (1915) 213–215. References to the use of the *gaṇḍī* are frequent in the *Mūlasarvāstivāda-vinaya*—see, as a sample, *Gilgit Manuscripts,* iii 2, 145, 156, 158; iii 3, 9; iii 4, 35, 36, 37, 81, 92; *Saṅghabhedavastu,* ii, 83; *Śayanāsanavastu and Adhikaraṇavastu,* 41, 55, 85, 106; etc. It is interesting to note that striking "la tablette du cloître . . . cette sorte de gong funèbre," also signaled the beginning of monastic funerals in Medieval Western monasteries (Gougaud, *Revue mabillon* [1929] 281, 290), and its function there marks the communal nature of the event; see Lemaitre, *Prieurs et prieurés dans l'occident médiéval,* 185: ". . . on sonne la claquoir (*tabula*) pour réunir les frères . . ."

28. *Gilgit Buddhist Manuscripts,* vi, fol. 852.3–852.5; *Gilgit Manuscripts,* iii 2, 126.17–127.3—Tibetan: *Derge,* 3, 210.2–210.4; *Tog,* 3, 275.5–276.1; *Peking,* 41, 280-5-4 to 280-5-6.

29. S. Lévi, "Les éléments du formation du Divyāvadāna," *TP* 8 (1907) 105–122, esp. 122: "De ce point de vue, la langue du Mūla Sarvāstivāda Vinaya prend, par ses étrangetés même, une importance exceptionnelle; elle montre le sanscrit de Pāṇini entraîné par la circulation de la vie réelle, en voie d'altération normale, sur les confins des pracrits . . ."; *Saṅghabhedavastu,* i, xx, n. 2.

30. Both here and in II and III below, the Tibetan translators appear to have construed the dead monk's speech as a rhetorical question. The Tibetan, in fact, looks like it might be translating an interrogative *mā* construction (cf. *BHSG,* §§ 42.12–42.16); in III, the final text in this series cited below, the manuscript itself has a negative in the parallel construction, but it is *na* not *mā.*

31. *Gilgit Manuscripts,* iii 2, 127.5 (*bhikṣavas tam abhinirhṛtya,* of the dead body of an ordinary monk); *Pravrajyāvastu,* fol. 12r.2 (*bahir api nirhṛtya,* of the dead body of the teacher Saṃjayin); *Divyāvadāna,* 281.30 (*śibikābhir nirharitvā,* of the dead body of Aśoka); *Avadānaśataka,* i, 272.1 (*sabrahmacāribhir . . . śarīrābhinirhāraḥ kṛtaḥ,* of the body of a dead monk); *Udāna,* 8.21 (*sarīrakaṃ mañcakaṃ āropetvā nīharitvā,* of the dead body of an ascetic); Pāli *Vinaya,* iv, 308 (*bhikkuniyo taṃ bhikkhuniṃ nīharitvā,* of the dead body of a nun); etc. There are, of course, other technical meanings for *abhinirhāra;* cf. M. H. F. Jayasuriya, "A Note on Pali *abhinīhāra* and Cognate Forms in the Light of Buddhist Hybrid Sanskrit," *Añjali. Papers on Indology and Buddhism,* O. H. de A. Wijesekera Volume (Peradeniya: 1970) 50–54.

32. J. Jain, *Life in Ancient India as Depicted in the Jain Canon and Commentaries. 6th Century* B.C. *to 17th Century* A.D., 2nd ed. (New Delhi: 1984) 281–284, esp. 283 where *nīharaṇa* is cited as the term for "the ceremony of taking out the dead."

33. *ādahanaṃ nītvā: Gilgit Manuscripts,* iii 2, 127.13 (*dur khrod du khyer te,* of the body of a monk); iii 2, 125.14 (*sreg tu khyer nas,* of the body of a monk); *śmaśānaṃ nītvā: Gilgit Manuscripts,* iii 2, 144.14 (*dur khrod du bsregs nas,* of the body of a monk); *tam ādāya dahanaṃ gataḥ: Gilgit Manuscripts,* iii 2, 118.15 (*de khyor te sreg tu dong ngo,* of the body of a monk). Cf. *Saṅghabhedavastu,* i, 70, 163; *Derge,* 10, 224ff, 444, 472; *Divyāvadāna,* 428; etc. It will, perhaps, be clear from even the small sample cited here that the Tibetan translations of the terms and phrases involved are neither consistent nor exact; cf. n. 38 below.

34. *Gilgit Buddhist Manuscripts,* vi, fol. 852.5–852.8; *Gilgit Manuscripts,* iii 2, 127.4–127.11—Tibetan: *Derge,* 3, 210.4–210.6; *Tog,* 3, 276.1–276.5; *Peking,* 41, 280-5-6 to 281-1-1.

35. G. Schopen, "Monks and the Relic Cult in the *Mahāparinibbāna-sutta,*" Ch. VI above.

36. On the meaning of the term *pūjā* and the kinds and range of activities it can refer to, see J. Charpentier, "The Meaning and Etymology of Pūjā," *IA* 56 (1927) 93–99, 130–136; L. de La Vallée Poussin, "Totémisme et Végétalisme," *Bulletins de la classe des lettres et des sciences morales et politiques, Académie Royale de belgique,* 5e série, T. XV (1929) 37–52; P. Thieme, "Indische Wörter und Sitten," *ZDMG* 93 (1939) 105–139, esp. 105–123; A. L. Basham, "The Evolution of the Concept of the Bodhisattva," *The Bodhisattva Doctrine in Buddhism,* ed. L. S. Kawamura (Waterloo: 1981) 19–59, esp. 35–36; G. E. Ferro-Luzzi, "*Abhiṣeka,* the Indian Rite that Defies Definition," *Anthropos* 76 (1981) 707–742; A. Ostor, *Puja in Society* (Lucknow: 1982); D. D. Malvania, "The Word Pūjā and Its Meaning," *Indologica Taurinensia* 14 (1987–1988) 269–273; etc.

37. See below n. 43.

38. T. W. Rhys Davids and W. Stede, *The Pali Text Society's Pali-English Dictionary* (London: 1921–1925) 698 s.v. *sarīra.* It is worth noting here that the handling of the term *śarīra-pūjā* by the Tibetan translators is far from satisfactory and a long way from their usual consistency. In this passage and in III cited below, *śarīra-pūjā* is translated by *ro la mchod pa, ro la mchod pa byas la,* and *ro la mchod pa byas; ro* means first "dead body, corpse, carcass," then "body," then "residue, remains, sediment." *Avadānaśataka,* ii, 272.2, however, which reads *śarīrābhinirhāraḥ kṛtaḥ / tato 'sya śarīre śarīra-pūjāṃ kṛtvā,* is translated *rus bu phyir phyung ngo / de nas de'i rus bu la rus bu'i mchod pa byas nas.* Here, then, where the first occurrence of *śarīra,* and almost certainly the second and third, can only mean "body," the Tibetan translates it in all three instances by *rus ba* which can only mean "small bone" or "bones in general." Again, especially in the first instance, *śarīra* cannot possibly mean "bone" since the context makes it certain that it refers to a newly dead "body" which has not even been removed from the monk's cell, let alone cremated. Likewise, in the *Mahāparinirvāṇa-sūtra,* there are several occurrences of the term *śarīra-pūjā* in passages narrating events that preceded the cremation; that is to say, prior to the time that there could have been any "bones" or "relics." At 36.2, where Ānanda asks what should be done with the body of the Buddha after his death, *śarīra-pūjāyām autsukyam āpadyemahi* is translated by *sku gdung la . . . mchod pa ji snyed cig brtson par bgyi lags* (similarly at 46.4); at 48.8, where the wandering Ājīvika tells Mahākāśyapa that the Buddha is dead and that his body was honored for seven days, *śarīre śarīrapūjā* is translated by *sku gdung la mchod pa bgyis pa;* but at 49.19, where Kāśyapa formulates his intention to personally repeat the *śarīra-pūjā* of the Buddha's body that had already been performed by the Mallas, he says: *yan nv ahaṃ svayam eva bhagavataḥ śarīrapūjāyām autsukyam āpadyeya,* and this is translated into Tibetan by *ma la bdag nyid kyis bcom ldan*

'das la mchod pa'i las bya'o snyam du spro ba bskyed nas. In other words, in the same text, *śarīra* is sometimes translated by *sku gdung,* which is the respect form of *rus* and means first of all—if not exclusively—"bone," in contexts where there could not yet have been any "bone"; or it is sometimes not translated at all: 49.19, where the Sanskrit text has "worship of the body of the Blessed One," the Tibetan has simply "worship of the Blessed One" himself. There are, moreover, numerous instances where we do not have the Sanskrit original, but where it was almost certainly *śarīra-pūjā.* Here too there is considerable variation: at *Derge,* 10, 480, for example, immediately after Śāriputra's death, a fellow monk is said to have *śā ri'i bu'i ring bsrel la lus kyis mchod pa byas te.* Context makes it virtually certain that this can only refer to funeral procedures, and it is very likely that the original read *śarīre śarīrapūjā,* but in spite of this the Tibetan literally means something like "performing the worship with the body on the *relics* of Śāriputra." Later in the same account—Derge, 10, 488—where again the original almost certainly had *śarīre śarīrapūjā,* and where the reference is undoubtedly to post-cremation remains, the Tibetan has *ring bsrel la ring bsrel gyi mchod pa bgyi'o.* In the account of the death of Mahāprajāpatī (*Derge,* 10, 224ff), we find *lus la mchod pa;* in the account of the death of Prasenajit (*Derge,* 10, 174), we find both *khog pa la mchod pa* and *lus la mchod pa;* in the account of the death of the Monk Gavāṃpati, *rus pa la rus pa'i mchod pa* (*Derge,* 10, 606)—in all these cases the original was almost certainly *śarīrapūjā* or *śarīre śarīrapūjā.* It is not impossible that a systematic survey of the Tibetan handling of the term might reveal meaningful patterns in what now appears to be confusion, but such a survey has yet to be done. It is also worth noting that, although rare, there are traces of the use of the term *śarīra-pūjā* to refer to honor directed toward post-cremational remains and not to a funereal procedure. This appears to be the case several times in the account concerning the remains of Śāriputra at *Derge,* 10, 488ff; likewise, at *Divyāvadāna,* 252.10, when Aśoka expresses his desire to honor the *stūpas* of the Buddha's famous disciples, the Sanskrit text has him say *teṣāṃ śarīrapūjāṃ kariṣyāmi;* J. Przyluski, *La légende de l'empereur Açoka (Açoka-avadāna) dans les textes indiens et chinois,* Annales du musée guimet, 32 (Paris: 1923) 257, however, translates the parallel passage in the *A-yü-wang-chuan* (*Taishō* 2042) as " 'Je veux maintenant honorer les *stūpa* des grands disciples . . . ' "; see also Schopen, "Monks and the Relic Cult in the *Mahāparinibbāna-sutta,*" Ch. VI above, 108ff. Note, finally, that the Sanskrit sources themselves do not always use the term *śarīra-pūjā;* cf. n. 70.

39. *Divyāvadāna,* 281.30 (note that for Vaidya's *śibikābhir nirharitvā śarīrapūjāṃ kṛtvā rājānaṃ pratiṣṭhāpayiṣyāma,* the text given in S. Mukhopadhyaya, *The Aśokāvadāna. Sanskrit Text compared with Chinese Versions* [New Delhi: 1963] 132.7, provides an important variant: *śivikābhir nirharitvā śarīrapūjāṃ kṛtvā dhmāpayitvā rājānaṃ pratiṣṭhāpayiṣyāma*—this reading makes it very clear that *śarīrapūjā* preceded cremation); *Derge,* 10, 174. The fact that known kings—including and especially Aśoka—did not receive the funeral of a *Cakravartin* only emphasizes the purely ideal, if not entirely artificial, character of both the idea and the description of such a funeral in the texts, as well as the fourfold classification of those "worthy of a *stūpa*"; cf. A. Bareau, *Recherches sur la biographie du buddha dans les sūtrapiṭaka et les vinayapiṭaka anciens: II. Les derniers mois, le parinirvāṇa et les funérailles,* T. II (Paris: 1971) 50ff; G. de Marco, *I "Kuṣāṇa" nella vita del Buddha. Per una Analisi del Rapporto tra Potere Politico e Religione nell' Antico Gandhāra,* Supplemento n. 34 agli *Annali* (Napoli: 1983) 47–54; etc.

40. *Gilgit Buddhist Manuscripts,* vi, fol. 852.8–852.10; *Gilgit Manuscripts,* iii 2, 127.12–127.18—Tibetan: *Derge,* 3, 210.7–211.2; *Tog,* 3, 276.5–277.1; *Peking,* 41, 281-1-1 to 281-1-3.

41. *Gilgit Manuscripts,* iii 2, 144.14; *Derge,* 10, 472.2ff; *Derge,* 10, 224.6ff; *Avadānaśataka,* i, 272ff; etc.—reference to both or either is not, however, invariably found in references to monastic funerals. Sometimes such references contain only phrases like *tam ādahane saṃskārya* or *tam ādahanaṃ nītvā saṃskārya* (*Gilgit Manuscripts,* iii 2, 118.16, 125.4), where a recitation of *Dharma* and transfer of merit are probably simply understood. For the importance of performing a "*pūjā* of the teacher (i.e. the Buddha)" (*śāstuś ca pūjā*) for a dying but not yet dead monk, see *Gilgit Manuscripts,* iii 2, 124.11ff. It is again worth noting the similar procedures stipulated in "les coutumiers monastiques" composed in the Medieval West: ". . . on annonce la nouvelle au chapitre et l'on fait aussitôt un office pour le défunt, avec sonnerie de cloches"; "les frères résidant dans cette dépendance (prieuré, prévôté, etc. . . .) font pour le mort ce qui se fait dans le monastère, c'est-à-dire l'office des morts pendant sept jours, avec glas le premier jour, distribution d'une pitance (*justicia*) pendant trente jours avec chant du psaume *Verba mea* (Ps. 141) et de cinq autres psaumes pour le défunt." See Lemaitre, *Prieurs et prieurés dans l'occident médiéval,* 185; Gougaud, *Revue mabillon* (1929) 281ff.

42. For what is probably still the best discussion of the subtleties sometimes involved in what is called the "transfer of merit," see J. Filliozat, "Sur le domaine sémantique de *puṇya,*" *Indianisme et bouddhisme. Mélanges offerts à Mgr. Étienne Lamotte* (Louvain-la-neuve: 1980) 102–116.

43. See—noting the language used to express such "transfers"—*Gilgit Manuscripts,* iii 1, 220.12 (*nāmnā dakṣiṇām ādiśeyam,* to *pretas* who were the deceased relatives of a group of laymen); *Gilgit Manuscripts,* iii 4, 181.5, 18; 182.12 (*nāmnā dakṣiṇām ādeśaya,* to deceased relatives); *Derge,* 10, 472.2ff (*yon bsngo zhing,* to a deceased monk); *Śayanāsanavastu and Adhikaraṇavastu,* 37.7 (*nāmnā dakṣiṇā ādeṣṭavyā* 37.11; *nāmnā dakṣiṇām uddiśasi,* both to deceased donors who had given *vihāras* to the Order); *Gilgit Manuscripts,* iii 4, 161.1 (*nāmnā dakṣiṇām ādekṣyati,* to deceased parents by a son); *Rab tu 'byuṅ ba'i gźi,* ii, 41.9 (*miṅ gis yon bsṅo ba byed par gyur cig,* to deceased parents by a son); for literature related to this *Vinaya,* see *Avadānaśataka,* i, 272.13 (*nāmnā dakṣiṇā ādiṣṭā,* to a deceased monk by the Buddha); *Divyāvadāna,* 1.23, 286.24; *Avadānaśataka,* i, 15.1, 197.3, 277.2; etc., all to deceased parents by a son. There are, as well, instances which use the same vocabulary but where the transfer is directed to living beings: *Saṅghabhedavastu,* i, 199.25 (*dakṣiṇā ādiṣṭā,* by the Buddha to his father); *Gilgit Manuscripts,* iii 4, 80 (*dakṣiṇādeṣṭavyeti,* connected with the *Poṣadha,* cf. the last verse of the *Mūlasarvāstivāda Prātimokṣa Sūtra: prātimokṣasamuddeśād yat puṇyaṃ samupārjitaṃ / aśeṣas tena lokoyaṃ maunīndraṃ padam āpnuyāt //* in A. C. Banerjee, *Two Buddhist Vinaya Texts in Sanskrit* [Calcutta: 1977] 56); *Mahāparinirvāṇa-sūtra,* 6.10, 6.13 (*nāmnā dakṣiṇām ādiśava; dakṣiṇām ādiśet,* to local devas). In his work on the Pāli *Petavatthu,* H. S. Gehman noted and carefully studied parallel expressions in "Ādisati, Anvādisati, Anudisati and Uddisati in the Petavatthu," *JAOS* 43 (1923) 410–421. In a short note written long before the Sanskrit text of the *Mūlasarvāstivāda-vinaya* was available, he also argued that expressions like *nāmnā dakṣiṇādeśana* in the *Avadānaśataka* were "Pālisms" in "A Pālism in Buddhist Sanskrit," *JAOS* 44 (1924) 73–75. But, in fact, it now appears that such expressions are much more firmly anchored in Sanskrit—especially Mūlasarvāstivāda—sources and are of limited and late occurrence in Pāli sources; they occur frequently only in texts like the *Petavatthu,* very rarely elsewhere: at *Aṅguttara,* iii, 43 (*petānaṃ dakkhiṇaṃ anuppadassati*), and once in the Pāli *Mahāparinibbāna-sutta* (I.31: *tāsaṃ dakkhiṇam ādise*—the same expression in the same verse also appears in the parallel accounts to the *Mahāparinibbāna* passage that are now found at *Udāna,* 85ff, and Pāli *Vinaya,* i, 228ff). This pattern of occurrence of

the expression *dakkhiṇam ādis-* in Pāli sources, noting especially its occurrence in the *Mahāparinibbāna-sutta,* parallels that of the term *śarīra-pūjā.* Both are firmly rooted and frequent in Mūlasarvāstivāda sources (see above n. 38), both are rare in anything but "late" Pāli sources, but both occur prominently in the Pāli *Mahāparinibbāna-sutta;* cf. J. P. McDermott, *Development in the Early Buddhist Concept of Kamma/Karma* (New Delhi: 1984) 41ff, although his views are not themselves free of problems. It is possible that we may have in both expressions indications of the influence of continental sources on canonical Pāli. It is also worth noting that at least the expression *dakṣiṇādeśana* is not limited to Mūlasarvāstivāda sources. In the *Sphuṭārthā Śrīghanācāra-saṃgraha-ṭīkā* of Jayarakṣita, for example, the term occurs and is provided with a "definition": *dakṣiṇādeśanañ ca dānagāthāpāṭhaḥ*, in Sanghasena, ed., *Sphuṭārthā Śrīghanācārasaṅgrahaṭīkā,* Tibetan Sanskrit Works Series, XI (Patna: 1968) 36.10: " 'Assignment of gift' is the reading of gift-verses" (J. D. M. Derrett, *A Textbook for Novices. Jayarakṣita's "Perspicuous Commentary on the Compendium of Conduct by Śrīghana,"* Pubblicazioni di Indologica Taurinensia, XV [Torino: 1983] 44). This work, it appears, is affiliated with the Mahāsāṅghika; cf. M. Shimoda, "The *Sphuṭārthā Śrīghanācārasaṅgrahaṭīkā* and the Chinese *Mahāsāṅghika Vinaya,*" *IBK* 39.1 (1990) 495–942. Finally, for some interesting suggestions concerning the background of the expression, see B. Oguibenine, "La dakṣiṇā dans le Ṛgveda et le transfert de mérite dans le bouddhisme," *Indological and Buddhist Studies. Volume in Honour of Professor J. W. de Jong on his Sixtieth Birthday,* ed. L. A. Hercus et al. (Canberra: 1982) 393–414.

44. Kane, *History of Dharmaśāstra,* Vol. IV, 257.

45. *Śrautakośa. Encyclopedia of Vedic Sacrificial Literature,* Vol. I, English Section; Part II (Poona: 1962) 1037.

46. This same congruency may also allow us a better understanding of some otherwise puzzling elements in the *Mahāparinirvāṇa-sūtra.* The Sanskrit version, for example, goes to some trouble to indicate that, although the funereal *śarīra-pūjā* had already been performed for the Buddha when Mahākāśyapa finally reached Kuśinagara, he nevertheless is made to repeat the entire procedure himself (49.18–49.20). This at first sight seems both odd and unnecessary. But it makes perfect sense if—as is not unlikely—the compiler of the text "knew" that Kāśyapa was the chief heir of the Buddha (cf. *Gilgit Manuscripts,* iii 1, 259–260), and if he "knew" that, for a monk to inherit, he must perform or participate in the funeral of the deceased. Seen from this point of view, Kāśyapa could not be what he was supposed to be unless he had performed the *śarīra-pūjā* or had participated in the funeral. Kāśyapa's role in the Pāli version of the text—although slightly less odd—can also be explained in this way.

47. R. F. Gombrich, *Precept and Practice. Traditional Buddhism in the Rural Highlands of Ceylon* (Oxford: 1971) 243.

48. Something similar has somewhat hesitantly been noted by Knipe in regard to Hindu funereal practice: "The doctrines of transmigration and liberation transformed the whole of ancient Indian speculation and practice, but the rites accorded the ancestors bear a stamp of rigorous antiquity. They appear to endure beside the newer sentiments of *saṃsāra* and *mokṣa.*" "The ritual world view of early vedic religion could abide through several strenuous periods via the directives of the *sūtras* and *śāstras* for individual funeral and ancestral rites, with remarkably little tampering from innovative doctrines, theologies, and cosmographies that gradually eroded the official, institutional structures of vedic religion. Although the concern shifted from the early vedic desire for a state of perpetual non-death or immortality to the dilemmas of *saṃsāra* and the ideal of *mokṣa,* the intention

of the *śrāddhas* survived, and the understanding of the passage of the deceased as a cosmogonic progression, with an individual's salvation dependent on the correct ritual activity of his descendants, permitted these archaic ceremonies for the dead to continue to the present day"; D. M. Knipe, "*Sapiṇḍīkaraṇa:* the Hindu Rite of Entry into Heaven," *Religious Encounters with Death. Insights from the History and Anthropology of Religions,* ed. F. E. Reynolds and E. H. Waugh (University Park and London: 1977) 111–124, esp. 112, 121–122.

49. Rockhill, *The Life of the Buddha and the Early History of His Order,* 112.

50. L. de La Vallée Poussin, "Staupikam," *HJAS* 2 (1935) 286-287.

51. A. Seidel, "Dabi," *Hôbôgirin,* sixième fascicule (Paris/Tokyo: 1983) 577f.

52. *Derge,* 10, 472.2-474.1; *Tog,* 9, 704.7–707.5; *Peking,* 44, 91-4-3 to 92-1-1. The footnote letters inserted into the text refer to the separate critical apparatus that follows it and in which variants—most of little consequence—are recorded.

53. This entire paragraph is made up of stereotypical phrases used to describe an orthodox union and birth; cf. *Gilgit Manuscripts,* iii 2, 1–2, 52; iii 4, 6, 15, 23, 24, 28, 29, 53; *Śayanāsanavastu and Adhikaraṇavastu,* 13; *Saṅghabhedavastu,* i, 27; *Rab tu 'byuṅ ba'i gźi,* ii, 7, 21, 23, 42; *Pravrajyāvastu,* 312; *Divyāvadāna,* 2; *Avadānaśataka,* i, 206, 261, 295; etc.

54. For the whole of what has been abbreviated here, see Feer, *Avadāna-çataka,* 3; *Pravrajyāvastu,* 16.

55. As with the Sanskrit texts from the *Cīvaravastu* treated above, so here in the Tibetan text the style is sometimes elliptical, and there is a considerable reliance on pronouns whose referents sometimes need to be drawn out.

56. The Sanskrit is cited from *Gilgit Manuscripts,* iii 2, 140.14.

57. For the Sanskrit underlying much of this paragraph, cf. *Gilgit Manuscripts,* iii 1, 285.17ff: (said of a monk bitten by a snake) *sa tathā vihvalo brāhmaṇagṛhapatibhir dṛṣṭaḥ / te kathayanti / bhavantaḥ katarasyâyaṃ gṛhapateḥ putra iti / aparaiḥ samākhyātam / amukasya iti / te kathayanti / anāthānāṃ śramaṇaśākyaputrīyāṇāṃ madhye pravrajitaḥ / yadi na pravrajito 'bhaviṣyat jñātibhir asya cikitsā kāritā abhaviṣyad iti /;* see also *Gilgit Manuscripts,* iii 1, ix.10, although the passage there involves considerable reconstruction. Note that our text has no word for "funeral," which I supply both here and below. A literal translation would be more like "would surely have performed the honors/ceremonies," "honors/ceremonies for a (deceased) monk are to be performed," etc. For Sanskrit phrases which might lie behind *rim gro byas par 'gyur ba,* etc., see below n. 70.

58. So de La Vallée Poussin, *HJAS* 2 (1935) 286, translates the Chinese. In a note he suggests the Chinese was translating *śarīra-pūjā,* but the Tibetan would not support this; cf. n. 38 above.

59. So de La Vallée Poussin, *HJAS* 2 (1935) 286; Seidel, *Hôbôgirin,* sixième fasc., 578.

60. So de La Vallée Poussin, *HJAS* 2 (1935) 286; Seidel, *Hôbôgirin,* sixième fasc., 578; cf. J. Przyluski, "Le partage des reliques du buddha," *MCB* 4 (1935–1936) 341–367, esp. 345–346.

61. It is virtually certain that Tibetan *yon bsngo zhing* here is translating some form of *dakṣiṇām ādiś-;* cf. *Mahāparinirvāṇa-sūtra,* 6.10: *nāmnā dakṣiṇām ādiśasva = yon sngo ba mdzad du gsol;* 6.13: *dakṣiṇām ādiśet = yon bsngo byas; Gilgit Manuscripts,* iii 2, 127.18: *dakṣiṇām uddiśya = yon bsngo ba byas nas;* etc.

62. Determining the precise referent of the term or title *Tridaṇḍaka* is not as easy as one might expect. Modern scholars, on the basis of good Chinese evidence (I-tsing, colophons from Tun Huang), have with differing degrees of certainty seen in *Tridaṇḍaka*

a reference to a specific text. *Taishō* 801, the text in question, has in fact been assigned in various Chinese sources two titles: *(Fo shuo) wu ch'ang ching,* "Sūtra (Spoken by the Buddha) on Impermanency," a title which has been taken as a translation of a Sanskrit title something like *Anityatā-sūtra,* and *San ch'i ching,* "Sūtra des Trois Ouvertures" or "les trois 'informations.' " Sometimes the second title is given as an alternative, sometimes the two titles are simply combined into one: *Fo shuo wu ch'ang san ch'i ching;* de La Vallée Poussin renders the Chinese corresponding to our *Kṣudraka* passage by "récite les trois 'informations', *K'i* [et] le Sūtra sur l'impermanence," *HJAS* 2 (1935) 287. *Taishō* 801, or the *Anityatā-sūtra,* would appear to be well suited for a funeral text; see the Sanskrit version edited in I. Yamada, "Anityatāsūtra," *IBK* 20.2 (1972) 1001–1996. It appears, moreover, from at least Takakusu's translation, that I-tsing says in his description of a monastic funeral in his *Record* that "while the corpse is burning . . . the 'Sūtra on Impermanence' (*Anitya-sūtra*) is recited" (Takakusu, *A Record of the Buddhist Religion as Practiced in India and the Malay Archipelago,* 81–82). Bareau, however, in summarizing the passage says only: "Un moine récite un bref sermon (*sūtra*) sur l'impermanence (*anityatā*) . . . ," *ACF* 1989–90, 636. In the account of the funeral of Mahāprajāpatī in the *Kṣudraka,* finally, the Buddha himself is said to have "expounded teachings connected with impermanence" (*mi rtag pa dang ldan pa'i chos dag bshad nas; Derge,* 10, 226.2). All of this would seem to argue for identifying the *Tridaṇḍaka* with the *Anityatā-sūtra.* But there are still other indications that would seem to suggest that the *Tridaṇḍaka* was not, in fact, a specific text but a kind of ritual formulary into which any given text could be inserted. Although I-tsing does not appear to refer to the *Tridaṇḍaka* in his description of a monastic funeral, he does refer to it elsewhere in his *Record* and his description of it is of considerable interest. Lévi has translated the passage as follows: "Dans les pays occidentaux, l'adoration des caitya et le service ordinaire se font à la fin de l'après-midi ou au crépuscule . . . Quand tout le monde est définitivement assis, un maître des sūtra monte sur le siège aux lions (*siṃhāsana*) et déclame *un peu de sūtra* . . . Quant aux textes sacrés qu'on récite, c'est surtout les Trois Ouvertures qu'on récite. C'est un recueil dû au vénérable *Ma ming* (Aśvaghoṣa). La première partie compte dix vers; l'objet du texte est d'exalter les Trois Joyaux. Ensuite vient un texte sacré proprement dit, prononcé par le Buddha en personne. Après l'hymne et le récitation, il y a encore plus de dix vers, qui ont trait à la déflexion des mérites (*pariṇāmanā*) et à la production du voeu (*praṇidhāna*). Comme il y a trois parties qui s'ouvrent successivement, on appelle ce texte sacré les Trois Ouvertures"; see S. Lévi, "Sur la récitation primitive des textes bouddhiques," *JA* (1915) 401–447, esp. 433–434; cf. Takakusu, *A Record of the Buddhist Religion as Practiced in India and the Malay Archipelago,* 152–153, and R. Fujishima, "Deux chapitres extraits des mémoires d'I-tsing sur son voyage dans l'inde," *JA* (1888) 411–439, esp. 416–418. This passage is important in at least two ways. First, the *Tridaṇḍaka* described here is not a specific text, but a set form of recitation consisting of three parts: (1) praise of the three precious things followed by (2) the recitation of "un texte sacré proprement dit" with the sequence concluded by, (3) a formal transfer of merit. The "texte sacré" is unspecified and can apparently be any text suitable to the occasion of the recitation. The second important thing that I-tsing's description indicates would point in the same direction. We have seen so far in the *Mūlasarvāstivāda-vinaya* that the recitation of the *Tridaṇḍaka* is one of the specified moments for the distribution of a deceased monk's estate, and that it is recited as a part of a monastic funeral. I-tsing's description, however, makes it clear that these were not the only ritual contexts in which the *Tridaṇḍaka* was used. His description would seem to indicate that it was also used during the daily "adoration des caitya et le service ordinaire," and to these ritual moments we can add others. The *Poṣadhavastu* of the *Mūlasarvāstivāda-vinaya,* for example, associates the recitation of the *Tridaṇḍaka* with the fortnightly communal recitation of the *Prātimokṣa,* which is often presented as the most important congregational ritual in Buddhist monasticism (see *Gilgit Manuscripts,* iii 4, 80.5, where details concerning the appropriate length of its recitation are given). This association is repeated in the *Bod rgya tshig mdzod chen mo,* which characterizes the *Tridaṇḍaka* as a procedure or method of practice connected with the Upoṣadha: *gso sbyong gi sbyor chog cig ste;* its description of the *Tridaṇḍaka* as a recitative formulary corresponds almost exactly to I-tsing's: . . . *phyag 'tshal ba'i rgyud / mdo 'don pa'i rgyud / bsngo ba'i rgyud de rgyud gsum dang ldan pa'i sgo nas tshul khrims rnam dag gi mdo la sogs pa'i chos bshad cing nyan par byed pa'o /* in Kraṅ dbyi sun, ed., *Bod rgya tshig mdzod chen mo,* Vol. I (Beijing: 1985) 577. Elsewhere in the *Mūlasarvāstivāda-vinaya,* moreover, the recitation of the *Tridaṇḍaka* is prescribed in the ritual required before cutting down a tree; see the text cited in K. Tokiya, "The Anityatā-sūtra Quoted in the Tibetan Version of a Mūlasarvāstivāda Text," *IBK* 34.1 (1985) 164; etc. It is, therefore, not just the structure of the *Tridaṇḍaka* as it is described by I-tsing, but also its use in a variety of different ritual contexts that suggests that it might well have been not a specific text but a specific set type of recitation or an established formulary into which any given *sūtra* text could be inserted. The Chinese identification of the *Tridaṇḍaka* with the *Anityatā-sūtra* may have resulted from the fact that I-tsing sent home the version of the formulary used for monastic funerals into which the *Anityatā* had been inserted and this came to be considered the only version. All of this will, of course, require further research to settle; so too will the attribution of the formulary to Aśvaghoṣa. For material bearing on both questions, see—in addition to the sources already cited—P. Demiéville, "Bombai," *Hôbôgirin,* Premier fasc. (Tokyo: 1929) 93ff; R. Sāṅkṛtyāyana, "Search for Sanskrit Mss. in Tibet," *JBORS* 24.4 (1938) 157–160; E. H. Johnston, "The *Tridaṇḍamālā* of Aśvaghoṣa," *JBORS* 25 (1939) 11–14; Lin Li-Kouang, *L'aide-mémoire de la vraie loi* (Paris: 1949) 303–305; L. Giles, *Descriptive Catalogue of the Chinese Manuscripts from Tunhuang in the British Museum* (London: 1957) 114–115; Durt, *Hôbôgirin,* cinquième fasc., 437; P. Demiéville, "Notes on Buddhist Hymnology in the Far East," *Buddhist Studies in Honour of Walpola Rahula,* ed. S. Balasooriya et al. (London: 1980) 50, n. 31; Seidel, *Hôbôgirin,* sixième fasc., 577–578; etc.

63. de La Vallée Poussin, *HJAS* 2 (1935) 287. Here again we have a case where what should be a straightforward referent turns out not to be so. The problems start with an old one. Tibetan translations almost never distinguish between *stūpa* and *caitya,* both terms almost always being rendered by *mchod rten;* there are apparent exceptions, but they are extremely rare—see the *Mchod rten gcig btab na bye ba btab par 'gyur pa'i gzungs* (*Peking,* 6, 151-2-2 to 151-3-2; 11, 168-4-8 to 164-5-8) where the transliteration *tsai tya* appears several times. The original that was translated in our passage by *mchod rten la phyag mi 'tshal nas* and *mchod rten la phyag 'tshal bar bya'o* cannot, therefore, be determined. There is also the fact that the Tibetan versions are not in agreement as to whether the text is referring to one or to several *mchod rtens:* the *Derge* has in the second occurrence *mchod rten la,* but both *Tog* and *Peking* have *mchod rten dag la* (de La Vallée Poussin translates the Chinese as singular). Both considerations may bear on an even more important point: we do not know to whom the *mchod rten* or *mchod rtens* belonged; we do not know whether the reference is to a *stūpa* or *stūpas* of the Buddha, or to the *stūpa* or *stūpas* of the local monastic dead—it is now clear that the latter were found in considerable numbers at a considerable number of mostly very early monastic sites in

India; cf. Schopen, "An Old Inscription from Amarāvatī," Ch. IX above; for some regional variation in regard to whether such structures were called *stūpas* or *caityas,* see 197 and n. 38. Taking this category into account it is, of course, not impossible that our text might be referring to a *stūpa* built for the deceased monk whose funeral has just been performed. It appears, however, that at least Mūlasarvāstivāda texts do not seem to link funereal activity *per se* with the erection of *stūpas* for the local monastic dead. In none of the numerous references to monastic funerals in Mūlasarvāstivāda literature that I know is there any reference to erecting a *stūpa.* In fact, the erection of *stūpas* for the local monastic dead is legislated separately in the *Mūlasarvāstivāda-vinaya*, not in an account of a funeral, but in an account concerning the post-funereal "relics" of Śāriputra (*Derge,* 10, 488ff). This would suggest, I think, that in this *Vinaya* funeral ceremonies and cult activity directed toward relics or reliquaries of the local monastic dead were conceived of as fundamentally different forms of religious behavior. (It is—in so far as I know—only in a few Pāli narrative passages that funeral ceremonies for local monks or nuns are directly linked with the erection of *stūpas* for them; cf. *Udāna,* 8.21; Pāli *Vinaya,* iv, 308.) [See now G. Schopen, "Ritual Rights and Bones of Contention: More on Monastic Funerals and Relics in the *Mūlasarvāstivāda-vinaya,*" *JIP* 22 (1994) 31–80.] In light of these considerations, it might be well to assume—until it can be shown otherwise—that *mchod rten (dag) la phyag 'tshal bar bya'o* in our passage refers to worshipping the *stūpa* or *stūpas* of the Buddha, and that such an act was the final moment of a monastic funeral. What "external" evidence we have also would seem to indicate that funeral activity and activity connected with *stūpas* were thought of as distinct. I-tsing in his *Record* refers to something "like a *stūpa*" for the local monastic dead, but he seems to indicate that such was not always erected and that when it was it was made an indeterminate time after the funeral: the monks, he says, "on returning [from the cremation] to their apartments, . . . cleanse the floor with powdered cow-dung. All other things remain as usual. There is no custom as to putting on a mourning-dress. They sometimes build a thing like a *stūpa* for the dead, to contain his *śarīra* (or relics). It is called a '*kula,*' which is like a small *stūpa,* but without the cupola on it"; see Takakusu, *A Record of the Buddhist Religion as Practiced in India and the Malay Archipelago,* 82; cf. Bareau, *ACF* 1989–1990, 636: "Après la crémation, on recueille les restes corporels (*śarīra*) et on élève sur eux un petit tumulus appelé *kula.* Celui-ci ressemble à un *stūpa,* mais on ne dresse pas de parasols (*chattra*) à roues (*cakra*) à son sommet . . ." For an attempt to identify what I-tsing calls a *kula* with what is found at a number of monastic sites in India, see G. Schopen, "Burial *Ad Sanctos* and the Physical Presence of the Buddha in Early Indian Buddhism," Ch. VII above, esp. 120. Note too that Rockhill's summary of our text is particularly unsatisfactory at this point: "Previously to being interred the body must be washed. A cairn or tchaitya (*mchod rten*) must be raised over the remains" (*The Life of the Buddha and the Early History of His Order,* 112). There is no justification in the text itself for his interpretation of either injunction: it is the monks who participated in the funeral who must wash, and the *mchod rten* is to be worshipped, not "raised."

64. I. B. Horner, *The Book of the Discipline,* Vol. I (Oxford: 1938) xvi–xvii.

65. Horner, *The Book of the Discipline,* Vol. I, xxix.

66. Horner, *The Book of the Discipline,* Vol. I, xv.

67. Ch. Malamoud, "Les morts sans visage. Remarques sur l'idéologie funéraire dans le brâhmanisme," *La mort, les morts dans les sociétés anciennes,* ed. G. Gnoli et J.-P. Vernant (Cambridge and Paris: 1982) 441–453, esp. 441, 445, 449.

68. L. Dumont, *Homo Hierarchicus. The Caste System and Its Implications,* completely revised English ed. (Chicago: 1980) 49–50.

69. Jain has recently argued that the "elaborate rules for disposing of the dead bodies of Jain monks" found in Jain literature are also early: "The material contained in the *Bhag{avatī} Ārā{dhanā}* belongs to the time of early Jainism when the division of Śvetāmbara and Digambara did not exist in the Jain *Saṅgha*" (J. Jain, "Disposal of the Dead in the Bhagavatī Ārādhanā," *JOIB* 38 [1988] 123–31. Though a late text, see the interesting description of "The Funeral of a Renouncer" in J. P. Olivelle, ed., *Saṃnyāsapaddhati of Rudradeva,* The Adyar Library Series, 114 [Madras: 1986] 63ff). It should be noted that the scholarly literature in regard to the date of the *Mūlasarvāstivāda-vinaya* is marked by ambivalence and seeming contradictions. Lamotte, for example, notably on the basis of the fact that this *Vinaya* contains a "prediction" relative to Kaniṣka and was not translated into Chinese until the eighth century, asserts that "on ne peut attribuer à cet ouvrage une date antérieure aux IVe–Ve siècles de notre ère" in *Histoire du bouddhisme indien,* 727. But Huber, already in 1914, had drawn very different conclusions from the presence of this prediction relative to Kaniṣka. He had said: "Ce petit fait vient s'ajouter à un certain nombre d'autres déjà connus qui tendent à montrer que le Vinaya des Mūla-Sarvāstivādins a subi un remaniement aux environs de l'ère chrétienne," and then added: "Sans discuter la date exacte du roi Kaniṣka, on peut dire que la mention de son nom nous reporte vers le même temps." See E. Huber, "Études bouddhiques III.—Le roi kaniṣka dans le vinaya des mūlasarvāstivādins," *BEFEO* 14 (1914) 19; Gnoli, *Saṅghabhedavastu,* i, xix, has more recently made much the same observation. Moreover, and again long before Lamotte, Lévi had already counseled against attributing too much significance to the date of the Chinese translation: "La date tardive de la traduction chinoise . . . ne doit pas non plus nous entraîner trop vite à tenir l'ouvrage pour récent" in *TP* 8 (1907) 115f. To this might be added the fact that dating the compilation of a work does not necessarily date its specific contents: "dans l'état fragmentaire de nos connaissances sur le bouddhisme indien, la date récente du document qui nous fait connaître une légende, ne permet nullement de conclure à la formation récente de la légende elle-même" (Huber, *BEFEO* 14 [1914] 17). This is made strikingly evident in regard to the *Mūlasarvāstivāda-vinaya* in another series of observations and investigations. Although he repeatedly characterizes the *Mūlasarvāstivāda-vinaya* as "tardif" or "le plus récent de tous les recueils disciplinaires," Bareau says as well that the form of the *stūpa* it describes appears to be the "most ancient" in A. Bareau, "La construction et le culte des stūpa d'après les Vinayapiṭaka," *BEFEO* 50 (1960) 233. Elsewhere, while still pointing to its "late" character, he says: ". . . d'après des études comparatives approfondies mais très partielles, le *Vinayapiṭaka* des Mūlasarvāstivādin paraît nettement plus archaïque que celui des Sarvāstivādin et même que le plupart des autres *Vinayapiṭaka*" (A. Bareau, *Les sectes bouddhiques du petit véhicule* [Paris: 1955] 154). More specifically, Lévi, in a detailed study of certain linguistic forms in the *Vinaya,* says for example: "L'interdiction de 'boire à la sangsue', promulgée d'abord dans un dialecte qui pratiquait l'adoucissement de la sourde intervocalique, est arrivée telle quelle aux rédacteurs du canon pali qui n'ont plus reconnu sous son altération le terme original; ainsi des autres écoles, à l'exception des Mūla-Sarvāstivādins, qui montrent encore sur d'autres points du canon une incontestable supériorité," *JA* (1912) 510; M. Hofinger, in his study of the Second Council, argues that the oldest extant accounts of these events are preserved in the *Mūlasarvāstivāda-* and *Mahāsāṅghika-vinayas* (M. Hofinger, *Étude sur le concile de vaiçālī* [Louvain: 1946] 235–241, 256); I myself have suggested that the account of the remains of the former

Buddha Kāśyapa found in the *Mūlasarvāstivāda-vinaya* appears from every angle to be earlier than the standardized, revised, and probably conflated accounts found in our other *Vinayas* in "Two Problems in the History of Indian Buddhism," Ch. II above, 28–29. If these divergent opinions and observations suggest a state of some uncertainty concerning the date of the *Mūlasarvāstivāda-vinaya,* then their presentation has succeeded in representing the actual state of our knowledge. We simply know very little that is definitive about it; the illusion, of course, is that we know anything more about the dates of our other *Vinayas,* including that preserved in Pāli. It does, however, seem that there is mounting evidence that the *Mūlasarvāstivāda-vinaya*—whatever its date or the degree of its "remaniement"—contains a good deal of very early material. The rules concerning monastic funerals may, in fact, be just another case in point.

70. For the Sanskrit translated by *rim gro bya ba,* see L. Chandra, *Tibetan-Sanskrit Dictionary* (New Delhi: 1961) 2268–2269, and note that Sanskrit *satkāra,* when not actually a "w.r. for *saṃskāra,*" can itself in one form or another mean "doing (the last) honour (to the dead), cremation of a corpse, funeral obsequies," "to pay the last honours to (acc.), cremate," etc.; M. Monier-Williams, *A Sanskrit-English Dictionary* (Oxford: 1899) 1134. As stated earlier, Sanskrit accounts of monastic funerals do not always use the expression *śarīra-pūjā:* at *Gilgit Manuscripts,* iii 2, 118.15, for example, we find *bhikṣavas tam ādāya dahanaṃ gatāḥ . . . bhikṣavas tam ādahane saṃskārya vihāram āgatāḥ;* at iii 2, 125.14: *bhikṣavas tam ādahanaṃ nītvā saṃskārya vihāram āgatāḥ.*

71. Although it contains some details not yet found in the texts, I-tsing's description of a monastic funeral also contains, in one form or another, the same basic elements; see Takakusu, *A Record of the Buddhist Religion as Practiced in India and the Malay Archipelago,* 81–82, and Bareau, *ACF* (1989–1990) 636.

72. It would appear from Jain's remarks in *Life in Ancient India as Depicted in the Jain Canon and Commentaries,* 281–284, and *JOIB* 38 (1988) 123–131, that the funeral of a dead Jain monk was by preference and, when at all possible, an exclusively monastic affair. But Jain sources explicitly legislate for contingencies: "The question of carrying the dead [monk] for disposal was rather complicated . . . If there were only one single monk and it was not possible for him to carry the dead, ascetics belonging to non-Jain religion or laymen should be called, or help should be taken from the members of the Mallagaṇa, the Hastipālagaṇa or the Kumbhakāragaṇa, or in the absence of these a village-headman, *cāṇḍalas,* people from degraded castes, sweepers, barbers and others should be approached." It is not impossible that the Buddhist *Vinayas* also contained such legislation and it simply has not been recognized as such. The well-known passage that we associate with the *Mahāparinirvāṇa-sūtra,* which has been taken wrongly to establish that "śarīrapūjā, the worship of relics, is the concern of the laity and not the bhikṣusaṃgha" (Schopen, "Monks and the Relic Cult in the *Mahāparinibbāna-sutta,*" now Ch. VI above, 100–101), may be, in fact, just such legislation. In the passage in question (Sanskrit 36.2–36.3; Pāli V.10), Ānanda asks how the funereal *śarīra-pūjā* for the Buddha could be performed, and the Buddha responds in the Sanskrit version: *alpotsukas tvam ānanda bhava śarīrapūjāyāḥ. prasannā brāhmaṇagṛhapataya etad āpādayiṣyanti.* All of the other known versions are essentially similar: Pāli, " 'ne soyez pas occupés (*avyāvaṭā tumhe hotha*) du culte [à rendre au] corps du Tathāgata' "; Chinese D, " 'ne vous souciez pas de cette affaire' "; Chinese A and C, " 'restez tranquilles' "; etc. All versions, as well, indicate essentially the same reason why Ānanda need not be concerned: " 'les pieux brahmanes et maîtres de maison (*gṛhapati*) s'en chargeront' "; all quotations are from Bareau, *Recherches sur la biographie du buddha dans les sūtrapiṭaka et les vinayapiṭaka anciens: II. Les derniers*

mois, le parinirvāṇa et les funérailles, T. II, 36–37. Previous interpretations of this passage—and they have been many—have, it seems, never asked why Ānanda should have been so concerned in the first place. Moreover, they have failed to take into account, among other things, that the *Mahāparinirvāṇa-sūtra* was almost certainly a piece of *vinaya;* that the Buddha's declaration came at almost the very end of the various *Vinayas* and certainly at the very end of the narrative time or internal chronology assumed by the canonical texts; and that—finally—Ānanda found himself, in so far as we can tell, alone. This would mean in terms of the *Mūlasarvāstivāda-vinaya,* for example, that by the time the reader or redactor of this *Vinaya* had reached this passage, he would have seen or inserted both sets of rules governing monastic funerals that we have looked at here and a host of narrative descriptions of monastic funerals, in all of which it was monks and monks alone who did and were explicitly directed to perform the funeral of a fellow-monk. But again, in so far as we can tell, Ānanda found himself alone or virtually so. He could not, therefore, fulfill the *vinaya* rule. This situation can explain well Ānanda's concern, the Buddha's assurance, and the sense of the passage: the Buddha was allowing an exception to the rule. This interpretation, although differing markedly from others, is perhaps worth pursuing. It is also perhaps worth noting that it—or some residual sense that Ānanda had indeed broken the rule—may also explain one of the charges brought against Ānanda by Mahākāśyapa at "the council of Rājagṛha." Among other things and in all versions, Ānanda is criticized, in fact charged with a fault (*duṣkṛta*), for having allowed apparently unauthorized individuals—nuns, laymen, and especially laywomen—to participate in what could only have been the funereal *śarīra-pūjā;* most of the versions emphasize that the women saw the Buddha's penis, and that could only have happened during the preparation of the body before it was wrapped. See, for the various accounts, J. Przyluski, *Le concile de rājagṛha. Introduction a l'histoire des canons et des sectes bouddhiques* (Paris: 1926–1928) 15, 50–51, 64, 153, 157, etc.

73. The role of ghosts, demons, etc., in the promulgation of *vinaya* rules would make an interesting topic of study. In both the Pāli *Vinaya* (i, 149ff) and the *Mūlasarvāstivāda-vinaya* (*Gilgit Manuscripts,* iii 4, 149ff), for example, problems with or the presence of *piśāca* or *amanuṣyas* are cited as legitimate causes for cutting short the rain-retreat, an act which otherwise was forbidden. Again in the Pāli *Vinaya* the case of a monk who had "a non-human affliction" (*amanussikābādha*) or was "possessed" prompted the Buddha to allow monks to eat raw flesh and drink blood (Pāli *Vinaya,* i, 202; I. B. Horner, *The Book of the Discipline,* Vol. IV [London: 1951] 274, n. 6); etc. It would appear, moreover, from Jain's remarks that many of the rules governing Jain monastic funerals were also connected with the fear of "ghosts": "If these rites are not followed, it is possible that some deity might enter the dead body, rise, play and create disturbances to the saṅgha" (*JOIB* 38 [1988] 127).

74. Unfortunately, the material studied here makes little specific reference to nuns, and in this it is probably typical of textual sources on the whole and unrepresentative of what actually occurred; see G. Schopen, "Monks, Nuns, and 'Vulgar' Practices," Ch. XI below, esp. 248ff. It is true, however, that none of the inscribed—and therefore certain—*stūpas* of the local monastic dead found at Indian monastic sites were erected for a nun; see Schopen, "An Old Inscription from Amarāvatī," now Ch. IX above. The subject requires, and will undoubtedly reward, future research.

CHAPTER XI

On Monks, Nuns, and "Vulgar" Practices

The Introduction of the Image Cult into Indian Buddhism

THERE IS A CURIOUS consistency in the way in which major doctrinal changes and innovations in the history of Indian Buddhism have been explained. Some variant of a single explanatory model has been used to account for such diverse phenomena as the initial split within the Buddhist community that produced the Mahāsāṅghika and the beginnings of Buddhist sectarianism, the appearance and growth of relic worship and the *stūpa* cult, and the appearance of the Mahāyāna, "celestial *bodhisattvas,*" the cult of images, and Buddhist tantric practices. The same model has been used, as well, to account for the disappearance of Buddhism from India.

It is equally curious that we owe the most recent and perhaps most clearly articulated statement of this model to a classicist working in "late antiquity." Brown, in talking about the rise of the cult of the saints in Latin Christianity, speaks of "a particular model of the nature and origin of the religious sentiment," which he calls the " 'two-tiered' model." In this model:

> The views of the potentially enlightened few are thought of as being subject to continuous upward pressure from habitual ways of thinking current among "the vulgar" . . .
>
> When applied to the nature of religious change in late antiquity, the "two-tiered" model encourages the historian to assume that a change in the piety of late-antique men, of the kind associated with the rise of the cult of saints, must have been the result of the capitulation by the enlightened elites of the Christian church to modes of thought previously current only

Originally published in *Artibus Asiae* 49:1–2 (1988–1989):153–168. Reprinted with stylistic changes with permission of *Artibus Asiae*.

> among the "vulgar." The result has been a tendency to explain much of the cultural and religious history of late antiquity in terms of drastic "landslips" in the relation between the elites and the masses. Dramatic moments of "democratization of culture" or of capitulation to popular needs are held to have brought about a series of "mutations" of late-antique and early medieval Christianity.[1]

That this view or "model" has become an almost unnoticed part of our scholarly method could be easily documented on every side. That it is deeply embedded in even the best standard works on Indian Buddhism is clear from any number of statements in Lamotte. The latter, under the heading "influence du milieu laïc," says, for example:

> Le bouddhisme n'est pas qu'une philosophie mystique à l'usage des candidats au Nirvāṇa. Ce fut aussi une religion qui sortit du cadre étroit des couvents pour se répandre à travers toutes les couches de la population. Il n'est pas douteux que, sur certains points de la doctrine et du culte, les religieux n'aient dû composer avec les aspirations des laïcs . . . les succès croissants de la propagande eurent pour effet de transformer le bouddhisme, de message philosophico-mystique qu'il était primitivement, en une véritable religion comportant un Dieu (plus exactement un buddha divinisé), un panthéon, des saints, une mythologie et un culte. Cette religion ne tarda pas à s'infiltrer dans les monastères et à influencer, peu ou prou, les savants docteurs.[2]

Later in the same work and at the end of his short discussion of the cult of images, Lamotte says:

> Dans l'ensemble, en face des exigences multipliées du sentiment populaire, la réaction cléricale n'a manqué ni de souplesse ni d'adresse . . . Dans la vie courante, les autorités spirituelles évitaient de prendre position, tolér-aient sans permettre, concédaient sans accorder . . .[3]

In fact, this attitude and the " 'two-tiered' model" has particularly affected our understanding of such things as the introduction of the cult of images into Indian Buddhism almost from the very beginning of the discussion. Sixty years ago Coomaraswamy said:

> . . . it may well be asked how it came to pass that Hinduism, Buddhism, and Jainism alike became "idolatrous" religions. The answer to this question was admirably expressed by Jacobi over forty years ago: 'I believe that this worship had nothing to do with original Buddhism or Jainism, that it did not originate with the monks, but with the lay community, when the people in general felt the want of a higher cult than that of their rude deities and demons, when the religious development of India found in Bhakti the supreme means of salvation. Therefore instead of seeing in the Buddhists the originals and in the Jainas the imitators, with regard to the

> erection of temples and worship of statues, we assume that both sects were . . . brought to adopt this practice by the perpetual and irresistible influence of the religious development of the people in India.[4]

That this model is still very much current can be seen in even the most recent discussions of the early image cult.[5]

The position here is an odd one. It starts with the assumption—another old one—that Indian Buddhism was a religion dominated by a religious elite. But then it almost immediately asserts that these "enlightened elites"—"les savants docteurs," "les autorités spirituelles," "the monks"—were apparently able only to react: change and innovation were apparently out of their hands and were the result of the pressure of popular, lay feeling; it was the laity, it seems, who stimulated change and innovation. But apart from the fact that this would have been an almost complete reversal of the role that "autorités spirituelles" have always had in Indian culture, every indication that we have in regard to the cult of images, for example, suggests something like the very opposite.

Precisely because it was a later innovation in Indian Buddhism, the development of the cult of images can be much more easily followed than many other, earlier developments. This is especially true of its introduction and its earlier phases at individual sites. By means of one of the most important and most unaccountably little-used sources for the history of Indian Buddhism, we are able to actually document the role of the Indian Buddhist monastic in this process. In fact, even a preliminary analysis of the large collection of donative inscriptions that have come down to us clearly indicates the preponderant place that the monks and nuns had in the entire enterprise. We might start late and with Sārnāth.

There are twenty-two image inscriptions from Sārnāth in which the donor is clear that date to the Kuṣān and Gupta periods. In fifteen of these, including the *very earliest,* the donor of the image is a monastic.[6] In only three is the donor specifically said to be a layman, and one of these is uncertain.[7] In four others, only the name of the donor is given without any indication of his status. Even if we assume that this last group were laymen, still there are more than twice as many monk donors as lay donors. The numbers for monastic donors are almost certainly far out of proportion with the actual number of monks in the general population. They are also in striking contrast with what we find at Sārnāth at the end of what Sahni calls "the Mediaeval Period": 1100–1200 C.E. Here we find six lay donors, and possibly two more, but not a single monk.[8] Monastics initiated and disproportionately supported the cult of images at Sārnāth in the early periods.

In the Western Cave Temples we can even more clearly watch the introduction of the cult of images. The caves at Ajaṇṭā were excavated in two main phases. In the early phase, which goes back to the first century B.C.E., there are no images. In the second phase, which started in the fifth century C.E., images were an integral part of the new excavations and were introduced into many of the older caves as well. Here, there is no doubt about who was responsible for their introduction. We have thirty-six donative inscriptions connected with images from Ajaṇṭā in which the status of the donor can be determined. In only three of these inscriptions are the donors laymen, and one of these cases is doubtful. The other thirty-three donors were all monks. Ninety-four percent of these images were given by monks.[9]

Although less overwhelming, the evidence from other cave sites in Western India always points in the same direction. Eighteen of our donative inscriptions from Kānheri record the gifts of laymen: caves, cisterns, seats, and so on. Seven show monks and nuns making the same kind of gifts. But although laymen never donated images, two additional inscriptions indicate that monks did. The two inscriptions from Kānheri connected with images both indicate they were given by monks.[10] Moreover, if Leese is right about "the earliest extant figures of the Buddha at Kaṇheri," it is worth noting that the figures she identifies resulted either entirely or in large part from the patronage of a group of five monks.[11] The pattern is very much the same at Kuda. Here eighteen inscriptions record the gifts of laymen: caves, cisterns, a bathing tank, and so on. In only one case did a layman give an image. There are six additional inscriptions from Kuda that record the gifts of monks: in two of these, monastic individuals donated caves; in one, the object given is unclear; the remaining three inscriptions all record the gifts of images by monks.[12] At both Kuda and Kānheri the images found are intrusive—they were not part of the original plan. They were introduced onto the site, and in five out of six cases they were introduced by monks. Many of the images at Ajaṇṭā were also intrusive, and virtually all of them were introduced by monks.

The monastic role in the cult of images is also apparent in the Kharoṣṭhī inscriptions—some quite early—from the Northwest. There are eighteen Kharoṣṭhī inscriptions in the old collection edited by Konow that record the gifts of images and in which the donor's name is preserved. Of these eighteen, more than two-thirds (or thirteen) record the gifts of monks.[13] When we add to these the image inscriptions that have been published recently, the figures change somewhat but not markedly. I know of nine newly discovered Kharoṣṭhī inscriptions connected with images, but in three of these the status of the donor is unclear or problematic.[14] In five others, the donors are lay persons, and in one—the *earliest* dated piece of Gandhāran sculpture—the donor is a monk.[15] It is worth noting that even if in all three of the new inscriptions in which the donor's status is unclear the donor is assumed to be a lay person, this would still mean that almost 60 percent of the inscribed images from Gandhāra now known were given by monks, and this figure, again, is certainly way out of proportion in terms of the percentage of monks in the total population. It is also worth noting that both of the earliest actually dated Gandhāran images were the gifts of monks.

Because images are much more frequently inscribed and much more frequently and precisely dated at Mathurā, Mathurān images are probably our most important single source of information on the cult of images, especially in its early phase. Here too, the monastic element disproportionately predominates. Of the twenty-six inscriptions published in Lüders' collection that record the gift of an image and preserve the donors' names, seventeen—or almost two-thirds—record the gifts of monks or nuns.[16] When we add the ten more recently published inscriptions in which the donors are clear[17] and the six inscriptions on early images found elsewhere (Kauśāmbī, Sārnāth, or Śrāvastī) but known to have come from Mathurā,[18] we arrive at a total of forty-two. Of these forty-two images, seventeen were donated by lay persons, but twenty-five by monks or nuns: here again, almost two-thirds. But because many of the Mathurān images are more precisely dated, we can make an even more precise chronological analysis of them.

Since the four image inscriptions assigned by Lüders to the Kṣatrapa period (*MI* nos. 1, 72, 80, 86) are not actually dated, our analysis will be limited to dated Kuṣān inscriptions on images of Mathurān origin in which the status of the donor is clear. (See Table 1. I include the two Kharoṣṭhī inscriptions dated in an early Kuṣān year, marked with an asterisk.)[19]

The first feature that strikes the eye is the proportionately high number of monastic donors: two-thirds of the donors of images in dated Kuṣān inscriptions were monks or nuns. But for the hazards of time, this number would have been higher. Only two of the Kuṣān image inscriptions recording the gift of lay persons lacked a year date and were therefore excluded from the analysis. But four of the inscriptions recording monastic gifts lacked such a date and had to be excluded. The second striking feature of our table is the clustering of monastic donors *at the very beginning of the period.*

Apart from one exception, every image set up in the first dozen years of the period was set up by a monk or a nun. The exception—number v in our table—is itself very doubtful. Lüders says "owing to the deplorable state of the inscription, the reading of the date is not absolutely reliable." Sahni reads it as year 30, and Lüders in a note says "it may have been 4 or 40."[20] There is a distinct possibility that it belongs much further down in our table. However this may be, we need go no further in our analysis to conclude that, on the basis of the actual evidence, the cult of images in the Kuṣān period—the earliest period we can actually reach—was almost entirely, and very probably exclusively, a monastically initiated and supported cult.

But these inscriptions can tell us even more about the individuals involved

Table 1. Status of Donors in Kuṣān Period: Inscriptions from Mathurā

	Kuṣān Year	*Type of Donor*	*Location*	*Source*
i	2	monastic	Kauśāmbī	*EI* 24, 210ff
ii	3	monastic	Sārnāth	*EI* 8, 173ff
iii	3[a]	monastic	Śrāvastī	*EI* 8, 181
iv	4	monastic	Mathurā	*EI* 34, 9ff
v	4 or 40?	lay	Mathurā	*MI* No. 172
vi	5*	monastic	Peshawar(?)	*BEFEO* 61, 54
vii	6	monastic	Kauśāmbī	*Central Asia in the Kushan Period,* Vol. II, 15
viii	8	monastic	Mathurā	*MI* No. 154
ix	14	lay	Mathurā	*MI* No. 81
x	16	monastic	Mathurā	*MI* No. 157
xi	17	lay	Mathurā	*MI* No. 150
xii	23	lay	Mathurā	*MI* No. 136
xiii	26	lay	Mathurā	*JIABS* 10.2, 101
xiv	31	monastic	Mathurā	*MI* No. 103
xv	32	monastic	Ahicchatra	*JASB* 21, 67
xvi	33	monastic	Mathurā	*MI* No. 24
xvii	39	monastic	Mathurā	*MI* No. 126
xviii	45	lay	Mathurā	*MI* No. 180
xix	46	lay	Mathurā	*JAIH* 13, 277ff
xx	51	monastic	Mathurā	*MI* No. 29
xxi	89*	monastic	Mamāne Ḍheri	*KI* LXXXVIII

[a]The year has not actually been preserved in this inscription, but since the same donor set up images in the years 2 and 6, the year 3 is a reasonable approximation; cf. the following discussion.

in this monastic innovation. If we set aside the doubtful lay inscription of the year 4 or 40, then we can see that the donors of five of the first Buddhist cult images known in India (i, ii, iii, vi, vii) had at least one more quality in common in addition to the fact that they were all monastics: these donors are all called *trepiṭakas,* those "who know the Three *Piṭakas,*" those who knew the whole of Buddhist sacred literature as it existed at the time. This would suggest that they were not average monks, but high ecclesiastics of wide religious knowledge.

It would also mean—as we shall see in greater detail in a moment—that the earliest dated cult images set up at a minimum of three major Buddhist sites in the Ganges Basin—at Sārnāth, Śrāvastī, and Kauśāmbī—and in Gandhāra (i, ii, iii, vi, vii), were set up by learned monastics, by individuals who "knew the Three *Piṭakas.*" It is also interesting to note that one of the two inscribed images introduced at Kānheri was the gift of a pupil of yet another *trepiṭaka,*[21] and that the donor of the other image dated in the year 4 at Mathurā (iv) was a companion monk to another monk who is called a "preacher of Dharma," a *dha{r}mma-{kathi}ka.* The connection between the beginnings of the image cult and learned monastics is everywhere, so to speak, carved in stone.

Yet other things about the donors of these early images emerge from their accompanying inscriptions. The latter indicate that at least five of these images were set up by a group of monastics who knew one another—perhaps intimately. They also allow us a rare insight into the life and multifarious relationships of one learned monk at the beginning of the Kuṣān period.

The learned monk, the *Bhikṣu* Bala "who knew the Three *Piṭakas,*" himself "caused to be set up" (*pratiṣṭhāpito*) an image in the third year of Kaniṣka at Sārnāth. This is a huge image, ten-feet high and three-feet wide. Both the stone it is made of and its style indicate that it came from Mathurā, which—as the crow flies—is 300 miles away. He "caused it to be set up" at Sārnāth "at the place where the Lord [i.e., the Buddha] used to walk" (*bhagavato caṃkame*); that is to say, on the "promenade, terrace, place for walking" at Sārnāth that local tradition apparently maintained the Buddha had actually used. He also provided this huge image with a large stone umbrella.[22] Some time before or after—the exact year is unsure—this same learned monk "caused to be set up" another image at Śrāvastī. This image is also huge—eleven-feet, eight-inches high—and it too was made in Mathurā, which—again, as the crow flies—is more than 200 miles away. At Śrāvastī also Bala caused this monumental image to be set up "at the place where the Lord used to walk." Here as well he provided the image with a stone umbrella.[23]

As Vogel has already said, all the evidence points to the fact that these were the first images set up at Śrāvastī and Sārnāth, two of the most important Buddhist sacred sites in India. It is, therefore, of considerable significance that the person responsible was at both places the same learned monk, and all of the evidence indicates that he alone was responsible, in spite of the fact that the cost of having the images made and having them transported must have been very great. There is no question about this in regard to the Śrāvastī image: although he attached two separate inscriptions to his gift—one on the base of the image and one on the umbrella shaft—Bala himself is the only donor mentioned. The inscription on the base reads:

{mahārājasya devaputrasya kaniṣkasya saṃ . . . di} 10 9 etaye purvaye bhikṣusya puṣya{vu}-
{ddhis}ya saddhy{e}vihārisya bhikṣusya balasya trepiṭakasya dānaṃ b{o}dhisatvo chātraṃ dāṇḍaś ca śāvastiye bhagavato caṃkame
kosaṃbakuṭiye acaryyāṇāṃ sarvastivādinaṃ parigahe

(*EI* 8 [1905–1906] 181)

[In the year [3] of the Great King, the Devaputra Kaniṣka, in the . . . the month of . . ., on the] 19th [day], on this date the gift of the Monk Bala, who knows the Three *Piṭakas* and is a companion of the Monk Puṣyavuddhi, [i.e.,] a *Bodhisattva,* an umbrella, and its shaft [were set up] in Śrāvastī, on the Blessed One's Promenade, in the Kosaṃbakuṭi, for the possession of the Sarvāstivādin Teachers.

Here, although Bala identifies himself in part by reference to a fellow monk—Puṣyavuddhi—that fellow monk is not associated with his gift. The gift is said to be Bala's alone. Note that what was almost certainly the first cult image set up at Śrāvastī—one of the most important of Buddhist sites—was not only given *by* a learned monk, it was also given *to* a group of learned monks, "the Sarvāstivādin Teachers."

The inscription on the umbrella shaft belonging to the Śrāvastī image, although very fragmentary at the beginning, almost certainly is worded exactly the same as the inscription on the base. No more. In this, the inscriptions on the Sārnāth image differ.

There are three separate inscriptions associated with the Sārnāth image: one on the umbrella shaft, which is the longest, one on the front of the image pedestal, and one on the back of the image between the feet. The last of these reads:

mahārajasya kaṇiṣ{kasya} saṃ 3 he 3 di 2{2}
etaye purvaye bhikṣusya balasya trepiṭa{kasaya}
bodhisatvo chatrayaṣṭi ca {pratiṣṭhāpito}

(*EI* 8 [1905–1906] 179)

The year 3 of the Great King Kaniṣka, the 3rd month of winter, the 22nd day. On this date, by the Monk Bala who knows the Three *Piṭakas*, a *Bodhisattva*, an umbrella, and its shaft were caused to be set up.

Here, Bala is the only donor mentioned. He alone is said to be responsible for setting up "the *Bodhisattva,* an umbrella, and its shaft." But the inscription on the front of the pedestal says that the *Bodhisattva* at least—the umbrella and shaft are not mentioned—was "caused to be set up" by Bala *mahākṣatrapena kharapallānena sahā kṣatrapena vanaṣparena,* which on the face of it means: "together with the Great Satrap Kharapallāna and the Satrap Vanaṣpara." The inscription on the shaft is even fuller. It records that the *Bodhisattva,* umbrella, and shaft were set up by the Monk Bala, who is here identified as "the companion of the Monk Puṣyavuddhi"—thus identifying the Bala of the Śrāvastī image with the Bala named here at Sārnāth. But it goes on to say that this was done "together with his mother and father, together with his preceptors and teachers, his companions and pupils, together with Buddhamitrā who knows the Three *Piṭakas,* together with the Satrap Vanaṣpara and Kharapallāna, and together with the Four Assemblies, for the welfare and happiness of all beings."

The situation appears somewhat contradictory here. The inscription on the back of the image says that Bala alone set up the image, umbrella, and shaft. The other two inscriptions say that the same act was done—following the usual interpretation of *saha*—"together with" a number of named individuals. The seeming contradiction turns on the interpretation of *saha:* if it is taken literally, the inscriptions recording the same event are saying different things; if it does not literally mean "together with," they are not. There are internal indications that seem to indicate that *saha* was not intended to be understood in its literal sense.

The last group mentioned in the shaft inscription according to the way Vogel has printed it, is "the Four Assemblies"; that is, "all monks, nuns, laymen, and laywomen." The universalistic character of this group is even clearer if we read *sahā ca sarvāhi pariṣāhi,* "and together with all assemblies," instead of *sahā ca(tu)hi pariṣāhi,* "together with the Four Assemblies." Vogel admits he hesitated between the two readings.[24] In fact, both are possible. But the important point here is that, in either case, it is very difficult to believe that the inscription intended to say that the image at Sārnāth was "caused to be set up" by Bala "together with"—*literally*—"all monks, nuns, laymen, and laywomen." In fact, several individuals and subgroups who would fall into the larger categories such as "monks" have already been specifically mentioned. It seems much more likely that the *saha* construction is used here—and perhaps everywhere in Buddhist donative inscriptions—as a means by which the donor can share the merit of his act by explicitly associating others with it. He shares or "transfers" the *act* rather than, as is frequent elsewhere, the *merit* resulting from it. The end result in either case is the same.[25]

Whether Bala's gift was literally made "together with" the groups or individuals named, or whether—as appears to be more likely the case—he chose to associate these groups or individuals with his meritorious act, it would seem obvious that he had a special relationship with them, especially with those he specifically names. The Satraps Vanaṣpara and Kharapallāna were clearly important local political figures, and it appears likely that the Monk Bala, like the Monk Buddhabhadra later at Ajaṇṭā, was "the friend of kings." Like Buddhabhadra again, he must also have been a man "of considerable wealth."[26] But the one other specifically named individual he associates with his act has no counterpart in Buddhabhadra's inscription. Bala specifically names, in addition to the Satraps, only Buddhamitrā: a woman—she is called here neither a nun nor a pupil—who "knows the Three *Piṭakas.*" This is of particular importance, both for what it reveals about Bala's preoccupations and for the fact that it establishes that he knew and apparently had a special relationship with a woman named Buddhamitrā who—like himself and apparently on the same footing—"knew the Three *Piṭakas*" or the whole of Buddhist canonical literature as it existed at the time. This, in turn, is important because it suggests that he probably knew the woman who, on at least two occasions—the year 2 and the year 6 of Kaniṣka—"caused to be set up" the first cult images at Kauśāmbī, yet another major Buddhist sacred site.

The earliest dated cult image set up at Kauśāmbī was, like Bala's images at Sārnāth and Śrāvastī, a very large standing image very probably made at Mathurā, which was more than 200 miles away. It, again like both Bala's images, was set up "on the promenade of the Blessed One, the Buddha" (*bhagavato buddhasa ca{ṃ}kame*). These facts alone would suggest that the installation of these three images—the first of their kind at these important sites—was the result of a patterned and coordinated effort: all three originated from the same place, and all three were set up on a "promenade" associated with the Buddha. This suggestion is further strengthened by the fact that the Kauśāmbī image was set up by a woman named Buddhamitrā who, according to the inscription, "knew the Three *Piṭakas.*" This Buddhamitrā, called here "a nun" (*bhikhuṇī*), can hardly be anyone else than the Buddhamitrā "who knows the Three *Piṭakas*" that Bala mentions in his inscription from Sārnāth. This same Buddhamitrā set up at least three separate images "on the promenade of the Blessed One" at Kauśāmbī: the first in the year 2, another in the year 6, and a third in an unknown year.[27]

The nature of the relationship between Bala and Buddhamitrā is curiously unstated. Buddhamitrā is the only specifically named individual—apart from the Satraps—whom Bala associates with his gift. But he does not say that she was a nun, nor does he indicate that she was his pupil. Buddhamitrā, although specifically mentioned by Bala, does not mention him at all in any of her three inscriptions. She indicates that she was a nun but gives no indication of whom her teacher was. This is of some significance, since it was a common practice already for monks or nuns to identify themselves by reference to the monastic who was their teacher. The association of Bala and Buddhamitrā with one another, as well as their association with Mathurā, is, however, both confirmed and given specificity by the donative inscription of yet another nun who seems to have carried on their joint project. This inscription records the fact that, in the year 33, a nun named Dhanavatī "caused to be set up" at Mathurā an image. Dhanavatī describes herself both as a nun and as "the sister's daughter of the nun Buddhamitrā, who knows the *Tripiṭaka,* the female pupil of the monk Bala, who knows the *Tripiṭaka*" (*bhīkṣusya balasya {t}repiṭakasya antevā{si}n(ī)y(e) {bhi}kṣuṇīye tre(pi-*

ṭi){kā}ye buddha{mi}trāy{e} bhāgineyīye, MI no. 24). Thirty years after Buddhamitrā set up her first image at Kauśāmbī, her maternal niece set up an image at Mathurā. The niece identified herself exclusively in terms of her relationship to Buddhamitrā, and identified Buddhamitrā in turn as a "pupil" of Bala. That neither of the latter made reference to Buddhamitrā's "pupilhood" is curious, but it is clear that their names were still linked by the generation that followed them.

If the connection between learned monastics and the beginnings of the image cult is everywhere apparent, it is even more specifically so in the Bala-Buddhamitrā inscriptions. We seem to see here something like an intentional, organized, even coordinated distribution of early images from a central point. The earliest cult images at three of the most important Buddhist sites in the Ganges Basin—Kauśāmbī, Śrāvastī, and Sārnāth—almost certainly came from Mathurā, where scholarly opinion is more and more inclined to locate the production of the first Buddha images.[28] The production, transportation, and installation of all these images—again, the first at these sites—was effected by at least two monastics who knew one another in one or more capacities. And both of these individuals were, in their contemporary idiom, very learned. All of the evidence suggests that these learned monastics were, in Basham's words, "propagandists for a new cult,"[29] and that this propaganda was effected in a systematic fashion. This can only mean that the only "autorités spirituelles" whom we have actual knowledge of, far from "taking no position," were the sponsors and initiators of one of the most radical and far-reaching innovations in Indian Buddhist cult practice. That some of these "autorités spirituelles" were women brings us to the last aspect of the question that we can deal with here.

If, because of an almost exclusive reliance on textual sources, our picture of the actual Indian Buddhist monk is more than a little skewed, the picture of the Indian Buddhist nun—for the same reason—has been almost obliterated. Oldenberg, for example, says:

> In number they [Buddhist nuns] were apparently far behind monks, and therefore it is to be doubted also, whether at any time there was inherent in the spiritual sisterhood a degree of influence which could be felt, bearing on the Buddhist community as a whole. The thoughts and forms of life of Buddhism had been thought out and moulded solely by men and for men.[30]

That this is off-the-mark on several counts can be surmised on the basis of what we have seen already of the nun Buddhamitrā: her activities at Kauśāmbī would almost certainly have had profound "influence" there "on the Buddhist community as a whole." It was she who introduced at Kauśāmbī the cult image. In fact, nuns, and laywomen as well, seem to have been very actively involved in the development of the "new cult." This will be easily apparent if we rewrite our table containing the data for the image cult connected with Mathurā in such a way as to show gender differences. (See Table 2.)

If we set aside the two Kharoṣṭhī inscriptions, we can note that, of the nineteen individuals associated with Mathurā who "caused images to be set up" in the Kuṣān period, six were monks, two were laymen, six were nuns, and five were laywomen. Nuns here, rather than being "far behind monks," had parity with them both in terms of numbers and in terms of learned titles. This parity was not new. It occurred before in the earlier inscriptions recording donations connected with the *stūpa*/relic cult at Sāñcī: there were at Sāñcī one hundred twenty-nine monk donors, and one hundred twenty-five nuns. At least four inscriptions from Sāñcī record the gift of a nun named Avisinā who is called one "who is versed in the *Sūtras,*"[31] and at least three nun donors at Sāñcī had "pupils" (*antevāsin*).[32] The figures for other early sites show a similar pattern: at Pauni there were three monk donors and five nuns;[33] at Bhārhut, sixteen nuns and twenty-five monks;[34] at Amarāvatī, twelve monk donors and twelve nun donors.[35] The one striking exception from the early period comes from our Kharoṣṭhī inscriptions: in Konow's collection there are sixteen monk donors but not a single nun. There are, as well, no nuns in the more recently published Kharoṣṭhī inscriptions. The reasons for this are not yet clear. It may well have to do with the fact that the geographic area from which our Kharoṣṭhī inscriptions came is precisely that area which has always been most open to foreign influence and occupation, and this influence and occupation may have determined a differ-

Table 2. Gender Differences of Donors in Kuṣān Period Inscriptions from Mathurā

	Kuṣān Year	*Donor*		*Kuṣān Year*	*Donor*
i	2	nun	xii	23	laywoman
ii	3	monk	xiii	26	layman
iii	(3)	monk	xiv	31	nun
iv	4	monk	xv	32	monk
v	4 or 40?	laywoman	xvi	33	nun
vi	5*	monk	xvii	39	nun
vii	6	nun	xviii	45	laywoman
viii	8	nun	xix	46	layman
ix	14	laywoman	xx	51	monk
x	16	monk	xxi	89*	monk
xi	17	laywoman			

ent attitude toward the participation of women in monastic lives.[36] But however this might eventually be explained, it is clear already that, in addition to geographical factors affecting the degree of participation of nuns in recorded Buddhist activities, there is a marked chronological component as well.

From the very earliest period up to and through the Kuṣān period, nuns were everywhere—apart from the Kharoṣṭhī area and Nāgārjunikoṇḍa—present as active donors in numbers similar to those of monks. When we move from the Kuṣān to the Gupta period (the fourth to fifth centuries C.E.), this pattern changes radically. Among the donors of images associated with Mathurā in the Kuṣān age, for example, there were, as we have seen, six monks and six nuns. But in the Gupta inscriptions from Mathurā, while there are six monk donors, there is only a single nun.[37] This marked drop in the number of nun donors at Mathurā occurred in conjunction with at least one other change that can be detected there: a new kind of monk appeared at Mathurā in the fourth to fifth centuries. Five of the six Gupta monk donors appear to have belonged to the same group. They all refer to themselves as *śākyabhikṣus*—a title unknown in previous periods.[38] That the presence of these monks is related to the decline or disappearance of nun donors is suggested as well at other sites, perhaps most dramatically at Ajaṇṭā and Sārnāth. At Ajaṇṭā there were thirty-three monastic donors of images, all of the fifth century, and every one of them was a monk. There was not a single nun. Of these thirty-three monks, at least twenty-five specifically referred to themselves as *śākyabhikṣus.*[39] The same pattern is found in the Gupta inscriptions from Sārnāth: there were thirteen monk donors of images but only a single nun. Here too eleven of the thirteen monk donors referred to themselves as *śākyabhikṣus.*[40]

Although the full details have yet to be worked out, it appears that the appearance or presence of monks calling themselves *śākyabhikṣus* everywhere in the fourth to fifth centuries C.E. occurred in conjunction with the marked decline or disappearance of the participation of nuns in recorded Buddhist religious activity. The fact that these *śākyabhikṣus* were almost certainly Mahāyāna monks may seem curious, but it appears that the emergence of the Mahāyāna in the fourth to fifth centuries coincided with a marked decline in the role of women of all kinds in the practice of Indian Buddhism.[41] What is important for us to note here, however, is that until that time—contrary to Oldenberg—nuns, indeed women as a whole, appear to have been very numerous, very active, and, as a consequence, very influential in the actual Buddhist communities of early India. The female monastics who, like their male counterparts, were so active in religious giving and the cults of relics and images were, again like their male counterparts, oftentimes of high ecclesiastical standing: they were "masters of the Three *Piṭakas,*" "versed in the *Sūtras*," and many of them had groups of disciples.

Before we formulate any general conclusions regarding the material we have seen so far, at least one point should be clearly emphasized. In dealing with the earliest phase of the image cult—primarily but not exclusively at Mathurā—I have intentionally restricted myself to inscribed, dated images in which the status of the donor is clear. The reasons for this are very simple: there are no images that can be proved to be earlier, and there are no earlier data on the donors of images. Whether these are *absolutely* the earliest images cannot, in fact, be known. But even if there were earlier images, they could not have been many, and, almost all would agree, they could not have been much earlier. It is, therefore, extremely unlikely that their inclusion would alter the pattern of patronage we have uncovered. In a rough sort of way this can actually be demonstrated. Although none of them are actually dated, Lüders assigns four image inscriptions to the Kṣatrapa period. In two of these, the status of the donor is unclear (nos. 72, 86); in one, the donor is a laywoman (no. 1); in the other, the donor is a monk (no. 80). (A fifth inscription, no. 155, cannot definitely be connected with an image.)

These same considerations apply with even greater force to true cult images. While there may have been earlier representations of the Buddha in human form in narrative or even decorative contexts, what evidence we have argues against any long-standing *Buddhist* tradition of monumental cult images in a medium other than stone.[42] Unquestionably, early monumental Buddhist cult images in stone—like those of Bala and Buddhamitrā at Sārnāth, Śrāvastī, and Kauśāmbī—presuppose not a previously established, Buddhist cult-image tradition, but an image tradition of a different kind:

> All these early images [in stone] from Mathurā and the surrounding area are closely related with the local *yakṣa* figures and with images of Kuṣāna emperors. They belong to the same world, where the concepts of overlordship, of fame and of fortune (*bhāga*) predominate . . . It has been pointed out that the standing Buddha image is really a replica of the earlier standing *yakṣa* or royal image, but lacking the regalia and insignia of royalty.[43]

Surely if there had been a prior tradition of any standing of Buddhist cult images in wood or clay, the stone images that we have would not still be borrowing so heavily from non-Buddhist models. The fact that our earliest extant monumental cult images in stone represent a tradition still groping for its own types and iconography, still working with non-Buddhist models, virtually precludes any long-standing development of *Buddhist* cult images in clay or wood. The monumental cult images we have in stone from Sārnāth, Śrāvastī, and elsewhere are probably the earliest that there were.

Although this is but a preliminary study of Buddhist donative inscriptions associated with images, still a number of points are already clear. We have seen that the first cult images at several major Buddhist sacred sites—Sārnāth, Śrāvastī, Kauśāmbī, Mathurā—in the early Kuṣān period were set up by learned nuns and monks. We have seen that the earliest dated images in the Northwest were the gifts of learned monks, that it was monks who introduced images of the Buddha into the monastic cave complexes at Kānheri, Kuda, and—massively—at Ajaṇṭā in the fourth to fifth centuries C.E., and that it was monks who donated new images in the fifth-century revitalization at Sārnāth. Although images were introduced at different times at different sites, they were almost always introduced by the same group everywhere: either monks or nuns. It would appear that the image and its attendant cult were major preoccupations of nuns and monks; that they everywhere introduced the cult and everywhere disproportionately supported it.[44] These were not the monks and nuns our textual sources have presented to us; but those monks and nuns, it is coming to be clear, were not in any case the real Indian monastics.

A picture of the actual Indian Buddhist monk and nun is gradually emerging; he and she differ markedly from the ideal monk and nun who have been presented on the basis of textual material alone. The actual monk, for example, unlike the textual monk, appears to have been deeply involved in religious giving and cult practice of every kind from the very beginning. He is preoccupied not with *Nirvāṇa* but, above all else, with what appears to have been a strongly felt obligation to his parents, whether living or dead. He is concerned as well, for example, with the health of his companions and teachers. He appears, in short, as very human and very vulnerable.[45] We do not yet understand him well by any means, but the work of Brown, with which we started the present essay, may not only provide us with an alternative model for change and innovation, it may also give us a clue concerning where we might begin to look in trying to understand this actual monk.

Speaking again about the cult of the saints in Latin Christianity, Brown says "it is not surprising, perhaps, that the cult of the patron saint spread most quickly in ascetic circles." In fact, although he has been criticized for using the term, he refers to "the remarkable generation of Christian leaders" from these circles as the *impresarios* of the cult: "for the *impresarios* of the new cult are precisely those who had taken on themselves the crushing weight of holiness demanded by the ascetic way of life."[46] As Brown himself notes, this suggests that change and innovation "come from a very different direction from that posited by the 'two-tiered' model" and that "the evidence of the pressure from 'mass conversions' "—compare Lamotte's "les succès croissants de la propagande" cited above—"has been exaggerated. Nor is there any evidence that the *locus* of superstitious practice lay among the 'vulgar'. Indeed, it is the other way round . . ."[47] Our donative inscriptions would suggest an Indian situation in the first centuries of the Common Era that was remarkably parallel in essentials: changes in cult practice came from, and were supported by, learned "ascetic circles." But the possible parallel may go further and may provide a partial explanation for the Indian case.

Brown again says: "For the *impresarios* of the cult of saints were studiously anxious men. Sulpicius and Paulinus shared the strong link . . . of having very recently and at no small cost of suffering and scandal, abandoned their previous social identities," and it was they who sought "the face of a fellow human being where an earlier generation had wished to see the shimmering presence of a bodiless power . . ."[48] Again there appear to be clear parallels in the Indian situation. The renunciation of the household life—especially for high-class brahmins—would have entailed the wrenching loss of their "social identity." To judge by the textual sources, it was a move fraught with difficulty and generated strong familial reactions.[49] To judge by the inscriptional sources, it created a disproportionately strong sense of anxiety in regard to their "abandoned" parents on the part of individual monks and nuns. These concerns, again, would have pressed particularly hard on monks from brahmin families, and it is precisely this group that apparently made up the majority of the Buddhist elite.[50] Although much else remains to be understood, it appears that it was this same group that introduced and promoted the cult of images, that sought "the face of a fellow human being where an earlier generation had wished to see the shimmering presence of a bodiless power."

Notes

1. P. Brown, *The Cult of the Saints. Its Rise and Function in Latin Christianity* (Chicago: 1981) 16–18.

2. *Histoire du bouddhisme indien,* 686–687.

3. *Histoire du bouddhisme indien,* 705.

4. A. K. Coomaraswamy, "The Origin of the Buddha Image," *The Art Bulletin* 9 (1927) 297; the quotation from Jacobi is from his *Gaina Sutras,* Sacred Books of the East, XXII (Oxford: 1884) xxi.

5. E.g., J. C. Huntington, "The Origin of the Buddha Image: Early Image Traditions and the Concept of Buddhadarśanapunyā," in A. K. Narain, *Studies in Buddhist Art of South Asia* (New Delhi: 1985) 27, 28, 35, etc.; S. L. Huntington, with contributions from J. C. Huntington, *The Art of Ancient India. Buddhist, Hindu, Jain* (New York and Tokyo: 1985) 124.

6. D. R. Sahni, *Catalogue of the Museum of Archaeology at Sārnāth* (Calcutta: 1914) B(a)1, B(b)59*, B(b)6o*, B(b)172*, B(b)175*, B(b)179*, B(b)293*, B(b)294*, B(b)295*, B(b)300*; H. Hargreaves, "Excavations at Sārnāth," *ARASI* 1914–15 (Calcutta: 1920) nos. XIV, XV, XVI*, XVII*, XVIII (123–127). Hargreaves' nos. XV, XVI, XVII have been reedited in J. M. Rosenfield, "On the Dated Carvings of Sārnāth," *ArA* 26 (1962) 11ff. Asterisks indicate *śākyabhikṣus*, cf. nn. 40 and 41.

7. Sahni, *Catalogue*, B(b)299[?], B(d)1; Hargreaves, *ARASI 1914–15,* no. XIX.

8. Certain: Sahni, *Catalogue,* B(d)13, B(d)20, B(e)1, B(e)10, B(f)15; possible: B(d)42; certain in Hargreaves, *ARASI 1914–15,* no. XXV; possible: nos. XXI, XXII—same donor in both.

9. Lay: G. Yazdani, *Ajanta,* Part II: Text (Oxford: 1933) no. 11 (64); *Ajanta,* Part III: Text (Oxford: 1946) no. IX.2 (89); M. K. Dhavalikar, "New Inscriptions from Ajaṇṭā," *ArO* 7 (1968) no. 3. Monastic: Yazdani, *Ajanta,* II: no. 9*; Yazdani, *Ajanta,* III: VI*, IX. 1*, .3*, .4*, .5*, .6*, .7*, .11*, .12; X.2, .3*, .7*, .8*, .9, .10*, .11*, .12*, .13*, .15*, .16*, .18, .19, .21; XVI.1*, .2*, .3*; *Ajanta,* Part IV: Text (Oxford: 1955) XXII*, XXVI.2*, .4*; Dhavalikar, "Inscriptions," nos. 4*, 5; D. C. Sircar, "Inscription in Cave IV at Ajanta," *EI* 33 (1960) 262 (uncertain).

10. J. Burgess, *Report on the Elura Cave Temples and the Brahmanical and Jaina Caves in Western India* (London: 1883) nos. 6, 7 (77).

11. M. Leese, "The Early Buddhist Icons in Kaṇheri's Cave 3," *ArA* 41 (1979) 83–93.

12. J. Burgess, *Report on the Buddhist Cave Temples and Their Inscriptions,* Archaeological Survey of Western India, Vol. IV (London: 1883). Lay: no. 7; monastic: nos. 8, 9, 10.

13. S. Konow, *Kharoshṭhī Inscriptions with the Exception of Those of Aśoka,* Corpus Inscriptionum Indicarum, Vol. II, Pt. 1 (Calcutta: 1929) nos. XXXVI.1, .2, .4, .5, .6, .7, .8; XL, XLII, XLIII, XLIV, LVIII, LXXXVIII. It should be noted that all but two of these inscriptions (nos. LVIII, LXXXVIII) come from only two sites. Nos. XL, XLII, XLIII, and XLIV are from Loriyān Tangai. The *stūpa* there has been assigned to "perhaps the second century A.D.," and the characters of the inscriptions are said to be "evidently late" (Konow, 106). Nos. XXXVI.1, .2, .4, .5, .6, .7, .8, all come from Jauliāñ, and the situation there is complicated. The images with which the inscriptions are associated, and the inscriptions themselves, have been assigned by Marshall to the second half of the fifth century C.E., but they are a part of the redecoration of much older *stūpas.* Konow, however, is inclined to think, on the basis of the oddly mixed paleography of the inscriptions, that "some of the inscriptions are copies of older ones, executed when the old images and decorations were restored or repaired" (92–93).

14. S. Konow, "Kharoṣṭhī Inscription on a Begram Bas-relief," *EI* 22 (1933–1934) 11–14; J. Brough, "Amitābha and Avalokiteśvara in an Inscribed Gandhāran Sculpture," *Indologica Taurinensia* 10 (1982) 65–70; A. K. Narain, "A Note on Two Inscribed Sculptures in the Elvehjem Art Center of the University of Wisconsin, Madison," *Indian Epigraphy. Its Bearing on the History of Art,* ed. F. M. Asher and G. S. Gai (New Delhi: 1985) 73–74.

15. Lay: G. Fussman, "Documents épigraphiques kouchans (II)," *BEFEO* 67 (1980) 54–55, 56–58; H. W. Bailey, "Two Kharoṣṭhī Inscriptions," *JRAS* (1982) 149; G. Fussman, "Deux dédicaces kharoṣṭhī," *BEFEO* 74 (1985) 34; G. Fussman, "Un buddha inscrit des débuts de notre ère," *BEFEO* 74 (1985) 43–45. Monk: Fussman, *BEFEO* 61 (1974) 54–58. This last inscription is dated in the year 5 "d'une ère qui ne peut être que l'ère de Kaniṣka" (Fussman). The assignment of the year has not been universally accepted (e.g., S. J. Czuma, *Kushan Sculpture: Images from Early India* [Cleveland and Bloomington: 1985] 198–199; K. Khandalavala, "The Five Dated Gandhāra School Sculptures and Their Stylistic Implications," *Indian Epigraphy. Its Bearing on the History of Art,* 68–69), although the arguments against it are not convincing.

16. H. Lüders, *Mathurā Inscriptions,* ed. K. L. Janert, Abhandlungen der Akademie der Wissenschaften in Göttingen, Philo.-Hist. Kl., Dritte Folge, Nr. 47 (Göttingen: 1961) nos. 4, 8, 24, 29, 41, 67, 80, 90, 103, 121, 126, 152, 154, 157, 179, 185, 186.

17. R. C. Sharma, *Buddhist Art of Mathurā* (Delhi: 1984) lay: 181, n. 41; 191, n. 63; 226, n. 153; 226, n. 154; 228, n. 159; monk: 223, n. 148; lay: P. R. Srinivasan, "Two Brahmi

Inscriptions from Mathura," *EI* 39 (1971) 10–12; B. N. Mukherjee, "A Mathura Inscription of the Year 26 and of the Period of Huviṣka," *JAIH* 11 (1977–1978) 82–84 (= R. C. Sharma, "New Buddhist Sculptures from Mathura," *Lalit Kalā* 19 [1979] 25–26; Sharma, *Buddhist Art of Mathurā,* 232, n. 169; G. Schopen, "The Inscription on the Kuṣān Image of Amitābha and the Character of the Early Mahāyāna in India," *JIABS* 10.2 [1987] 99–134); B. D. Chattopadhyaya, "On a Bi-scriptual Epigraph of the Kuṣaṇa Period from Mathura," *JAIH* 13 [1980–1982] 277–284 (cf. B. N. Mukherjee, "A Note on a Bi-scriptual Epigraph of the Kuṣaṇa Period from Mathurā," *JAIH* 13 [1980–1982] 285–286); monk: D. C. Sircar, "Brahmi Inscriptions from Mathurā," *EI* 34 (1961–1962) 9–13.

18. Ahicchatrā: D. Mitra, "Three Kushan Sculptures from Ahichchhatrā," *Journal of the Asiatic Society,* Letters, 21 (1955) 67; Sārnāth: J. Ph. Vogel, "Epigraphical Discoveries at Sarnath," *EI* 8 (1905–1906) 173–179; Śrāvastī: T. Bloch, "Two Inscriptions on Buddhist Images," *EI* 8 (1905–1906) 180–181, and his "Inscription on the Umbrella Staff of the Buddhist Image from Sahet Mahet," *EI* 9 (1907–1908) 290–291; Kauśāmbī: K. G. Goswami, "Kosam Inscription of the Reign of Kanishka, the Year 2," *EI* 24 (1938) 210–212 (cf. A. Ghosh, "Kosam Inscription of Kanishka," *IHQ* 10 [1934] 575–576; Ghosh reads the date "the 22nd (?) year of Mahārāja Kaniṣka"); G. Sharma and J. Negi, "The Saka-Kushans in the Central Ganga Valley (Mainly a Review of the New Data from Kausambi)," *Central Asia in the Kushan* Period, Vol. II, ed. B. G. Gafuron et al. (Moscow: 1975) 15ff. In all of these inscriptions, the donors are monastics.

19. Several images fairly certainly of Mathurān origin and having low-numbered year dates have been excluded because of the uncertainty concerning the date or the identity of the king referred to in them. This is the case, for example, with the two inscriptions—assigned to the Kuṣān period—on images found at Sāñcī but thought to have come from Mathurā; cf. J. Marshall, A. Foucher, and N. G. Majumdar, *The Monuments of Sāñchī,* Vol. I (Delhi: 1940) 385–387, nos. 828 and 830; J. M. Rosenfield, *The Dynastic Arts of the Kushans* (Berkeley: 1967) 112; A. L. Basham, *Papers on the Date of Kaniṣka, Submitted to the Conference on the Date of Kaniṣka, London, 20–22 April, 1960* (Leiden: 1968) 108ff, 267ff, 283, 290–291. This is also the case with the image from Bodh-Gayā dated in the year 64; cf. B. M. Barua, "A Bodh-Gayā Image Inscription," *IHQ* 9 (1933) 417–419, etc.

20. Lüders, *Mathurā Inscriptions,* 200 and n. 6.

21. Burgess, *Report on the Elura Cave Temples,* no. 6 (77).

22. Vogel, *EI* 8 (1905–1906) 173ff.

23. Cf. note to Table 1 and Bloch, *EI* 8 (1905–1906) 180–81, *EI* 9 (1907–1908) 290–291.

24. Vogel, *EI* 8 (1905–1906) 176, s.v. L9.

25. Cf. G. Schopen, "Two Problems in the History of Indian Buddhism," Ch. II above, 36ff.

26. W. Spink, "Ajanta: A Brief History," *Aspects of Indian Art. Papers Presented in a Symposium at the Los Angeles County Museum of Art, October 1970,* ed. P. Pal (Leiden: 1972) 51; Yazdani, *Ajanta,* IV, 114–118.

27. See the sources cited for Kauśāmbī in n. 18 above.

28. On the wide distribution of Mathurān images, see J. E. van Lohuizen-de Leeuw, "Gandhāra and Mathurā: Their Cultural Relationship," *Aspects of Indian Art,* 39 and notes; J. E. van Lohuizen-de Leeuw, "New Evidence with Regard to the Origin of the Buddha Image," *South Asian Archaeology 1979,* ed. H. Härtel (Berlin: 1981) 393–394.

29. A. L. Basham, "The Evolution of the Concept of the Bodhisattva," *The Bodhisattva in Buddhism,* ed. L. S. Kawamura (Waterloo: 1981) 30.

30. H. Oldenberg, *Buddha: His Life, His Doctrine, His Order,* trans. W. Hoey (London: 1882) 381; or *Buddha, sein Leben, seine Lehre, seine Gemeinde* (Berlin: 1881) 389–390.

31. Marshall et al., *Sāñchī,* Vol. I, nos. 304, 305, 540, 680.

32. Marshall et al., *Sāñchī,* Vol. I, nos. 118, 645, 804.

33. S. B. Deo and J. P. Joshi, *Pauni Excavation (1969–70)* (Nagpur: 1972). Monks: nos. 5, 7, 8; nuns: nos. 9, 12, 13, 14, 21.

34. H. Lüders, *Bharhut Inscriptions,* Corpus Inscriptionum Indicarum, Vol. II, Pt. 2, ed. E. Waldschmidt and M. A. Mahendale (Ootacamund: 1963) 2 and nn. 1 and 2.

35. C. Sivaramamurti, *Amaravati Sculptures in the Madras Government Museum* (Madras: 1977). Monks: nos. 5, 10, 11, 19, 30, 33, 34, 38, 63, 99, 112, 113; nuns: 31, 62, 68, 69, 70, 74, 80, 83, 93, 96, 99, 100. A number of these inscriptions record joint donations.

36. The inscriptions from Ikṣvaku Nāgārjunikoṇḍa would be another exception, but they are atypical in several other ways as well; cf. G. Schopen, "Filial Piety and the Monk in the Practice of Indian Buddhism," Ch. III above, 63–64.

37. Monks: Lüders, *Mathurā Inscriptions,* nos. 67, 152, 179, 185, 186; Sharma, *Buddhist Art of Mathurā,* 223, n. 148; nuns: Lüders, *Mathurā Inscriptions,* no. 8.

38. The exception is Sharma, *Buddhist Art of Mathurā,* 223, n. 148. On the *śākyabhikṣus* and the emergence of the Mahāyāna in the fourth to fifth centuries C.E., see M. Shizutani, "On the Śākyabhikṣu as Found in Indian Buddhistic Inscriptions," *IBK* 2 (1952) 104–105 (in Japanese); and his "Mahāyāna Inscriptions in the Gupta Period," *IBK* 19 (1962) 355–358; H. Sarkar, *Studies in Early Buddhist Architecture of India* (Delhi: 1966) 106–107; G. Schopen, "Mahāyāna in Indian Inscriptions," *IIJ* 21 (1979) 1–19; Schopen, "The Inscription on the Kuṣān Image of Amitābha and the Character of the Early Mahāyāna in India," *JIABS* 10.2 (1987) 99–137.

39. All those marked with an asterisk in n. 9 above.

40. All those marked with an asterisk in n. 6 above; the single nun is in Hargreaves, *ARASI 1914–15,* no. XIV.

41. The possible connection between the emergence of the Mahāyāna and the decline and disappearance of the nun has not been made before, but it—like the fourth to fifth century emergence of the Mahāyāna itself—requires much fuller study. I am now working on a larger project involving both. In general, the nun in Buddhist epigraphy has received little attention; see B. C. Law, "Bhikshunis in Indian Inscriptions," *EI* 25 (1940) 31–34; A. S. Altekar, "Society in the Deccan during 200 B.C.–A.D. 500," *JIH* 30 (1952) 63ff; A. M. Shastri, *An Outline of Early Buddhism (A Historical Survey of Buddhology, Buddhist Schools and Sanghas Mainly Based on the Study of Pre-Gupta Inscriptions)* (Varanasi: 1965) 141–144; S. Nagaraju, *Buddhist Architecture of Western India (c. 240 B.C.–c. A.D. 300)* (Delhi: 1981) 32.

42. Cf. Huntington in *Studies in Buddhist Art of South Asia,* 23–58, where conjecture, especially but not exclusively in regard to texts, is very much in evidence.

43. D. L. Snellgrove, *The Image of the Buddha* (Paris and Tokyo: 1978) 53–54.

44. It is equally clear that the sectarian affiliation of these monks and nuns has little, if any, bearing on their association with the image cult. While the monks promoting the cult in the fourth to fifth centuries at Ajaṇṭā, Sārnāth, and Mathurā were predominately Mahāyāna monks, those involved in the same cult at Śrāvastī, Kauśāmbī, Mathurā, etc., in the Kuṣān period almost certainly were not. The widespread assumption that connects the image cult with the Mahāyāna is simply not well founded; cf. Schopen, "Mahāyāna in Indian Inscriptions," 16, n. 7; D. Snellgrove, *Indo-Tibetan Buddhism. Indian Buddhists and Their Tibetan Successors,* Vol. I (Boston: 1987) 49.

45. Cf. Schopen, "Filial Piety and the Monk in the Practice of Indian Buddhism," now Ch. III above, and "Two Problems in the History of Indian Buddhism," now Ch. II above, 30ff. In the first of these earlier pieces especially I have not always distinguished clearly between monk and nun donors and have used the term "monk" when I should have used the term "monastic." The degree of concern for their parents on the part of nuns as a separate category is therefore not clearly discernible there.

46. Brown, *The Cult of the Saints,* 30, 57, 67; for the criticism, see J. Fontaine, "Le culte des saints et ses implications sociologiques. Réflexions sur un récent essai de Peter Brown," *Analecta Bollandiana* 100 (1982) 17–41, esp. 23ff.

47. Brown, *The Cult of the Saints,* 32.

48. Brown, *The Cult of the Saints,* 63–64, 51.

49. A. Bareau, "Les réactions des families dont un membre devient moine selon le canon bouddhique pali," *Malalasekera Commemoration Volume,* ed. O. H. de A. Wijesekera (Colombo: 1976) 15–22.

50. B. C. Gokhale, "The Early Buddhist Elite," *JIH* 43 (1965) 391–402.

CHAPTER XII

The Buddha as an Owner of Property and Permanent Resident in Medieval Indian Monasteries

PROBABLY ALL WOULD AGREE that understanding the way in which the person of the Buddha was understood is central to any attempt to characterize the Indian groups that came to coalesce around that person. In fact, understanding how that person was understood or perceived has, it appears, oftentimes determined how a great many other matters were understood. The old Anglo-German school of Pāli scholarship, for example, saw the Buddha as a kind of sweetly reasonable Victorian Gentleman. Such a view dominated not only the scholarly world, but as Almond has recently shown,[1] the popular press of the day. It is, therefore, hardly surprising that the "religion" attributed to him was understood as an orderly system of sweetly reasonable, rational Victorian ethics, a system that—significantly—was seen to carry an implicit "native" criticism of the actual, observable religions of nineteenth century India, and to point up their "decline."[2]

This view, like virtually every other one that followed it, was built up almost exclusively from a particular, if not peculiar, selected reading of literary sources. The later views, the views of the so-called Franco-Belgian school, in this regard at least differed not at all. They treated later sources, to be sure, but still literary sources only. They took seriously the works of the later Vasubandhu, of Asaṅga and Haribhadra—works of the early medieval and medieval periods. They determined, for example, that "the extreme Mahāyāna reduced the Buddha to two elements: . . . indescribable reality and the suprarational intuition of this reality"; that the Buddha was understood to have not one, but two, three, or—eventually—four bodies, each thought of in ever-increasing abstract terms; that, finally, the real Buddha was thought to be "the Dharmakāya which has no flesh or blood or bones."[3] In light of this understanding of the Buddha, the Buddhism of this period was understood as a collection of loosely connected, increasingly convo-

---

Originally published in *Journal of Indian Philosophy* 18 (1990):181–217. Reprinted with stylistic changes with permission of Kluwer Academic Publishers.

luted systems of abstract theory. This understanding still confronts the neophyte when he or she approaches the standard textbooks dealing with Mahāyāna Buddhism.

It is at least curious that this particular Buddhology, based as it is almost exclusively on a narrowly limited corpus of highly specialized literature, has persisted in virtually all of the work done by modern scholars on the medieval period. It is curious because, already sixty years ago, de La Vallée Poussin—a man whose knowledge of Buddhist scholastic literature has probably not yet been equaled—unequivocally declared it to be incomplete and merely partial. At the end of his long discussion "sur les corps du Bouddha," itself largely taken up with the beginnings of the increasingly abstract conceptions of the early medieval period, de La Vallée Poussin said: "La description des théories abstraites n'est qu'une partie, non négligeable, de l'histoire de la bouddhologie."[4] Buddhist Studies has been slow to realize the implications of this, and many other, observations scattered throughout the still-astounding body of work left by this Belgian scholar.

Because of this slowness, the "abstract theories" have by default been left to stand as the sole representatives of medieval Buddhist conceptions of the Buddha, and this, in turn, has left an almost permanent distortion of the doctrinal record, a distortion that would require the availability of other sources to remove. But such sources—at least some of them—have been available for a very long time, and de La Vallée Poussin, at the head of the same discussion already referred to, had already pointed us in a promising direction: "la vénération des corps," he said, "occupe une place notable dans l'épigraphie."[5] De La Vallée Poussin was referring here primarily to the various "hymns" (*stava*) found, not commonly it now appears, in Buddhist inscriptions. But he was, at least, still pointing to an important source, a source which we too might do well to consider, although with a broader and less self-consciously literary selection.[6]

There are considerable numbers of Buddhist donative records and land grants that have survived from the medieval period.[7] We might look at a sample of these—and it is *only* a sample—paying particular attention to their language, to what they say about both the Buddha's location and about where he was thought to be and to what they say about his role in the transactions being recorded.

Earlier inscriptions already contain some hints of what is to come, but they are somewhat ambiguous or can, at least, be understood in more than one way. An inscribed first century slab from Kauśāmbī that has the Buddha's footprints carved on it says, for example: "(this) slab was caused to be made . . . in the residence of the Buddha, in the Ghoṣitārāma" (. . . *budhāvāse ghoṣitārāme . . . śilā kā(ritā)*).[8] Given the traditions that assert that the Buddha had actually lived on occasion at Kauśāmbī, the "residence of the Buddha" referred to here may not refer to a *current* residence, but to a structure or room where the Buddha was thought to have *formerly* resided.[9]

Similarly, the inscription on a faceted stone pillar from Mithouri that "may be assigned to the 2nd Century A.D." may also be interpreted in more than one way. It says the donor "caused an umbrella to be set up for the Blessed One, the Pitāmaha, the Fully and Completely Awakened One, in the Saptaparṇṇa Monastery" (. . . *saptaparṇṇa-vihāre bhagavat-pitāmahasya samyaksaṃbuddhasya . . . cha{traṃ pra}tiṣṭhāpayati).*[10] Although, in the end, the differences in possible meaning may be small, the inscription can be understood to be saying either that the umbrella was set up for the Buddha who was himself in the monastery, or it may be saying that the umbrella itself was set up in the monastery *for* the Buddha without specifying where the latter actually was. But even this second interpretation would suggest, at least, that things intended "for," or at least "belonging to," the Buddha were "set up" in this monastery.

If, however, the language of these and a small number of other early inscriptions remains ambiguous and not altogether explicit, the same cannot be said of a large number of inscriptions and land grants that belong to the medieval period. Starting from the fourth to fifth centuries, the language of inscriptions becomes ever increasingly unambiguous and straightforward in regard to the Buddha's location, his proprietorship, and his permanent residency in local monasteries. The fifth century inscriptional record of the foundation of Cave XVI at Ajaṇṭā, for example, explicitly refers to this cave as the "excellent dwelling to be occupied by the Best of Ascetics"; that is, the Buddha (*udāraṃ . . . veśma yatī{ndra-sevyam}*),[11] but this cave is not a "shrine" or *caityagṛha.* It is a *vihāra* containing seventeen residential cells, only one of which—the central cell in the back wall—seems to have been intended for the Buddha.[12] Moreover, in spite of the fact that this cave—Cave XVI—was intended to provide residential quarters for monks, while the closely contemporaneous Cave XXVI was a *caityagṛha,* both are referred to by the same term: *veśman,* "dwelling."[13]

If the Ajaṇṭā text locates the Buddha in monastic living quarters, a fifth or sixth century inscription from Cave VI at Kuda provides us with an early instance of his being the recipient of real property. It says:

> This is the gift of the Śākyabhikṣu Saṃghadeva. And having here attached the Cheṃdina field it is given to the Buddha as capital for lamps. Whoever would disrupt [this endowment] would incur the five great sins.
>
> *deyadharmmoyaṃ śākyabhikṣoḥ saṃghadevasya atra ca cheṃdinakhetra{ṃ} badhvā dīpamūlya-buddhasya dattaṃ {//} yo lopaye{t} pa{ṃ}ca-mahāpātakaba{saṃ}yukto bhave{t}.*[14]

While the full technical sense of *badhvā* is not entirely clear, I have translated it as "having attached," intending by that some of the legal sense of the English phrase. It is, however, clear from the imprecation that we are dealing with an ongoing endowment. It is equally clear that the field was given directly to the Buddha, and that the profit realized from it was to be applied to his service.

Equally interesting—although from a somewhat different angle—are two fifth- or sixth-century copperplate land grants, one from Bāgh in Madhya Pradesh, the other from Gunaighar in Bengal. The first of these records the gift of a village that was "to be used" to provide perfumes, incense, and flowers, and the like "*for* the Blessed One, the Buddha," *and* to provide the requisites for the monks, both of whom—the language of the record makes clear—were thought to reside "in the monastery called Kalāyana . . . caused to be constructed by Dattaṭaka" (*dattaṭaka-kārita-kalāyana-vihāre. . . bhagavato buddhāya gandhadhūpa-mālyabalisatropayojyaḥ . . . āryya-bhikṣu-saṅghasya cāturddiśābhyāgatakasya cīvara-piṇḍapāta-glāna-pratyaya-śeyyāsana-bhaiṣajya-hetor . . .*)[15] This "monastery" is almost certainly Cave II, the cave in which the plate was found. It, like Cave XVI at Ajaṇṭā, was a residential *vihāra* having twenty-one cells, the central cell in the back wall being reserved for the Buddha.[16]

Although, geographically speaking, it was written a long way from Bāgh, the Gunaighar grant is quite similar. It records the gift of five clearly delimited parcels of land:

> for the perpetual employment, three times a day, of perfumes, flowers, lamps, incense, etc., for the Blessed One, the Buddha, (who is) in the monastery in the Aśrama of Avalokiteśvara, which is the property of the community of irreversible Mahāyāna monks received through just this Teacher [Śāntideva], and for the provision of robes, bowls, beds, seats, medicines, etc., for the community of monks (in the monastery).
>
> *-āryyāvalokiteśvarāśrama-vihāre anenaivācāryyeṇa pratipādita-* [read: *-te*] *māhāyānika-vaivarttika-* [read: *-āvaivarttika-*] *-bhikṣu-saṃghanām* [read: *-ānām*] *parigrahe bhagavato buddhasya satataṃ triṣkālaṃ gandha-puṣpa-dīpa-dhūpādi-pra{varttanāya} {ta}sya bhikṣusaṃghasya ca cīvara-piṇḍapāta-śayanāsana-glāna-pratyayabhaiṣajyādi-paribhogāya.*[17]

As in the land grant from Bāgh, the grammatical structure of the Gunaighar grant would seem to indicate that the locative phrase situates *both* the Blessed One, the Buddha, *and* the community of monks in the same establishment, and the donors' intention seems to have been to provide for both. These two land grants have—as their very name implies—something else in common. Like most of the remaining inscriptions that will be cited here, these are not religious texts or panegyrics. Both the Bāgh and Gunaighar grants are legal documents authorizing and recording the transfer of property. Their language, therefore, in regard to this transfer, is not likely to have been casual but must have been chosen to articulate specifically perceived and legally acknowledged realities.

Much the same sort of evidence as is found at Bāgh and Gunaighar occurs also in the rich collection of Buddhist land grants from Valabhī in Gujarat, even when—and that not infrequently—the vocabulary used is somewhat different. We find, for example, in a grant of Dharasena II dated to 575 C.E. that two villages were given, in part:

> for the sake of furthering the activity—through flowers, incense, perfumes, lamps, oils, etc.—of/for the Blessed Ones, the Buddhas, in the monastery of the worthy Śrī Bappa which the Ācārya-Bhadanta-Sthiramati had caused to be built.
>
> *ācāryya-bhadanta-sthiramati-kārita-śrī-bappa-pādīya-vihāre bhagavatāṃ buddhānāṃ puṣpa-dhūpa-gandha-dīpa-tailādi-kriyotsarppaṇārthaṃ.*[18]

Elsewhere in the Valabhī grants the same expression is applied to monks in a given monastery, the only difference being that their activity is "furthered" through robes, bowls, and the other monastic requisites: *-vihāre nānādigabhyāgatāṣṭādaśa-nikāyābhyantarāryya-bhikṣu-saṅghāya grāsācchādana-śayanāsana-glāna-bhaiṣajyādi-kriyotsarppaṇārthaṃ.*[19]

When taken together, statements of this sort would seem to suggest that the Valabhī grants were intended to provide for the needs of two groups, both of which appear to have been thought of as residing in the local monasteries: Buddhas and monks. Although their specific needs might differ, it appears to have been thought that both groups must be provided for, and both were conceptually considered residents of a single kind of establishment. This, of course, must strike us as odd because we think of the members of the two groups as conceptually and completely different, and we are not in the habit of thinking that the Buddha—let alone several Buddhas—actually lived in any seventh century monastery in Valabhī or anywhere else for that matter. But the wording of these grants, and all of the records we have seen and will see further on, suggests that their drafters thought otherwise. Modern scholars have seen in these and similar passages references to what we call "images." But although this may be correct from at least our own culturally limited frame of reference, and although the concrete referent in these passages may, in fact, have been an object of stone that we would call an "image," the drafters of these grants and all the inscriptions we will deal with here never use a word that could—however unsuitably—be translated as "image." They talk about "*persons*," not objects; and these "*persons*"—like the monks who are also to be provided for—always live in monasteries.[20]

But if medieval records consistently locate these "*persons*" in monasteries, some of them specify even more precisely that location. Yet another Valabhī grant of Dhruvasena I appears to provide us one such instance:

{ā}cāryya-bhadanta-buddhadāsa-kārita-vihāra-kutyāṃ pratiṣṭāpita-bhagavatāṃ ssamya{ksaṃbu}-{ddhānāṃ buddh}-ānām gandha-dhūpa-puṣpa-dīpa-tailopayogi . . . catur-ddiś-ābhyāgatobhaya-vihāra-prativāsi-bhikṣu-saṅghasya {pi}ṇḍapāta-śayanāsana-glāna-pratyaya-bhaiṣajya-pariṣkāropayogārtthaṃ ca pra{tip}āditaḥ {//}.*[21]

Given for the acquisition of perfumes, incense, flowers, lamps, oils, etc., for the Blessed Ones, the Fully and Completely Awakened Buddhas established in the chamber in the monastery built by the Ācārya-Bhadanta-Buddhadāsa . . . and for the acquisition of the requisites—bowls, beds, seats, and medicines—for the community of monks dwelling in the monastery from the four directions.[22]

There are at least two points worth noting here. First, the Buddhas are specifically said to be "established" not just in the monastery, but "in the chamber (*kuṭī*) in the monastery." The specificity intended here, however, seems oddly incomplete: although the text as it now stands seems to want to indicate a precise location, it uses a generic term without further qualification, and which "chamber" was intended does not now appear to be indicated. This oddity, taken together with both epigraphical and textual parallels, would seem to suggest that we have here a scribal error and that the intended reading was almost certainly *gandha-kuṭyāṃ*. In the only other occurrences of the term *kuṭī* in the Valabhī grants, for example, the term always occurs in compound with a preceding *gandha-*: a grant of Śīlāditya III reads *gandha-kuṭī* [read: *-kuṭyāṃ?*] *ca bhagavatāṃ buddhānāṃ pūjā-snapana-gandha-dhūpa-puṣpādi-paricaryyārthaṃ,* "for serving the Blessed Ones, the Buddhas, and (or, in) the Perfume Chamber with worship, baths, perfumes, incense, flowers, etc.";[23] in a recently published plate of Dharasena IV, the grant is said to be in part *gandhakuṭyāś ca khaṇḍa-sphuṭita-pratisaṃskaraṇāya,* "for repairing the cracks and breaks in the Perfume Chamber. . . ."[24] Not only do these passages support the emendation suggested above for the grant of Dhruvasena I but they indicate that the *gandhakuṭī* was an established and important element of the monasteries at Valabhī. Moreover, we have—as we shall see—a significant amount of evidence that indicates that this was the case as well in a considerable number of medieval Buddhist monasteries elsewhere in India,[25] and we know that "the Perfume Chamber' " was supposed to be the central cell in a Buddhist monastery reserved as the residence of the Buddha himself.

The second point to be noted is that our passage says that the Buddhas were "established" (*pratiṣṭ{h}āpita-*) in the monastery, but the monks were "dwelling" (*prativāsi-*) in it. This verbal difference may be thought to be significant, and perhaps it is. However, it is important to remember that the first meaning of *prati* $\sqrt{}$*sthā* is "to stand, stay, abide, dwell," and that the causative—which we have here—has marked tones of "permanence," "fixity," and "continued existence over time." *Prati* $\sqrt{}$*3. vas,* on the other hand, need imply none of this and is not infrequently used in the sense of "to lodge, receive as a guest." The Buddhas, then, may have been considered the only permanent residents of a monastery.

It is also worth noting, as shown in these passages, the Valabhī grants frequently refer to Buddhas in the plural. This may be because there actually were several, or we may have here—as Sircar, for example, has suggested we have elsewhere—"the plural number signifying *gaurava* (venerableness)," the *pluralis majestaticus.*[26] Although the use of the plural predominates, the fact that the use of the singular in virtually the same context and construction is not rare may well argue for the plurals being plurals of respect. In any case, references to a plurality of Buddhas are not infrequently found in Indian inscriptions from very early on.[27]

The language of the Valabhī grants provides us, then, with important information on monastic conceptions of the Buddha in medieval Gujarat, but this, of course, is not the only area for which we have records from this period. A roughly contemporaneous record from Nālandā, for example, provides us with a particularly striking instance of the language of personal presence in a form that we have not yet seen. The record in question, the Stone Inscription of Yasovarmmadeva, has been variously dated to the sixth or eighth century.[28] It is written in an elaborate *kāvya* style and as a consequence is not always easy to interpret. It would appear that its primary purpose was to record a series of benefactions made by the son of a royal minister. Among these is a "permanent endowment" specifically said to be "for the Blessed One, the Buddha" (*akṣaya-nīvikā bhagavate vuddhāya*); the same donor provided the monks with food and gave to "the sons of the *Śākya*" a *layana,* a "residence" or "house." The most interesting statement, however, occurs as a part of the concluding imprecation and constitutes a clear warning:

> Whoever would create an obstacle to this gift which is to last as long as the created world (he should know that) the Conqueror in person, the Blessed One, dwells always here within on the Diamond Throne.
>
> *yo dānasyāsya kaścit kṛtajagadavadher antarāyaṃ vidadhyāt sākṣād vajrāsanastho jina iha bhagavān antarasthaḥ sadāste* /[29]

The language is very strong here, and the sense of personal presence (*sākṣād, iha*) and permanent abiding (*sadāste*) is pronounced. Although the style of our record sometimes makes it difficult to understand, this much is certain. It is equally certain that the permanent endowment was given directly to the Buddha himself, and reasonably certain that the place wherein the Blessed One is said to "always" dwell was the *layana* or "residence" that had been given to the monks.[30]

Yet other forms of expression involving both the sense of legal recognition and personal presence are found in other grants. In the Toramāṇa Inscription from the Salt Range in the Punjab, for example, which Sircar dates to the sixth century, the statement that seems to have been intended as a description of the primary act being recorded reads:

> This religious gift, the establishment of a monastery for the Community of Monks from the Four Directions which is headed by the Buddha.
>
> *buddha-pramukha* [read: *-khe*] *cāturdiśe bhikṣusaṃghe deyadharmo {'}ya{ṃ} vihāra-pratiṣṭhāpana.*[31]

Fortunately, we have a fairly good idea of how such an expression would have been understood from both literary sources and contemporary or near-contemporary epigraphical records.

Strikingly similar expressions occur throughout both Pāli and Sanskrit canonical literature in passages that, of course, narrate events that are supposed to have occurred while the Buddha was very much alive and a living presence. Some of these passages are so commonplace as to be clichés. In a typical passage describing the feeding of the Buddha and his disciples, for example, that group is described as *buddhapramukhaṃ bhikṣusaṃghaṃ* or *buddhapamukhaṃ bhikkhusaṃghaṃ,* "the community of monks headed by the Buddha."[32] T.W. Rhys Davids translates one such passage in the *Mahāparinibbāna-sutta* by: "And the Exalted One robed himself early, took his bowl with him, and repaired, with the brethren [*saddhiṃ bhikkhusaṃghena*], to the dwelling-place of Sunīdha and Vassakāra . . . and with their own hands they set the sweet rice and the cakes before the brethren with the Buddha at their head [*buddhapamukhaṃ bhikkhusaṃghaṃ*].[33] Equally interesting is another passage from the same text. Ambapāli's gift of the "mango grove" is there expressed in the following form: *imāhaṃ bhante ārāmaṃ buddhapamukhassa bhikkhusaṃghassa dammīti. paṭiggahesi bhagavā ārāmaṃ;* "Reverend," Ambapāli says, "I give this grove to the community of monks with the Buddha at their head. The Blessed One accepted the grove."[34] That the monastic recipients of gifts of food and real property should be described in this way in texts narrating events set during the lifetime of the Buddha is not surprising. Such a description says nothing more than that the actual community that received these gifts was headed by the still-living Buddha, and that it was he—explicitly at least in the case of Ambapāli's grove—who accepted or took possession of them. But if that is what *buddhapamukhassa bhikkhusaṃghassa* means in other Buddhist texts, it is hard to see how *buddha-pramukhe cāturdiśe bhikṣusaṃghe* could mean anything essentially different in the Toramāṇa Inscription, an inscription that shows clear signs of having been authored by someone familiar with even the most technical textual definitions of the Buddha.[35] It is hard to argue that the conception changed if the expression remained constant, regardless of how much time intervened.

Much the same point is reached if we look at epigraphical usage. At the end of an inscription from Nāgārjunikoṇḍa that makes provision for the maintenance, etc., of a *devakula* or temple, the body charged with the ultimate responsibility for seeing that the work was done is called the *seṭhi-pamakha* [= Skt. *śreṣṭhi-pramukha*] *-nigamo,* "the council of citizens headed by the banker."[36] Similarly, in a sixth-century land grant from Andhra Pradesh, the order transferring the land is addressed to the *rāṣṭrakūṭa-grāma-vṛddha-pramukha-viṣaya-(ni)vāsinaḥ,* "to the inhabitants of the district headed by the elders of the village and district officer"[37]

The Nāgārjunikoṇḍa inscription and the Andhra land grant are, of course, describing corporate or legal entities with a particular structure. But the fact that a Buddhist monastic community could be described in the same way in a document like the Toramāṇa Inscription dealing in part with the transfer of property would seem to suggest that it, too, was considered to be organizationally similar. This, in turn, would mean that if "the council of citizens" were legally or corporately recognized as headed "by the banker," the sixth-century Buddhist monastic community in the Salt Range must have been thought of as legally or corporately headed "by the Buddha." Moreover, in the same way the council and particularly its head, were charged with the responsibility for making sure the provisions of the gift were fulfilled, the monastery whose erection was recorded in the inscription of Toramāṇa must have been intended for *both* the monastic community and, particularly, its corporate head. Finally—and perhaps most significantly—these epigraphical parallels appear to indicate that the designation *-pramukha* was never applied "symbolically," but always referred to actual individuals holding certain responsible positions.

This corporate or legal language continued to be used for a very long time, and when it was not used, it was not infrequently replaced with an even more interesting turn of phrase. It was used, for example, in a twelfth century inscription from Śrāvastī recording the grant of six villages together with "all water and dry land, mines of iron and salt, repositories (i.e., ponds) of fish, etc.," within their boundaries. These six villages are said to be granted to:

> *śrīmaj-jetavana-mahāvihāra-vāstavya-buddha-bhaṭṭāraka-pramukha-parama-ārya-(ś)ākyabhikṣu-saṃghāya* . . .[38]
>
> The Community of Excellent Venerable Śākya-Monks which is headed by the Lord Buddha who resides in the Great Monastery in the Illustrious Jetavana.

or:

> The Community of Excellent Venerable Śākya-Monks headed by the Lord Buddha which resides in the Great Monastery in the Illustrious Jetavana.

However this long compound is nuanced, it seems fairly certain that ownership of the villages in question was being transferred to the monastic community as a corporate group, that, in terms of the transfer, the Buddha was considered to be the legal head of the group, and that both the Buddha and the monastic community were thought to reside in the same monastery. This last point, at least, again draws support from the living arrangements reflected in the ground plan of the monastery in question. Monastery 19 is described as having "an open courtyard in the centre surrounded by rows of [residential] cells on all sides . . . The central chamber in the row facing the entrance forms the shrine and is situated directly opposite the main entrance-gate, so that the statue that it enshrined was the first object coming to the view of the visitor . . ."[39]

This same sense of personal presence and of ownership by the Buddha however, is by no means restricted to passages in which he is designated as *-pramukha* of the community. We have already seen one instance—the Yasovarmmadeva Inscription—in which this vocabulary does not occur. An early ninth-century copperplate grant of Devapāla from Nālandā is yet another. In this grant we find the gift of five villages being made, in part, to provide the resident Buddha with an income:

> *suva{rṇṇa}dvīpādhipama{hā}rājaśrībālaputradevena dūtakamukhena vayam vijñāpitāḥ yathā mayā śrīnālandāyām vihāraḥ kāritas tatra bhagavato buddhabhaṭṭārakasya prajñāpāramitādisakaladharmmanetrīsthānasyāyārthe . . . pratipādit{ā}ḥ*[40]

> We, being requested to by the Mahārāja, the Illustrious Bālaputradeva, the king of Suvarṇṇadvīpa, through an ambassador, (declare): 'As I have had constructed a monastery in Illustrious Nālandā [the previously mentioned villages] . . . are granted for the sake of providing an income to the Blessed One (residing) there, the Worshipful Buddha, the Storehouse of All Methods of Dharma, the Perfection of Wisdom, etc.'

As in the Yasovarmmadeva Inscription, the sense of presence is clear: the Buddha in question is "*there*" (*tatra*) in the monastery. As in the Yasovarmmadeva Inscription where a permanent endowment is given directly to the resident Buddha, here too the Buddha himself is provided with an "income" (*āya*) in his own right and not as the head of the *Saṅgha.* The implication here is that some of these villages are transferred directly to the Buddha himself, that he himself owns them. This again is very clear in yet other copperplate grants.

In the so-called Larger Leiden Plates, for example, the wording is straightforward. These plates—which date to the eleventh century—record the gift of a village *atiramaṇīyañ cūḷāmaṇivarmma-vihāram adhivasate buddhāya,* "to the Buddha residing in the surpassingly beautiful Cūḷāmaṇivarma Monastery" in Nāgapaṭṭinam.[41] Here again, there is no reference to the Buddha as the head of the monastic community, and the village is given to him directly as an individual; he and he alone became the "owner" by the terms of the grant. Here too, the explicit wording of the grant leaves no room to doubt that the Buddha himself was thought to actually reside in the specifically named monastery. It is, moreover, worth noting that there was official, *external* recognition of the Buddha's legal ownership of land, even in non-Buddhist records that record gifts similar to those recorded in both the Nālandā Grant of Devapāla and the Larger Leiden Plates. A Chandella copperplate grant of the twelfth century, for example, records the donation of a village to a number of brāhmaṇas. But it explicitly excludes from the grant five *halas* of land within the village that already belonged to the Buddha: *deva-śrī-bauddha-satka-pañcahalāni bahiḥkṛtya.*[42]

The last examples we might look at refer—like some of the Valabhī grants—to the *Gandhakuṭī*, "the Perfume Chamber." Sircar, for example, has noted that originally the term *Gandhakuṭī* referred to "the room occupied by the Buddha at Śrāvastī, but later indicated the Buddha's private chamber in any Buddhist establishment,"[43] and Edgerton has noted literary uses that seem "to imply that any monastery might be provided with one."[44] The epigraphical sources confirm both.

The earliest inscriptional reference to the *Gandhakuṭī* occurs in a label from Bhārhut, and it is clear that here the term is applied to the original chamber at Śrāvastī.[45] But the epigraphical sources also indicate that from the fourth or fifth century on, the *Gandhakuṭī* was an established part of Buddhist monastic establishments everywhere. There is a third- or fourth- century reference to a *Gandhakuṭī* in the inscriptions from Ghaṇṭaśala;[46] a late-fourth-century reference in an inscription from Hyderabad to the *Gandhakuṭī* in the monastery named after Govindarāja, the founder of the Viṣṇukuṇḍi dynasty;[47] references in inscriptions from Ajaṇṭā,[48] Kānheri,[49] and Kauśāmbī[50]—all probably dating from around the fifth century; several references in inscriptions from Sārnāth dating from the fourth or fifth century to the eleventh,[51] and from Bodh-Gayā[52] covering much the same period; references from Valabhī (sixth or seventh century),[53] for Kurkihar (ninth to eleventh centuries),[54] and from Nālandā.[55] Both the geographical and the chronological range of these references establish that a large number of Buddhist monasteries had, in the medieval period, a private chamber reserved for the Buddha. In addition, some of these references make it very clear that these private chambers were formally recognized as distinct organizational components of their monasteries and had specifically titled monks or groups of monks attached to them.

The monk donor in the Hyderabad inscription, for example, is called a *gaṃdhakuṭī-vārika,* and we have a reasonably good idea of what this might have meant from a series of similarly constructed monastic titles, all of which have *-vārika* as the final element. Literary sources know, for instance, *bhājana-vārika,* "(monks) in charge of receptacles," *pānīya-vārika,* "(monks) in charge of beverages," *upadhi-vārika,* "(monks) in charge of physical properties," or a "beadle, or provost of a monastery," etc.[56] Titles ending in *-vārika,* would appear, then, to have been used to designate the monk or monks who were officially in charge of important administrative and material areas or aspects of a functioning monastery. To judge by his title, a *gandhakuṭī-vārika* must have been a similar official, a monk or the monk "in charge of the Perfume Chamber." The fact that such an office was formally instituted and acknowledged would argue for the importance this chamber had in the life of the community, and would seem to indicate that it was already a fully integrated institutional element of medieval Buddhist monasteries. The same conclusions would seem to follow from the fact that references to "monks in charge of the Perfume Chamber" are found not only in Andhra Pradesh, but also at such widely separated sites as Kānheri and Nālandā: in a fourth or fifth-century donative record from the former site, the monk donor is called a *mahā-gandhakuṭī-vārika,* "one who is in charge of the Great Perfume Chamber";[57] from the latter come a number of interesting sealings, two of which refer to two distinct groups of *gandhakuṭī-vārikas.* The first of these reads:

> *śrī-nālandāy(āṃ) śrī-bālāditya-gandhakuḍī-vārika-bhikṣū(ṇām)*[58]
>
> Of/for/belonging to the monks in charge of the Perfume Chamber of Śrī-Bālāditya at Śrī-Nālandā.

and the second:

> *śrī-nā-dharmapāladeva-gandha-kuṭī-vārika-bhikṣūṇā(ṃ)*[59]
>
> Of/for/belonging to the monks in charge of the Perfume Chamber of Dharmapāladeva at Śrī-Nālandā.

These sealings are, however, important not just because they help to establish the wide geographic spread of the *Gandhakuṭī* as a formally recognized component of Buddhist monastic establishments; they also indicate that in at least some cases it was not a single monk who was charged with the oversight of the Perfume Chamber but a group of monks. They confirm, as well, the fact that different individual monasteries at a single site each had its own *Gandhakuṭī* and suggest that, like the monasteries themselves, these *Gandhakuṭīs* could be individually named after their chief sponsors or donors. Finally, the mere existence of these sealings would suggest that within the monastery, the *Gandhakuṭī* functioned as a distinct and individual entity that either owned its own movable property or had its own official correspondence with other monasteries or concerns. In fact, the two primary uses of such sealings appear to have been either to mark ownership of the property to which they were attached, or to "vouch for the genuineness" of the letters or documents that were sent or circulated under their seal.[60]

But if the sealings from Nālandā indicate that the *Gandhakuṭī* as a corporate entity either owned its own property or had its own official correspondence, yet another type of sealing indicates that this was true as well for the individual who resided in it. Several specimens of such sealings have been found at Sārnāth—Marshall and Konow refer to "a number" of them in their report for the year 1907,[61] and Hargreaves recorded two more.[62] These sealings have all been dated to the sixth or seventh century, and the text on all of them is essentially the same:

śrī-saddharmmacakkre mūla-gandhakuṭyāṃ bhagavataḥ

Although the meaning of this seems to be straightforward, the treatment of the text has been somewhat disingenuous. Vogel, for example, has translated it as:

at the Saddharmacakra in the principal Gandhakuṭī of the Lord.[63]

But Vogel's translation—suggesting as it does that it is the *Gandhakuṭī* that is "of the Lord"—violates what little syntax the sealing provides and differs markedly from his translation of other similarly constructed texts on other sealings. A seal-die from Kasia, for example, which has a legend with virtually the same grammatical construction, reads *śrī-viṣṇudvīpavihāre bhikṣusaṅghasya.* Here, Vogel takes the final inflected form for what it most obviously is—an independent genitive—and translates the legend as "of the community of friars at the Convent of Holy Viṣṇudvīpa."[64] Bearing in mind that "an independent genitive is used . . . on seals and personal belongings to name the owner of the object,"[65] the sense of the Kasia legend is clear: the document or property to which the sealing was attached was "of," "from," or "belonged to" the monks in the Viṣṇudvīpa Monastery. In light of this Kasia legend, and others like it, the sense of the Sārnāth sealing must almost certainly be the same and must almost certainly be translated:

of/belonging to the Blessed One in the original Perfume Chamber in the Śrī-Saddharmacakra (Monastery).

Understood in this way, these Sārnāth sealings—which date from the sixth or seventh century—would seem to indicate that it was not just the monks attached to the *Gandhakuṭī* who owned their own property or carried on their own distinct official business. The same apparently was true of "the Blessed One in the original Perfume Chamber." The language of the legend and what we know of the function of such sealings would seem to allow little room for other conclusions. Moreover, by using the designation "original," these sealings would seem to suggest that—as Marshall and Konow noted long ago—"there were also other *gandhakuṭīs* in Sārnāth,"[66] that at Sārnāth, as at Nālandā and probably at Kānheri,[67] there were several. But if nothing else, these sealings provide us with yet another kind of evidence indicating that the Buddha was thought to have been a current resident and an abiding presence in medieval Buddhist monasteries. The language of the sealings makes it clear that the Blessed One himself was thought to be *in* the Perfume Chamber. It was this location and it alone that was noted on these sealings, sealings whose mere existence would seem to indicate that the Blessed One resident in the Perfume Chamber had certain active functions that required an official documentation. In fact, these sealings of the Blessed One are like—perhaps more than anything else—those that contemporary living kings attached to their land grants and other official records.[68]

The apparent emphasis on the Blessed One's presence in the *Gandhakuṭī* is not, however, found at Sārnāth only on these sealings. It is expressed, as well, in at least one donative record from the site. The record occurs on an old rail-pillar that appears to have been recut and reused as a lampstand in the Gupta period. Although now fragmentary, its restoration is fairly sure. It reads:

> *deyadharmmo yam paramopā- / -sika-sulakṣmaṇāya mūla- / {gandhakuṭyāṃ bha}-gavato buddhasya / pradīpaḥ*[69]

> This is the religious gift of the excellent laywoman Sulakṣmaṇā: a lamp for the Blessed One, the Buddha, in the original Perfume Chamber.

When the laywoman Sulakṣmaṇā gave a lamp to the Buddha, apparently she did not think of him as gone or unlocatable but as present in and available at the Perfume Chamber, the cell or room reserved for him in the monastery. In this she perhaps differed from the authors of medieval Buddhist *śāstras;* or, at least, from the views they formally stated. But as we have seen, she differed very little from a large number of other donors, or from those fully literate and probably monkish scribes who throughout the medieval period likewise appear to have had no doubts about where the Buddha was.

Sulakṣmaṇā's record—in fact medieval epigraphic material as a whole—appears then to provide us with conceptions of the Buddha that otherwise have not been noted, conceptions that are embedded in and underlie a whole series of legal or quasi-legal documents connected in the main with the transfer of property, and conceptions that differ markedly from those that are articulated in formal Buddhist literary and doctrinal sources of much the same period. These epigraphical conceptions are, moreover, not limited to a specific region but are pan-Indian. They are expressed from the fifth century on in "documents" from Andhra Pradesh, Bihar, and Bengal, from Uttar Pradesh and Maharastra, and from Gujarat and the Punjab. These are conceptions that—without the usual exaggeration implied in the phrase—can be said to occur everywhere.

This epigraphical material is, however, sometimes fragmentary, sometimes elusive, and not infrequently difficult to interpret. Fortunately, we are not without some means to test our interpretation. If the interpretation of the epigraphical material presented above is correct—if the Buddha was actually thought to reside in monasteries—then we should find, for example, clear evidence in monastic architecture of accommodations being provided for him. Moreover, if the Buddha was considered to be an actual individual within the monastic community that owned or had a claim to certain property, we should expect to find at least some rulings or regulations within the monastic codes or *Vinayas* to confirm this. Happily, we find both, and in fact a bit more, but none of this can be treated in detail here. We can simply note, for example, that the *Mūlasarvāstivāda-vinaya*—the one *Vinaya* for which we have some evidence of use in medieval Indian monastic communities[70]—contains numerous passages that explicitly treat the Buddha as a juristic personality and describe the appropriate procedures for dealing with *buddhasantaka,* "that which belongs to the Buddha."

Typical of such passages is that in the *Adhikaraṇa-vastu* where pearls are given "one part for the Buddha, one part for the *Dharma,* and one part for the *Saṅgha*" (*ekaṃ buddhāya ekaṃ dharmāya ekaṃ saṃghāya*), and where the Buddha is made to specify how each part is to be used:

> *ato yo buddhasya bhāgas tena gandhakuṭyām pralepaṃ dadata; yo dharmasya sa dharmadharāṇām pudgalānāṃ; yaḥ saṃghasya taṃ samagraḥ saṃgho bhajayatu,*[71]
>
> what of this is the Buddha's share, with that you should plaster the Perfume Chamber; what belongs to the *Dharma,* that is for the persons preserving the *Dharma;* what belongs to the *Saṅgha,* the entire *Saṅgha* should share that!

Likewise, in a *Cīvara-vastu* passage dealing with the distribution of the estate of a wealthy layman who had intended to become a monk but who had died before he could do so, we find:

> *suvarṇaṃ ca hiraṇyaṃ cānyacca kṛtākṛtaṃ trayo bhāgāḥ kartavyāḥ; eko buddhasya, dvitīyo dharmasya, tṛtīyaḥ saṃghasya. yo buddhasya tena gandhakutyāṃ keśanakha-stūpeṣu ca khaṇḍachuṭṭaṃ pratisaṃskartavyam; yo dharmasya tena buddhavacanaṃ lekhayitavyaṃ siṃhāsane vā upayoktavyam; yaḥ saṃghasya sa bhikṣubhir bhājayitavyaḥ*[72]
>
> The coined and uncoined gold and other worked and unworked metal is to be divided into three shares—one for the Buddha, a second for the *Dharma,* a third for the *Saṅgha.* With that which belongs to the Buddha, the dilapidation and damage in the Perfume Chamber and on the hair and nail *stūpas* is to be repaired; with that which belongs to the *Dharma,* the word of the Buddha is to be copied, or it is to be used on the Lion Throne; that which belongs to the *Saṅgha* should be shared by the monks.

Elsewhere in the *Cīvara-vastu* a similar threefold division is to be effected, and it is said *buddhasantakena buddhapūjā vā gandhakutyāṃ stūpe vā navakarma kartavyam,*[73] "with that belonging to the Buddha, worship of the Buddha is to be performed, or new work in the Perfume Chamber or on the *stūpa* is to be undertaken." Yet another passage from the *Cīvara-vastu* refers to two distinct categories of real wealth that belong to the Buddha and indicates that both could be drawn on to finance *pūjās* of the Buddha undertaken for sick or dying monks. The monastic community could use—among other things—"that belonging to the perpetual endowment for the Buddha" (*buddhākṣayanīvisantakaṃ*), or they could "sell" (*vikrīya*) an "umbrella or flag or banner or jewel on the *tathāgata-caitya* or in the Perfume Chamber" (*tathāgata-caitye vā gandhakuṭyāṃ vā chatraṃ vā dhvajaṃ vā patākā vā ābharaṇakaṃ vā*); in either case, the funds obtained were then to be used to attend to the sick or dying monk and to perform a *pūjā* of the Teacher on his behalf (*upasthānaṃ kartavyaṃ śāstuś ca pūjā*). Should the latter recover, he is to be told "that belonging to the Buddha was used for you" (*yad buddhasantakaṃ tavopayuktam iti*), and he should make every effort to repay it (*tena yatnam āsthāya dātavyam*).[74] There is, finally, at least one passage in the *Vinaya-kṣudraka-vastu* where the otherwise fairly consistent, anachronizing language of these passages appears to break down, and the "share" apparently belonging to the Buddha appears to be specifically assigned to an "image." Here, in the account of events surrounding the housing of Śāriputra's relics, the text says the monks received precious jewels and pearls but did not know how they should be distributed. In response to the situation, the Buddha is made to say:

> *bud dud gang yin pa de dag ni shing 'dsam bu'i grib ma na bzhugs pa'i sku gzugs la dbul bar bya'o / gzhan yang chung shas shig ni shâ ri'i bu'i mchod rten de'i bcos legs bya bar bzhag la lhag ma ni dge 'dun tshogs pas bgo bar bya'o / de de bzhin gshegs pa'i mchod rten gyi ma yin gyi / shâ ri'i bu'i mchod rten gyi yin te / de lta bas na 'gyod par mi bya'o /*[75]

> Which are for the Buddha, those are to be given to the image which is sitting in the shadow of the *jambu* tree. A small part is to be put aside to repair the *stūpa* of Śāriputra. The remainder is to be divided by the community of monks—this does not belong to the *stūpa* of the *Tathāgata,* it belongs to the *stūpa* of Śāriputra: therefore, there is no fault [in the latter usage].

The translation of the first clause given here is tentative. I do not know what *bud dud* means, although this reading appears in all of the Kanjurs available to me: the Peking, Derge, and Tog Palace.[76] Context and similar passages suggest that it might be the equivalent of *buddhasya, buddhasantaka,* or *bauddha,* and I have translated it accordingly. It may, however, be the name of a specific gem or precious jewel. But in either case, the passage indicates that a "share" of valuable property was explicitly assigned to an "image." An instance of just such an image may be had in the headless figure discovered at Sāñcī that bears on its base a Kuṣān inscription indicating, it seems, that it is "a stone (image depicting) the 'Jambu-shade' (episode) of the Bhagavat (Śākyamuni)" (*bhagava-{sya} . . . sya jambuchāyā-śīlā*).[77]

These passages and others like them scattered throughout the *Mūlasarvāstivāda-vinaya* deserve and require a thorough study; they need to be studied in light of the similar passages and conceptions signaled by Gernet in *Vinayas* extant now only in Chinese;[78] they need to be studied further in connection with medieval Indian land grants and inscriptions that make explicit provision for copying texts.[79] For the moment, though, we need only note that the *Vinaya* that may well have governed the majority of medieval monastic communities in eastern India, and perhaps as well those residing at Ajaṇṭā and similar sites, contains exactly what we would expect if our interpretation of the epigraphical material is correct. It contains explicit rules that acknowledge, at the very least, the juristic personality and presence of the Buddha within the midst of the monastic community that it envisions. It contains explicit rules concerning the property and real wealth owned by this "person." And it contains specific directions concerning the central accommodations provided for him. This Buddha, at least, was a force and a factor in almost every aspect of everyday medieval monastic life.

What is almost unavoidably indicated by the epigraphical material and monastic codes is, however, only confirmed more fully by what we know about the development of Buddhist monastic architecture. Dehejia says "the early rock-cut caves of western India . . . are all Buddhist monasteries. Each site consists of one or more *caityas*—chapels for congregational worship—and several *vihāras* which were residential halls for the monks."[80] What needs to be emphasized however, is that although each early site necessarily had both "chapels" and residential quarters, they were kept spatially and architecturally distinct and each separated one from the other. The Buddha resided, as it were,[81] in his own separate quarters, in the *stūpa* housed in a separate excavation that was used for public and "congregational worship." Exactly the same pattern occurs at the much less numerous and much less well-preserved early structural sites. For example, even though the earliest monastic residential quarters at the Dharmarājikā at Taxila face the "Great *Stūpa*," they are separated from it.[82] This pattern becomes even clearer in the Taxila area with somewhat later *vihāras*. They are typically quadrangular structures having an open court surrounded by rows of residential cells, usually on all four sides. The main entrance to these monasteries almost always faces directly—and, if possible, is symmetrically aligned with—the main *stūpa*, which is outside of and separated from the monastic residential quadrangle.[83] There are, of course, some variations and some movement toward a different arrangement—attempts toward tentatively drawing the two types of "residence" into a tighter intimacy. Sometimes the *stūpa* is placed in the middle of the residential court, and although remaining distinct, it is surrounded by the living quarters of the monks.[84] But these attempts remain tentative and pale in comparison with a major rearrangement that began to appear everywhere in the fifth century—at exactly the time that we start to get clear epigraphical references to the Buddha as an actual resident of Indian monasteries.

Vogel was perhaps the first to sense the significance of this rearrangement, first at Kasia,[85] then at Bāgh, where he alludes at least to its possible connection with the *Gandhakuṭī.*[86] It has, however, been most fully studied at the Western Cave sites in several works by Dhavalikar. Dhavalikar notes that in the early Western Caves "the standard *vihāra* plan from the beginning consisted of a squarish hall with cells in side and back walls," and that the *caityagṛha,* "the shrine proper for the congregation" was separate from the *vihāra,* which "was for the residence of monks." Then, through a reconstructed sequence the details of which may or may not be entirely acceptable, he clearly shows that the later *vihāras,* too, "were squarish pillared halls, with cells in side and back walls," but they now also had "a shrine in the centre of the back wall containing a Buddha image. The vihāra," he now says, "also thus served the purpose of a shrine."[87] He also notes "that by the middle of the fifth century the typical . . . plan of the shrine-cum-vihara was completely standardized."[88] We have already noted this "plan" at the *vihāra* Cave XVI at Ajaṇṭā, *vihāra* Cave II at Bāgh, Monastery 19 at Śrāvastī, and Monastery I at Nālandā—all sites from which we have contemporary inscriptional records that speak of the Buddha as residing *in* these specific monasteries. Two additional very clear structural examples of this "shrine-cum-*vihāra*" plan are provided by Sirpur Monastery[89] and Monastery 1 at Ratnagiri.[90]

This plan—both pervasive and standardized after the fifth century—is not difficult to describe. It was achieved by only a slight modification of the typical layout for early Buddhist monasteries: structural examples were formerly quadrangular structures surrounding an open court with rows of residential cells on all four sides, or, occasionally, on only three. But in this new plan, what would have previously been only another monastic residential cell in the middle of the back wall facing the main entrance has been architecturally set apart as a very special room. The old plan had been altered to accommodate a new and equally special resident: the Buddha has moved into private monastic quarters. This new addition is, however, in at least one important sense, only a return to a much earlier tradition, and, in a sense, the Buddha has only reoccupied his old quarters.

In the *Śayanāsana-vastu* a householder in Vārāṇasī named Kalyāṇabhadra asks permission of the Buddha to build a *vihāra* for "the disciples of the Blessed One" (*bhagavataḥ śrāvakāṇāṃ vihāraṃ kārayeyam iti*). The Buddha grants permission, but Kalyāṇabhadra is presented as not knowing how such a structure should be made. At this point the Buddha is made to give specific instructions:

> *bhagavān āha: yadi trilayanaṃ kārayasi madhye gandhakuṭiḥ kārayitavyā dvayoḥ pārśvayor dve layane; evaṃ triśāle nava layanāni; catuḥśāle madhye dvārakoṣṭhakābhimukhaṃ gandhakuṭiḥ dvārakoṣṭhakapārśvayor dve layane.*[91]

> The Blessed One said: if you have three cells made, the Perfume Chamber is to be made in the middle, the two (other) cells on each side; likewise, if there are nine cells in three wings; in a quadrangular (*vihāra*) the Perfume Chamber (is to be placed) in the middle (of the back wall) facing the main entrance, two cells on each side of the entrance.

That these instructions constitute a virtually exact description of what Dhavalikar called "the shrine-cum-vihara" plan—a plan found almost everywhere after the fifth century—is probably obvious. We need only note that this correspondence between *vinaya* rule and actual groundplan allows us to label more precisely the special cell in the middle of the back wall of post-fifth-century Buddhist monasteries: although called by Dhavalikar and others simply a "shrine," it could hardly have been intended as anything other than the *Gandhakuṭī.* This means, of course, that the monastic architects at Ajaṇṭā, Bāgh, Nālandā, and numerous other post-fifth-century sites provided—exactly like Kalyāṇabhadra in early Benares and Anāthapiṇḍika at Śrāvastī—special accommodations in their monasteries that were reserved for the Buddha himself. It was apparently in such monastic quarters that, from the fifth to the fourteenth centuries, the Buddha was thought to live.[92]

There may, however, be one final bit of archaeological evidence that further confirms what epigraphical, architectural, and *vinaya* sources all suggest. If the "images" housed in medieval monastic *Gandhakuṭīs* were cognitively classified with the living Buddha, if such stone Buddhas were actually thought to *live* in these establishments, they also—at least occasionally, and in spite of their unusually hardy constitutions—must have *died* there. The remains of such "dead" Buddhas—if, again, our interpretation is correct—should have been treated not as mere objects; they should have been treated as the mortuary remains of any other "dead" Buddha had been treated.

And that, it seems, is exactly what occurred. When Marshall opened a ninth- or tenth-century *stūpa* at Śrāvastī, he did not find human remains. Instead, he found the remains of an old and broken image, an image that was probably made in the Kuṣān period at Mathurā.[93] This was not an isolated find. In *Stūpa* no. 9 at the same site yet another similar broken image had been deposited. This *stūpa* was "also of the Medieval Period," although the image was much older.[94] Marshall noted at least three additional instances of such "burials" in the medieval *stūpas* at Sāñcī[95] and still other instances at Sārnāth.[96] More recently, yet another instance was discovered at the latter site.[97] Marshall, more than forty years ago, had already drawn a first, obvious conclusion: ". . . the burial of older cult statues, whole or fragmentary, in Buddhist *stūpas* is a practice which appears to have been common during the medieval age."[98] It would seem then, again in "the medieval age," that the remains of dead images were ritually treated and permanently housed exactly like the mortuary remains of dead Buddhas; that, in fact, the equivalence of image and actual person that we have noted held not just during the life of the image but in its death as well.[99]

If nothing else, the convergence here of these distinct, and very different kinds of sources is remarkable. Epigraphical, architectural, *vinaya,* and archaeological sources all come together toward the same point: all document in different ways a conception of the Buddha that was very widely and very deeply held. This conception is important for the history of Indian religion because it is—in many respects—strikingly similar to the conception of divinity which predominates in medieval Hindu Temple Religion and raises, therefore, the question of the relationship, chronological and otherwise, between the two.[100] But it is also important—and perhaps most interesting—because it tells us a great deal that we otherwise could not know about "the abstract theories" concerning the "person" of the Buddha. It confirms and gives specificity to the wisdom of de La Vallée Poussin's observation: "the abstract theories" were, indeed, "one part," but "only one part of the history of Buddhology" or the conception of the Buddha. That part, to be sure, was not "insignificant," but it was, apparently, not unduly significant either. Bearing in mind that our inscriptions, for example, did not express the views of the masses, but were obviously written by literate individuals familiar with Buddhist doctrines of the day, it would appear that "the abstract theories"—which, significantly, were being developed at virtually the same time—had little, if any, direct *detectable* influence on a large segment of even the already limited number of literate members of the Buddhist society of their day, most of whom were probably monks.

This is particularly striking if we bear in mind that two of the sites that have produced some of the fullest epigraphical documentation for the conception of the Buddha as a permanent monastic resident were, during the period from which this documentation comes, the two most important centers of Buddhist scholasticism in Northern India. I-tsing, for example, says that in his day (the seventh century), "After having studied this commentary [the *Kāśikāvṛtti*], students begin to learn composition in prose and verse, and devote themselves to logic (*hetuvidyā*) and metaphysic (*abhidharmakosha*) . . . Thus instructed by their teachers and instructing others they pass two or three years, generally in the Nālandā monastery in Central India, or in the country of Valabhī (Walā) in Western India." These two places, he says, "are like Chin-ma, Shih-ch'ü, Lung-men and Ch'ue-li"—the foremost seats of learning in China.[101] May says:

> Quant à l'idéalisme proprement dit, il connaît, parallèlement à l'école des

> logiciens, une brillante floraison: il se scinde en deux écoles principales . . . L'une, est l'école de Valabhī . . . L'autre école, celle de Nālandā, eut une destinée brillante et devint le plus important centre d'études bouddhiques dans les derniers siècles du bouddhisme indien.[102]

The synchronism between, for example, both the epigraphical and architectural sources and the development of the abstract theories points us, as well, toward another curious observation: language expressing the personal presence and permanent abiding of the Buddha began to appear explicitly in inscriptions at almost exactly the same time—the fourth or fifth century—as monastery ground plans began to show that specific and elaborate accommodations were beginning to be provided for the Buddha in Indian monasteries. But both of these phenomena began to appear, then, at or during the period when some of the most abstract theories concerning the person of the Buddha were beginning to take definitive shape. This, of course, would suggest that all three developments were not unrelated, but specifying the nature of the relationship is not easy. Several possibilities present themselves. It is conceivable that the security, if you will, of dwelling in daily domestic intimacy with the Buddha provided a certain freedom of thought on the theoretical level—that increased etherealization and abstraction were possible precisely because the domestic presence of the Buddha was firmly established. It is conceivable, as well, that the abstract theories constituted a kind of minority report and were, in fact, a reaction to the apparently pervasive sense of the Buddha's personal presence, that they were in intent, at least, an attempt at reformation. It is also conceivable, finally, that the reaction went in the opposite direction: the increasing emphasis on the abiding presence of the Buddha, and the architectural efforts to assure daily domestic contact with him, were fueled by the anxieties engendered by the increasingly abstract and ethereal character of current theoretical discussions. All of these are possibilities but all have one thing in common: they all indicate that any attempt to assess the actual historical significance of Buddhist *śāstric* notions must take into account a far broader range of sources than has heretofore been considered. They remind us—if such a reminder be required—that Indian Buddhism is very much more than the sum of its *śāstras.*

Notes

1. P. C. Almond, *The British Discovery of Buddhism* (Cambridge: 1988) esp. 77–79. The first half of Ét. Lamotte, "La légende du Buddha," *RHR* 134 (1948) 37–71, contains a still-useful sketch of the changing scholarly perceptions of the historical Buddha.

2. Almond, *The British Discovery of Buddhism,* 70–77. Curiously, it was also explicitly argued that the promotion of archaeological work could provide a useful critique of

nineteenth-century "Brahmanism" by showing that "Brahmanism, instead of being an unchanged and unchangeable religion which has subsisted for ages, was of comparatively modern origin, and had been constantly receiving additions and alterations. . . ." see A. Imam, *Sir Alexander Cunningham and the Beginnings of Indian Archaeology* (Dacca: 1966) 39–41.

3. L. de La Vallée Poussin, *Vijñaptimātratāsiddhi. Le siddhi de Hiuan-tsang,* T. II (Paris: 1929) 762–813, esp. 774, 776, 788–791.

4. de La Vallée Poussin, *Vijñaptimātratāsiddhi,* T. II, 811.

5. de La Vallée Poussin, *Vijñaptimātratāsiddhi,* T. II, 763.

6. de La Vallée Poussin does refer to the "invocation" of at least one inscription, but his example is non-Indian, and he does not pursue the possibilities further. In fact, similar "invocations" or *maṅgalas* are frequently found at the head of several varieties of the more elaborate types of Buddhist inscriptions, and they constitute a rich potential source for future study. A cursory study of some of the epithets applied to the Buddha in pre-Gupta inscriptions has been published by A. M. Shastri, "The Legendary Personality of the Buddha as Depicted in Pre-Gupta Indian Inscriptions," *The Orissa Historical Research Journal* 8 (1960) 168–176, reprinted with few alterations as 22–35 of A. M. Shastri, *An Outline of Early Buddhism (A Historical Survey of Buddhology, Buddhist Schools and Sanghas Mainly Based on the Study of Pre-Gupta Inscriptions)* (Varanasi: 1965).

7. "Medieval" is used here in a very broad and very loose sense to cover the period from the fifth to about the fourteenth century C.E.—cf. A. L. Basham, *The Wonder That was India,* 3rd rev. ed. (New York: 1967) xxi–xxii. This periodization reflects the fact that what is usually called—using an unsatisfactory dynastic terminology—the "late Gupta" represents not an end, but the beginnings of a number of new developments in the form and content of Indian Buddhist inscriptions. For a recent attempt to catalog the Buddhist inscriptions of this period, although already now somewhat outdated, see Shizutani Masao, *Indo bukkyō himei mokuroku* (Kyoto: 1979) 159–232.

8. A. Ghosh, "Buddhist Inscription from Kausambi," *EI* 34 (1961–1962) 14–16. The inscription is fragmentary and its interpretation consequently not sure.

9. Cf. E. J. Thomas, *The Life of Buddha as Legend and History,* 3rd ed. (London: 1949) 115, n. 2: "It is doubtful if Buddha ever went so far west as Kosambī. There were later important monasteries there, and this is sufficient to explain the existence of legends attached to it."

10. P. R. Srinivasan, "Two Brahmi Inscriptions," *EI* 39 (1971 but 1985) 123–128.

11. V. V. Mirashi, *Inscriptions of the Vākāṭakas,* Corpus Inscriptionum Indicarum, Vol. V (Ootacamund: 1963) 103–211, esp. 109, line 18. The reading is in part a reconstruction but is fairly sure; cf. *{ya}ti* as a title of the Buddha in line 1 of this same inscription, and note that he is also referred to elsewhere at Ajaṇṭā as *munīndra-* (Cave XVII inscription [Mirashi] 127, line 28).

12. For the plan of Cave XVI, see J. Fergusson and J. Burgess, *The Cave Temples of India* (London: 1880) pl. xxxiii, 1; see also the discussion and plans in W. Spink, "Ajaṇṭā's Chronology: The Crucial Cave," *ArO* 10 (1975) 143–169, and W. Spink, "The Splendours of Indra's Crown: A Study of Mahāyāna Developments at Ajaṇṭa," *Journal of the Royal Society of Arts* 122, no. 5219 (1974) 743–767, esp. 758–760 and figs. 13a–13d.

13. For the Cave XXVI inscription, see G. Yazdani, *Ajanta,* Part IV: Text (London: 1955) 114–118, vs. 14. What in vs. 14 is called a *veśma* is called a *śaila-gṛhaṃ . . . śāstuḥ,* "a stone residence . . . for the Teacher," in vs. 6, and a *sugatā{layaṃ},* "a house for the Sugata," in vs. 13.

14. J. Burgess, *Report on the Buddhist Cave Temples and Their Inscriptions,* Archaeological Survey of Western India, Vol. IV (London: 1883) 86, no. 10.

15. V. V. Mirashi, *Inscriptions of the Kalachuri-Chedi Era,* Corpus Inscriptionum Indicarum, Vol. IV, Pt. 1 (Ootacamund: 1955) 19–21, esp. 20, line 5ff. I have omitted here, and in a number of the grants quoted below, the portion explicitly providing for the maintenance and upkeep of the monastery. Such a provision is a common, even a standard, element in land grants to Buddhist monasteries. The failure to take this into account in specific regard to the Bāgh grant has, unfortunately, affected Spink's attempt to date the caves. Spink argues in part that the presence of such a provision in the Bāgh grant indicates that Subandhu actually made "repairs" to the caves and that they were, therefore, excavated earlier than had been previously thought. But the provision, of course, need not imply any of this; see W. M. Spink, "Bagh: A Study," *Archives of Asian Art* 30 (1976/1977) 53–84, esp. 54, 56, 58, 83. It might also be noted that Mirashi's translation of the grant is not free of problems. The key phrase "for the Blessed One, the Buddha," has, for example, been entirely omitted.

16. For the plan of Cave II at Bāgh, see J. Marshall et al., *The Bagh Caves in the Gwalior State* (London: 1927) pl. I.

17. D. C. Bhattacharyya, "A Newly Discovered Copper-plate from Tippera [the Gunaighar Grant of Vainyagupta: The Year 188 Current (Gupta Era)]," *IHQ* 6 (1930) 45–60; D. C. Sircar, *Select Inscriptions Bearing on Indian History and Civilization,* Vol. I, 2nd rev. ed. (Calcutta: 1965) 340–345; P. K. Agrawala, *Imperial Gupta Epigraphs* (Varanasi: 1983) 113–116. The preservation of the plate is not entirely satisfactory, nor is anything certain known about the monastery referred to, the plate being an accidental find; see, however, F. M. Asher, *The Art of Eastern India, 300–800* (Delhi: 1980) 16, 32, 63. The identity of the *Ācārya* Śāntideva mentioned in this record also remains unclear.

18. G. Bühler, "Further Valabhī Grants," *IA* 6 (1877) 9–12, esp. 12, line 3. The Sthiramati of this record has been persistently identified with the Yogācāra author of the same name; see S. Lévi, "Les donations religieuses des roi de Valabhī," *Bibliothèque de l'école des hautes-études, sciences religieuses, études de critique et d'histoire,* 2° série, 7° vol. (1896) 75–100, reprinted in *Mémorial Sylvain Lévi* (Paris: 1957) 218–234, esp. 231; Y. Kajiyama, "Bhāvaviveka, Sthiramati and Dharmapāla," *WZKS* 12–13 (1968–1969) 193–203; etc.

19. G. Bühler, "Grants from Valabhī," *IA* 5 (1876) 204–221, esp. 207, line 7.

20. This, of course, is not to say that words for "images" do not occur in Buddhist records and inscriptions of this period. They do occur, but not commonly; see, for example, the seventh to eighth century inscription from Nālandā in D. C. Sircar, "Nalanda Inscription of King Prathamasiva," *EI* 39 (1971 but 1985) 117–122, esp. 122, line 10 (*bhagavato buddhasya bimbaṃ*), line 12 (*pratikṛtir . . . śās{tu}r*). The occurrence of such terms in a small number of medieval inscriptions may or may not point to the not unlikely possibility that different groups had different conceptions of these "objects," but terms like *bimba, pratikṛti, pratimā,* etc. must be much more fully studied and much more carefully nuanced before this will become clear; to translate them all automatically and indiscriminately as "image" is, to say the least, not helpful. For some remarks on the patterned occurrence and nonoccurrence of the term *pratimā* in the pre-Gupta inscriptions from Mathurā, see G. Roth, "The Physical Presence of the Buddha and its Representation in Buddhist Literature," in M. Yaldiz and W. Lobo, eds., *Investigating Indian Art. Proceedings of a Symposium on the Development of Early Buddhist and Hindu Iconography Held at the Museum of Indian Art, Berlin, in May 1986* (Berlin: 1987) 306, n. 8, and the sources

cited there. For the Khotanese terms *pratābimbaa* (Skt. *pratibimba*) and *pe'ma, pema, paima* (Skt. *pratimā*) and some interesting material illustrating Khotanese conceptions of Buddhist "images," see H. W. Bailey, "The Image in Gaustana," in N. A. Jayawickrama, ed., *Paranavitana Felicitation Volume* (Colombo: 1965) 33–36: "The Buddhas were conceived to be in these images. Thus we have the Khotanese verse *ramanī tcaṣū paima bīsai jīsta bai'ysa,* 'the deva Buddha resident in the delightful splendid image' "; etc. These Khotanese conceptions are particularly interesting because they are articulated in sources that are broadly contemporaneous with a considerable number of the Indian inscriptions cited here. See also n. 39 below. Although further afield, see H. Delahaye, "Les antécédents magiques des statues chinoises," *Revue d'esthétique* 5 (1983) 45–53, and the very interesting paper by B. Frank, "Vacuité et corps actualisé: la problème de la presence des 'personnages vénérés' dans leurs images selon la tradition du bouddhisme japonais," *JIABS* 11.2 (1988) 53–86.

21. Th. Bloch, "An Unpublished Valabhī Copper-plate Inscription of King Dhruvasena I," *JRAS* (1895) 379–384, esp. 383, line 18.

22. Note that Lévi, "Les donations religieuses des roi de Valabhī," 232, identifies the *Ācārya* Buddhadasa with the scholastic of the same name who "était l'élève d'Asaṅga."

23. D. B. Diskalkar, "Some Unpublished Copper-plates of the Rulers of Valabhī," *JBomBRAS* 1 (1925) 13–64, esp. 63, line 53. This text is faulty, and it is not impossible that the intended reading was *-kutyāṃ,* not *-kuṭī.* In any case *-kuṭī* is, as it stands, almost certainly a scribal error. In form it could only be either a stem form without grammatical marker or a nominative singular. Context and syntax, however, make the second alternative virtually impossible.

24. P. R. Srinivasan, "Two Fragmentary Charters of Maitraka Dharasena IV," *EI* 35 (1970 but 1976) 219–224, esp. 223, line 8.

25. See below 268ff.

26. D. C. Sircar, *Epigraphic Discoveries in East Pakistan* (Calcutta: 1973) 11; 62, line 9; D. C. Sircar, "Jagadishpur Plate of the Gupta Year 128," *EI* 38 (1970 but 1979) 247–252, esp. 249. In the passage he is dealing with here, Sircar sees a reference to a Buddhist establishment, but it might very well be Jain; cf. S. Siddhanta, "The Jagadishpur Copper Plate Grant of the Gupta Year 128 (A.D. 447–448)," *Journal of the Varendra Research Museum* 1 (1972) 23–37. If the record is in fact referring to Jain *Arhats,* its language would provide an early and striking Jain parallel to what we find in Buddhist records from Valabhī and elsewhere. An equally early and more certainly Jain parallel may be seen in K. N. Dikshit, "Paharpur Copper-Plate Grant of the [Gupta] Year 159," *EI* 20 (1929–1930) 59–64: *kāśika-pañca-stūpa-nikāyika-nigrantha-śramaṇācāryya-guhanandi-śiṣya-praśiṣyādhiṣṭhita-vihāre bhagavatām arhatāṃ gandha-dhūpa-sumano-dīpādy-arthan . . .,* etc. Asher (*The Art of Eastern India,* 15) has expressed some doubt about the Jain character of this record, but the epithet *pañca-stūpa-nikāyika-* makes it virtually certain that it is Jain; see A. K. Chatterjee, *A Comprehensive History of Jainism {up to 1000 A.D.}* (Calcutta: 1978) 105–106. The mere fact that it is not always easy to distinguish Buddhist and Jain inscriptions of this sort is, however, in itself significant.

27. See G. Schopen, "The Inscription on the Kuṣān Image of Amitābha and the Character of the Early Mahāyāna in India," *JIABS* 10.2 (1987) 99–134, esp. 105–106, 121–122.

28. H. Sastri, "Nalanda Stone Inscription of the Reign of Yasovarmmadeva," *EI* 20 (1929–1930) 37–46; H. Sastri, *Nalanda and its Epigraphic Material,* MASI, No. 66 (Delhi: 1942) 78–82; D. C. Sircar, *Select Inscriptions Bearing on Indian History and Civilization,*

Vol. II (Delhi: 1983) 229–232; S. M. Mishra, "The Nālandā Stone Inscription of the Reign of Yaśovarmadeva—A Fresh Appraisal," *Studies in Indian Epigraphy* 3 (1977) 108–115.

29. Sastri, *EI* 20 (1929–1930) 44, line 9.

30. The last assertion at least may, perhaps, draw some support from the fact that the inscription of Yasovarmmadeva "was found buried in the debris of the southern verandah of the old *vihāra*—now called Monastery I" at Nālandā. Sastri says of this *vihāra* and the others in the eastern row: "The [monastic] quadrangles had a projecting porch on one side which gave the entrance to the monastery . . . Directly opposite to the entrance was the shrine wherein the principal image of Tathāgata was enthroned as we see in Monastery No. 1 where the chapel still preserves the remains of a colossal figure of the Buddha . . ." (*Nalanda and Its Epigraphic Material,* 22). What this means, of course, is that Monastery I—in fact, all the *vihāras* in the eastern row—had exactly the same basic layout as Cave XVI at Ajaṇṭā and Cave II at Bāgh: although all were primarily intended as monastic residences and consisted of individual residential cells, each had the central cell in the back wall specially reserved for the Buddha. For the layout at Nālandā, see pl. 23 in B. Kumar, *Archaeology of Pataliputra and Nalanda* (Delhi: 1987) esp. 181–182. On the uncertainties concerning the second half of the verse quoted above, see Sastri, *EI* 20 (1929–1930) 39 and n. 1; 46, n. 3; etc.

31. G. Bühler, "The New Inscription of Toramana Shaha," *EI* 1 (1892) 238–241, esp. 240, line 6; Sircar, *Select Inscriptions,* Vol. I, 422–424. Bühler's notes to his edition reflect the curious character of the language of this record: "a mistake," "a monstrous form," "utterly wrong," "the utter loss of all feeling for the rules of the language"; cf. É. Senart, "L'inscription du vase de Wardak," *JA* (1914) 581.

32. T. W. Rhys Davids and J. E. Carpenter, eds., *The Dīgha Nikāya,* Vol. II (London: 1903) 88, 97, etc.; E. Waldschmidt, ed., *Das Mahāparinirvāṇasūtra,* T. II (Berlin: 1951) 152 (6.9), 188 (12.4), 256 (26.15), etc.; cf. G. von Simson, *Zur Diktion einiger Lehrtexte des buddhistischen Sanskritkanons* (München: 1965) 16.7, 16.9, 16.11, etc.; J. S. Speyer, ed., *Avadānaçataka,* Vol. I (St. Petersbourg: 1906) 9.8, 58.5, 64.9, etc.

33. T. W. and C. A. F. Rhys Davids, *Dialogues of the Buddha,* Pt. II (London: 1910) 93.

34. Rhys Davids and Carpenter, *Dīgha,* ii, 98.

35. Among the various epithets applied to the Buddha in the Toramāṇa Inscription we find, for example, *daśabalabalinacatuvaiśāradyacatasrapratisaṃ[vidā]aṣṭādaśāveṇīkādbhutadharmasamanvāgatasya sarvasatvavatsalamahākāruṇikasya* (Bühler, *EI* 1 [1892] 240, lines 5ff). These qualities or characteristics are not only textual, but were involved in "the controversy about the nature of the *āveṇikabuddhadharmas* . . . reflected in a number of important Sanskrit Buddhist scholastic texts"; see Y. Bentor, "The Redactions of the *Adbhutadharmaparyāya* from Gilgit," *JIABS* 11.2 (1988) 21–52, esp. 25–26 and notes.

36. D. C. Sircar, "More Inscriptions from Nagarjunikonda," *EI* 35 (1963) 1–36, esp. 7, line 7; cf. D. C. Sircar, "Note on Nagarjunikonda Inscription of 333 A.D.," *EI* 38 (1969 but 1971) 183–185.

37. S. S. Ramachandra, "Hyderabad Museum Plates of Prithivi-Sri-Mularaja," *EI* 38 (1969 but 1971) 192–195, esp. 194, line 15. For some earlier instances of the use of the term *-pramukha,* see H. Lüders, *Mathurā Inscriptions* (Göttingen: 1961) §§47–51 (all of which are associated with what Lüders translates as "the commissioners of the Community": *saṅghaprakṛtān[ā]ṃ bh[ad]raghoṣa-pramukhā(nāṃ),* "the commissioners of the Community headed by Bhadraghoṣa," etc.), and §27.

38. D. R. Sahni, "Saheth-Maheth Plate of Govinda-Chandra [Vikrama-]Samvat 1186," *EI* 11 (1911–1912) 20–26, esp. 24, line 20.

39. M. Venkataramayya, *Śrāvastī* (New Delhi: 1956) 13–15. Khotanese material again provides some interesting parallels. First of all, according to Bailey, "In Khotanese texts the Sanskrit *pramukha* 'chief' is used in various dialectal forms as the title of the head of a Buddhist monastery (*vihāra*)"; see H. W. Bailey, "Iranica," *BSOAS* 11 (1943–1946) 2. Elsewhere, Bailey cites as examples *tcarmaja prramāha maledaprañа,* "Maledaprañа principal [*pramukha*] of Tcarma," and—notably—*drūttīrai prraumāha' ttathāgatta śrībhadra,* "the Tathāgata Śrībhadra principal [*pramukha*] of Dro-tir"; see H. W. Bailey, "Hvatanica IV," *BSOAS* 10 (1940–1942) 921. Bailey's second example would seem to explicitly designate a Buddha as the head of a monastery. Notice too the invocation to P. 2026 treated in the same paper (894–895) where Buddhas dwelling in two local communities are referred to: "Homage, reverence to the Buddha dwelling in Brrūya; homage, reverence to the Buddha in Khāṃhyape." For even more generalized uses of *pramukha* as a monastic title in Khotanese and in Tibetan sources dealing with Khotan, see H. W. Bailey, *Indo-Scythian Studies. Being Khotanese Texts,* Vol. IV (Cambridge: 1961) 24 (7), 82ff; H. W. Bailey, *The Culture of the Sakas in Ancient Iranian Khotan* (Delmar: 1982) 66, both dealing with a letter in which several monks are referred to by name with titles: *Dvipiṭaka Ācārya Pramukha* Yaśaḥ-prajña, *Tripiṭaka Ācārya Pramukha* Puṇya-mitra, etc.); R. E. Emmerick, *Tibetan Texts Concerning Khotan* (London: 1967) 60.3, 137 (*par-mog = pramukha*).

40. H. Shastri, "The Nalanda Copper-plate of Devapala-deva," *EI* 17 (1923–1924) 310–327, esp. 322, line 38; Sastri, *Nalanda and Its Epigraphic Material,* 92–102, esp: 98, line 38.

41. K. V. Subrahmanya Aiyer, "The Larger Leiden Plates (of Rajaraja I)," *EI* 22 (1933–1934) 213–266, esp. 242, lines 83–84.

42. R. B. Hiralal, "Four Chandella Copper-plate Inscriptions," *EI* 20 (1929–1930) 125–136, esp. 130, line 14; see also R. K. Dikshit, "Land-grants of the Chandella Kings," *Journal of the Uttara Pradesh Historical Society* 23 (1950) 228–251, esp. 239.

43. D. C. Sircar, *Some Epigraphical Records of the Medieval Period From Eastern India* (New Delhi: 1979) 32.

44. *BHSD,* 209.

45. H. Lüders, *Bharhut Inscriptions,* Corpus Inscriptionum Indicarum, Vol. II, Pt. 2, rev. E. Waldschmidt and M. A. Mehendale (Ootacamund: 1963) 107–108 (B 34).

46. J. Ph. Vogel, "Prakrit Inscriptions from Ghantasala," *EI* 27 (1947–1948) 1–4, esp. 3, A and B. The same inscriptions were published some twenty years later as recent discoveries and without reference to Vogel in M. S. Sarma, "Some Prākṛit Inscriptions from Ghaṇṭaśāla," *Epigraphia Āndhrica* 2 (1979) 1–3. None of these inscriptions contain a date. Two of them are virtually identical and record the construction of a "stone *maṇḍapa* with a *gandhakuṭī,* a railing (*vedikā*) and a *toraṇa.*"

47. P. V. P. Sastry, "Hyderabad Prakrit Inscription of Govindaraja Vihara," *JESI* 11 (1984) 95–100. This inscription is poorly edited here and must be studied again. For now, the readings marked "[ed.]" in the notes are to be preferred. The donor in this record, a monk, is called among other things *goviṃdarāja-vihārasa gaṃdhakuṭi-vārika,* the sense of which has been misunderstood; see below n. 56.

48. Mirashi, *Inscriptions of the Vākāṭakas,* 120–129 (no. 27), esp. 127, line 27. This is the "Inscription in Ajaṇṭā Cave XVII." It records the "construction" of, among other things, a *Gandhakuṭī* but because it is badly preserved and fragmentary there is some uncertainty about which of the extant excavations at Ajaṇṭā it refers to.

49. J. Burgess, *Report on the Elura Cave Temples and the Brahmanical and Jaina Caves in Western India* (London: 1883) 77 (no. 6). The inscription records the gift of a *śākyabhikṣu*

(*śākya-* has been inadvertently omitted from the reading published here but is easily read in the facsimile, pl. LI); this monk is also called *mahāgandhakuṭī-vārika;* cf. below, 269ff.

50. G. R. Sharma, "Excavations at Kauśāmbī, 1949–1955," *Annual Bibliography of Indian Archaeology,* Vol. XVI (Leyden: 1958) xliv: "Inscription on a lotus-shaped lamp (pl. Vc and d). The inscription records the donation of the lotus-shaped lamp by Bhikṣu Pradipta for the use in the Gandhakuṭī of the monastery." Although the bibliography of B. Ch. Chhabra's work published in *Svasti Śrī Dr. B. Ch. Chhabra Felicitation Volume,* ed. K. V. Ramesh et al. (Delhi: 1984) lists the "Ghoshitarama Terracotta Lamp Inscription" and says it was "published twice in English and once in Sanskrit," it gives no further details and I have yet to locate it. In the photograph published by Sharma the whole inscription is not clearly readable.

51. E. Hultzsch, "The Sarnath Inscription of Mahipala," *IA* 14 (1885) 139–140; and see below nn. 61, 62, and 69.

52. B. Indraji, "An Inscription at Gayā Dated in the Year 1813 of Buddha's Nirvana, with Two Others of the Same Period," *IA* 10 (1881) 341–347, esp. 342, line 13; Th. Bloch, "Notes on Bodh Gayā," *ARASI 1908–09* (Calcutta: 1912) 139–158, esp. 153, line 1; R. D. Banerji, *The Palas of Bengal,* Memoirs of the Asiatic Society of Bengal, Vol. V, No. 3 (Calcutta: 1915) 35, line 3; D. C. Sircar, "Three East Indian Inscriptions of the Early Medieval Period," *JAIH* 6 (1972–1973) 39–59.

53. See above nn. 21, 23, and 24.

54. A. Banerji-Sastri, "Ninety-three Inscriptions on the Kurkihar Bronzes," *JBORS* 26 (1940) 236–251, esp. nos. 31 and 32.

55. See below nn. 58 and 59.

56. *BHSD,* 477 s.v. *vārika.* Edgerton cites as the usual Tibetan equivalent *zhal (l)ta pa,* "guard, superintend(ent)." Curiously, this Buddhist material has not been taken into account in an exchange between Sircar and S. P. Tewari concerning the meaning of *vārika* in inscriptions. See S. P. Tewari, "A Note on Varika of the Inscriptions," *JESI* 9 (1982) 34–36 (also in Tewari, *Contributions of Sanskrit Inscriptions to Lexicography* [Delhi: 1987] 208–211); D. C. Sircar, "The Designation 'Varika'," *Vajapeya: Essays on Evolution of Indian Art and Culture. Prof. K. D. Bajpai Felicitation Volume,* Vol. I, ed. A. M. Sastri et al. (Delhi: 1987) 111–112. The Buddhist usage clearly favors Sircar.

57. See n. 49 above.

58. Sastri, *Nalanda and Its Epigraphic Material,* 38 and n. 4 (S.I. 675).

59. Sastri, *Nalanda and Its Epigraphic Material,* 43 (S.I. 730), but accepting the emendation proposed in P. V. B. Karunatillaka, "The Administrative Organization of the Nālandā Mahāvihāra from Sigillary Evidence," *The Sri Lanka Journal of the Humanities* 6.1 and 2 (1980) 62. See also the more general discussion on 61–64 of the term *vārika.* There is a third sealing published in Sastri (40, S.I. A, 357) that refers to a *Gandhakuṭī,* but it does not contain the term *vārika: śrīdevapāla-gandhakuḍyāṃ.*

60. See Sastri, *Nalanda and Its Epigraphic Material,* 27, for example. It is a pity that in one of the very few studies connected with the *Gandhakuṭī* the title *gandhakuṭīvārika* and a considerable number of other things have been so carelessly treated. J. S. Strong, "Gandhakuṭī: The Perfumed Chamber of the Buddha," *History of Religions* 16 (1977) 390–406, referring to the Kānheri inscription (n. 18 above), cites the title as "*gandhakuṭī-bhārika.*" This, of course, is wrong and had he actually checked the work he cites as his primary source—Lüders' list in *EI* 10 (1909–1910) no. 989—he would have seen that it was so. "*Gandhakuṭī-bhārika*" is an invention of S. Dutt (*Buddhist Monks and Monasteries in India* [London: 1962] 149), which is nowhere attested, and certainly not at Kānheri.

The form found at Kānheri is, as given by Lüders, "*mahāgandhakuṭīvārika?*," the question mark reflecting the uncertainty expressed in Burgess (n. 49 above) concerning the possibility of reading-*cārika* instead of -*vārika,* an uncertainty that was removed by the publication of the Nālandā seals. In both Lüders and Burgess the title is translated as "the guardian of the great gandhakuṭī," but because, apparently, Strong wants the title to "confirm" a story in the *Avadānaśataka* about a monk sweeping the *Gandhakuṭī*, Strong himself invents a quotation that he attributes to Dutt: He says that the title means "according to Sukumar Dutt, a 'monk in charge of keeping the sanctuary clean'." What Dutt actually says is " . . . *Gandhakuṭī-bhārika* who was in charge of the sanctuary (Lüders, no. 989 at Kanheri) and probably had to keep it clean and make arrangements for the daily worship." The Nālandā material, long available, should have indicated to Dutt and Strong how unlikely it was that the term referred to a janitor. Strong says of the *Gandhakuṭī* that it was "never itself a canonical tradition, figuring only sporadically in a few popular texts." But unless he wants to argue that the *Mūlasarvāstivāda-vinaya* is not "canonical," this is contradicted in one of his own notes. In his n. 19 he says: ". . . there are two references to the *gandhakuṭī* in the Vinaya of the Mūlasarvāstivādins"; he then cites, probably only by coincidence, the only two passages that occur in Bagchi's index, and adds: "the first of these is just a passing reference: the second specifies the location of the *gandhakuṭī* as being in the middle of the monastery. Together they add little to the Pāli materials we have reviewed . . ." There are several problems here. First, there are many more references to the *Gandhakuṭī* in the *Mūlasarvāstivāda-vinaya* than the two in Bagchi's index. This is clear from the fact that the passage he refers to as "just a passing reference" is only one of a series of passages indicating that certain kinds of material possessions and moveable wealth that "belonged" to the Buddha had to be lodged in or used on the *Gandhakuṭī* and that—since such wealth frequently consisted of items like jewels and pearls—the *Gandhakuṭī* was not only a central unit in the monastic economy but also one of the wealthiest. See *Gilgit Manuscripts,* iii 2, 142.10, 143.12, 146.3; *Gilgit Manuscripts,* iii 4, 210.4; *Śayanāsanavastu and Adhikaraṇavastu,* 68.22; and below. More could be added here, but it is probably clear that few of the facts and perhaps even less of the interpretation in Strong's paper can be taken with confidence.

61. J. H. Marshall and S. Konow, "Sārnāth," *ARASI 1906–07* (Calcutta: 1909) 97. See also J. H. Marshall and S. Konow, "Excavations at Sārnāth 1908," *ARASI 1907–08* (Calcutta: 1911) 66.

62. H. Hargreaves, "Excavation at Sārnāth," *ARASI 1914–15* (Calcutta: 1920) 127.

63. J. Ph. Vogel, "Seals of Buddhist Monasteries in Ancient India," *Journal of the Ceylon Branch of the Royal Asiatic Society,* N.S. 1 (1950) 27–32, esp. 27.

64. Vogel, "Seals of Buddhist Monasteries in Ancient India," 30.

65. G. Fussman, "Numismatic and Epigraphic Evidence for the Chronology of Early Gandharan Art," *Investigating Indian Art,* ed. M. Yaldiz and W. Lobo (Berlin: 1987) 80.

66. Marshall and Konow, *ARASI 1906–07,* 99.

67. The presence of more than one *Gandhakuṭī* at Kānheri is at least suggested by the designation *mahā-gandhakuṭī-vārika* (above n. 48), "the superintendent of the *Great Gandhakuṭī,*" the specificity added by the *mahā-* being otherwise unnecessary.

68. See, for example, H. Shastri, "The Nalanda Copper-plate of Devapaladeva," *EI* 17 (1923–1924) 310–327, esp. 310, where the seal reads simply *śrī-devapāladevasya,* "of the Illustrious Devapāladeva," and D. C. Sircar, "Lucknow Museum Copper-plate

Inscription of Surapala I, Regnal Year 3," *EI* 40 (1973 but 1986) 4–16, esp. 5, which reads *śrīśūrapāladevasya,* "[this] belongs to the Illustrious Śūrapāladeva."

69. The text cited here is that found in D. R. Sahni, *Catalogue of the Museum of Archaeology at Sārnāth* (Calcutta: 1914) 211. A second similar inscription on yet another recut pillar was also found at the site. It reads: *deyadharmmo yaṃ paramopa- / -{sa}ka-kīrtteḥ {mūla-ga}ndhaku- / {tyāṃ pra}dī{p . . . ddhaḥ}* (also Sahni, 211). What remains of both inscriptions, taken together with the sealings already discussed, allows for a fairly certain restoration.

70. The most direct evidence comes, of course, from Gilgit. To judge by the manuscript material recovered from this site, the monastic community at Gilgit was governed by this *Vinaya,* although the rest of the literature it had available was primarily—although not exclusively—Mahāyāna. See O. von Hinüber, "Die Erforschung der Gilgit-Handschriften (Funde buddhistischer Sanskrit-Handschriften, I)," *Nachrichten der Akademie der Wissenschaften in Göttingen I. Philo-Hist. Klasse,* Jahrgang 1979, Nr. 12 (Göttingen: 1979) 329–359; O. von Hinüber, "Die Bedeutung des Handschriftenfundes bei Gilgit," *ZDMG,* Supplement V, XXI. Deutscher Orientalistentag vom 4 bis. 29 März 1980 in Berlin (Wiesbaden: 1982) 47–66; etc. That virtually the same situation is mirrored in the Tibetan Kanjur—primarily Mahāyāna *sūtra* literature, but only the *Mūlasarvāstivāda-vinaya*—would seem to argue for the pervasiveness of this *Vinaya* in the primarily Mahāyāna Indian communities from which Tibet got its Buddhism, and may, in fact, suggest that this was the standard *Vinaya* in Eastern India at the time. I-tsing, *A Record of the Buddhist Religion as Practised in India and the Malay Archipelago,* points in the same direction. More specifically, his remarks suggest the importance of this *Vinaya* at Tāmralipti and Nālandā (the latter, incidentally, has produced the only epigraphic reference I know to the Mūlasarvāstivāda; see S. L. Huntington, *The "Pāla-Sena" Schools of Sculpture* [Leiden: 1984] 225–226, no. 34). There are, moreover, indications of a connection between this *Vinaya* and Ajaṇṭā: J. Przyluski, "La roue de la vie à Ajaṇṭā," *JA* (1920) 313–331; M. Lalou, "Trois récits du dulva reconnus dans les peintures d'Ajaṇṭā," *JA* (1925) 333–337; M. Lalou, "Notes sur la décoration des monastères bouddhiques," *Revues des arts asiatique* 5.3 (1930) 183–185; D. Schlingloff, *Studies in the Ajanta Paintings. Identifications and Interpretations* (Delhi: 1987) 14, 34, 70–71, 77–78, 153, etc.

71. *Śayanāsanavastu and Adhikaraṇavastu,* 68.9ff.

72. *Gilgit Manuscripts,* iii 2, 143.10. This passage—like a number of other passages from the *Mūlasarvāstivāda-vinaya*—has been incorporated by I-tsing in his *Record;* see J. Takakusu, *A Record of the Buddhist Religion as Practised in India and the Malay Archipelago* (London: 1896) 192.

73. *Gilgit Manuscripts,* iii 2, 146.3.

74. *Gilgit Manuscripts,* iii 2, 124.1ff. There are a number of textual problems in the passage as a whole—Dutt, for example, makes several emendations—and the Tibetan translation (*Peking,* 41, 280-3-6ff) differs here, as it frequently does, just enough so that it does not provide a sure guide. However, the general sense of the passage is not in doubt.

75. *Peking,* 44, 95-3-5ff.

76. Given the not infrequent difficulty in distinguishing *d/ng,* especially but not exclusively, in the Peking edition, it is not impossible to read *bud dung,* etc. *Dung* can mean "a kind of shell or conch." [See G. Schopen, "Ritual Rights and Bones of Contention: More on Monastic Funerals and Relics in the *Mūlasarvāstivāda-vinaya,*" *JIP* 22 (1994) 59–60 for a much better discussion of the term.]

77. J. Marshall, A. Foucher, and N. G. Majumdar, *The Monuments of Sāñchī,* Vol. I

(Delhi: 1940) 385–386; Vol. III, pl. 124b. The inscription is fragmentary and has given rise to somewhat different interpretations. Two interesting studies of this "episode"—the so-called "First Meditation"—have recently been published: H. Durt, "La 'visite aux laboureurs' et la 'méditation sous l'arbre *jambu*' dans les biographies sanskrites et chinoises du buddha," *Indological and Buddhist Studies. Volume in Honour of Professor J. W. de Jong on His Sixtieth Birthday,* ed. L. A. Hercus et al. (Canberra: 1982) 95–120, and D. Schlingloff, "Die Meditation unter dem Jambu-Baum," *WZKS* 31 (1987) 111–130 (118, n. 32: "Die Inschrift [on the Sāñcī figure] vermeldet die Errichtung einer Statue des Erhabenen, der sich auf einem Steinsitz (?) unter dem Schatten des Rosenapfelbaumes befindet"). The passage cited above is not the only one in the *Mūlasarvāstivāda-vinaya* to refer to this image; see *Gilgit Manuscripts,* iii 2, 142.1: *yaṣṭa{yo yā} āyatās tā jambūcchāyikāḥ pratimāyā dhvajavaṃśāḥ kārayitavyāḥ,* and Takakusu, *A Record of the Buddhist Religion,* 190.

78. J. Gernet, *Les aspects économiques du bouddhisme dans la société chinoise du ve au xe siècle* (Paris: 1956) esp. 61–70, 149–162. Gernet, given his primary focus, justifiably paid little attention to the *Mūlasarvāstivāda-vinaya:* "Le Vinaya des Mūlasarvāstivādin, traduit au début du viiie siècle par Yi-tsing, et venu trop tard n'a pu avoir sur la constitution des institutions monacales autant d'influence que les précédents"; 62, n. 1. See also A. Bareau, "La construction et le culte des stūpa d'après les Vinayapiṭaka," *BEFEO* 50 (1960) 229–274, esp. 230, 242–243, 244, 256–257; A. Bareau, "Indian and Ancient Chinese Buddhism: Institutions Analogous to the Jisa," *Comparative Studies in Society and History* 3.4 (1961) 443–451. For traces of similar ideas in the Pāli *Vinaya,* see G. Schopen, "The *Stūpa* Cult and the Extant Pāli *Vinaya,* "Ch. V above, esp. 89–90; and, for the strong continuance of such ideas in Mahāyāna *sūtra* literature, G. Schopen, "Burial *Ad Sanctos* and the Physical Presence of the Buddha in Early Indian Buddhism," Ch. VII above, esp. 128–131. See, finally, for some brief remarks on some of these ideas in the *Abhidharmakośa* and *Mahāvibhāṣā,* M. Hofinger, "Le vol dans la morale bouddhique," *Indianisme et bouddhisme. Mélanges offerts à Mgr. Étienne Lamotte* (Louvain-La-Neuve: 1980) 177–189, esp. 185.

79. See, for example, from Valabhī, G. Bühler, "Additional Valabhī Grants, Nos. IX–XIV," *IA* 7 (1878) 66–72, esp. 67, line 5: . . . *tasya gandhapuṣpadhūpadīpatailādikriyotsarppaṇārthaṃ saddharmmasya pustakopakra . . . ānādeśasamatvāgatāṣṭādaśanikāy{ābhyantarā}ryyabhikṣu{saṃgha}sya cīvirapiṇḍapā{ta} . . . -vihārasya ca khaṇḍasphuṭitaviśīrṇṇapratisaṃskāraṇārtham . . .;* from Nālandā, Shastri, *EI* 17 (1923–1924) 322, line 38: . . . *bhagavato buddhabhaṭṭārakasya. . . āyārthe. . . cāturddiśāryabhikṣu-saṅghasya balicarusatracīvarapiṇḍapātaśayanāsanaglānapratyaya-bhaiṣajyādyarthaṃ dharmaratnasya lekhanādyarthaṃ vihārasya ca khaṇḍasphuṭitasamādhānārthaṃ;* from Kailan, D. C. Sircar, "The Kailan Copper-plate Inscription of King Śrīdhāraṇa Rāta of Samataṭa," *IHQ* 23 (1947) 221–241, esp. 239, line 22: . . . *bhagavatas tathāgataratnasya gandhadhūpadīpa-mālyānulepanārthan tadupadiṣṭamārggasya dharmmasya lekhanavācanārtham āryasaṅghasya ca cīvarapiṇḍapātādivividhopacārārtha. . . .* All of these make clear provision for copying texts as well.

80. V. Dehejia, *Early Buddhist Rock Temples. A Chronology* (London: 1972) 71.

81. On the Buddha as a living presence in his *stūpa* and relics, see Bareau, "Le construction et le culte des stūpa d'après les Vinayapiṭaka," 269: "D'autre part, la participation du *stūpa* au caractère sacré des reliques et de la personne du Buddha ou du saint tend à personnaliser le monument . . . le *stūpa* est plus que le symbole du Buddha, c'est le Buddha lui-même"; Schopen, "Burial *Ad Sanctos* and the Physical Presence of the Buddha in Early Indian Buddhism," Ch. VII above; and Schopen, "On the Buddha and His Bones," Ch. VIII above.

82. J. Marshall, *Taxila. An Illustrated Account of Archaeological Excavations carried out at Taxila under the Orders of the Government of India between the Years 1913 and 1934,* Vol. I (Cambridge: 1951) 275.

83. Marshall, *Taxila,* Vol. I, 315, 316, 317, 318, etc.

84. Marshall, *Taxila,* Vol. I, 365.

85. J. Ph. Vogel, "Excavations at Kasiā," *ARASI 1906–07* (Calcutta: 1909) 44–67, esp. 48–49.

86. Marshall et al., *The Bagh Caves in the Gwalior State,* 27–28.

87. M. K. Dhavalikar, *Late Hinayana Caves of Western India* (Poona: 1984) 79, 3. Dhavalikar uses here and elsewhere "Hīnayāna" to refer to "early" caves and "Mahāyāna" to refer to the "later" caves. I have avoided these sectarian usages in the belief that their accuracy has yet to be fully demonstrated.

88. M. K. Dhavalikar, "Evolution of the Buddhist Rock-cut Shrines of Western India," *JASBom* 45/46 (1970/1971) 50–61, esp. 53; see also M. K. Dhavalikar, "The Beginnings of Mahayana Architecture at Ajanta," *Madhu. Recent Researches in Indian Archeology and Art History. Shri M. N. Deshpande Festschrift,* ed. M. S. Nagaraja Rao (Delhi: 1981) 131–38.

89. A. Ghosh, ed., *Indian Archaeology 1954–55—A Review* (New Delhi: 1955) 24–26, esp. fig. 6.

90. D. Mitra, *Ratnagiri (1958–61),* MASI, No. 80 (New Delhi: 1981) Vol. I, 152ff, esp. fig. 8. It should, perhaps, be noted that the central cell in the back wall of Cave II at Bāgh houses a *stūpa,* not an image. This, however, may only represent a formal, and not a conceptual difference in the articulation of the sense of the Buddha's presence; see n. 81 above. The question needs further study.

91. *Śayanāsanavastu and Adhikaraṇavastu,* 10.20ff.

92. That constructional activity at Buddhist monastic sites was under the supervision of specifically designated monks is clear from both literary and inscriptional sources; see M. Njammasch, "Der *navakammika* und seine Stellung in der Hierarchie der buddhistischen Klöster," *Altorientalische Forschungen* 1 (1974) 279–293. For the construction of the *Gandhakuṭī* at Śrāvastī in Pāli sources, see V. Fausbøll, *The Jataka,* Vol. I (London: 1877) 92.21 (*so majjhe dasabalassa gandhakuṭiṃ kāresi*).

93. J. H. Marshall, "Excavations at Saheth-Maheth," *ARASI 1910–11* (Calcutta: 1914) 11–12 and pl. VIa; see also D. R. Sahni, "A Buddhist Image Inscription from Śrāvastī," *ARASI 1908–09* (Calcutta: 1912) 133–138.

94. Marshall, "Excavations at Saheth-Maheth," 12 and pl. VIb.

95. Marshall et al., *The Monuments of Sāñchī,* Vol. I, 47–49.

96. Marshall and Konow, "Excavations at Sārnāth, 1908," 68, etc.

97. A. Ghosh, ed., *Indian Archaeology 1962–63—A Review* (New Delhi: 1965) 97, 107; cf. M. C. Joshi, "Studies in Early Indian Art in Uttar Pradesh and Neighbouring Areas: Summary and Suggestions," *Archaeology and History. Essays in Memory of Shri A. Ghosh,* ed. B. M. Pande and B. D. Chattopadhyaya, Vol. II (Delhi: 1987) 495–506, esp. 501 and pl. 134.

98. Marshall et al., *The Monuments of Sāñchī,* 47.

99. The above remarks should not be taken to imply that all "images" found in *stūpas* are to be interpreted in this way. There are some instances where other ideas—although not unrelated—appear to be intended. See, for example, the carefully arranged set of images found in the core of the main *stūpa* at Devnimori in R. N. Mehta and S. N. Chowdhary,

Excavation at Devnimori (A Report of the Excavation conducted from 1960 to 1963) (Baroda: 1966) 49ff.

100. See as a sampling for the aspects which have most concerned us here: A. B. Keith, "The Personality of an Idol," *Journal of Comparative Legislation and International Law,* 3rd series, 7 (1925) 255–257; J. N. Banerjea, *The Development of Hindu Iconography* (Calcutta: 1956) esp. 36–107; G.-D. Sontheimer, "Religious Endowments in India: The Juristic Personality of Hindu Deities," *Zeitschrift für vergleichende Rechtswissenschaft* 67 (1965) 44–100; J. D. M. Derrett, "The Reform of Hindu Religious Endowments," *South Asian Politics and Religion,* ed. D. E. Smith (Princeton: 1966) 311–336; H. von Stietencron, "Orthodox Attitudes Towards Temple Service and Image Worship in Ancient India," *Central Asiatic Journal* 21 (1971) 126–138; D. L. Eck, *Darśan. Seeing the Divine Image in India,* 2nd rev. ed. (Chambersburg: 1985).

101. J. Takakusu, trans., *A Record of the Buddhist Religion as Practised in India and the Malay Archipelago,* 176–177.

102. J. May, "La philosophie bouddhique idéaliste," *Asiatische Studien / Études asiatiques* 25 (1971) 256–323, esp. 298.

Index of Archaeological Sites and Inscriptions

Index of Texts

Index of Words, Phrases, and Formulae

Index of Subjects

Amitābha, 39–40, 53 n. 89, 53 n. 90

darśan, 116–117, 137 n. 9, 138 n. 10
de la Vallée Poussin, L., 8, 101, 149, 205, 259, 277
dhāraṇīs, 120–122, 142 n. 31
Dharmaśāstra, 214, 219
disposal of the dead, 8–9, 72, 92–93, 96 n. 19, 105, 115ff, 194 n. 6, 204ff
donative formulae, 5, 6, 7, 35–36, 37–38, 39, 40–41, 42, 51 n. 82, 51 n. 83, 52 n. 85, 52 n. 86, 52 n. 87, 53 n. 88, 54 n. 95, 55 n. 98, 57–63, 69, 77, 115, 167, 170–171, 172, 246

I-tsing, 120, 225 n. 19, 232 n. 62, 234 n. 63, 236 n. 71, 277, 286 n. 70, 286 n. 72

juristic personality of the Buddha, 272–274

Lamotte, Ét., 5–7, 18 n. 29, 24, 25, 27, 41–42, 144, 168, 239, 252

Mahāyāna, 31, 32, 36, 37ff, 52 n. 83, 54 n. 94, 81, 85, 96 n. 18, 99, 129, 148, 150, 188, 202 n. 97, 238, 250, 256 n. 38, 256 n. 41, 256 n. 44, 258, 259, 261, 286 n. 70, 288 n. 87
manuscript traditions, 1, 16 n. 5, 25, 91, 96 n. 23, 136 n. 6, 203 n. 111
monastic titles, 24, 30–31, 32, 34, 35, 36, 44 n. 5, 44 n. 7, 45 n. 8, 49 n. 42, 49 n. 45, 54 n. 95, 62, 63, 65, 77, 78, 93, 107, 117, 138 n. 11, 139 n. 12, 139 n. 13, 159, 165, 169, 174, 175, 176, 186–188, 189, 190, 191, 202 n. 103, 210, 211, 212, 243, 244, 245, 247, 248, 249, 250, 268, 269, 283 n. 39

nirvāṇa in inscriptions, 36, 39, 64
nuns, 248–250

Oldenberg, H., 30, 185, 204, 248, 250

personal property owned by monks, 3–4

religious acts undertaken for the dead, 35, 36, 37, 38, 59, 61–62, 63
Rhys Davids, T.W., 8, 100, 185, 204

"schools" in inscriptions, 26, 37ff, 51 n. 83, 52 n. 85, 80, 93, 159, 167–168, 195 n. 25, 245
stūpas / relics, 28, 29, 30, 32, 33, 34, 76, 77, 96 n. 19, 100, 103–104, 106, 108, 115, 199ff, 126–128, 128–131, 148–164, 160, 165ff, 179–180, 197 n. 38, 198 n. 50, 218, 233 n. 63, 272, 273, 276–277

transfer of merit, 6–7, 19 n. 31, 36ff, 54 n. 95, 78–79, 213, 221, 229 n. 42, 246